DATE DUE			
SEP 2 31S			
MAR 02 91'S			

WITHDRAWN

The History of Accounting

This is a volume in the Arno Press collection

The History of Accounting

Advisory Editor
Richard P. Brief

Editorial Board
Gary John Previts
Stephen A. Zeff

*See last pages of this volume
for a complete list of titles*

ADVANCED ACCOUNTING

Lawrence R[obert] Dicksee

ARNO PRESS

A New York Times Company

New York — 1976

Editorial Supervision: SHEILA MEHLMAN

———◆———

Reprint Edition 1976 by Arno Press Inc.

Reprinted from a copy in The American Institute
  of Certified Public Accountants Library

THE HISTORY OF ACCOUNTING
ISBN for complete set: 0-405-07540-5
See last pages of this volume for titles.

Manufactured in the United States of America

———◆———

Library of Congress Cataloging in Publication Data

Dicksee, Lawrence Robert, 1864-1932.
    Advanced accounting.

    (The History of accounting)
    Reprint of the 1903 ed. published by Gee, London.
    1. Accounting.   I. Title.   II. Series.
HF5635.D53   1976   657'.046   75-18464
ISBN 0-405-07547-2

ADVANCED ACCOUNTING

BY

LAWRENCE R. DICKSEE, M.Com., F.C.A.

(of the firm of SELLARS, DICKSEE & CO.)

(Professor of Accounting at the University of Birmingham.)

WITH

AN APPENDIX

ON

THE LAW RELATING TO ACCOUNTS

BY

J. E. G. DE MONTMORENCY, B.A., L.L.B. (Cantab.)

(of the Middle Temple, Barrister-at-Law)

LONDON :

GEE & CO., Printers and Publishers, 34 Moorgate Street, E.C.

—

1903.

BY THE SAME AUTHOR.

———

"AUDITING : A PRACTICAL MANUAL FOR AUDITORS." (Fifth Edition)

"BOOKKEEPING FOR ACCOUNTANT STUDENTS." (Fourth Edition)

"BOOKKEEPING FOR COMPANY SECRETARIES." (Second Edition)

"BOOKKEEPING EXERCISES FOR ACCOUNTANT STUDENTS" -

"GOODWILL, AND ITS TREATMENT IN ACCOUNTS." (Second Edition)

"BANKRUPTCY TRUSTEE'S ESTATE BOOK." (Second Edition) -

"PROFITS AVAILABLE FOR DIVIDEND" - - -

"AUCTIONEERS' ACCOUNTS" - - - -

"SOLICITORS' ACCOUNTS" - - - -

———

GEE & CO., Printers and Publishers, 34 Moorgate Street, London, E.C.

CONTENTS.

PREFACE

THE present work was commenced upwards of two years ago, and was at that time primarily undertaken with a view to assisting candidates for the Final Examination of the Institute of Chartered Accountants to attain the high standard of knowledge which has been set at those Examinations during the past few years. The pressure of other business, however, materially interfered with its rapid progress at that time, and, in the meanwhile, there has been a general awakening on the part of both business men and educationalists to the importance of Accounting, which has, it is thought, still further emphasised the desirability of such a work being issued as soon as possible.

The subject of Accounting has been included in the curriculum of the University of Birmingham for the Faculty of Commerce, and a very complete knowledge of the science is required on the part of all candidates for its Commercial degrees. The University of London has introduced " Accountancy and Business Methods " as an optional subject in connection with its Science degrees in the Economics section. Instruction in the subject has also been arranged for by the newly founded Victoria University of Manchester, and a knowledge of Accounting will doubtless be required on the part of candidates for its degrees in Commerce. Other provincial Universities have also been established during the past year, and these doubtless in due course will create Faculties of Commerce, which, in their turn, will serve to still further diffuse a thorough knowledge of Accounts. The subject of Advanced Accounting has also been included in the scheme of instruction undertaken by the Commercial Education Committee of the London Chamber of Commerce ; while the standard in Accounts required by examiners for the Institute of Chartered Accountants, and other organised bodies of professional Accountants throughout the United Kingdom, is steadily becoming more and more exacting.

It has been my privilege to be in no small degree associated with this movement, by being called upon to impart instruction in Accounts in connection with certain of these undertakings, and as a result I have been led to the belief that a work dealing adequately with the whole range of subjects embraced would meet a want that has hitherto been experienced doubtless by other teachers besides myself. It might perhaps be thought that a work designed upon these comprehensive lines could not be equally suitable, and equally useful, to both Accountant Students and others, who, while desiring a knowledge of Accounts, had yet no intention of entering the profession of accountancy. But, inasmuch as the object is in all cases presumably to acquire a thorough knowledge of the science of Accounts, it is thought that the requirements of these various classes of Students, if not absolutely identical, have at least very much in common, and are therefore capable of being served from the same source. In the case of Accountant

Students, their reading will naturally to a large extent be supplemented by practical experience, which, (if properly guided) is perhaps the best teacher of all. In the case of others, it must be the aim of the teacher to, so far as lies in his power, supply the place of such practical instruction, for this is a task which, it is thought, cannot be successfully accomplished by any book.

It has throughout been my aim to handle the matter in such a manner that the reader may be inspired with a real interest in a subject which is in many quarters thought to be absolutely uninteresting. If this object has been achieved, the Student will have already made a great step towards a mastery of the science of Accounting ; and it is perhaps safe to say that until such an interest has been aroused his progress is not likely to be rapid. If, in this endeavour to popularise an admittedly unpopular subject, I have occasionally fallen into inaccuracies of expression, I can only hope that these will be kindly pointed out to me by my readers, and I promise that their suggestions shall receive my best attention in any subsequent edition.

I should like to take this opportunity of expressing my thanks to those practitioners who have already so kindly assisted me with suggestions and information. In particular are my acknowledgments due to Mr. ADAM MURRAY, F.C.A., Mr. ROGER N. CARTER, F.C.A., Mr. CHAS. E. BRADLEY, F.C.A., and the Hon. Secretaries of the various Chartered Accountants Students' Societies in Great Britain, who have supplied me with the material upon which Chapters XXII. and XXIII. are founded.

The Appendix on the Law relating to Accounts, by Mr. J. E. G. DE MONTMORENCY, B.A., LL.B., will, I trust, be found as interesting and as instructive to my readers as it has already proved to myself, and will, I venture to hope, materially help to make the present work acceptable to Lawyers as well as to Students of Accounts. The second Appendix has been added for the convenience of those who may wish to use the work as a text-book. The questions have, for the most part, been extracted from the papers set from time to time at the Examinations of the Institute of Chartered Accountants, but also comprise some that have been set by the Joint Examining Board of Chartered Accountants in Scotland, and some set by the Author at Examinations held by the Chartered Institute of Secretaries, the University of Birmingham, the London School of Economics, and other bodies. It is hoped, therefore, that they will be found of a thoroughly representative character.

LAWRENCE R. DICKSEE.

COPTHALL HOUSE, LONDON, E.C.

September 24th 1903.

CHAPTER I.

INTRODUCTION.

THE object of the present work is to combine, within the limits of a volume of reasonable size, such information with regard to the theory and practice of accounting as will enable, or at least assist, the reader to attain the standard fixed by such examinations as those of the Institute of Chartered Accountants (Final), the Society of Accountants and Auditors (Final), the University of Birmingham (Bachelor of Commerce), University of London (Bachelor of Science [Economics]), and the like. That the requisite information may' be obtained from books already published is not denied, but to obtain it from such sources would involve consulting a relatively large number of different works, from each of which the desired portion would have to be selected, while many existing publications, which are in other respects excellent, are defective by reason of not being sufficiently up-to-date to meet present requirements. From what has been said, however, it will be seen that the present volume lays no claim to absolute originality, but it is hoped that—if only on the grounds of economy, of both time and money—it will be found to meet the requirements of those who desire to obtain (without unnecessary expenditure of either commodity) a thorough knowledge of the higher branches of accounting. It is hardly to be expected that this result can be achieved in its entirety, save by those whose practical experience with the subject has been fairly considerable; but the effort has been made in the present work to study the requirements not merely of the practical man who desires further guidance and assistance in the formulation of his ideas upon a thoroughly sound theoretical basis, but also the student in accounts who, while bereft of the advantages that can be derived only from actual practice, yet finds it necessary to acquire a sound mastery of the subject as a whole.

In a work of this description, it is manifestly unnecessary to—at the waste of valuable space—weary the reader with detailed explanations upon quite elementary matters. A reasonable amount of knowledge on his part (such as might readily be obtained by a perusal of Parts I. and II. of the author's "Bookkeeping for Accountant Students") has therefore been assumed; but because it has been found that many who have arrived at this standard are yet somewhat deficient on many elementary principles of fundamental importance, some space has been devoted to the consideration of certain matters that might be regarded as not properly belonging to the study of advanced bookkeeping. These elementary questions are, however, passed over as quickly as possible, and are merely introduced for the sake of avoiding any risk of misconception as to the manner in which the more advanced problems are handled. It is hoped, therefore, that while the present work will be found sufficiently exhaustive, it will at the same time not impose too great a strain upon the patience of the advanced student.

It is perhaps desirable to add a word as to the manner in which the subject has been handled. The chapters dealing chiefly with questions of principle follow the normal lines, although numerous paragraph headings have been introduced to facilitate

B

subsequent reference. Those chapters, however, which explain actual operations in practical book-keeping are in each case illustrated by *pro formâ* problems introducing the various points to be elucidated. By this means it is hoped that an additional practical value may be given to the work.

In conclusion, it may be added that while a complete knowledge of every point mentioned is not essential to the thorough understanding of each particular section of the subject, yet to a very large extent it is impossible for the higher problems of bookkeeping to be thoroughly grasped by those who have not studied the less difficult applications of the science. It follows therefore that the fullest benefits can only be derived from each individual chapter after a careful study of all those that precede it. At the same time, it should be stated that the various chapters have been framed with a view to facilitating ready reference with regard to any particular point on which information may be sought, and it is therefore hoped that the work may be found of value to the practical man of business as well as to the student who has sufficient leisure to study the subject exhaustively.

CHAPTER II.

CAPITAL AND REVENUE.

THE proper distinction between Capital and Revenue items is one of the most important matters in connection with accurate accounting, and as time goes on, and the tendency is for business operations to become continually more complex, the importance of this distinction becomes increased rather than reduced. The reader who has been in the habit of preparing Balance Sheets and Profit and Loss Accounts from a Trial Balance will probably hardly need to be reminded that this operation consists in the sorting out of the various Ledger Balances under the two headings of "Capital" and "Revenue," the Capital items being collected together in the form of a Balance Sheet, while the Revenue items are collected into another account, which may be variously named "Trading Account," "Profit and Loss Account," "Revenue Account," &c., and which may (for purposes of convenience) be described by the generic term "Revenue Account." Simple as this operation may seem from the point of view of the practical bookkeeper, it is hardly overstating the case to say that most of the errors of principle that are perpetrated in practice arise from the lack of ability, or a lack of desire, to strictly discriminate between Capital and Revenue items ; hence the vast importance of a clear understanding upon this point. This understanding may, it is thought, be ·best acquired by dealing with the subject upon systematic lines.

EXAMPLE OF A SINGLE SHIP.

One of the most ancient (and therefore one of the simplest) modes of transacting business is through the agency of a ship. Our first example may therefore be appropriately sought in this direction. Shortly stated, the position of affairs here is that the proprietors agree to find among them a certain sum of money, which is thought sufficient for the purposes of their undertaking. The amount of money so found by them is described as the Capital of the venture, and from the point of view of the undertaking (that is to say, in the books of the ship) it is regarded as a receipt upon Capital Account. The bulk of the money so raised would be spent in acquiring the desired vessel, and the amount so expended comes under the heading of "Capital Expenditure." There will, however, be further Capital Expenditure necessary before the ship can start upon its first voyage, in thoroughly fitting it out after it leaves the builders' hands, and in placing on board the necessary stores, &c., to enable it to take the sea. At the moment that the ship has been fully equipped it may be said that Capital Expenditure ceases, and any surplus of Capital Receipts over Capital Expenditure up to that date may be regarded as the "Working Capital"—that is to say, the excess of the moneys adventured by the proprietors over and above those necessary for the equipping of their undertaking, which is deemed necessary to enable it to engage in its business operations without being unduly handicapped by want of capital. At this stage the actual trading operations commence, which will involve the receipt (on "Revenue Account") of various sums earned for freight, passage money, &c., and the expenditure incurred in the process of earning these moneys, e.g., Wages, Consumption of Stores, Coal, Port

Dues, and the like. When the voyage has been completed, and all outstanding accounts collected, or paid, as the case may be, the result (after replacing stores consumed, and the like, and bringing them up to the same level as before) will be that the available cash balance is either more or less than the original working capital. Any excess of the cash balance over the working capital will represent profit earned, and any deficiency there may be will represent loss incurred during the voyage. The problem is, from most points of view, quite simple, in that at the completion of each voyage it is possible to strike a balance of accounts, leaving practically no balances outstanding as representing uncompleted transactions. There is, however, a point that must be carefully borne in mind—namely, that this method of arriving at the profit depends for its accuracy upon the assumption that such payments have been made and charged up against Revenue as will make good any wastage that may have taken place in the original equipment of the undertaking. This wastage may be roughly divided under two headings—consumption of specific stores which may be readily replaced by the purchase of others, and the indirect operations of wear and tear and lapse of time, which detract from the value of the assets represented by Capital Expenditure, but which cannot be conveniently made good by the immediate expenditure of a corresponding sum. This latter class of indirect wastage is known as "Depreciation." The true profits of an undertaking cannot be ascertained without first of all charging against Revenue the amount of loss sustained under the heading Depreciation, but in this particular instance it is usual to ignore Depreciation, because it is thought undesirable to allow large sums of money (such as will be necessary to rehabilitate the Capital assets) to remain indefinitely in the hands of the ship's manager; but when this course is pursued, it is important to bear in mind that the Revenue Account, omitting as it does to provide for Depreciation, *does not show the true profit earned ;* while, on the other hand, the Capital assets,

being retained in the books at a figure exceeding their actual value, are *over*-stated to a corresponding extent.

ADDITIONAL CAPITAL EXPENDITURE.

The same principles apply to all other classes of undertakings, but it is rarely that they arise in quite so simple a form, because with most concerns the expenditure on Capital Account, instead of ceasing before the Revenue Account is opened, is continually being added to for the sake of extending or improving the original undertaking. Examples coming under this heading are afforded by gas works, water works, railways, and the like. In these cases Capital Expenditure and expenditure upon Revenue Account have, of necessity, to some extent to be incurred simultaneously ; but there is as a rule no difficulty in keeping the Capital Expenditure distinct from the outset, and in any case the principles already enunciated will apply. Only that expenditure which is incurred with a view to completing or perfecting the equipment of the undertaking, and thus increasing its capacity to earn revenue, may be properly charged as Capital Expenditure : all other expenditure must be debited to Revenue.

And as with these undertakings Capital Expenditure will be continually taking place, so, on the other hand, will capital assets be continually wearing out, and having to be replaced in order to keep the undertaking as a whole in a proper state of working efficiency. The cost of these replacements must in all cases be charged against Revenue, and (so far as it goes) it will take the place of provision for Depreciation. If the various assets wear out, and have to be replaced very quickly, the expenditure upon renewals will very closely approximate to the actual wastage caused by Depreciation ; in practice, however, there will always be some margin, because a certain amount of wastage must necessarily take place before expenditure can be usefully incurred upon renewals and repairs. Even in these cases, therefore, some allowance for Depreciation is necessary in addition to the actual expenditure, if the

Revenue Account is to show the true profit of the undertaking.

CAPITAL ASSETS.

From what has been stated, it will be seen that all expenditure that may properly be regarded as Capital Expenditure must be represented by more or less tangible assets, whereas nothing remains to represent expenditure that has been incurred upon Revenue Account. The expenditure under both headings is, in bookkeeping, represented by a debit balance in the Ledger, and the ultimate test of the reality of Capital Expenditure is as to whether there exists an asset which may be said to still represent the expenditure incurred.

When, however, a shrinkage in the value of assets has occurred, owing to causes outside the ordinary operations of carrying on the business, it would not be proper to debit such wastage to Revenue Account, for if such a wastage or loss as this were to be debited to Revenue Account the actual result of the trading operations would be obscured. If thought desirable, such losses of Capital may be made good by specifically allocating profits on Revenue Account for that purpose, but under no circumstances does the law require this to be done before profits are divided among the proprietors of the undertaking, and in any event it is desirable that the accounts should clearly distinguish between proper expenditure *on* Revenue Account, and such incidental losses on Capital Account as may have occurred. It thus follows that Capital assets may decrease in value without Revenue being affected in consequence. So long, however, as these assets are not realised, such shrinkage can at best be only an estimated item, and it is therefore usual to ignore it in the accounts. Hence, in accounts, there is not necessarily any very intimate connection between the actual intrinsic value of Capital assets at any given moment and the value at which they appear in the books of account. The proper basis for our present purpose may be taken to be the cost price, subject only to deduction for such Depreciation as may be properly charged against Revenue. *Per contra* estimated increases in the value of Capital assets should be likewise disregarded.

FIXED & FLOATING ASSETS.

The justification for thus ignoring fluctuations in the value of Capital assets is that these assets have been acquired, and are being permanently retained, not with a view to their being eventually realised at a profit in the ordinary course of business, but with a view to their being *used* for the purpose of enabling trading profits to be made in other ways. For example there is no fixed connection between the realisable value of a ship and its earning capacity; and in the case of a factory, its value to the undertaking depends merely upon the accommodation that it offers, and is entirely irrespective of any speculative rise or fall that may have taken place in the value of land or building materials. Similarly, the value of machinery to a business depends upon the amount of work that can be turned out, and not upon the market price of iron or steel at that particular time. For practical purposes, therefore, these fluctuations may fairly be said to be of no account, and in any event it is quite an open question whether, pending a realisation (which is not contemplated), any more reliable basis of value could be adopted than the actual cost in the first instance.

In the case, however, of assets which it is not intended to retain and utilise in the business (as, for example, Stock, Book Debts, or temporary investments), a wholly different question arises. Here, if the accounts are to be upon a sound basis, it is important not to lose sight of the fact that the whole object of the business is to convert these items into cash at the earliest possible moment, or at any moment that may be thought convenient. In every case therefore the intrinsic value at the moment is clearly a potent factor, and any shrinkage that may have taken place must consequently be regarded as a realised loss, if the accounts are to be kept upon a sound basis, and as such it must be deducted from the value of the asset and debited to Revenue. *Per contra* appreciations in the value of these floating assets might with equal propriety be credited to Revenue ; but as, pending actual realisation, there must always be a doubt as to whether any such appreciation has actually occurred, it is only prudent to postpone taking credit for the assumed profit until such time as it has been actually earned. A further argument in support of this method of treatment is afforded by the consideration that the proper time to take credit for a profit on the realisation of floating assets would certainly appear to be the time when such realisation is effected. These points will, however, be found further discussed later on.

APPRECIATION OF FLOATING ASSETS.

It has already been stated that under no circumstances should appreciation in the value of fixed assets be credited to Revenue, while appreciation in the value of floating assets should under normal circumstances not be taken credit for until actual realisation. With regard to the latter, however, a few exceptions arise. Certain assets by their nature regularly and consistently increase in value in exactly the same way (and for the same reasons)

that most assets decrease in value with equal regularity. Two examples under this heading will, it is thought, be sufficient. (1) *Reversions*, that is to say, an asset which represents the holder's title to receive a sum of money at some fixed or determinable future date. As the future date approaches, the present value of the reversion naturally increases, and, in the case of an undertaking whose regular business it is to purchase such assets, Revenue may properly be credited with the actual appreciation from time to time, provided a reasonable margin be reserved for contingencies. Life insurance policies may for this purpose be treated as reversions. (2) When the asset represents freehold or leasehold property, to the possession of which the owner will be entitled at the expiration of a tenancy under which he receives a rent less than the true annual value of the property. Here the annual appreciation in value is income as much as the rent that is actually received ; but unless a large number of similar properties are held, it is generally thought convenient to postpone taking credit for the amount of such increase until the expiration of the existing tenancy, when the capital value of the property might fairly be written up and Revenue be credited with the excess.

PROBLEM.—A capitalist purchases the freehold of a house of the annual value of £150, subject to a lease at £50 per annum, having unexpired term of five years. How much should he pay for the freehold in order to give him a return of 5 per cent. on his money, and what is the value of the property at the end of each successive year during the term of the lease ?

What is actually purchased in this case is an immediate annuity of £50 per annum (which at 5 per cent. is worth £1,000), and a reversion to a further annuity of £100 per annum, commencing 5 years hence. The value of this reversion at 5 per cent. is £1,567·052 ; the total amount to be paid for the freehold would therefore be £2,567·052, say, £2,567 1s.

The present value of a reversion of a perpetuity of £1 1s., under the 5 per cent. Tables, is as follows :—

5 Years Deferred	..	..	..	..	£15·67052
4 ,, ,,	..	..	..	..	16·45405
3 ,, ,,	..	..	..	..	17·27675
2 ,, ,,	..	..	..	..	18·14059
1 ,, ,,	..	..	..	..	19·04762

At the end of the first year, therefore, the property may be written up to the value of a reversion deferred four years, at the end of the second year to the value of a reversion deferred three years, and so on. This gives the value of the freehold property as follows :—

At Date of Purchase	..	..	..	..	..	..	..	£2,567·052
At End of First Year	..	..	..	..	..	..	..	2,645·405
,, Second Year	..	..	..	..	..	..	..	2,727·675
,, Third Year	..	..	..	..	..	..	..	2,814·059
,, Fourth Year	..	..	..	..	..	..	..	2,904·762
,, Fifth Year	..	..	..	..	..	..	..	3,000·000

NOTE.—The above calculation does not, of course, take into account whatever provision may be necessary for depreciation owing to the deterioration of the fabric of the buildings. This, however, is a separate question, and can only be determined after careful enquiry into the condition of the structure and the class of materials and workmanship employed in its erection.

SUMMARY.

To sum up the contents of this chapter, it may be stated that " Capital Receipts " are sums contributed to an undertaking, and intended to be permanently left in that undertaking for the sake of enabling it to carry on its business. " Capital Expenditure " is that expenditure *bonâ fide* incurred for the sake of acquiring, extending, or completing the equipment of the undertaking, with a view to placing it upon a revenue-earning basis, or to improving its revenue-earning capacity. " Working Capital " is the excess of " Capital Receipts " over " Capital Expenditure." " Capital Expenditure " is represented by assets—" fixed " or " floating." " Fixed Assets " are those which form a part of the permanent equipment of the undertaking, which, as such, are not intended for realisation. " Floating Assets " are those assets which in the ordinary course of business are continually changing, and which are intended either for consumption in the ordinary process of manufacture or trading operations, or for sale, and such intermediate forms (Book Debts, Bills Receivable, &c.) as they may take in the process of conversion into cash. Cash and all forms of temporary investment are also included under this heading. " Revenue Receipts " are those which properly arise out of the business operations of the undertaking—*i.e.*, earnings. Unless the business is upon a cash basis there will, however, always be some discrepancy between the actual earnings and the receipts in respect thereof, and the proper item to credit to Revenue Account will be the true earnings for the period, rather than the actual receipts in cash. Revenue Expenditure consists of all those expenses incurred in connection with the earning of Revenue, including Depreciation of Fixed and Floating Assets. There will, however, always be a difference between Revenue Expenditure and payments on Revenue Account, for (disregarding the fact that such payments may be made in advance, or may be in arrear) there will often be no cash payments to represent provision for Depreciation, unless the whole of the provision that is necessary under this heading has been made by actual renewals or repairs during the period in question. If, however, a " Sinking Fund " is created to provide for the renewal of wasting assets, provision for Depreciation will be a cash payment.

PROBLEM.—Classify the debit and credit balances of the following undertakings under their proper headings of Capital and Revenue:—

    (*a*)   A Ship,

    (*b*)   A Gas Company,

    (*c*)   A Railway Company,

    (*d*)   A Colliery,

    (*e*)   An Ordinary Commercial Undertaking.

(*a*) A SHIP.

DEBIT BALANCES.

Capital Expenditure on Fixed Assets	Capital Expenditure on Floating Assets (deficiencies in which must be made good out of Revenue)	Revenue Expenditure
Cost of Ship Cost of Structural Improvements	Coals Stores Provisions, &c. Sundry Debtors Investments Cash	Wages Port Dues Insurance Repairs and Renewals Coals, Stores, and Provisions consumed (Depreciation) Interest Dividends to Proprietors

CREDIT BALANCES.

Receipts on Capital Account—Fixed Liabilities	Receipts on Capital Account—Floating Liabilities	Receipts on Revenue Account
Moneys received from Proprietors (including Premiums) Moneys received from Holders of Debenture Stock, Mortgages and Bonds.	Outstanding Liabilities for Stores, &c., purchased, and Expenses incurred Undivided Profits Unallocated provision for Assets	Freights earned Passage-money earned Other Income

(*b*) A GAS COMPANY.

DEBIT BALANCES.

Capital Expenditure on Fixed Assets	Capital Expenditure on Floating Assets (deficiencies in which must be made good out of Revenue)	Revenue Expenditure
Lands secured Buildings, Plant, Machinery, &c. Mains, Meters, and Service Pipes Cost of promoting Special Acts	Coals Coke, Tar, and other Residual Products Sundry Stores Debtors for Gas and Residuals supplied, &c. Investments Cash	Coals and other Materials used in manufacture Wages incurred in manufacture and distribution of Gas, and lighting Repairs and Maintenance of Works, Plant, Mains and Meters General Establishment Charges Law Costs Parliamentary Charges (Oppositions) Depreciation of Leaseholds Interest Bad Debts Dividends to Proprietors

CREDIT BALANCES.

Receipts on Capital Account—Fixed Liabilities	Receipts on Capital Account—Floating Liabilities	Receipts on Revenue Account
Moneys received from Proprietors (including Premiums) Moneys received from holders of Debenture Stock, Mortgages, and Bonds	Debts due for Materials supplied and Expenses incurred Undivided Profits Unallocated Provision for Losses	Sale of Gas Rent of Meters Sale of Residual Products Rents Received Transfer Fees Other Income

(c) A RAILWAY COMPANY.

DEBIT BALANCES.

Capital Expenditure on Fixed Assets	Capital Expenditure on Floating Assets (deficiencies in which must be made good out of Revenue)	Revenue Expenditure
Expenditure on Lines open for Traffic Expenditure on Lines in course of Construction Expenditure on Rolling Stock Subscriptions to other Railways Expenditure on Docks, Steamboats, &c.	General Stores Accounts due from other Companies Accounts due from Clearing House Accounts due from Post Office Sundry Outstanding Accounts Investments Cash	Maintenance of Permanent Way, &c. Locomotive Power Carriage and Wagon Repairs Traffic Expenses General Charges Law Charges Preliminary Expenses Compensation Rates and Taxes Government Duty Interest on borrowed Money Dividends to Proprietors

CREDIT BALANCES.

Receipts on Capital Account—Fixed Liabilities	Receipts on Capital Account—Floating Liabilities	Receipts on Revenue Account
Moneys received from Proprietors (including Premiums) Moneys received from Creditors on Fixed Loans or issue of Debenture Stock (including Premiums)	Debts due to other Companies Amount due to Clearing House Sundry Liabilities for Purchases and Expenditure Temporary Loans Lloyd's Bonds Insurance Funds Undivided Profits Unallocated Provision for Losses	Receipts from Passengers, Parcels, &c. Mails Merchandise Live Stock Minerals Rents Transfer Fees Dividends on Shares in other Companies

(d) A COLLIERY COMPANY.

DEBIT BALANCES.

Capital Expenditure on Fixed Assets	Capital Expenditure on Floating Assets (deficiencies in which must be made good out of Revenue)	Revenue Expenditure
Cost of acquiring Property, Buildings, Plant and Machinery Cost of developing and opening up Property	Stores Sundry Debtors Cash Overpaid Royalties	Stores Consumed Wages of getting and handling Coal Carriage Depreciation of Rolling Stock Interest (including that paid under Hire-Purchase Agreements) Dividends to Proprietors

CREDIT BALANCES.

Receipts on Capital Account—Fixed Liabilities	Receipts on Capital Account—Floating Liabilities	Receipts on Revenue Account
Receipts from Shareholders, Debenture-holders, and Mortgagees (including Premiums)	Sundry Creditors for Goods supplied and Expenses incurred Undivided Profits Unallocated Provision for Losses	Sale of Coals Rents Transfer Fees Other Income

(e) A COMMERCIAL COMPANY.

DEBIT BALANCES.

Capital Expenditure on Fixed Assets	Capital Expenditure on Floating Assets (deficiencies in which must be made good out of Revenue)	Revenue Expenditure
Land and Buildings Plant and Machinery Fixtures, Fittings, and Furniture	Raw Materials Unfinished Goods Sundry Debtors Investments Cash	Raw Materials Consumed Expenses of Manufacture (including Wages) Expenses of distribution (including Wages) Rent, Rates, and Taxes General Establishment Charges Depreciation Interest and Discount Dividends to Proprietors

CREDIT BALANCES.

Receipts on Capital Accounts—Fixed Liabilities	Receipts on Capital Account—Floating Liabilities	Receipts on Revenue Account
Receipt from Proprietors, Debenture-holders, and Mortgagees Premiums on issue of Shares or Debentures	Outstanding Creditors Unallocated Provision for Losses Undivided Profits	Sales of Goods Discounts Transfer Fees Miscellaneous Receipts

CHAPTER III.

THE ORGANIZATION OF ACCOUNTS.

UNDER this heading may be included those arrangements which are designed to, as far as possible, ensure the accuracy and regularity of accounts in all respects. A system of accounts may be well designed to meet the requirements of any particular undertaking, and may yet fail to achieve its purpose through slackness on the part of those on whom the duty of supervision devolves. This failure may arise from the work being allowed to get into arrear, or through errors (whether inadvertent or fraudulent) being allowed to arise. Whatever the exact cause may be, the result will as a rule be the same—a loss will be experienced, and in addition the reputation of the business may suffer. The subject is therefore one of very considerable importance to all who are interested in accounts.

The designing of a proper system of accounts is, from our point of view, a purely theoretical matter: the practical adaptation of that system to the record of the transactions of the undertaking—and its adaptation upon regular and systematic lines, with a view to avoiding irregularities and losses of all kinds—comes under the heading of "Organisation," an essentially practical matter, which is now being dealt with.

It goes without saying that, however much trouble may be taken by those responsible for the record of business transactions, errors will occasionally arise. The object of a proper system of organisation is to detect these errors at the earliest possible moment, thus reducing to a minimum the inconvenience or

loss that they might occasion. Shortly stated, the only means of detecting errors of any kind is by careful checking, and a proper system of organisation will always provide for the checking of every item of work in connection with accounting, and particularly in connection with Invoices, Statements of Account, Returns, and the like, which are issued to third parties.

AUDITS, PROFESSIONAL AND "STAFF."

All such checking as that just described may, from one point of view, be regarded as auditing. Save in the case of the smallest undertakings, a distinction may very properly be made between that portion of the work upon which it is desirable to employ skilled accountants who are entirely independent of the administrative staff, and that part which (under suitable supervision) may be equally well performed by the staff itself. Many items may, in point of fact, be better checked by the staff than by independent Auditors, on account of the greater familiarity of the former with the actual facts involved. At the same time, if the system of check is to be complete, it is important that there should be a clear understanding as to what work is to be performed by each, and this is best accomplished by allowing the outside Auditor to organise the whole system of internal check. This is the more desirable, in that the experience of the Auditor will enable him to organise such a system more effectively than could be reasonably expected on the part of one who has received no special training in that direction; but, the system once organised, the duty of seeing that it is actually carried out, in precisely the same manner as was originally designed, may to a large extent be left to the chief of the counting-house.

From some points of view the matters dealt with in this chapter are intimately connected with those discussed in Chapter XVII., which deals with various classes of fraud, and the methods to be adopted for their prevention and detection. In the majority of cases where fraud has occurred, the attempt will have been made to conceal it by means of false entries, and it should be the aim of every system of internal check, or audit, to detect these falsifications at the earliest possible moment. So long, however, as this point is clearly understood the two matters may, it is thought, be most conveniently dealt with separately.

The general aim of every system of internal check is to provide for the detection of all errors in accounts, of whatsoever description, and the best means of doing so is to make at least two persons responsible for every entry that occurs, and also for the proper record of every transaction that has taken place. In order not to make undue demands upon the time of more important persons, the system must be so arranged that relatively unimportant matters are checked in detail by those occupying a comparatively subordinate position ; and, in order that the work when so arranged may be properly performed, it is important not merely that some responsible person should supervise it, and see that every detail of the system is duly carried out by the prescribed persons, but also that the duties of the various persons concerned be changed about from time to time. This latter is especially important as a safeguard against collusion. In the case of comparatively small undertakings, it is sometimes difficult to arrange matters upon this footing, on account of the smallness of the staff, or of that portion of the staff which can be relied upon for purposes of internal check. In such cases, however, it is usually practicable for the principal himself to do something in the direction indicated ; if

a proper system be formulated, this might readily be done without making undue claims upon the principal's time, and the professional audit may be so arranged as to cover the whole scheme of internal check in general terms, and to supply in detail those parts which are lacking in the staff audit. The exact point where the staff audit should leave off and the professional audit commence cannot be indicated in general terms, as the matter is to a large extent one of expediency. The professional audit must in all cases be sufficiently full to enable the Auditor to satisfy himself not merely of the general correctness of the accounts, but also of their correctness in detail ; but so long as it is sufficiently full to ensure this object, the balance of advantage lies in throwing as much responsibility as possible upon the staff audit, because (for the reasons already stated) those who are actually in touch with the transactions engaged upon are better capable of verifying the detailed records than those whose only knowledge of the transactions is such as may be gained from the records themselves.

PRO FORMA RULES.

The following is a short, and necessarily incomplete, summary of the various matters that should ordinarily be provided for when organising a set of accounts and designing a system of internal check with regard thereto. Naturally, however, it will in many cases require elaboration at one point or another.

(1) All cash received to be paid into the bank daily, a due record being kept of who is responsible for the handling of the same.

(2) No one having the handling of money should have the control of any books of account other than the corresponding Cash Book. (If practicable, the cashier should not even write up the Cash Book.)

(3) All payments, other than Petty Cash payments, to be made by cheque.

(4) The Petty Cash Book should be kept on the "Imprest" system, under the supervision of the chief cashier.

(5) No person entrusted with the receipt of moneys should be authorised to make any payments out of the monies so received by him.

(6) Counterfoil (or other) Receipt Books should be used to acknowledge all monies received.

(7) Proper vouchers should be received for all payments made. It is *not* desirable that these should be upon a uniform form supplied to the payees.

(8) All cash balances should be regularly and systematically verified daily, and a permanent record kept of the daily balances. The balance of every Bank Account should be verified at least once a week.

(9) All Ledgers should be rendered "self-balancing," and their balance frequently tested by someone in authority. The detailed postings should be checked by someone independent of the Ledger-keeper. Trade Ledgers should be balanced at least once a month, and other Ledgers at least once a quarter.

(10) An adequate system of Stock Accounts and Cost Accounts should be provided.

(11) A proper system of checking all invoices for goods received by several independent persons should be instituted, and rigorously carried out.

(12) In the same way, adequate safeguards should be taken to ensure that no goods leave the premises without being first charged up as Sales.

(13) Similar precautions should be taken with regard to the Returns and Allowances, both inwards and outwards,

(14) All trade payments should—before being made—be systematically checked, and passed by several independent persons.

(15) There should be a constant supervision of the Book Debts, and especially of those overdue, in order to ensure that no losses are incurred, through carelessness or dishonesty.

(16) In order to as far as possible guard against this, every time the Sold Ledgers are balanced a verified list of all accounts more than a certain number of days overdue should be submitted to the chief of the counting-house, and by him to one of the principals for further instructions.

(17) Special precautions should be taken with regard to all payments made by cash (*e.g.*, Wages), with a view to ensuring the accuracy with which the lists of amounts due have been compiled. Several different persons should be made individually responsible for *each* part of the work.

CONCLUSION.

It is, perhaps, desirable to again repeat that no system of organisation can be really effective which does not, in addition to making two persons responsible for everything, so systematise matters as to make it impossible for any member of the staff to make any entries whatever in the books which are not, for the time being, in his keeping. If mistakes and frauds are to be avoided, it is important that there should be no doubt as to who is responsible for the entries appearing from time to time in each book, and also as to who is responsible for the checking of those entries and the seeing that they completely record the transactions. If these very useful precautions be neglected there is practically nothing to prevent either inadvertent or fraudulent mistakes from remaining undetected.

CHAPTER IV.

METHODS OF BALANCING.

IT is assumed that the reader is fully acquainted with the general particulars of double-entry bookkeeping, and the manner in which the accuracy of the Ledger postings may be tested by the agreement of the Trial Balance. It is, however, desirable to discuss the various methods by which the balancing of a large set of books may be simplified, and also the means by which a set of books that have not been completely kept by double-entry may be balanced.

" SELF-BALANCING " LEDGERS.

Where the business is sufficiently large to render the employment of more than one Ledger desirable, it is very convenient to be possessed of some means of balancing each Ledger independently of the rest. This is desirable for two reasons: (1) Trade Ledgers should be balanced at frequent intervals, so that any mistakes that have occurred may be speedily rectified, while it is convenient that the whole set of Ledgers should be balanced so often. (2) In the event of the Trial Balances of the books as a whole not agreeing, it is a great saving of time to be able to *localise* the error in one particular Ledger, and so confine further investigation to that point.

The general principle of " Self-Balancing " Ledgers cannot be said to form part of " advanced " bookkeeping, and as, moreover, it has been fully described in the author's " Bookkeeping for Accountant Students " it is not now proposed to go over the same ground again; suffice it to say that in order to make each Ledger self-balancing it must be made to contain within itself a two-fold record

of every transaction that it covers. This, of course, involves posting to each separate Ledger numerous items which, although necessary to complete the double-entry, would not be included in that Ledger unless it *were* desired to render it self-balancing. All these additional items are (so far as possible) condensed into totals to save labour, and—having been so condensed—are posted to one general account, called the " Adjustment Account."

Where, however, there are two, or more, Ledgers, it is desirable that one of the series should contain the " key " to all the rest. It is usual to select for this purpose a Ledger kept by one of the most responsible employees—*i.e.*, either the Private Ledger or the Nominal Ledger. In this Ledger, instead of having only *one* Adjustment Account to complete the double-entry of that Ledger, a separate Adjustment Account is opened in respect of *every* other Ledger. The particular Adjustment Account selected for the posting of what may be termed the " redundant entries " being in each case the one relating to the Ledger which contains in detail the *other half* of the transaction. For example, assuming the Nominal Ledger is the one containing all the " keys," purchases are posted to the debit of this Ledger, which—unless it be self-balancing—contains no corresponding credit: to render it self-balancing the monthly totals of the Purchases are posted to the credit of an Adjustment Account, and the " Bought Ledger Adjustment Account " is selected for that purpose because the contra entry to the Purchases is posted in detail to the credit of the Bought Ledger. If there were two or more

Bought Ledgers, a separate Adjustment Account would be opened in the Nominal Ledger for each. There would, however, be no difficulty in ascertaining how much of the total purchases had been posted in detail to each separate Bought Ledger Adjustment Account, as each would have its own Bought Book, or, at all events, separate columns in the Bought Book would be appropriated to each.

The following example will suffice to clear up any doubts as to the precise application of the principles already described :—

PROBLEM.—The following Balance Sheet and Profit and Loss Account have been prepared from the books of the British Motor Car Company, Limited. These books included Bought, Sold, and Private Ledgers, each of which was " self-balancing." Show the Trial Balance of each separate Ledger as it would have appeared in the books before any provision had been made for bad and doubtful debts or depreciation :—

BALANCE SHEET, 31st December 1900.

Liabilities.	£	s	d	£	s	d	Assets.	£	s	d	£	s	d
Capital Account, 100,000							Building, Plant, Machinery,						
Shares of £1 each ...	100,000	0	0				etc....	60,000	0	0			
Less Calls in Arrear ...	462	0	0				Less Depreciation ...	1,200	0	0			
				99,538	0	0					58,800	0	0
Trade Creditors, viz :—A...	540	0	0				Debtors, viz. :—G.	47	10	0			
B...	50	0	0				H.	12	0	0			
C...	75	0	0				I.	160	10	0			
D...	920	0	0				J.	21	0	0			
E...	55	0	0				K.	110	0	0			
F...	62	0	0										
				1,702	0	0		351	0	0			
Profit and Loss Account ...				18,060	0	0	Less Provision for Bad						
							and Doubtful Debts	36	0	0			
											315	0	0
							Stock-in-Trade				45,645	0	0
							Cash				14,540	0	0
				£119,300	0	0					£119,300	0	0

Dr.   PROFIT AND LOSS ACCOUNT for the Year ended 31st December 1900.   Cr.

To Rent, Salaries, and General Expenses ...	£2,500	By Gross Profit as per Trading Account ...	£22,000
„ Directors' Fees	1,000	„ Balance from last year's Account... ...	796
„ Depreciation	1,200		
„ Bad Debts	36		
„ Balance ... ... '	18,060		
	£22,796		£22,796

THE BRITISH MOTOR CAR COMPANY, LIM. *Bought Ledger Trial Balance*, 31st December 1900.	Dr. £ s d	Cr. £ s d
A.		540 0 0
B.		50 0 0
C.		75 0 0
D.		920 0 0
E.		55 0 0
F.		62 0 0
Private Ledger Adjustment Account	1,702 0 0	
	£1,702 0 0	£1,702 0 0

THE BRITISH MOTOR CAR COMPANY, LIM. *Sold Ledger Trial Balances.* 31st December 1900.	Dr. £ s d	Cr. £ s d
G.	57 10 0	
H.	12 0 0	
I.	160 10 0	
J.	21 0 0	
K.	110 0 0	
Private Ledger Adjustment Account		351 0 0
	£351 0 0	£351 0 0

The British Motor Car Company, Lim.

Private Ledger Trial Balance, 31st December 1900.

	Dr.			Cr.		
	£	s	d	£	s	d
Share Capital Account				100,000	0	0
Sundry Shareholders	462	0	0			
Bought Ledger Adjustment Account				1,702	0	0
Sold Ledger Adjustment Account	351	0	0			
Buildings, Plant, Machinery, &c.	60,000	0	0			
Stock-in-trade	45,645	0	0			
Cash	14,540	0	0			
Rent, Salaries, and General Expenses	2,500	0	0			
Directors' Fees	1,000	0	0			
Trading Account				22,000	0	0
Profit and Loss Account ..				796	0	0
	£124,498	0	0	£124,498	0	0

THE "CONSTRUCTION" OF ADJUSTMENT ACCOUNTS.

In practice it frequently arises that it is desired to balance the various Ledgers separately, although the system of accounts has not anticipated this contingency, and no Adjustment Accounts have been provided. What has to be done in such a case is to *construct* Adjustment Accounts from the materials available. Supposing, for instance, it is desired to balance the Sold Ledger separately, and no Sold Ledger Adjustment Account exists, the procedure will be upon the following lines :—

The entries in the Sold Ledger will come under the following headings :—(1) Opening Balances, (2) Sales, (3) Sales Returns, (4) Cash, (5) Closing Balances, and probably some (or all) of the following :—(6) Interest, (7) Discount, (8) Bad Debts, (9) Bills Receivable, (10) Bills Dishonoured, (11) Transfers to other Ledgers. The Opening Balances are probably known from schedules already in existence ; if not, they must be carefully extracted, and a schedule prepared showing the total balances standing in the Ledger at the commencement of the current period. The total Sales can be readily arrived at from the Day Book, and the Sales Returns from the Returns Book. The Cash will be found upon the debit side of the Cash Book : if a separate Sold Ledger Cash Book exists (or there is a separate column for Sold Ledger items in the General Cash Book) this total can be readily arrived at, but, if not, the cash received must be analysed. The Discount will probably be the total of the "Discount" column on the debit side of the Cash Book, but care must be taken to see that no extraneous item has been included. The Bills Receivable will be the total of the Bills Receivable Book for the current period. The only items that remain to be considered are Bad Debts and Interest. These can be best arrived at by referring to the corresponding accounts in the Nominal Ledger, which will readily show the amount of Bad Debts written off and the amount of Interest charged to customers during the current period. These various figures can then be put together in the form of an Adjustment Account, and the balance shown by such an account should, of course, agree with the total of the Sold Ledger balance at the close of the period.

EXAMPLE :—

| Dr. | SOLD LEDGER ADJUSTMENT ACCOUNT. | Cr. |

	£	s	d		£	s	d
To Balances standing at commencement of current period, as per Schedule				By Cash received, as per analysis of Cash Book ..			
„ Sales, as per Day Book Totals				„ Discounts allowed, as per Cash Book			
„ Bills returned, as per analysis of Bills Received Account				„ Returns, as per Returns Book .. .. '			
„ Interest, as per Interest Account				„ Bills receivable, as per Bills Received Book ..			
„ Transfers from other Ledgers				„ Transfers to other Ledgers			
„ Difference in Books (if any)				„ Bad Debts, as per Bad Debts Account			
				„ Difference in Books (if any)			
				„ Balances standing at close of current period, as per Schedule			
	£				£		

BALANCING SINGLE=ENTRY BOOKS.

In many cases the same course can with advantage be pursued, even in connection with Ledgers that have only been kept by single-entry; but in some cases it will be found to be impracticable, as, for instance, when the Bought Ledger has been posted up direct from invoices, which are either filed away or pasted into a Guard Book in such a manner that it is practically impossible to add them. In such cases the best course to pursue is to call back the postings *from* the Ledger into the various subsidiary books so far as they go. If the Cash be called back into the Cash Book before the Private and Nominal Ledgers have been checked, it becomes a comparatively simple matter to extract from the Cash Book the total of the Bought Ledger Cash, for all that has to be done is to extract from the Cash Book the items upon the credit side that have been ticked off against the Bought Ledger. The Bills Payable and Discounts can be ticked off in the same manner, and there will still remain unticked in the Bought Ledger the Purchases and Purchase Returns. It is then necessary to go through the Bought Ledger, page by page, and extract therefrom all the items that have not been ticked. Probably the only unticked items on the debit side will be Returns, and the only unticked items upon the credit side Purchases; but care must be taken to separate any special items, so that they may be taken out in a separate total. This last remark applies especially to transfers from (or to) other Ledgers, seeing that these figures will also be required to assist in the balancing of those other Ledgers.

TABULATING THE LEDGERS.

When the number of accounts in any Ledger is not very numerous, but the postings to the Ledgers include a great number of different classes of items, it is sometimes more convenient to go straight through the Ledger and "tabulate" all the entries appearing upon each account. The following example clearly illustrates what is meant in this connection. Care must, however, be taken to see that the totals of the various analytical columns agree with the corresponding totals of "Goods," "Cash," "Discount," &c., as otherwise, although the Ledger may itself balance, it cannot be grafted upon the other Ledgers so as to enable them to balance as a whole.

PROBLEM.—Given a set of books kept by single-entry, with instructions to prove their accuracy by double-entry (but not by creating a new set of books), how would you proceed? Deal in the manner you suggest with the following accounts :—

JOHN SMITH

1900				£	s	d	1900				£	s	d
Nov. 1.	To Balance	..	..	..	7	10	0	Nov. 16.	By Cheque	..	..	..	17	0	0
,, 10.	,, Goods	..	..	..	10	0	0	,, 16.	,, Allowance to Returns	..	..	2	0	0
,, 11.	,, Carriage	..	..	..	1	10	0	,, 30.	,, Goods	..	..	..	25	0	0
,, 30.	,, Bill	..	..	..	20	0	0							

PETER BROWN.

					£	s	d						£	s	d
Nov. 2.	To Cheque	..	..	..	3	0	0	Nov. 1.	By Balance	..	..	..	13	0	0
,, 7.	,, do.	..	..	..	5	0	0								
,, 1.	,, Returns	..	..	..	6	0	0								

THOMAS JONES.

					£	s	d						£	s	d
Nov. 10.	To Goods	..	..	..	5	0	0	Nov. 11.	By Cheque	..	..	..	5	0	0
,, 12.	,, Cheque returned	..	..	5	0	0									
,, 14.	,, Charges	..	..	..	1	1	0								

MATTHEW SMITH.

					£	s	d						£	s	d
Nov. 1.	To Balance	..	..	..	60	0	0	Nov. 29.	By Acceptance	..	..	..	150	0	0
,, 10.	,, Goods	..	..	..	30	10	0								
,, 10.	,, Carriage	..	..	..	1	10	0								
,, 29.	,, Cheque	..	..	..	60	0	0								

GEORGE ROBINSON.

					£	s	d						£	s	d
Nov. 6.	To Cheque	..	..	..	45	0	0	Nov. 1.	By Balance	..	..	..	90	0	0
,, 8.	,, Charges	..	..	..	4	10	0								
,, 15.	,, Cheque	..	..	..	30	0	0								
,, 20.	,, Goods	..	..	..	100	0	0								

ARTHUR SHAW.

					£	s	d						£	s	d
Nov. 10.	To Goods	..	..	..	70	0	0	Nov. 16.	By Returns	..	..	..	22	0	0
,, 10.	,, Carriage	..	..	..	7	0	0	,, 16.	,, Allowance	..	..	..	10	0	0
,, 10.	,, Charges	..	..	..	2	0	0	,, 30.	,, Cheque	..	..	..	47	0	0

The Ledger Accounts should be " tabulated " as shown upon the following page.

Cr.

Name	Balance 1/11/00 £ s d	Cash £ s d	Returns & Allowances £ s d	Goods £ s d	Bills £ s d	Balance (Dr.) 30/11/00 £ s d	Total £ s d
J. Smith		17 0 0	2 0 0	25 0 0			44 0 0
P. Brown	13 0 0					1 0 0	14 0 0
T. Jones		5 0 0				6 1 0	11 1 0
M. Smith					150 0 0	2 0 0	152 0 0
G. Robinson	90 0 0					89 10 0	179 10 0
A. Shaw		47 0 0	32 0 0				79 0 0
	£103 0 0	£69 0 0	£34 0 0	£25 0 0	£150 0 0	£98 11 0	£479 11 0

Dr.

Name	Balance 1/11/00 £ s d	Goods £ s d	Carriage £ s d	Bills £ s d	Cash £ s d	Returns & Allowances £ s d	Charges £ s d	Balance 30/11/00 (Cr.) £ s d	Total £ s d
J. Smith	7 10 0	10 0 0	1 10 0	20 0 0				5 0 0	44 0 0
P. Brown					8 0 0	6 0 0			14 0 0
T. Jones		5 0 0			5 0 0		1 1 0		11 1 0
M. Smith	60 0 0	30 10 0	1 10 0		60 0 0				152 0 0
G. Robinson		100 0 0			75 0 0		4 10 0		179 10 0
A. Shaw		70 0 0	7 0 0				2 0 0		79 0 0
	£67 10 0	£215 10 0	£10 0 0	£20 0 0	£148 0 0	£6 0 0	£7 11 0	£5 0 0	£479 11 0

PROFIT AND LOSS ACCOUNTS · BY SINGLE-ENTRY.

Occasionally it happens that it is desired to compile an account in the form of a Trading and Profit and Loss Account, while (on account of the great expense and trouble involved) it is deemed inexpedient to balance the books by double-entry in the manner explained in the preceding paragraphs. Such a state of affairs often arises in connection with appeals against assessments for Income Tax, when the Commissioners require a Profit and Loss Account to be produced. But the system now about to be explained cannot be recommended for any other purpose, inasmuch as although it shows results in the *form* of a Profit and Loss Account, the account when prepared is—unlike Profit and Loss Accounts compiled by double-entry—no check whatever upon the accuracy of the bookkeeping.

Shortly stated, the system consists of analysing the cash into Cash Received from customers, Cash paid for Goods, Business Expenditure under various convenient headings, and other Special Items, so that the analysis as a whole may be absolutely agreed with the Cash Book. Stock must, of course, be taken at the commencement and end of the period, or if the opening stock is unknown it must be estimated upon the best available basis, and the accuracy of the resulting account will be entirely dependent upon the accuracy of this estimate. Assuming, however, that the opening and closing Stocks are known, the Sales are arrived at by adding to the Cash received from customers the closing Sold Ledger Balances and deducting the opening Sold Ledger Balances; the figure of Purchases is obtained by adding the closing Bought Ledger Balances to the Cash paid for goods, and deducting therefrom the opening Bought Ledger Balances, while in the same manner the various items of Business Expenditure are adjusted by outstandings at the opening and close of the period, so as to obtain the Expenditure incurred during the current period, whether actually paid or not. These

C 2

figures being arrived at, they are put together in the form of a Profit and Loss Account in the usual way.

The following example gives such a "con-structed" Trading and Profit and Loss Account in tabular form. It need hardly be stated, however, that only the right-hand column upon each side would be submitted to the Income Tax Commissioners.

Dr.   TRADING AND PROFIT AND LOSS ACCOUNT, for the Year ended 31st December 1901.   Cr.

	Cash Paid during 1901	Out-standing 31 Dec. 1901	Total	Out-standing 1 Jan. 1901	Net Total		Cash Received during 1901	Out-standing 31 Dec. 1901	Total	Out-standing 1 Jan. 1901	Net Total
	£ s d	£ s d	£ s d	£ s d	£ s d		£ s d	£ s d	£ s d	£ s d	£ s d
To Stock 1/1/01 ..	..		..	..	8,000 0 0	By Sales .. ..*	21,000 0 0	3,835 0 0	24,885 0 0	4,885 0 0	20,000 0 0
„ Purchases ..	9,300 0 0	7,000 0 0	16,300 0 0	6,800 0 0	9,500 0 0	„ Stock, 31/12/01	..	..	..	..	8,550 0 0
„ Wages ..	6,070 0 0	150 0 0	6,220 0 0	120 0 0	6,100 0 0						
„ Carriage and Freight ..	1,170 0 0	180 0 0	1,350 0 0	150 0 0	1,200 0 0						
„ Gross Profit ..	..	..	..	..	3,750 0 0						
					£ 28,550 0 0						£ 28,550 0 0
To Rent, &c. ..	300 0 0	75 0 0	375 0 0	75 0 0	300 0 0	By Gross Profit ..	..	..	..	..	3,750 0 0
„ Travelling Expenses	450 0 0	..	450 0 0	..	450 0 0						
„ Trade Expenses	480 0 0	50 0 0	530 0 0	30 0 0	500 0 0						
„ Discounts ..	255 0 0	122 0 0	377 0 0	97 0 0	280 0 0						
„ Bad Debts ..	200 0 0	..	..	..	200 0 0						
„ Net Profit ..	..	..	..	..	2,020 0 0						
	£ 18,525 0 0			£	3,750 0 0		£ 21,000 0 0			£	3,750 0 0

Dr.   CASH ANALYSIS   Cr.

	£ s d		£ s d
To Balance, 1 January 1901 ..	1,225 0 0	By Payments for Goods ..	9,300 0 0
„ Receipts from Customers ..	20,545 0 0	„ „ Wages ..	6,070 0 0
		„ „ Carriage ..	1,170 0 0
		„ „ Rent ..	300 0 0
		„ „ Travelling Expenses ..	450 0 0
		„ „ Trade Expenses	480 0 0
		„ Drawings	2,400 0 0
		„ Balance, 31 December 1901	1,600 0 0
	£ 21,770 0 0		£ 21,770 0 0

* Note :—The Discounts allowed and Bad Debts written off must be added to the cash actually received (£20,545) to arrive at this item, so as to arrive at the total amount by which the debits to the Sold Ledger have been reduced during the year.

CHAPTER V.

BRANCH ACCOUNTS, ETC.

THE system of rendering each separate Ledger of a set of books "self-balancing" by means of Adjustment Accounts is, it will be remembered, that each Self-balancing Ledger completes the double entry of every transaction therein recorded, and so contains within itself all the materials for a Trial Balance of its own. The sub-division of the Ledger is in all cases dictated by convenience; but, as has already been said under the head of "Balancing," the division ordinarily follows some classification of the nature of the transactions. Where, however, a business is carried on in two or more departments, it is sometimes found convenient to make a sub-division according to these departments, so that the Ledgers might be divided into "Head Office," "Department A," "Department B," &c., instead of into the more general divisions of "Private Ledger," "Sold Ledger," "Bought Ledger," &c. It will be readily perceived, however, that whatever the system of dividing up the transactions may be, it is still quite easy to make each Ledger self-balancing by means of Adjustment Accounts.

BRANCH ACCOUNTS.

It therefore follows that if an undertaking has a branch away from the Head Office, and yet the whole of the bookkeeping is done *at* the Head Office, there is no difficulty in keeping all the transactions of the Branch in a separate Ledger at the Head Office, in making that separate Ledger self-balancing, and in incorporating the results of the Branch into the accounts periodically prepared in connection with the undertaking, as a whole. This point being grasped, it will be seen that it is really quite immaterial *where* the Branch Ledger, and its various subsidiary books, are kept. These Branch books might just as well be kept at the Branch itself, if such a course were equally convenient, and it makes no difference whatever to the system of bookkeeping where the books of the Branch (or, for that matter, of any Branch) are kept. They all form part of *one system* of bookkeeping, and by means of the Adjustment Accounts work into the Head Office books, just as though all the Ledgers were kept at the Head Office.

When the Ledgers are kept at the Branches, it is, however, usual for the Adjustment Account in the Branch Ledger to be called "Head Office Account," and for the various Adjustment Accounts in the Head Office books to be identified with the various Branches. But this is only a variation of name, and involves no new principle. Another variation that frequently occurs, which also is dictated solely by convenience, is that remittances passing from the Head Office to the Branch, and from the Branch to the Head Office, are generally posted in both Ledgers to a separate Remittance Account, instead of being posted direct to the Adjustment Account, so that no entries whatever take place in the Adjustment Account except when the books are periodically balanced and closed. This last-named modification is by no means always observed, but it will be found particularly convenient when dealing with foreign branches where questions of exchange arise.

The following example, which deals (in totals) with the transactions for six months of an undertaking carrying on business at three branches, while the main accounts are kept at the Head Office, further illustrates the principle already described.

PROBLEM.—The Wholesale Provision Company has a number of Retail Branches which are supplied from the Depôt, but they keep their own Sales Ledgers, receive Cash against Ledger Accounts, and pay in the whole of their Cash every day to Head Office. They send out their own Statements of Accounts monthly. All Wages and Branch Expenses are drawn by cheque from Head Office on the imprest system.

From the following particulars, supplied by each Branch, show the Branch Accounts in the Head Office Books, and then incorporate the whole into one General Trial Balance and Profit and Loss Account.

	A. £	B. £	C. £
Six Months' Sales to 30th June 1901	2,700	2,600	2,300
Return Inwards	20	24	16
Allowance to Customers	5	4	6
Cash received on Ledger Accounts	2,380	2,400	2,000
R. M. Sales	1,420	1,250	1,300
Stock at commencement	540	480	500
Stock at end	620	580	480
Debtors, January 1st 1901	1,250	1,200	1,100
Debtors, June 30th 1901	1,530	1,262	1,378
Bad Debts	15	10	—
Goods received from Depôt, less Returns	2,120	2,060	2,000
Rent and Taxes paid	80	70	75
Wages and Sundry Expenses	380	356	350

ACCOUNTS IN HEAD OFFICE BOOKS.

Dr.   "A." BRANCH ACCOUNT.   Cr.

1901		£ s d	£ s d	1901		£ s d	£ s d
Jan. 1	To Balance, viz. :—			June 30	By Cash—Ledger Accounts		2,380 0 0
	Debtors	1,250 0 0		"	" " R. M. S.		1,420 0 0
	Stock	540 0 0		"	" Balance down, viz. :—		
			1,790 0 0		Debtors	1,530 0 0	
June 30	" Goods		2,120 0 0		Stock	620 0 0	
	" Cash, Rates		80 0 0				2,150 0 0
	" Do. Wages		380 0 0				
	" Profit transferred to Profit and Loss Account		1,580 0 0				
			£5,950 0 0				£5,950 0 0
July 1	To Balance down, viz. :—						
	Debtors	1,530 0 0					
	Stock	620 0 0					
			2,150 0 0				

Dr.   "B." BRANCH ACCOUNT.   Cr.

1901		£ s d	£ s d	1901		£ s d	£ s d
Jan. 1	To Balance, viz. :—			June 30	By Cash—Ledger Accounts		2,400 0 0
	Debtors	1,200 0 0		"	" " R. M. S.		1,250 0 0
	Stock	480 0 0		"	" Balance down, viz. :—		
			1,680 0 0		Debtors	1,362 0 0	
June 30	" Goods		2,060 0 0		Stock	580 0 0	
	" Cash—Rates		70 0 0				1,942 0 0
	" Do. Wages		356 0 0				
	" Profit transferred to Profit and Loss Account		1,426 0 0				
			£5,592 0 0				£5,592 0 0
July 1	To Balance down, viz. :—						
	Debtors	1,362 0 0					
	Stock	580 0 0					
			1,942 0 0				

Dr.   "C." BRANCH ACCOUNT.   *Cr.*

1901		£ s d	£ s d	1901		£ s d	£ s d
Jan. 1	To Balance, viz. :—			June 30	By Cash—Ledger Accounts ..	..	2,000 0 0
	Debtors	1,100 0 0		"	" " " R. M. S.	..	1,300 0 0
	Stock	500 0 0	1,600 0 0	"	" Balance down, viz. :—		
June 30	" Goods	..	2,000 0 0		Debtors	1,378 0 0	
"	" Cash—Rates	..	75 0 0		Stock	480 0 0	1,858 0 0
"	" Do. Wages	..	350 0 0				
"	" Profit transferred to Profit and Loss Account	..	1,133 0 0				
			£5,158 0 0				£5,158 0 0
July 1	To Balance down, viz. :—						
	Debtors .. .. :— ..	1,378 0 0					
	Stock	480 0 0	1,858 0 0				

Dr.   CAPITAL ACCOUNT.   *Cr.*

		£ s d	£ s d	1901		£ s d	£ s d
			•	Jan. 1	By Balance, made up as follows :—		
					A. Branch	1,790 0 0	
					B. "	1,680 0 0	
					C. "	1,600 0 0	
					Stock at Head Office	6,180 0 0	11,250 0 0

Dr.   CASH ACCOUNT.   *Cr.*

1901		£ s d	£ s d	1901		£ s d	£ s d
June 30	To A Branch—Ledger Accounts ..	2,380 0 0		June 30	By A. Branch—Rates	80 0 0	
"	" " " . R. M. Sales ..	1,420 0 0	3,800 0 0	"	" B. " "	70 0 0	
"	" B " Ledger Accounts ..	2,400 0 0		"	" C. " "	75 0 0	225 0 0
"	" " " " R. M. Sales ..	1,250 0 0	3,650 0 0	"	" A. " Wages	380 0 0	
"	" C " Ledger Accounts ..	2,000 0 0		"	" B. " "	356 0 0	
"	" " " " R. M. Sales ..	1,300 0 0	3,300 0 0	"	" C. " "	350 0 0	1,086 0 0
			£10,750 0 0	"	" Balance down	..	9,439 0 0
July 1	To Balance down	..	9,439 0 0				£10,750 0 0

Dr.   GOODS ACCOUNT.   *Cr.*

1901		£ s d	£ s d	1901		£ s d	£ s d
Jan. 1	To Stock, Balance on hand ..	..	6,180 0 0	June 30	By A. Branch	..	2,120 0 0
			£6,180 0 0	"	" B. "	..	2,060 0 0
				"	" C. "	..	2,000 0 0
							£6,180 0 0

| Dr. | | PROFIT AND LOSS ACCOUNT. | | Cr. |

	£ s d	£ s d		£ s d	£ s d
			By Transfer from Branch A.	1,580 0 0	
			" " " " B.	1,426 0 0	
			" " " " C.	1,133 0 0	
					4,139 0 0

TRIAL BALANCE, 30th June 1901.

	Dr. £ s d	Cr. £ s d
Branch A.	2,150 0 0	
" B.	1,942 0 0	
" C.	1,858 0 0	
Cash	9,439 0 0	
Capital		11,250 0 0
Profit and Loss Account		4,139 0 0
	£15,389 0 0	£15,389 0 0

Note.—For the sake of simplicity Head Office Transactions have been excluded, so far as is possible, consistently with completing the double-entry record.

A more elaborate example, showing how the accounts of the Head Office, a Factory, and two Trading Branches are combined, is instanced by the following example, at the foot of which appears the combined Balance Sheet and Profit and Loss Account in the form in which they would probably be presented to shareholders.

PROBLEM.—The X. Y. Z. Manufacturing Company, Limited, has a share capital of £75,000 in 7,500 shares of £10 each, all issued and fully paid. It manufactures goods for sale at its two Branches (here referred to as A. and B. respectively), which sell goods of the Company's manufacture only. From the annexed Trial Balance of the books at the Head Office (where the private or general books are kept) and at the Factory and Branches, construct an Account to show respectively the result of the manufacturing and the gross profit at each Branch, also a Balance Sheet.

NOTES.

The Stocks on the 31st December 1898 were :—

						£ s d
Factory	...	...	...	...	...	...	9,177 5 7
Branch A	...	...	...	...	...	...	4,590 3 8
" B	...	...	...	...	...	...	1,922 5 5

Allow depreciation for one year to 31st December 1898 on the following items of the 1st January 1898 at the rates indicated :—

Factory Machinery, etc.	...	...	...	...	...	10 per cent.
Branch Fixtures, etc.	...	...	...	...	...	5 "

(No depreciation to be written off Head Office Furniture, etc.).

THE X·Y·Z. MANUFACTURING COMPANY, LIMITED.—TRIAL BALANCE, 31st December 1898.

Dr.	Head Office. £ s d	Factory. £ s d	Branch A. £ s d	Branch B. £ s d
Freehold Premises—				
Factory	50,000 0 0			
Branch A.	10,000 0 0			
,, B.	10,000 0 0			
Goodwill	30,000 0 0			
Machinery, Fixtures, Furniture, &c., as at 1st January 1898—				
Head Office	500 0 0			
Factory	7,500 0 0			
Branch A.	2,000 0 0			
,, B.	1,500 0 0			
Bankers	6,790 1 6			
Cash Balance ..	16 2 6	135 9 2	89 3 2	58 1 8
Stocks (1st January 1898) ..		10,216 5 9	3,218 1 6	2,190 6 7
Purchases (Net)		76,516 2		
Wages		41,316 2 8		
Factory Manager's Salary ..		1,000 0 0		
Salaries and Wages ..			3,516 9 6	3,022 3 4
Carriage to Branches ..		2,517 6 9		
Rates and Taxes ..		316 2 9	569 7 6	452 9 2
Salaries and Office Expenses	3,519 6 8			
Sundry Expenses		517 6 8	3,017 9 2	1,869 4 6
Goods from Factory ..			75,267 3 2	45,350 0 2
Bad Debts			679 8 1	1,029 2 2
Debtors			9,620 2 9	5,730 2 3
Factory (Current Account)	2,333 1 11			
Branch B. do. ..	3,672 3 10			
Head Office do.			4,914 3 3	
Income Tax	650 0 0			
Directors' Fees	1,500 0 0			
Auditors' Fees	105 0 0			
Debenture Interest ..	2,000 0 0			
	£132,085 16 5	£132,534 16 6	£100,891 8 1	£59,701 9 10

Cr.	Head Office. £ s d	Factory. £ s d	Branch A. £ s d	Branch B. £ s d
Share Capital	75,000 0 0			
Debentures, 4 per cent. ..	50,000 0 0			
Creditors..	550 10 0	9,584 11 3	176 7 6	359 2 6
Goods to Branch A. ..		75,267 3 2		
Do. B. ..		45,350 0 2		
Sales			100,715 0 7	55,670 3 6
Profit and Loss (Balance of previous year's Profit)	1,621 3 2			
Head Office (Current Account)		2,333 1 11		3,672 3 10
Branch A. (Current Account)	4,914 3 3			
	£132,085 16 5	£132,534 16 6	£100,891 8 1	£59,701 9 10

Dr.   MANUFACTURING AND TRADING ACCOUNT, for the Year ended 31st December 1898.   Cr.

	FACTORY £ s d	BRANCH A. £ s d	BRANCH B. £ s d	TOTAL £ s d		FACTORY £ s d	BRANCH A. £ s d	BRANCH B. £ s d	TOTAL £ s d
To Stock, 1st Jan. 1898 ..	10,216 5 9	3,218 1 6	2,190 6 7	15,624 13 10	By Sales ..	120,617 3 4	100,715 0 7	55,670 3 6	156,385 4 1
„ Purchases ..	76,516 2 9	75,267 3 2	45,350 0 2	76,516 2 9	„ Stock, 31st Dec. 1898	9,177 5 7	4,590 3 8	1,922 5 5	15,689 14 8
„ Wages and Salaries ..	42,316 2 8	3,516 9 6	3,022 3 4	48,854 15 6					
„ Gross profit carried down ..	745 17 9	23,303 10 1	7,029 18 10	31,079 6 8					
	£129,794 8 11	£105,305 4 3	£57,592 8 11	£172,074 18 9		£129,794 8 11	£105,305 4 3	£57,592 8 11	£172,074 18 9
To Carriage ..	2,517 6 9	..	..	2,517 6 9	By Gross profit brought down ..	745 17 9	23,303 10 1	7,029 18 10	31,079 6 8
„ Rates and Taxes ..	316 2 9	569 7 6	452 9 2	1,337 19 5	„ Balance, being loss for the year..	3,354 18 5			
„ Sundry Expenses .	517 6 8	3,017 9 2	1,869 4 6	5,404 0 4					
„ Bad Debts .	..	679 8 1	1,029 2 2	1,708 10 3					
„ Depreciation	750 0 0	100 0 0	75 0 0	925 0 0					
„ Balance, being profit for the year	..	18,937 5 4	3,604 3 0	19,186 9 11					
	£4,100 16 2	£23,303 10 1	£7,029 18 10	£31,079 6 8		£4,100 16 2	£23,303 10 1	£7,029 18 10	£31,079 6 8

BALANCE SHEET, 31st December 1898.

LIABILITIES.

	HEAD OFFICE £ s d	FACTORY £ s d	BRANCH A. £ s d	BRANCH B. £ s d	TOTAL £ s d
Share Capital	75,000 0 0				75,000 0 0
Debentures	50,000 0 0				50,000 0 0
Creditors	550 10 0	9,584 11 3	176 7 6	359 2 6	10,670 11 3
Current Accounts	4,814 3 3	3,083 1 11	..	3,747 3 10	..
Profit and Loss Account	..	..	18,937 5 4	3,604 3 0	13,033 6 5
	£130,364 13 3	£12,667 13 2	£19,113 12 10	£7,710 9 4	£148,703 17 8

ASSETS.

	HEAD OFFICE £ s d	FACTORY £ s d	BRANCH A. £ s d	BRANCH B. £ s d	TOTAL £ s d
Premises	70,000 0 0				70,000 0 0
Goodwill	30,000 0 0				30,000 0 0
Machinery, &c.	10,575 0 0				10,575 0 0
Stock	..	9,177 5 7	4,590 3 8	1,922 5 5	15,689 14 8
Debtors	..	..	9,620 2 9	5,730 2 3	15,350 5 0
Cash at bank	6,790 1 6			..	6,790 1 6
Cash in hand	16 2 6	135 9 2	89 3 2	58 1 8	298 16 6
Current Accounts	6,830 5 9		4,814 3 3		..
Profit and Loss Account	6,153 3 6	3,354 18 5			..
	£130,364 13 3	£12,667 13 2	£19,113 12 10	£7,710 9 4	£148,703 17 8

Note.—In practice it would be more convenient for the Machinery Accounts to be kept in the books of the respective branches, thus avoiding the necessity of making the necessary adjustments for depreciation through the Current Accounts.

SUMMARISED BALANCE SHEET, 31st December 1898.

Liabilities.	£ s d	£ s d	Assets.	£ s d	£ s d
Capital Account (7,500 shares of £10 each, fully paid up)	..	75,000 0 0	Goodwill	..	30,000 0 0
Debentures	..	50,000 0 0	Premises	..	70,000 0 0
Creditors	..	10,670 11 3	Machinery, Fixtures, Furniture, &c. ..	..	10,575 0 0
Profit and Loss Account :—			Stock-in-Trade	..	15,689 14 8
Balance from last Account	1,621 3 2		Debtors	..	15,350 5 0
Net Profit for the Year (as per Profit and Loss Account)	11,412 3 3		Cash at Bank	6,790 1 6	
		13,033 6 5	„ in hand	298 16 6	
					7,088 18 0
		£148,703 17 8			£148,703 17 8

Dr. SUMMARISED PROFIT AND LOSS ACCOUNT, for the Year ended 31st December 1898. *Cr.*

	£ s d		£ s d
To Head Office Salaries and Office Expenses	3,519 6 8	By Gross Profit	19,186 9 11
„ Income Tax	650 0 0		
„ Directors' Fees	1,500 0 0		
„ Auditor's Fees	105 0 0		
„ Debenture Interest	2,000 0 0		
„ Balance, being Net Profit for the Year	11,412 3 3		
	£19,186 9 11		£19,186 9 11

FOREIGN BRANCHES.

The method of recording the transactions occurring at various Branches of the same business having now been described, there remain to be considered those points which must be borne in mind in connection with the application of this principle to the accounts of a Branch situated abroad, where the transactions (or the majority of them) naturally take place in the currency of that country, and not in English money.

If the exchange value of the foreign currency never varied, the problem would, of course, be a most simple one, as in that case a certain number of dollars, francs, &c., would always represent the same amount expressed in sterling; but, as a matter of fact, there is no such fixed exchange value, and indeed differences of exchange arise in practice in connection with remittances between Great Britain and its dependencies abroad where the English coinage is employed. These latter differences, however, relate solely to remittances, and may therefore be treated as being merely the commission charged (or allowed) by bankers for forwarding money to a distant place, and may be conveniently treated in the books as ordinary cash discounts, without otherwise disturbing the system already described.

In the case of foreign currencies, however, the position is different. The essence of the problem is that while profits are, for the most part, earned in one currency, they have to be distributed among shareholders (or partners) in another; while the working capital of the undertaking (or the bulk of it) is, for the time being, invested in assets which are only realisable in the foreign currency. Add to these the facts that the rate of exchange is frequently altering, and sometimes varies within very considerable limits, and the further fact that the intrinsic value of the foreign currency is often far less than even its exchange value, and it will be seen that the problem is one that requires the most careful consideration, if it is to be treated so that the accounts may accurately show the position of affairs.

In the majority of cases it will be found that while the proprietors reside in Great Britain, and profits have to be divided there, the bulk of the fixed and floating assets are held in a foreign country; while—with the exception of such liabilities as debentures, mortgages, &c.—most of the debts of the undertaking would be due in the foreign country and payable in foreign currency. The undertaking itself, however, is a British one; and the accounts which are required to show its position from time to time have to be submitted in British currency. Very little consideration will suffice to show that the method so ordinarily adopted of converting the Foreign Trial Balance, and incorporating it in the Head Office books, at a uniform rate of exchange cannot in the nature of things produce correct results.

For instance, with Anglo-Indian undertakings it is common practice to regard the rupee as being worth 1s. 6d., and to convert the Indian Trial Balance at this assumed rate of exchange. The result is that while fixed assets (which might properly be brought into the accounts at cost, less depreciation) are probably upheld at a considerably lower figure, debts due to the undertaking and payable in rupees, together with any cash balances in India, are stated in the accounts at a figure considerably in excess of the amount that could possibly be realised in sterling if they could be all collected and the total cash (in rupees) remitted home. While, *per contra*, the local liabilities are stated at a sterling figure in excess of the amount that would have to be sent out from home in order to extinguish them. This system is also equally misleading in connection with the Trading and Profit and Loss Accounts, seeing that all the Revenue items—*i.e.*, the aggregate of the transactions representing income and expenditure during the current period—are stated at amounts in excess of the actual value in English money of these transactions. It will thus be seen that by this method fixed assets are probably under-stated, liabilities are over-stated, floating assets are under-stated, and the amount of all Revenue items is exaggerated. Under some circumstances it may so happen that the various items of assets and liabilities so balance each other that the aggregate result is approximately, if not actually correct; but it can only be quite by chance that such a result should be produced. The general custom is to provide for the admitted inaccuracy of the result as a whole by a general Reserve to cover the loss on exchange. This may, of course, answer the purpose of preventing the final figure of net profit being over-stated, and so dividends being paid out of Capital; but it must be clear that, whatever the advantages of the system on the score of simplicity, it is in its nature quite inaccurate and unworthy of adoption, except perhaps in connection with isolated transactions undertaken by concerns that do not habitually trade abroad.

The only system that can give really reliable and accurate results is one that recognises that in the case of such undertakings the foreign currency, instead of being a definite expression of value, is only the "medium" temporarily employed at the Branch for the record of the transactions in such a form that they can be afterwards considered upon their respective merits by the Head Office when the Foreign Trial Balance is periodically remitted home.

PROBLEM.—Explain how the following Trial Balance of the books of a Branch in New York should be incorporated in the Head Office Accounts :—

TRIAL BALANCE, 31st December 1901.

Head Office Account	..	..	..	..	..		$20,000
Remittance Account	..	..	..	..	..	$5,000	
Cash	..	..	..	..	..	4,260	
Debtors	..	..	..	..	..	7,500	
Creditors	..	..	..	..	..		1,000
Fixtures and Fittings	..	..	..	..	..	1,740	
Stock (on 1st January 1901)	..	..	..	..	..	4,650	
Purchases	..	..	..	..	..	16,210	
Sales	..	..	..	..	..		28,430
Trade Expenses	..	..	..	..	..	4,600	
Discounts	..	..	..	..	..		250
Bills Receivable	..	..	..	..	..	5,720	
						$49,680	$49,680

Stock on 31st December 1901, $4,800.

Assume that rate of exchange on 31st December 1901 is 5, that the average for the year is 4·98, and that the rate on 1st January 1901 (and before) is 5·05.

In the Head Office Books the following balances appear :—

New York Branch	..	..	..	..	..	£3,960 7 10 *debit*
Remittance Account..	..	..	..	..	..	1,004 0 0 *credit*

First convert the dollars into sterling; fixed assets at same rate as before; floating assets and liabilities at current rate; Revenue items at average rate ; the remittances at actual rate; the Adjustment Account at same rate as before (=figure in Head Office Books) :—

NEW YORK TRIAL BALANCE,
31st December 1901.

	£ s d	£ s d
Head Office Account		3,960 7 10
Remittance Account (amount realised)	1,004 0 0	
Cash	852 0 0	
Debtors	1,500 0 0	
Creditors		200 0 0
Fixtures and Fittings	344 11 1	
Stock (1st January 1901)	920 15 10	
Purchases	3,255 0 5	
Sales		5,708 16 8
Trade Expenses	923 15 8	
Discounts		50 4 0
Bills Receivable	1,144 0 0	
Difference in Exchange		24 14 6
	£9,944 3 0	£9,944 3 0

Stock (31st December 1901), £960.

Then pass the following Journal entries in the Head Office Books:—

JOURNAL, 1901.

31st December.				£ s d	£ s d
Remittance Account ..	..	..	..	1,004 0 0	
To New York Branch Account	..	..	..	..	1,004 0 0
New York Trading Account ..	..	..	..	5,099 11 11	
To New York Branch Account	..	..	..	..	5,099 11 11
Viz. :—Stock (1st January 1901)		£920 15 10			
Purchases	..	5,255 0 5			
Trade Expenses	..	923 15 8			
		£5,099 11 11			
New York Branch Account ..	..	..	..	6,743 15 2	
To New York Trading Account	..	..	..	..	6,743 15 2
Viz. :—Sales	..	£5,708 16 8			
Stock (31st December 1901)		960 0 0			
Discounts	..	50 4 0			
Profit on Exchange	..	24 14 6			
		£6,743 15 2			
New York Trading Account ..	..	..	..	1,644 3 3	
To Profit and Loss Account	..	..	..	..	1,644 3 3
(Being Profit on New York Branch transferred.)					

The Ledger Accounts in the Head Office Books will then appear as follows:—

Dr.   NEW YORK BRANCH ACCOUNT.   Cr

1901		£ s d	£ s d	1901			£ s d	£ s d
Jan. 1	To Balance		3,960 7 10	Dec. 31	By Remittance Account.. ..			1,004 0 0
Dec. 31	„ New York Trading Account		6,743 15 2	„ „	New York Trading Account			5,099 11 11
				„ „	Balance down, viz :—			
					Cash		852 0 0	
					Debtors		1,500 0 0	
					Bills Received		1,144 0 0	
					Fixtures		344 11 1	
					Stock..		960 0 0	
							4,800 11 1	
					Less Creditors		200 0 0	
								4,600 11 1
			£10,704 3 0					£10,704 3 0
1902								
Jan. 1	To Balance		4,600 11 1					

Dr.   REMITTANCE ACCOUNT.   Cr.

1901		£ s d	1901 (various Dates)		£ s d
Dec. 31	To New York Branch Account	1,004 0 0		By Cash	1,004 0 0

Dr.   NEW YORK TRADING ACCOUNT.   Cr.

1901		£	s	d	1901		£	s	d
Dec. 31	To New York Branch Account, Stock (1st January 1901)	920	15	10	Dec. 31	By New York Branch Account Sales ..	5,708	16	8
„	„ New York Branch Account, Purchases	3,255	0	5	„	„ „ „ Stock ..	960	0	0
„	„ „ „ Trade Expenses	923	15	8	„	„ „ „ Discounts	50	4	0
„	„ Profit and Loss Account: Net Profit	1,644	3	3	„	„ „ Profit on Exchange	24	14	6
		£6,743	15	2			£6,743	15	2

Dr.   PROFIT AND LOSS ACCOUNT.   Cr.

			1901		£	s	d
			Dec 31	By New York Trading Account	1,644	3	3

Note.—Had the erroneous system of adhering to one fixed rate of exchange been adopted, the profit of the New York Branch would have appeared to be £1,604 (at 5, the rate of the day), or £1,611 0s. 11d. (at 4·98, the average rate)—a difference of 2½ and 2 per cent. respectively.

DEPARTMENTAL ACCOUNTS.

Another branch of the class of accounts already considered in this chapter relates to the division of the business into separate Departments, usually (but not necessarily) situated under the same roof. The various departments of a large undertaking are usually under separate management, and for this reason (if for no other) it is desirable that the accounts should be framed so that the results achieved by each may be separately shown. Even in smaller undertakings there are numerous, and obvious, advantages to be derived from the employment of Departmental Accounts.

These accounts differ from those connected with Branches, in that the customers of one Branch may be—and very likely are—customers of all Branches: it will therefore be very undesirable to keep separate Sold Ledgers in respect of each department. For the like reason there is usually no advantage to be obtained from a departmental division of the Bought Ledger Accounts: it is far better that each Personal Account should record the whole of the transactions entered into with each particular person. With regard to the Nominal Accounts, however, this is not the case, the balance of advantage lying in so analysing all the sources of income and expenditure as to enable, at all events, a separate Trading Account to be prepared for each department, if not a separate Profit and Loss Account as well.

So far as the Purchases are concerned this can be readily done by adopting a tabular form of Bought Book, and separate Pay Sheets for the wages paid in respect of each department. A convenient form of Bought Book is shown overpage, the various items in the Total column being posted to the credit of the various Personal Accounts in the Bought Ledger, while the totals of the various Analytical columns are posted monthly to the debit of separate Purchases Accounts opened in respect of each Department.

BOUGHT BOOK.....................................19....

Date	Invoice No.	Name	B.L. Fo.	Total of Invoices	Department A.	Department B.	Department C.	Department D.	Department E.	Department F.
				£ s d	£ s d	£ s d	£ s d	£ s d	£ s d	£ s d

A similar form of ruling may (if desired) be employed for the analysis of Sales, but it frequently happens that these are far too numerous for this to be the most expeditious mode of procedure. The invoices for goods sold—whether on credit or for cash—should be prepared in the Sales Departments, in duplicate, by means of a carbon sheet. In the case of Cash Sales, the duplicate will pass in the first instance to the Cashier, and the number and amount be entered upon the Cash Sheet, so that the Cashier's money may be checked. The duplicate is then passed on to the Counting House, which also receives direct from the Selling Department the duplicates of the bills representing Credit Sales. As each bill is numbered consecutively, and a summary of the numbers and amounts kept in the Selling Department, there is no difficulty in tracing the loss or destruction of a bill, should it occur. The Credit Sales duplicates are passed on to the Sales Ledger clerks, who write them up in their respective Day Books, and then hand them to the Dissecting Clerk; while the Cash Sales duplicates are written up in the Cash Sales Book by the Chief Cashier's assistant, and then also handed to the Dissecting Clerk. It is the duty of the latter to analyse both the Credit and the Cash Sales of each day, giving each Department credit for its sales; the Dissecting Clerk's total for the day's Credit Sales must agree with the Day Book totals, while his total for the Cash Sales must agree with the total Cash received by the Chief Cashier from the Departmental Cashiers. The entries in this Analysis Book thus form the medium for posting to the credit of Sales Accounts opened for each Department the Day's Sales of that Department, both on credit and for cash. (c. f. Chap. XVIII).

It not infrequently happens that one of the Departments may have occasion to purchase from another, as, for instance, the Dressmaking from the Drapery Department. In such a case the Drapery Department treats the Dressmaking Department as an ordinary customer (save that, as a rule, the goods would be charged at trade or cost price), while the Dressmaking Department hands over the invoice to the Counting House as an invoice respecting goods purchased by it in the ordinary way. At the end of each month the total goods sold by each Department to other Departments is ascertained, and a transfer made debiting the Sales Account and crediting the Purchases Account of the Selling Department with that amount. The reason for treating these transfers as *deductions from Purchases*, instead of as Sales is because they do not bear the ordinary Gross Profit, and it is desired to remove any element that might tend to disturb the percentage of gross profit realised upon actual sales. Establishment expenses of all kinds would be debited to Nominal Accounts in the usual way. As a rule, these expenses would be transferred to a combined Profit and Loss Account, which would stand credited with the gross profit earned by each Department. Sometimes, however, it is thought more convenient to charge the whole—or some—of these Expenses to the Departmental Accounts, in which case the charge might be either by way of apportioning the total expenditure, when ascertained; or the departments (or some of them) may be charged a fixed sum per annum, in which case that sum is debited to them and credited to the various general Nominal Accounts concerned.

The following example shows the form in which the accounts would be prepared of a business divided into three departments, two of which are Trading Departments and the third a Manufacturing Department.

PROBLEM.—The following is the Trial Balance of the books of A. B. at 30th June 1901 :—

	£ s d	£ s d	£ s d
Sundry Debtors ...		1,520 0 0	
„ Creditors ...			1,346 0 0
Plant and Machinery ...		1,050 0 0	
Bills Payable ...			329 0 0
„ Receivable ...		108 0 0	
Shares in Imperial Land Company, Lim....		250 0 0	
Capital Account ...			1,625 0 0
Cash in hand...		22 0 0	
Bank Overdraft ...			532 0 0
Bad Debts ...		46 0 0	
Stock at 30 June 1900—			
Department A	£790 0 0		
„ B	320 0 0		
„ C	400 0 0		
		1,510 0 0	
Purchases—			
Department A	2,851 0 0		
„ B	821 0 0		
„ C	2,021 0 0		
		5,693 0 0	
Sales—			
Department A	3,075 0 0		
„ B	1,563 0 0		
„ C	3,540 0 0		
			8,178 0 0
Wages Productive, Department B		419 0 0	
Salaries and Wages Unproductive		322 0 0	
Drawings ...		210 0 0	
Advertising ...		251 0 0	
Dividend on Shares ...			25 0 0
Interest to Bank ...		76 0 0	
Commission ...		142 0 0	
Rent, Rates, and Insurance		111 0 0	
Discounts and Allowances		129 0 0	
Depreciation ...		132 0 0	
Carriage ...		103 0 0	
General Expenses ...		70 0 0	
Stationery ...		25 0 0	
Discounts on Purchases			154 0 0
		£12,189 0 0	£12,189 0 0

D

The Stock at 30th June 1901 amounted to—Department A, £1,005 ; Department B, £365 ; Department C, £305. Provide 2½ per cent. for discount on Book Debts, £75 for Reserve for loss through bad debts, and adjust in the year the proportions of the following :—

(1) Fire Insurance Premiums paid to 25th March £1902, £44. (2) Rent of works for quarter ended 24th June 1901, £45. (3) Telephone rental due and paid 30th November 1901, £20.

Prepare (a) Trading Accounts for the Departments A, B, and C. (b) Profit and Loss Account. (c) Balance Sheet.

The following adjusting entries are necessary before finally closing the books :—

JOURNAL, 1901.

30th June.		£ s d	£ s d
Suspense Account.. .. .. *Dr.*		41 6 8	
To Rent, Rates, and Insurance		..	33 0 0
„ General Expenses		..	8 6 8
(Being proportions paid in advance—viz., say, three-fourths of £44 equals £33; five-twelfths of £20 equals £8 6s. 8d.)			
Rent, &c., Account .. .. *Dr.*		45 0 0	
To Suspense Account		..	45 0 0
(Being one quarter's rent of Works due Midsummer last.)			
Discounts and Allowances .. .. *Dr.*		38 0 0	
To Reserve for Discounts		..	38 0 0
(Being 2½ per cent. on Sundry Debtors, £1,520, reserved to cover Cash Discounts.)			
Bad Debts .. .. *Dr.*		75 0 0	
To Reserve for Bad and Doubtful Debts		..	75 0 0
(Being provision for possible loss by reason of Doubtful Debts.)			

Dr.   TRADING ACCOUNT for the Year ended 30th June 1901.   *Cr.*

	Dept. A.	Dept. B.	Dept. C.		Dept. A.	Dept. B.	Dept. C.
	£ s d	£ s d	£ s d		£ s d	£ s d	£ s d
To Stock : 30th June 1900 ..	790 0 0	320 0 0	400 0 0	By Sales	3,075 0 0	1,563 0 0	3,540 0 0
„ Purchases	2,851 0 0	821 0 0	2,021 0 0	„ Stock: 30th June 1901	1,005 0 0	365 0 0	305 0 0
„ Wages	..	419 0 0	..				
„ Gross Profit, transferred to Profit and Loss Account	439 0 0	368 0 0	1,424 0 0				
	£4,080 0 0	£1,928 0 0	£3,845 0 0		£4,080 0 0	£1,928 0 0	£3,845 0 0

Dr.   PROFIT AND LOSS ACCOUNT for the Year ended 30th June 1901.   Cr.

	£ s d	£ s d		£ s d	£ s d
To Rent, Rates and Insurance	123 0 0		By Gross Profit from Trading Account:—		
„ Wages and Salaries..	322 0 0		A Department	439 0 0	
„ Advertising	251 0 0		B „	368 0 0	
„ Carriage .. „	103 0 0		C „	1,424 0 0	2,231 0 0
„ Commission	142 0 0		„ Dividend on Shares		25 0 0
„ Stationery	25 0 0		„ Discounts on Purchases		154 0 0
„ General Expenses	61 13 4	1,027 13 4			
„ Bank Interest..	76 0 0				
„ Bad Debts	121 0 0				
„ Discounts and Allowances..	167 0 0	364 0 0			
„ Depreciation		132 0 0			
„ Balance (being net profit for the year) transferred to Capital Account		886 6 8			
		£2,410 0 0			£2,410 0 0

BALANCE SHEET, 30th June 1901.

Liabilities.		£ s d	£ s d	Assets.		£ s d	£ s d
CAPITAL ACCOUNT :—				Plant and Machinery (less Depreciation)			1,050 0 0
Balance, 1st July 1900		1,625 0 0		Stock in Trade			1,675 0 0
Net Profit, per Profit and Loss Account		886 6 8		Bills Receivable			108 0 0
		2,511 6 8		Sundry Debts	..£1,520 0 0		
Less Drawings		210 0 0	2,301 6 8	Less Reserve for Discounts	£38 0 0		
Bills Payable			1,346 0 0	„ Reserve for Bad Debts	75 0 0	113 0 0	1,407 0 0
Sundry Creditors			329 0 0	Shares in Imperial Land Co., Lim.			250 0 0
Bank Overdraft			532 0 0	Cash in hand			22 0 0
Suspense Account			3 13 4				
			£4,512 0 0				£4,512 0 0

D 2

CHAPTER VI

TABULAR BOOKKEEPING.

THE term "Tabular Bookkeeping" is generally applied to a special form of Ledger, but it is equally applicable to books of first entry, and the advantages of the system may be as often introduced at this point as in connection with Ledgers. Any form of account book which is provided with several columns, in order to facilitate the classification of the transactions recorded, may be properly stated to come under this heading.

TABULAR CASH BOOK.

Probably the commonest example of the employment of tabular bookkeeping is the ordinary three-column Cash Book, which provides separate columns for the record of transactions with the Bank, with the Office Cash, and Discounts. The advantages of this form of book are too well known to call for any detailed comment. It may, however, be pointed out that, while the ordinary three-column Cash Book is a very rudimentary form of tabular bookkeeping, so far as it goes it well illustrates the advantages which the system offers, as applied to books of first entry. More elaborate examples of tabular Cash Books are found when it is thought desirable to provide for the separate balancing of several Ledgers without introducing subsidiary Cash Books for each. Another—and perhaps more generally used—form is that which enables a large number of detailed postings to be dispensed with, periodical totals being substituted therefor. In extreme cases (as, for example, in the accounts of non-trading charitable institutions, the accounts of trustees in bankruptcy, and the like) the necessity for the employment of a Ledger may be entirely obviated by the employment of a tabular Cash Book. An example of such a book will be found in Chapter XIV., which deals with Bankruptcy and Insolvency Accounts. Another form, which may be usefully described here in greater detail, is the ordinary Cash Book, from which Ledger postings are made in detail, with a large number of analytical columns, which are added with a view to enabling the various Ledgers to be balanced separately, and also with a view to reducing to a minimum the number of detailed postings that have to be made to certain accounts in which numerous transactions occur. The following example, which gives the *pro formâ* ruling of a Cash Book suitable to a large Building Society, clearly shows how this may be accomplished. The only entries posted in detail into the General Ledger will be those entered in the column marked "General Ledger." The others will be posted to the proper accounts in the General Ledger (many of which, it will be observed, are "Adjustment Accounts") in daily totals only, the detailed postings being made to the various subsidiary Ledgers—viz., "Advances Ledger," "Paid-up Share Ledger," "Investment Share Ledger," and "Depositors' Ledger." The receipts in respect of "Fines" afford an example of a class of transaction which frequently occurs, and which is only posted in total in order to save clerical labour: the fines received would, of course, have to be also entered in the various departmental Ledgers, but they would there be recorded in memo. only, as in no way affecting the balances outstanding on the various members' accounts.

EXAMPLE:

FORM OF TABULATED CASH BOOK SUITABLE FOR A BUILDING SOCIETY.

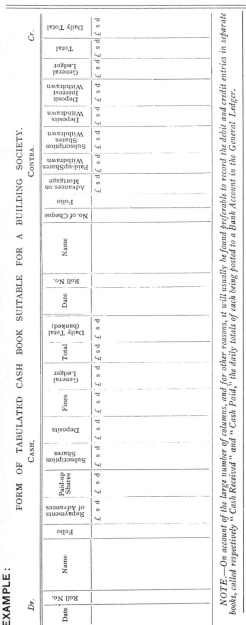

NOTE.—On account of the large number of columns, and for other reasons, it will usually be found preferable to record the debit and credit entries in separate books, called respectively "Cash Received" and "Cash Paid," the daily totals of each being posted to a Bank Account in the General Ledger.

Before leaving this branch of the subject, it may be added that in many trading concerns it will be found convenient to add an extra column upon each side of the Cash Book for the record of Cash Sales and Cash Purchases respectively, as by this means postings, in weekly or monthly totals, may be substituted for a large number of detailed postings upon each side. Similarly, if transactions in Bills are very numerous, it will often be found convenient to add an additional pair of columns for "Bills Payable" and "Bills Receivable" respectively, more especially if the Bill Book be extended into a "Bill Ledger," as in that case the Bill Ledger may be readily balanced separately.

TABULAR JOURNAL.

Passing on to other books of first entry, the ordinary form of Purchases Book, with Analysis columns for each department, is, of course, an example of Tabular Bookkeeping, and the ordinary form of Bill Book is another example. It is, however, only thought necessary to illustrate one form of ruling under this heading, as showing the development of which the tabular system is capable. The form given overpage will be found particularly useful to Agents and others who have occasion to buy, or sell, goods, or to incur expenses on behalf of numerous other persons, as it automatically ensures the debiting of some person or persons with the full amount of each liability incurred. It is, of course, purely a question of convenience whether the accounts to be debited be placed in columns and the accounts to be credited in lines, or whether the accounts to be credited be placed vertically and the accounts to be debited horizontally. In practice, however, it will generally be found desirable to place the largest number upon horizontal lines, with a view to reducing to a minimum the number of columns required.

EXAMPLE :

FORM OF EXPENSES JOURNAL

suitable for Agents, etc.

Date	No. of Invoice	Account to be Credited	Fo.	Amount of Invoice	Accounts to be Debited					
					A	B	C	D	E	F
				£ s d	£ s d	£ s d	£ s d	£ s d	£ s d	£ s d
					Fo.	Fo.	Fo.	Fo.	Fo.	Fo.

TABULAR LEDGER.

The most important developments of the Tabular System are, however, to be found in connection with Ledgers. Leaving upon one side the rudimentary forms of Tabular Ledger that have already been mentioned, the varieties in general use may be divided into two classes. The first class is suitable for the record of transactions when the number of Personal Accounts is very considerable, and when only one such transaction occurs with each person during a specified limit of time. These conditions apply to Rent Accounts, the Rate Accounts of Local Authorities, Subscription Accounts of various Societies, Accounts for Gas, Water, Electric Light, Telephone Rent, and the like. In all these cases the number of separate Personal Accounts required is so considerable that a Ledger kept upon the ordinary lines could not be very readily balanced, and the tabular form, each page of which is capable of being balanced separately, is therefore more convenient. The essential principle is that of dividing the Ledger into pages (or groups of pages), not according to the transactions with each of the various persons concerned, but according to the date, or period, covered by these transactions. That is to say, a folio (or, if necessary, a number of folios) is set aside to record *all* the transactions of a certain nature during a certain prescribed *period ;* the period will naturally vary according to the nature of the undertaking, but whatever period may be covered, *all* the transactions that occur within that time (and which are of such a nature as to be recorded in this Ledger at all) are entered upon the page (or series of pages) dealing with that particular period. These pages are ruled in columnar form, so that a separate line may be devoted to each person, and a separate column to each class of transaction that may have to be recorded ; or sometimes it may be convenient to reverse the process, and to assign a column to each Personal Account and a line to the record of each separate item in that account. As a rule, however, the first-named is the more usual course. It is not thought necessary to give numerous examples of Tabular Ledgers coming under this heading. The following will clearly explain the working of the system, whatever may be the exact nature of the transactions to be recorded.

EXAMPLE :

FORM OF TABULAR LEDGER (Suitable for a Water Company).

Arrears 31/12/02	C.B. Fo.	Arrears Coll'ct'd	Ref. No.	No. in Street and Name	Rate'ble Value	Annual Rent (for Water)	Extras	C.B. Fo.	Amount Rec'iv'd	Allowances, Vacancies, and Bad Debts		Arrears 31/12/03	(The like particulars for 1904)	(The like particulars for 1905)	Arrears 31/12/05
										Fo. A/c	Amount				
£ s d		£ s d			£ s d	£ s d	£ s d		£ s d		£ s d	£ s d			£ s d

NOTES :—A separate line to be devoted to each Account.
The name of each Street to be written across the column marked "No. in Street and Name," and the various accounts in that Street to be written thereunder.
If the rate is payable half-yearly, two lines should be devoted to each Account.

It will be seen that, under this system, the total of each of the various columns is capable of being agreed with known facts, and these totals having been so agreed, the exact balancing of the Ledger as a whole follows as a matter of course, if the various additions and cross-additions have been correctly made. If any difference occurs it must be due to a mistake in addition, and that mistake can be readily located on to a single page. Tabular Ledgers may therefore be very easily balanced exactly, even if the number of separate accounts should run into several thousands.

From what has been stated, it will be seen that Tabular Ledgers have their limitations, and that the form so far described is only suitable when there is but one debit (or possibly two) to be made to each person during the period covered by the Ledger opening. Up to a certain extent, the application of the Tabular System may be slightly extended to deal with exceptional cases by leaving three or four lines to an account; but, speaking generally, if there is more than one debit to an account in each period, the system is not suitable. There is, however, nothing (save the question of convenience) to prevent the period selected for a Ledger opening being made as short as may be thought desirable, but the considerable labour of re-writing all the names each time a new set of folios has to be brought into operation naturally imposes a limit upon development in this direction.

An especial advantage of Tabular Ledgers is that, inasmuch as a great number of Personal Accounts lie upon the same folio, and as the state of each account can be very readily perceived, this system affords great facilities for the collection of outstanding debts. Under some circumstances, therefore, it may be thought desirable to extend the system in directions which *primâ facie* do not appear to be very suitable—*e.g.*, to the accounts (or some portion of the accounts) of ordinary traders whose dealings with their customers are at frequent, but irregular intervals. The Tabular System may be applied to the requirements of such cases by the employment in the first instance of a Subsidiary Ledger to *collect* the various entries to the debit of each customer, the totals being then transferred into the Tabular Ledger when a periodical statement of accounts is rendered. This form of Tabular Ledger is very suitable to such undertakings as Collieries, which as a rule render daily invoices in quantities only, the monthly statement of account being the only priced invoice which is forwarded to the customer. In such a case the Subsidiary Ledger might record the various deliveries to the debit of the customer in quantities only, and the Tabular Ledger might be brought into play to record the actual debit in money when the monthly statement is sent out. As such monthly statements would under normal circumstances be supplied at stated intervals, a Tabular Ledger devoting a separate set of pages to each month might be found useful in this connection.

Another form of Tabular Ledger that is sometimes handy to the professional man is one which deals with all bills delivered to clients. A considerable proportion of these bills will doubtless be settled by remittances within a comparatively short space of time, and these may be definitely disposed of in the Tabular Ledger at once. Others, however, will remain outstanding for longer, or will have to be settled " in account " with other transactions, and these, inasmuch as they cannot be conveniently dealt with under the Tabular System, might be readily transferred from the Tabular Ledger to another upon the old-fashioned lines, and there dealt with in due course. If the number of transfers that had to be made for these reasons was inconsiderable, the employment of a Tabular Ledger would undoubtedly be found advantageous, in that, while involving somewhat less labour than the writing up of a Bill Book and the posting of the various items to Ledger Accounts, it enables the collection of outstanding accounts to be far more readily supervised than would be the case with the old-fashioned Ledger. A form of ruling designed to meet these requirements is given overpage.

EXAMPLE :

COSTS LEDGER for the Quarter Half-Year ended..................19..

Date of Account Rendered	Name of Client and Matter	Press Copy L.B. Fo.	Balance brought forward £ s d	Amount of A/c render'd during curr't period £ s d	Total Amount Due £ s d	Date Received	C.B. Fo.	Amount Received £ s d	Ledger Fo.	Amount Trans-ferred £ s d	Balance carried forward £ s d	Disburse-ment Ledg'r Fo.	Amount Received £ s d	Disburse-ments included in charges £ s d	Net Charges £ s d

Another development of the Tabular System with regard to Ledgers is often applied (although perhaps unconsciously) to the Nominal Ledger, or to Nominal Accounts in a Private (or General) Ledger. With a view to keeping the number of different Nominal Accounts within reasonable limits, it is often customary to post somewhat different classes of expenditure to the same account; *e.g.*, under the heading of General Expenses, or Trade Expenses, the most diverse items will often be included. Further classification of these various items is probably unnecessary for the purpose of compiling the usual Profit and Loss Account; but for statistical purposes totals of detailed expenditure under different classes may be required, which, with the normal form of Ledger, can only be obtained by " dissecting " the various Nominal Accounts. If, however, each of these accounts be provided with several Money columns, this dissection may be made continuously as the Ledger is posted, and is not merely readily available at the close of the financial year, but also at any time up to date. Tabular Nominal Ledgers upon these lines are especially convenient where a great number of separate Trading Accounts are desirable for the different departments. They will also be found useful to merchants in connection with Consignment Accounts of more than ordinary complexity, to publishers who may wish to show separately the results of each work produced, and to others.

The second main type of Tabular Ledger differs essentially from the preceding. Hitherto a form has been dealt with which greatly facilitates the handling of a large number of individual accounts, but which is not suitable where there are a great number of transactions at irregular intervals with the same person, or where the necessity arises to dissect in considerable detail the total debit to the Personal Account. If, however, the position of affairs is reversed, and a very detailed analysis of the total debits is required without any very great number of Personal Accounts being affected, the Tabular System may still be applied with advantage. The most notable instance of such application is in connection with the accounts of hotels, where the debits to the various visitors have to be dissected over a great number of Nominal Accounts. Here, however, the inevitable limitation of the Tabular System retains its hold to this extent, that only one entry of exactly the same kind can be conveniently recorded upon the same Ledger opening. Consequently, in order to meet the requirements of the altered position, it becomes necessary to reduce the period that can be covered by a single opening of the Ledger, the ordinary period covered in the case of an Hotel Ledger kept upon the Tabular System being a single day. The shortness of this period does not, however, cause any very serious inconvenience, because in any event the majority of visitors do not make a protracted stay, and their accounts will therefore under any circumstances only cover a comparatively short space of time; and because, further, the exigencies of this particular industry necessitate the Personal Account of each visitor being invariably kept up to date hour by hour, which would be impossible unless the Ledger were also used as a book of first entry. The form ordinarily adopted under these circumstances is thus upon the lines of the example shown overpage. In comparatively small hotels it is desirable, if possible, to make the Ledger openings of sufficient size to cover all the transactions of one day; but if there are more than about 30 visitors at a time this is impracticable, and two or more openings must be employed and the cross-totals carried forward. The totals of the Nominal Accounts may be either carried forward from day to day and posted direct into the Nominal Ledger monthly, or they may be abstracted daily into a Summary Book, and from there posted monthly into the Nominal Ledger. As a rule, the latter will be found the most convenient course to pursue, both because it reduces the number of cross-casts and on account of the utility of the Summary Book for statistical purposes.

EXAMPLE:

VISITORS' LEDGER.

THURSDAY, JANUARY 1, 1903.

Room No....	1	2	3	4	5	6	7	8	9	10	11	12	13	14	15	16	17	Daily Total	Brought Forward	Carried Forward
Name..	T. Smith	P. Jameson		P. Ransom	O. Jones															
	£ s d	£ s d	£ s d	£ s d	£ s d	£ s d	£ s d	£ s d	£ s d	£ s d	£ s d	£ s d	£ s d	£ s d	£ s d	£ s d	£ s d	£ s d	£ s d	£ s d
DEBITS.—																				
Balance bt. Forward																				
Apartments	0 5 0	0 5 0		0 5 0	0 3 0													0 18 0		0 18 0
Boarders																				
Breakfast	0 2 6	0 2 6		0 2 6	0 2 6													0 9 6		0 9 6
Luncheons	0 2 6	0 1 9		0 2 0	0 2 6													0 8 9		0 8 9
Dinners	0 4 0	0 4 0		0 4 6														0 12 6		0 12 6
Desserts and Ices																				
Sandwiches																				
Tea and Coffee																				
Soups																				
Suppers																				
Servants' Board																				
Wine																				
Spirits & Liquors	0 2 6			0 3 6	0 1 6													0 7 6		0 7 6
Ales, Stouts, etc.																				
Minerals																				
Cigars																				
Newspapers																				
Postage																				
Paid Out																				
Washing	0 1 0	0 1 0		0 1 0																
Carriage	0 1 0	0 1 0		0 1 6	0 1 0															
Billiards				0 1 0																
Stationery																		0 4 0		0 4 0
Attendance																		0 2 6		0 2 6
Baths																				
Fire and Lights																				
Total	0 15 6	0 16 9		1 0 0	0 10 6													3 2 9		3 2 9
CREDITS.—																				
Overcharges																				
Cash Received				0 1 0	0 10 6													0 10 6		0 10 6
Ledger Account	0 15 6																			
Balance car. Forward		0 16 9		1 0 0														2 12 3		2 12 3
Total	0 15 6	0 16 9		1 0 0	0 10 6													3 2 9		3 2 9

Tabular Ledgers upon somewhat the same lines as the preceding may be used by many domestic tradesmen with advantage, and are in point of fact in very general use in the Dairy and Bakery trades. Occasionally it may be found advantageous to employ some modification of the Tabular System in connection with the accounts of Butchers, Grocers, and others, and in this connection it should be remembered that the abolition of the Day Book effects a very material saving of clerical labour, which will go far towards compensating for any additional trouble that the keeping of the Ledger may entail. The accurate keeping of a Tabular Ledger requires, however, a certain amount of technical training on the part of the bookkeeper, which may often militate against its employment by traders of this description.

SUMMARY.

To sum up, it will be observed that under favourable circumstances the Tabular Ledger greatly facilitates the keeping of accounts upon such lines that they are always up to date and may be readily balanced exactly, while at the same time it especially lends itself to a detailed analysis of Nominal Accounts, which is generally very desirable and often absolutely essential. A very important application of the system arises in connection with the issue of Capital by Joint-Stock Companies, and the issue of Loans by Local Authorities. This, however, will be found to be dealt with separately in Chapter IX. The careful student will doubtless be able to imagine circumstances, other than those enumerated, in which the adoption of the Tabular System, either to books of first entry or to Ledgers, is very desirable. It is, however, well to add a word by way of caution as to the circumstances under which this system is *not* applicable. Shortly, it may be stated that when the transactions occur at irregular intervals, and are of such a nature that

they require to be recorded in the Ledger in considerable detail, and in particular when (owing to the nature of the business) it is essential to be able to follow the transactions with each separate person in the order of their occurrence, the Tabular System is inapplicable. It may be also added that, save for the purpose already mentioned in connection with a Nominal Ledger, the Tabular System cannot with advantage be applied to either Real or Nominal Accounts, as it is essential that these should be recorded in the Ledger with a certain amount of detail attached to each item. It is also desirable to avoid any form of Tabular Bookkeeping which involves the mixing up of cash entries with entries that have nothing to do with cash. Consequently a book of first-entry upon Tabular lines which deals, under appropriate columns, with *all* transactions, whether cash or otherwise, is an undesirable one, in spite of the fact that it is very frequently adopted by both solicitors and auctioneers. The danger of employing this form of book in such cases is that, if entries not relating to cash should be placed in the Cash columns, or if cash entries should not be placed in the Cash columns, serious mistakes may easily arise, and also, unless the entries are very carefully verified, frauds might remain undetected. If the Tabular System be applied to books of first-entry it is important that each of such books should in the first instance be so arranged as to only deal with transactions of a more or less similar class. For example, Goods Bought, Goods Sold, Bills Receivable, Bills Payable, and Cash, may each form a suitable subject for a book of first-entry upon Tabular lines ; but no two, or more, of these should be combined in the same book. It is all the more important to emphasise this point, because the combination already referred to undoubtedly effects a material saving of clerical labour, which would be extremely advantageous did it not involve even more serious disadvantages.

CHAPTER VII.

STOCK ACCOUNTS, AND STORE ACCOUNTS.

IN some old-fashioned works upon bookkeeping *pro formâ* examples of a merchant's accounts will be found, in which each separate parcel of goods is provided with a separate Ledger Account, which is debited with the cost and credited with the proceeds realised upon the sale of that parcel. With accounts so kept, the gross profit is arrived at by bringing together the credit balances of these various accounts, and the exact manner in which the total gross profit has been earned can be readily perceived. It is safe to say, however, that it is only in very theoretical text-books that anything of the kind can be really attempted. Even if the amount of detailed work involved did not render the cost of carrying out such a system prohibitive, there are very few businesses in which it would be practicable to so ear-mark the goods bought and sold as to thus keep tally of them from the moment that they came into the place to the moment that they went out again. Some traders who deal in articles of considerable value—*c.g.*, jewellers—are, however, compelled to keep a very strict account of their stock. But although the principle previously described is to some extent followed, no attempt is made to open a separate Ledger Account in respect of each article, the Tabular System being employed instead, which effects an enormous saving of time, and, moreover, enables the actual position of affairs at any time to be more readily appreciated.

But although it is the exception rather than the rule for a strict account to be kept of the various commodities bought, sold, and consumed, in all cases, *some* sort of an account is necessary to avoid waste and to detect leakage. The various plans adopted, suited to the requirements of different undertakings, will be considered in the present chapter.

JEWELLERS' STOCK ACCOUNTS.

It has already been stated that jewellers and others dealing in articles of considerable intrinsic value keep an accurate account of such articles upon the Tabular System. These Stock Accounts form no part of the system of double-entry, but are supplemental thereto, confirming both the Gross Profit and the Stock-in-Hand, and enabling any discrepancies in either to be fully traced. The stock is usually, in the first instance, grouped under convenient general headings, and a separate Stock Book, or a separate section in the same Stock Book, employed for each. A convenient form of ruling is that given overpage, although the special requirements of each business may involve some slight modification.

EXAMPLE :

JEWELLERY STOCK BOOK.

Department......................   From...............190.. to................190..

Reference No.	Date	Description of Article	From whom Bought	Invoice Reference	Stock on hand ......19..	Purchases during period	Cost Price of Goods Sold	Day Book Reference	Selling Price of Goods Sold	Stock on hand ......19..
					£ s d	£ s d	£ s d		£ s d	£ s d

The working of this book will, it is thought, be perceived without difficulty. At the commencement of each financial period the amount of Stock-in-Hand (as per inventory) is entered up in the Money column provided for that purpose. The purchase invoices are next analysed, and particulars inserted in the " Purchases " column of all additions to stock, reference being made in the column provided for that purpose to the invoice, or to the folio in the Invoice Book. The total of this column for any period should agree with the total Purchases, as shown by the Invoice Book, and in order to check the accuracy of the Stock Book these totals should be agreed at least monthly. Each article as put into stock is provided with a Reference Number (which agrees with the Stock Book number), so that the salesmen can at all times ascertain the cost thereof and where it was purchased. Whenever goods are sold—whether for cash or on credit—the Reference Number is noted in the Cash Sales Book (or the Day Book, as the case may be), and from these books the third and fourth Money columns of the Stock Book are compiled. The fourth Money column contains the price realised for the goods, and the total of this column should be agreed monthly with the Sales effected. In the third column is inserted the cost price of the goods as sold—that is to say, whenever the selling price of an article is inserted in the fourth column the cost

price is simultaneously inserted in the third column. It may be added that this column is not always employed in practice ; but it is especially convenient because the difference between the third and fourth columns at any time represents the gross profit on goods sold, and should be capable of exact agreement with the gross profit arrived at from financial books, while the difference between the first and second columns added together and the third column should at all times equal the cost price of the goods remaining on hand. At the close of the period these differences are extended into the last column, which should agree exactly with the inventory prepared at stock-taking. The more valuable commodities will, of course, require checking much more frequently than the annual stock-taking, and it will be seen that this system lends itself to the stock of the more expensive classes of goods being verified at any time—if necessary daily.

In every case there will probably be some articles stocked of a comparatively small value, which it is not thought desirable to check in such detail as that described. These will be grouped under convenient descriptions, and all articles of the same description might be marked with the same reference number, provided, of course, their cost and selling prices were the same. In other cases it may be thought sufficient to keep tally in quantities only ; but this is not recommended, as the amount of trouble saved is no compensation for the loss of a direct and absolute check, which is inevitable if there be any material departure from the sytem of marking each item of the stock with a reference number. If the cheaper items of the same value be grouped, a sufficient "compression" of the system will be effected to reasonably answer all practical purposes.

CELLAR STOCK BOOKS.

Another class of stock which it is generally desirable to check in full detail is that contained in the cellars of wine merchants, hotel keepers, &c. Here, however, it is not generally either practicable or desirable that the Stock Accounts should deal with money. In the case of wine merchants, the blending and bottling operations would make such calculations a matter of considerable intricacy, while *per contra* the selling price would by no means necessarily be the same to every customer, and would probably vary considerably according to the quantity booked at the time the sale was effected. With hotel keepers the need for a careful check upon the money does not exist in connection with the check upon the stock, in that the same person would never under any circumstances be responsible for both stock and money; while the Gross Profits are not cut so fine as to make it worth while to compile detailed information as to the amount of profit earned upon each bottle sold. Cellar Stock Accounts are accordingly simplified in some respects; but, on the other hand, the transactions are probably very much more numerous, so that greater difficulty arises in checking them with the financial books from time to time. It is best, therefore, to provide a separate column for each day of the month, so that the amount taken out of the cellar upon each day may be separately agreed. The purchases will be much more rare in comparison, and one column per month will therefore suffice, particularly if a Date column be added to facilitate reference. A convenient form of Cellar Stock Book is given below:—

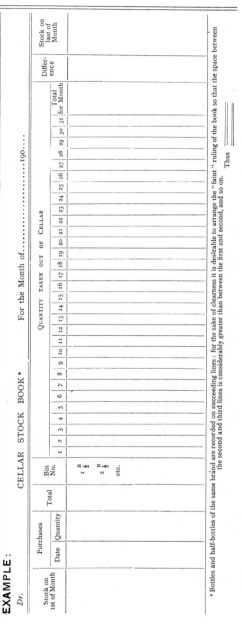

EXAMPLE:

CELLAR STOCK BOOK *

Dr. For the Month of............................190....

* Bottles and half-bottles of the same brand are recorded on succeeding lines: for the sake of clearness it is desirable to arrange the "faint" ruling of the book so that the space between the second and third lines is considerably greater than between the first and second, and so on. Thus

BULK STOCK BOOK.

The form of Stock Book given above relates exclusively to bottles and half-bottles. With regard to liquor kept in bulk, a somewhat different form of book will be found preferable. Here the number of different items of which tally has to be kept is probably not very numerous, while the number of transactions in respect of each item may be considerable. For example, the contents of a butt will not by any means necessarily be completely exhausted before fresh liquor is put into it; and, indeed, it is probable that as a rule such butts would be continually replenished, partly with a view to improving the quality and partly with a view to keeping it uniform over an extended period. The Tabular System does not lend itself to the record of transactions of this description, and it is best, therefore, to fall back upon the ordinary old-fashioned Ledger Account, opening a separate account in respect of each butt, debiting it with all quantities put in, and crediting it with all quantities taken out. Additions which are direct purchases may be conveniently entered in black ink (with the necessary reference to the invoice), while additions extracted from other sources already in stock should be inserted in red ink. *Per contra* quantites taken out *not* for immediate sale should be also entered in red ink, the corresponding debit being either to the Ledger Account of another butt, or (if the quantities have been bottled) to the debit side of the Cellar Stock Book; while if the quantities have been sold without being bottled, the entry should be made in black ink and the reference passed to the Day Book. As all the transactions in the present work are dealt with from a bookkeeping point of view, it is unnecessary to more than mention in passing that, wherever blending operations are undertaken, they should be performed by someone entirely trustworthy, so that accurate accounts may be kept of any *increase* in the bulk arising from the addition of water. The stock in bulk can only be actually ascertained by periodical gauging, and as a rule it is not convenient that this should take place at very frequent intervals. The result is that the check upon liquids in bulk is at all times necessarily somewhat incomplete, more especially bearing in mind the fact that a certain amount of wastage must be allowed for on account of evaporation.

BAR STOCKS.

On the other hand, when stock has to be kept of the contents of bars, or other places where bulk is "broken" through the goods being sold by the glass or other measure, no waste ought to occur, as in measuring out liquids full measure is never given, so that at least the whole of the nominal contents of the receptacle ought to be accounted for. These remarks apply even where what is called "full measure" is the custom, because a liquid measure is never absolutely drained, so that the amount that goes out of a liquid measure is never quite so much as its theoretical contents. Liquid stocks thus possess a tangible advantage over solid stocks, which, when sold by weight, must in all cases be slightly over measure, in order to afford the "turn of the scale"; and the smaller the quantities sold at a time, the greater the wastage arising from this cause will be. With regard to the checking of bar stocks generally, it is not practicable to employ any tabular form of Stock Book, because it is practically impossible to keep a strict account of the price of the various items sold. A far simpler and equally effective method is to take an inventory of the contents of the Bar at frequent intervals, say once a week at least, and to charge up the contents at selling price. Any additions to stock during the week should be added to the original inventory at selling price, and the difference between the figure so arrived at and the selling price valuation of the stock on hand at the end of the week should represent the cash takings of the Bar during the period. It is not usual to discuss any small discrepancies, either one way or the other; but bar-keepers who continually show a deficiency of stock are superseded.

GENERAL TRADE STOCKS.

In the preceding paragraph a method of keeping an accurate check upon stock without going into details has been described. This system is, however, only applicable (a) Where the selling price never varies. (b) Where it is practicable to take stock at comparatively frequent intervals. (c) Where wastage is trifling. To the majority of undertakings none of these conditions apply. In most cases the selling price varies to some extent, according to the quantity sold at a time, e.g., dozens are sold at a lower price than single articles, while, moreover, the amount of stock necessary to carry on a satisfactory trade is frequently so considerable that it is practically impossible to take stock, save at such rare intervals that—for this particular purpose—it does not afford a sufficiently immediate safeguard against peculation. Moreover, in many cases the amount of waste necessarily incidental to the trade renders it practically impossible to keep a very strict account of the stock in items. All these considerations, however, so far from removing the necessity for a reliable check, tend to make one of even greater importance, more especially when the business is of such magnitude that the proprietors do not attend personally to every detail. A system that is very general among large traders is that of keeping a check upon the operations of a department by means of statistical accounts, compiled upon the basis of an assumed percentage of Gross Profit. The operations of the business as a whole are split up into " departments," each of which is probably in the hands of a departmental manager, who is entrusted with the purchase of goods for his department, and generally responsible for the results it shows. It is known in advance what Gross Profit *ought* to be earned upon the sales of each department, and very frequently the manager's remuneration depends to some extent upon this percentage being earned. The analysis of purchases and sales into departments has already been explained, and the reader will thus perceive that it is a very simple matter to compile statistical Stock Accounts in con-

nection with each department, either weekly or monthly, as may be preferred. At the commencement of the financial year, the Stock Account starts with the actual ascertained stock, as per the stock-taking of that date. The additions to stock can be ascertained from the purchases analysis. What, however, is not exactly known is the cost price of the goods sold—that is, of the figure that has to be credited to the Stock Account in order that the balance from time to time may show the cost of the goods remaining in stock. The cost price of goods sold may, however, be estimated by deducting from the actual Sales the estimated percentage of Gross Profit, and so long as the Gross Profit actually earned equals this percentage, the statistical accounts will be compiled upon a correct basis, and the stock at the end of the financial period will agree with the actual Stock-in-Hand at that date. Any discrepancy between these two figures will indicate a corresponding inaccuracy in the estimated Gross Profit. That is to say, if the actual stock is less than the estimated stock, the actual Gross Profit must be correspondingly less than the estimate, and *vice versâ*.

It may at first sight appear that there is but little gained by preparing such Stock Accounts at frequent intervals, seeing that they can only be verified when an actual stock-taking takes place. It must be remembered, however, that any inaccuracy in the balance of Stock represents an equal inaccuracy in the balance of Gross Profit, and a careful scrutiny of either will thus enable a check to be kept upon the other. It is not merely in connection with the Gross Profit that a strict check can be kept upon departmental managers, past experience will have shown the proper ratio of the Stock at any period of the year to the Sales, and any increase in the estimated stock over what is regarded as a fair normal stock at that time of year would be carefully scrutinised. Should the Stock at any time appear too heavy, the manager will be closely questioned as to how the increase arose, and it must be borne in mind that it is not open to him to question the accuracy of the estimated figure of stock without throwing an equal doubt upon the question as to whether he is selling the goods of his department at the proper rate of profit. For example, if three months after stock-taking the stock of a particular department appears to be £500 more than is thought to be necessary, it is not open for the manager to protest that in point of fact his stock is not larger than usual, unless at the same time he is prepared to admit that his Gross Profit for the past three months is £500 less than it would have been had he realised the proper percentage of Gross Profit. It will thus be seen that figures compiled upon this basis are of the utmost value to those who have sufficient knowledge of the trade and the circumstances to utilise them to advantage.

It need hardly be stated that these figures, being purely estimates, are kept entirely separate from the financial books. For convenience sake they are usually compiled in tabular form, one set of accounts showing the results of all the departments upon an opening, and another set dealing separately with the accounts of each department, the figures of succeeding years being placed in successive columns, so that the statistics covering an extending period may be conveniently compared. At the foot of each year are inserted in red ink the differences between the estimated results and those shown by the actual stocktaking. so that the information afforded by these statistics may be complete. The following examples show suitable rulings for these purposes. They are, however, of course subject to considerable modification, according to the exact nature of the business carried on.

EXAMPLES: MONTHLY STOCK ACCOUNTS for the Year ended 28th February 1902.

		Dept. "A." (10%)	Dept. "B." (15%)	Dept. "C." (15%)	Dept. "D." (10%)	Dept. "E." (15%)	Dept. "F." (25%)	Dept. "G." (8%)	Dept. "H." (12½%)
		£ s d	£ s d	£ s d	£ s d	£ s d	£ s d	£ s d	£ s d
1901 Mar. 1 31	Actual Stock	2,000 0 0	6,000 0 0						
	Purchases ..	720 0 0	100 0 0						
		2,720 0 0	6,100 0 0						
"	Net Sales	500 0 0	300 0 0						
"	Estimated Stock .. &c., &c.	2,220 0 0	5,800 0 0						
1902 Feb. 22 28	Estimated Stock ..	2,460 0 0	6,270 0 0						
	Purchases ..	390 0 0	90 0 0						
		2,850 0 0	6,360 0 0						
"	Net Sales	600 0 0	300 0 0						
"	Estimated Stock ..	2,250 0 0	6,060 0 0						
	Actual Stock ..	2,170 0 0	6,075 0 0						
	Difference Over ..	..	15 0 0						
	" Under ..	80 0 0							

MONTHLY DEPARTMENTAL STOCK ACCOUNTS, from 1900-1 to 1903-4, Department "A," Gross Profit, 10 %.

Date		1900-1901	1901-1902	1902-1903	1903-1904
		£ s d	£ s d	£ s d	£ s d
Mar. 1 31	Actual Stock		1,840 0 0	2,000 0 0	
	Purchases..		600 0 0	720 0 0	
			2,440 0 0	2 720 0 0	
"	Sales ..	492 0 0	..	555 11 1	
	Less 10 %	49 4 0	442 16 0	55 11 1	500 0 0
April 1	Estimated Stock		1,997 4 0	2,220 0 0	
	&c. to end of year.				

STORES ACCOUNTS.

It is convenient to observe a distinction between the accounts kept as a check upon goods that are bought for the purposes of re-sale (*i.e.*, the stock of traders), and goods that are bought for the purpose of being used in manufacture (*i.e.*, the raw materials, or stores, of manufacturers). The former have been described as " Stock Accounts " and the latter may be conveniently known as " Stores Accounts." To some extent the same general principles apply to both, but with Stores Accounts certain special considerations are involved, in that these accounts are usually required to provide part of the data necessary to compile accurate accounts of the *cost* of manufactured articles. It is necessary, therefore, not merely to be able to keep a check upon the amount of each separate stores in hand, and also to be able to show in a convenient form the amount consumed in respect of each separate contract, or each separate lot of goods or articles manufactured. This latter use of Stores Accounts is fully described in Chap. XIX., which deals with " Cost Accounts," but the particular requirements in connection with the matter will to some extent modify the keeping of the Stores Accounts themselves. Hence the necessity of referring to the subject here.

As a preventive of waste, the chief requirements in connection with Stores Accounts is that they should be kept under as many headings as are necessary to enable each of the various classes of Stores to be separately treated ; so that in case of need the value of Stores-in-hand—as shown by the Stores Account—may be readily verified, without its being necessary to take an inventory of the *whole* of the Stores. For example, in a gas works, a separate account would be kept in respect of " Mains," and in a large concern this would be sub-divided so that each size of main would be kept separately. By this means, if any doubt arises as to the accuracy of the accounts, they can be readily tested by taking an inventory of the amount of that particular commodity in hand ; so that any discrepancy disclosed may be traced at the time, instead of it being necessary to wait until it is practicable for stock to be taken- of the whole of the stores. This sub-division of the Stores under headings has also the very important advantage that the balances of the various Stores Accounts afford an invaluable index of the quantity of materials in stock, so that others may be ordered when those in hand are approaching exhaustion. It may safely be said that the more detailed the sub-division upon these lines, the more useful the Stores Accounts will be found to be ; but regard must, of course, be had to what is practicable, in view of the expense that an ideally perfect set of accounts would involve.

Enough has been stated to show that the general principle involved is that of recording transfers to the debit of a large number of different jobs, runnings, or contracts, for Stores consumed, from the credit a large number of different classes of Stores, and the most convenient method of recording these transfers will to a great extent depend upon the number of different accounts involved. In all cases the original record of the transfer will be a Requisition, requesting the store-keeper to hand over certain stores, to be charged up to such-and-such accounts. The Requisitions will naturally deal with quantities only, and not with the value of the goods required. As a rule, however, the Stores Accounts will be most conveniently kept in money, although in some cases as an additional check they may be advantageously kept in both money and quantity. Under these circumstances much depends upon a suitable form of Requisition. The following is a typical specimen, subject of course to modifications to meet the precise requirements of each case :—

EXAMPLE :

THE EUREKA MANUFACTURING CO., LIM.

STORES REQUISITION No......

To the Store-keeper.   Please supply the following, viz.—

Stores Ledger Folio	Quantity	Description	A/c.	Price	Value	Cost Ledger Folio
					£ s d	

To be charged up to contract No...... ....
...............190......   *Superintendent.*

All Requisitions should in the first instance be bound up in counterfoil books, so that a permanent record may be kept in case the sheet itself should get mislaid or destroyed, and they should be consecutively numbered so that attention may be at once drawn to the absence of one, and enquiries instituted accordingly. These sheets should be priced out and extended by the store-keeper, so that a proper value may be placed upon every commodity issued, and when this portion of the work has been properly checked the work of recording the transfer may be pursued. In some cases it will be sufficient to treat the Requisitions in the same manner as a bank treats its cheques—that is, they may be made to serve as the posting medium to the debit of the work and to the credit of the Stores, without being first recorded in any book of original entry (*c.f.* Chap. XVIII.). The Ledger postings will then in each case contain a reference to the number of the Requisition, and the Ledger folios would be put on the latter so as to show that it had been posted to both debit and credit. Where, however, issues of Stores are numerous, this practice would be inconvenient, because it would involve a large number of postings to the Ledger Accounts, whereas it is convenient that the Ledger Accounts should be kept as condensed as practicable in order that the general effect may be more closely followed. Under these circumstances the intervention of a Tabular Journal becomes desirable, and the following ruling will sufficiently explain what is here intended.

EXAMPLES:

STORES JOURNAL (Credit Stores Accounts).

No. of Requisition	"A" A/c.		"B" A/c.		"C" A/c.	"D" A/c.	"E" A/c.	"F" A/c.	"G" A/c.	"H" A/c.
	Quantity	Value	Quantity	Value						
		£ s d		£ s d	£ s d	£ s d	£ s d	£ s d	£ s d	£ s d

STORES JOURNAL (Debit Contract Accounts).

No. of Requisition	No. 1	No. 2	No. 3	No. 4	No. 5	No. 6	No. 7	No. 8	No. 9	No. 10
	£ s d	£ s d	£ s d	£ s d	£ s d	£ s d	£ s d	£ s d	£ s d	£ s d

By tabulating the results as before indicated, the number of postings to each account can be limited to one per day, or one per week, as may be found most convenient, while the accuracy of the tabulation can be tested, because the total of the tabulations to the credit of stores for any period should, of course, exactly equal the total of the tabulations to the debit of the various jobs.

It should be explained here that the debit postings are in practice frequently made not in the Store-keeper's Office, but in the Cost Office. That, however, in no way affects the principle already described, although naturally in such a case it becomes necessary either to frame the Requisitions so that they are capable of *division* between the two departments, or else for them (or the Journal) to be passed on from one department to the other, so that each may record that part of the transactions which concerns it.

In order that no mistakes may arise through issues of stores being credited to the wrong Stores Account —such a mistake may easily occur, if the clerks entering up the Requisitions do not themselves have the handling of the stores—it is desirable that the store-keeper actually issuing the goods should mark the sheets with a letter or number indicating the exact account affected. A set of rubber stamps will be found very convenient for this purpose.

The debits to the various Stores Accounts are, of course, prepared from the purchase invoices. Care must, however, be taken to see that the totals are agreed at frequent intervals.

E 2

CHAPTER VIII.

PARTNERSHIP ACCOUNTS.

BOOKKEEPING, as applied to businesses carried on by single persons, records the transactions between—and the relative position of—the business and outside persons, and also of the business and its proprietor. In the case of a partnership, there are two or more proprietors, and the bookkeeping has to be modified accordingly. The essential principles, however, remain the same. The excess of the assets over the outside liabilities at any time are still the "Capital" of the business; but as it is desired not merely to keep account of the transactions between the business and outsiders, but also on account of the transactions between the business and its partners, a separate "Capital Account" has to be kept for each partner, which (if the books are correctly and completely written up) will invariably show the amount due to (or from) that partner from (or to) the business.

NATURE OF PARTNERSHIP.

A partnership is defined by the Partnership Act, 1890, as "the relation which subsists between per-"sons carrying on a business in common with a view "of profit." The exact relationship between the partners is covered by the general law; subject, however, to such modifications thereto as may have been mutually agreed upon. These modifications usually take the form of Partnership Articles, which are commonly (but not necessarily) under seal. The partnership agreement need not, however, be in writing, and so long as the agreement can be established it is binding on all parties thereto. So far as the accounts are concerned, the principal points

in connection with the general law are that each partner is entitled to share equally in the profits of the firm; but before arriving at such profits, interest at the rate of 5 per cent. must be credited to each partner for *loans* made by him to the business with the consent of the other partners, although no interest is payable upon partners' capital. In the absence of an agreement to the contrary, any partner can at any time terminate the partnership.

CONDITIONS OF PARTNERSHIP AGREEMENTS.

These general conditions are usually supplemented and varied as follows:—

(1) The amount of Capital to be contributed by each partner is stated, and it is generally provided that such Capital bears interest at the rate of 5 per cent. per annum.

(2) The amount that each partner is entitled to draw periodically on account of profits is limited.

(3) It is provided that proper books of account shall be kept, such as are used among persons carrying on a similar class of business.

(4) That the books shall be kept on the partnership premises, and that all partners shall have access thereto.

(5) It is further provided that at least in every year, upon a date named, a "general account" shall be made of all the partnership property, showing the exact position of the firm; and that such account when prepared shall be signed by all the partners, and thereupon shall be binding upon them all—save that, if any manifest error is discovered within three months from the date of such signing, it shall be corrected.

(6) It is usual also to provide for the assessment of the amount to be paid to a retiring partner, or to the representatives of a deceased partner, in respect of Goodwill.

In practice, it frequently happens that disputes arise between partners, or between surviving partners and the representatives of a deceased partner, on account of the insufficiency, or ambiguity, of the terms of the partnership agreement.

It is recommended, therefore, that, in addition to the foregoing, additional clauses should be inserted to the following effect:—

(1) That the firm's accounts shall be periodically audited by a Chartered Accountant. It is desirable where practicable that the name of the Accountant selected should be inserted in the partnership deed, as then a majority of the partners cannot change the Auditor, although, of course, he can still be changed by the unanimous decision of *all* the partners.

(2) The accounts to be kept upon a proper system of Double Entry, to be approved by the Auditor.

(3) All differences or disputes upon matters of account to be referred to Auditor, whose decision shall be binding upon all parties.

(4) Provision should be made for the charging of interest upon all drawings in excess of the prescribed amount, and for allowing of interest upon any excess of the authorised drawings over the actual amount withdrawn.

(5) On the death or retirement of a partner it is necessary, under the general law, to take stock and to balance the books in order to ascertain the respective positions of the partners. To avoid the trouble and inconvenience that this would cause, it is generally desirable to insert a clause providing that the share of the outgoing partner in the profits of the current broken period shall be computed upon the average of the three preceding years. A clause to this effect should, however, only be inserted when the profits do not fluctuate considerably, as otherwise serious injustice might be done by excluding the results of the broken period.

(6) The exact *mode* of paying out the outgoing partner should be provided, and, where practicable, this amount should be payable by instalments extending over such a period as not to seriously cripple the business; or, in the alternative, a policy of " survivorship insurance " should be effected at the cost of the firm.

BALANCING PARTNERSHIP BOOKS.

It is not anticipated that the reader will find any difficulty in preparing the usual accounts from a Trial Balance of the books of the firm, but for the sake of completeness the following example is appended:—

PROBLEM.—Prepare a Profit and Loss Account and Balance Sheet from the following Trial Balance of X. Y. & Co.'s books, extracted at 31st December 1896, covering six months' operations.

	£	£
Cash at Bankers	2,640	
Petty Cash in hand	3	
Sales		16,123
Stock in hand 1st July 1896	2,741	
Returns (Customers' Returns for the half-year)	330	
Discount allowed Customers	938	
Bills Receivable in hand	182	
Sundry Debtors	5,272	
Purchases	8,403	
Discount allowed on Purchases		390
Wages	1,404	
Reserve for Bad and Doubtful Debts		540
Reserve for Discounts on Book Debts		197
Sundry Creditors		1,970
Buildings	4,384	
Patent Rights	50	
Loan on Mortgage		4,500
Rent, Rates, and Taxes	106	
Advertising	463	
Traveller's Salary	431	
Carriage	394	
Bad Debts written off	101	
Plant and Machinery	2,672	
Repairs	84	
C. G.—Capital Account (Balance 1st July 1896)		6,110
C. G.—Drawing Account	1,200	
S. G.—Capital Account (Balance 1st July 1896)		2,952
S. G.—Drawing Account	720	
Interest on Loans	124	
Reserve Account—Patent Royalties received in advance..		500
Royalties on Patents attributable to the half-year to 31st December 1896		40
Trade and General Expenses	502	
Depreciation written off Buildings	23	
Depreciation written off Plant, &c.	155	
	£33,322	£33,322

The Stock-in-Trade on hand at 31st December 1896 is valued at £3,275. No Interest on Capital or withdrawals is to be provided for.

The Profits are to be apportioned as follows :—

C. G., five-eighths ; S. G., three-eighths.

Dr.   TRADING ACCOUNT for the 6 months ended 31st December 1896.   **Cr.**

	£ s d	£ s d		£ s d	£ s d
To Stock, 1st July 1896	..	2,741 0 0	By Sales	16,123 0 0	
„ Purchases	..	8,403 0 0	_Less_ Returns	330 0 0	
„ Carriage	..	394 0 0			15,793 0 0
„ Wages .. .. :	..	1,404 0 0	„ Stock, 31st December 1896 ..	..	3,275 0 0
„ Gross Profit transferred to Profit and Loss Account	..	6,126 0 0			
		£19,068 0 0			£19,068 0 0

Dr.   PROFIT AND LOSS ACCOUNT for the 6 months ended 31st December 1896.   **Cr.**

	£ s d	£ s d		£ s d	£ s d
To Rent, Rates, and Taxes	106 0 0		By Gross Profit as per Trading Account	..	6,126 0 0
„ Trade and General Expenses ..	502 0 0		„ Royalties on Patents..	..	40 0 0
„ Advertising	463 0 0		„ Discounts on Purchases	..	390 0 0
„ Traveller's Salary	431 0 0	1,502 0 0			
„ Repairs	84 0 0				
„ Depreciation of Buildings ..	23 0 0				
„ Do. Plant, &c. ..	155 0 0	262 0 0			
„ Bad Debts	101 0 0				
„ Interest on Loans	124 0 0				
„ Discounts allowed	938 0 0	1,163 0 0			
„ Balance (being Net Profit for the half-year) transferred to Capital Accounts, viz. :—					
C. G., ⅝ths share	2,268 2 6				
S. G., ⅜ths share	1,360 17 6	3,629 0 0			
		£6,556 0 0			£6,556 0 0

BALANCE SHEET, 31st December 1896.

Liabtlities.	£ s d	£ s d	_Assets._	£ s d	£ s d
Capital Account, viz. :—			Buildings, _Less_ Depreciation	..	4,384 0 0
C. G., Balance 1st July 1896 .. .. .. £6,110 0 0			Plant and Machinery, _Less_ Depreciation	..	2,672 0 0
Less Drawings .. 1,200 0 0			Patent Rights	..	50 0 0
	4,910 0 0		Stock-in-Trade	..	3,275 0 0
Add Share of Net Profit 2,268 2 6			Bills Receivable	182 0 0	
		7,178 2 6	Sundry Debtors	5,272 0 0	
S. G., Balance 1st July 1896 .. .. .. £2,952 0 0				5,454 0 0	
Less Drawings .. 720 0 0			_Less_ Reserve for Discount and Bad and Doubtful Debts	737 0 0	
	2,232 0 0				4,717 0 0
Add Share of Net Profit 1,360 17 6			Cash at Bankers	2,640 0 0	
		3,592 17 6	Petty Cash in hand	3 0 0	
					2,643 0 0
Loan on Mortgage	..	10,771 0 0			
Sundry Creditors	..	4,500 0 0			
Reserve for Royalties paid in advance	..	1,970 0 0			
		500 0 0			
		£17,741 0 0			£17,741 0 0

NOTES.—(1) _Returns should be deducted, so as to show a net figure of Sales or Purchases._ (2) _Cash Discounts should appear in the Profit and Loss Account, not in the Trading Account._ (3) _The item " Royalties " may be a liability, but is more likely to be a source of income, especially as £500 appears to have been received in advance._ (4) _A special Reserve—e.g., for Discount or Bad Debts—should be deducted from the items in respect of which it is made, and not shown as a liability._

ADJUSTING ACCOUNTS KEPT BY SINGLE-ENTRY.

Rather more trouble may be experienced in cases where the books have only been kept by single entry. Under these circumstances the only method of arriving at the profit for the current period is to prepare a "Statement of Assets and Liabilities," which (in normal cases) will show a surplus of assets. This Surplus is the amount of Capital in the business at the date when the statement is prepared, and is consequently the combined capital of the partners as at that date. The balance of each separate partner's Capital Account is arrived at by adding to the above balance the amount drawn out by all the partners during the current period, and the total sum arrived at is the surplus that *would have been* in hand had no monies been withdrawn. If from this total be deducted the amount standing to the credit of all the partners on Capital Account at the commencement of the period, the difference must be the accretions of capital during the period—*i.e.*, the Net Profit. The following is a simple example, showing clearly how such a problem should be dealt with :—

PROBLEM.—A., B. & C. are partners in the firm of X., Y. & Co., whose books are kept by single entry. At 30th November 1900 the balance in favour of the firm was £14,080, thus :—

				£
A.	..	..	..	6,080
B.	..	..	..	5,000
C.	..	..	..	3,000
				£14,080

At 30th November 1901 their assets amounted to £47,250, and their liabilities to £33,297, the balance in favour of the firm being thus £13,953.

Profits and losses are divisible as follows: Five-tenths to A., three-tenths to B., and two-tenths to C. Their drawings during the year have been as follows :—

				£
A.	..	..	..	1,207
B.	..	..	..	820
C.	..	..	..	600

What are the amounts at the credit of their accounts respectively at 30th November 1901 after providing interest on capital at 5 per cent. ? And show how the amounts are arrived at.

STATEMENT OF AFFAIRS, 30th November 1901.

	£ s d	£ s d		£ s d	£ s d
Sundry Liabilities		33,297 0 0	Sundry Assets		47,250 0 0
Balance down (being Capital of the firm on 30th Nov. 1901)		13,953 0 0			
		£47,250 0 0			£47,250 0 0
Capital on 30th Nov. 1900, A.	6,080 0 0				
B.	5,000 0 0		Balance down..		13,953 0 0
C.	3,000 0 0	14,080 0 0	Drawings: A.	1,207 0 0	
			B.	820 0 0	
			C.	600 0 0	2,627 0 0
Interest on Capital for the year A. ..	304 0 0				
B. ..	250 0 0				
C. ..	150 0 0	704 0 0			
Balance (being net profit for the year ended 30th Nov. 1901) A.	898 0 0				
B.	538 16 0				
C.	359 4 0	1,796 0 0			
		£16,580 0 0			£16,580 0 0

Dr.   PARTNERS' CAPITAL ACCOUNTS (CONDENSED).   Cr.

		A	B	C			A	B	C
		£ s d	£ s d	£ s d	1900 Dec. 1	By Balance	£ s d 6,080 0 0	£ s d 5,000 0 0	£ s d 3,000 0 0
1900 Nov. 30	To Drawings	1,207 0 0	820 0 0	600 0 0	1901 Nov.30	„ Interest on Capital..	304 0 0	250 0 0	150 0 0
„	„ Balance down	6,075 0 0	4,968 16 0	2,909 4 0	„	„ Share of Profit ..	898 0 0	538 16 0	359 4 0
		£7,282 0 0	£5,788 16 0	£3,509 4 0			£7,282 0 0	£5,788 16 0	£3,509 4 0
					1901 Dec. 1	By Balance .. :.	6,075 0 0	4,968 16 0	2,909 4 0

NOTE.—Results arrived at by single-entry should always be proved as far as possible, as there is not—as in double-entry—any automatic check upon their clerical accuracy. The proof is as follows :—The adjusted Capital Accounts show as balances £6,075 + £4,968 16s., + £2,909 4s. = £13,953. This is the same as the Capital of the firm as a whole, as shown by the Statement of Affairs. The Capital of all the Partners taken together must always equal the Capital of the firm.

As already stated, the practice of keeping books by single entry is never to be recommended, particularly in the case of a partnership; but as the problem frequently arises in practice, it is well to consider an adjustment of Partnership Accounts, in which the circumstances are somewhat more involved than the preceding.

Such a problem is given below, and will well repay careful attention and perusal :—

PROBLEM.—On the 31st December 1895, A.'s liabilities amounted to £2,000, and his assets to £3,500. On the 1st January 1896, he admitted B. into partnership on the terms that A.'s capital was to be agreed at £1,500; that B. should not be called upon to find any capital; that profits should be divided between the partners in the proportions of two-thirds to A. and one-third to B.; that B.'s drawings should be limited to £400 a year until such time as A. had been paid the premium which it was agreed that he should receive in consideration of the partnership. This premium is fixed at £575, to be paid from year to year out of the excess of B.'s share of profits over his drawings, interest at the rate of 5 per cent. per annum being charged by A. on the balance outstanding from time to time. The firm only kept their books by single entry, but statements of their assets and liabilities were prepared at the end of each year as follows :—

	Liabilities.		Assets.
1896	£3,600	.. ..	£5,300
1897	2,400	.. ..	4,000
1898	3,500	.. ..	5,200
1899	3,200	.. ..	6,700
1900	3,000	.. ..	6,000

A.'s drawings during the five years were as follows :—

1896	..	..	..	..	..	£725
1897	..	..	..	..	..	850
1898	..	..	..	..	..	1,000
1899	..	..	..	..	..	1,000
1900	..	..	..	..	..	1,600

B. only drew out his agreed maximum of £400.

You are required to show (a) the Capital Accounts of the partners for the five years, allowing interest at 5 per cent. per annum, and (b) a Statement showing the Account between A. and B. in respect of Goodwill.

Dr. — STATEMENT OF AFFAIRS (Condensed) 1896-1900. — **Cr.**

	1896	1897	1898	1899	1900		1896	1897	1898	1899	1900
	£ s d	£ s d	£ s d	£ s d	£ s d		£ s d	£ s d	£ s d	£ s d	£ s d
Liabilities ..	3,600 0 0	2,400 0 0	3,500 0 0	3,200 0 0	3,000 0 0	Assets	5,300 0 0	4,000 0 0	5,200 0 0	6,700 0 0	6,000 0 0
Balance down (being Capital of the firm at close of the year) ..	1,700 0 0	1,600 0 0	1,700 0 0	3,500 0 0	3,000 0 0						
£	5,300 0 0	4,000 0 0	5,200 0 0	6,700 0 0	6,000 0 0	£	5,300 0 0	4,000 0 0	5,200 0 0	6,700 0 0	6,000 0 0
Capital o firm at commencement of the year	1,500 0 0	1,700 0 0	1,600 0 0	1,700 0 0	3,500 0 0	Balance down ..	1,700 0 0	1,600 0 0	1,700 0 0	3,500 0 0	3,000 0 0
Interest on Capital	75 0 0	85 0 0	80 0 0	85 0 0	175 0 0	Drawings: A. ..	725 0 0	850 0 0	1,000 0 0	1,000 0 0	1,600 0 0
Balance (being net profit for the year) ..	1,250 0 0	1,065 0 0	1,420 0 0	3,115 0 0	1,325 0 0	Do. B. ..	400 0 0	400 0 0	400 0 0	400 0 0	400 0 0
£	2,825 0 0	2,850 0 0	3,100 0 0	4,900 0 0	5,000 0 0	£	2,825 0 0	2,850 0 0	3,100 0 0	4,900 0 0	5,000 0 0
Division of above Profits: A. ..	833 6 8	710 0 0	946 13 4	2,076 13 4	883 6 8						
B. ..	416 13 4	355 0 0	473 6 8	1,038 6 8	441 13 4						
£	1,250 0 0	1,065 0 0	1,420 0 0	3,115 0 0	1,325 0 0						

Dr. — "A" CAPITAL ACCOUNT (Condensed). — **Cr.**

	1896	1897	1898	1899	1900		1896	1897	1898	1899	1900
	£ s d	£ s d	£ s d	£ s d	£ s d		£ s d	£ s d	£ s d	£ s d	£ s d
To Drawings ..	725 0 0	850 0 0	1,000 0 0	1,000 0 0	1,600 0 0	By Balance: 1st Jan. ..	1,500 0 0	1,700 0 0	1,645 0 0	1,700 0 0	3,500 0 0
" Balance: 31st Dec. ..	1,700 0 0	1,645 0 0	1,700 0 0	3,500 0 0	2,972 18 8	" Interest on Capital ..	75 0 0	85 0 0	82 5 0	85 0 0	175 0 0
						" Share of Profits	833 6 8	710 0 0	946 13 4	2,076 13 4	883 6 8
						" Transfer from B. on a/c. of Goodwill ..	16 13 4	..	26 1 8	638 6 8	14 12 0
£	2,425 0 0	2,495 0 0	2,700 0 0	4,500 0 0	4,572 18 8	£	2,425 0 0	2,495 0 0	2,700 0 0	4,500 0 0	4,572 18 8

Dr. — "B" CAPITAL ACCOUNT (Condensed). — **Cr.**

	1896	1897	1898	1899	1900		1896	1897	1898	1899	1900
	£ s d	£ s d	£ s d	£ s d	£ s d		£ s d	£ s d	£ s d	£ s d	£ s d
To Balance: 1st Jan.	..	..	45 0 0	..	..	By Balance: 1st Jan. ..	..	..	..	..	..
" Drawings ..	400 0 0	400 0 0	400 0 0	400 0 0	400 0 0	" Interest on Capital	..	..	..	..	..
" Interest on Overdraft ..	..	..	2 5 0	..	..	" Share of Profits	416 13 4	355 0 0	473 6 8	1,038 6 8	441 13 4
" Transfer to A. ..	16 13 4	..	26 1 8	638 6 8	14 12 0	" Balance: 31st Dec. ..	..	45 0 0	..	..	..
" Balance: 31st Dec. ..	..	..	..	..	27 1 4						
£	416 13 4	400 0 0	473 6 8	1,038 6 8	441 13 4	£	416 13 4	400 0 0	473 6 8	1,038 6 8	441 13 4

Dr. — "B" IN A/c WITH "A" IN RESPECT OF GOODWILL (Condensed).* — **Cr.**

	1896	1897	1898	1899	1900		1896	1897	1898	1899	1900
	£ s d	£ s d	£ s d	£ s d	£ s d		£ s d	£ s d	£ s d	£ s d	£ s d
To agreed Premium ..	575 0 0	..	..	..	..	By Amount credited as paid on account..	16 13 4	..	26 1 8	638 6 8	14 12 0
" Balance: 1st Jan.	..	587 1 8	616 8 10	621 3 7	13 18 1	" Balance: 31st Dec. ..	587 1 8	616 8 10	621 3 7	13 18 1	..
" Interest for the year ..	28 15 0	29 7 2	30 16 5	31 1 2	0 13 11						
£	603 15 0	616 8 10	647 5 3	652 4 9	14 12 0	£	603 15 0	616 8 10	647 5 3	652 4 9	14 12 0

NOTE.—These Problems are rather troublesome to solve, as the smallest error vitiates the figures of every subsequent year. It is best, therefore, to complete the Statement of Affairs for the whole period before attempting to compile the Capital Accounts of the various partners : these should then be compiled, taking care to see that the closing balances added together agree each year with the total capital of the firm, as shown in the Statement of Affairs.

* It must be clearly understood that this Account cannot be included in the books of the firm, which show the relation of each partner to the business but *not* the relations of the partners *inter se.* The Account must, however, be compiled as a memorandum, in order to know the amount due from B. to A., in respect of Goodwill from time to time, and also when the whole amount is cleared off.

DISSOLUTION OF PARTNERSHIP.

It is, however, chiefly in connection with Dissolutions that problems most distinctive of this particular class of accounts arise. Accounts upon a dissolution of partnership may require adjustment in one of two ways:—

   (a) One, or more, of the partners may continue the business, and pay out the retiring partner, or partners.

   (b) The assets of the firm may have to be realised, and—after payment of the firm's debts—the surplus distributed among the partners in proportion to their respective interests.

PAYING OUT RETIRING PARTNER.

The first problem is for many reasons the simpler. The outgoing partner is then paid such sum as may have been agreed upon, the payment being either in cash or spread over a period. The continuing partners will probably continue to use the books of the firm, and it then becomes necessary to consider the entries that require to be made in these books to adjust them to the altered position of affairs.

The following example shows alternative methods of dealing with this problem:—

PROBLEM.—On the 31st December 1901 the Balance Sheet of A. and B. stood as follows:—

				£	s	d					£	s	d
A. Capital Account	..		..	1,500	0	0	Premises	..	..	..	250	0	0
B. do. do.	..		..	1,000	0	0	Stock	..	..	..	200	0	0
Sundry Creditors	..		..	500	0	0	Sundry Debtors	..	..	2,000	0	0
							Cash	..	..	..	550	0	0
				£3,000	0	0					£3,000	0	0

A. buys out B., agreeing to pay him £1,600 for his share of the assets and goodwill of the business as it stands, £400 being paid at once, and the balance to be paid in three months' time.

You are required to show the Balance Sheet of A. as at 1st January 1902 (after the transaction has been carried through), and also the Capital Accounts of A. and B.

Dr.   **"A." CAPITAL ACCOUNT.**   Cr.

1901		£	s	d	1901						£	s	d
Dec. 31	To Balance down	2,100	0	0	Dec. 31	By Balance					1,500	0	0
						„ Goodwill					600	0	0
		£2,100	0	0							£2,100	0	0
					1902								
					Jan. 1	By Balance					£2,100	0	0

Dr.   **"B." CAPITAL ACCOUNT.**   Cr.

1901		£	s	d	1901						£	s	d
Dec. 31	To Transfer to "B" Account	1,600	0	0	Dec. 31	By Balance					1,000	0	0
					„	„ Goodwill					600	0	0
		£1,600	0	0							£1,600	0	0

Dr.								"B."				Cr.

1901 Dec. 31	To Cash					£ s d 400 0 0	1901 Dec. 31	By Transfer from "B" Capital Account ..	£ s d 1,600 0 0
"	" Balance down	..	..	..	..	1,200 0 0			
						£1,600 0 0			£1,600 0 0
							1902 Jan. 1	By Balance	1,200 0 0

BALANCE SHEET, 1st January 1902.

Liabilities.						£ s d	Assets.						£ s d
"A." Capital Account	..	..	..	..	..	2,100 0 0	Goodwill ..	..	..	..	..	..	1,200 0 0
"B." ..	..	..	..	..	..	1,200 0 0	Premises ..	..	..	..	..	..	250 0 0
Sundry Creditors	..	..	..	..	..	500 0 0	Stock ..	..	..	..	..	..	200 0 0
							Sundry Debtors..	..	..	..	..	..	2,000 0 0
							Cash ..	..	..	..	..	..	150 0 0
						£3,800 0 0							£3,800 0 0

NOTE.—If preferred, the Goodwill Account might be written off, reducing " A.'s " Capital Account to £900. A shorter way of recording the transaction is to credit " B " with £600 (the amount required to adjust the balance of his account with the agreed purchase-price), and debit " A.'s " Capital Account with the same amount. No Goodwill Account will then be raised.

TRANSFER OF BUSINESS.

Closely allied with the foregoing is the case of a sole trader selling his business as it stands to another, who wishes to continue using the same books. This problem is perfectly simple, if it be borne in mind that the Capital Account of the outgoing proprietor *primâ facie* shows the amount due to him from the business. If necessary, the balance of that account must be adjusted, so as to agree with the purchase-price that the vendor is about to receive; and, the sale being effected, the account remains open in the Ledger until the purchase-price has been actually paid. But from the date of the sale it of course ceases to be a "Capital" Account, the late proprietor now becoming merely a creditor of the business. The following example makes this position of affairs clear.

PROBLEM.—On the 31st December 1901, A. D. prepared a Balance Sheet of his business as follows :—

Liabilities.				£ s d	Assets.			£ s d
Capital	..		..	1,000 0 0	Premises ..	..	..	200 0 0
Sundry Creditors	..		..	500 0 0	Stock ..	..	..	300 0 0
					Book Debts	..	..	900 0 0
					Cash at Bank	..	..	100 0 0
				£1,500 0 0				£1,500 0 0

On the 1st January 1902 he transferred the business to his son C. D., who paid him £400 for the Goodwill, Premises, and Stock, and agreed to discharge the liabilities, and to collect and account for the Book Debts, subject to a commission of 2½ per cent. The balance at bank was retained by the father. C. D. opened a new Bank Account with a balance of £1,000, out of which he paid the £400 premium to his father. He decided to continue using the same books.

You are required to show (1) C. D.'s starting Balance Sheet, after the transfer had been effected and the premium paid, (2) C. D.'s Capital Account, and (3) the closing of the Capital Account of A. D.

Dr.   "A. D." CAPITAL ACCOUNT.   **Cr.**

1902		£	s	d	1901		£	s	d
Jan. 1	To Cash	100	0	0	Dec. 31	By Balance	1,000	0	0
"	" do. per "C. D."	400	0	0	1902				
"	" Balance transferred to "A. D." Account..	900	0	0	Jan. 1	" Goodwill	400	0	0
		£1,400	0	0			£1,400	0	0

"A. D."   **Cr.**

					1902		£	s	d
					Jan. 1	By Balance from "A. D." Capital Account	900	0	0

Dr.   " C. D." CAPITAL ACCOUNT.   **Cr.**

					1902		£	s	d
					Jan. 1	By Cash	1,000	0	0

BALANCE SHEET, 1st January 1902.

Liabilities.	£	s	d	Assets.	£	s	d
"C. D." Capital Account	1,000	0	0	Goodwill	400	0	0
"A. D." (in respect of Book Debts)	900	0	0	Premises	200	0	0
Sundry Creditors	500	0	0	Stock	300	0	0
				Book Debts	900	0	0
				Cash at Bank	600	0	0
	£2,400	0	0		£2,400	0	0

NOTE.—The taking over of the liabilities is exactly balanced by the taking over of the Premises and Stock, the £400 is thus paid entirely in respect of Goodwill. If it is preferred to open a Goodwill Account, the £400 must be debited to "C. D.'s" Capital Account, reducing the balance to £600. It is best not to anticipate the 2½ per cent. Commission on the realisation of Book Debts, but to debit it to "A. D.'s" Account as and when remittances on account are made.

REALISATION ACCOUNTS.

The method of closing the books and adjusting the Capital Accounts of the various partners when the business is discontinued and the assets realised, is shown in the next example. It should be stated, however, that in practice the Bought and Sold Ledgers would probably be discontinued as from the date of dissolution. If the Private Ledger is "self-balancing," the balances outstanding on the Sales Ledger Account and the Bought Ledger Account respectively at the date of the dissolution would be brought down in full detail, instead of being in total only, so that the payment of the creditors and the realisation of the book debts might be perceived from a perusal of the Private Ledger alone. Or, if these creditors and debtors are very numerous, the better plan would be to adhere to the system of totals in the Private Ledger and to supplement the Adjustment Account by new Tabular Ledgers for creditors and debtors respectively, ruled in the form shown on the following page.

Ledger Folio	Name	Address	Ledger Balance	Date Paid	C. B. Folio	Cash	Discounts and Allowances	Remarks
			£ s d			£ s d	£ s d	

It will be perceived that the "Realisation Account" shown in the following example is for all practical purposes upon the same lines as an ordinary Profit and Loss Account. Often, however, the method is adopted of transferring the balance standing upon all the various assets accounts to the debit of the Realisation Account as at the date of the dissolution. These assets accounts are thus closed at once, and the cash realised on the disposal of the various assets is then posted direct to the credit of the Realisation Account. This last-named method is preferable where only a comparatively small number of accounts are involved, and is therefore specially suitable for problems arising at examinations. Whichever method be adopted, however, the balance of the Realisation Account will be the same—viz., loss (or profit) on the realisa-tion—and this balance must be transferred to the Capital Accounts of the various partners; each partner bearing his share of the loss (or profit) in the proportions that may have been already agreed.

In the absence of a special agreement to the contrary, all partners share both profits and losses equally, quite irrespective of the amount of capital standing to their credit; but if it has been agreed that profits are to be shared in any other proportion, losses must be borne in the same proportion as profits were to have been, unless there is a special agreement that they are to be borne in a different proportion.

The following example shows in full the entries necessary to close the books of a firm and adjust the accounts of the various partners:—

PROBLEM.—J., H., and B. are partners; their interests in the profits of the firm are one-half, three-eighths, and one-eighth respectively. On December 31 1892 the partnership terminates, and the Balance Sheet is as follows:—

			£					£
Sundry Creditors	...	...	3,550	Cash at Bankers...	...	...	250	
J., Capital Account	...	...	3,500	Bills Receivable ...	...	...	300	
H., Capital Account	...	...	1,500	Book Debts	...	...	...	6,000
B., Capital Account	...	...	1,000	Stock ...	...	...	...	1,000
				Lease ...	...	...	...	500
				Plant and Machinery	...	...	1,500	
			£9,550					£9,550

On June 30 1893, when the affairs of the firm have been liquidated, it is found that the assets have realised £400 less than the values on the Balance Sheet of December 31 1892, viz., Book Debts, £100 less; Lease, £150 less; and Plant and Machinery, £150 less.

The expenses of winding-up the business amount to £90, and the partners are entitled to interest at 5 per cent. per annum upon their Capital Accounts. Show how to close the books at June 30 1893, giving each partner's account, with the balance ultimately found to be payable to him.

Dr.   CASH AT BANKERS.   *Cr.*

1893		£	s	d	1893		£	s	d
Jan. 1	To Balance	250	0	0	June 30	By Creditors	3,550	0	0
June 30	,, Bills Receivable	300	0	0	,,	,, Liquidation expenses	90	0	0
,,	,, Book Debts	5,900	0	0	,,	,, Balance down	5,510	0	0
,,	,, Stock	1,000	0	0					
,,	,, Lease	350	0	0					
,,	,, Plant, &c.	1,350	0	0					
		£9,150	0	0			£9,150	0	0
July 1	To Balance down	£5,510	0	0					

Dr.   J. (CAPITAL ACCOUNT).   *Cr.*

1893		£	s	d	1893		£	s	d
June 30	To Realisation Account—Loss ..	320	0	0	Jan. 1	By Balance	3,500	0	0
,,	,, Balance down	3,267	10	0	June 30	,, Interest	87	10	0
		£3,587	10	0			£3,587	10	0
					July 1	By Balance down	£3,267	10	0

Dr.   H. (CAPITAL ACCOUNT).   *Cr.*

1893		£	s	d	1893		£	s	d
June 30	To Realisation Account—Loss ..	240	0	0	Jan. 1	By Balance	1,500	0	0
,,	,, Balance down	1,297	10	0	June 30	,, Interest	37	10	0
		£1,537	10	0			£1,537	10	0
					July 1	By Balance down	£1,297	10	0

Dr.   B. (CAPITAL ACCOUNT).   *Cr.*

1893		£	s	d	1893		£	s	d
June 30	To Realisation Account—Loss ..	80	0	0	Jan. 1	By Balance	1,000	0	0
,,	,, Balance down	945	0	0	June 30	,, Interest	25	0	0
		£1,025	0	0			£1,025	0	0
					July 1	By Balance down	£945	0	0

Dr.   BILLS RECEIVABLE.   *Cr.*

1893		£	s	d	1893		£	s	d
Jan. 1	To Balance	300	0	0	June 30	By Cash	300	0	0

Dr.	SUNDRY CREDITORS.					Cr.	
1893 June 30	To Cash	£ s d 3,550 0 0	1893 Jan. 1	By Balance		£ s d 3,550 0 0	

Dr.	BOOK DEBTS.					Cr.	
1893 Jan. 1	To Balance	£ s d 6,000 0 0	1893 June 30 ,, ,,	By Cash .. .. ,, Realisation Account		£ s d 5,900 0 0 100 0 0	
		£6,000 0 0				£6,000 0 0	

Dr.	STOCK.					Cr.	
1893 Jan. 1	To Balance	£ s d 1,000 0 0	1893 June 30	By Cash		£ s d 1,000 0 0	

Dr.	LEASE.					Cr.	
1893 Jan. 1	To Balance	£ s d 500 0 0	1893 June 30 ,, ,,	By Cash .. .. ,, Realisation Account		£ s d 350 0 0 150 0 0	
		£500 0 0				£500 0 0	

Dr.	PLANT AND MACHINERY.					Cr.	
1893 Jan. 1	To Balance	£ s d 1,500 0 0	1893 June 30 ,, ,,	By Cash .. .. ,, Realisation Account		£ s d 1,350 0 0 150 0 0	
		£1,500 0 0				£1,500 0 0	

Dr.	REALISATION ACCOUNT.				Cr.	
1893 June 30 ,, ,, ,, ,, ,,	To Loss on Book Debts .. .. ,, do. Lease .. .. ,, do. Plant, &c. .. .. ,, Cash, Liquidation Expenses.. ,, Interest, J. .. .. .. ,, do. H. .. .. .. ,, do. B.	£ s d 100 0 0 150 0 0 150 0 0 90 0 0 87 10 0 37 10 0 25 0 0	1893 June 30	By Loss on Realisation, transferred to— J. .. .. .. £320 H. .. .. .. 240 B. .. .. .. 80 ———	£ s d 640 0 0	
		£640 0 0			£640 0 0	

NOTE.—*Under ordinary circumstances, interest upon Capital is not payable after the date of dissolution unless by special arrangement ; but the wording of the problem suggests the existence of a special arrangement between the partners.*

ORDER OF DISTRIBUTION OF ASSETS.

Another point that must be carefully borne in mind is the provision contained in the Partnership Act, 1890, as to the *order* in which the proceeds of the various assets are to be applied, in the event of a dissolution. This order is as follows: —

(1) In payment of the debts of a firm to outside creditors.

(2) In repayment to each partner of amounts *lent* by him to the firm, if any.

(3) In repayment to each partner of the Capital contributed by him to the firm.

(4) The surplus (if any) to be divided in the same proportion as profits are divisible.

This rule sometimes gives rise to the misconception that, in the event of a deficiency of assets, those partners who have advanced money to the firm have a preferential claim upon all assets remaining after the outside creditors have been satisfied, and that in the event of there not remaining sufficient to repay capital in full the balance must be applied in the form of a dividend of so much in £ upon the capital contributed by each partner. As a matter of fact, this view is quite incorrect. Partners are liable to make good *inter se* whatever losses have been incurred. If the assets are not sufficient to repay capital, as well as loans and outside creditors, there must necessarily have been a loss, and each partner is liable to repay to the firm his share of such loss. As a matter of fact, however, it is not usual to require each partner to find his share in cash, and then to refund him the whole of his capital intact; what is done is to debit each partner's *account* with his proportion of the loss, and only to ask him for a further contribution in the event of his Capital Account (when so adjusted) showing a debit balance.

In the following example the Capital Account of one of the partners shows a debit balance, which is made good by a transfer from his Loan Account. This example is included, as showing that the order of distribution stated in the Partnership Act, 1890, has under some circumstances the effect that one partner may find that he does not receive back even his loans in full, while another may receive back not only his loans, but also a portion of his capital. The golden rule to be observed in all these cases is that, in order to adjust the accounts of the various partners, *it is invariably necessary to ascertain the final balance of profit (or loss) up to the date of distribution, and to credit (or debit) each partner with his respective share, in the proportions in which it has been agreed that profits (or losses) are to be borne.* This is entirely irrespective of the amount of capital, or loans, that each partner may have put into the business.

PROBLEM.—A. and B. are partners sharing profits equally. Their capital, as it appears in the books of the partnership on the 30th June 1901 (the date on which they dissolve partnership), is A. £2,000, and B. £500. The total amount owing by the firm is £5,000, which includes £1,000 due to A. on Loan Account, and £500 due to B. on Loan Account. The whole of the assets of the firm realised £6,000.

Prepare accounts closing up the partnership, and show the position in which the partners stand with each other.

Dr.   REALISATION ACCOUNT.   Cr.

1901		£ s d	1901		£ s d
June 30	To Amount of assets at this date as per books	7,500 0 0	July 1	To Cash, total amount realised on assets	6,000 0 0
			,,	,, Loss, apportioned thus :— A. .. .. £750 0 0 B. 750 0 0	1,500 0 0
		£7,500 0 0			£7,500 0 0

Dr.   SUNDRY CREDITORS.   Cr.

1901 July 1	To Cash	£ s d £3,500 0 0	1901 June 30	By Amount as per Balance Sheet	£ s d £3,500 0 0

Dr.   A. (LOAN ACCOUNT).   Cr.

1901 July 1	To Cash	£ s d £1,000 0 0	1901 June 30'	By Amount as per Balance Sheet	£ s d £1,000 0 0

Dr.   B. (LOAN ACCOUNT)   Cr.

1901 July 1 „	To Transfer from Capital Account „ Cash	£ s d 250 0 0 250 0 0 £500 0 0	1901 June 30	By Amount as per Balance Sheet	£ s d 500 0 0 £500 0 0

Dr.   A. (CAPITAL ACCOUNT).   Cr.

1901 July. 1 „	To Share of Loss .. .. .. „ Cash	£ s d 750 0 0 1,250 0 0 £2,000 0 0	1901 June 30	By Amount as per Balance Sheet	£ s d 2,000 0 0 £2,000 0 0

Dr.   B. (CAPITAL ACCOUNT).   Cr.

1901 July 1	To Share of Loss	£ s d 750 0 0 £750 0 0	1901 June 30 July 1	By Amount as per Balance Sheet „ Transfer to Loan Account, being deficiency of Capital which B. is liable to make good	£ s d 500 0 0 250 0 0 £750 0 0

Dr.   CASH.   CONTRA.   Cr.

1901 July 1	To Proceeds of realisation ..	£ s d 6,000 0 0 £6,000 0 0	1901 July 1 „ .,	By Sundry Creditors .. .. „ A. (Loan Account) .. .. „ B. (balance of Loan Account) „ A. (Capital Account)	£ s d 3,500 0 0 1,000 0 0 250 0 0 1,250 0 0 £6,000 0 0

NOTE.—For convenience it has been assumed that the realisation of the estate was completed on 1st July 1901.

F

CALCULATION OF INTEREST.

When, on a dissolution, one partner goes out and another continues the business, the question of interest frequently arises in practice, although (in the absence of a special agreement) all calculation of interest ceases at the date of dissolution, even if the partnership articles provide for interest on capital. When the continuing partner also continues the old books, the adjustment of this problem can usually be best effected by raising an Account Current *outside* the books altogether.

The following example will show what is meant better than any general explanation:—

PROBLEM.—M. & N. being equal partners agree to dissolve as from 31st December 1900, and the following is their position:—

They owe creditors £960, they have debtors £3,600, and office effects £200. M. is to realise the debts, to pay the liabilities, to take over the office effects at £180, to allow N. £500 for his share of goodwill, and to pay him his proportion as realised. The debts realise less by £80, and after payment of creditors they are realised at an average date of six months from the date of dissolution. M. pays N. £1,000 at the end of three months, and the balance at the end of twelve months, with interest at 5 per cent. per annum.

What must he then pay?

Dr.					N., IN ACCOUNT WITH M.				Cr.
			Interest	Cash				Interest	Cash
1901			£ s d	£ s d	1901			£ s d	£ s d
Mar. 31	To Cash		37 10 0	1,000 0 0	Jan. 1	By Half-Share of Office Effects taken over by M. at £180..		4 10 0	90 0 0
Dec. 31	„ Balance of Interest		24 0 0			„ Half-Share of Goodwill ..		25 0 0	500 0 0
„	„ Balance down (being amount due to N., including Interest)		..	894 0 0	June 30	„ Half Share of Proceeds of Book Debts, less amount due to Creditors (£3,520 − £960=£2,560)		32 0 0	1,280 0 0
					Dec. 31	„ Interest to date		..	24 0 0
			£61 10 0	£1,894 0 0				£61 10 0	£1,894 0 0
					1902				
					Jan. 1	By Balance down		..	894 0 0

AVERAGE DUE DATE.

The problem just considered suggests that, of the numerous items making up the debts received and the liabilities paid, the "average date" of settlement was the 30th June 1901. This question of average date frequently arises in connection with interest calculations, as affording in many instances by far the simplest method of computing the actual amount of interest to be taken into account. The present seems therefore a suitable opportunity for explaining how such calculations are made.

For the sake of simplicity, only a limited number of items will be assumed. Let us suppose that the Book Debts collected are made up as follows:—

1901	£
April 10	1,000
„ 11	120
July 19	1,400
Sept. 2	1,000
	——£3,520

and that the liabilities paid consist of the following items :—

	1901	£
March	21	100
April	11	260
May	15	300
Nov.	26	300
		——£960

The rule to adopt is as follows :—Take any convenient date (preferably one of the dates recorded in the example), multiply each amount by the number of days intervening between the date selected and the date of that item. Add the products together, and divide by the total of the original amounts. The result will be the number of days between the average date and the date originally selected, so that the latter can by this means be readily ascertained. Having thus ascertained independently the average date of receiving the book debts, and the average date of discharging the liabilities, the combined average may be obtained in the same manner ; save that the date selected must be one different from either average date, and the products must be deducted instead of added together, and then divided by the difference between the average amounts. The full working is shown below, which (combined with the above description) will make the method of procedure clear. Working from the 31st December 1900—

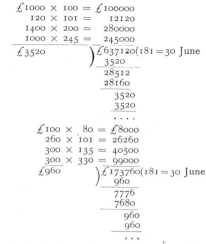

The shortest way of ascertaining a " combined " average date is as follows :—

CHAPTER IX.

COMPANY ACCOUNTS.

IT is proposed in the present chapter to consider those problems in accounting which are peculiar to companies registered under the Companies Acts, 1862 to 1900, or incorporated by special Act of Parliament. The treatment of companies' accounts in other respects is dealt with elsewhere, and with a few obvious exceptions all the chapters in this work apply to the accounts of companies as much as to those of other undertakings. Speaking generally, for the purposes of the present chapter, the books of companies may be divided into two sections—viz., those that deal with the detailed accounts of the various shareholders and debenture-holders, and those that deal with the ordinary financial transactions of the undertaking. As, however, these two sections to some extent record the same transactions (although from different points of view), it will be convenient, when dealing with each particular problem, to first explain the method of recording it in the financial books, and afterwards those entries which are necessary in the subsidiary Share Books.

ISSUE OF CAPITAL.

In the nature of things one of the earliest transactions upon which a company embarks is the issue of capital. The term " Capital," properly speaking, can be applied only to Shares ; but inasmuch as the entries in respect of the issue of Debentures, or Debenture Stock, follow upon much the same lines, it will be convenient to explain the procedure simultaneously. In the case of private syndicates and other similar undertakings—which, while securing the benefits of registration with limited liability,

are owned by a very small number of proprietors—no very special treatment becomes necessary in connection with the issue of Capital. In such cases separate Share Ledgers are only necessary to meet the requirements of the statutes, and it will be found convenient to record all the various transactions fully in the financial books, opening a Personal Account for each shareholder, which will be debited with the amount from time to time called up upon his shares and credited with the amount which he pays thereon. Under normal circumstances, however, the number of shareholders in a company is so considerable that it is not convenient to include their various Personal Accounts in the financial books. A separate Share Ledger is therefore employed, and "Total Accounts" only are kept in the General Ledger. These total accounts are for all practical purposes "Adjustment Accounts." The exigencies of the case point, as a matter of convenience, to two sets of such Adjustment Accounts being employed, one set to check the accuracy of the Ledgers with regard to the number of shares issued under each class and the amount called up thereon, and the other set to check the amount due, or in arrear, from time to time from the shareholders whose accounts are kept in detail in each separate Ledger. A separate account must invariably be kept in the General Ledger recording the amount from time to time called up upon each class of Shares, Stock, or Debentures issued, as the information under this heading has a fundamental bearing upon the financial aspect of the undertaking, and must therefore be shown in detail in its periodical Balance

Sheets. The amount due from time to time from individual investors need not, however, necessarily be shown in the same detail. This is rather a question of practical expediency. Separate totals must, of course, be shown of the arrears due from shareholders and the arrears due from debenture-holders; but it is not necessary for either of these totals to be further split up, unless the number of Personal Accounts is so considerable as to render this course desirable with a view to facilitating the exact balancing of the detailed records in the Share and Debenture Ledgers respectively. So far as stock-holders are concerned, stock being invariably fully paid-up, no arrears can arise, and no special difficulty will therefore occur under this heading.

The most convenient method of recording entries in connection with the issue of Capital is perhaps best shown by way of the following :—

PROBLEM.—A Company formed to acquire an established business issues ordinary capital £100,000 in £10 shares, payable £1 on application, £2 on allotment, and the balance three months after allotment; preference capital £50,000 in £10 shares, payable in the same manner; and £50,000 in debentures of £100 each, payable 10 per cent. on application, and the balance on allotment. The whole (other than the shares taken by the vendor) was subscribed, allotted, and duly paid up.

Make Journal entries relating to the issue of the capital.

		JOURNAL.	Dr.	Cr.
			£ s d	£ s d
Jan.	15	Application Account (O. S.) .. .. To Ordinary Share Capital Account .. .. (Being £1 per share on 6,000 Ordinary Shares allotted this day)	6,000 0 0	.. 6,000 0 0
Jan.	15	Allotment (O. S.) .. .. To Ordinary Share Capital Account .. .. (Being £2 per share on 6,000 Ordinary Shares allotted this day)	12,000 0 0	.. 12,000 0 0
Apr.	15	Call Account (O. S.) .. .. To Ordinary Share Capital Account .. .. (Being £7 per share on 6,000 Ordinary Shares, as per Minute of this date)	42,000 0 0	.. 42,000 0 0
		(Similar entries for 5,000 Preference Shares)		
Jan.	15	Sundry Debenture-holders .. .. To Debentures Account .. .. (Being amount payable on 500 £100 Debentures issued this day)	50,000 0 0	.. 50,000 0 0

NOTE.—It will be seen that in this case separate " Application," " Allotment," and " Call " Accounts are opened for each class of shares to facilitate separate balancing by stages ; if, however, there is not likely to be any serious difficulty in balancing, one general " Shareholders' Account " would suffice. This latter method is shown in connection with the debenture issue.

The detailed record of applications from investors, and of the subsequent allotments and the collection of instalments due, involves transactions of a somewhat special nature on account of the very considerable number of Personal Accounts that have usually to be kept, and also because the exigencies of the case require that these accounts should be prepared against time, and therefore upon such a system as will readily enable them to be always kept up to date. These special requirements are met by a combination of the " Tabular System " with the " Slip System " of accounts. A general outline of the Tabular System has already been given in Chapter VI., while in Chapter XVIII. will be found a description of the Slip System. Inasmuch, however, as its application for the present purpose involves only a quite rudimentary knowledge of the system, it is thought that the reader will experience no difficulty in grasping the following description without waiting to acquire a thorough mastery of the Slip System in all its numerous developments. The essential feature of the Slip System is to employ the same record for two or more different purposes in accounting, and for the present purpose it is not necessary to go beyond this point. For the sake of clearness, the following description is confined to the issue of a particular class of capital—e.g., Ordinary Shares. The same procedure will, however, apply to every other class of Share Capital, and also to Debenture issues; while in connection with issues of Stock, it is only necessary to add that, as a rule, stock is not issued, save in exchange for fully paid-up shares; but in the event of its being issued direct, the collection of the various instalments making such Stock fully paid will invariably be recorded in the Application and Allotment Sheets, so that thereafter no record becomes necessary, other than the amount of stock standing to the credit of each separate investor. When a simultaneous issue is being made for two or more different classes of capital, the various issues should be kept separate ab initio, both because the transactions are essentially separate, and also for the sake of facilitating balancing by keeping the work divided into well-defined sections. To guard against the confusion that would arise from entries being recorded under the *wrong* sections, it is, however, desirable that all papers and documents of every description should be clearly distinguishable, either by being printed upon distinctively tinted paper, or being clearly headed in differently coloured inks.

With these preliminary observations the detailed explanation of the issue of Capital may be proceeded with. The initial record in connection with these transactions is the letter of application received from the investor, which should in all cases be upon the prescribed form. This form will vary in detail, according to the requirements of the case, but should always consist of two separate parts, the upper containing the actual application (and showing *inter alia* the name, address, and occupation of the applicant, the number of shares applied for, and

the amount deposited upon such application), while the second part—which is detachable—should consist of the Bankers' receipt for the deposit paid on application. The first part will be lodged with the Company's Bankers, and will be received by the Company from its Bankers at convenient intervals, varying naturally according to the heaviness of the subscription list. From this part the preliminary records are made. The second section (*i.e.*, the receipt for deposits) will be retained by the various applicants, and eventually given up by them in exchange for share certificates if an allotment takes place, or for a cheque returning the deposit in the event of no allotment taking place. From the Application Forms, as received from the Company's Bankers, the "Application and Allotment Sheets" are written up. The forms will be numbered consecutively as received, and entered upon separate sheets corresponding to the initial letters of the applicants' surnames; or in the case of a very heavy list there may be a further sub-division on the "vowel-index" principle, which will divide the applications into 130 sections, five for each letter of the alphabet. This portion of the work should be kept as closely up to date as possible from hour to hour, and once every day at least while the subscription list is open the total of the column headed "Deposits Received on Applications" should be agreed with the amount accounted for by the Bankers in the Bank Pass Book. The exact form of Application and Allotment Sheet will vary somewhat, according to the conditions of the proposed issue. Speaking generally, it is desirable that the Sheets (which are in tabular form) should record the Personal Accounts of the various applicants up to as late a date as possible, with a view to simplifying the records that will have to appear later in the Share Ledger. On the other hand, the tabular form of Ledger is unsuitable from the moment when any extensive transfers of shares are likely to take place, and therefore in practice it is rarely possible to employ the Tabular System up to the point when the shares become fully paid. Alternative forms, suitable for different circumstances, are given below, and it will, of course, be understood that anything intermediate between these two forms will be practicable, if suited to the special requirements of the case.

EXAMPLES:

ORDINARY SHARES.

APPLICATIONS AND ALLOTMENTS SHEET (Suitable when the whole of the Capital is called up quickly).

No. of Application	Name of Applicant	Address	Occupation	No. of Shares Applied for	Deposits Received on Applications £ s d	C.B. Fo.	Remarks	Proposed Allotment	No. of Shares Allotted	No. of Allotment Letter	Distinctive Numbers of Shares Allotted From	To	Amount due on Allotment £ s d	Cash Received in Payment of Allotment Money £ s d	C.B. Fo.	No. of Letter of Regret	Cash Returned on Applications Declined £ s d	C.B. Fo.	Amount of Call due......19.. £ s d	Cash Received in Payment of Call £ s d	C.B. Fo.	Total Amount paid up £ s d	Share Ledger Fo.	No. of Share Certificate

ORDINARY SHARES.

APPLICATIONS AND ALLOTMENTS SHEET (Suitable when the whole of the Capital is not called up quickly).

No. of Application	Name of Applicant	Address	Occupation	No. of Shares Applied for	Deposits Received on Applications £ s d	C.B. Fo.	Remarks	Proposed Allotment	No. of Shares Allotted	No. of Allotment Letter	Distinctive Numbers of Shares Allotted From	To	Amount due on Allotment £ s d	Cash Received in Payment of Allotment Money £ s d	C.B. Fo.	No. of Letter of Regret	Cash Returned on Applications Declined £ s d	C.B. Fo.	Total Amount paid up £ s d	Share Ledger Fo.	No. of Share Certificate

A careful perusal of the above forms will show that when the results of the various sheets are summarised, as they should be from time to time, the total of the columns showing the aggregate amount of deposits received should agree with the amount accounted for by the Company's Bankers. The total amount of shares allotted should agree with the actual allotment made, and therefore with the entries made in the General Ledger through the medium of the Journal. The total amount of the column marked " Amount Payable on Allotment " should agree with the balance of the corresponding Allotments Account in the General Ledger on the date when the allotment takes place, and so on. If the first form of Application and Allotment Sheets be used, the only particulars required in the Share Ledger will be the number (quantity) and the distinctive numbers of the shares standing in the name of each shareholder; but if, at the date of opening the Share Ledger, the shares are not fully paid, then each shareholder's Personal Account in the Share Ledger must also show the amount called up on his shares, and the amount (if any) in arrear thereon. The aggregate amount of such arrears must agree with the balance of the corresponding Calls Account in the General Ledger. From the date that the Share Ledger is opened the Application and Allotment Sheets must be definitely closed. They should then be bound up for future reference when required, and from that time occupy the place occupied by any ordinary Ledger which has been used up and superseded by a new one.

The form of Share Ledger that is most convenient will naturally vary to some extent, according to the form of Application and Allotment Sheets that have been used. The following forms correspond with the two forms of Application and Allotment Sheets already given. Intermediate forms can be readily designed from these where necessary.

EXAMPLES:

FORM OF SHARE LEDGER (for fully paid Shares).

(*Surname*) .... (*Christian Name*) ....

(*Address*)..

(*Occupation*)................................

ORDINARY SHARES of £—— each (Fully paid-up).

		Shares Disposed of					Shares Acquired			Balances	
		Distinctive Numbers					Distinctive Numbers				
Date	Folio	From	To	No. of Shares	Date	Folio	From	To	No. of Shares	Date	No. of Shares

FORM OF SHARE LEDGER (for Shares not fully paid).

(*Surname*) .... (*Christian Name*) ....

(*Address*) ....

....

(*Occupation*) ....

ORDINARY SHARES of £—— each.

Dr.					CASH ACCOUNT.			Cr.
Date	Particulars	Amount per Share called up	Folio	Amount due	Date	Particulars	Folio	Amount paid
				£ s d				£ s d

SHARE ACCOUNT.

		Shares Disposed of					Shares Acquired				Balances	
		Distinctive Numbers					Distinctive Numbers					
Date	Folio	From	To	No. of Shares	Date	Folio	From	To	No. of Shares	Date	No. of Shares	

The above forms contain all the information that is prescribed in the statutory "Register of Members." It is not therefore necessary that the latter should be kept as a separate book; but, if thought desirable, a separate Register may readily be provided, and such a course is sometimes preferred, as it avoids the disadvantage of offering to all comers information which is not specifically required by statute.

A "Stock Ledger" will be upon the same lines as a Share Ledger; but, owing to the altered circumstances, certain variations occur, and it is therefore thought desirable to give the following form of ruling suitable under the altered circumstances:—

EXAMPLE:

FORM OF STOCK LEDGER.

(Surname)............... (Christian Name)..............

(Address) ....

....

(Occupation)..........

ORDINARY STOCK.

Stock Disposed of			Stock Acquired			Balances	
Date	Fo.	Amount	Date	Fo.	Amount	Date	Amount
		£ s d			£ s d		£ s d

CALLS.

When the whole of the Capital issue is called up before the Share Ledger is opened, the Calls made from time to time are entered in the column, or columns, provided for that purpose in the Application and Allotment Sheets (*vide* form on page 71), and the monies received in payment of such Calls are also posted to these Sheets from the Cash Book. If, however, the Share Ledger is opened before the whole of the Capital is called up, a special "Call Book" has to be provided. This, however, will be ruled in the same manner as the simplest form of Day Book, and therefore requires no detailed description. It may be mentioned in passing that if Capital receipts are entered in detail in the General Cash Book, it is desirable to provide an additional (inside) column for the record of details, so that only the periodical totals may be posted into the General Ledger. Save, however, in the case of comparatively small companies, it is usually more convenient to employ a subsidiary Cash Book for the record of these receipts, the daily totals only appearing in the General Cash Book; and where there are several different classes of shares, it will generally be found desirable to open a special banking account in respect of *each*, and to employ a subsidiary Cash Book for monies received in respect of each class. In intermediate cases, however, one Subsidiary Cash Book will suffice; but, if so, separate columns should be provided in that Cash Book for each class of Capital, with a view to facilitating the sectional balancing of the Ledgers.

SHARE CERTIFICATES.

For the purposes of this work, it is unnecessary to discuss in detail the duties of a Company Secretary, other than those which arise directly out of the accounts. It may be mentioned in passing, however, that at about this stage Share Certificates will have to be issued, to be delivered up in exchange for Allotment Letters and Bankers' receipts for instalments of Capital paid. It is convenient that a column should be added to the Application and

Allotment Sheets for the record of the consecutive numbers of these certificates : and if transfers are likely to be numerous, it will be found to be far more satisfactory to provide. a form of Certificate that allows of the distinctive numbers being placed in the *margin*, rather than to employ a form which requires the distinctive numbers to be inserted in the body of the Certificate, as the latter form is very inconvenient if several groups of shares have to be placed on the same Certificate. In the case of Stock certificates, such a difficulty does not arise, as no distinctive numbers are required, and the aggregate amount of stock need never be stated in more than one figure. For example, if it becomes necessary to register £1,500 stock in the name of A., which has been acquired by him from, say, five different stock-holders, the Certificate will only be for "£1,500 stock," whereas if 1,500 shares have been acquired from five different shareholders, there will probably be at least five groups of distinctive numbers, and perhaps considerably more.

TRANSFERS,

whether of Shares, Debentures, or Stock, in no way affect the financial position of the Company, and therefore involve no entries whatever in the financial books. Naturally, however, they involve the entry of corresponding records in the Share, Debenture, or Stock Ledgers, as the case may be. These entries are made through the medium of a Register of Transfers, a book which is in the nature of a Journal, kept (for the sake of convenience) upon tabular lines. The following is a fuller form of ruling than is perhaps generally adopted, but the additional columns will in all cases be found to facilitate the rapid record of transactions, while at the same time avoiding as far as possible the risk of errors. The additional columns for the number of the old Certificate and the numbers of the new Certificates will be found particularly useful in practice.

EXAMPLE :

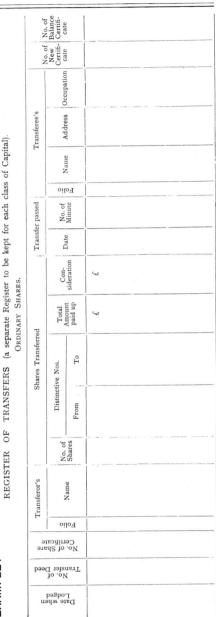

REGISTER OF TRANSFERS (a separate Register to be kept for each class of Capital).

ACQUISITION OF PROPERTY.

In the majority of cases a new Company is formed for purposes which include the acquisition of some specific property or business, or of several such, with a view to working them thereafter. Accordingly what are known in bookkeeping as "opening entries" are of very common occurrence in connection with Company Accounts, and even when a Company is formed with what may be termed a "clean slate"—that is to say, without being tied down to the acquisition of any specific property for the purpose of carrying out its objects—it will doubtless in the near future have to enter into such a transaction in some form or another. Consequently "opening entries" of some kind will almost invariably have to be made in the books of a Company during the earlier stages of its career. These opening entries differ only in form from those with which the reader is doubtless already acquainted in connection with elementary bookkeeping exercises. Whenever property is acquired, the account, or accounts, that are set aside to record transactions in such property are debited with the cost price thereof, and the Personal Account of the Vendor is credited. This elementary principle of bookkeeping holds good for large as well as for small transactions. The basis of the transaction will be a contract, under seal, entered into by the Company, under which for a certain specified consideration it agrees to acquire certain specific property. Such a contract is, as a rule, confirmatory to a preliminary contract previously entered into between the Vendor and a trustee on behalf of the Company, the object of such preliminary contract being to give the Company a "firm option" to purchase. It need hardly be stated, however, that such a preliminary contract is not essential, and that its only object is to bind the Vendor until such time as the Company is in a position to contract for itself. A short way of recording such a transaction would be to debit

accounts representing the various assets acquired, and to credit accounts representing the various liabilities (if any) taken over, and the various classes of consideration given by way of purchase-price. In practice, however, such a mode of accounting would be inconvenient—first, because the consideration is not invariably wholly given at the time that the contract becomes binding; and, secondly, because the actual consideration that passes in practice will never be exactly the same as the nominal consideration named in the contract. The causes of these differences, and the best method of dealing with them in accounts is shown in detail in Chapter X., for our present purposes, therefore, it may be assumed, for the sake of simplicity, that the actual consideration that passes *is* the same as the nominal consideration.

As at the date of the execution of the contract of purchase, a Journal entry should be made, crediting the Vendors with the nominal purchase consideration and debiting the various assets acquired. If (as is very frequently the case) the contract of sale includes the taking over of the Vendor's liabilities by the Company, then, of course, accounts must be opened and credited with the amount of such liabilities, and the credit to the Personal Account of the Vendor will be reduced to a corresponding extent. As, and when, the purchase-money is paid, the Vendor's account will be debited; and when the whole purchase-price has been paid no balance will remain outstanding on the Vendor's account.

If the whole of the purchase-price is agreed to be discharged in cash, the payment of the Vendor is a very simple matter, and will be recorded in the books by means of postings to the debit of the Vendor's account from the credit side of the Cash Book. As a rule, however, only a portion of the purchase-price is so discharged, and in some cases the Vendor agrees to receive nothing whatever in

Cash. The purchase-consideration is, as a rule, discharged either wholly or partially by the issue of Shares or Debentures, credited as fully-paid up; that is to say, Shares or Debentures which involve upon the allottee no liability to pay to the Company the face-value thereof. Such " paper " consideration is regarded as being valid payment, and although in many cases the purchase-price may be swollen to compensate for the non-payment of Cash, in other cases it may be actually reduced by this process, because the consideration is known to have an intrinsic value considerably in excess of par. Prior to the passing of the Companies Act, 1900, the issue of " fully-paid " Shares was beset by numerous restrictions, which not infrequently resulted in considerable hardship to the allottees, or to subsequent transferees to whom a legal knowledge of the circumstances might be imputed. Under the Companies Act, 1900, however, it was provided that so long as Shares are duly paid for, they need not necessarily be paid for in cash ; all that is now necessary is that, when it is sought to avoid the liability to pay for such Shares in cash, a contract reciting the whole of the circumstances under which the allottee claims such Shares as fully paid-up must be filed with the Registrar of Joint Stock Companies within one month from the date of the allotment of such Shares. This contract should invariably be prepared by the Company's Solicitors, and need not therefore be discussed in these pages. From the point of view of the accounts, all that is necessary is that there should have been such a contract, that its execution should have been duly authorised by the Directors, and that such authorisation should have been recorded in the Company's Minute Book. The Journal entry recording the transaction should refer to the contract, and also to the Minute authorising its execution. The nature of the entry is that it debits the Vendor with the nominal value of the consideration paid to him, and credits such value to the accounts opened to record the amount called up from time to time on the various classes of Shares or Debentures issued. With these preliminary remarks the exact nature of the opening entries of a Company will be readily understood from a study of the following—

PROBLEM.—A Company, under a contract dated 1st January 1903, takes over as a going concern the business of A. Jones. The purchase-price is agreed at £100,000, payable as to £50,000 in Ordinary Shares of £1 each, £25,000 in 6 per cent. Preference Shares of £1 each, and the balance in cash.

The assets consist of Freehold Land and Buildings, £16,000 ; Plant and Machinery, £42,000 ; Stock-in-Trade, £37,000 ; Book Debts, £51,000. The liabilities are Sundry Creditors on Open Account, £27,000 ; Bills Payable, £19,000.

The completion of sale takes place on 12th January 1903.

Show, by means of Journal entries, the necessary entries in the financial books of the Company, disregarding the apportionment of outstandings (*vide* Chapter X.) :—

JOURNAL, 1903.

	£	s	d	£	s	d
1st January.						
Freehold Land and Buildings	16,000	0	0			
Plant and Machinery	42,000	0	0			
Stock-in-Trade	37,000	0	0			
Sold Ledger Account	51,000	0	0			
To A. Jones				146,000	0	0

(*Being Property, as described above, acquired from Mr. A. Jones, as per contract of this date between him and the Company ; vide Minute No. —.*)

	£	s	d	£	s	d
A. Jones	46,000	0	0			
To Bought Ledger Account				27,000	0	0
„ Bills Payable				19,000	0	0

(*Being Liabilities, as above described, taken over from Mr. A. Jones, under contract of this date between him and the Company ; vide Minute No. —.*)

	£	s	d	£	s	d
12th January.						
A. Jones	100,000	0	0			
To Ordinary Share Capital Account				50,000	0	0
„ 6 per cent. Preference Share Capital Account				25,000	0	0
„ Cash				25,000	0	0

(*Being 50,000 Ordinary Shares of £1 each, Nos. 8-50,007 and 25,000 6 per cent. Preference Shares of £1 each, Nos. 150,001-175,000, allotted to A. Jones as fully paid-up, in pursuance of contract between him and the Company, dated 1st inst., filed with the Registrar of Joint-Stock Companies this day : also Cash paid him, being balance of consideration under such contract ; vide Minute No. —.*)

Before leaving this subject, it is desirable to draw attention to two modifications that sometimes arise in practice. (1) Occasionally the Share consideration paid to the Vendor will take the form of *partly* paid-up Shares, instead of fully paid-up Shares. In such a case, the Vendor will be debited, and the Share Capital Account credited, with the amount agreed to be regarded *as* paid-up upon the Shares in question ; and therefore Calls, up to the nominal value of the Shares, may be made by the Company thereafter. The issue of partly paid-up Shares is, for practical purposes, restricted to " reconstructions," which are considered fully in Chapter XVI. (2) Occasionally the agreed purchase-consideration will be satisfied by an issue of fully paid-up Shares amounting in all to a smaller sum. So long as it is perfectly clear that the assets acquired by the Company are worth the nominal value attached to them, the effect of such an arrangement as this is that the Vendor's Shares are issued to him " at a premium," and the proper treatment of premiums is explained hereafter. There is, as a rule, no inducement to unduly inflate the purchase-consideration, because an *ad valorem* stamp duty has to be paid thereon ; but if the Shares issued to the Vendor in satisfaction of purchase-price are not worth more than par, a serious question may arise as to whether the real facts of the case are not that the actual cost price *to the Company* of the assets acquired by it is less than the price stated in the contract of sale. In such a case, it would not be proper to debit the various assets' accounts with anything in excess of the actual cost price, and it may therefore become necessary to go behind the letter of the contract of sale, ascertain the true facts, and (for purposes of accounting) reduce the purchase-price accordingly. Such cases are, however, not very likely to often occur in practice.

FORFEITURE OF SHARES.

Under most Articles of Association, the power is reserved to the Company to forfeit any of the Shares upon which Calls may remain unpaid for more than a prescribed length of time. This power can, however, only be exercised after due notice has been given to the registered holder of such Shares. In order to clearly understand the necessary entries to be made on a forfeiture taking place, it is important to appreciate the state of the books at that date. From time to time the Share Capital Account will show as a credit balance the aggregate amount called up upon all Shares that may have been issued, while the Allotment Account (or Calls Account, as the case may be) will show as a debit balance the amount in arrear. The effect of forfeiture is to forfeit all the *rights* of the then holder of such Shares and to reduce *pro tanto* the issued Capital of the Company. Accordingly, when Shares are forfeited, the credit balance of the Share Capital Account must be reduced by the amount called up on such Shares as have been forfeited. The act of forfeiture does not extinguish the liability of the late shareholder, and therefore at first sight it might appear to be unnecessary to write off the debit balance on the Allotment (or Calls) Account; but inasmuch as such balance is in all probability a Bad Debt, the moment of forfeiture would appear to be the proper time to write this fictitious asset out of the books, and in any event it can no longer be correctly described as the amount due from a member of the Company. Therefore, in so far as the amount called up upon the Shares forfeited represents an amount due on such Shares, it should be credited to the Allotment (or Calls) Account, and the difference, which represents the amount actually received by the Company on the Shares that have been forfeited, should be transferred to a "Forfeited Shares Account." If the arrears of Calls are ultimately recovered after forfeiture they should be also credited to the Forfeited Shares Account. The Directors of a Company have power to from time to time re-issue such Shares as may have been forfeited, and, if they be re-issued at par, the entries in the financial books will be in all respects upon the same lines as though the Shares so re-issued formed part of a new issue; but the Directors may, if they think it in the interest of the Company, re-issue such Shares at any discount, not exceeding the amount previously received from the original shareholder. The amount standing to the credit of the Forfeited Shares Account is available to make good this Discount, and must be re-transferred from the Forfeited Shares Account to the credit of Applications and Allotments Account. Any balance that may then remain outstanding on the credit of the Forfeited Shares Account represents a Premium received on Shares, and may be treated accordingly.

PROBLEM.—The Directors of a Company pass a resolution on 13th July 1903 forfeiting 100 Ordinary Shares of £1 each, upon which a deposit of 2s. 6d. per Share has been received, but upon which the 7s. 6d. due on allotment and a further call of 5s. per Share remain unpaid. On the same date they re-issue the Shares to one of their number, credited with 15s. per Share paid-up thereon, for £70. Show, in Journal form, the necessary entries in the financial books of the Company.

JOURNAL, 1903.

13th July.						£ s d	£ s d
Share Capital Account ..	..	..	..	..	..	75 0 0	
To Allotment Account ..	..	..	..	..	..	..	37 10 0
,, Call Account ..	..	..	..	..	..	..	25 0 0
., Forfeited Shares Account	..	..	..	..	..	..	12 10 0
(*Being* 100 *Shares, No. — to —, standing in the name of* ———, *forfeited this day for non-payment of Calls, vide Minute No. —*).							
Forfeited Shares Re-issued Account	..	..	..	..	..	75 0 0	
To Share Capital Account	..	..	..	..	..	..	75 0 0
Cash ..	..	..	..	..	..	..	70 0 0	
Forfeited Shares Account ..	..	..	..	..	..	5 0 0	
To Forfeited Shares Re-issued Account	..	..	..	..	..	..	75 0 0
(*Being* 100 *Shares, No. — to —, re-issued to* ———, *credited with* 15s. *per Share paid-up, for* £70, *vide Minute No. —.*)							

In the Share Books of the Company the best way of dealing with forfeitures is to pass an entry through the Register of Transfers, transferring such Shares from the name of the original holder to a " Forfeited Shares Account," and upon their re-issue to transfer them back from the Forfeited Shares Account into the name of the new holder. In order to complete the record which vouches the entries in the Register of Transfers, it is desirable that a slip should be inserted in the proper place in the Guard Book where transfers are filed, fully recording the facts and the authority for the entries made.

ISSUE OF SHARES AT A PREMIUM.

Sometimes an issue of Shares is made under such circumstances that subscribers are required, in addition to paying up the face value of such Shares, to pay a Premium (or Bonus) to the Company in consideration of receiving the privilege of an allotment. In the Share Books the best method of dealing with such premiums is to provide an additional column on the Application and Allotment Sheets for the amount due in respect of such Premiums. There is no occasion to divide the Cash columns in the same way, as, if the whole amount due is not paid, the first monies received would be allocated as being in respect of the Premium charged. Such Premium would invariably be received before the entries are transferred to the Share Ledger, and consequently the ordinary form of ruling for the Share Ledger will still be all that is required. In the financial books the Applications and Allotments Account must be debited with the total amount due on allotment, including Premiums; but the amount of such Premiums, instead of being credited to the Share Capital Account, should be credited to a Premiums Account, as shown in the following : —

PROBLEM.—A Company offers for subscription 100,000 Shares of £1 each, at a premium of 2s. 6d. per Share, payable 5s. on application, 7s. 6d. on allotment, and the balance one month after allotment. Show the necessary entries in the financial books of the Company, assuming that the subscription list opened on 14th July 1903, that applications were then received for 120,000 Shares, and that the Company went to allotment on the following day.

Dr.   SHARE CAPITAL ACCOUNT.   Cr.

			£	s	d
	1903 July 15	By Application Account	12,500	0	0
	"	" Allotment Account	37,500	0	0
	"	" Call Account	50,000	0	0

Dr.   APPLICATION ACCOUNT.   Cr.

1903 July 15	To Share Capital Account	£ 12,500	s 0	d 0	1903 July 14	By Cash	£ 30,000	s 0	d 0
"	" Premium Account	12,500	0	0					
"	" Cash	5,000	0	0					

Dr.   ALLOTMENT ACCOUNT.   Cr.

1903 July 15	To Share Capital Account	£ 37,500	s 0	d 0	1903 July —	By Cash	£ 37,500	s 0	d 0

Dr.   CALL ACCOUNT.   Cr.

1903 Aug. 15	To Share Capital Account	£ 50,000	s 0	d 0	1903 Aug. —	By Cash	£ 50,000	s 0	d 0

Dr.	PREMIUM ACCOUNT.		Cr.
	1903 July 15	By Application Account	£ s d 12,500 0 0

Dr.	CASH.		CONTRA.		Cr.
1903 July 14 — Aug. —	To Application Account .. .. „ Allotment Account .. .. „ Call Account	£ s d 30,000 0 0 37,500 0 0 50,000 0 0	1903 July 15	By Application Account (deposits returned) ..	£ s d 5,000 0 0

The question as to how Premiums should eventually be treated is, from some points of view, still an open one, it never having been expressly decided whether or not such Premiums are legally available for distribution by way of dividend. It would appear, however, to be doubtful whether they can be legally so distributed, and it is therefore thought desirable that, instead of following the usual practice of transferring Premiums to Reserve Fund, they should be retained permanently to the credit of "Premiums Account," and shown as a separate item upon the Liabilities' side of the Balance Sheet. In Companies whose accounts are kept upon the "Double-Account System" (*vide* Chapter XII.) all Premiums received are treated as part of the Capital Receipts of the Company.

DEBENTURES.

As has already been stated, the entries in connection with the issue of Debentures, or Debenture Stock, follow upon exactly the same lines as those already explained in connection with the issue of Shares or Stock. It remains to be added, however, that whereas the latter cannot be issued at a Discount and are irredeemable, the former may be issued at a Discount, and may be issued upon such terms that they are redeemable, either by notice, or at the expiration of a certain definite period. The proper entries in connection with the issue of Debentures at a Discount and the redemption of Debentures have therefore still to be considered.

ISSUE OF DEBENTURES AT A DISCOUNT.

The entries in this case are naturally the converse of the issue at a Premium, with the result that "Discounts Account" must be debited, and "Applications Account" credited with the amount agreed to be deducted from the nominal value of the Debentures as an inducement to subscribers. The position is thus in many respects analogous to an issue of partly-paid Shares. In the detailed Debenture books the most convenient method is to provide a special column on the Application and Allotment Sheets for the amount agreed to be considered as allowed off the nominal value of the Debentures allotted, and no entries need appear in connection with the matter in the Debenture Ledger.

The proper treatment of the debit balance on the "Discounts Account" varies according to the terms of the issue. It is perhaps desirable, however, to mention in passing that a special Discounts Account should be opened in respect of each such issue, and that under no circumstances should these Discounts be confused with the ordinary Discounts allowed by the Company in the course of its trading operations. If the Debentures are irredeemable, the debit balance of the Discounts Account will only become a realised loss in the event of the Company going into liquidation, and it would therefore not be improper to permanently include it upon the Assets' side of the Balance Sheet, or to deduct it from the liability under Debentures appearing upon the Liabilities'

G

side; but although such treatment might be permissible, it would undoubtedly be preferable for the loss to be written off over a term of years, in the same manner as it is usual to gradually write off Preliminary Expenses. If, on the other hand, the Debentures are redeemable, then clearly the amount of the Discounts allowed upon the issue will become a realised loss on the date when such Debentures become redeemable, and under these circumstances it is essential that the loss should be written off, out of Revenue, during the period of such issue. For example, if the Debentures be redeemable in seven years' time, then one-seventh of the aggregate Discount allowed should be written off against Profits each year.

REDEMPTION OF DEBENTURES.

In the Debenture books the best method of dealing with Debentures redeemed is, through the medium of the Register of Transfers, to transfer such Debentures as are redeemed from time to time to a "Debentures Redeemed Account." In the financial books the entries are not, as a rule, sufficiently numerous to make it worth while to adopt any abbreviated method, and it will therefore in general answer all practical purposes if Debentures Account be debited, and Cash credited, with the amount paid to Debenture-holders from time to time in redemption of these liabilities. If, however, the number of Debenture-holders renders some form of abbreviated entry desirable, the detailed particulars of the various payments may appear in an inner column of the Cash Book, and the total only may be posted to the debit of the Debentures Account. In exchange for the monies so paid, the original Debenture Bonds should, of course, be received

from the Debenture-holders, and submitted to the Auditors as vouchers for the respective payments.

CONVERSIONS AND SPLITS.

Conversions of fully-paid Shares into Stock, or of Stock of one denomination into Stock of another denomination, and the "splitting" of Shares or Stock into two denominations, are transactions that do not often occur in connection with registered Companies, but they are comparatively common with railway companies and other undertakings incorporated by special Act of Parliament. The authority for such transactions will, of course, under these circumstances be obtained by a supplementary Act, or from a provision already made in the existing Private Act. When Shares are converted into Stock, the entries in the financial books are of quite a simple kind, all that is necessary being to reduce the credit balance on the appropriate Share Capital Account and to credit a corresponding sum to the new Stock Account. If the nominal amount of the new Stock be *less* than the amount paid up upon the old Shares, the new Stock has been issued at a Premium; if the nominal amount be more, the new Stock has been issued at a Discount. Under these circumstances, however, the Discount is usually "capitalised," and not gradually written off out of profits. In the departmental books it will generally be found best to open an entirely new Stock Ledger, and to close up the old Share Ledger; and as the number of Personal Accounts is generally very considerable, it will usually be found convenient to pass these transfers through a specially designed "Conversion Journal" ruled somewhat as follows:—

EXAMPLE :

FORM OF CONVERSION JOURNAL (Shares into Stock).

Old Shares								New Stock		
Share Ledger Folio	No. of Shares	Distinctive Nos.		No. of Old Certificate	Name	Address	Occupation	Amount	Stock Ledger Folio	No. of New Certificate
		From	To							
								£ s d		

When Stock of one description is converted into Stock of another (as, for example, when 5 per cent. Stock is converted into 4 per cent. Stock), the capital value of the Stock will usually be increased *pro ratâ*, so that the income actually paid to the Stockholders may remain the same. In effect, therefore, the new Stock is issued at a discount. In other respects it follows the same lines as those already indicated, save that the Conversion Journal will require some slight modification, so far as the ruling of the left-hand side is concerned.

The commonest form of "splitting" is when uniform Shares or Stock are split up into Preference and Ordinary Shares or Stock. If the amount of new Shares (or Stock) issued in exchange for the old is, in the aggregate, equal to the nominal amount of old Shares (or Stock) the new issue is at par; but if—as is very often the case—£100 of the Stock is split up into £100 Preference Stock *and* £100 Ordinary Stock, the new issue is, of course, at a Discount of 50 per cent. Such "Splits" are not uncommon when the market price is greatly in excess of the nominal value, and it is desired (for purposes of convenience) to effect a closer approximation of the two.

REGISTRATION OF PROBATE OR LETTERS OF ADMINISTRATION.

There is a very general misapprehension with regard to the consequences that ensue upon the death of a registered holder of Shares, Debentures, or Stock. It is frequently insisted that the investment must be forthwith transferred into the names of the legal personal representatives of the deceased holder, and that it is only after such transfer has been effected that the latter are competent to dispose of the investment. From the point of view of the Company, there is no objection to this plan, which incidentally has the effect of increasing the revenue from Transfer Fees; but it cannot be insisted upon, and in the case of partly-paid Shares is altogether indefensible, in that it seeks to place upon the legal personal representatives of the deceased shareholder a personal liability for unpaid capital that cannot be legally enforced. The legal personal representatives (whether they be the executors named in the will of the deceased, or the administrators appointed by the Court to administer his estate) are entitled, on production of the probate, or letters of administration as the case may be, to have their title to deal with the investment registered, without any transfer being made into their names personally; and thereafter they may at any time execute a transfer in favour of a purchaser of such Shares. Until such transfer is executed, any Calls that may be due, or become due, are payable out of the estate of the deceased; but the executors or administrators are not personally liable to pay Calls, should the estate be deficient. The proper entry to make in the Share Ledger notifying the title of the legal personal representatives of a deceased shareholder is as follows:—

Probate granted to A. of ———— ——, and B. of ————————,

on ———— 19—. Registered, ———————— 19—. X. Z., Secretary.

Many Companies charge a half-a-crown fee for making such an entry, and, as a rule, such fee is paid without demur; but inasmuch as this registration is not a transfer, no fee can be charged for its record, save in the unlikely event of the Company's Articles of Association making express provision therefor.

PAYMENT OF DIVIDENDS.

In the case of an undertaking owned by a sole trader, or a private firm, the profit shown from time to time by the Profit and Loss Account is forthwith transferred to the Capital Account of the proprietor, or, in the case of a firm, it is divided into shares previously agreed upon, and the Capital Accounts of the various partners are credited each with his respective share. In the case of a Company, however, the profit cannot be divided (save to a limited extent, when the payment of interim dividends is authorised) until the shareholders in general meeting have passed a resolution dealing with the matter. Accordingly the accounts that have to be submitted for approval at such general meeting must show to the credit of Profit and Loss Account whatever balance is at the disposal of the shareholders. Unless, therefore, some special modification of book-keeping were to be introduced, the Profit and Loss Account of each successive year would fail to show the actual results of that year's operations, because those results would be obscured by the balance of profit brought forward from the previous period and its disposition during the current period. It is there-

fore usual at the date of balancing, instead of bringing down the amount of net profit as a credit balance, to forthwith transfer it to another account (which is variously called "Net Revenue Account," "Net Profit and Loss Account," "Profit and Loss Appropriation Account," &c.), and whatever disposition the shareholders may order of the amount standing to the credit of this latter account is recorded by entries to the debit thereof. That the Net Revenue Account may be kept in a concise form it is convenient that the entries to the debit should be made in totals through the Journal to the various accounts affected, upon the lines shown in the following example:—

PROBLEM.—The X. Company, Lim. on making up its accounts to 31st December 1902, shows a balance available for distribution of £7,567 12s. 2d. At the Annual General Meeting, held on 7th April 1903, it is resolved to declare a dividend on the 40,000 Preference Shares (£1 each) of 5 per cent., and also a dividend of 10 per cent. (free of income tax) on the 40,000 Ordinary Shares of £1 each. £1,000 is to be transferred to Reserve Fund, and the balance carried forward. Show the Ledger Accounts, detailing the appropriation of divisible profits.

Dr.   NET REVENUE ACCOUNT.   Cr.

1903		£ s d	1903		£ s d
April 7	To Preference Dividend	2,000 0 0	Jan. 1	By Balance forward..	7,567 12 2
"	" Ordinary Dividend	4,000 0 0			
"	" Reserve Fund	1,000 0 0			
"	" Balance down	567 12 2			
		£7,567 12 2			£7,567 12 2
			1903 April 8	By Balance forward..	567 12 2

Dr.   PREFERENCE DIVIDEND ACCOUNT.   Cr.

1903		£ s d	1903		£ s d
April 12	To Cash	1,877 1 8	April 7	By Net Revenue Account ..	2,000 0 0
"	" Income Tax	122 18 4			
		£2,000 0 0			£2,000 0 0

Dr.   ORDINARY DIVIDEND ACCOUNT.   Cr.

1903		£ s d	1903		£ s d
April 12	To Cash	4,000 0 0	April 7	By Net Revenue Account ..	4,000 0 0

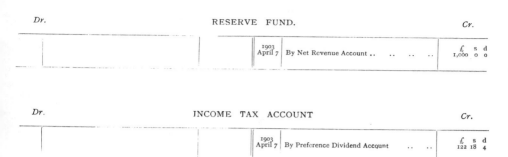

Dr.   RESERVE FUND.   Cr.

| | | 1903 April 7 | By Net Revenue Account .. .. | £ s d 1,000 0 0 |

Dr.   INCOME TAX ACCOUNT   Cr.

| | | 1903 April 7 | By Preference Dividend Account .. .. | £ s d 122 18 4 |

NOTE.—(1) *As a rule it is convenient to open a separate Bank Account for each dividend.* (2) *The £122 18s. 4d. transferred to the credit of Income Tax Account is available to reduce the sum directly chargeable against profits in respect of Income Tax paid by the Company. It represents (approximately) £500 at 1s. 2d., and £1,500 at 1s. 3d. in the £.*

For information upon the important subject of Income Tax, the reader is referred to Chapter XIII. It may be mentioned here, however, that when any classes of shareholders are limited to a maximum dividend, such dividends must invariably be paid after deducting Income Tax at the current rate. Income Tax must also be deducted from interest paid to Debenture-holders. As to whether or not Income Tax is deducted from holders of the most deferred class of Shares is immaterial, and will depend upon the wording of the resolution declaring the dividend; but, unless otherwise provided, Income Tax must be deducted in this case also. But, whether Income Tax be deducted from the amount actually paid to shareholders or not, the Company will have been assessed upon its profits, and individual shareholders need not therefore again pay Income Tax on the dividends received by them, whether or not any specific deduction has been made from such dividends as representing Income Tax. The best method of dealing with entries with regard to Income Tax in a Company's accounts will, however, be better appreciated after the subject itself has been more fully discussed, and the matter will therefore be left over until the conclusion of Chapter XIII.

REDUCTION OF CAPITAL.

The Companies Acts provide that under certain circumstances a Company may, with the approval of the Court, reduce its Capital either by returning to shareholders money not actually required for the purposes of the undertaking, or by writing off ascertained losses. The convenience of being able to effect a reduction of Capital in the first-named case is sufficiently obvious to call for no detailed discussion, although it may be mentioned in passing that instances of its application rarely occur in practice. With regard to the second case, the ability to write off ascertained losses (whether a balance to the debit of Profit and Loss Account, representing an accumulated loss on Revenue Account, or a shrinkage in the value of fixed assets, which represents a loss on Capital Account), provided proper steps be taken to protect the interests of creditors and all minorities of shareholders, is equally convenient, on the assumption that until such losses have been made good no dividends can be declared. Numerous cases that have come before the Courts during recent years throw, however, considerable doubt upon the dictum that at one time used to be regarded as unquestionable, that no dividends could be legally declared so long as a debit balance remained outstanding on Profit and Loss Account, and under these circumstances the object of providing machinery for the reduction of Capital is somewhat obscure. For the purposes of this work, however, it is unnecessary to pursue such a subject in detail. It is sufficient to show the entries necessary in the books of a Company to give effect to a reduction of Capital when such a reduction has been authorised. The following example will clearly explain the procedure in such cases:—

PROBLEM.—The H. K. Company, Lim., having a capital of £1,000,000, divided into 100,000 Shares of £10 each, £5 per Share called up, obtains leave to reduce its capital to £250,000 by writing £100,000 off the value of its properties and returning £150,000 in cash to its shareholders. The capital of the Company (when reduced) will be £250,000, divided into 100,000 Shares of £2 10s. each, fully paid up.

Show by means of Journal entries the necessary entries in the Company's books.

JOURNAL.

Share Capital Account	£250,000	
To Cash	..	£150,000
„ Property Account	..	100,000
(Being in reduction of the capital of the Company, as per scheme passed by the shareholders at General Meeting held on the ——————— 19—, and confirmed by the Court under order dated ————— 19—, sanctioning a return to shareholders of £1 10s. per share in cash, and the writing down of Property Account by the sum of £100,000.)		

NOTES.—(1) *The cash return will be treated like a dividend, so far as detailed entries are concerned.* (2) *Each account in the Share Ledger should be marked with a rubber stamp, recapitulating the terms of the reduction scheme.* (3) *The Share Certificates should be called in and exchanged for Certificates for an equal number of fully paid-up Shares of £2 10s. each.*

CHAPTER X.

VENDORS' ACCOUNTS.

IN the course of the present chapter it is proposed to consider in detail those adjustments, or apportionments, of accruing income and expenditure that have to be taken into account as between vendor and purchaser when a property changes hands.

Taking first of all the comparatively simple case of the sale of a house, or a piece of land, a contract to purchase such property for an agreed price is, as usually drawn up, a contract to pay an agreed price on the date named for the completion of the sale, the vendor agreeing to defray all expenses appertaining to the property up to the date of the sale, and the purchaser agreeing to give the vendor credit for all payments made by him on account of the property that have been made in advance. If the purchase-money, as so adjusted, is not actually paid on the date named for completion, interest thereon must be paid to the vendor up to such date as completion actually takes place.

The payments which the vendor has to discharge up to the date of completion comprise all payments which are properly chargeable against the property about to be conveyed, such as Rent, Rates, and Taxes. Repairs would certainly not be included as a matter of course, and the vendor should therefore make no payments in respect of repairs without first obtaining the purchaser's consent, together with his express agreement to allow such payments in account. Fire insurance is a permissible payment in the case of leasehold property, as the lease will in such cases invariably include a covenant that the lessee is to keep the premises insured against fire. As a matter of business practice, however, fire insurance up to a reasonable amount will always be allowed as a payment. As the reader will be aware, these various outgoings are not paid from day to day, but at fixed intervals, and consequently it usually follows that at the date of completion certain of these charges have been actually paid in advance, in which case the vendor is entitled to credit for the amount so paid in advance, and that certain other charges have not been paid up to the date of completion. The charges in arrear must accordingly be debited to the vendor in account, thereby reducing the amount that the purchaser will have to pay to the vendor on completion. With these preliminary explanations no difficulty will be experienced in understanding the following problem, which represents a fairly typical case :—

PROBLEM.—Give a *pro formâ* account showing how the exact amount due to the Vendor on completion of a sale of property is arrived at, assuming that the date fixed for completion was the 29th December 1902, and that the completion actually took place on 21st February 1903.

Dr.						PURCHASER IN ACCOUNT WITH VENDOR.				Cr.
		£ s d	£ s d				£ s d	£ s d		
1902 Dec. 29	To Purchase-price, as per Contract of Sale		5,000 0 0	1902 Dec. 29	By Ground Rent from 26th to 29th December 1902, 4 days at £50 per ann. (*less* tax at 1/3 in the £)		0 10 3			
"	" Fire Insurance paid in advance to 25th March 1903, 86 days at £3 15s. per ann.	0 17 8		"	" Poor Rate for the 6 months ending 25th March 1903, 86 days at £12 per 6 months		5 3 1			
"	" General District Rate paid in advance to 31st December 1902, 2 days at £30 10s. per 6 months	0 6 11		"	" Property Tax for the Year ending 5th April 1903, 97 days at £16 per ann.		4 5 0			
			1 4 7					9 18 4		
				"	" Balance down			4,991 6 3		
			£5,001 4 7					£5,001 4 7		
Dec. 29	To Balance down		4,991 6 3	1903 Feb. 21	By Cash			5,027 11 1		
1903 Feb. 21	" Interest to date of completion, 54 days at 5% per ann.		36 4 10							
			£5,027 11 1					£5,027 11 1		

NOTES.—(1) *The date up to which apportionment has to be made will be fixed by the contract of sale.*

(2) *If—as is usual, unless the sale be to a Company about to be formed—a deposit has been paid by the Purchaser, it should be credited in this account.*

(3) *On completion the Vendor must produce receipts for* (a) *Rent paid to 25th December* 1902, (b) *Fire Insurance paid to 25th March* 1903, (c) *General District Rate paid to 31st December* 1902, (d) *Poor Rate paid to 29th September* 1902, *and* (e) *Property Tax paid to 5th April* 1902.

(4) *Interest on the balance of £4,991 6s. 3d. will be charged up to the actual date of payment.*

SALE TO A COMPANY.

As has already been stated in the previous chapter, certain apportionments have in practice invariably to be made when an existing business is sold to the Company. If possible, unquestionably the most straightforward manner of carrying the transaction through would be to prepare a Balance Sheet of the business as at the date of completion, in which case the necessary apportionments will be made automatically in the ordinary course of balancing the books. Such a method, however, although very desirable, can but rarely be carried into effect, because the accurate balancing of the books of a going concern necessarily occupies time, and would thus cause delay in the completion of the purchase. Moreover, the provisional contract of sale generally fixes the date upon which the business (together with the benefit of all outstanding contracts) is to be transferred to the Company, while at the date of executing such provisional contract it is impossible to fix an exact date for the completion of the purchase. The usual custom, therefore, is for the undertaking to be conveyed to the Company as from a certain fixed date, the company paying interest on the purchase-money from that date forward. Whatever date may be fixed as the time from which the transfer is to be deemed as having taken place, the vendor is entitled to all profits accruing up to that date, while all profits accruing subsequently are the property of the purchasing Company. It is important to bear in mind, however, that although subsequent profits accrue to the purchasing Company, the latter can only divide among its shareholders such profits as may have accrued since the date when it was authorised to carry on business. Any profits arising between the date of sale and the date when the Company is entitled to commence business must be capitalised; that is to say, that amount must be applied towards the reduction of the figure of cost at which the assets acquired stand in the books of the Company. This is, of course, only reasonable, as in fixing the purchase-price the vendor will doubtless have taken into account the probable amount of profits accruing between the date of the sale and the date of completion, and will have increased the purchase-price accordingly. In order, therefore, to arrive at the true purchase-price this loading must be deducted. If the assets acquired by the Company include the item of Goodwill, this should, as a rule, be the first item to be written down; but if nothing be included for Goodwill, then some fixed asset—preferably the most permanent—should be the one to be reduced. It is, however, perfectly permissible to set off interest on purchase-money against accruing profits, with a view to avoiding the necessity of charging against Revenue Account interest accruing prior to the date upon which the Company is entitled to commence business.

If there be but a slight interval of time between the date of the preliminary contract of sale and the date of completion, these apportionments of accrued profits will probably raise no very vital question, and may even represent a negligible quantity; but cases are by no means infrequent in which (owing probably to some delay in the flotation of the Company) an interval of six or nine months may have elapsed, and in such cases the matter is of very considerable importance. It may be quite impossible for the Directors of the new Company to determine exactly what profits had accrued up to the date when the Company was entitled to commence business and what profits have accrued subsequently; but the responsibility will rest upon them to make a proper apportionment, and they must therefore act reasonably in the matter. A rough-and-ready division of the total profits according to time would not usually be a reasonable apportionment. A better method would be to apportion the Gross Profit between the two periods according to the total Sales in each, and to apportion the expenses chargeable against Gross Profits directly according to time. This method would give a very accurate result in the case of most businesses; but if the percentage of Gross Profit earned at different periods of the year was unequal, that fact would undoubtedly have to be taken into consideration in determining the apportionment of Gross Profit.

The following problems will, it is thought, clear up all remaining points that properly arise under this heading, and will at the same time serve to further explain those that have already been mentioned in general terms.

PROBLEM.—On 3rd January 1903 A. agrees to sell his business as a going concern to an approved Company about to be formed by a promoter X. The sale is to take effect as from 31st December 1902, and the agreed purchase-price is made up as follows :—

Goodwill	...	...	...	...	...	£20,000
Plant and Machinery	...	...	...	...	...	12,500
Freehold Land and Buildings	...	...	...	...	18,750
Stock-in-Trade	...	...	...	...	...	21,970
Book Debts and Bills Receivable (guaranteed by A. to produce)	...	31,000
						104,220
Less Trade Liabilities (guaranteed by Vendor not to exceed)	...	14,220
						£90,000

It is further agreed that the completion shall take place during 1903, and that pending completion A. is to be entitled to interest at 6 per cent. per annum, A. in the meanwhile to carry on the business as Trustee for the Company.

X. registers the British Manufacturing Company, Lim., on 26th March 1903. The Company duly goes to allotment, and on 1st May 1903 it is authorised to commence business. It is accordingly arranged to complete the purchase on the 8th May 1903. A. supplies an account showing—

(1) Receipts from 1st January to 8th May 1903, £24,175.

(2) Payments   ,,   ,,   ,,   ,,   £19,620.

(3) Book Debts amounting to £39 are admitted to be irrecoverable.

(4) The Liabilities outstanding on 31st December 1902 are admitted to have been under-stated by £25.

Assuming that A. opened new Trade Ledgers on 1st January 1903, show the entries now necessary in the Company's General Ledger, assuming the completion to be duly carried through on 8th May 1903, and 80,000 fully paid-up Shares then allotted to A. in part satisfaction of purchase-price, the balance being paid in cash.

Dr.   GOODWILL   ACCOUNT.   Cr.

1903 May 1	To A. ..	£ s d 20,000 0 0		

Dr.   PLANT   AND   MACHINERY.   Cr.

1903 May 1	To A. ..	£ s d 12,500 0 0		

Dr.   FREEHOLD   LAND   AND   BUILDINGS.   Cr.

1903 May 1	To A. ..	£ s d 18,750 0 0		

Dr.   STOCK-IN-TRADE.   Cr.

1903 May 1	To A. ..	£ s d 21,970 0 0		

Dr.   SOLD   LEDGER   ACCOUNT.   Cr.

1903 May 1	To A. ..	£ s d 31,000 0 0	1903 May 8	By A. ..	£ s d 39 0 0

Dr.   BOUGHT   LEDGER   ACCOUNT.   Cr.

		1903 May 1	By A. ..	£ s d 14,220 0 0
		,, 8	,, ,,	25 0 0

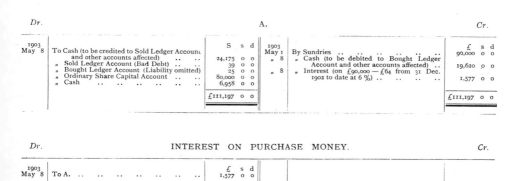

Dr.		A.				Cr.
1903 May 8	To Cash (to be credited to Sold Ledger Account and other accounts affected) ..	£ s d 24,175 0 0	1903 May 1	By Sundries	£ s d 90,000 0 0	
"	Sold Ledger Account (Bad Debt)	39 0 0	" 8	" Cash (to be debited to Bought Ledger Account and other accounts affected) ..	19,620 0 0	
"	Bought Ledger Account (Liability omitted)	25 0 0	" 8	" Interest (on £90,000 — £64 from 31 Dec. 1902 to date at 6 %)	1,577 0 0	
"	Ordinary Share Capital Account	80,000 0 0				
"	Cash	6,958 0 0				
		£111,197 0 0			£111,197 0 0	

Dr.		INTEREST ON PURCHASE MONEY.			Cr.
1903 May 8	To A.	£ s d 1,577 0 0			

PROBLEM.—Taking the facts stated in the previous problem, assuming that the books of the British Manufacturing Company, Lim., are balanced on 31st December 1903, and that the accounts for the year show the following result, how would you deal with the net profit?—

Gross Profit	...	...	...	...	£18,720
General Expenses		...	...	...	5,290
Directors' Fees, &c.		...	...	...	700
Depreciation of Plant and Machinery at 10 per cent.					
Do.	Land and Buildings, at 2 per cent.				

The first step is to apportion the gross profit equitably between the two periods. Assuming that it has been earned at a regular rate, and that from 1st January to 30th April the Sales were £60,000, and from 1st May to 31st December they were £140,000, then the gross profit earned since 1st May may be assumed to be $\frac{7}{10}$ths × £18,720 = £13,104. The Profit and Loss Account from 1st May to 31st December then stands as follows:—

Gross Profit	..	..	..	..	..	..		£13,104 0 0
General Expenses ($\frac{2}{3}$ × £5,290)	..	..	..	..	£3,536 13 4		
Directors' Fees, &c.	..	..	..	..	..	700 0 0		
Depreciation of Plant	..	..	..	..	..	826 13 4		
" Land	..	..	..	..	..	250 0 0		
							5,313 6 8	
The Net Profit available for dividend is thus	..	..	..				£7,790 13 4

The total net profit for the year is £11,105; therefore £3,314 6s. 8d. must be held over. This may be applied (1) towards paying £1,577 due to A. for interest, (2) towards writing down Preliminary Expenses or Goodwill Account.

CHAPTER XI.

EXECUTORSHIP ACCOUNTS.

GENERAL CONSIDERATIONS.

HITHERTO most writers upon Executorship Accounts have enlarged upon the highly technical nature of this branch of bookkeeping, and as a consequence the impression is very prevalent that the proper keeping of Executorship Accounts is a matter of the greatest intricacy, which is only properly understood by a comparatively small number of persons. It may be, and probably is, quite true that few people are thoroughly versed in the proper treatment of Executorship Accounts, but this is less due to any inherent difficulty presented by the subject itself than to systematic attempts to make a "mystery" of that which is after all but a quite ordinary matter.

The object of every properly designed system of bookkeeping is to adapt itself to the special requirements brought about by the nature of the particular classes of transactions that have to be recorded, and no properly designed system will present greater variations from the normal type than are necessary to meet the requirements of these special transactions. It follows, therefore, that no material departure from the ordinary system of bookkeeping can be justified that is not *necessitated* by the particular circumstances arising from the transactions that have to be recorded in the books. If the matter be viewed in this light, it must be admitted that there is nothing very exceptional in the transactions that have to be recorded in executorship matters.

NATURE OF TRANSACTIONS.

Avoiding details of a purely legal nature, it may be stated that the transactions that have to be recorded by executors relate to (1) the keeping of a strict account of the property of which the Testator died possessed ; (2) realising such property and—after payment of all proper debts, duties, and expenses—distributing the surplus in such manner as the testator may have decreed. In the majority of cases, such distribution takes place as soon as possible ; but sometimes the terms of the Will require the whole, or a portion, of the estate to be invested, and the income derived therefrom to be applied for the benefit of one or more persons, called "life-tenants," until the happening of some event, when the estate (or some specified fraction thereof) is bodily handed over to the life-tenants, or some of them, or to some other parties. Strictly speaking, these last conditions, where a portion of the estate is held in trust, form no part of "Executorship Accounts," but relate rather to the accounts of Trustees ; but it is convenient to deal with all transactions connected with the estates of deceased persons under this general heading.

For that reason also it is well to point out here that, in the absence of a Will, the general law of succession applies, and the estate is distributed in accordance with that general law ; while if the Will makes no provision as to who is to be held entitled to any particular portion of the estate, there is an intestacy so far as that particular portion is concerned, and it is dealt with accordingly.

Where there is no Will there can be no Executors, for Executors are appointed under the Will; and occasionally it will be found that even a Will omits to provide for the appointment of Executors. In all such cases application must be made to the Court, who will appoint whomsoever it thinks proper to " administer " the estate, and so far as the accounts are concerned the accounts of that Administration are for all practical purposes the same as Executorship Accounts.

It will thus be seen that, speaking generally, the class of transactions involved in Executorship Accounts consists of the getting in of assets and distributing them among the persons entitled thereto; while in some cases, instead of their being immediately distributed, the assets (or a portion of them) are invested in suitable securities, and the income derived therefrom is distributed among the persons entitled thereto (*cestuis que trustent*). There is thus absolutely nothing about the transactions themselves rendering Executorship Accounts distinctive from other classes of accounts. Transactions involving the realisation and distribution of an estate are also common to bankruptcy, company liquidation, &c.; while accounts relating to investments that are held more or less permanently, and to the collection and distribution of the income derived therefrom, present no essentially new feature because the original capitalist happens to have died, and the collection and distribution therefore devolves upon his representatives. Hitherto, therefore, no reason has been found in the nature of the transactions themselves that calls for any peculiar modification of the ordinary system of bookkeeping, as applied to ordinary commercial accounts.

SPECIAL REQUIREMENTS.

There are, however, certain forms and returns that have to be submitted to the Inland Revenue authorities, and there is always the possibility that at some future time the Executors' accounts may have to be submitted to, and passed by, the Court of Chancery. It is therefore important that any

system of bookkeeping that may be adopted be one that readily lends itself to these requirements; but this does not of itself appear to justify such a radical departure from all the principles of sound bookkeeping as is involved by the adoption of the so-called " cash system " which is so generally in use where solicitors, instead of accountants, have the conduct of matters. A simple Cash Account has, of course, the merit of simplicity, and where only a few transactions have to be recorded it is quite adequate for the requirements of the situation; but accounts upon a cash basis do not lend themselves conveniently to an exhaustive examination at some future date of *all* the transactions of the executors. This much must be admitted by the advocates of the " cash system," who even go so far as to put it forward as one of the advantages of their method that it obviates the necessity for numerous adjusting entries, showing the difference of the original valuation of the assets and the amount they eventually realised. Seeing that the Executors are *primâ facie* responsible for the advantageous realisation of all property passing through their hands, it will be seen that, however much the accounts may be simplified, they cannot fail to be seriously defective if they omit to record one of the most important points affecting the due discharge of the Executor's duties—viz., the shrinkage (or appreciation) on the realisation of the various items of property for which he is accountable. It has been further argued that accounts kept upon the " cash system " are preferred by the Rules of the Supreme Court. It is no doubt true that the Chancery Division of the High Court of Justice, in all cases, requires a Cash Account to be passed; but every adequate system of bookkeeping requires a proper Cash Account to be kept, and the mere fact that the Court is not up to date in its requirements does not dispose of the fact that the Cash Account is not, in itself, a complete record of all transactions. From the point of view of the accountant, there is this further advantage in the general adoption of the ordinary commercial system, that the accounts, being kept upon the same fundamental principles as all other classes of accounts, present only differences upon necessary points of detail, which can be readily grasped so soon as the requirements of the situation are duly appreciated. Unquestionably the *chief* requirement is a set of accounts that, even 50 years hence if need be, will be perfectly intelligible to all parties interested and their professional advisers; and it can hardly be going too far to say that this end is more likely to be achieved by adopting the only system that has been found adequate to meet the requirements of business men, than by adhering to a system which —while still regarded as sufficient by the High Court of Justice—has remained without alteration and improvement ever since that Court existed. It has been thought desirable in the first place to clear the ground by pointing out the inadequacy of the system of accounts so generally favoured by lawyers; but this having now been done, the proper treatment of this section of accounts can be proceeded with without further delay.

CASH BOOK.

The most convenient form of Cash Book for Executorship Accounts is unquestionably one having separate columns in respect of Capital and Income. The balance of the Capital columns then shows the amount of Capital that for the time being is not invested, while the balance of the Income columns shows the amount of Income in hand that has not been distributed. Of course if, under the terms of the Will, no one has a life-interest in the Estate (that is to say, no one is entitled to receive certain payments out of Income, and out of Income alone) there is no occasion to observe any distinction between Capital and Income, and accordingly the Income columns may be omitted from the Cash Book and the Income Account from the Ledger, all monies received by way of Income being then credited direct to the Estate Account.

All monies received should invariably be banked intact, and all payments made by cheque. If a Petty Cash Book be necessary, it should be kept upon the "imprest" system, so that eventually *all* cash payments may pass through the Cash Book and then be posted into the Ledger. A separate Bank Account should invariably be kept in connection with the Estate; and if the executors are, under special directions contained in the Will, carrying on the business of the deceased, a separate account should be kept in respect of the business transactions.

The chief advantages of the double-column Cash Book is that, if it be written up from day to day, it provides all the information that the Executors would require to have constantly before them, so that the Ledger may be posted up at more convenient intervals. This is especially desirable where the Ledger is kept by an Accountant, and not by the Executors themselves. The double-column Cash Book has also the further advantage that it offers a check upon the accuracy of the Income Account in the Ledger, seeing that the balance of the Income columns in the Cash Book should always agree with the Income Account in the Ledger.

THE JOURNAL.

In many cases the employment of a Journal for Executorship Accounts is unnecessary. Unless absolutely necessary a Journal is actually undesirable, as it is especially important that the fullest possible detail should be contained in the Ledger itself, while if a Journal be employed there is always the temptation to make "bare" entries in the Ledger, and include whatever explanation may be thought necessary in the Journal only. In many cases there would be no scope for the use of a Journal, except in connection with the opening entries, and these can quite conveniently be made by way of transfers in the Ledger from the Estate Account to the various other accounts concerned. Where, however, the Estate is a complicated one, and a considerable number of distributions "in kind" amongst beneficiaries take place, the employment of a Journal may be found a great convenience. But under no circumstances should its use be allowed to reduce the amount of detailed explanation appended to all entries in the Ledger itself.

THE LEDGER.

Concerning the Ledger, the only point that calls for special attention is that in the case of Investments separate columns should be provided for "Capital" and "Income," and a further column upon each side for "quantities" of stocks or shares, so that the amount invested from time to time may be readily perceived, even if frequent realisations of investments take place at varying prices.

All monies received by way of Income should be posted from the Cash Book to the account recording the Investment, where they will appear in the Income column upon the credit side of the account. When the books are periodically balanced, the credit balances of the Income columns on each Investment Account should be transferred to the Income Account. At interim balances (that is to say, when the books are merely being balanced periodically, and not at a time when an apportionment has to be made) all accruing interest should be disregarded, as the Executors are not accountable to the Beneficiaries for income until it is received, and it is convenient that the books should disclose what the Executors are accountable for, rather than the exact position of the estate, which latter is of little consequence, save when there is a change of life-tenants, or a distribution of the Estate (or some portion of it) has to be made. Moreover, an accurate Balance Sheet, showing the exact position of the estate, can never be prepared without taking into account fluctuations in the value of the various investments, and it would be ridiculous to adjust these from time to time when such readjustments could mean nothing, and would only serve the purpose of complicating the accounts.

OPENING THE BOOKS.

In ordinary commercial bookkeeping, the first step to be taken, when opening a set of books in respect of a new business, is to compile a Statement of Affairs, showing the financial position to date, and then to raise the various necessary accounts in the Ledger in accordance with that Statement. It is submitted that exactly the same procedure should be observed in connection with Executorship Accounts.

The Inland Revenue authorities, from whom the Executors obtain the grant of Probate which authorises them to deal with the estate of the testator, require that a statement shall be submitted to them—in the prescribed form—of the affairs of the testator as at the date of his death. This statement must be verified by affidavit, and may very fairly be taken as the starting point for the Executors' books, seeing that it discloses under oath the whole estate passing into the hands of the Executors, for which they are accountable to the beneficiaries. If at any subsequent time it should be found that the original estimate of the position was a mistaken one—whether by way of over or under-estimate—an affidavit has to be filed with the Inland Revenue authorities, setting forth the full facts, and claiming a return of over-paid duty, or paying the under-paid duty, as the case may be. If therefore these affidavits, and the accounts in support thereof, be followed, it will be seen that they necessarily afford the most reliable and the best possible basis for opening the Executorship Accounts.

It is not proposed in the present work to consider in detail executorship law, or the duties leviable in executorship matters. The former would be quite foreign to the subject of this work, and the latter vary so from time to time that no detailed consideration of them could be expected to apply for more than a very limited space of time. The general principles, however, will doubtless remain constant, and it is unlikely in the extreme that any alteration in the law will be effected that will render the form of accounts here advocated either inapplicable or inconvenient.

ESTATE DUTY ACCOUNT.

The form of Estate Duty Account at present in force is given on pages 97 to 104, and the various blanks have been filled in in accordance with the assumed facts of a typical case, which, it is thought, will sufficiently explain the leading features in connection with this particular class of accounts. This account should be carefully studied in conjunction with the explanatory notes and instructions supplied by the Inland Revenue authorities, and the reader will then be in a position to consider further the best method of opening the books in accordance with the position there disclosed.

PROBLEM.—X. died on 30th November 1900, his Estate on that date being as follows:—

	£
Cash in House ...	10
Cash at Bank ...	1,000
Household Furniture ...	500

Leasehold Property valued at £1,000 (let at £60 a year, rent payable half-yearly, 30th June and 31st December, paid to 30th June 1900).

Freehold Property (hitherto in deceased's occupation) 2,000

30 £10 Shares in the Mont Blanc Ice Company, Lim., quoted at £15 per Share (dividend for the year ended 31st December 1900, 10 per cent., paid 31st December 1901).

£1,000 5 per cent. Debentures East Western Railway Company, Lim., quoted at £160 per cent. (interest payable half-yearly 31st June and 31st December).

X. was partner in a business, and accounts were taken at the date of his death showing his share to be:—Capital, £4,000; share of profit to date of death £550, less drawings to same date £450. Debts due from deceased at the date of his death amounted to £300, and the funeral expenses were £100.

Prepare an Account for Probate, and show upon what amount duty was payable, the account being rendered on 31st March 1901.

ACCOUNT No. 1.

Personal Property situate in the United Kingdom, and Real Property situate in England, for or in respect of which the Grant is to be made.

The Property situate in Scotland and Ireland respectively should be so marked.

FIRST PART.—Personal Property.

No Foreign Property should be included in this Account.

(A) Published Quotations or Brokers' Certificates, or letters from the Secretaries of the Companies, showing the market price at the date of death, should be attached (*).

Where there is not sufficient space to insert all the particular details of the different items, a separate schedule should be annexed.

(B) The name or names of the banks should be stated.

(C) If the power or Interest was derived under a Will, state name and date of death of the Deceased, but if under a Deed, state the date, together with names and addresses of the Trustees, and if the Deed has been already produced give the official reference appearing upon it.

(D) Annex a schedule of such specific articles bequeathed for national or *quasi*-national purposes as are within the purview of sect. 15 (2) of the Finance Act, 1894. See Clauses 28 and 35 of Form A—2. State the value in each case, and whether the Treasury has remitted the Estate duty thereon, and if not whether it is intended to apply for remission.

Annex also a schedule of such specific articles settled to be enjoyed in kind in succession by different persons as are within the purview of sect. 20 (1) of the Finance Act, 1896. See Clauses 29 and 36 of Form A—2. State the value in each case, and whether the Treasury has authorised the application of the section to them, and if not whether it is intended to apply for authorisation. State also whether the property has yet been sold, or is in the possession of a person now competent to dispose of it.

(E) If there is a valuation, it should be annexed. The Commissioners reserve the right to require the separate value of each item to be stated, and in the case of pictures the names of the artists.

(F) State date from which profits are computed.

(G) A valuation must be annexed.

(H) These words to be cancelled where the amount is actually ascertained.

	Nominal Value of Stocks	Market Price of Stocks at date of Death (*)	Gross Principal Value at date of Death
	£ s d		£ s d
Stocks or Funds (including Exchequer Bills) of the United Kingdom, viz.:—			
Stocks, Funds, or Bonds of Foreign Countries, or of British Dependencies and Colonies, transferable in the United Kingdom, viz.:—			
Proprietary Shares or Debentures of Public Companies (A)—			
30 £10 Shares in Mont Blanc Ice Co., Lim.	300 0 0	15	450 0 0
£1,000 5% Debentures East Western Railway Co., Lim. ..	1,000 0 0	160	1,600 0 0

Dividends and Interest declared and accrued due, in respect of the above Investments, *as per statement annexed*, to date of death .. ..

(NOTE.—Unless stocks and shares are quoted ex. div., the market price includes accruing dividends and interest.)

Cash in the House			10 0 0
Cash at the Bankers (B) { (1) on Drawing Account, and Interest (if any) thereon to date of death { (2) on Deposit, and Interest thereon to date of death			1,000 0 0
Money out on Mortgage, and Interest thereon to date of death, *as per statement annexed*			
Money out on Bonds, Bills, Promissory Notes, and other Securities, and Interest thereon to date of death, *as per statement annexed*			
Book Debts			
Other Debts, *as per list annexed*			
Unpaid Purchase Money of Real and Leasehold Property contracted in lifetime of the Deceased to be sold			
Deceased's interest in proceeds of sale of Real Property directed to be sold by settlement or by will of some other person whether actually sold or not, estimated at (C)			
Personal Property over which the Deceased had and exercised by will an absolute power of appointment (C)			
Policies of Insurance, and Bonuses (if any) thereon, on the life of the Deceased, *as per statement annexed*			
Saleable value of Policies of Insurance and Bonuses (if any) on the life of any person other than the Deceased, *as per statement annexed*			
(D) Household Goods, Pictures, China, Linen, Apparel, Books, Plate, Jewels, Carriages, Horses, &c.—			500 0 0
If sold, realised gross £			
(E) If unsold, estimated at £ 500 0 0			
Stock-in-Trade, Live and Dead Farming Stock, Implements of Husbandry, &c.—			
If sold, realised gross £			
If unsold, estimated at £			
Goodwill of Business, if taken over at a price .. .. £			
If valued according to custom of trade .. .. .. £			
If neither, estimated at .. .. £			
(viz.,..........years' purchase of net profits.)			
(F) Profits of Business from..........1...... to date of death			
(G) Ships and Shares of Ships registered at Ports in the United Kingdom, and Profits of same to date of death, *as per statement annexed* (H), estimated at			
The Deceased's share in Real and Personal Property as a Partner in the Firm of X. & Y.			
as per Balance Sheet annexed, signed by the surviving Partners.. If none, estimated at			4,100 0 0

* Market Price of Stocks, &c.—When there is a published quotation, a price one quarter up from the lower to the higher of the official "closing prices" should be adopted as an estimated price. For example:—Where the "closing prices" were "98—100," the market price is $98 + \frac{100-98}{4} = 98\frac{1}{2}$. Where the death occurred on a Sunday, or other day for which no prices are available, the price for the day before should be taken.

Carried forward .. .. £   7,660   0   0

H

(I) No Mortgage Debt created or *incurred* by the Deceased himself is to be deducted unless such debt was created or incurred *bona fide* for full consideration in money or money's worth wholly for the Deceased's own use and benefit.

(K) If the interest was derived under a will, state name and date of death of the Deceased; but if under a Deed state the Date, together with names and addresses of the Trustees, and if the Deed has been already produced give the official reference appearing upon it.

(L) All Interests in Expectancy in personal property, whether veste 1 or contingent, should be included, whether or not the property is chargeable with Estate duty, on the Deceased's death as passing under the earlier disposition.

(M) But where the Deceased was entitled to the interest expectant upon his own death, or upon the death of another person who survives him, and Estate duty is payable upon the corpus or the property on the Deceased's death, the Interest in Expectancy is not also chargeable with Estate duty on Deceased's death as part of his free Estate. Although, as it is in fact part of his free Estate, its value must be looked at for the purposes of the Probate Court. The Interest in Expectancy should be brought into this Affidavit, and be taken out again in the Summary on p. 102.

(N) *No deduction is to be taken here unless Treasury authority has been first obtained.*

ACCOUNT No. 1 (First Part)—*continued.*

	Gross Principal Value at date of Death
	£ s d
Brought forward	7,660 0 0

Leasehold Property (for years) *as per detailed description subjoined or annexed.—*

Giving—
  1. Particular description.   If sold, realised gross £
  2. Term unexpired at date of death.   If unsold, estimated at £ 1,000 0 0
  3. Gross rents, where let, or if not let, either the gross assessment to property tax (not the *reduced assessment for collection of Income Tax*, under Finance Act, 1894, s 35) or *gross* (not rateable) assessment to Poor Rate.   Less (I) a Mortgage Debt of .. £   £ 1,000 0 0
  4. The Ground Rent.   due from the Deceased and created by an Indenture dated the....day of........1....,
  5. The nature and amount of the yearly outgoings paid by the Lessee as owner.   for which the said Leasehold Property is the sole security.   1,000 0 0

Rents of the Deceased's own Real and Leasehold Property due prior to the death, but not received by the Deceased, (H) estimated at   ..   ..

Apportionment of the rents of the Deceased's Real and Leasehold Property to date of death (H) estimated at 25 0 0

(K) Income accrued due, but not received prior to the death, arising from Real and Personal Property of which the Deceased was Tenant for life, or for any less period, viz. ....
....

Apportionment of such Income to date of death   ..   ..

The Deceased's Interest (L) expectant upon the death of ....
now aged....................years, under the Will of..
proved...or under a Settlement dated the
.......................day of...1...., and made between
....
(setting out the parties to the Deed) in the Property (M) set out in the statement annexed, and of which Fund the present Trustees are ....

(K) Other Personal Property not comprised under the foregoing heads, viz. ....
....

(a) Gross Personal Property in First Part of Account No. 1	£	8,685 0 0
N.B.—(a) is the "gross value" which is to be carried to par. 3 on page 1*.		
(b) Deduct Total of First and Second Parts of Schedule No. 1	£	400 0 0
N.B.—(b) is the "aggregate amount" which is to be carried to par. 5 on p. 1*.		
(c) Net Personal Property in First Part of Account No. 1	£	8,285 0 0
N.B.—(c) is the reduced "value" which is to be carried to par. 5 on page 1*.		
(d) Deduct (N) specific articles [see note (D) on page 97] whereon Estate duty is either not payable at all, or is not now payable	£	
(e) Balance remaining	£	8,285 0 0
(f) Deduct net Settled Personal Property (if any) in Account No. 1 (First Part), *in so far as the same is not fully aggregable with the free property.* [See Clauses 33 & 34 (particularly the last part of Clause 33 (3)) of the Form A—2]	£	
(g) Balance remaining	£	8,285 0 0

N.B.—(g) is the amount of "Personal Property [Account No. 1 (First Part)]" which is to be carried to Part I. of the Summary.
(f) is to be carried to Part II. of the Summary.   £   8,685 0 0

ACCOUNT No. 1—*continued.*   Second Part.—Real Property in England.
For use *only* where the Deceased died on or after the 1st January 1898.

(Note.—This Account is NOT *to include land of copyhold tenure or customary freehold where an admission, or any act by the lord of the manor, is necessary to perfect the title of a purchaser from the customary tenant.)*

Interests in expectancy in Real Property, where the circumstances are otherwise appropriate, should be included here, as well as interests in possession. Particulars, as in the case of interests in expectancy in Personal Property (see First Part above), should be furnished.

(C) See Note (C) on page 97.

	Gross *Annual* Value at date of Death	Gross *Principal* Value at date of Death
		£ s d
Real Property in ENGLAND vested in the Deceased without a right in any other person to take by survivorship		2,000 0 0
(The particulars of that part of the property in respect of which the duty is to be now paid are stated in the First Part of the Account No. 5, and of that part of the property in respect of which the duty is not to be now paid in an "appropriate account" marked ....)		
(C) Real Property in ENGLAND over which the Deceased executed by will a general power of appointment		
(The particulars of that part of the property in respect of which the duty is to be now paid are stated in the Third Part of the Account No. 5, and of that part of the property in respect of which the duty is not to be now paid in an "appropriate account" marked ....)		
N.B.—This is the "gross value" which is to be carried to par. 6 on page 1*. .. .. £		2,000 0 0

To be signed by the persons making oath or affirmation }
                   Total of First and Second Parts   ..   £   10,685 0 0
N.B.—This, where the deceased died on or after the 1st January 1898, is the "aggregate gross value" which is to be carried to par. 7 on page 102.
Where the Deceased died before that date, the total of the *First* Part will be such "aggregate gross value."

---

* This page has not been reproduced, as it does not affect the accounts.

SCHEDULE No. 1.

FIRST PART.—An account of the debts due, and owing from the Deceased, to persons resident in the United Kingdom, or due to persons resident out of the United Kingdom, but contracted to be paid in the United Kingdom, or charged on property situate within the United Kingdom.

Where the debts on the Deceased's personal property exceed the value thereof, and the deficiency is a proper deduction for Estate duty purposes against the Deceased's real property, deduction of such deficiency may be taken in Schedule No. 5.

N.B.—WHERE THE SPACE IS INSUFFICIENT, THE ACCOUNT OR SCHEDULE SHOULD BE CONTINUED ON A SEPARATE SHEET.

	Name and Address of Creditor	Description of Debt (This should include the date and short particulars of any security for the Debt.)	Amount
NOTE.—See Clauses 52 to 54 of the Form A—2 as to what debts may *not* be deducted. A STATEMENT OF ANY DEBTS PAYABLE BY LAW OUT OF THE PERSONAL PROPERTY IN ACCOUNT No. 1, BUT WHICH CANNOT BE DEDUCTED AGAINST ESTATE DUTY, SHOULD BE ANNEXED TO THE SCHEDULE BY WAY OF RIDER. *Where a debt is claimed to be due to the husband or wife, or any other member of the Deceased's family, a full explanation should be given, and evidence of the debt should be annexed.* A mortgage debt not created by the Deceased himself but charged on real property which was acquired by the Deceased subject to the mortgage is primarily payable out of such real property and must not be deducted here. A mortgage debt created by the Deceased himself on his real property, but which is payable by his heir or his devisee under " Locke King's Act," 17 & 18 Vict. c. 113, is a debt in respect of which reimbursement may be claimed and must not be deducted here, unless such reimbursement cannot be obtained. A debt for payment of which the Deceased was surety only must not be deducted, unless the executor has already paid it, and cannot recover it from the original debtor. Where the debt is for " money lent " or " overdraft " to a Bank, the date of the loan and the particulars of the security, if any, given, or, if none, the facts relied on, as showing that the debt is legally recoverable, should be stated.		[Full particulars to be inserted here.]	£ s d 300 0 0
			£ 300 0 0

SECOND PART.—An account of the funeral expenses of the Deceased.

NOTE.—The cost of mourning or tombstone cannot be deducted.	Toombes & Son, Undertakers	£ s d 100 0 0
		£ 100 0 0
To be signed by the persons making oath or affirmation	Total of First and Second Parts .. £	400 0 0

ACCOUNT No. 2.

Personal or moveable property situate abroad, which is not saleable or transferable in the United Kingdom.

NOTE.—Property saleable or transferable in the United Kingdom should be included in Account No. 1 as " Personal Property situate *in* the United Kingdom."

	Particulars and Local Situation of the Property	Principal Value at date of Death
It should be clearly shown how the value of the property expressed in English money is arrived at.		
	Gross Value .. .. £ Deduct Total of Schedule No. 2 .. £	
To be signed by the persons making oath or affirmation	Net Value .. .. £ N.B.—This is the amount to be carried to Summary.	

SCHEDULE No. 2.

An account of the debts due and owing from the Deceased to persons resident out of the United Kingdom, other than debts contracted to be paid in the United Kingdom or charged on property situate within the United Kingdom, which have been deducted in the above Schedule No. 1.

	Name and Address of Creditor	Description of Debt (This should include the date and short particulars of any security for the debt.)	Amount
See Clauses 52 to 54 of the Form A—2 as to what debts may *not* be deducted, AND SEE FIRST TWO NOTES TO SCHEDULE No. 1. Deduction may be here claimed (*a*) of any duty payable in any *foreign* country by reason of the Deceased's death in respect of property situate in that *foreign* country and included in the Account No. 2, and (*b*) of an amount not exceeding 5 per cent. on the value of any property in the Account No. 2, representing *additional* expense incurred in administering or realising such property by reason of its being situate *out of the United Kingdom*.			£ s d
	To be signed by the persons making oath or affirmation		£

H 2

_____deceased.

ACCOUNTS Nos. 3 (A) AND 3 (B).

3 (a). An account of the PERSONAL property, whether in possession or reversion, OTHER THAN THAT IN THE ACCOUNTS Nos. 1 and 2, of which the Deceased at the time of h.... death was *competent to dispose* within the meaning of the Finance Act, 1894 [see Sec. 22 (2) (a)], but of which ..he did *not* dispose. *The duty on this property* MUST BE PAID *on the delivery of this Affidavit.*

3 (b). An account of money which the Deceased had, at the time of h.... death, a general power to charge on real property whether the power was exercised by h.... will or not. *The duty on this property* MUST BE PAID *on the delivery of this affidavit.*

Short material particulars of Disposition conferring the Power, with date of and names of any Parties to any Deed, and name of any Testator, and date of Probate of his Will	Particulars of Property (A separate statement should be attached giving full particulars, as in Account No. 5 on page 101, of any Leaseholds for years.)	Principal Value at date of Death
		£ s d
3 (a)		
	Gross Value .. .. £	
	† Deduct Debts and Incumbrances upon Leaseholds .. £ († A separate statement marked Schedule No. 3 (a) should be attached, giving full particulars as in Schedule No. 5 on page 101.)	
	Net Value .. .. £ N.B.—This is the amount to be carried to Summary (see Note).	
3 (b) (i.) Where the power was exercised		
(ii.) Where the power was not exercised		
To be signed by the persons } making oath or affirmation }	N.B.—This is the amount to be carried to Summary .. £	

ACCOUNT No. 4.

An account of OTHER PERSONAL property passing on the Deceased's death (including Leaseholds for years in which the Deceased's interest was less than an absolute interest), *whereon the Estate duty is* ELECTED TO BE paid *on the delivery of this Affidavit.*

Title to Property Date and short material particulars of Disposition, with date of and names of Parties to any Deed, and name of any Testator, and date of Probate of his Will. The names and addresses of the beneficiaries should also be given, together with their relationship (a) to the Deceased, and (b) to the predecessor from whom the property is derived	Particulars of Property (A separate statement should be attached giving full particulars, as in Account No. 5 on page 101, of any Leaseholds for years.)	Principal Value at date of Death
		£ s d
	Gross Value .. .. £	
	† Deduct Debts and Incumbrances upon Leaseholds .. £ († A separate statement marked Schedule No. 4 should be attached giving full particulars as in Schedule No. 5 on page 101.)	
	Net Value .. .. £ N.B.—This is the amount to be carried to Summary (see Note).	

ACCOUNT No. 5.

An Account of REAL Property passing on the Deceased's Death, *whereon the Estate duty is* ELECTED TO BE PAID *on the delivery of this affidavit.*

PARTICULARS OF REAL PROPERTY

TITLE UNDER WHICH THE PROPERTY PASSES ON THE DEATH OF THE DECEASED.	Description of property, including situation, tenure, quantity, tenants' names, and nature of tenancy, and distinguishing between arable, meadow, pasture, orchards, gardens, woods, moors, commons, wastes, pleasure grounds, building land, &c.	Rental, if let, or gross (not rateable value for the poor rate, if unlet and not assessed to property tax.	Value for property tax. State the gross assessment (and not the reduced assessment for collection of Income Tax under Finance Act 1894, s. 35)	Nature of deductions from the gross annual value. Tenants' outgoings should not here be deducted unless paid by owner	Amount of Deductions	Net Annual Value	Number of Years purchase as estimated	Estimated principal value at date of death, at gross amount realised, if since sold and date of completion of sale.
Date and short material particulars of disposition, with date of any deed, and names of parties thereto, and name of any testator or intestate, and date of probate of his will or grant of administration. The names and addresses of the beneficiaries should also be given, together with their relation (if any) to the deceased, and (b) the predecessor from whom the property is derived.		£ s d	£ s d		£ s d	£ s d		£ s d
								2,000 0 0
FIRST PART.—Real Property passing under the Deceased's will or intestacy, other than the property in Second Part (below)	[Full particulars to be recorded here.]							
England— Scotland and Ireland—								
SECOND PART.—Land of copyhold tenure or customary freehold, passing as in First Part (above) where an admission or act by the Lord of the Manor is necessary to perfect the title of a purchaser from the customary tenant								
THIRD PART.—Real property over which the Deceased executed by will a general power of appointment, other than the property in Fourth Part (below)								
England— Scotland and Ireland—								
FOURTH PART.—Land as in Second Part (above) over which the Deceased executed a power as in Third Part (above)								
FIFTH PART.—Real Property passing under other titles, viz.—								
To be signed by the person making oath or affirmation								

Gross value..................£
Deductions in Schedule No. 5................£
Net value.............£
N.B.—This is the amount to be carried to Summary (see Note)............£

Observe.—As to Agricultural property, see Clause 46 of Form A—2.

If the real property include unlet fishing or sporting rights, church patronage, timber, unlet building land, mines, or other property which has no annual value, or the annual value whereof is no criterion of the principal value, full details of the property is licensed it should be expressly so stated, and the particulars of the lease and other lettings should be fully set out.

Generally, as to all property, all such particulars should be furnished as are requisite to arrive at the principal value.

NOTE.—If any part of the property in this Account is *not fully aggregable with the Deceased's free property*, a separate statement should be annexed showing (a) the amount *fully aggregable with the free property*, (b) the amount of any property which *would be* fully aggregable with the free property, but is *not* because of any other unsettled property is, by reason of its small value, an "Estate by itself." [See Clause 34 of the Form A—2], (c) the amount of any "Estate by itself," and, WHERE THE DEATH AND THEREON OR AFTER THE 15TH APRIL 1900, (d) the amount of any "settled property," liable to limited aggregation. The several amounts should be separately carried to the Summary. See Clauses 33 to 36 of the Form A—2 as to aggregation.

SCHEDULE No. 5.

An account of the debts and incumbrances upon the Real property in Account No. 5. (See Clauses 52 to 54 of the Form A—2 as to what debts and incumbrances may *not* be deducted, AND SEE FIRST NOTE TO SCHEDULE NO. 1.) *Where the debts on the Deceased's real property exceed the value thereof, and the deficiency is a proper deduction for Estate duty purposes against the Deceased's personal property, deduction of such deficiency may be taken in Schedule No. 1.*

Nature of debt or incumbrance and by whom created	Short material particulars of security, with date of and names of parties to any deed, and name of any testator, and date of Probate of his will.	Short particulars of property charged, to identify it in above account.	Names and addresses of persons to or in whom the debt or incumbrance is now due or vested	Amount of debt or incumbrance
				£ s d

To be signed by the person making oath or affirmation

Total .. £

....deceased.

SUMMARY OF AFFIDAVIT.

This Summary is not on oath, and if wrong may be amended without the Affidavit being resworn.

PART I.—THE DECEASED'S FREE PROPERTY AND PROPERTY FULLY AGGREGABLE THEREWITH.

(As to Aggregation, see Clauses 33 to 36 of the Form A—2.)

FIRST TABLE.—For determining Rate of Estate Duty	Net Value of Property		THIRD TABLE.—For determining AMOUNT of Estate Duty and interest to be now Paid			
	Personal	Real		£	s	d
	£ s d	£ s d				
I. Personal Property [Account No. 1 (First Part)]	8,285 0 0		A.—Estate Duty on the net value of the PERSONAL Property (XX.), adjusted (*) if necessary (XXI.), at the appropriate rate (XV.) of 4 per cent. .. £	331		
II. " " [" " 2]						
III. " " [" " 3 (a)]			*Deduct* duty payable in any British possession, to which sec. 20 of the Finance Act, 1894, applies by reason of the Deceased's death, in respect of Property situate in such possession. (The deduction is not to exceed the amount of the Estate Duty to be now paid on the Property in respect of which such duty is payable) .. .. .. £			
IV. " " [" " 3 (b)]						
V. " " [" " 4]						
VI. Real " " [" " 5]		2,000 0 0				
VII. Total net values of Personal and Real property, respectively, in Accounts Nos. 1 (First Part), 2, 3 (a), 3 (b), 4, and 5	8,285 0 0	2,000 0 0				
VIII. *Deduct* value of Interests in Expectancy in Property on the corpus whereof Estate duty is payable on the Deceased's death under the earlier disposition, provided that the Property is itself *fully aggregable with the free property, but not otherwise.* [See note (M) at page 98.] Deduct no other Interests in Expectancy here £			Net duty .. .. £	331	8	0
			Deduct duty paid or payable, to which sec. 21 of the Finance Act, 1896, applies, in respect of the property. (The deduction is not to exceed the amount of the Estate Duty to be now paid on the property in respect of which such duty has been paid or is payable) .. .. .. £			
IX. Total net values of Personal and Real Property, respectively, in Accounts Nos. 1 (First Part), 2, 3 (a), 3 (b), 4, and 5, for determining Rate of Estate Duty..	8,285 0 0	2,000 0 0	Net duty .. [.. £	331	8	0
X. *Add* other Property *fully aggregable with free property* [See par. 14 of Affidavit, and marginal notes 18 and 19 on page 2(not reproduced)], passing on the Deceased's death in respect of which Estate duty is NOT to be paid on this Affidavit £			*Add* 3 per cent. per annum interest thereon, from day after death, viz., 30th November 1900, till date of delivery of affidavit, viz., 31st March 1901, both days inclusive, i.e.,........years and 91 days ..	4	2	8
XI. Total net values of Personal and Real property respectively .. .. .. £	8,285 0 0	2,000 0 0				
XII. Carry down into "*Personal*" column from No. XI. the total value of Real Property £	2,000 0 0		Total duty and interest (Personal Property) .. £	335	10	8
XIII. Total net value of Personal and Real Property .. .. £	10,285 0 0		B.—Estate Duty on the net value of the REAL Property (XX.), adjusted (*) if necessary (XXI.), at the appropriate rate (XV.) of 4 per cent.			
XIV. This is No. XIII., but "adjusted," if adjustment is necessary [Read Note (*) on page 104] £	10,285 0 0		Whole duty .. .. .. £80 0 0 } ½th or ¹⁄₁₀th thereof .. .. £ }	80	0	0

XV. The appropriate RATE of Estate Duty [See clause 70 of Form A—2] is........per cent. [Read footnote (†) on this page.]			[Read Note (‡) on page 104.]			
SECOND TABLE.—For determining Value on which Estate Duty or an instalment thereof is to be now paid.	Net Value of Property		*If the Deceased has been dead more than a year* [Read Note (§) on page 104], *and the whole duty is to be now paid—*			
	Personal	Real				
	£ s d	£ s d	*Add* 3 per cent. per annum interest upon the whole duty, from day after expiration of 12 months after death till date of delivery of affidavit, both days inclusive, i.e.,..........years and .... days			
XVI. Values as in No. VII. above.	8,285 0 0	2,000 0 0				
XVII. *Deduct* value, or a proportion thereof, of Interests in Expectancy such as are mentioned in note (M) on page 98, whether the Property itself *is or is not fully* aggregable with the free property, *including* any deducted at No. VIII. above [Read Note (**) on page 104] .. £			*But if only the instalments due are to be now paid—*			
XVIII. Balance .. .. £	8,285 0 0	2,000 0 0	*Add* 3 per cent. per annum interest upon *whole* duty from day after expiration of 12 months after death till date when *last overdue* instalment was payable, both days inclusive, i.e.,............years and ....months .. .. .. £			
XIX. *Deduct* value of *other* Interests in Expectancy, in respect of which Estate duty is payable, but is elected to be paid when the Interest falls into possession :— Account No......£........ } " " ......£........ } £			*Add* 3 per cent. per annum interest upon amount of *overdue* instalments, from day after date when *last overdue* instalment is payable till date of delivery of affidavit, both days inclusive, i.e.,......days £			
XX. Net values of Personal and Real Property, respectively, for determining Amount of Estate Duty .. .. £	8,285 0 0	2,000 0 0	Total duty and interest (Personal and Real) } Property .. ..] £	415	10	8
XXI. This is No. XX., but "adjusted," if adjustment is necessary [Read Note (*) on page 104] £	8,285 0 0	2,000 0 0				

[Continued on page 103]

  † If Deceased died *before* 9th April 1900, the *adjusted* value at XIV. determines the rate of Duty.

  If Deceased died *on or after* 9th April 1900, then if the free and unsettled property, by reason of its value, is an "Estate by itself" [See Clause 34 of the Form A—2], the value at XIII. determines the Rate of Duty. But if the free and other unsettled property is not an "Estate by itself" the Rate is to be thus arrived at :—

    (a) Value at XIII. above   .. .. £

    (b) Total value of "settled property" liable to limited aggregation   .. .. £

    (c) Totals of (a) and (b)   .. .. £

    (d) The appropriate Rate for (a), treated as an "Estate by itself," is   .. ..per cent.

    (e) The appropriate Rate for (c), treated as fully aggregable property is   .. ..per cent.

    (f) If (e) exceeds (d), (d) is to be raised one-half per cent., and the resulting Rate, viz., ...per cent. is the appropriate Rate for (a). But if (e) is equal to (d), then (d) is the appropriate Rate for (a).

PART II.—Property not FULLY Aggregable with the Deceased's Free Property.

Each "Estate by itself," or "Settled Property" liable to limited aggregation, should be separately shown. If the spaces provided are not sufficient, additional statements in similar form should be annexed.

FOURTH TABLE.—For determining RATE of Estate duty on an "Estate by itself."

No. of Account	Whether Real or Personal	Value of "Estate by itself"	
		Actual	As adjusted (*) where necessary
		£ s d	£ s d
I.			
II.	The appropriate RATE of Estate duty [see Clause 70 of Form A—2] is ....per cent.		

NOTE.—If the property passes in equal shares to more than one person, and each share is an "Estate by itself," Tables Fourth and Seventh or Eighth should be filled up in respect of one share only, and the amount of the duty and interest so ascertained in respect of one share should be multiplied by the number of shares to ascertain the total amount payable. Where the shares are unequal, each share should be separately shown.

Number of separate "Estates" .. .. ..

Total duty and interest in respect thereof .. .. £

FIFTH TABLE.— For determining RATE of Estate duty on "Settled Property" liable to limited aggregation.

No. of Account	Whether Real or or Personal	Value of "Settled Property"
		Actual
		£ s d
I.		
II.	The appropriate RATE of Estate duty [see Clause 70 of Form A—2] is .... per cent.	

NOTE.—The appropriate RATE of Estate duty at II. above is to be thus arrived at :—
(a) The total net principal value of all property liable to Estate duty on the Deceased's death, as disclosed by this affidavit .. .. .. £
(b) *Deduct* the value of any property forming an "Estate by itself" £
(c) There remains the total value of the property which is liable to either full or limited aggregation .. £
(d) The appropriate Rate for the "Settled Property," treated as an "Estate by itself," is .. ..per cent.
(e) The appropriate Rate for (c), treated as fully aggregable property, is .. ..per cent.
(f) If (e) exceeds (d), (d) is to be raised one-half per cent., and the resulting Rate, viz., ...per cent. is the appropriate Rate for the "Settled Property." But if (e) is equal to (d), then (d) is the appropriate Rate.

SIXTH TABLE.—For determining RATE of Estate duty on property which would be fully aggregable with the Free and other unsettled property, were not such Free and other unsettled property an "Estate by itself."

No. of Account	Whether Real or Personal	Value of Property	
		Actual	As adjusted (*) where necessary
		£ s d	£ s d
I.			
II.	The appropriate RATE of Estate duty [see Clause 70 of Form A—2] is ....per cent.		

NOTE.—The appropriate RATE of Estate duty at (II.) above is to be thus arrived at :—
(a) Value at (I.) above .. .. £
(b) Add value of other property liable to full aggregation .. ..£
(c) Total value of property liable to full aggregation .. ..£
(d) Add value of "Settled Property" liable to limited aggregation .. ..£
(e) Total value of property liable to full and limited aggregation .. ..£
(f) The aggregate Rate for (c), treated as an "Estate by itself," is .. ..per cent.
(g) The appropriate Rate for (e), treated as fully aggregable property, is .. ..per cent.
(h) If (g) exceeds (f), (f) is to be raised one-half per cent., and the resulting Rate for (a). But if (g) is equal to (f), then (f) is the appropriate Rate.

SEVENTH TABLE.—[For Personal Property.] For determining AMOUNT of Estate duty and interest to be now PAID on the "Estate by itself," referred to in Fourth Table, or the "Settled Property" referred to in Fifth Table, or the property referred to in Sixth Table.

A.—Estate duty on the net value of the PERSONAL Property (I.), adjusted (*) if necessary, at the appropriate rate (II.) of ....per cent. .. .. .. £

Deduct duty payable in any British Possession, to which Section 20 of the Finance Act, 1894, applies, by reason of the Deceased's death, in respect of property situate in such possession. (The deduction is not to exceed the amount of the Estate duty to be now paid on the property in respect of which such duty is payable .. £
•Net duty £

Deduct duty paid or payable, to which Section 21 of the Finance Act, 1896, applies, in respect of the property. (The deduction is not to exceed the amount of the Estate duty to be now paid on the property in respect of which such duty has been paid or is payable.) .. £
Net duty £

Add 3 per cent. per annum interest thereon, from day after date of death, viz., ...I...., till date of delivery of affidavit, viz.,..............190.., both days inclusive, *i.e.,*..........years and........days .. £

Total duty and interest (Personal Property) .. £

EIGHTH TABLE.—[For Real Property.] For determining AMOUNT of Estate duty and interest to be now PAID on the "Estate by itself," referred to in Fourth Table, or the "Settled Property" referred to in Fifth Table, or the property referred to in Sixth Table.

B.—Estate duty on the net value of the REAL Property (I.), adjusted (*) if necessary, at the appropriate Rate (II.) of ....per cent.
‡ { Whole duty .. .. £............... } £
{ ½th or ⅕th thereof .. .. £............... }

If the Deceased has been dead more than a year (§) and the whole duty is to be now paid—

Add 3 per cent. per annum interest upon the whole duty from day after expiration of 12 months after death till date of delivery of affidavit, both days inclusive, *i.e.,* ....years and................days .. £

But if only the instalments due are to be now paid—

Add 3 per cent. per annum upon *whole* duty, from day after expiration of 12 months after death till date when *last overdue* instalment was payable, both days inclusive, *i.e.,*..............years and................months.. £
Add 3 per cent. per annum interest upon amount of *overdue* instalments, from day after date when *last overdue* instalment was payable till date of delivery of affidavit, both days inclusive, *i.e.,*..............days .. £

Total duty and interest (Real Property) .. .. £

* ‡ § See the Notes on page 104.

NOTE.—The Estate duty in respect of Annuities provided by the Deceased otherwise than by his will, which are referred to in Section 2 (1) (d) of the Finance Act, 1894, may be paid by four annual instalments [see Clause 63 of the Form A—2]. No interest is chargeable for the first year after the Deceased's death. If the duty, or a part thereof, is to be now paid, adapt the Fourth and Eighth Tables to meet the case.

If an "Estate by itself," or "Settled Property" liable to limited aggregation, or a fully aggregable property, consists partly of Personal Property and partly of Real Property, adapt the Tables to meet the case.

.... deceased.

* *Where the Deceased died on or after the 9th April 1900, the duty is chargeable upon the exact net principal value of the Estate, both as regards rate and amount of duty.*

Where the Deceased died on or after the 1st July 1896, but before the 9th April 1900, the net principal value of the Estate should be *decreased* to an even multiple of £10, except that where the net value exceeds £100, and does not exceed £200, the duty is £1.

Where the Deceased died after the 1st August 1894, but before the 1st July 1896, the net principal value of the Estate should be *increased* to an even multiple of £10.

See Clause 72 of the Form A—2 for more detailed information.

The values, so *adjusted*, where necessary, should be written in the spaces provided (XIV. and XXI.) below the true values (XIII. and XX.), and the rate of duty, and amount of duty and interest, should be computed upon the *adjusted* values, and not upon the true values.

Real property directed to be sold at or after the Deceased's death, whether actually sold or not, is to be treated as REAL property.

** If the property, the subject of the Interest in Expectancy, forms an "Estate by itself," or is "Settled Property" liable to limited aggregation, and is chargeable at the *same* or a *higher* rate of Estate duty than the *fully* aggregated "one estate," deduct at No. XVII. the *whole* value of the Interest in Expectancy. But if the "Estate by itself" or "Settled Property," liable to limited aggregation, is chargeable at a *lower* rate, then deduct only so much of the value of the Interest as represents that lower rate. Thus, if the "Estate by itself," or "Settled Property" liable to limited aggregation, is chargeable at 2 per cent., and the *fully* aggregated "one estate" at 3 per cent., deduct two-thirds, and if the rates are 3 per cent. and 7 per cent. respectively, deduct three-sevenths, and so on. If payment of the duty which still remains to be paid is elected to be deferred until the interest falls into possession, then deduct the *remaining* part of the value (in the above examples, one-third and four-sevenths respectively) at No. XIX.

‡ If at the time of the delivery of this affidavit *not more than* 12 months has expired since the date of the Deceased's death, carry out the whole duty, or ⅘th or 7/10th of it, according as the duty is to be paid in one sum, or by yearly or by half-yearly instalments. No interest is chargeable.

§ Where at the time of the delivery of this affidavit *more than* 12 months has expired since the date of the Deceased's death, the duty on the Real property, whether it is paid in one sum or by instalments, is chargeable with interest. The interest is chargeable upon the *whole* unpaid duty, from 12 months after the Deceased's death, up to the date of payment of the duty or of an instalment thereof, although part only of the duty may be overdue. See Clause 62 of the Form A—2. Where the duty is elected to be paid by instalments, and payment is not made on a date when an instalment becomes payable, the interest upon the whole duty is to be calculated up to the date when the last overdue instalment was payable, and interest from that date is to be calculated upon the *overdue* instalments.

PART III.—Total of Parts I. and II, of Summary.

		Rate
Part I.—Total duty and interest .. .. £		
NOTE. — The total amount paid on each "Estate by itself," or "Settled Property" liable to limited aggregation, or property liable to full aggregation, and the rate should be separately shown. (Annex a schedule if the space is insufficient.)	„ II. { Total duty and interest (Personal) .. .. £ / „ „ „ (Real) .. .. £	
Total duty and interest paid on this Affidavit .. .. £		

RECEIPT FOR DUTY AND INTEREST.

Here state the name and full address of the person who pays the duty.	....

1.	2.
A. G.	**Received** the.....................day of................. ...., 190....,
	the sum of ....
Comptrolled and Registered for	....Pounds,
	....shillings and...........................pence, for
.... ,, ... ,, ...	*Estate Duty* and Interest thereon.
	....
	for Commissioners of Inland Revenue.
....	
for Accountant-General of Inland Revenue.	£.............. ,, ... ,, ...
	This receipt does not imply that the amount of duty is not subject to rectification.

For use at Chief Office.

These stamps do not imply that the Rates of duty are not subject to rectification.

PARTNERSHIP ACCOUNTS.

It should be noted that when a person who has been in business by himself dies, the Estate Duty Account contains full and detailed particulars of *all* his assets and liabilities, both with regard to his business and in respect of his private affairs. Where, however, the partner of a firm dies, the assets and liabilities of the firm do not come into the Estate Duty Account at all. In their place must be stated, as a separate asset, the deceased's share in real and personal property as a partner in the firm, his share being, of course, represented by the amount standing to the credit of his Capital Account in the firm's books after they have been adjusted up to the date of death. If anything is payable to the executors of the deceased partner as his share of the goodwill of the business, it is, of course, included in this amount.

DUTY ON REAL AND PERSONAL ESTATE.

Both Real and Personal Estate are liable to Estate Duty, and the rate at which the duty is levied depends upon the aggregate net value of both Estates added together. It is important, however, to bear in mind that, while in the ordinary course the Executors may very likely pay the duty out of the Personal Estate, that proportion of it which is in respect of the Real Estate is a deduction from the Real Estate itself, and must not be *charged* against the Personal Estate. This point is, of course, only of practical importance, if the persons entitled to the Real Estate (or the Residue thereof) are not the same as the persons entitled to the Residue of the Personal Estate. The same principle applies to Legacy Duty, when it is payable by the Estate and not by the Legatee.

APPORTIONMENT.

Although it is not intended in this work to discuss the law with regard to executorships and administrations, it is impossible to altogether ignore the question of Apportionment. It will, however, be treated from a bookkeeping point of view—that is to say, its practical effect will be considered in detail—while the reader must be referred to some legal text-book for information as to exactly when to apply the rules here laid down.

Speaking generally, the executors are accountable for the estate of the deceased as from the date when he died; and where any portion of that estate represents money laid out at interest in undertakings making a regular return of income by way of rent, interest, or dividend, the income accruing up to the date of death represents part of the *capital* of which the deceased died possessed. This is of importance in two ways. (1) Duty has to be paid upon the value of the estate at the date of death, and therefore accruing income has to be included in the amount upon which duty is payable. (2) Persons entitled to the income derived from the estate (or any portion of it) are not entitled to all the *cash* that may be received by way of income after that date, but merely to the proportion that represents income accrued since the date of death. An apportionment has therefore to be made of the income accruing partly before and partly after the death of the testator.

This seems the most convenient place to draw attention to the fact that where a specific investment is bequeathed, the legatee is entitled to that investment as from the date of death, together with the benefit of all income accruing *from that date;* but the income accruing due on the investment up to the date of death is part of the general estate. It must be noted that a bonus, or surplus profits, accruing after the death of the deceased is subject to apportionment. Moreover, dividends and bonuses declared during the life of the deceased are part of his estate, even if paid after his death.

In making these apportionments, it is proper to regard the whole of the actual date of death as being after the decease of the testator, even though in point of fact he died quite late on that day. The law on this point, however, does not appear to be perfectly clear. It is to be noted that a posthumous child born *after* the next rent day from the death of his father is entitled, under 10 & 11 Will. III., c. 16, to the intermediate profits of the *settled* land: the profits of a *descended* estate, on the other hand, belong to a posthumous child only from the date of his birth—*i.e.,* on the above rule—including the whole of his birthday.

Income tax at the current rate must, of course, be deducted from all income before arriving at the amount that is to be apportioned.

In spite of the foregoing, it cannot be too strongly impressed upon the reader that when securities having a current market value are included in the Estate Duty Account at mid-market price, it is *not*—save in certain special circumstances—necessary to add to this value any further amounts as representing the accruing income up to date, unless the market price is quoted as being *ex div.* A moment's reflection will show the reason for this. The market price is the price at which the investment can be bought or sold at the date in question, and unless the price is expressly quoted *ex div.* anyone purchasing on that date would acquire the benefit of all accruing interest or dividend; so that, if the investment could have been sold at the date of death, the total amount receivable in respect of it would be the market price, and not the market price *plus* a further sum for income accrued to date. It is not, however, by any means every class of investment earning income for which market prices are quoted, and where the valuation included in the Estate Duty Account is upon any other basis, the proportion of income accruing must be separately accounted for. But whether the accruing income is separately accounted for, or included in the capital sum as part of the market price, the first dividend receivable after the date of death *must in all cases be apportioned*, so that only the proportion earned after death may be credited to Income Account, the proportion earned up to the date of death being applied towards the reduction of the value at which the investment stands in the books. This is, of course, as it should be, seeing that the market price will naturally fall when the dividend is paid, unless outside circumstances influence it in the opposite direction.

In many undertakings it is customary to pay dividends half-yearly, or at even more frequent intervals. The apportionment in such cases must be upon the footing that the dividend earned during the whole year accrued day by day, and is the aggregate of the interim and final dividends declared in respect of that year, the amounts received as interim dividend being regarded as merely payments on account, and treated as such in the calculation of the apportionment. A share in the profits of a private partnership is not apportionable.

PROBLEM.—A. died on 31st March 1900, leaving amongst other estate, the following investments :—

   1,000   £10 Shares, fully paid, in James Cope & Co., Lim., at 19.
   1,500   ,,   ,,   George Tosh & Co., Lim., at 21.
   350   ,,   ,,   John Tribe & Co., Lim., at 12.

Each Company's financial year ended on 30th June.

James Cope & Co.. Lim., paid quarterly interim dividends on 1st December, 1st March, and 1st June, at 7½ per cent. per annum; George Tosh & Co., Lim., a half-yearly interim dividend at the rate of 5 per cent. per annum; while John Tribe & Co. paid no interim dividend.

When the accounts of the three Companies were made up, dividends for the year at the rate of 10 per cent. were declared by each, the balance for the year to be payable on 1st September.

How would you deal with these in the books of the trust ?

The total dividends received are as follows :—

						£	s	d	£	s	d
J. Cope & Co., Lim.	1st Dec. ..	..	..	..	..	187	10	0			
	1st Mar. ..	..	..	..	..	187	10	0			
	1st June ..	..	..	..	..	187	10	0			
	1st Sept. ..	..	..	..	..	437	10	0			
									1,000	0	0
G. Tosh & Co., Lim.	1st Mar. ..	..	..	..	..	375	0	0			
	1st Sept. ..	..	..	..	..	1,125	0	0			
									1,500	0	0
J. Tribe & Co., Lim.	1st Sept. ..	..	..	..	..				350	0	0
Total for the year ended 30th June		..	..	..	..				£2,850	0	0

The Apportionment works out as follows (taking months instead of days, and disregarding income tax):—

	Already received on a/c of Capital	Proportion of receipts since death on a/c of Capital	Proportion of receipts since death on a/c of Income
	£ s d	£ s d	£ s d
J. Cope & Co., Lim.	375 0 0	375 0 0	250 0 0
G. Tosh & Co., Lim.	375 0 0	750 0 0	375 0 0
J. Tribe & Co., Lim.	..	262 10 0	87 10 0
	£750 0 0	£1,387 10 0	£712 10 0

Dr. SHARES OF £10 EACH IN JAMES COPE & CO., LIM. **Cr.**

		No. of Shares	Capital	Income			No. of Shares	Capital	Income
			£ s d	£ s d				£ s d	£ s d
1900 Mar. 31	To Estate Account ..	1,000	19,000 0 0		1900 June 1 Sept. 1	By Cash .. .. " "	..	187 10 0 187 10 0	375 0 0

Dr. SHARES OF £10 EACH IN GEORGE TOSH & CO., LIM. **Cr.**

		No. of Shares	Capital	Income			No. of Shares	Capital	Income
			£ s d	£ s d				£ s d	£ s d
1900 Mar. 31	To Estate Account ..	1,500	31,500 0 0		1900 Sept. 1	By Cash	..	750 0 0	375 0 0

Dr. SHARES OF £10 EACH IN JOHN TRIBE & CO., LIM. **Cr.**

		No. of Shares	Capital	Income			No of Shares	Capital	Income
			£ s d	£ s d				£ s d	£ s d
1900 Mar. 31	To Estate Account ..	350	4,200 0 0		1900 Sept. 1	By Cash	..	262 10 0	87 10 0

Dr. ESTATE ACCOUNT. **Cr.**

		£ s d			£ s d
			1900 Mar. 31 " "	By 1,000 Shares of £10 each in J. Cope & Co., Lim. .. .. " 1,500 Shares of £10 each in G. Tosh & Co., Lim. .. .. " 350 Shares of £10 each in J. Tribe & Co., Lim.	19,000 0 0 31,500 0 0 4,200 0 0

Dr.		CASH.			CONTRA.			Cr.
			Capital	Income			Capital	Income
1900			£ s d	£ s d			£ s d	£ s d
June 1	To J. Cope & Co., Lim., Interim Dividend		187 10 0					
Sept. 1	„ J Cope & Co., Lim., Final Dividend		187 10 0	375 0 0				
„	„ G. Tosh & Co., Lim., Final Dividend		750 0 0	375 0 0				
„	„ J. Tribe & Co., Lim., Final Dividend		262 10 0	87 10 0				

WHEN APPORTIONMENT IS MADE.

An apportionment having once been made as at the date of the death of the Testator, all further sums received by way of income are treated as being Income in respect of the period up to and including the date of such receipt, and are distributed accordingly. When, therefore, the Executors' books are balanced from time to time, no account is taken of accruing Income.

If occasion should arise for an investment to be realised, and the proceeds re-invested in another class of security, only the sums *actually received as representing interest or dividend* are treated as Income, although this may have the effect of increasing, or reducing, the normal income for the period under review. The reason for ignoring Apportionment upon a change of investment is that the Apportionment Act, 1870, does not provide for an apportionment being made under such circumstances, and the Court cannot recognise an apportionment under any circumstances, unless it comes within the terms of the Act. It will thus be seen that there is scope for a Trustee, by frequent changes of investments, either to materially increase the income of a life-tenant, or to materially reduce it. Under such circumstances, however, any of the parties concerned might (and doubtless would) apply to the Court for redress; and the Court, if satisfied that the action of the Trustee was not *bonâ fide*, would make such order as it thought just under the circumstances, which would probably be in the form of an order for the Trustee to make good the damages caused out of his own pocket, without giving him any right to recover from the party who had benefited. Abuses of this description are thus not likely to occur often.

But although no apportionment is made between Capital and Income when investments are changed, upon the happening of any event (except apparently —save in the case of tithe—on the death of an incumbent of a living) under which the interest of the life-tenant *ceases*—as, for instance, on the death of a life-tenant, or her re-marriage (if a widow), and if the Will so provides—an apportionment must be made, so as to arrive at the balance of income due to the late life-tenant up to the date when his (or her) interest in the income ceased. The reason for this is that the life-tenant is entitled to the whole of the income earned from the date of the death of the testator up to the time when, for any reason, the interest of such life-tenant ceases.

From this may be deduced the general rule that no apportionment is ever made, except when a different person becomes entitled to the income, or when the income (*e.g.*, a terminable annuity or rent-charge) ceases. But, as already stated, apportionment does not always occur, even in these cases. The same rule must, of course, be applied where there are several life-tenants and the interest of one ceases: an Apportionment of the whole income must be made up to that date, so as to arrive at the exact balance due to the late life-tenant.

PROBLEM.—The Estate of W. Quits, deceased, vested in trustees, consisted of property and investments producing the following income during the year 1898 :—

Yearly Rents.	Half-yearly Payments due.	Received Less-Tax.*
£210	Feb. 20th and Aug. 20th	7 days after due
150	June 20th and Dec. 20th	10 ,,
90	March 20th and Sept. 20th	2 ,,

Loans on Mortgage.	Rate of Interest.	Interest due half-yearly.
£10,000	3 per cent.	Jan. 20th and July 20th
6,000	4 per cent,	April 20th and Oct. 20th

Interest, less Tax,* was received in each case the day following that on which it became due.

The widow (who was entitled to the income during her life) died on the 20th July 1898, having been paid on account of the income received as above stated :—

$$£200 \text{ on March 1st.}$$
$$100 \text{ on April 1st.}$$
$$100 \text{ on July 1st.}$$

After the widow's death the income was divisible between a son and daughter in equal shares.

Write up the following Accounts for the year, showing what sums were due to the beneficiaries on the 31st December 1898 :—

(1) Income Account.
(2) Widow's Account.
(3) Son's Account.
(4) Daughter's Account.

Dr.   INCOME ACCOUNT.   **Cr.**

1898		£ s d	£ s d	1898		£ s d
June 30	To Widow	..	495 0 0	Jan. 21	By Cash	150 0 0
Dec. 31	„ Widow, apportionment to 20 July, viz.—			Feb. 27	„ Do.	105 0 0
	July 20 Interest (the whole)..	150 0 0		Mar. 22	„ Do.	45 0 0
	Aug. 20 Rent (⅚ of £105) ..	87 10 0		April 21	„ Do.	120 0 0
	Sept. 20 Do. (⅔ of £45) ..	30 0 0		June 30	„ Do.	75 0 0
	Oct. 20 Interest ½ of £120 ..	60 0 0		July 21	„ Do.	150 0 0
	Dec. 20 Rent (⅙ of £75) ..	12 10 0	340 0 0	Aug. 27	„ Do.	105 0 0
„ „	„ Son	77 10 0		Sept. 22	„ Do.	45 0 0
„ „	„ Daughter	77 10 0	155 0 0	Oct. 21	„ Do.	120 0 0
				Dec. 30	„ Do.	75 0 0
			£990 0 0			£990 0 0

Dr.   WIDOW'S ACCOUNT.   **Cr.**

1898		£ s d	1898		£ s d
Mar. 1	To Cash	200 0 0	June 30	By Income Account	495 0 0
April 1	„ Do.	100 0 0	„ „	„ Do.	340 0 0
July 1	„ Do.	100 0 0			
Dec. 31	„ Balance down	435 0 0			
		£835 0 0			£835 0 0
			1898 Jan. 1	By Balance down	435 0

Dr.   SON'S ACCOUNT.   **Cr.**

			1898		£ s d
			Dec. 31	By Income Account	77 10 0

* Divisions of Income may be made by months instead of days, and deductions for Income Tax omitted.

Dr.			DAUGHTER'S ACCOUNT.			Cr.
		1898 Dec. 31	By Income Account			£ s d 77 10 0

SPECIFIC LEGACIES.

A Specific Legacy (according to Lord Selborne) is the bequest of "something which a testator, identifying it by a sufficient description, and manifesting an intention that it should be enjoyed in the state and condition indicated by that description, separates in favour of a particular legatee from the general mass of his personal estate." If it should so happen that at the time of his death the testator was not possessed of any property answering to the description contained in the will, the bequest lapses altogether: its place is not taken by a pecuniary legacy of the corresponding assumed value. On the other hand, a Specific Legacy is not liable to abate, if there be a deficiency of assets, with the general legacies. Specific Legacies are best dealt with in the books as though they were pecuniary legacies satisfied in kind, instead of in cash. That is to say, the property specifically bequeathed should in the first instance be credited to Estate Account and debited to a special account dealing with that class of property. When it is ascertained that the estate is sufficient to pay debts and costs without having recourse to this property, an entry can be passed debiting Estate Account and crediting the specific legatee with the amount at which that property is valued in the books. When the legacy is actually handed over a further transfer should be made, from the credit of the Property Account to the debit of the Specific Legatee's Account.

If the Specific Legacy be an investment bearing interest, or producing rents, it is important to bear in mind that the income accrued due up to the date of the testator's death belongs to the general estate, and not to the specific legatee. The latter is, however, entitled to all income accrued since the date of death, even although—owing to delay in the handing over of the legacy—that income may in the meantime have been received by the Executors. Moreover, it has been held that bonuses declared after the testator's death on shares specifically bequeathed belong to the specific legatee, and are therefore not subject to apportionment.

GENERAL LEGACIES.

Pecuniary Legacies can only be paid provided the estate produces sufficient to provide in the first instance for all debts, duties and expenses, and also for all Specific and Demonstrative Legacies. If, however, there be a special direction that a legacy for a fixed sum is "immediately payable," that may be regarded as a Specific Legacy to the extent of entitling the Legatee to a preference over the other pecuniary Legatees.

From the bookkeeping point of view, the total amount of pecuniary Legacies should be debited to Estate Account and credited to Legacies Account—in the latter the various names of the Legatees should, of course, be stated separately. As the legacies are paid, Cash Account is credited and Legacies Account debited, so that by the time all the legacies are paid, no balance remains upon the Legacies Account. Unless the Bequest be expressly declared to be "free of legacy duty," whatever duty may be payable on the legacy must be deducted from the amount paid to the Legatee, and accounted for to the Inland Revenue authorities. The cash postings to the debit side of the Legacy Account will thus consist of the various payments to the Legatees (*less* duty), and a further payment to the Inland Revenue authorities in respect of the Legacy Duty so deducted. If, however, the Legacy Duties (or any of them) have to be paid out of the Estate, a corresponding transfer must be made from the debit of Estate Account to the credit of Legacies Account, in order to balance the latter.

DEMONSTRATIVE LEGACIES.

Reference must be made to a class of legacies that combine the characteristics of both Specific and General Legacies—that is to say, legacies that are not liable to abate with the general legacies, or to ademption or lapse. Such legacies are called Demonstrative Legacies, and usually consist of bequests of money with reference to a particular fund for their payment, or more generally may be defined as legacies of quantity with reference to a particular source of distribution on which the Legatee has a lien. A gift of a specific number of sheep out of a specific flock, or of a specific number of shares out of a specific fund, would be Demonstrative Legacies. From the bookkeeping point of view, such legacies may be classed with Specific Legacies.

ANNUITIES.

A Bequest not infrequently takes the form of an annuity payable during the lifetime of the Beneficiary. This may be provided for in the accounts in any one of the three following ways (unless, of course, the Will contains special directions with regard to the matter) : —(1) By payment out of the general Income of the Estate from year to year. (2) By setting aside and " ear-marking " special securities and applying the interest received thereon towards the payment of the Annuity during the life-

time of the Annuitant, re-transferring the securities back to the general Estate on the death of the Annuitant. (3) By purchasing an Annuity out of Capital, either from the Government or a Life Insurance Office. It may be noted that when money is bequeathed to be invested in the purchase of an annuity for the life of the Legatee, it is a vested legacy, and the Legatee can elect whether to take the sum itself or to have an annuity purchased therewith.

The following examples show the bookkeeping entries in connection with each method. It must be borne in mind, however, that when either the second or third method is adopted, the proportion of Annuity accruing from the date when the Annuity commenced up to the date when it is otherwise provided for must be paid out of the estate, as shown in the first method.

PROBLEM.—A. died on 5th November 1900, leaving *inter alia* an annuity of £50 per annum to B., aged 60, and an annuity of £50 per annum to C., aged 72, both free of Legacy Duty. The executors elect to provide for C.'s annuity by setting aside £1,818 3s. 4d. of 2¾ per cent. Consols, which are purchased *ex div.* on 5th January 1901, at 105. They provide for B. by the purchase of an annuity of £50 per annum from the North British and Mercantile Company on 31st December 1900, for which they pay £623 14s. 2d. C. dies on 5th July 1901.

Show the necessary entries in Journal form.

JOURNAL.

31st December 1900.	£	s	d	£	s	d
Estate Account	623	14	2			
To B. Annuity Account				623	14	2
B. Annuity Account	623	14	2			
To Cash				623	14	2

Being provision for an annuity of £50 per annum to be paid to B. by the North British and Mercantile Insurance Company, commencing 1st January 1901.

	£	s	d	£	s	d
Income Account	7	13	8			
To B. Annuity Account				7	13	8
B. Annuity Account	7	13	8			
To Cash				7	13	8

Being payment to B. of proportion of annuity from 5th November 1900 to date : 56 days at £50 per annum.

5th January 1901.	£	s	d	£	s	d
Estate Account	1,911	10	0			
To Annuity for C. Trust Account				1,911	10	0
2¾ per cent. Consols	1,911	10	0			
To Cash				1,911	10	0

Being provision for an annuity of £50 per annum to C., by purchase of £1,818 3s. 4d. Consols at 105 (Brokerage, £2 7s. 6d.)

	£	s	d	£	s	d
Income Account	8	7	1			
To C. Account				8	7	1
C. Account	8	7	1			
To Cash				8	7	1

Being payment to C. of proportion of annuity from 5th November 1900 to date : 61 days at £50 per annum.

5th April.								
Cash	..	..	..	..	..	..	12 10 0	
To 2¾ per cent. Consols	..	..	..	..	..	..		12 10 0
C. Account	..	..	..	..	..	..	12 10 0	
To Cash	..	..	..	..	..	..	..	12 10 0
Being quarter's dividend on Consols received, and handed over to C.								
5th July.								
Cash	..	..	..	..	..	..	12 10 0	
To 2¾ per cent. Consols	..	..	..	..	..	..		12 10 0
C. Account	..	..	..	..	..	..	..	
To Cash	..	..	..	..	..	..	12 10 0	12 10 0
Being quarter's dividend on Consols received, and handed over to C.								
Annuity for C. Trust Account	..	..	..	..	..	1,911 10 0		
To Estate Account	..	..	..	..	..	..	..	1,911 10 0
Being provision for annuity to C., re-transferred to General Estate upon death of C. this day.								

Legacy Duty is payable on the cash value of the annuity, arrived at by tables provided by the Inland Revenue authorities. The actual payment is made by four annual instalments, but if the annuitant dies in the interim no further instalments are payable. Unless the annuity is left free of Legacy Duty, these instalments are deducted from the annuity payments.

INTEREST ON ADVANCES.

It frequently occurs that Executors (or Trustees) are authorised to make advances to Beneficiaries on account of their respective shares of the Residue of the Estate. Such Advances generally bear interest. As a matter of bookkeeping, this interest must be debited to the respective Beneficiaries and credited to Estate Account, thus increasing the balance of the latter that is available for distribution.

PROBLEM.—A. B. died on 5th April 1901, leaving among other assets £50,000 of 2¾ per cent. Consols (valued at 93½), which he bequeathed to his nephews C., D., and E. His Trustees were directed to sell the Stock and to divide the proceeds; the dividends on the Stock to the date of Sale, and any interest received up to the date of division free of duty and expenses or deduction of any kind on the dividends, among his three nephews, in the proportion of half to C., one-third to D., and one-sixth to E. The Stock was sold on 5th October 1901, ex-dividend, at 93, the price and dividends from the date of death were received on that day and deposited in Bank, and the Brokerage and Charges were, as directed, paid out of the General Trust Estate. The dividend due 5th July was received on 5th October along with the dividend due on that day. The Trustees had power, out of the General Trust Estate, to make Advances to the Beneficiaries to account of their shares to an amount not exceeding £7,500 each, said Advances to be equalised as between the Beneficiaries themselves, with interest at 4 per cent., but no interest was to be payable by them to the General Trust Estate. The Trustees advanced to C. on 30th April 1901 £5,000, and on 29th May £2,500; to D. on 15th May £1,000, and on 1st June £3,000; and to E. on 20th June £6,000, and on 15th July £500.

Frame a State of Progressive Interest on the Advances, and prepare a scheme of division showing the exact amount payable to each Beneficiary on 15th December 1901. Calculate Interest on the Bank Deposit at 2½ per cent. Leave out fractions of a penny.

Dr.   TRUST IN FAVOUR OF C., D., AND E. ACCOUNT.   *Cr.*

1901		£ s d	1901		£ s d
Oct. 5	To 2¾ % Consols Account—Loss on Sale ..	250 0 0	April 5	By 2¾ % Consols Account	46,750 0 0
Dec. 15	„ C. Account	23,801 17 7	Oct. 5	„ Do. Interest to date	687 10 0
„	„ D. „	15,867 18 5	Dec.15	„ Interest Account..	416 5 2
„	„ E. „	7,933 19 2			
		£47,853 15 2			£47,853 15 2

Dr.   2¾ % CONSOLS ACCOUNT.   *Cr.*

1901		Stock £ s d	Capital £ s d	Income £ s d	1001		Stock £ s d	Capital £ s d	Income £ s d
April 5	To Trust in favour of C., D., and E.	50,000 0 0	46,750 0 0		Oct. 5	By Cash (2 quarters dividend) ..	..	..	687 10 0
Oct. 5	„ Do. — Half-year's dividend to date ..	..	..	687 10 0	„	„ Do. (Sale of Consols) ..	50,000 0 0	46,500 0 0	
					„	„ Trust Account —Loss on Sale	..	250 0 0	
		£50,000 0 0	£46,750 0 0	£687 10 0			£50,000 0 0	£46,750 0 0	£687 10 0

Dr.   C. ACCOUNT.   *Cr.*

1901		£ s d	1901		£ s d
Apr. 30	To Cash	5,000 0 0	Dec.15	By Trust Account	23,801 17 7
May 29	„ „	2,500 0 0			
Dec. 15	„ Interest	180 0 0			
„	„ Cash	16,121 17 7			
		£23,801 17 7			£23,801 17 7

Dr.   D. ACCOUNT.   *Cr.*

1901		£ s d	1901		£ s d
May 15	To Cash	1,000 0 0	Dec.15	By Trust Account	15,867 18 5
June 1	„ „	3,000 0 0			
Dec. 15	„ Interest	87 15 7			
„	„ Cash	11,780 2 10			
		£15,867 18 5			£15,867 18 5

Dr.   E. ACCOUNT.   *Cr.*

1901		£ s d	1901		£ s d
June 20	To Cash	6,000 0 0	Dec.15	By Trust Account	7,933 19 2
July 15	„ „	500 0 0			
Dec. 15	„ Interest	124 14 3			
„	„ Cash	1,309 4 11			
		£7,933 19 2			£7,933 19 2

Dr.   BANK DEPOSIT ACCOUNT.   *Cr.*

1901		£ s d	1901		£ s d
Oct. 5	To Cash	47,187 10 0	Dec.15	By Cash	47,211 5 4
Dec. 15	„ Interest	23 15 4			
		£47,211 5 4			£47,211 5 4

ι

Dr.	INTEREST ACCOUNT.				Cr.
1901 Dec. 15	To Trust Account	£ s d 416 5 2	1901 Dec. 15 " " "	By C. .. .. " D. .. .. " E. .. .. " Bank Deposit Account	£ s d 180 0 0 87 15 7 124 14 3 23 15 4
		£416 5 2			£416 5 2

Dr.	CASH.			CONTRA.	Cr.
1901 Oct. 5 " Dec. 15	To 2¾ % Consols—Interest .. .. " Do. Proceeds of Sale .. " Bank Deposit Account	£ s d 687 10 0 46,500 0 0 47,211 5 4	1901 April 30 May 15 June 1 " 20 July 15 Oct. 5 Dec. 15 " "	By C.—Advance .. .. " C. Do. .. .. " D. Do. .•.. .. .. .. " E. Do. .. .. " E. Do. .. .. " Bank Deposit Account .. .. .. " C. .. .. " D. .. .. " E.	£ s d 5,000 0 0 1,000 0 0 2,500 0 0 3,000 0 0 6,000 0 0 500 0 0 47,187 10 0 16,121 17 7 11,780 2 10 1,309 4 11
		£94,398 15 4			£94,398 15 4

RESIDUARY LEGATEES.

As it is practically impossible for a testator to know the exact value of the property that he will leave behind him at his death, it is usual to appoint a Residuary Legatee, or Residuary Legatees, who are entitled to receive the surplus or residue of the personal estate after payment of all prior claims. If no Residuary Legatee can be ascertained from the terms of the Will, there is an intestacy in respect of the Residue, which accordingly goes to the next-of-kin. The ultimate distribution of the Residue may be either in cash, or in kind : that is to say, the whole Estate may be realised, and the cash balance distributed among those entitled to the Residue, or the Estate in its existing form· may be divided among them. If the various Residuary Legatees are, owing to their different relationship to the deceased, liable to legacy duty at different rates, each must pay the duty upon his respective share of the Residue, even although it may have been expressly bequeathed to him " free of legacy duty." The words " free of legacy duty " have no meaning as applied to the Residue, seeing that after the distribution of the Residue there remains no general Estate out of which legacy duty could possibly be paid.

An Executor has power, even though no express authority be given him for that purpose in the Will, to agree with a Residuary or other general Legatee to appropriate a specific portion of the Estate to him. Moreover, where a residuary trust fund is settled by Will, upon trust for several persons and their families, the trustees have power, *virtute officii*, to appropriate specific investments to any of the settled shares before the period of final division without making any corresponding appropriation to other shares. The principle upon which executors and trustees under a Will which contains a trust for sale and conversion have power to appropriate any specific part of the Residuary Estate towards satisfaction of a legacy or share of the Residue, is that they have power to sell the particular asset to the Legatee, and to set off the purchase-money against the legacy. This doctrine is not confined to pure Personal Estate, but extends to chattels real, such as leaseholds, and, it would seem, to Real Estate which is subject to a trust for sale and conversion. The accounts must, of course, show such appropriations and settings-off in full detail.

A common form of Bequest in connection with Residue, where the testator leaves children who are minors, is one in the nature of a direction that it is to be held in trust for the benefit of the children until such time as they come of age, or, in the case of daughters, until such time as they become of age or marry (with the consent of their guardian), whichever event may happen first. It is not unusual, but, as we have seen, not really essential, to endow the executor with a discretion enabling him to determine the share of each child as he becomes entitled to it absolutely. In these cases of appropriation an accurate Balance Sheet must be prepared each time one of the children becomes entitled to his share, all accruing interest apportioned up to date, and the accounts adjusted so that the balance of the Estate Account and Income Account respectively show the exact estimated value of the Capital in hand and the Income accrued up to date. The accounts of each of the children (which represent the amounts to which they are respectively entitled) are correspondingly adjusted, and the account of the one who is entitled immediately to receive his share is debited with the corresponding amount of cash. A portion of the Estate is realised, if necessary, to produce that sum; or, by arrangement with the Legatee, specific securities may be handed over at an agreed price, instead of actual cash passing.

The following example shows clearly the various entries in connection with transactions of this description :—

PROBLEM.—An Estate consisting of £10,000 in 2¾ per cent. Consols, purchased at 110, is held in trust for A and B., who are to receive the income during their minority, each being entitled to receive his (half) share of the Capital on his coming of age. The income has been regularly divided up to 5th July 1901. On 28th September 1901 A. came of age; £5,000 Consols were accordingly sold for cash at 93 (less Brokerage £6 5s.), and the proceeds handed to him.

Show the accounts in the Trustee's Ledger.

Dr.   TRUST IN FAVOUR OF A. ACCOUNT.   Cr.

1901		Capital £ s d	Income £ s d	1901		Capital £ s d	Income £ s d
Sept.28	To Consols Account — Loss on Realisation	856 5 0		Sept. 1	By Balance	5,500 0 0	
Oct. 5	„ Cash	4,643 15 0		Oct. 5	„ Interest on Consols ..		34 7 6
„	„ „		34 7 6				

Dr.   TRUST IN FAVOUR OF B. ACCOUNT.   Cr.

1901		Capital £ s d	Income £ s d	1901		Capital £ s d	Income £ s d
Oct. 5	To Cash		34 7 6	Sept. 1	By Balance	5,500 0 0	
				Oct. 5	„ Interest on Consols		34 7 6

Dr.   2¾% CONSOLS ACCOUNT.   Cr.

1901		Stock £ s d	Capital £ s d	Income £ s d	1901		Stock £ s d	Capital £ s d	Income £ s d
Sept. 1	To Balance	10,000 0 0	11,000 0 0		Sept.28	By Cash	5,000 0 0	4,643 15 0	
Oct. 5	„ A.—Interest ..			34 7 6	„	„ Loss on Sale of Consols to pay out A: transferred to his account		856 5 0	
„	„ B. „ ..			34 7 6	Oct. 5	„ Cash			68 15 0

NOTE.—*There being only one investment it is convenient to add Income columns to the accounts of A. and B. rather than to open an Income Account. For the same reason it becomes unnecessary to re-value B's. share of the estate : this can be conveniently left standing at cost. As the £5,000 Consols are sold ex-dividend, A. will, of course, be entitled to half the dividend received on the 5th October 1901.*

I 2

INSUFFICIENT ASSETS.

The ultimate disposal of the Residue has already been dealt with. It remains, however, to be explained what procedure must be adopted when, instead of there being a Residue, the Estate is insufficient to provide for all the bequests made by the will.

In a work of this description it is not necessary to discuss the order of precedence of the various debts due on the death of the Testator when the Estate is insolvent, beyond stating that if the general Personal Estate not specifically bequeathed is insufficient to pay the Debts then the real estate not specifically bequeathed must bear the deficiency ; if there be no Real Estate (or it be insufficient), the General Pecuniary Legacies must abate *pro ratâ*, or, if necessary, be abandoned entirely. Devised and Residuary Real Estate and Specific Legacies contribute rateably on the failure of the General Legacies to meet the deficiency.

Assuming, however, that there is sufficient to pay all Debts, Costs, and Specific Legacies, but not sufficient to pay the Pecuniary Legacies, then the latter must all abate *pro ratâ*, unless the Will, or any rule of law, indicates any special order of priority. An Executor, however, is entitled to a preference in respect of any Debt due to him by the Deceased, as against other creditors of equal degree ; but this right does not make him a " secured creditor " within the meaning of Section 10 of the Judicature Act, 1875.

When the Estate is not sufficient to pay Legacies in full, Legacy Duty is, of course, only paid upon the reduced, and not upon the full, amount.

PROBLEM.—A Testator dies leaving Personal Estate worth £10,000, and Real Estate worth £25,000. He specifically bequeaths £2,000 Personalty and £10,000 Realty to his niece W. His Debts amount to £2,000 and the pecuniary Legacies to £5,000. The residue of both Personal and Real Estates is left to X. The Executorial Expenses (including all duties payable by the estate) amounted to £3,500. All Legacies were left free of Legacy Duty. Raise accounts showing ultimate amount received by X.

Dr.   PERSONAL ESTATE ACCOUNT.   Cr.

	£ s d	£ s d		£ s d	£ s d
To Cash : Executorship Expenditure, &c. ..	3,500 0 0		By Sundry Assets		10,000 0 0
Less Estate Duty on Real Estate, and Legacy Duty on Bequest of Realty	1,300 0 0	2,200 0 0	„ Transfer from Real Estate Account to make up amount required to pay Legacies, &c.		1,200 0 0
„ Do. Debts due by Deceased		2,000 0 0			
„ Do. Specific Bequest to W.		2,000 0 0			
„ Do. Pecuniary Legacies		5,000 0 0			
		£11,200 0 0			£11,200 0 0

Dr.   REAL ESTATE ACCOUNT.   Cr.

	£ s d		£ s d
To Cash : Specific Bequest to W.	10,000 0 0	By Sundry Assets	25,000 0 0
„ Do. Estate Duty	1,000 0 0		
„ Do. Legacy Duty	300 0 0		
„ Transfer to Personal Estate Account	1,200 0 0		
„ Cash : Residue to X.	12,500 0 0		
	£25,000 0 0		£25,000 0 0

NOTE.—It makes no difference in this instance, but when different persons are entitled to the Residue on Personal and Real Estates respectively, it is important to see that each is charged with its due proportion of the Duties paid.

RESIDUARY ACCOUNT.

It has already been stated that Residuary Legatees have to pay Legacy Duty, if their relationship to the deceased be such as to render them liable to this duty. The amount upon which duty is payable is arrived at by preparing a Residuary Account, which must be in the prescribed form, and verified by affidavit. The form at present in use is shown below. It will be seen that it differs from the form of the Estate Duty Account, chiefly in that it deals (so far as possible) with actual realisations instead of estimated values, and that it is brought up to date, all payments made before arriving at the Residue being deducted from the Corpus, while all income received since the date of death is added.

PROBLEM.—Taking the Estate of X. shown on page 96, assume that the testator bequeathed £25 to each of his Executors A. and B., who were strangers in blood, that the Leasehold Property was bequeathed absolutely to his Widow, and the Residue to his Widow in trust for life, and afterwards in equal shares to his Partner Y. and his Brother Z. Assume that Mrs. X. died on 31st May 1901, that the remainder of the Estate was realised on that day, the Freeholds fetching £2,000 net, the Furniture £450, the Shares £14 10s. each, and the Debentures £165 (net). Assume, further, that all rents, dividends, &c., are received in due course, all debts and legacies paid on 30th June, and the Residuary Account made up on that date

Prepare (a) The Executors' Cash Book and Ledger.

(b) The Residuary Account.

Dr.		CASH.			CONTRA.		Cr.
		Capital	Income			Capital	Income
1900		£ s d	£ s d	1901		£ s d	£ s d
Nov. 30	To Estate Account	1,010 0 0		Mar. 31	By Estate A/c. : Estate Duty ..	411 8 0	4 2 8
Dec. 31	„ E. & W. Ry. Co., Lim., ½ yr's interest (less tax) ..	19 15 0	4 0 0	June 30	„ Do.— Executorship Exps.	4 2 8	
1901				„	„ Debts due at death (sundry accounts)	300 0 0	
Jan. 31	„ Leasehold Property, ½ yr's rent (less tax)	23 13 11	4 16 1	„	„ Funeral Expenses (Toombes & Son)	100 0 0	
„	„ Mont Blanc Ice Co., Lim., yr's dividend to 31/12/00 (less tax)	26 3 2	2 6 10	„	„ Legacies A/c. A. (less duty) ..	22 10 0	
May 31	„ Household Goods, &c., proceeds of sale	450 0 0		„	„ Do. B. „ ..	22 10 0	
„	„ Mont Blanc Ice Co., Lim., sale of Shares @ £14 10s. ..	435 0 0		„	„ Income A/c., Exctors. Mrs. X.		21 17 2
„	„ E. & W. Ry. Co., Lim., sale of Debentures @ £165 ..	1,630 7 0	19 13 0	„	„ Residue A/c. Y. (less duty) ..	3,973 4 9	
„	„ X. & Y., in payment of deceased's interest per Y. ..	4,100 0 0		„	„ Do. Z. „ ..	4,282 5 5	
„	„ Freehold Property	2,000 0 0		„	„ Legacy Duties	578 18 3	
				„	„ Leasehold Properties A/c.: proportion of Rent from 30/11/00 to 31/12/00 due to Executors., Mrs. X.	..	4 16 1
		£9,694 19 1	£30 15 11			£9,694 19 1	£30 15 11

Dr.   ESTATE ACCOUNT.   **Cr.**

		£ s d	£ s d			£ s d	£ s d
1900 Nov. 30	To Debts due at Death		300 0 0	1900 Nov. 30	By Mont Blanc Ice Co., Lim. ..		450 0 0
"	" Funeral Expenses		100 0 0	"	" East Western Railway Co., Lim.		1,600 0 0
1901 Mar. 31	" Cash: Estate Duty		411 8 0	"	" Cash		1,010 0 0
"	" Do. Executorship Expenses		4 2 8	"	" Household Goods		500 0 0
"	" Balance down		9,869 9 4	"	" Share in firm of X. & Y. ..		4,100 0 0
				"	" Leasehold Property		1,025 0 0
				"	" Freehold Property ..		2,000 0 0
			£10,685 0 0				£10,685 0 0

		£ s d	£ s d				£ s d
1901 May 31	By Difference on realisation of Household Goods		50 0 0	1901 Mar. 31	By Balance		9,869 9 4
June 30	" Legacies' Account: A. ..	25 0 0		May 31	" Difference on Mont Blanc Ice Co., Lim.		11 3 2
"	" Do. B. ..	25 0 0		"	" Difference on E. W. Ry. Co., Lim.		50 2 0
"	" Specific Legacies' Account, Mrs. X.		1,001 6 1				
"	" Residue Account		8,829 8 5				
			£9,930 14 6				£9,930 14 6

Dr.   £10 SHARES IN MONT BLANC ICE COMPANY, LIM.   **Cr.**

		Shares	Capital	Income			Shares	Capital	Income
			£ s d	£ s d				£ s d	£ s d
1900 Nov. 30	To Estate Account	30	450 0 0		1901 Jan. 31	By Cash : Dividend for year ended 31st December 1900	..		2 6 10
1901 May 31	Estate Account, difference on Realisation	..	11 3 2		May 31	" Cash—Sale of Shares ..	30	26 3 2 435 0 0	
"	Income Account	..		2 6 10					
			£461 3 2	£2 6 10				£461 3 2	£2 6 10

Dr.   £100 5% DEBENTURES IN EAST WESTERN RAILWAY COMPANY, LIM.   **Cr.**

		No.	Capital	Income			No.	Capital	Income
			£ s d	£ s d				£ s d	£ s d
1900 Nov. 30	To Estate Account	10	1,600 0 0		1900 Dec. 31	By Cash—½-year's Interest..	..	19 15 0	4 0 0
1901 May 31	" Estate Account, difference on Realisation.. ..	..	50 2 0		1901 May 31	" " —Sale of Debentures	10	1,630 7 0	19 13 0
"	" Income Account	..	..	23 13 0					—3 0
			£1,650 2 0	£23 13 0				£1,650 2 0	£23 1

Dr.   SHARE IN FIRM OF "X. & Y."   **Cr.**

		£ s d			£ s d
1900 Nov. 30	To Estate Account	£4,100 0 0	1901 May 31	By Cash : Per "Y."	£4,100 0 0

Dr. LEASEHOLD PROPERTY ACCOUNT (giving full details). Cr.

		£ s d	£ s d			£ s d	£ s d
1900 Nov. 30 1901 May 31	To Estate Account .. .. .. „ Cash—Mrs. "X."—Income accrued since death on Property specifically bequeathed to her	1,025 0 0 ..	 4 16 1	1900 Dec. 31 1901 May 31	By Cash : Rent .. .. „ Mrs. "X."—Property specifically bequeathed to her, handed over this day	23 13 11 1,001 6 1	4 16 1
		£1,025 0 0	£4 16 1			£1,025 0 0	£4 16 1

Dr. FREEHOLD PROPERTY ACCOUNT (giving full details). Cr.

		£ s d			£ s d
1900 Nov. 30	To Estate Account	£2,000 0 0	1901 May 31	By Cash : Proceeds of Sale	£2,000 0 0

Dr. HOUSEHOLD GOODS, &c. Cr.

		£ s d			£ s d
1900 Nov. 30	To Estate Account	500 0 0	1901 May 31 „	By Cash : Net Proceeds of Sale .. .. .. „ Estate Account : Difference on Realisation	450 0 0 50 0 0
		£500 0 0			£ 500 0 0

Dr. LEGACY DUTIES ACCOUNT. Cr.

		£ s d			£ s d
1901 Nov. 30	To Cash : Commissioners of Inland Revenue ..	578 18 3	1901 June 30 „ „ „	By Legacies Account : A. .. .. „ Do. B. .. .. „ Residue Account : Y. .. .. „ Do. Z.	2 10 0 2 10 0 441 9 5 132 8 10
		£578 18 3			£578 18 3

Dr. DEBTS DUE AT DEATH. Cr.

		£ s d			£ s d
1901 June 30	To Cash (in detail)	£300 0 0	1900 Nov. 30	By Estate Account (in detail)	£300 0 0

Dr. FUNERAL EXPENSES. Cr.

		£ s d			£ s d
1901 June 30	To Cash : Toombes & Son	£100 0 0	1900 Nov. 30	By Estate Account	£100 0 0

| Dr. | | | | LEGACIES ACCOUNT. | | | | Cr. |

1901		£ s d	£ s d	1900		£ s d	£ s d
June 30	To Cash : A.	22 10 0		Nov. 30	By Estate Account, viz. :—		
"	" Legacy Duty	2 10 0	25 0 0		A.	25 0 0	
"	" Cash : B.	22 10 0			B.	25 0 0	50 0 0
"	" Legacy Duty	2 10 0	25 0 0				
			£50 0 0				£50 0 0

| Dr. | | | SPECIFIC LEGACIES ACCOUNT. | | | Cr. |

1901		£ s d	1901		£ s d
May 31	To Leasehold Property Account	£1,001 6 1	May 31	By Estate Account : Mrs. X.	£1,001 6 1

| Dr. | | | INCOME ACCOUNT. | | | Cr. |

1901		£ s d	1901		£ s d
March 31	To Cash : Interest on Estate Duty	4 2 8	May 31	By Mont Blanc Ice Co., Lim.	2 6 10
June 30	" " Executors, Mrs. X., being income accrued up to date of her death ..	21 17 2	"	" East Western Railway Co., Lim.	23 13 0
		£25 19 10			£25 19 10

| Dr. | | | | RESIDUE ACCOUNT. | | | | Cr. |

1901		£ s d	£ s d	1901		£ s d	£ s d
June 30	To Cash : Y.	3,973 4 9		June 30	By Estate Account, viz. :—		
"	" Legacy Duty	441 9 5	4,414 14 2		Y.	4,414 14 2	
"	" Cash : Z.	4,282 5 5			Z.	4,414 14 3	8,829 8 5
"	" Legacy Duty	132 8 10	4,414 14 3				
			£ 8,829 8 5				£ 8,829 8 5

FORM No. **3.** INLAND REVENUE. [**Form of Residuary Account.**

Here state the Name and Address of the Person who forwards this Account. } ....

All Personal Estate, and also, where mixed up with the Personal Estate, all Moneys arising from the sale, mortgage, or other disposition of all Real Estate directed by Will to be sold, &c., are to be accounted for upon this Form, for the purpose of having the Legacy Duty assessed pursuant to the Legacy Duty Act, 1796 (36 Geo. III. c. 52) ; the Legacy Duty Act, 1805 (45 Geo. III. c. 28) ; the Stamp Act, 1815 (55 Geo. III. c. 184), and the Succession Duty pursuant to the Customs and Inland Revenue Act, 1888 (51 & 52 Vict. c. 8), and the Finance Act, 1894 (57 & 58 Vict. c. 30).

Where the Personal Estate is not chargeable with Legacy Duty, the proceeds of sale of Real Estate directed to be sold should be accounted for upon the Form No. 8 ; as also where moneys arising from the sale of Real Estate do not form part of the General Estate but are separately given.

The Account, when filled up *in duplicate*, should be transmitted to the Secretary, Estate Duty Office, Somerset House, London, W.C.

OBSERVE.—Money should not be remitted until the account has been delivered by the parties and the amount payable and the mode of payment have been notified to them.

DIRECTIONS.

Executors and Administrators, before the Retainer of any part of the Property to their own use, are to deliver the particulars thereof, and pay the duty thereon within 14 Days after, under the Penalty of treble the value of the Duty.

All Rents, Dividends, Interest, and Profits arising from the Personal Estate of the Deceased, or from the Real Estate directed by will to be sold, &c., subsequently to the time of the death, and all accretions thereon down to the time of retainer, must be considered as part of the Estate, and be accounted for accordingly.

| REGISTER | of the Year 1 , | Folio | Affidavit. |

‡ Please read the Instructions printed above.

*Here state the Name and Address of the Executor or Administrator.

An Account ‡ of the Personal Estate, and of Moneys arising out of the Real Estate of X., who died on the 30th day of November One Thousand Nine Hundred ....exhibited by * Y. and Z.

the Executors (or) Administrator........ of the Deceased, (or) Trustee...... of the Real Estate directed by the Will to be sold, &c., acting under the Will (or) Letters of Administration [with Will annexed] of the effects of the Deceased proved in, or granted by, the Registry of the Probate Division of the High Court of Justice, on the 30th day of June 1901.

No. 1. No. 2.

	Description of Property	Date of Sale, if Sold	Money received and Property converted into Money	Value of Property not converted into Money
Money and Property converted into Money are to be inserted in Column No. 1, and the date when converted when converted affixed.	Cash in the House	.	£ s d 10 0 0	£ s d
	Cash at the Bankers	..	1,000 0 0	
† Property not converted into Money is to be valued at the time of retainer, and its value so ascertained inserted in Column No. 2, and Inventories and proper Valuations must be produced.	†Furniture, Plate, Linen, China, Books, Pictures, Wearing Apparel, Jewels, and Ornaments	31 May '01	450 0 0	
	†Wine and other Liquors..			
	†Horses and Carriages, Farming Stock, and Implements of Husbandry			
	†Stock-in-Trade			
	†Goodwill, &c., of Trade or Business..			
	Life Assurance Policies			
As to apportionment of Rents and other income see the Apportionment Act, 1870 (33 & 34 Vic., c. 35).	Rents due at the Death of the Deceased	..	23 13 11	
	Mortgages and Interest due at the Death			
	Bonds, Bills, Notes, and Interest due at the Death			
	Book and other Debts			
	Canal Shares, viz. :—			
The Shares not converted into Money are to be valued at the market price of the day of retainer. If there be Shares in many Companies it may be convenient to insert the total amount or value in this Account, and annex a Statement of the particular Shares. (*See foot of next page for Rule for ascertaining market price*).	Railway Shares, viz. :— East Western Railway Company, 5% Debentures .. Interest thereon due at Death	31 May '01 ..	1,630 7 0 19 15 0	
OBSERVE.—If this Account is delivered in connection with a life tenant's death, and the required particulars cannot be fully stated, the existing fund, together with any sums advanced and taken out of trust, should be brought in, and a statement should be annexed giving all the information available.	Other Shares, viz.:— Mont Blanc Ice Company, Lim. .. .. .. Dividend thereon due at Death	31 May '01 ..	435 0 0 26 3 2	
	The Stocks or other Securities of British Colonies, viz.:—			
	Ships or Shares of Ships			
	Carried forward.. ..	..	£3,594 19 1	

			No. 1.	No. 2.
	Description of Property.	Date of Sale, if Sold	Money received and Property converted into Money	Value of Property not converted into Money

NOTE. — If there should not be room in this Form for the particulars of any description of Property, the Total only of the amount or value of such Property is to be inserted here, and the particulars are to be stated on a separate paper.

The Stocks unconverted are to be valued at the market price of the day on which they are retained for the use of the residuary legatee. (*See footnote*.)

	£ s d		£ s d
Brought forward..	..	3,594 19 1	
	£ s d	Price of Stocks	
Exchequer Bills			
Bank Stock			
East India Stock			
East India Bonds			
3 per cent. Consols..			
3 per cent. reduced			
New 3 per cents.			
2¾ per cent. Consols			
2¾ per cent. reduced			
2½ per cent. reduced			
Dividends on the above Stocks Due at the Death			
The Stocks or Public Securities of Foreign States, viz. :—			
Property which the Testator had power to appoint as he thought fit, viz. :—			
Property not comprised within the above description, viz. :— Interest in firm of X. and Y.	..	4,100 0 0	
Leasehold Property directed to be sold, *as per statement of particulars annexed*			
Real Property directed to be sold, *as per statement of particulars annexed* ..	31 May '01	2,000 0 0	

OBSERVE. — Was the deceased possessed for life or otherwise of any *Real or Leasehold* property, other than that brought into this Account? Reply.............. (Say " Yes " or " No.")

Insert the Total of Column No. 1 in Column No. 2				9,694 19 1
Total of Property.. ..				£9,694 19 1

PAYMENTS.	£ s d	
Probate or Administration	411 8 0	
Funeral Expenses	100 0 0	
Expenses attending Executorship or Administration	4 2 8	
†Debts on Simple Contract, Rent and Taxes, Wages, &c., due at the Death of the Deceased, *as per Statement annexed*	3 0 0 0	
†Debts on Mortgage, with Interest (if any) due at the Death..		
†Debts on Bonds and other Securities, with ditto		
Pecuniary Legacies *as per Statement annexed*	50 0 0	
‡ purchased on the of at		

†A Statement of these Deductions, *signed by the Executor or Administrator*, is to be annexed.

‡ Here state the particulars of any other lawful payments and of the Funds or other Securities purchased and when.

*Where there is a published quotation, a price one quarter up from the lower to the higher of the official "closing prices" should be adopted as an estimated price. For example:—Where the "closing prices" were 98—100, the market price is $98 + \frac{100-98}{4} = 98\frac{1}{2}$. Where the day of retainer was a day for which no prices are available, the price for the day before should be taken.

	£ s d
(*Deduct the Total of the Payments from the Total of the Property* .. ..)	865 10 8
Net Amount of Property carried forward ..	£8,829 8 5

To show BALANCE *of* CASH, *if any.*

Total of Column No. 1 ..	£9,694 19	1
Total of Payments	865 10	8
Cash Account ..	£8,829 8	5

No. 3.

<table>
<tr><td></td><td>£ s d</td></tr>
<tr><td>Net amount of Property brought forward ..</td><td>8,829 8 5</td></tr>
</table>

NOTE.—Upon reversions falling in, state the date of the death of the Tenant for Life.

Separate Papers are to be annexed to the Account to show how these Totals are made up.

* If the Cash balance has borne interest, the actual amount earned should be brought in. If it has not, but could have done so, interest at 3 per cent. per annum should be brought in.

INTEREST, DIVIDENDS, RENTS, &c., SINCE THE DEATH.

Rents of Real and Leasehold Estates directed to be Sold to the time of Sale, if Sold; if not, to the date of this Account

Dividend on the Stocks and Funds Sold to the time of Sale and of those remaining Unsold, including the last Dividends ..

Interest on Exchequer Bills Sold or Paid off to the time of Sale or Payment, and of those remaining Unsold, to the date of this Account ..

Interest on Bonds, Mortgages, and other Securities Paid off, to the Day of Payment and of those outstanding, to the date of this Account ..

*Interest on £ being the Balance of Cash in Hand as on the other side, to the date of this Account

Income of Canal, Railway, and other Shares, to the time of Sale, and of those remaining Unsold, and on other Property, yielding an Income not included in any of the above Items, to the date of this Account

The value of the Benefit accruing to the Executor or other Person entitled to the Residue from the Interest of Money or Dividends of Stock retained to answer vested or contingent Legacies, payable at a future day without the intermediate Interest or Dividends

	£ s d
	25 19 10
Total ..	8,855 8 3

PAYMENTS OUT OF INTEREST, &c.

	£ s d
Interest on Mortgages, Bonds, and other Securities, due from the Estate	
Interest on Pecuniary Legacies ..	
Payments on account of Annuities	
Other Payments, if any, viz.	
Interest on Estate Duty	4 2 8
Net Income paid to Mrs. X.	21 17 2

Deduct the Total Amount of these Payments from the foregoing Total ..

	25 19 10
Balance ..	8,829 8 5

A Schedule of Particulars of these Deductions to be annexed.

DEDUCTIONS FROM RESIDUE.

	£ s d
Debts still due from the Estate	
Retained to pay Outstanding Legacies	
Total Deductions ..	
Net Residue ..	8,829 8 5

Deduct any Portion of the Residue not liable to Duty, or for which Duty is paid on separate Receipts, viz. .. ..

Residue on which Duty is chargeable	8,829 8 5

No. 1. DECLARATION. No. 2.

(1) State whether this Sum is the whole or what part of the Residue. (2) Insert the Christian and Surnames of the Residuary Legatees or next of Kin, and (3) their Relationship or Consanguinity, in the words of the Act, as set forth on the other side.

This portion to be used with either form of declaration.

FOR USE IN ALL CASES EXCEPT AS IN No. 2.

I (or) We do declare that the foregoing is a just and true Account, and I (or) We offer to pay the sum of £573 18s. 3d. for the Legacy Duty, at the rate of 10 per cent. and 3 per cent. respectively upon the sums of £4,414 14s. 2½d., being (1) each one half of the said Residue and Moneys to which

I am (or) We are entitled and which I (or) We intend to retain to my (or) our own use, and for the use of (2) Y. and Z. in equal shares, the former being a stranger to, and the latter being (3) a brother of the Deceased.

Dated this day of 1901.

FOR USE ONLY WHERE THE TESTATOR DIED AFTER 30TH JUNE 1888, AND BEFORE 2ND AUGUST 1894, and then only where the Residue comprises real Estate directed to be sold as well as Personal Estate.

I (or) We do declare that the forgoing is a just and true Account, and I (or) We offer to pay the sum of £ , of which £

is the *Legacy* Duty at per cent. on £ the proportion representing Personal Estate, and £ is the *Succession* Duty at per cent. on £ the proportion representing Real Estate, to which

Y.
(*Here sign the Account*)..................................
Z.

Rates of Legacy Duty payable on Legacies, Annuities, and Residues, by the Stamp Act, 1815 (55 Geo. III. c. 184), and the Customs and Inland Revenue Act, 1888 (51 & 52 Vict. c. 8).

NOTE.—If the Deceased died on or after the 1st June 1881, every Pecuniary Legacy or Residue or Share of Residue, although not of the amount or value of £20, is chargeable with Duty; Customs and Inland Revenue Act, 1881 (44 & 45 Vict. c. 12), s. 42.

The description of the Residuary Legatee, or next of Kin, is to be in the following words of the Act.	On Real Estate, if the Deceased died *before* 1st July 1888, or if Estate Duty under the Finance Act, 1894, has been paid upon the property, and on Personal Estate.	On Apportioned Value of Real Estate where Deceased died *on or after* 1st July 1888, and Estate Duty under the Finance Act, 1894, has not been paid upon the property.
* Children of the Deceased, and their Descendants, or the Father or Mother, or any Lineal Ancestor of the Deceased, or the Husbands or Wives of any such Persons ..	1 per Cent.	1½ per Cent.
Brothers and Sisters of the Deceased, and their Descendants, or the Husbands or Wives of any such Persons ..	3 do.	4½ do.
Brothers and Sisters of the Father and Mother of the Deceased, and their Descendants, or the Husbands and Wives of any such Persons ..	5 do.	6½ do.
Brothers and Sisters of a Grandfather or Grandmother of the Deceased, and their Descendants, or the Husbands or Wives of any such Persons ..	6 do.	7½ do.
Any Person in any other Degree of Collateral Consanguinity, or Strangers in Blood to the Deceased ..	10 do.	11½ do.

* Persons otherwise chargeable with Legacy Duty at the rate of 1 per cent. are exempt in respect of any Legacy, Residue, or Share of Residue, payable out of, or consisting of any Estate or Effects according to the value whereof duty shall have been paid on the Affidavit or Inventory, in conformity with the Customs and Inland Revenue Act, 1881, or where Estate Duty under the Finance Act, 1894, has been paid upon the value of the Property, and the same passes under the Deceased's Will or Intestacy.

The Husband or Wife of the Deceased is not subject to Legacy Duty.

Relations of the Husband or Wife of the Deceased are chargeable with Legacy Duty at the rate of 10 per cent. or 11½ per cent., as the case may be, unless themselves related in blood to the Deceased.

OBSERVE.—Interest at the rate of 3 per cent. per annum is chargeable upon Legacy and Succession Duty in arrear, under the provisions of the Finance Act, 1896 (59 & 60 Vict. c. 28), s. 18 (2).

CHAPTER XII.

THE DOUBLE-ACCOUNT SYSTEM.

THE second chapter of this work was devoted to an explanation of the essential difference between Capital and Revenue, and it was also there shown that both receipts and expenditure upon Capital Account were capable of a further subdivision—the receipts into "fixed liabilities" and "floating liabilities," and the expenditure into "fixed assets" and "floating assets." It is now necessary to consider the matter in further detail, with a view to explaining the nature and operations of the Double-Account System.

NATURE OF DOUBLE-ACCOUNT SYSTEM.

In the first place, it will perhaps be convenient to state what the Double-Account System is *not*. Students of accounting not infrequently are under the impression that the Double-Account System is synonymous with the Double-Entry System. This however (as will be seen later on), is a complete misapprehension. Another common form of error is to suppose that the Double-Account System is a peculiar system of accounts which especially distinguishes between Capital and Revenue. The proper distinction between Capital and Revenue is a fundamental principle of *every* system of accounting. A Trial Balance summarises all Ledger balances into one general account, and the operation known as "closing the books" consists in the separation of the Capital items from the Revenue

items. The latter are focussed together into the Revenue Account, which in practice is often subdivided into sections (headed respectively "Trading Account," "Profit and Loss Account," "Net Profit Account," &c.), while the Ledger balances remaining after this operation has been concluded—*i.e.*, the Capital items—are brought together in the form of a Balance Sheet. The process of closing the books up to this point is identical under all systems of bookkeeping. The distinction between the Double-Account System and the Single Account System lies mostly in the form that the Balance Sheet takes. As has already been pointed out, the Revenue Account is, for purposes of convenience, frequently divided into sections : the first section showing the results of manufacturing (or of buying and selling, as the case may be) ; the second section reducing the Gross Profit shown by the preceding section to the Net Profit by the charging up of all establishment expenses ; and the third section showing the ultimate disposition, or division, of such Net Profit. In connection with most undertakings, it is found to sufficiently well answer all practical purposes to frame the Balance Sheet as an undivided whole ; but with regard to some undertakings, it is thought convenient to divide it into two sections, the first of which comprises "fixed assets" and "fixed liabilities" (along with the balance of Working Capital) ; while the second section contains the

"Floating Assets," the "Working Capital," and the "Floating Liabilities." Undertakings which divide their Balance Sheet upon these lines are said to be kept upon the "Double-Account System."

If any attempt were being made in this work to deal with the subject of accounting upon an historical basis, it would be necessary to discuss in detail the origin of the Double-Account System, and a complete discussion of the matter would probably reach to considerable lengths. For present purposes, however, such an inquiry is hardly necessary, although perhaps a few words upon the subject will not be out of place. The Double-Account System is probably the creation of lawyers, rather than of accountants, and its object would appear to be to direct special attention to the importance of keeping a strict account of the expenditure of monies received by the creation of Fixed Liabilities; that is to say, from the issue of Capital to Shareholders or Debenture-holders. The system is applied almost exclusively to companies that have been incorporated by special Act of Parliament to work public undertakings—such as Railways, Gas Companies, Water Companies, Electric Light Companies, and the like—in connection with which it has been made an express condition of authorising the Company to raise capital that such capital should be expended in certain specified directions. The Double-Account System will enable even those who are unacquainted with scientific bookkeeping to readily discern to what extent monies received from Shareholders and Debenture-holders have been applied in the acquisition of Fixed Assets, and this would appear to be the principal, if not the sole, reason for employing this particular form of accounts. Another point to be borne in mind in connection with this subject is that, prior to the introduction of electrical undertakings in commerce, those concerns which were required to frame their accounts upon the Double-Account System possessed in common the important factor that, while they were required to carry on their undertaking permanently at least as much for the public good as for the benefit of investors, the Fixed Assets which they acquired were in the nature of things extremely numerous, so numerous indeed that the cost of from time to time replacing them as they wore out would (roughly speaking) automatically average itself as a fairly level charge against the profits of each successive year: consequently—in view of the fact that such replacements of worn-out assets must necessarily take place, in order to enable the concern to continue its business—it was considered that it would be a more certain and sounder basis for the accounts, to require such provision for the replacement of worn-out Fixed Assets to be made directly out of Revenue, than to charge Revenue with an estimated provision for Depreciation and to allow successive replacements of assets to be capitalised as and when they were effected.

LIMITATIONS OF DOUBLE-ACCOUNT SYSTEM.

This idea, ingenious as it undoubtedly is, would appear to have emanated from a lawyer rather than an accountant. One seems to trace in it the well-known affection of the Chancery Division for a Cash Statement, as well as its rooted distrust of all accounts framed upon any other basis; while the system, although approximately accurate under most circumstances, omits to provide for several contingencies that could hardly have escaped the notice of the trained accountant. To some extent, this subject may be more profitably discussed under the heading of "Depreciation and Reserves," which is fully dealt with in Chapter XX., but the following points may be usefully mentioned here:—

(1) Assuming that for a period of, say, 50 years, the total amount of expenditure necessary to keep the Fixed Assets of an undertaking in a proper state

of working efficiency was £50,000, then as a matter of fact the sum of £1,000 ought to be charged against each year's revenue in order to arrive at the true net profit for that year, and this remark applies as much to the first year of the undertaking's existence as to the ·fiftieth. Under the Double-Account System, however, if only actual expenditure on replacements be charged against Revenue, it is clear that during the first few years the payments under this heading will be smaller than the average expenditure of £1,000. Consequently, if the Double-Account System be strictly applied in its entirety, the true Net Profits of the undertaking during the first few years of its existence will, as a matter of course, be over-stated. This defect is in practice generally obviated by debiting to Revenue, not the actual expenditure incurred, but an estimated annual expenditure: for example, taking the case already cited, if the proper annual charge for renewals be estimated at £1,000, but the actual expenditure during the first year were only £400, then, instead of debiting Revenue Account with but £400 for renewals, Revenue Account would be debited with £1,000 and a " Provision for Renewals Account " credited with the corresponding sum. The Provision for Renewals Account would be debited with the actual expenditure incurred (£400), and the credit balance of £600 would be brought forward into the Balance Sheet taken out at the end of the first year as a Floating Liability. By this means the over-stating of Net Profits may be avoided, while still retaining the *form* of the Double-Account System. It will be seen, however, that the *principle* of the Double-Account System is no longer retained in its entirety.

(2) If the Double-Account System be rigidly adhered to, the aggregate amount of Capital Expenditure can only be altered as actual extensions of the original work are undertaken. The cost of replacement of Fixed Assets will be in all cases charged against Revenue, no matter whether such replacements cost more or less than the original expenditure under the same heading. From whichever point of view the matter be regarded, this seems hardly reasonable. The Single Account System— *i.e.*, the ordinary commercial system of accounting— charges the cost of assets against Revenue during the period that such assets are of use to the undertaking, the annual charge being so framed that by the time these assets are useless the whole of their cost has been written off, leaving the undertaking free to purchase, out of Capital, further new assets to take their place. If the new assets cost more than the old ones that have now been worn out, the result of this operation will be that the actual Capital Expenditure will be increased *pro tanto ;* while *per contra* if the cost of such assets has been reduced, the aggregate capital expenditure would be lessened to a corresponding extent. This is as it should be, for it makes the charges against Revenue for Depreciation of Fixed Assets dependent upon the actual cost of the Fixed Assets that are then in existence. With the Double-Account System, on the contrary, if, for example, a gas-main has become worn-out and has to be replaced, the cost of such replacement is charged against Revenue. If the cost of making and laying mains has increased since the Company was formed, the result will be that the Capital Expenditure of the Company stands at a lower figure than the actual expenditure incurred in Fixed Assets then in existence, with the result that an unfair charge has been made against Revenue Account ; if, on the other hand, the cost of materials and labour has decreased since the Company first came into existence, the result will be that the whole cost of the original assets that are now worn out has not been made good out of Revenue by the time they have been removed and replaced by others of equal utility, and under these circumstances, of course,

Revenue Account is favoured at the expense of Capital Account. The effect of this rigid adherence to the Double-Account System is to discourage replacements and renewals in localities where the cost has risen, and to somewhat unduly encourage them in localities where the cost has fallen. And although, in point of fact, instances of a Fixed Asset being replaced by another of an exactly similar description are perhaps rare, the same principles will, of course, apply where enlargements are contemplated, as only that portion of the new work which represents an improvement in the working efficiency or capacity of the old work can, under the Double-Account System, be treated as Capital Expenditure. In practice, business men have to some extent reduced matters to a reasonable level by departing from the strict letter of the Double-Account System. For example, in Australia—where the cost of engineering work is at the present time considerably less than it was when railways were first started on that continent—the usual practice is to gradually write down the actual expenditure as the high-priced old assets become worn-out and are replaced by lower costing assets of equal efficiency; while in this country, where the cost of engineering work shows a tendency to continually increase, the initial Capital Expenditure is indirectly written up as the Fixed Assets are renewed by charging Capital with more than its strictly fair proportion of the aggregate cost when renewals and enlargements take place simultaneously.

(3) Perhaps the weakest feature of the Double-Account System as a whole is that, while it provides for all necessary renewals being made good out of Revenue, a provision which (as has already been explained) to a large extent obviates the necessity of providing for Depreciation, it omits to take into account what may be styled as expenditure upon *abandoned objects*. Under any sound business system of accounting Fixed Assets that have become useless for the purposes of the business, or which are no longer used for its purposes, should in all cases be written down to the actual realisable value, and the amount that has to be then written off would be charged against Revenue. Under the Double-Account System, however, nothing has to be charged against Revenue until a renewal of the original assets takes place. If the assets are being continually used, such renewal cannot, of course, be very considerably delayed beyond the proper time; but if the assets have altogether fallen out of use, expenditure upon their renewal may be indefinitely postponed, and thus in fact losses which have actually occurred will not be charged against Revenue. For example, if a siding, or a station, be abandoned, it will, under the Double-Account System, still enter into the total of Capital Expenditure, even although it may be possessed of no value, either intrinsic or as a means of earning revenue; while, disregarding such extreme cases, the actual amount to be charged against the profits of any one year for renewals may be easily modified to a large extent by deferring expenditure which is really necessary to make good a shrinkage in value that has actually taken place. To some extent this risk is obviated by the fact that the Fixed Assets of such undertakings must be kept in a reasonable state of efficiency to enable them to carry on their work without accident, and to some extent also the certificates required from the permanent officials of the Company, that the assets of their respective departments are in proper working order, may also be regarded as a safeguard; but there is a considerable margin of difference between such deterioration as makes the continued working of an asset dangerous, and such deterioration as may have a marked effect upon its true value, while the certificates of permanent officials (being, in the nature of things, but the expression of an individual opinion) also leave room for a certain amount of latitude.

APPLICABILITY OF DOUBLE-ACCOUNT SYSTEM.

It has already been stated that the Double-Account System has been prescribed by Parliament as being applicable to the accounts of certain specific undertakings. Its use in practice is, however, by no means necessarily confined to these. All undertakings working upon similar lines may, with equal convenience, employ the Double-Account System ; and so long as its rules be interpreted with a reasonable amount of intelligence and latitude in cases where a strict application would unfairly favour either Capital or Revenue, the system may be well applied, not merely to the accounts of Railway, Gas, Water, and Electric Light Companies, but also to Tramway, Canal, Shipping, Telephone, and Mining Companies, and to Companies owning property from the letting of which they derive a regular income. The system is, however, unsuitable to undertakings which from time to time sell a portion of their Fixed Assets (or those assets which under ordinary circumstances would be regarded as " fixed "), as, for example, a Land Development Company, which after spending money upon the acquisition of land and upon draining and road-making, disposes of it in plots for building purposes.

Speaking generally, it is, as has already been stated, a distinctive feature of the Double-Account System that it does not provide directly for the Depreciation of Fixed Assets. There is, however, no difficulty in employing the Double-Account *form* while yet writing down Fixed Assets to provide for Depreciation ; but under such circumstances it is not obvious what advantages remain, as perhaps the solitary advantage of employing the Double-Account System at all is that it shows clearly the actual Capital Expenditure that has been incurred upon Fixed Assets from time to time, regarding such figure of cost as being a more useful item of information than any hypothetical valuation of assets which have not been realised, and which it is not intended to realise in the ordinary course of business operations.

CHAPTER XIII.

INCOME TAX.

IT is not proposed to deal exhaustively in this work with the law relating to Income Tax. The subject is one that could only be discussed adequately at a far greater length than is here available, and it may be added that it would be inconsistent to discuss the law of Income Tax fully without according the same treatment to many other branches of law which affect accounts more or less directly. The present moment would, moreover, be a particularly inopportune one for the purpose of considering Income Tax law in detail, inasmuch as a Parliamentary Committee has recently been appointed to inquire into the whole matter with a view to further legislation. It is therefore only reasonable to suppose that considerable alterations will be effected in the near future. Be that as it may, however, the law determining the method of making assessments for Income Tax is outside the scope of the present work: it is proposed here merely to deal with those portions of the subject that directly affect the accounts, as such.

Broadly speaking, Income Tax is a charge against business profits, but one that is (as a rule) not based directly upon the amount of such profits. Generally, the tax is paid directly to the official collector; but inasmuch as the rule obtains of taxing all income, as far as possible, at its source, the tax is sometimes paid by those from whom the profits have been received, in which case they have the right to deduct it from the profits paid over by them. The most common examples of Income Tax so paid indirectly occur in connection with the payment of rent, interest, and dividends. The tax is in such cases calculated on the exact amount paid, usually at the rate current during the period in which the income was earned, subject, however, to the proviso that the person making the deduction has never the right to deduct Income Tax which he has not actually paid to the official collectors, and subject to the further proviso that the amount actually deducted as tax must not exceed the current rate upon the amount payable.

For example, a tenant who pays rent to his superior landlord is frequently called upon to pay Income Tax assessed under Schedule " A " (or " Property Tax," as it is commonly called): from the next subsequent payment of rent to the superior landlord it is competent for him to deduct the tax so paid by him, provided that the assessment under Schedule " A " does not exceed the amount of rent actually payable. If, however, the assessment exceeds the rent, tax on the rent only may be deducted. Thus, if the rent actually paid be at the rate of £100 per annum, and the assessment be upon £83 6s. 8d. (£100 less ⅙th allowed for repairs, &c.), the whole tax so paid may be deducted from the next payment of rent. If, however, the assessment be for less than £83 6s. 8d., the amount of tax actually paid can alone be deducted, as the tenant is not entitled to make any profit out of the Income Tax; if, on the other hand, the assessment be for more than £83 6s. 8d., only the tax on £83 6s. 8d. may be deducted from the rent paid to the landlord, and the balance of such tax must be borne by the tenant. This, on reflection, will be found to be perfectly reasonable, as, if the assessment be higher than the rent, the presumption is that the rent is less than the true annual value of the premises, and therefore that the tenant has himself a beneficial interest in the premises.

Tax may be deducted from annual interest, or any other similar payment, by the person making such payment, and will in all cases be at the rate current during the time that the payments accrued due. If there has been an alteration in the rate of tax during that period, a corresponding apportionment must be made. The same remarks apply to dividends, save that the dividends paid by certain classes of undertakings are required to bear deduction for Income Tax at the rate current when the dividend is actually paid. All sums so deducted for Income Tax must be duly accounted for by the party making the deduction to the Inland Revenue authorities, except when such payments are made out of profits which have already been fully assessed. Thus, if a Company has been fully assessed on its profits under Schedule "D," it is under no obligation to account to the Inland Revenue, in addition, for tax deducted from interest on debentures, dividends on shares, &c., because the profits out of which such payments have been made are included in the Company's assessment under Schedule "D."

Leaving upon one side such items as those already alluded to, on which Income Tax is paid by the recipient of the income indirectly, the amount actually payable in respect of Income Tax under Schedule "D" will never exactly agree with the actual profits earned, partly because certain proper charges against profits are not allowed by the Income Tax authorities as deductions from income, and partly because certain deductions and abatements are allowed by the Income Tax authorities which are not trade expenses, but perhaps chiefly because the assessment under Schedule "D" will not be on the profits of any single year but upon the average profits for the last three completed years— or, in the case of a new business, on the average profits since such business was commenced. It should further be borne in mind that the Government year closes on the 5th April, and that Income Tax is usually demanded, and paid, during the month of January. An undertaking, therefore, which closes its books in the latter part of the calendar year will usually at the date of its Balance Sheet have a liability in respect of Income Tax accruing due; while an undertaking which closes its books in the first three months of the year will usually have paid Income Tax up to the subsequent 5th of April, and therefore in advance. This is a matter that should always be borne in mind when calculating the outstanding liabilities and payments made in advance for Balance Sheet purposes.

Unless the question of Income Tax be carefully considered, there is often a danger of the first half-year's, or year's, profits of a new undertaking being overstated by omitting to take into account the accruing liability in respect of Income Tax. It is thought that the best plan is to debit Income Tax Account as a matter of course with tax at the current rate on the profits earned during that period which are liable for taxation, the amount so charged being credited to an "Income Tax Suspense Account." This latter account should be debited with all Income Tax paid, and at each successive Balance Sheet the balance on the Suspense Account may be adjusted if necessary.

In the case of Limited Companies, a very considerable portion of the tax actually paid will be recovered from debenture-holders and preference shareholders, and perhaps also from holders of ordinary shares. In such cases it is clear that the Company itself will

K 2

only have to actually bear the Income Tax on those profits which remain undivided, and on such sums as may represent the difference between the amount of the assessment and the true profits for the period. The amount to be actually debited to Profit and Loss Account should be reduced accordingly. It is desirable, however, if the exact charge cannot be determined in advance, to debit the first Profit and Loss Account with a sufficient sum, so that there may be a slight reserve in hand. This is important, in that it will generally be found, as time goes on, that tax has to be paid on a sum considerably in excess of the true profits. The following problem will, it is thought, clearly explain the working of all the points already referred to :—

PROBLEM.—A Limited Company commenced business on 1st July 1895. It balanced its books annually and the following are the results shown :—

	Balance of Profit and Loss Account		Deductions not allowed for Income Tax purposes		Income Tax paid by Company		Dividends declared (from which Tax was deducted)
1895-6	... £3,800	...	£600	...	£100	...	£3,000
1896-7	... 5,600	...	700	...	100	...	5,000
1897-8	... 4,600	...	700	...	175	...	5,000
1898-9	... 2,800	...	600	...	175	...	3,000

Show the net amount to be charged against each year's profits for Income Tax, and the Income Tax Suspense Account for the four years.

Dr.   INCOME TAX SUSPENSE ACCOUNT.   Cr.

1896		£ s d	1896		£ s d
Jan. 1	To Cash	100 0 0	June 30	By Income Tax Account (8d. in the £ on £4,400)	146 13 4
June 30	„ Balance	46 13 4			
		£146 13 4			£146 13 4
1897			1896 July 1	By Balance	46 13 4
Jan. 1	To Cash	100 0 0	1897 June 30	„ Income Tax Account (8d. in the £ on £6,300)	210 0 0
June 30	„ Balance	156 13 4			
		£256 13 4			£256 13 4
1898			1897 July 1	By Balance	156 13 4
Jan. 1	To Cash	175 0 0	1898 June 30	„ Income Tax Account (8d. in the £ on £5,300)	176 13 4
June 30	„ Balance	158 6 8			
		£333 6 8			£333 6 8
1899			1898 July 1	By Balance	158 6 8
Jan. 1	To Cash	175 0 0	1899 June 30	„ Income Tax Account (8d. in the £ on £3,400)	113 6 8
June 30	„ Balance	96 13 4			
		£271 13 4			£271 13 4
			1899 July 1	By Balance	96 13 4

Dr.   INCOME TAX ACCOUNT.   Cr.

			£ s d				£ s d
1896 June 30	To Income Tax Suspense Account		146 13 4	1896 June 30 "	By Dividend Account .. .. " Profit and Loss Account		100 0 0 46 13 4
			£146 13 4				£146 13 4
1897 June 30	To Income Tax Suspense Account		210 0 0	1897 June 30 "	By Dividend Account .. .. " Profit and Loss Account		166 13 4 43 6 8
			£210 0 0				£210 0 0
1898 June 30	To Income Tax Suspense Account		176 13 4	1898 June 30 "	By Dividend Account .. .. " Profit and Loss Account		166 13 4 10 0 0
			£176 13 4				£176 13 4
1899 June 30	To Income Tax Suspense Account		113 6 8	1899 June 30 "	By Dividend Account .. .. " Profit and Loss Account		100 0 0 13 6 8
			£113 6 8				£113 6 8

NOTE.—The balance to credit of Income Tax Suspense Account on the 30th June in each year represents (a) *the liability for Tax accruing since 5th April previous;* (b) *provision to compensate for the fact that the assessment is on the three years' average.*

RETURNS FOR INCOME TAX.

The preparation of accounts for submission to the Inland Revenue authorities comes properly under the heading of accounting, and must therefore be dealt with in the present work, in spite of the fact that the basis of such assessments will in all probability be altered in the near future. Such accounts are chiefly required in connection with assessments under Schedule " D," to which, therefore, our comments may be confined. The basis of such assessments is (as has already been stated) the profits of the last three completed years. Returns are ordinarily required about June. If, therefore, the usual period of balancing be, say, the 30th June, the assessment for the year ended 5th April 1904 will be on the average profits for the three years ended 30th June 1903. If, however, the accounts are generally balanced at the end of December, the basis would be the accounts for the three years ended 31st December 1902. Occasionally an undertaking will, for one reason or another, alter the date of its periodical accounts; for example, a concern which up to the 31st December 1901 had regularly closed its books at the end of the calendar year, might again take out a Balance Sheet on the 30th June 1902, and thereafter balance its books regularly at the end of June. In such a case, the proper basis for the assessment for the year 1903-4 would be the three and a-half years ended 30th June 1903.

It is the duty of every business concern to prepare, in or about the month of June, a return for Income Tax purposes, and, if the return be accepted, the assessment will be upon the basis of such return. No accounts are required to accompany the return; but inasmuch as the person making it has to at the same time make a statutory declaration as to its truth, it is clear that (if called upon) he should be in a position to substantiate his figures. Under no circumstances should a return be based upon estimates. If no proper accounts have been prepared in the past, and it is now impossible to compile them, no return should be made. There is no statutory provision compelling persons to make a return of their income for purposes of taxation; but if no such return be made (or if the Commissioners do not accept the return) they will make such an assessment as they may think fit, and unless the party assessed gives due notice of appeal, the assessment cannot be set aside. In such a case, the tax due under the assessment must be paid during the first three months of the ensuing calendar year; but, immediately *after* the 5th April following, the party may claim to have refunded to him the amount of tax overpaid, if he can satisfy the authorities that the amount actually paid by him is in excess of the amount upon which he was legally liable.

If notice of an appeal be given, the party assessed must attend before the Commissioners at the appointed time for the purpose of supporting his appeal. He cannot be compelled to produce either books or accounts upon such an occasion, but unless he produces proper accounts (and, if called upon so to do, the books from which they were compiled) his appeal is not likely to be granted. It is usual for the evidence that will be submitted to the Commissioners to be first submitted to the Surveyor, and such a course facilitates matters from both points of view, as it may remove all necessity for the appellant to appear before the Commissioners. It is desirable that the Surveyor should be consulted as to the form which he wishes the accounts to take. Most Surveyors prefer to have submitted to them copies of the last three years' Profit and Loss Accounts exactly as they have been compiled for the purposes of the business, along with three supplementary accounts, adding to the net profit shown by the previous ones those items which are not allowed as deductions for Income Tax purposes, and deducting those items upon which tax has already been paid, thus arriving at a corrected figure. Some Surveyors, on the other hand, prefer to have placed before them, in the form of a simple Profit and Loss Account, a statement showing on the one hand all sources of taxable income, and upon the other all deductions that may be properly made therefrom, in order to arrive at the profits assessable. The ultimate result is, of course, the same in every case, but it is desirable to prepare the accounts in the form preferred by each individual Surveyor. The following examples will show clearly how both forms should be prepared. Only one year's figures are given here. In practice, it is convenient to place the three years' figures in separate columns upon the same sheet, as this not only saves time, but also enables the figures to be more readily compared.

EXAMPLE:

(A).

Dr.　　　PROFIT AND LOSS ACCOUNT, for the Year ended 31st December 1902.　　　Cr.

	£	s	d		£	s	d
To Rent	120	0	0	By Gross Profit	3,500	0	0
„ Rates, Taxes, and Insurance	55	0	0	„ Discounts	150	0	0
„ Bank Interest and Charges	80	0	0	„ Dividends from Public Companies	120	0	0
„ Depreciation	120	0	0				
„ Interest on Mortgage	80	0	0				
„ Income Tax	100	0	0				
„ Interest on Capital	215	0	0				
„ Balance, being Net Profit	3,000	0	0				
	£3,770	0	0		£3,770	0	0

	£	s	d		£	s	d
To Dividends from Public Companies (already taxed at source)	120	0	0	By Net Profit, as above	3,000	0	0
„ Annual Value of Premises used solely for business purposes	225	0	0	„ Rent	120	0	0
„ Profits Assessable for Income Tax (subject to such allowance as the Surveyor may, in his discretion, make for wear and tear of Plant and Machinery)	3,290	0	0	„ Depreciation	120	0	0
				„ Interest on Mortgage	80	0	0
				„ Income Tax	100	0	0
				„ Interest on Capital	215	0	0
	£3,635	0	0		£3,635	0	0

(B).

STATEMENT OF PROFITS FOR ASSESSMENT FOR INCOME TAX, for the Year ended
Dr.   31st December 1902.   *Cr.*

	£	s	d		£	s	d
To Annual Value of Premises used solely for business purposes	225	0	0	By Gross Profit	3,500	0	0
„ Rates, Taxes, and Insurance	55	0	0	„ Discounts	150	0	0
„ Bank Interest and Charges	80	0	0				
„ Balance, being Profits Assessable (subject to allowance for wear and tear, as in " Example A ")	3,290	0	0				
	£ 3,650	0	0		£3,650	0	0

REPAYMENTS OF TAX.

Applications for repayment of tax overpaid will arise not merely when there has been an unexpected falling off in profits, but also when (*inter alia*), through an oversight, the applicant has omitted to claim deduction for life insurance premiums, or an abatement on the ground that his income from all sources amounts to less than £700 per annum. It need hardly be stated that it is always desirable that these deductions should be made upon the return where possible. If, however, the life insurance policy has been taken out since the return was made, an application for repayment is clearly the only remedy open to the taxpayer. The application is considered in due course by the Surveyor, who will call for such evidence in support of the facts therein stated as he may consider proper; and, if the claim be allowed, the applicant will in due course receive a money order for the amount of tax overpaid direct from the Inland Revenue authorities at Somerset House. Accompanying the money order will be a form to be used by him for any similar application he may have to make at the close of the next year, such subsequent application having to be made direct to Somerset House. This practice is especially convenient to those who receive all, or the bulk of, their income from various sources with the Income Tax deducted, as it is then only by application for repayment that they are able to obtain the benefit of deductions for life assurance, or of such abatements as they may be entitled to in the case of small incomes.

It has already been stated that Income Tax is assessed in advance, and (frequently) also paid somewhat in advance. If, at the end of the current year, it be found that the amount upon which tax has been paid exceeds the assessable profits for the past three years, *including the year of assessment*, the difference, or overcharge, may be recovered on application to the proper authorities. In the case of a declining business, therefore, a corrected return should always be prepared upon these lines, with a view to ascertaining whether it is not possible to obtain repayment of tax overpaid. Thus, in the case of a concern which for the year 1903-4 paid Income Tax on the average profits for the three years ended 30th September 1902, if on the preparation of the accounts for the year ended 30th September 1903 it should be found that there has been a loss, or that the average profits for the three years ended 30th September 1903 are less than the amount upon which tax was paid for the year ended 5th April 1904, then application must be made for the repayment of the excess. The actual working of this principle (which is comprised in Section 133 of the Income Tax Act, 1842) is clearly shown in the following

PROBLEM.—In the month of June 1902 A. B. & Co. made a return of profit for Income Tax Assessment under Schedule D, for the year ending 5th April 1903. The amount was £9,000, being the average of the three years ended 31st December 1901, namely :—1899, £9,000 ; 1900, £10,000 ; and 1901, £8,000. The assessment was duly made, and the tax on £9,000 paid in January 1903. Some months later, when the accounts for the year 1902 were made up, the taxable profit for that year was ascertained to be £6,900. State what adjustment and relief A. B. & Co. are entitled to, and how such relief is to be obtained ; also state what difference it would have made in the amount of the relief if the profits of the three years ended 31st December 1901 had been : for 1899, £13,800 ; 1900, £6,200 ; 1901, £7,000.

Under Section 133 of the Income Tax Act, 1842, on A. B. & Co.'s proving to the satisfaction of the Commissioners by whom the assessment was made that their profits and gains for 1902 were as stated, the Commissioners would have it in their power to cause the assessment to be amended, and to certify under their hands to the Commissioners for Special Purposes at the chief office of Inland Revenue in England the amount of the sum overpaid upon such first assessment. Such last-mentioned Commissioners would then issue an order, directed to the Receiver-General of Stamps and Taxes, or to an officer for the receipt and collection of the duties granted under the Income Tax Act of 1842, or to a distributor or a sub-distributor of stamps, for the repayment of the sum overpaid.

On the production of such order the sum overpaid would be repaid, and a receipt therefor endorsed by A. B. & Co. on the order

In ascertaining the amount to be refunded, attention must be paid to the 6th Section of 28 & 29 Vict., c. 30, which provides no reduction or repayment is to be made unless the profits of the year of assessment are proved to be less than the profits for one year on the average of the last three years, including the said year of assessment ; nor shall any such relief extend to any greater amount than the difference between the sum on which the assessment has been made, and such average profits for one year as aforesaid.

Now, in the first case, the average profits for one year on the average of the last three years, including the year of assessment, would be £8,300, and the difference between it and the sum of £9,000 (on which the assessment has been made) should be £700.

Thus :—

Tax paid in January 1903 (£9,000 @ 1/3) =	..		..	£562	10 0

Average Profits—

1900	..	£10 000	
1901	..	8 000	
1902	..	6 900	
		£24,900	

Average, £8,300.

Tax on £8,300 (@ 1/3) =	..	..	..	518	15 0
Amount overpaid	..	..	..	£43	15 0

In the second case, as the average profits, reckoning in the same year of assessment, are but £6,700, there will therefore be no repayment, as they are less than the profits for the year of assessment—viz., £6,900.

Forms upon which application for repayment of tax must be made should be obtained from the Surveyor in whose district the applicant *resides*, but as, unlike forms for returns, they cannot be very readily obtained by the public, copies of two of the more representative forms at present in use are reproduced on the following pages.

EXAMPLE :   (TRUSTEES, &c.)

THIS FORM is to be used by a Trustee who claims Repayment of Income Tax for the FIRST time. When filled up it should be sent to the Surveyor of Taxes for the District in which the Claimant resides. The Name and Address of the Surveyor may be obtained from the Local Collector of Taxes.

Where Repayment is NOT claimed for the first time, the Form sent with the last order of repayment should be used, but if it has been lost or mislaid, application should be made to the Secretary of Inland Revenue (Claims' Branch), Somerset House, London, W.C., for another Form. In making the application, the date when the last Repayment was obtained should be stated, and, if possible, the official number of the Order.

No. 44. Trustees, &c.	INCOME TAX.—EXEMPTION CLAIM, 1 -1 INCOME NOT EXCEEDING £160.	Registered No. of Claim.

N.B.—*A Trustee can claim only for Minors, a Person Incapacitated, or a Married Woman permanently separated from Her Husband.*

1. Here state name or names of person or persons for whom Claim is made.
2. State whether Minor (see questions on back of Form), Person incapacitated or Married Woman permanently separated from her husband.
3. State whether Trustee, Agent, &c.
4. Describe Deed or Will under which Trust created or otherwise.
5. State FULL address of office.

I declare that the following is a true account of the Income from EVERY SOURCE for the year ending 5th April, 1   , of 1...........................

...........................who 2...........................

and for whom I am 3...................under 4...........................

and I therefore claim to be repaid the sum of £   :   :   at the Money Order Office at 5...........................

Order No.

B (Trustees)—Allowed for

£   s.   d   to

CLAIMANT'S SIGNATURE } at full length.   ....

N.B.—A Lady must state, after Signature, whether Widow or Spinster.

CLAIMANT'S Full Postal Address {...........................
...........................Date...........................190 .

This Space MUST NOT be filled up by the Claimant.

Particulars of the TOTAL INCOME of the Person on whose behalf the Claim is made, from EVERY SOURCE WHETHER TAXED OR NOT, for the Year from 6th April 1   , to 5th of April 1   .

No. 1. Income derived from Dividends on Stock inscribed in the books of the Bank of England or from English Government Annuities. (For these no Certificate of Deduction is required.)

Name or Description of Stock or Annuity & whether the Dividends are paid by post or through Bankers	Name or Names (in due order) in which the Stock stands. If in Chancery, the correct Title of the Suit (which appears at the head of each Draft issued by the Chancery Pay or Accountant-General's Office) should be given instead. Claimants should take a note of the Title of the Cause when each Draft is received, also whether in English or Irish Funds.	Amount thereof, and if part of larger sum, state also larger sum	Month and Year when Dividend or Annuity due from which deduction made	Annual Amount of Income from each source	Amount of Income Tax paid on, or deducted from each source of Income
		£ s d		£ s d	£ s d

No. 2. Income NOT DERIVED from any of the sources referred to in No. 1. (Collectors' Receipts or Certificates required as per Instructions on the back hereof, except for British, Irish, Colonial or Indian Government Pay or Pension.)

Total Amount of Income from all sources and Income Tax thereon   .. £

No. 3. Particulars of DEDUCTIONS FROM INCOME, such as GROUND RENT, INTEREST, &c. If there be none state "None." (See note 13 on back of this Form.) | Annual Amount |
| £   s   d |

Total Deductions and Income Tax thereon   ..   .. £

Total Amount of Income from all sources after Deductions, and of } Income Tax claimed to be returned   ..   .. } £

Having examined the preceding Claim, I certify that the Claimant appears to be entitled to exemption from Income Tax, and to be repaid the sum of £   :   :   Given under my hand, this   day of   190

District...........................   ....Surveyor.

We Certify that the Claimant named on the other side, having proved to our satisfaction that the whole of the Income of the person on whose behalf the claim is made, estimated according to the Acts for granting Duties on Profits arising from Property, Professions, Trades, and Offices, does not exceed the Sum of One Hundred and Sixty Pounds per Annum, is entitled to exemption from Income Tax.

Given under our hands, this

day of 190	*Commissioners for* *General Purposes.*

INSTRUCTIONS.

1. *When the Claim is on behalf of a Minor or Minors, the following Questions must be answered and signed by the Trustee :—*

QUESTIONS.   ANSWERS.

a. Has the Minor, or have the Minors, a vested, *i.e.*, an absolute Interest in the property, or only a contingent Interest, *i.e.*, depending on the occurence of some specific event ? If the latter, particulars of the contingency should be stated.

b. Is the Income expended for Education or for Maintenance ? If the Interest be contingent, the sum expended must be stated, and the claim restricted to the tax on that sum.

Signature
of
Trustee

2. **No claim for Repayment of Income Tax on the ground that the Income from all sources does not exceed £160 a year can be allowed, unless it be made within three years after the end of the year of Assessment to which the claim relates. 10th Sec., 23rd Vic. cap. 14.**

3. **The Penalty for fraudulently concealing or untruly declaring the Income is £20 and treble the Duty chargeable.**

4. In filling up the Form on the other side, the Claimant must set forth fully in Divisions Nos. 1 and 2 every source of Income whether taxed or not, with the amount derived from each source. The Income of a Married Woman living with her Husband is deemed by the Income Tax Acts to be his Income (notwithstanding any Settlement or the provisions contained in the Married Women's Property Act, 1882), and the particulars thereof must be included in the Husband's claim. Where, however, the total joint Income of a Husband and Wife does not exceed £500, and such total Income includes profits of the Wife from any business carried on or exercised by means of her own personal labour, and the rest of the total Income or any part thereof arises or accrues from profits of a business carried on or exercised by means of the Husband's own personal labour, and unconnected with the business of the Wife, the profits of the Wife may (under the Act 60 & 61 Vict. cap. 24) be treated as a separate Income, and a separate claim may be made in respect thereof. Any Income of the Husband, however, arising or accruing from the business of his Wife or from any source connected therewith must be regarded as part of the Income of the Wife.

5. **If the Income be** from Lands, Tenements, or Hereditaments, state the precise situation of each property, with the name of the occupier, and the amount of the annual rent or value, and who bears the cost of repairs. If the person on whose behalf the claim is made resides in his own house, the Annual Value thereof must be entered in Division No. 2. Receipts by the Local Collector of Income Tax should be attached to the claim.

6. Profits from the occupation of land are to be estimated at one-third of the full amount of rent and tithe.

7. If the Income be from the Public Funds, English Government Annuities, Dividends on Colonial or Corporation Stocks inscribed in the books of, and payable by, the Bank of England, the directions in Division No. 1 must be complied with; and no vouchers are required for these items.

8. If from an Office, state the name of the Office.

9. If from Trade, Profession, or Employment, state the nature thereof, where carried on, and the particulars of the assessment.

10. If from Dividends or Interest arising from Money invested in any Stock, Shares, or otherwise (except in the Stock of the Bank of England and those mentioned in No. 7), Certificates must be attached showing the amount of Dividends or Interest applicable to the period for which the claim is made.

11. If from Annuities, Interest of Money, or other property not coming under any of the foregoing heads, state fully the particulars, including the name and address of the person by whom paid. Certificates, signed by the persons who deducted the Income Tax, must be securely attached to the claim.

12. When the Certificates are not in the name of the Claimant, it should be stated whether the person or persons named are Trustees, or otherwise.

13. If the Income be subject to deduction in respect of Ground Rent, Interest, Annuity, or other Annual Charge, the particulars thereof must be set forth in Division No. 3, so as to show the amount of Annual Payment or Payments charged upon the Income, whereby the same is diminished. The Income Tax on any such charges relating to the property on which repayment is sought must be deducted from the claim, being recoverable from the persons to whom such charges are paid. **If there be none, state " None."**

14. A Claim may be made as soon as the Income of the year has been received, but only one Claim should be made for each year.

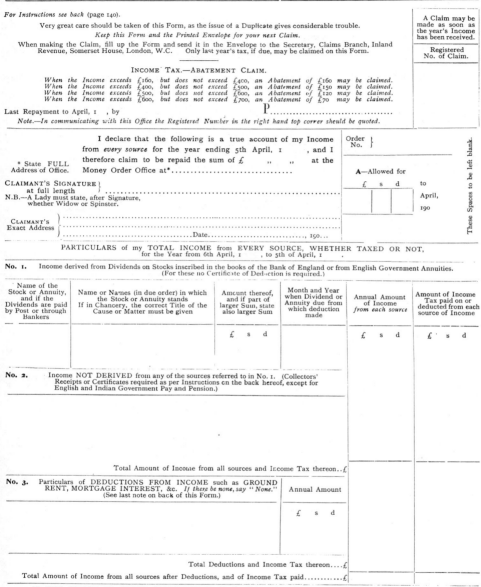

Very great care should be taken of this Form, as the issue of a Duplicate gives considerable trouble.

Keep this Form and the Printed Envelope for your next Claim.

When making the Claim, fill up the Form and send it in the Envelope to the Secretary, Claims Branch, Inland Revenue, Somerset House, London, W.C.   Only last year's tax, if due, may be claimed on this Form.

A Claim may be made as soon as the year's Income has been received.

Registered No. of Claim.

INCOME TAX.—ABATEMENT CLAIM.

When the Income exceeds £160, but does not exceed £400, an Abatement of £160 may be claimed.
When the Income exceeds £400, but does not exceed £500, an Abatement of £150 may be claimed.
When the Income exceeds £500, but does not exceed £600, an Abatement of £120 may be claimed.
When the Income exceeds £600, but does not exceed £700, an Abatement of £70 may be claimed.

Last Repayment to April, 1   , by   P..

Note.—In communicating with this Office the Registered Number in the right hand top corner should be quoted.

I declare that the following is a true account of my Income from *every source* for the year ending 5th April, 1   , and I therefore claim to be repaid the sum of £   ,,   ,,   at the Money Order Office at*...........................

* State FULL Address of Office.

CLAIMANT'S SIGNATURE }
at full length   } ....
N.B.—A Lady must state, after Signature, whether Widow or Spinster.

CLAIMANT'S } ....
Exact Address { ....
) ....Date.........................., 150...

Order }
No.   }

A—Allowed for

£   s   d   to
April,
190

These Spaces to be left blank.

PARTICULARS of my TOTAL INCOME from EVERY SOURCE, WHETHER TAXED OR NOT,
for the Year from 6th April, 1   , to 5th April, 1   .

No. 1.   Income derived from Dividends on Stocks inscribed in the books of the Bank of England or from English Government Annuities.
(For these no Certificate of Deduction is required.)

Name of the Stock or Annuity, and if the Dividends are paid by Post or through Bankers	Name or Names (in due order) in which the Stock or Annuity stands If in Chancery, the correct Title of the Cause or Matter must be given	Amount thereof, and if part of larger Sum, state also larger Sum	Month and Year when Dividend or Annuity due from which deduction made	Annual Amount of Income *from each source*	Amount of Income Tax paid on or deducted from each source of Income
		£ s d		£ s d	£ s d

No. 2.   Income NOT DERIVED from any of the sources referred to in No. 1. (Collectors' Receipts or Certificates required as per Instructions on the back hereof, except for English and Indian Government Pay and Pension.)

Total Amount of Income from all sources and Income Tax thereon..£

No. 3.   Particulars of DEDUCTIONS FROM INCOME such as GROUND RENT, MORTGAGE INTEREST, &c. *If there be none, say "None."* (See last note on back of this Form.)

Annual Amount

£   s   d

Total Deductions and Income Tax thereon....£

Total Amount of Income from all sources after Deductions, and of Income Tax paid...........£

IF THE SPACES BE FOUND INSUFFICIENT the Details may be written upon a sheet of paper, but the TOTALS must always be entered in this form.

INSTRUCTIONS.

1. **No claim for Repayment of Income Tax can be allowed, unless it be made within three years after the end of the year of Assessment to which the claim relates. 10th Sec., 23rd Vic., Cap. 14.**

2. **The Penalty for fraudulently concealing or untruly declaring the Income is £20 and Treble the Duty chargeable.**

3. In filling up the Form on the other side, the Claimant must set forth fully in Divisions Nos. 1 and 2 every source of Income, whether taxed or not, with the amount derived from each source. The Income of a Married Woman living with her Husband is deemed by the Income Tax Acts to be his Income (notwithstanding any Settlement or the provisions contained in the Married Women's Property Act, 1882), and the particulars thereof must be included in the Husband's claim. Where, however, the total joint Income of a Husband and Wife does not exceed £500, and such total Income includes profits of the Wife from any business carried on or exercised by means of her own personal labour, and the rest of the total Income or any part thereof arises or accrues from profits of a business carried on or exercised by means of the Husband's own personal labour, and unconnected with the business of the Wife, the profits of the Wife may (under the Act 60 and 61 Vict., cap. 24), be treated as a separate Income, and a separate claim may be made in respect thereof. Any Income of the Husband, however, arising or accruing from the business of his Wife or from any source connected therewith must be regarded as part of the Income of the Wife.

4. If the Income be from Lands, Tenements, or Hereditaments, state the precise situation of each property, with name of the occupier, and the amount of the annual rent or value, and who bears the cost of repairs. If the Claimant resides in his own house, the Annual Value thereof must be entered in Division No. 2. Receipts by the Local Collector of Income Tax must be attached to the claim.

5. Profits from the occupation of Land are to be estimated at one-third of the full amount of rent and tithe.

6. If the Income be from the Public Funds, English Government Annuities, Dividends on Colonial or Corporation Stocks inscribed in the books of, and payable by, the Bank of England, the directions in Division No. 1 must be complied with ; and no vouchers are required for these items.

7. If from an Office, state the name of the Office.

8. If from Trade, Profession, or Employment, state the nature thereof, where carried on, and the particulars of the assessment

9. If from Dividends or Interest arising from Money invested in any Stock, Shares, or otherwise (except in the Stock of the Bank of England or those mentioned in No. 6), Vouchers must be attached showing the amount of Dividends or Interest applicable to the period for which the claim is made.

10. If from Annuities, Interest of Money, or other property not coming under any of the foregoing heads, state fully the particulars, including the name and address of the person by whom paid. Certificates, signed by the persons who deducted the Income Tax, must be securely attached to the Claim.

11. When the Certificates are in other name or names than that of the Claimant, it should be stated whether the person or persons named are Trustees, or otherwise.

12. If the Income be subject to deduction in respect of Ground Rent, Mortgage Interest, Annuity, or other Annual Charge, the particulars thereof must be set forth in Division No. 3, so as to show the amount of Annual Payment or Payments charged upon the Income, whereby the same is diminished. The Income Tax on any such charges is recoverable from the persons to whom such charges are paid. **If there be none, state "None."**

CHAPTER XIV.

BANKRUPTCY AND INSOLVENCY ACCOUNTS.

THE special points arising in connection with the accounts relating to the estates of insolvent persons have their origin in the statutory requirements made upon persons administering these trusts.

STATEMENTS OF AFFAIRS.

Under normal conditions the object of any system of bookkeeping is to produce, at regular intervals, or whenever required, a statement showing the financial position at that date in the form of a Balance Sheet, and also an account showing—in a summarised form, and classified under convenient headings—the various sources of income, expenditure, or loss, that have contributed to the alteration of the position as contrasted with the previous occasion. The latter account is frequently divided into several sections, which are known collectively as a Profit and Loss Account or Revenue Account.

When an estate is found to be insolvent, somewhat similar accounts are prepared; but, owing to the special circumstances of the case, certain alterations of detail are found to add materially to their value for the purposes for which they are then required. In place of a Balance Sheet, showing upon the one hand the assets and upon the other the liabilities (the excess of the former over the latter being the proprietor's Capital), the statement that is required is one that will afford unsecured creditors some idea of the amount of their claims in the aggregate, and of the net amount of assets available to meet them. Consequently the Balance

Sheet form is varied so that all assets pledged as security for liabilities appear, not as assets, but as deductions from the claims of secured creditors. If a creditor be fully secured, the *surplus* value of the asset after liquidating his claim alone appears as an asset; while if a creditor be partially secured, the unsecured balance of his claim alone appears as a liability ranking against the general estate. There are also certain classes of creditors who are by law entitled to be paid in priority to the general body of creditors, and the claims of these are stated separately and deducted from the assets, so that a Statement of Affairs so compiled shows upon the one hand the total unsecured liabilities that are expected to rank against the estate for dividend, and upon the other the net total of " free " estate, which (subject to loss on realisation and costs) is available for distribution among creditors. The excess of the former figure over the latter is the Deficiency which the insolvent person has to account for.

To enable this Deficiency to be accounted for, some modification of the ordinary form of Profit and Loss Account must be provided. This modified account (which is called a " Deficiency Account ") differs chiefly from the ordinary Profit and Loss Account in that it starts with an opening balance, representing the amount of surplus assets of the insolvent (or the deficiency of assets, as the case may be) at some previous period. To this figure are added all sources of profit or gain that increase the total amount that has to be accounted for, while upon the other side are included the insolvent's personal expenditure, and (under suitable headings) all losses incurred by him, so that the balance of the account is the Deficiency shown in the Statement of Affairs.

In order to show more clearly the precise difference between the ordinary Balance Sheet and Profit and Loss Account upon the one hand, and the statutory form of Statement of Affairs and Deficiency Account in bankruptcy on the other, the following example is appended :—

PROBLEM.—(a) From the following Trial Balance as on 31st December 1901 prepare Balance Sheet, Trading Account, Profit and Loss Account, and Partners' Capital Accounts :—

	£	£
A. Capital 1st January 1901		150
B. " " "		3,000
Sales		6,250
Purchases	6,100	
Rent	150	
Salaries	450	
General Expenses	750	
Bad Debts	1,250	
Stock-in-Trade 1st January 1901	1,400	
Fixtures	150	
Bills Receivable	100	
Lease of Premises (held by Bank)	700	
Bills Payable		500
Trade Creditors		1,250
Book Debts	500	
Bank (Loan)		1,050
C. for Rent due		75
Salaries due (one month)		48
Cash at Bank	110	
A. Drawings	300	
B. "	363	
	£12,323	£12,323

Stock on 31st December 1901, £1,750. Five per cent. interest to be credited on Partners' Capital Accounts.

(b) Assuming that A. and B. begin business on 1st January 1901, draw up front sheet of Statement of Affairs and Deficiency Account in the form provided under the Bankruptcy Acts, allowing for a further liability on Bills discounted estimated to rank for dividend at £2,000.

(A).   BALANCE SHEET, 31st December 1901.

Liabilities.	£ s d	£ s d	Assets.	£ s d	£ s d
Capital Account:—B.			Lease of Premises	..	700 0 0
Balance, 1st January 1901	3,000 0 0		Fixtures	..	150 0 0
Interest	150 0 0		Stock-in-Trade	..	1,750 0 0
	3,150 0 0		Bills Receivable	..	100 0 0
Less Drawings £363 0 0			Book Debts	..	500 0 0
Share of Loss .. 1,128 15 0			Cash at Bank	..	110 0 0
	1,491 15 0		Capital Account:—A. (overdrawn).		
Bank Loan	..	1,658 5 0	Drawings	300 0 0	
Bills Payable	..	1,050 0 0	Share of Loss	1,128 15 0	
Trade Creditors	..	500 0 0		1,428 15 0	
Sundry Creditors	..	1,250 0 0	*Less* Credit Balance 1/1/01 £150 0 0		
		123 0 0	Interest 7 10 0		
				157 10 0	1,271 5 0
		£4,581 5 0			£4,581 5 0

Dr.   TRADING ACCOUNT, for the Year ended 31st December 1901.   Cr.

	£	s	d		£	s	d
To Stock : 1st January 1901	1,400	0	0	By Sales	6,250	0	0
„ Purchases	6,100	0	0	„ Stock : 31st December 1901	1,750	0	0
„ Gross Profit, transferred to Profit and Loss Account	500	0	0				
	£8,000	0	0		£8,000	0	0

Dr.   PROFIT AND LOSS ACCOUNT, for the Year ended 31st December 1901.   Cr.

	£	s	d	£	s	d		£	s	d	£	s	d
To Rent	150	0	0				By Gross Profit from Trading Account ..				500	0	0
„ Salaries	450	0	0				„ Balance, being Loss for the Year, viz.—						
„ General Expenses	750	0	0				A.	1,128	15	0			
„ Bad Debts	1,250	0	0				B.	1,128	15	0			
				2,600	0	0					2,257	10	0
„ Interest on Capital :—A.	7	10	0										
„ Ditto B.	150	0	0										
				157	10	0							
				£2,757	10	0					£2,757	10	0

(For answer to Problem (b) see overpage.)

(B).

THE BANKRUPTCY ACTS, 1883 AND 1890.

(¹) High Court of
Justice or the County
Court of ....,
holden at..........

In the (¹)

𝔍𝔫 𝔅𝔞𝔫𝔨𝔯𝔲𝔭𝔱𝔠𝔶.

Re A. and B.

STATEMENT OF AFFAIRS.

Court of

No.   of 1902.

To THE DEBTOR.—You are required to fill up, carefully and accurately, this Sheet, and the several Sheets A, B, C, D, E, F, G, H, I, J, and K, showing the state of your affairs on the day on which the Receiving Order was made against you, viz., the first day of January 1902.

Such Sheets, when filled up, will constitute your Statement of Affairs, and must be verified by Oath or Declaration.

Gross Liabilities	LIABILITIES (as stated and estimated by Debtor)	Expected to Rank	ASSETS (as stated and estimated by Debtor)	Estimated to produce
£ s d		£ s d		£ s d
	Unsecured Creditors, as per list (A)	1,750 0 0	Property, as per list (H), viz.:—	
		£ s d	(a) Cash at Bankers (claimed by Bank)	
	Creditors fully secured as per list (B)		(b) Cash in hand	
	Estimated value of Securities ..		(c) Cash deposited with Solicitor for costs of Petition	
	Surplus		(d) Stock-in-Trade (cost £ 〕	1,750 0 0
	Less amount thereof carried to Sheet C		(e) Machinery	
			(f) Trade Fixtures, Fittings, Utensils, &c.	150 0 0
	Balance thereof to *contra* ..		(g) Farming Stock..	
		£ s d	(h) Growing Crops and Tenant Right	
	Creditors partly secured, as per list (C)	1,050 0 0	(i) Furniture	
	Less estimated value of Securities	810 0 0	(j) Life Policies	
			(k) Other Property, viz.:—	
	Liabilities on bills discounted other than Debtor's own acceptances for value, as per list (D), viz.:—	240 0 0		
		£ s d	Total as per list (H)	1,900 0 0
	On accommodation bills as drawer, acceptor, or indorser		Book Debts, as per list (I), viz.:—	
	On other bills, as drawer or indorser	2,000 0 0	Good	500 0 0
		2,000 0 0		£ s d
			Doubtful	
	Of which it is expected will rank against the estate for dividend	2,000 0 0	Bad	1,250 0 0
	Contingent or other liabilities as per list (E) .. .. ..£			1,250 0 0
			Estimated to produce	
	Of which it is expected will rank against the estate for dividend ..		Bills of Exchange or other similar Securities, on hand, as per list (J) .. £100 0 0	
		£ s d	Estimated to produce	100 0 0
	Creditors for Rent, &c., recoverable by distress as per list (F)	75 0 0	Surplus from Securities in the hands of Creditors fully secured (per *contra*)	
	Creditors for Rates, Taxes, Wages, &c., payable in full, as per list (G)	48 0 0		2,500 0 0
	Sheriff's Charges payable under Section 11 of the Bankruptcy Act, 1890, estimated at		Deduct Creditors for distrainable Rent, and for preferential Rates, Taxes, Wages, Sheriff's Charges, &c. (*per contra*)	123 0 0
	Deducted *contra* .. .. ..£	123 0 0		2,377 0 0
			Deficiency explained in statement (K)	1,613 0 0
		£ 3,990 0 0		£ 3,990 0 0

I,   of

in the County of   , make oath and say, that the above Statement and the several lists hereunto annexed, marked A, B, C, D, E, F, G, H, I, J, and K, are to the best of my knowledge and belief a full, true, and complete statement of my affairs on the date of the above-mentioned Receiving Order made against me.

Sworn at ....
in the County of ....
this.......... *day of* ....190....,
before me, ...

Signature...

A.—UNSECURED CREDITORS.

The names to be arranged in alphabetical order and numbered consecutively, creditors for £10 and upwards being placed first.

No.	Name	Address and Occupation	Amount of Debt	Date when contracted		Consideration
				Month	Year	
			£ s d			
	[Full particulars to be set out here.]					

NOTE.—*The prescribed Form contains the following note :*—

(1) When there is a *contra* account against the Creditor less than the amount of his claim against the Estate, the amount of the Creditor's claim and the amount of the *contra* account should be shown in the third column, and the balance only be inserted under the heading " Amount of Debt " thus :—

Total amount of claim ... ... £ : :
Less contra account ... ... £ : :
£ : :

No such set-off should be included in Sheet " I."

(2) The particulars of any Bills of Exchange and Promissory Notes held by a Creditor should be inserted immediately below the name and address of such Creditor.

B.—CREDITORS FULLY SECURED.

No.	Name of Creditor	Address and Occupation	Amount of Debt	Date when Contracted		Considera-tion	Particulars of Security	Date when given	Estimated value of Security	Estimated Surplus from Security
				Month	Year					
			£ s d						£ s d	£ s d

C.—CREDITORS PARTLY SECURED.

No.	Name of Creditor	Address and Occupation	Amount of Debt	Date when Contracted		Considera-tion	Particulars of Security	Month and year when given	Estimated value of Security	Balance of Debt Unsecured
				Month	Year					
			£ s d						£ s d	£ s d

I.

D.—LIABILITIES OF DEBTOR ON BILLS DISCOUNTED OTHER THAN HIS OWN ACCEPTANCES FOR VALUE.

No.	Acceptor's Name, Address, and Occupation	Whether liable as Drawer or Indorser	Date when due	Amount		Holder's Name, Address, and Occupation (if known)	Amount expected to rank against Estate for Dividend
				Accommodation Bills	Other Bills		
				£ s d	£ s d		£ s d

(NOTE.—Ordinary " Bills Payable " are included in Schedule " A."   Only Bills for which the Debtor is liable as DRAWER *or* ENDORSER *appear in this Schedule.)*

E.—CONTINGENT OR OTHER LIABILITIES.

[Full particulars of all Liabilities not otherwise Scheduled to be given here.]

No.	Name of Creditor or Claimant	Address and Occupation	Amount of Liability or Claim	Date when Liability incurred		Nature of Liability
				Month	Year	
			£ s d			

F.—CREDITORS FOR RENT, &c., RECOVERABLE BY DISTRESS.

No.	Name of Creditor	Address and Occupation	Nature of Claim	Period during which claim accrued due	Date when due	Amount of Claim	Amount recoverable by Distress	Difference ranking for Dividend (To be carried to List A)
						£ s d	£ s d	£ s d

G.—PREFERENTIAL CREDITORS FOR RATES, TAXES, AND WAGES.

No.	Name of Creditor	Address and Occupation	Nature of Claim	Period during which Claim accrued due	Date when due	Amount of Claim	Amount payable in full	Difference ranking for Dividend (To be carried to List A)

H.—PROPERTY.

Full particulars of every description of Property in possession and in reversion as defined by Section 168 of the Bankruptcy Act, 1883, not included in any other List, are to be set forth in this List.

Full Statement and Nature of Property	Estimated to Produce
	£ s d
(a) Cash at Bankers	
(NOTE.—If anything is due to Bankers they have a lien on all monies in their hands.)	
(b) Cash in Hand	
(c) Cash deposited with Solicitor for Costs of Petition	
(d) Stock-in-Trade at .. .. (Cost £ : :) ..	1,750 0 0
(e) Machinery at	
(f) Trade Fixtures, Fittings, Utensils, &c., at	150 0 0
(g) Farming Stock at	
(h) Growing Crops and Tenant Right at	
(i) Household Furniture and Effects at..	
(j) Life Policies	
(k) Other Property (*state particulars*), viz. :—	
Lease of Premises	700 0 0

NOTE.—In practice a fair realisable value should be placed on all assets. In this example the book-values have been shown to facilitate comparison with the Balance Sheet previously given.

I.—DEBTS DUE TO THE ESTATE.

No.	Name of Debtor	Residence and Occupation	Amount of Debt			Folio of Ledger or other Book where Particulars to be found	When contracted		Estimated to Produce	Particulars of any Securities held for Debt
			Good	Doubtful	Bad		Month	Year		
			£ s d	£ s d	£ s d				£ s d	

NOTE.—The prescribed Form contains the following :—

If any Debtor to the Estate is also a Creditor, *but for a less amount than his indebtedness*, the gross amount due to the Estate and the amount of the *contra* account should be shown in the third column, and the balance only be inserted under the heading " Amount of Debt " thus:—

Due to Estate .. .. .. £ : :
Less *contra* account .. .. £ : :

£ : :

No such claim should be included in Sheet " A."

J.—BILLS OF EXCHANGE, PROMISSORY NOTES, &c., AVAILABLE AS ASSETS.

No.	Name of Acceptor of Bill or Note	Address, &c.	Amount of Bill or Note	Date when due	Estimated to Produce	Particulars of any Property held as Security for Payment of Bill or Note
			£ s d		£ s d	

K.—DEFICIENCY ACCOUNT.

	£ s d	£ s d		£ s d	£ s d
Excess of Assets over Liabilities on the (1) first day of January 1901 (if any).. ..		3,150 0 0	Excess of Liabilities over Assets on the (1) ......day of.................1..... (if any)		
Net Profit (if any) arising from carrying on business from the (1) ....day of............ 1......, to date of Receiving Order, after deducting usual trade expenses			Net Loss (if any) arising from carrying on busin·ss from the (1) First day of January 1901, to date of Receiving Order, after deducting from profits the usual trade expenses (*)		2,100 0 0
Income or Profit from other sources (if any) since the (1) ....day of............1....			Bad Debts (if any) as per Schedule " I " (2)..		2,000 0 0
Deficiency as per Statement of Affairs		1,613 0 0	Expenses incurred since the (1) First day of January 1901, other than usual trade expenses, viz., household expenses of selves and (3)		663 0 0
			(4) Other Losses and Expenses (if any)—		
			Surplus as per Statement of Affairs (if any)		
Total amount to be accounted for .. (5) £		4,763 0 0	Total amount accounted for .. .. (5) £		4,763 0 0

Each Sheet must be signed and dated by the Debtor, thus—

Signature...

Dated.. 1.................

NOTES.—(1) This date should be 12 months before date of Receiving Order, or such other time as Official Receiver may have fixed.
    (2) This Schedule must show when debts were contracted.
    (3) Add " wife and children " (if any), stating number of latter.
    (4) Here add particulars of other losses or expenses (if any), including Depreciation in the value of stock and effects or
        other property as estimated for realisation, and liabilities (if any), for which no consideration received.
    (5) These figures should agree.

PRIVATE ARRANGEMENTS.

It does not, of course, follow that every insolvent person who calls his creditors together has first had a Receiving Order made against him, and become amenable to the bankruptcy laws and regulations. The accounts submitted to private meetings of creditors do not, therefore, come strictly under the foregoing rules, but very much the same class of information will be required by the creditors attending the meetings, and as a rule, therefore, the bankruptcy forms are followed very closely, the only noticeable difference being that as a rule " Cash Creditors " are shown separately from " Trade Creditors," and full particulars of the Cash Creditors' claims are given, so that it may be readily perceived how much of the claims consist of principal, how much of interest, and to whom the money is owing. It is also usual to append a full list of the Trade Creditors for the information of those interested. On the other hand, no particulars of

---

* *Interest on Capital has been eliminated. Compare with Profit and Loss Account on page 143.*

the assets are given, other than the short particulars appearing upon the summarised Statement of Affairs.

In bankruptcy the filing of a proper Deficiency Account is compulsory, but in the case of private arrangements with creditors it is often not insisted upon. Where given, however, it usually follows the bankruptcy form, save that the sides are transposed so as to follow more closely an ordinary Profit and Loss Account form, in which the losses appear upon the debit and the gains upon the credit side.

TRUSTEES' CASH ACCOUNTS

Trustees in bankruptcy are required to keep and to periodically file detailed accounts of their receipts and payments. These accounts must be filed in duplicate. One copy is in tabular form, and provides columns for all the principal sources of receipts and classes of payments, while the other consists merely of the total columns of the more detailed account. Examples of both these forms are given below.

EXAMPLE:

ACCOUNTS 2.

RECEIPTS.   PAYMENTS.

Date	Particulars	Total	Drawn from Bank	Debts Collected	Property Realised	Receipts from Securities held by Creditors	Other Receipts	Date	Particulars	Voucher Nos. (in red).	Total
		£ s d	£ s d	£ s d	£ s d	£ s d	£ s d				£ s d

Left-hand side.]

PAYMENTS.

Paid into Bank	Costs of Realisation								Allowance to Debtor	Preferential Creditors (Section 40) and Rent	Payments to Redeem Securities	Dividends Paid	Other Payments
	Board of Trade and Court Fees	Law Costs of Petition (including £5 stamp.)	Law Costs after Receiving Order	Commission on Realisation and Distribution		Charges of Auctioneer, Accountant, Shorthand Writer, etc., as taxed	Notices in Gazette and Local Paper	Incidental Expenses, including Possession					
				Board of Trade	Trustee								
£ s d	£ s d	£ s d	£ s d	£ s d	£ s d	£ s d	£ s d	£ s d	£ s d	£ s d	£ s d	£ s d	£ s d

[Right-hand side.

EXAMPLE:　　　　　　　　THE BANKRUPTCY ACT, 1883.

Accounts 2 B.
Copy of Estate Cash }　　*In the*　　　　　*Court of*　　　　　No.　　　of 18
Book for Filing. ｝
RE　　　　　　　　　　　　　　　ESTATE CASH BOOK.

Date	Receipts	Total	Drawn from Bank	Date	Payments	Voucher No.	Total	Paid into Bank
		£　s　d	£　s　d				£　s　d	£　s　d

TRUSTEE'S TRADING ACCOUNT.

In cases where the Trustee is carrying on the business, he is required to file monthly a Trading Account kept in the prescribed form, which differs from the ordinary Trading Account in that it is merely an account of cash receipts and payments relating to the carrying on of the business. Where a separate Trading Account is kept, the monthly totals only need be shown in the general Cash Account, instead of the full details being given twice over.

The following is the form prescribed:—

EXAMPLE:　　　　　　THE BANKRUPTCY ACTS, 1883 & 1890.

In the　　　　　　　　　Court of
In Bankruptcy.　　　　　　　　　　　　　　　No.　　　of 19
　　　　　Re　　　　　　　the Trustee of the Property of the Bankrupt in

account with the Estate.
Dr.　　　　　RECEIPTS.　　　　　　　　　　　PAYMENTS.　　　　　*Cr.*

Date		£　s　d	Date		£　s　d

....................................*Trustee.*
Date....................................19

We have examined this Account with the Vouchers and find the same correct, and we are of opinion the expenditure has been proper.

Dated this　　　　　　　　　　　　day of　　　　　　　　19

.... } *Committee of Inspection.*

.... } [*Or Member of the Committee of Inspection.*]

....

SUMMARISED ACCOUNT OF RECEIPTS AND PAYMENTS.

When the estate has been completely realised and distributed the Trustee can apply for his release; but before doing so he must forward to each creditor who has proved, and to the debtor, a summarised account of all his receipts and payments in the prescribed form. A similar account has to be forwarded to all creditors each time a dividend is declared. When more than one account is sent out, the second and subsequent accounts do not each begin where the preceding one left off, but each is a complete statement of receipts and payments up to date.

The following example shows the form of account employed:—

EXAMPLE :

THE BANKRUPTCY ACTS, 1883 AND 1890.

In the High Court of Justice.

IN BANKRUPTCY.   No.   of 19 .

IN THE MATTER of A. C. and B. C. trading as " The C. Company," lately carrying on business at   Road

and   Street, both in the County of London, as   the said

A. C. residing at   Road,   in the County of London, and the said B. C

residing at   Road,   in the County of London.

(Under Receiving Order, dated the   day of   19).

Dr.   STATEMENT, showing position of Estate at date of declaring Third Dividend.   Cr.

	Estimated to produce per Debtor's Statement	Receipts			Payments
To Total Receipts from date of Receiving Order, viz. :—	£ s d	£ s d			£ s d
Cash in hand	79 10 4	69 10 4	By Board of Trade and Court Fees (including Stamp of £5 on Petition)..		57 10 3
Cash deposited with Solicitor	10 0 0	10 0 0		£ s d	
			Law Costs of Petition	20 0 6	
Stock-in-Trade	1,200 0 0	} 1,071 5 6	Other Law Costs	112 11 6	
Fixtures and Fittings	25 0 0				134 12 0
Provident Association Bond	30 0 0	35 11 8	Trustee's remuneration as fixed by the Committee of Inspection, viz. :—		
Book Debts and Trading Receipts	2,377 0 0	1,625 8 4		£ s d	
Surplus from Securities	87 7 0	20 16 5	5 per cent. on £2,361 12s. 1d. Assets realised ..	118 1 7	
Receipts per Trading Account			2½ per cent. on £1,749 8s. 1d. Assets distributed in Dividend	43 14 8	
Other Receipts	..	5 0 0			161 16 3
			Special Manager's charges		
			Person appointed to assist Debtor under sec. 70 of Bankruptcy Act, 1883		7 7 0
Total	£ 3,808 17 4	2,837 12 3	Auctioneer's charges as taxed		139 5 4
			Other charges		87 10 11
			Costs of possession..		
Less :			Cost of notices in Gazette and local papers ..		3 9 6
Deposit returned to Petitioner			Incidental outlay		64 7 9
Payments to Redeem Securities			Total cost of realisation		655 19 0
Costs of Execution			Allowance to Debtor		34 13 0
Payments per Trading Account	..	223 3 7	Creditors, viz. :—	£ s d	
			Preferential	110 19 11	
			Unsecured First Dividend of 4/- in the £ on £6,361 9s. 8d.	1,272 5 10	
			2nd Dividend of 1/- in the £	318 1 6	
			3rd Dividend now declared of 6d. in the £ ..	159 0 9	
			The Debtor's estimate of amount expected to rank for dividend was £5,916 13s. 1d.		
					1860 8 0
			Balance		63 8 8
Net realisations	£ 2,614 8 8				£ 2,614 8 8

By s. 72 (2) of the Bankruptcy Act, 1883, it is provided that " if one-fourth in number or value of Creditors dissent from the resolution, or the bankrupt satisfies the Board of Trade that the remuneration is unnecessarily large, the Board of Trade shall fix the amount of the remuneration."

Assets not yet realised estimated to produce £50.

The outstanding Assets consist of Book Debts, owing under hiring Agreements, and are of very doubtful character, and the estimate of £50 must be regarded as approximate only. The debts are payable by small instalments. The balance is reserved to provide the dividends (already declared), upon a claim which is expected to rank, but is not yet proved.

Creditors can obtain any further information by inquiry at the office of the Trustee.

Dated this   day of   19 .

          X. Z., *Trustee,*

             999 Cheapside, London, E.C.

PRIVATE ARRANGEMENTS.

In private arrangements, also, it is usual, every time a dividend is declared, to forward to each creditor an account of receipts and payments upon the same lines as that prescribed in bankruptcy, although in practice the form is frequently departed from in matters of detail.

Section 25, Sub-section 2 (*b*), of the Bankruptcy Act, 1890, provides that every trustee under a private arrangement shall, within thirty days from the 1st January in each year, transmit to the Board of Trade an account of his receipts and payments as such Trustee. The prescribed forms are given below; the accounts must be verified by affidavit. There is no provision for the payment over by the Trustee of unclaimed dividends in the case of private arrangements.

EXAMPLE:

Trustee's Account
of Receipts and Payments.

THE BANKRUPTCY ACT, 1890.   No.......

IN THE MATTER OF A DEED OF ARRANGEMENT.

| *Between* | | | | | *and his Creditors.* | | |

Dated the   day of   19 .   Registered the   day of   19

Trustee.

ACCOUNT OF RECEIPTS AND PAYMENTS.

Pursuant to Section 25 of the Bankruptcy Act, 1890.

Receipts				Payments			
Date	Of whom Received	Nature of Receipt	Amount	Date	To whom Paid	Nature of Payment	Amount
			£ s d				£ s d

*Here set out particulars of any outstanding estate, and the estimated value thereof.

NOTE.—The outstanding Estate consists of*

EXAMPLE:

Trustee's Trading
Account.

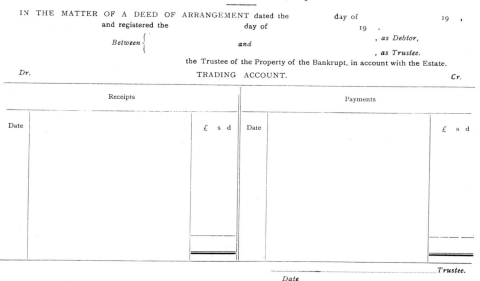

THE BANKRUPTCY ACT, 1890.

IN THE MATTER OF A DEED OF ARRANGEMENT dated the   day of   19   ,
and registered the   day of   19   .

Between {   *and*   , *as Debtor,*
                                                                                       , *as Trustee.*

the Trustee of the Property of the Bankrupt, in account with the Estate.

Dr.   TRADING ACCOUNT.   *Cr.*

Date	Receipts	£ s d	Date	Payments	£ s d

.... *Trustee.*
Date ....

*To be inserted if the Accounts have been audited by a Committee of Inspection.   *We have examined this Account with the Vouchers, and find the same correct, and we are of opinion the Expenditure has been proper.

Dated this   day of   19   .

....
Committee of Inspection [or, *Member of the Committee of Inspection*].

BANKRUPTCY OF FIRMS.

When a Receiving Order is made against a firm the estates of all the partners pass into bankruptcy, and the Trustee appointed of the joint estate becomes also the Trustee of each of the separate estates. These various estates must be all administered separately, but any surplus that there may be upon any of the separate estates must be handed over to the joint estate and distributed among the joint creditors until such time as they have received 20s. in the £, together with interest at 4 per cent. from the date of the Receiving Order. After this has been done, whatever surplus may remain upon any separate estate is handed back to that particular debtor. If, on the other hand, there should happen to be a surplus on the joint estate, it is divisible among the separate estates in proportion to the respective interests of the partners as though no Receiving Order had been made; but, of course, the surplus is handed over to the separate estates and applied towards the payment of the separate liabilities, so that no one of the debtors can receive back anything out of either joint or separate estate until the whole of the joint creditors and the whole of the creditors of his separate estate have been paid in full with interest. Partners are not, however, liable for the payment in full of the separate debts of their co-partners.

The forms of account are precisely the same as those already indicated. It should be mentioned, however, that where any separate estate does not produce sufficient to cover costs, it is competent for the Trustee, with the consent of the Committee of Inspection of the joint estate, to pay these costs out of the joint estate, so that to this extent one partner may be indirectly made liable for the costs of administering the estate of a co-partner.

The following example will serve to clearly show the proper treatment when assets belonging to separate estates have been pledged as security for the firm's debts : —

PROBLEM.—(a) From the following particulars construct the respective Balance Sheets of the firm of I., C. & A., and of the several partners :—

PARTICULARS *re* I., C. & A.

3rd April 1897.

	£	s	d
Trade Creditors, Joint Estate, unsecured	31,280	0	0
Cash Creditors, Joint Estate, unsecured	6,642	0	0
Cash Creditors, Joint Estate, collaterally partly secured by Policies of Assurance	9,015	0	0
On the life of I., worth	1,615	0	0
On the life of C., worth	738	0	0
Cash Creditors, Joint Estate, fully secured	10,435	0	0
They holding Securities belonging to the Firm, worth	14,395	0	0
Liabilities on Bills discounted, considered good	1,340	0	0
Preferential Creditors of Joint Estate	2,128	0	0
Tradesmen's Claims on Separate Estate of I.	697	0	0
Cash Creditors on Separate Estate of I.	2,578	0	0
They holding as security Freehold Property of his, worth ...	3,000	0	0
Tradesmen's Claims on Separate Estate of C.	119	0	0
Tradesmen's Claims on Separate Estate of A.	190	0	0
Cash Creditors of A., unsecured	510	0	0
Cash at Bank at credit of Joint Estate	1,050	0	0
Cash in hand do.	843	0	0
Debtors do.	2,975	0	0
Stock do.	30,155	0	0
Fixtures and Furniture do.	1,400	0	0
Household Furniture, Separate Estate of I.	1,000	0	0
Do. do. C.	1,000	0	0
Do. do. A.	500	0	0
Reversionary Interest under Will of John Smith, deceased, Separate Estate of A., worth	200	0	0
I. had overdrawn his Account with the Firm by...	4,500	0	0
C. „ „ „	3,000	0	0
A. „ „ „	1,182	0	0

(b) Show (in condensed form) the Statements of Affairs of the firm and the three separate partners.

(A).

I., C. & A.'s BALANCE SHEET, 3rd April 1897.

Liabilities.	£ s d	£ s d	Assets.	£ s d	£ s d
Trade Creditors	..	31,280 0 0	Cash at Bank	..	1,050 0 0
Cash Creditors	..	6,642 0 0	Cash in hand	..	843 0 0
Ditto (partly secured) ..	9,015 0 0		Debtors	..	2,975 0 0
Estimated value of			Stock	..	30,155 0 0
securities	2,353 0 0		Fixtures and Furniture	..	1,400 0 0
		6,662 0 0	Surplus from Securities (as per		
Ditto (fully secured) ..	10,435 0 0		contra)	..	3,960 0 0
Estimated value of			Partners' Accounts overdrawn,		
securities	14,395 0 0		viz. :—		
			I.	2,885 0 0	
Surplus (as per			C.	2,262 0 0	
contra) ..	3,960 0 0		A.	1,182 0 0	
					6,329 0 0
Liabilities on Bills discounted ..	1,340 0 0				
Estimated to rank for	..	—			
Preferential Creditors	..	2,128 0 0			
		£46,712 0 0			£46,712 0 0

I.'s BALANCE SHEET, 3rd April 1897.

Liabilities.	£ s d	£ s d	Assets.	£ s d	£ s d
Tradesmen's Claims	..	697 0 0	Household Furniture	..	1,000 0 0
Cash Creditors (fully secured) ..	2,578 0 0		Surplus from Securities	..	422 0 0
Estimated value of			Life Policy (deposited with creditors		
securities	3,000 0 0		of joint estate)	1,615 0 0	
Surplus (as per					
contra) ..	422 0 0		Deficiency	..	2,160 0 0
Amount due to firm of I., C. & A. ..	..	2,885 0 0			
		£3,582 0 0			£3,582 0 0

C.'s BALANCE SHEET, 3rd April 1897.

Liabilities.	£ s d	£ s d	Assets.	£ s d	£ s d
Tradesmen's Claims	..	119 0 0	Household Furniture	..	1,000 0 0
Amount due to firm of I., C. & A. ..	..	2,262 0 0	Life Policy (deposited with creditors		
			of joint estate)	738 0 0	
			Deficiency	..	1,381 0 0
		£2,381 0 0			£2,381 0 0

A.'s BALANCE SHEET, 3rd April 1897.

Liabilities.	£ s d	£ s d	Assets.	£ s d	£ s d
Tradesmen's Claims	..	190 0 0	Household Furniture	..	500 0 0
Cash Creditors	..	510 0 0	Reversionary Interest under Will of		
Amount due to firm of I., C. & A. ..	..	1,182 0 0	John Smith (decd.)	..	200 0 0
			Deficiency	..	1,182 0 0
		£1,882 0 0			£1,882 0 0

(B).

STATEMENT OF AFFAIRS.

Re I., C. & A.

Gross Liabilities	LIABILITIES (as stated and estimated by debtor)	Expected to rank	ASSETS (as stated and estimated by debtor)	Estimated to produce
£ s d		£ s d	Property, as per list (H), viz.:—	£ s d
37,922 0 0	Unsecured Creditors, as per list (A)	37,922 0 0	(a) Cash at Bankers	1,050 0 0
10,435 0 0	Creditors fully secured, as per list £ s d		(b) Cash in hand	843 0 0
	(B) 10,435 0 0		(d) Stock-in-trade (cost £) ..	30,155 0 0
	Estimated value of Securities .. 14,395 0 0		(e) Machinery	
			(f) Trade fixtures, fittings, utensils, &c. ..	1,400 0 0
	Surplus 3,960 0 0		(k) Other property, viz.:—	
	Less amount thereof carried to		Estimated surplus from separate	
	Sheet (C)		Estate of I. .. .. :. ..	725 0 0
			Ditto C.	881 0 0
	Balance thereof to contra .. £3,960 0 0			
9,015 0 0	Creditors partly secured, as per list (C) 9,015 0 0		Total as per list (H)	35,054 0 0
	Less estimated value of Securities 2,353 0 0	6,662 0 0	Book Debts, as per list (I), viz.:—	
			Good	2,975 0 0
	Liabilities on Bills discounted, other than debtors' own acceptances for value, as per list (D), viz.:— £ s d		Surplus from Securities in the hands of Creditors fully secured (per contra)	3,960 0 0
	On Accommodation Bills as drawer, acceptor, or indorser			41,989 0 0
1,340 0 0	On other Bills, as drawer or indorser 1,340 0 0		Deduct Creditors for distrainable Rent, and for preferential Rates, Taxes, Wages, Sheriff's charges, &c. (per contra)..	2,128 0 0
	£1,340 0 0			39,861 0 0
	Of which it is expected will rank against the Estate for dividend		Deficiency explained in Statement (K)	4,723 0 0
	Creditors for Rates, Taxes, Wages, £ s d &c., payable in full, as per list			
2,128 0 0	(G) 2,128 0 0			
	Deducted contra £2,128 0 0			
£60,840 0 0		£44,584 0 0		£44,584 0 0

STATEMENT OF AFFAIRS.

Re I.

Gross Liabilities	LIABILITIES.. (as stated and estimated by debtor)	Expected to rank	ASSETS (as stated and estimated by debtor)	Estimated to produce
£ s d		£ s d		£ s d
697 0 0	Unsecured Creditors as per list (A)	697 0 0	Property as per list (H), viz.:—	1,000 0 0
	Creditors fully secured, as per list £ s d		(i) Furniture	
2,578 0 0	(B) 2,578 0 0			
	Estimated value of Securities .. 3,000 0 0			
	Surplus 422 0 0		Total as per list (H)	1,000 0 0
	Less amount thereof carried to sheet (C)..		Surplus from Securities in the hands of Creditors fully secured (per contra)	422 0 0
	Balance thereof to contra .. £422 0 0			
	Surplus (to Joint Estate)	725 0 0		
£3,275 0 0		£1,422 0 0		£1,422 0 0

STATEMENT OF AFFAIRS.

Re C.

Gross Liabilities	LIABILITIES (as stated and estimated by debtor)	Expected to rank	ASSETS (as stated and estimated by debtor)	Estimated to produce
£ s d 119 0 0	Unsecured Creditors as per list (A) .. .. Surplus (to Joint Estate)	£ s d 119 0 0 881 0 0	Property, as per list (H), viz. :— (i) Furniture	£ s d 1,000 0 0
£119 0 0		£1,000 0 0	Total as per list (H)	£1,000 0 0

STATEMENT OF AFFAIRS.

Re A.

Gross Liabilities	LIABILITIES (as stated and estimated by debtor)	Expected to rank	ASSETS (as stated and estimated by debtor)	Estimated to produce
£ s d 700 0 0	Unsecured Creditors as per list (A)	£ s d 700 0 0	Property, as per list (H), viz. :— (i) Furniture .. .. (k) Other property, viz. :— Reversionary Interest under Will of John Smith (decd.)	£ s d 500 0 0 200 0 0
£700 0 0		£700 0 0	Total as per list (H)	£700 0 0

COMPOSITIONS.

When a composition is accepted, and the debtors continue trading, a " paper " profit is made by them upon carrying through the arrangement. In partnership cases the rights of the partners *inter se* must, of course, be considered, as shown in the following

PROBLEM.—M. & N. being in difficulties, effect an arrangement with their creditors under which the estate is to vest in a Trustee to be realised ; 15s. in the £ paid to the creditors, and the balance (if any) returned to the debtors after payment of costs. The creditors' claims amounted to £1,700. M.'s capital was £500 in credit, N.'s £250 overdrawn. M. handed a further £100 to the Trustee out of his private estate to further secure the payment of the composition. The partnership assets were :—Cash, £50 ; Debtors, £750 (produced £700) ; Machinery, Plant, and Furniture, £800 (realised £400) ; and Stock £350 (sold for £150). Raise the following Accounts :—(1) Firm's Balance Sheet ; (2) Trustee's Cash Account (the whole costs were £75) ; (3) Realisation Account ; (4) Creditor's Account ; (5) Profit and Loss Account ; (6) M.'s Capital Account ; and (7) N.'s Capital Account.

(1)

BALANCE SHEET.

Liabilities.	£ s d	£ s d	Assets.	£ s d
Capital Accounts :—			Machinery, Plant, &c.	800 0 0
M. in credit	500 0 0		Stock-in-Trade	350 0 0
N. overdrawn	250 0 0		Debtors	750 0 0
		250 0 0	Cash	50 0 0
Creditors		1,700 0 0		
		1,950 0 0		£1,950 0 0

(2)
Dr.   TRUSTEE'S CASH ACCOUNT.   Cr.

Receipts.	£	s	d	Payments.	£	s	d
To Cash	50	0	0	By Costs	75	0	0
„ Book Debts	700	0	0	„ Creditors, composition of 15s. in the £	1,275	0	0
„ Machinery, Plant, &c.	400	0	0	„ Balance	50	0	0
„ Stock-in-Trade	150	0	0				
„ Amount received from M.	100	0	0				
	£1,400	0	0		£1,400	0	0
To Balance	£50	0	0				

(3)
Dr.   REALISATION ACCOUNT.   Cr.

	£	s	d		£	s	d
To Sundry Assets	1,950	0	0	By Cash	1,300	0	0
				„ Profit and Loss Account	650	0	0
	£1,950	0	0		£1,950	0	0

(4)
Dr.   CREDITORS' ACCOUNT.   Cr.

	£	s	d		£	s	d
To Cash	1,275	0	0	By Balance	1,700	0	0
„ Profit and Loss Account	425	0	0				
	£1,700	0	0		£1,700	0	0

(5)
Dr.   PROFIT AND LOSS ACCOUNT.   Cr.

	£	s	d					£	s	d
To Realisation Account	650	0	0	By Creditors' Account				425	0	0
„ Expenses	75	0	0	„ Balance, viz. :—						
				M.	£150	0	0			
				N.	150	0	0			
								300	0	0
	£725	0	0					£725	0	0

(6)
Dr.   M.—CAPITAL ACCOUNT.   Cr.

	£	s	d		£	s	d
To Profit and Loss Account	150	0	0	By Balance	500	0	0
„ Balance down	450	0	0	„ Cash Paid to Trustee	100	0	0
	£600	0	0		£600	0	0
				By Balance down	£450	0	0

(7)
Dr.   N.—CAPITAL ACCOUNT.   Cr.

	£	s	d		£	s	d
To Balance	250	0	0	By Balance down	400	0	0
„ Profit and Loss Account	150	0	0				
	£400	0	0		£400	0	0
To Balance down	£400	0	0				

CHAPTER XV.

LIQUIDATION ACCOUNTS.

IN many respects the accounts in Company Liquidations follow the lines already laid down by the chapter on Bankruptcy and Insolvency Accounts. The statutory provisions, however, modify these to some extent, while the right of shareholders *inter se*—particularly where there is a surplus—claim special consideration.

DIFFERENT CLASSES OF LIQUIDATION.

There are three modes of liquidation applicable to companies. (1) Voluntary liquidation. (2) Voluntary liquidation under the supervision of the Court. (3) Compulsory liquidation.

VOLUNTARY LIQUIDATION.

With regard to the first, it need only be said that the winding up is conducted by a liquidator appointed by the shareholders, and that the procedure is one involving a minimum amount of formalities. There is no statutory necessity for a Statement of Affairs and Deficiency Account, or—to speak more accurately—the late officers of the Company cannot be called upon to prepare one. When, therefore, it is thought desirable to compile such a Statement for the information of creditors, the work devolves upon the liquidator.

It is usual, but not compulsory, for the liquidator every time he declares a dividend to forward therewith an account of his receipts and payments since the commencement of the liquidation. Such account should be as nearly as possible upon the same lines as similar accounts in Bankruptcy.

If the winding-up continues for more than one year, the liquidator is required by Section 139 of the Companies Act, 1862, to summon a General Meeting of the Company at the end of the first year and at the end of each succeeding year, or as soon thereafter as may be convenient, and to lay before such meeting an account showing his acts and dealings, and the manner in which the winding-up has been conducted. The account referred to in this section is an ordinary Account of Receipts and Payments, no special form being provided.

When the winding-up of the Company has been completed, the liquidator is required to summon a final meeting of the Company, and to submit thereto his final account. Again, no special form is prescribed, and it should therefore be upon the same lines as the preceding, save, of course, that as it is a final account it should show the ultimate disposal of all monies that have been received. All vouchers should be produced for inspection. The view is held in some quarters that the shareholders at this meeting vote the liquidator's remuneration, and that consequently this item cannot be included in the final accounts. This is a mistake. The shareholders are not required to vote the liquidator's remuneration. It merely rests with them to approve the account; and if they do so, the approval of the account as a whole constitutes of course an approval of every item contained therein. If they disapprove, the practical effect is that the final meeting has not been " held," and consequently the Company cannot be dissolved under the provisions of

Section 143 of the Companies Act, 1862. The meeting can, however, be adjourned from time to time, to admit of the accounts being amended to the satisfaction of the contributories. Beyond this purely negative power, the only course open to the contributories (or any one of them) is to apply to the Court under Section 138 of the Companies Act, 1862, when the Court will make whatever order it thinks just. Under Section 25 of the Companies Act, 1900, any creditor has a like power to apply to the Court, should he be dissatisfied with the remuneration paid to the liquidator, or with any other matter arising out of the liquidation.

The following is an example of a liquidator's final account:—

PROBLEM.—The Welsh Mining Company, Lim., goes into voluntary liquidation on the 30th June 1901 with Trade liabilities £1,200, Cash liabilities £1,050, Rent owing £75, Wages and Rates £56. Debentures £2,000. On the debentures six months' interest at 6 per cent. per annum was due on the date of the winding-up resolution. After a lapse of six months the leasehold property, &c., are sold for £3,600, and some small rents have come in amounting to £27 10s., whilst a minimum rent of leasehold at £150 per annum has been growing due since the date of winding-up. Make up the Liquidator's final account, allowing £45 3s. 6d. for Law Costs and Outlays, and for Liquidator's remuneration 3 per cent. on realisation, and 2 per cent. on distribution to unsecured creditors, and show the dividend payable.

THE WELSH MINING COMPANY, LIM. (in Liquidation).

ACCOUNT OF LIQUIDATOR'S RECEIPTS AND PAYMENTS

Dr.   To Date of Final Meeting.....................................1902.   Cr.

	£ s d	£ s d		£ s d	£ s d
To Proceeds of Realisation of Property..	3,600 0 0		By Law Costs and Outlays ..		45 3 6
„ Rents Received	27 10 0		„ Liquidator's Remuneration, viz.:—	..	
		3,627 10 0	3 % on £3,627 10s. realised ..	108 16 6	
			2 % on £1,125 distributed ..	22 10 0	
					131 6 6
(NOTE:—(1) *The rent, although*			Total costs of Winding-up ..	..	176 10 0
not strictly preferential, would			„ Preferential and Secured Creditors:—		
have to be paid in full before			Wages and Rates	56 0 0	
the property could be transferred			Rent (one year)..	150 0 0	
to a purchaser unencumbered.			Debentures	2,000 0 0	
(2) *Interest on debentures would*			Debenture Interest (one year) ..	120 0 0	
run to date of repayment).					2,326 0 0
			„ Unsecured Creditors:—		
			First and final Dividend of 10s. in		
			the £ upon £2,250	..	1,125 0 0
		£3,627 10 0			£3,627 10 0

LIQUIDATION UNDER SUPERVISION.

So far as the accounts are concerned, the provisions here are in all respects the same as in the case of a voluntary liquidation conducted without the supervision of the Court, save that the liquidator's remuneration is fixed by the Court, and subject, of course, to any special directions that the Court may give with regard to the rendering of accounts.

COMPULSORY LIQUIDATIONS.

The procedure when the Court makes an order for a Company to be wound up is entirely different from the preceding. In the first place, instead of the liquidator being appointed by the shareholders, the Official Receiver becomes *ipso facto* provisional liquidator immediately upon the passing of the order for the winding-up. It is the duty of the directors to submit to this official a Statement of Affairs, prepared in the prescribed form, which follows very closely the lines prescribed for Statements of Affairs in Bankruptcy. A printed copy of this statement (*i.e.*, of the "front sheet" and the Deficiency Account) is forwarded by the Official Receiver to every shareholder and every creditor, and it is of interest to note that the practice is to include in that form only those items in the prescribed form against which figures actually appear. That is to say, no "blank" items are included. The following example shows clearly the prescribed form, and the method of filling it up; but for the sake of completeness, every item has been included, even where no such assets or liabilities arise in the example given.

PROBLEM.—From the following prepare a Statement of Affairs and Deficiency Account of A., B. & Co., Lim., as on 31st December 1901, under the Companies (Winding-up) Act, 1890. The capital consists of 7 Founders' Shares of £10 each, £5 per Share called up and paid and 20,000 Ordinary Shares of £1 each, all called up :—

	£.	£
Debtors (Good)	8,175	
„ (Doubtful) estimated to produce 50 per cent.	3,160	
„ (Bad)	1,874	
		13,209
Buildings, Engines, &c., valued at		10,672
Unsecured Creditors		10,267
Secured Creditor, holding Mortgage of Buildings, &c.		7,175
Partly secured Creditors (security £1,500) ...		4,203
Liabilities on Bills Discounted (£280 to rank) ...		1,700
Bills Receivable—£350 valued at		280
Managing Director's Salary, owing for five months ...		250
Weekly Wages unpaid		180
Calls on Ordinary Shares unpaid (estimated to produce £50)...		85
Uncalled Capital—seven £10 Shares, £5 unpaid ...		35
Bank Account overdrawn		19
Cash in hand		7

M

In the High Court of Justice.

COMPANIES (WINDING-UP).

IN THE MATTER OF THE COMPANIES ACTS, 1862 to 1898.

AND

* Insert full name of Company.

IN THE MATTER OF * A. B. & COMPANY, LIMITED.

STATEMENT OF AFFAIRS on the 31st day of December 1901, the date of the Winding-up Order.

(I.) AS REGARDS CREDITORS.

Gross Liabilities	Liabilities	Expected to Rank	Assets	Estimated to Produce
£ s d	Debts and Liabilities, viz. :—	£ s d	(a) Property, as per list " H," viz. :—	£ s d
10,536 0 0	(a) Unsecured Creditors, as per (State number) list " A "	10,536 0 0	(a) Cash at Bankers .. .. (b) Cash in Hand	7 0 0
7,175 0 0	(b) Creditors fully secured £ s d (not including Debenture Holders) as per list " B " 7,175 0 0 Estimated value of Securities 10,672 0 0		(c) Stock-in-Trade .. .. .. (Estimated Cost, £ : :) (d) Machinery .. .. (e) Trade Fixtures, Fittings, Utensils, &c. .. (f) Investments in Shares, &c. .. (g) Loans on Mortgage .. .. .. (h) Other Property, viz. :—	
	Estimated surplus £ 3,497 0 0 Carried to list " C " £			7 0 0
	Balance to contra (d) £ 3,497 0 0		(b) Book Debts, as per list " I," viz. :— Good	8,175 0 0
4,203 0 0	(c) Creditors partly secured, as per list " C " .. .. 4,203 0 0 Less estimated value of Securities 1,500 0 0		£ s d Doubtful.. .. .. 3,160 0 0 Bad 1,874 0 0	
	Estimated to rank for Dividend ..	2,703 0 0	£5,034 0 0	
	(d) Liabilities on Bills Discounted £ s d other than the Company's own acceptances for value, as per list " D " .. .. 1,700 0 0 Of which it is expected will rank for Dividend	280 0 0	Estimated to produce .. .. (c) Bills of Exchange or other similar £ s d securities on hand, as per list " J ".. 350 0 0 Estimated to produce	1,580 0 0
1,700 0 0	(e) Other Liabilities, as per list £ s d " E " .. .. .. Of which it is expected will rank against the Assets for Dividend ..		(d) Surplus from Securities in the hands of Creditors fully secured (per contra) (b) .. .. (e) Unpaid Calls. as per list " K " .. £85 0 0	280 0 0 3,497 0 0
	(f) Loans on Debenture Bonds, £ s d as per list " F " deducted contra..		Estimated to produce .. .. Estimated Total Assets .. .. Deduct Loans on Debenture Bonds secured on the Assets of the Company as per contra (f)	50 0 0 13,589 0 0
180 0 0	(g) Preferential Creditors for Rates, Taxes, Wages, &c., as per list " G " deducted contra.. .. .. .. 180 0 0		Estimated Net Assets .. .. .. Deduct Preferential Creditors, as per contra (g)	13,589 0 0 180 0 0
	Estimated Surplus (if any) after meeting Liabilities of Company, subject to cost of Liquidation	£13,519 0 0	Estimated Amount available to meet Unsecured Creditors subject to cost of Liquidation .. Estimated Deficiency of Assets to meet Liabilities of the Company, subject to cost of Liquidation ..	13,409 0 0 110 0 0
£23,794 0 0		£13,519 0 0		£13,519 0 0

The Nominal Amount of Unpaid Capital liable to be called up to meet the above Deficiency is £35.

(II.) AS REGARDS CONTRIBUTORIES.

	£ s d	£ s d		£ s d
Capital Issued and Allotted, viz. :— 7 Founders' Shares of £10 per Share .. (7 Shareholders).			Estimated Surplus as above (if any) subject to costs of Liquidation	
Amount called up at £5 per Share, as per list " L "	35 0 0			
20,000 Ordinary Shares of £1 per Share .. (420 Shareholders).				
Amount called up at £1 per Share, as per list " M "	20,000 0 0			
......Preference Shares of £.... per Share (....Shareholders).				
Amount called up at £......per Share, as per list " N "..				
(a) Add par- (a) ticulars of any other capital.	£20,035 0 0			
Less Unpaid Calls estimated to be irre- coverable	35 0 0			
Add Deficiency to meet Liabilities as above		20,000 0 0 110 0 0	Total Deficiency as explained in Statement " O "	20,110 0 0
		£20,110 0 0		£20,110 0 0

I,...of...make oath and say that the foregoing Statement and the several Lists hereunto annexed marked "A," "B," "C," "D," "E," "F," "G," "H," "I," "J," "K," "L," "M," "N," and "O (1), O (2)," are, to the best of my knowledge and belief, a full, true, and complete statement of the affairs of the above-named Company, on the.................day of.................................1   , the date of the winding-up order.

Sworn at...

in the County of.....................................

this.............day of......................1

Before me.......................................

....

Signature ....

LIST "A."—UNSECURED CREDITORS.

The Names to be arranged in alphabetical order and numbered consecutively, Creditors for £10 and upwards being placed first.

NOTES.—1. When there is a contra account against the Creditor, less than the amount of his claim against the Company, the amount of the Creditor's claim and the amount of the contra account should be shown in the third column, and the Balance only be inserted under the heading "Amount of Debt," thus:—

$$£ \quad s \quad d$$

Total amount of Claim .. ..
Less: Contra Account .. ..
No such set-off should be included in List "I."

2. The particulars of any Bills of Exchange and Promissory Notes held by a Creditor should be inserted immediately below the name and address of such Creditor.

3. The names of any Creditors who are also Contributories, or alleged to be Contributories, of the Company must be shown separately, and described as such at the end of the List.

No.	Name	Address and Occupation	Amount of Debt	Date when Contracted		Consideration
				Month	Year	
			£ s d			

LIST "B."—CREDITORS FULLY SECURED (NOT INCLUDING DEBENTURE HOLDERS).

No.	Name of Creditor	Address and Occupation	Amount of Debt	Date when Contracted		Consideration	Particulars of Security	Date when given	Estimated Value of Security	Estimated Surplus from Security
				Month	Year					
			£ s d						£ s d	£ s d

LIST "C."—CREDITORS PARTLY SECURED.

(State whether also Contributories of the Company.)

No.	Name of Creditor	Address and Occupation	Amount of Debt	Date when Contracted		Consideration	Particulars of Security	Month and Year when given	Estimated Value of Security	Balance of Debt Unsecured
				Month	Year					
			£ s d						£ s d	£ s d

M 2

List "D."—LIABILITIES OF COMPANY ON BILLS DISCOUNTED OTHER THAN THEIR OWN ACCEPTANCES FOR VALUE.

No.	Acceptor's Name, Address, and Occupation	Whether liable as Drawer or Indorser	Date when due	Amount	Holder's Name, Address, and Occupation (if known)	Amount expected to rank for Dividend
				£ s d		£ s d

List "E."—OTHER LIABILITIES.

Full particulars of all Liabilities not otherwise Scheduled to be given here.

No.	Name of Creditor or Claimant	Address and Occupation	Amount of Liability or Claim	Date when Liability incurred		Nature of Liability	Consideration	Amount expected to rank against Assets for Dividend
				Month	Year			
			£ s d					£ s d

List "F."—LIST OF DEBENTURE-HOLDERS.

The Names to be arranged in alphabetical order and numbered consecutively.
SEPARATE LISTS must be furnished of holders of each issue of Debentures, should more than one issue have been made.

No.	Name of Holder	Address	Amount	Description of Assets over which Security extends
			£ s d	

List "G."—PREFERENTIAL CREDITORS FOR RATES, TAXES, SALARIES, AND WAGES.

No.	Name of Creditor	Address and Occupation	Nature of Claim	Period during which Claim accrued due	Date when due	Amount of Claim	Amount payable in full	Difference ranking for Dividend
						£ s d	£ s d	£ s d

List " H."—PROPERTY.

Full particulars of every description of property not included in any other lists are to be set forth in this list.

Full Statement and Nature of Property	Estimated Cost	Estimated to Produce
	£ s d	£ s d
(a) Cash at Bankers		
(b) Cash in hand		
(c) Stock in Trade, at		
(d) Machinery, at		
(e) Trade Fixtures, Fittings, Office Furniture, Untensils, &c.		
[State particulars] (f) Investments in Stocks or Shares, &c.		
[State particulars] (g) Loans for which Mortgage or other security held		
(h) Other Property, viz. :—		

List " I."—DEBTS DUE TO THE COMPANY.

The names to be arranged in alphabetical order, and numbered consecutively.

NOTE.—If any Debtor to the Company is also a Creditor, but for a less amount than his indebtedness, the gross amount due to the Company and the amount of the Contra Account should be shown on the third column, and the balance only be inserted under the heading " Amount of Debt," thus :—

Due to Company   ..   ..   £   s   d
Less : Contra Account   ..   ..
No such claim should be included in Sheet "A."

No.	Name of Debtor	Residence and Occupation	Amount of Debt			Folio of Ledger or other book where particulars to be found	When Contracted		Estimated to Produce	Particulars of any Securities held for Debt
			Good	Doubtful	Bad		Month	Year		
			£ s d	£ s d	£ s d				£ s d	

List " J."—BILLS OF EXCHANGE, PROMISSORY NOTES, &c., ON HAND AVAILABLE AS ASSETS.

No.	Name of Acceptor of Bill or Note	Address, &c.	Amount of Bill or Note	Date when due	Estimated to Produce	Particulars of any Property held as Security for Payment of Bill or Note
			£ s d		£ s d	

List " K."—UNPAID CALLS.

Con-secutive No.	No. in Share Register	Name of Shareholder	Address and Occupation	No. of Shares held	Amount of Call per Share unpaid	Total Amount due	Estimated to realise
					£ s d	£ s d	£ s d

List " L."—LIST OF FOUNDERS' SHARES.

Con-secutive No.	Register No.	Name of Shareholder	Address	Nominal Amount of Share	No. of Shares held	Amount per Share called up	Total Amount called up
						£ s d	£ s d

List " M."—LIST OF ORDINARY SHARES.

No.	Register No.	Name of Shareholder	Address	Nominal Amount of Share	No. of Shares held	Amount per Share called up	Total Amount called up
						£ s d	£ s d

List " N."—LIST OF PREFERENCE SHARES.

Con-secutive No.	Register No.	Name of Shareholder	Address	Nominal Amount of Share	No. of Shares held	Amount per Share called up	Total Amount called up
						£ s d	£ s d

LIST "O. (1)." DEFICIENCY ACCOUNT.

(1) Deficiency Account where Winding-up Order made WITHIN THREE YEARS OF formation of Company.

	£ s d		£ s d	£ s d
I. Gross Profit (if any) arising from carrying on business from date of formation of Company to date of Winding-up Order	1,267 0 0	I. Expenses of carrying on business from date of formation of Company to date of Winding-up Order, viz.:—		
			£ s d	
		Salaries and Wages	2,500 0 0	
		Rent, Rates, and Taxes.. ..	1,000 0 0	
		Miscellaneous Trade Expenses	288 0 0	
		Depreciation written off in Company's Books	10,000 0 0	
		Interest on Loans	..	13,738 0 0
II Deficiency as per Statement of Affairs..	20,110 0 0	II. Bad Debts (if any) as per List "I." (1)		3,804 0 0
		III. Directors' Fees from date of formation of Company to date of Winding-up Order		1,250 0 0
		IV. Dividends paid (if any) from date of formation of Company to date of Winding-up Order ..		2,500 0 0
		V. Losses on investments realised from date of formation of Company to date of Winding-up Order (exclusive of depreciation written off as above), viz. (4)		
		VI. Depreciation on Property not written off in Company's Books, viz. (4)		
		VII. Other Losses and Expenses (if any) (2) from date of formation of Company to date of Winding-up Order, viz. (4)		
		VIII. Unpaid calls .. as per List "K"	£ s d 85 0 0	
		Less: Amount taken credit for in front sheet as estimated to be realised therefrom } do.	50 0 0	
		Balance estimated as irrecoverab		35 0 0
Total amount to be accounted for .. (3)	£21,377 0 0	Total amount accounted f .. .. (3)		£21,377 0 0

Each Sheet must be signed and dated thus :—

NOTES.—(1) This list must show when debts were contracted.
(2) Here add particulars of other losses or expenses (if any) and liabilities (if any) for which no consideration received.
(3) These figures should agree.
(4) Where particulars are numerous they should be inserted in a separate Schedule.

Signature.....................................

Dated............................●●●●●●190

LIST " O. (2)." DEFICIENCY ACCOUNT.

(2) Deficiency Account where Winding-up Order made MORE THAN THREE YEARS AFTER formation of Company.

	£ s d		£ s d
I. Excess of Assets over Capital and Liabilities on the (1) day of 18 (if any) as per Company's Balance Sheet		I. Excess of Capital and Liabilities over Assets on the (1) day of 18 (if any), as per Company's Balance Sheet ..	
		II. Expenses of carrying on business from the (1) day of 18 viz. :—	
		£ s d	
II. Gross profit (if any) ari ing from carrying on business from the (1) day of 18 ..		Salaries and Wages .. .. Rent, Rates, and Taxes .. .. Miscellaneous Trade Expenses.. Depreciation written off in Company's Books .. .. .. Interest on Loans	
		III. Bad Debts (if any) as per List "I." (2).. ..	
III. Deficiency as per Statement of Affairs		IV. Directors' Fees from the (1) day of 18	
		V. Dividends paid (if any) since the (1) day of 18	
		VI. Losses on Investments realised since the (1) day of 18 exclusive of Depreciation written off as above, viz. (4)..	
(Note the difference here, as compared with Form " O. (1)." At the date of its formation a Company has neither Assets nor Liabilities (although of course it may subsequently adopt liabilities incurred before that date) ; if, however, the account does not date back to the date of registration, a starting balance must be taken into account, as in the Bankruptcy Form, which see.)		VII. Depreciation on Property not written off in Company's Books, viz. (4)	
		VIII Other Losses and Expenses (if any) (3) since the (1) day of 18 viz. (4)	
		£ s d	
		IX. Unpaid calls .. as per List " K." *Less*: Amount taken credit for in front sheet as estimated to be realised therefrom, as per List " K."	
		Balance estimated as irrecoverable	
Total amount to be accounted for.. .. (5) £		Total amount accounted for .. .. (5) £	

NOTES.—(1) Three years before date of Winding-up Order.

     (2) This List must show when debts were contracted.

     (3) Here add particulars of other losses or expenses (if any) and liabilities (if any) for which no consideration received.

     (4) Where particulars are numerous they should be inserted in a separate Schedule.

     (5) These figures should agree.

List "P."—IN SUBSTITUTION FOR SUCH OF THE LISTS NAMED "A" TO "O" AS
WILL HAVE TO BE RETURNED BLANK.

List	Particulars, as per Front Sheet	Remarks *Where no particulars are entered on any one or more of the Lists named "A" to "O" the word "Nil" should be inserted in this column opposite the particular List or Lists thus left blank.*
A	Unsecured Creditors	
B	Creditors fully secured (not including debenture-holders)	
C	Creditors partly secured	
D	Liabilities on Bills discounted other than the Company's own acceptances for value	
E	Other liabilities	
F	Loans on Debenture Bonds	
G	Preferential Creditors for rates, taxes, wages, &c.	
H	Property	
I	Book Debts	
J	Bills of Exchange or other similar securities on hand	
K	Unpaid Calls	
L	Founders' Shares	
M	Ordinary Shares	
N	Preference Shares	
O	Deficiency Account	

Signature.....................................

*Dated.....................................*190

Meetings of creditors and of contributories respectively are convened by the Official Receiver, and at these meetings the permanent liquidator of the Company is appointed. If the creditors and contributories do not agree upon a liquidator, the Court makes the appointment. An Official Receiver may be permanently appointed as liquidator. The accounts to be kept by the liquidator in a compulsory liquidation are upon the same lines as in bankruptcy. That is, they are restricted to an account of cash receipts and payments, kept in the prescribed form, and supplemented by a Trading Account where the business of the Company is carried on pending realisation. As in bankruptcy, the liquidator is required to pay all monies received into an account opened for that purpose at the Bank of England, unless special leave has been given for an account to be opened at a local bank.

The prescribed forms of Cash Book, Cash Account, and Trading Account are as follow:—

EXAMPLE:

Companies (Winding-up) Act, 1890.

IN THE_____COURT.

Companies Liquidation No._____of 1_____

CASH BOOK.

*In the matter of*_____

COMPANY'S CASH BOOK.

RECEIPTS.

PAYMENTS.

Date	Particulars	Total	Drawn from Bank	Debts Collected	Property Realised	Receipts from Securities held by Creditors	Calls	Other Receipts	Date	Particulars	Voucher Nos. (in red)	Total
		£ s d	£ s d	£ s d	£ s d	£ s d	£ s d	£ s d				£ s d

Left-hand side.]

PAYMENTS.

Paid into Bank	Costs of Realisation									Preferential Creditors and Rent	Payments to redeem Securities	Dividends Paid	Repayments to Contributories	Other Payments
	Board of Trade and Court Fees	Law Costs of Petition	Law Costs after Winding-up Order	Remuneration of Manager and Liquidator	Official Receiver's Com. on Assets Realised, and Amount Distributed in Dividend or Paid to Contributories	Charges of Auctioneer, Accountant, Shorthand Writer, etc., as taxed	Notices in *Gazette* and Local Paper	Incidental Expenses, including Possession						
£ s d	£ s d	£ s d	£ s d	£ s d	£ s d	£ s d	£ s d	£ s d		£ s d	£ s d	£ s d	£ s d	£ s d

[Right-hand side.

EXAMPLE :

Cash Book ⎰
Filing Copy ⎱   THE COMPANIES (WINDING-UP) ACT, 1890.

  In the   Court

  In the matter of   No.   of 1

                                    CASH BOOK.

Date	Receipts	Total	Drawn from Bank	Date	Payments	Voucher No.	Total	Paid into Bank
		£ s d	£ s d				£ s d	£ s d

EXAMPLE :

No. 3.

LIQUIDATOR'S TRADING ACCOUNT.

Insert here the name of the Company.

Insert here the name of the Liquidator.

the Liquidator of the above-named Company in account with the Estate.

[SEE OVER.

Dr.   RECEIPTS

DATE		£	s	d

This margin is reserved for binding, and should not be written across.

PAYMENTS. *Cr.*

DATE		£ s d

This margin is reserved for binding, and should not be written across.

(*Date*)............................ ....*Liquidator.*

RETURNS TO BOARD OF TRADE.

Under Section 15 of the Companies (Winding-up) Act, 1890, every liquidator is required to forward to the Board of Trade a Statement of Accounts in connection with each company of which he is the liquidator, whether it be wound up voluntarily or by order of the Court, both at the conclusion of the liquidation and at the end of each year during which the liquidation continues. The prescribed forms are given on the following pages, and will be readily understood.

EXAMPLE :

No. 75.

No. of } _____
Company }

Form of Statement of Receipts and Payments and General Directions as to Statements.

(1.) Every Statement must be on sheets 13 inches by 16 inches. Size of Sheets

(2.) Every Statement must contain a detailed account of all the liquidator's realisations and disbursements in respect of the Company. The Statement of Realisations should contain a record of all receipts derived from assets existing at the date of the winding-up order or resolution and subsequently realised, including balance in Bank, Book Debts and Calls Collected, Property Sold, &c. ; and the account of disbursements should contain all payments for costs and charges, or to creditors, or contributories. Where property has been realised, the gross proceeds of sale must be entered under realisations, and the necessary payments incidental to sales must be entered as disbursements. These accounts should not contain payments into the Companies Liquidation Account or payments into or out of Bank, or temporary investments by the liquidator, or the proceeds of such investments when realised, which should be shown separately :— Form and contents of Statement

(a) by means of the Bank Pass Book ;

(b) by a separate detailed statement of moneys invested, and investments realised.

Interest allowed or charged by the Bank, Bank commission, &c., and profit or loss upon the realisation of temporary investments, should, however, be inserted in the accounts of realisations or disbursements, as the case may be. Each receipt and payment must be entered in the account in such a manner as sufficiently to explain its nature. The receipts and payments must severally be added up at the foot of each sheet, *and the totals carried forward from one account to another without any intermediate balance, so that the gross totals shall represent the total amounts received and paid by the liquidator respectively.*

(3) When the liquidator carries on a business, a Trading Account must be forwarded as a distinct account, and the totals of receipts and payments on the Trading Account must alone be set out in the Statement. Trading Account

(4.) When dividends or instalments of compositions are paid to creditors, or a return of surplus assets is made to contributories, the total amount of each dividend or instalment of composition, or return to contributories, actually paid, must be entered in the Statement of Disbursements as one sum ; and the liquidator must forward separate accounts showing in lists the amount of the claim of each creditor and the amount of dividend or composition payable to each creditor, and of surplus assets payable to each contributory, distinguishing in each list the dividends or instalments of composition and shares of surplus assets actually paid, and those remaining unclaimed. Each list must be on sheets 13 inches by 8 inches. Dividends, &c.

(5.) Credit should not be taken in the Statement of Disbursements for any amount in respect of liquidator's remuneration, unless it has been duly allowed by resolution of the Company in general meeting or by order of Court.

LIQUIDATOR'S STATEMENT OF ACCOUNT.

Pursuant to Section 15 of the Companies (Winding-up) Act, 1890.

Name of Company_____

_____

Nature of proceedings (whether wound up by }
  the Court, or under the supervision of } _____
  the Court, or voluntarily).. .. .. }

Date of commencement of winding-up_____

Date to which Statement is brought down_____

Name and Address of Liquidator _____

_____

This Statement is required in duplicate.

N

LIQUIDATOR'S STATEMENT OF ACCOUNT

REALISATIONS

Date	Of whom received	Nature of Assets Realised	Amount
			£ s d
		Brought forward ..	
		Carried forward ..	

This margin is reserved for binding, and should not be written across.

pursuant to S. 15 of the Companies (Winding-up) Act, 1890.

DISBURSEMENTS.

Date	To whom paid	Nature of Disbursements	Amount
			£ s d
		Brought forward ..	
		Carried forward ..	

* NOTE.—No balance should be shown on this Account, but only the total Realisations and Disbursements, which should be carried forward to the next Account.

[TURN OVER]

N 2

ANALYSIS OF BALANCE.

	£	s	d
Total Realisations	,,	,,	
„ Disbursements	,,	,,	
Balance ..	,,	,,	

The Balance is made up as follows:—

1. Cash in hands of Liquidator .. .., ,,

                               £   s   d

2. Amounts invested by Liquidator .. .. .. ,, ,,
   (*as per separate account herewith*)
  Less Amounts realised from same .. .. ,, ,,

        Balance of amount invested ..   ,, ,

                             £   d

3. Total Payments into Bank including Balance at date of
   commencement of winding-up
   (*as per Bank Book*) .. .. .. ,, ,
   Total withdrawals from Bank .. .. .. ,, ,,

                       Balance at Bank ,, ,,

4. Amount in Companies' Liquidation Account .. .. ,, ,,

                Total Balance as shown above £ ,, ,,

NOTE.—The Liquidator should also state—

(1.) The amount of the estimated assets and
    liabilities at the date of the commence-
    ment of the winding-up .. ..
          { *Assets .. £
             *Liabilities .. £

    * The amount stated should be, respectively, the assets available for dividend (*i.e.*, not charged to secured creditors or debenture-holders) and the unsecured liabilities ranking for dividend.

(2.) The total amount of the capital paid
    up at the date of the commence-
    ment of the winding-up .. ..
          { Paid up in cash .. £
            Issued as paid up other-
             wise than for cash .. £

(3.) The general description and
    estimated value of out-
    standing assets (if any) ..

(4.) The causes which delay
    the termination of the
    winding-up .. ..

(5.) The period within which the winding-
    up may probably be completed ..

EXAMPLE:

No. 75 E.

No. of Company_____

SUMMARY OF LIQUIDATOR'S ACCOUNTS
[UNDER RULE 127 B (2)].

No. of Company_____

Nature of proceedings (whether wound up by the Court or under the super-vision of the Court, or voluntarily) ...

Date of commencement of winding up ...   .

Date to which Statement is brought down   ...   .

Name and Address of Liquidator   .

(To be forwarded in Duplicate).

ACCOUNT of Realisations and Disbursements pursuant to

From   I

RECEIPTS.

	£	s	d
Amount of calls (if any) realised			
Amount of other assets realised			
Interest on investments made by the liquidator			
Trading receipts			
Other receipts			
£			

3,

of

the liquidator of the above-named company, make oath and say that the above statement is a full and true

summary of my receipts and payments in the winding-up of the company from the   day of

I   , to the   day of   I   ; that

all dividends, instalments of composition, and shares of surplus assets which have remained unclaimed or

undistributed for six months have been paid into the Companies' Liquidation Account, and that the minimum

balance of other money representing unclaimed or undistributed assets which I have had in my hands or under

Section 15 of the Companies (Winding-up) Act, 1890.

To   1   .

PAYMENTS.

	£	s	d
Amount paid to secured creditors			
Amount paid to preferential creditors			
Amount paid to unsecured creditors			
Amount returned to contributories			
£			
Costs, namely :—			
(a) Law costs			
(b) Liquidators's remuneration			
(c) Other costs			
Trading payments			
Other payments			
£			

my control during the six months immediately preceding the date to which the above statement is brought down is £

Sworn at

this   day of   1

                Before me,

NOTE.—The Liquidator should also state—

(1.) The amount of the estimated liabilities at the date of
    the commencement of the winding-up ..   ..

(2.) The general description and estimated value of out-
    standing assets (if any) ..   ..

(3.) The causes which delay the termination of the
    winding-up ..   ..

(4.) The period within which the winding-up may probably
    be completed ..   ..

	£	s	d
Invested			
(5.) The balance of realised funds .. .. { In Bank			
In Hand			
Total .. .. £			

It should be added that all unclaimed dividends in voluntary liquidations must be paid into the Companies' Liquidation Account at the Bank of England, and a detailed return thereof submitted to the Board of Trade. All monies that have been in the hands of a voluntary liquidator for twelve months must also be paid into this account, and can only be drawn out again as required for the purposes of the liquidation. The necessary forms, both for paying in and drawing out, are issued by the Board of Trade, and it is important that the directions given on these forms be carefully observed, if it is desired to avoid delay in obtaining the repayment of monies from the Companies' Liquidation Account.

RETURNS TO SHAREHOLDERS.

Where a surplus remains in the liquidator's hands after payment of all costs and creditors' claims, it must be distributed among the shareholders in accordance with their respective rights. These rights are covered by the Company's Memorandum and Articles of Association. If the Memorandum and Articles make any special class (or classes) of shares preferential as regards capital, these must be paid in full before any surplus is available for distribution among shareholders who are not so preferred. For example, Preference Share Capital must usually (although not necessarily always) be returned in full before anything is returned on account of Ordinary Share Capital; but no arrears of preference dividend are payable until *all* Capital has been returned in full, because dividends upon shares are only payable out of profits.

Theoretically, all unpaid Capital should be called up by the liquidator before adjusting the rights of contributories. For example, uncalled Ordinary Capital might require to be called up to enable a repayment of Capital to be made to the holders of Preference Shares. In practice, however, calls are never made unnecessarily, and consequently the Capital would not be called up if it were clear at the outset that it would immediately afterwards have to be returned to the *same* shareholders. Thus, if the assets have realised sufficient to enable Preference Capital to be returned in full, any Capital uncalled on Ordinary Shares would not usually be called up, because when received it would merely have to be returned to the ordinary shareholders again. An exception to this rule arises, however, where a different amount has been called up upon groups of the *same* class of shares. For example, where some Ordinary Shares are fully paid and others only partly paid up, in order to adjust the rights of the ordinary shareholders *inter se* it may be necessary to call up a part of the uncalled Capital. From most points of view, the shareholders of a Company may be regarded as co-partners, and as under the heading of Partnership Accounts it was shown that upon a final adjustment it was necessary to charge each partner with his proper share of the loss incurred, or to credit each partner with his proper share of the profit earned, as the case may be, so in Companies, shareholders of a like class must, at the final adjustment, be left losing (or gaining) the same amount per share. The following example shows clearly the working out of the general principle already described : —

PROBLEM.—In the voluntary winding-up of the Barclutha Electric Light Company, Lim. (whose undertaking has been purchased by the local authority), the Liquidator having realised all the assets finds that the funds on hand amount to £10,525. These are subject to the Liquidator's remuneration and costs of liquidation, including estimated cost of closing the liquidation, which together amount to £745.

	£
The amounts due to Creditors are :—	
Preferable Debts	285
Ordinary Creditors	4,320

The Capital of the Company is as follows :—
Preference Shares having a preference as to Capital, as well as
to dividends :—

	£
500 Shares of £10 each fully paid up	5,000
Ordinary Shares :—	
2,000 Shares of £10 each fully paid up	20,000
2,500 Shares of £10 each £8 per Share paid up... ...	20,000

With the exception of the provision that the 500 Preference Shares have a preference as to capital, as well as to dividends, there are no special provisions in the Memorandum or Articles of Association as to the distribution of the assets in a winding-up.

Draw up a scheme showing the order in which the Liquidator, in accordance with his duty, should apply the realised funds, and state the mode in which he should adjust the rights of the different classes of shareholders among themselves, showing the actual results in figures.

THE BARCLUTHA ELECTRIC LIGHT COMPANY, LIM. (IN LIQUIDATION).
ACCOUNT OF LIQUIDATOR'S RECEIPTS AND PAYMENTS
To date of Final Meeting.................190....

	£ s d	£ s d		£ s d	£ s d
To Realisation of Assets :— (Show details)			By Costs of Liquidation :— (Show details)		745 0 0
„ Proceeds of Call of £1 per Share on 2,500 Ordinary Shares of £10 each, making same £9 per Share paid up ..		10,525 0 0	„ Creditors paid in full :— Preferential Claims .. .. .. Unsecured Claims	285 0 0 4,320 0 0	
	..	2,500 0 0			4,605 0 0
			„ Return to Shareholders :— Preference Shares, 500 Shares of £10 each, fully paid, returned in full ..	5,000 0 0	
			Ordinary Shares, 2,000 Shares of £10 each, fully paid, return of 23/- per Share	2,300 0 0	
			Ordinary Shares, 2,500 Shares of £10 each, £9 per Share paid, return of 3/- per Share	375 0 0	7,675 0 0
		£13,025 0 0			£13,025 0 0

NOTE.—*Shareholders of the same class must leave off losing, or gaining, the same amount per Share. In this case all the holders of Ordinary Shares lose £8 17s. od. per Share. If any Shareholders failed to pay the call made by the Liquidator, their Shares would be forfeited, and they would not participate in the final return in respect of those Shares.*

RECONSTRUCTIONS AND AMALGAMATIONS.

Cases frequently arise under which part, or all, of the assets of a Company in liquidation are sold to another Company, and the purchase-price received, either wholly or partly, in fully (or partly) paid up shares in that Company. Sometimes the purchasing Company also takes over the liabilities of the Company in liquidation. As a rule, such an arrangement was foreseen at the time that the vendor Company went into liquidation, and the scheme is commonly described as a " Scheme for Reconstruction." The term is, however, not a legal one, and does not very accurately describe what takes place, seeing that the old Company is not in fact " reconstructed," or " revivified," but wound up and dissolved in the usual way; while the purchasing Company is legally an entirely different undertaking, although it is often registered under the same (or some very similar) name. Several problems of some intricacy arise in connection with Reconstructions, but these are best considered in a separate chapter.

CHAPTER XVI.

RECONSTRUCTIONS AND AMALGAMATIONS.

IT has already been stated that the term "Reconstruction" is usually (although somewhat inaccurately) applied to a scheme under which a Company goes into liquidation for the express purpose of selling the whole, or some portion, of its undertaking to another Company formed for that specific object. The term is also generally used where such an arrangement is effected, even although it was not in contemplation at the date when the Vendor Company went into liquidation. Where, however, the undertaking of a Company is sold to another Company already in existence, the process is described as an "Amalgamation," and the latter term is also used to describe the arrangement under which the undertakings of two or more Companies are combined, even although the purchasing Company may be specially formed to carry the arrangement into effect.

RECONSTRUCTIONS.

In spite of these distinctions between Reconstructions and Amalgamations, however, the necessary accounts in connection with each process are very similar. So far as the accounts of the Vendor Company are concerned, it is probable that, in practice, the books would not be actually closed, as it is generally thought desirable to keep the books as they stood up to the date of liquidation, and for the Liquidator to keep his own accounts quite separate. None the less is it important that the actual nature of the transactions should be fully understood by the reader, and this will doubtless best be done by following the entries that would be necessary to completely close the books, were it thought desirable to do so.

Naturally, the closing entries have much in common with the corresponding entries in the case of a partnership that is completely wound up. A variation, however, occurs in that the chief—if not the only—return to the shareholders will be in the form of fully (or partly) paid-up shares in the new Company. To enable such a distribution to be effected, the first step is to adjust the rights of contributories *inter se*, and for that purpose to "settle" a List of Contributories. As regards the latter, the formalities prescribed by statute must be duly observed. With regard to the former, it need only be mentioned that, as in the case of ordinary liquidations so in reconstructions, the rights of contributories *inter se* must be "adjusted," and for this purpose it is necessary that the same amount *per share* should be called up upon all shares of the same class. The proceeds of the Calls so made will, of course, increase to a corresponding extent the cash balance available for distribution among the contributories as a whole.

So far as the purchasing Company is concerned, the position of affairs is quite simple, and differs in no way from that of any ordinary Company acquiring a going concern. The mere fact that the Vendor is the Liquidator of a Company, instead of a firm or a promoter, makes no difference whatever in the form of the necessary opening entries.

These preliminary remarks will enable the reader to trace without difficulty the working out of the following problem, which relates to a comparatively simple state of affairs :—

PROBLEM.—The " B " Company goes into voluntary liquidation on 30th September 1901. Its assets appear in the books as follows :—

Cost of Properties	£150,000
Machinery and Stores	12,000

Its liabilities are £25,000, and its Capital (fully paid-up) £200,000. The assets are sold to the " C " Company, Lim., for £100,000, payable in Shares of that Company of £1 each, credited with 16s. 8d. per Share paid, and £30,000 in cash, which just suffices to pay the liabilities and liquidation costs.

(a) Close the books of the " B " Company.

(b) Show the opening entries in the books of the " C " Company.

(a) On the 30th September 1901 the Balance Sheet of the " B " Company stood as follows :—

BALANCE SHEET, 30th September 1901.

Liabilities.	£	s	d	Assets.	£	s	d
Capital	200,000	0	0	Property	150,000	0	0
Creditors ..	25,000	0	0	Machinery and Stores	12,000	0	0
				Profit and Loss Account	63,000	0	0
	£225,000	0	0		£225,000	0	0

In Journal form the closing entries would be as follow :—

JOURNAL, 1901.

30th September.	£	s	d	£	s	d
Realisation Account	162,000	0	0			
To Property				150,000	0	0
„ Machinery and Plant				12,000	0	0
" C " Company	130,000	0	0			
To Realisation Account ..				130,000	0	0
Realisation Account	5,000	0	0			
To Liquidation Costs ..				5,000	0	0
Profit and Loss Account ..	37,000	0	0			
To Realisation Account ..				37,000	0	0
Cash	30,000	0	0			
Shares in " C " Company (120,000 of £1 each, 16s. 8d. per Share paid)	100,000	0	0			
To " C " Company				130,000	0	0
Creditors	25,000	0	0			
Liquidation Costs	5,000	0	0			
To Cash ..				30,000	0	0
Capital Account	100,000	0	0			
To Profit and Loss Account ..				100,000	0	0
Capital Account	100,000	0	0			
To Shares in " C " Company ..				100,000	0	0
(Being a distribution at the rate of 3 " C " Shares (16s. 8d. per Share paid up) for each 5 Shares held in the " B " Company.)						

(b) The opening entries in " C " Company's Journal are as follow :—

JOURNAL, 1901.

30th September	£	s	d	£	s	d
Property Account	113,000	0	0			
Machinery and Stores..	12,000	0	0			
Preliminary Expenses	5,000	0	0			
To Liquidator of " B " Company				130,000	0	0
Liquidator of " B " Company	130,000	0	0			
To Cash				30,000	0	0
„ Share Capital Account (120,000 Shares of £1 each, issued with 16s. 8d. per Share paid up, as per contract dated —1901, adopted —1901, filed —1901).				100,000	0	0

Assuming that the " C " Company has issued the remainder of its Capital (say, 30,000 Shares) for cash, and that all Shares are fully paid up, the Balance Sheet of the " C " Company will appear as follows :—

BALANCE SHEET.

Liabilities.	£	s	d	Assets.	£	s	d
Share Capital :				Property (at cost)	113,000	0	0
150,000 Shares of £1 each fully paid ..	150,000	0	0	Machinery and Stores	12,000	0	0
				Cash	20,000	0	0
				Preliminary Expenses	5,000	0	0
	£150,000	0	0		£150,000	0	0

NOTES.—(a) *The purchase price is £130,000, payable in Cash and Shares ; as the Shares are only partly paid up, the number issued is increased proportionately.* (b) *It is assumed (1) that the Machinery and Stores are worth their book value, otherwise the cost of the property would be increased pro ratâ ; (2) That the " B " Company has paid the costs of registering the " C " Company, in which case the £5,000 is best treated as Preliminary Expenses ; it might, however, be added to the cost of property instead.*

" ABSORPTIONS. "

Where an undertaking as a whole is sold to an already existing Company, the closing of the Vendor Company's accounts is upon the same lines as in a Reconstruction, while the opening entries in the purchasing Company's accounts involve no new principle. A practical variation, however, arises in that as a rule the business that is being bought and sold is a valuable one, so that instead of the transactions resulting in a loss being realised by the shareholders of the Vendor Company there is usually a profit. Such profit may arise from any one of the following causes, or from all :—

(a) From the price paid for Goodwill being in excess of the amount (if any) at which that item stands in the books of the Vendor Company.

(b) From the fact that Reserves which the Vendor Company has in the past thought it prudent to maintain need no longer be regarded as liabilities in the accounts.

(c) From the fact that the intrinsic value of the shares received in payment (or part payment) of the purchase-price is in excess of their nominal value.

Per contra the entries in the books of the Purchasing Company recording the purchase may require any (or all) of the following points to be borne in mind :—

(a) The purchase-price paid may exceed the value of the tangible assets acquired (or the excess of such tangible assets over the liabilities taken over).

(b) It is necessary that at all events the floating assets taken over should not be entered in the books at a figure in excess of their actual value.

(c) The shares of the purchasing company may (in fact) be issued at a premium, or at a discount.

A careful perusal of the following example will enable the proper treatment in connection with all these various points to be traced. It only remains to be stated that unless the contract of sale expressly states that the Purchasing Company takes over the liabilities of the Vendor Company, these liabilities must be paid by the latter; but where property passing is specifically charged with the repayment of certain liabilities, it can only be conveyed subject to the charge, so that in such cases the liability would have to be taken over, unless special arrangements were made for its redemption.

PROBLEM.—The Rufus Iron and Steel Company, Lim., of Birmingham, is purchased or absorbed by the Blackrod Iron and Steel Company, Lim., of Darlington, on 31st December 1901, and is afterwards carried on as a Branch Works only. The consideration for the purchase or absorption is the discharge of the Debenture Debt at a premium of 10 per cent. and a payment in cash of £7 10s., and the exchange of three £1 Shares in the Blackrod Company, of the market value of £2 10s. per Share for every Share in the Rufus Company.

The following is the Balance Sheet of the Rufus Company when taken over :—

BALANCE SHEET.

Liabilities.		Assets.	
	£		£
Capital—60,000 £10 Shares fully paid ...	600,000	Land and Buildings	189,855
Debenture Stock	280,000	Plant and Machinery, &c.	435,492
Sundry Creditors	39,754	Patterns and Drawings	5,000
Workmen's Savings Bank	21,205	Patents	9,577
Insurance Fund	10,000	Work in Progress and Stocks on hand ...	211,452
Reserve Fund	65,000	Furniture and Fittings	1,444
Revenue Balance	5,662	Cash in hand	120
		Cash at Bankers	77,396
		Sundry Debtors	91,255
	£1,021,621		£1,021,621

(a) Make the necessary closing entries in the books of the Rufus Company.

(b) Open the books of the Blackrod Company, so far as they relate to these transactions.

(A).   JOURNAL, 1901.

31st December.	£	s	d	£	s	d
Realisation Account	1,021,621	0	0			
To Sundry Assets (specified)	..			1,021,621	0	0
Cash	758,000	0	0			
Shares in Blackrod Co. (180,000 Shares of £1 each, fully paid, valued at 50s. per Share)	450,000	0	0			
To Realisation Account	..			1,208,000	0	0
Realisation Account	28,000	0	0			
To Debentures (premium on redemption)	..			28,000	0	0
Insurance Fund	10,000	0	0			
Reserve Fund	65,000	0	0			
Revenue Balance	5,662	0	0			
To Realisation Account	..			80,662	0	0
Debentures	308,000	0	0			
To Cash	..			308,000	0	0
Sundry Creditors	39,754	0	0			
Workmen's Savings Bank	21,205	0	0			
To Cash	..			60,959	0	
Share Capital	600,000	0	0			
Realisation Account	239,041	0	0			
To Cash	..			389,041	0	0
,, Shares in Blackrod Co. (being a distribution of 12s. 11¼d. (nearly) in the £ in cash, and 15s. in the £ in Shares of the Blackrod Co.)	..			450,000	0	0

(B).   JOURNAL, 1901.

31st December.	£	s	d	£	s	d
Land and Buildings	189,885	0	0			
Plant and Machinery, &c.	435,492	0	0			
Patterns and Drawings	5,000	0	0			
Patents	9,577	0	0			
Work in Progress and Stocks on hand	211,452	0	0			
Furniture and Fittings	1,444	0	0			
Cash in hand	120	0	0			
Cash at Bank	77,396	0	0			
Sundry Debtors	91,255	0	0			
To Liquidator of Rufus Company	..			1,021,621	0	0
Liquidator of Rufus Company	1,021,621	0	0			
To Cash (for Debenture Debt)	..			308,000	0	0
,, Do.	..			450,000	0	0
,, Share Capital A/c (180,000 Shares of £1 each, issued as fully paid as per contract dated vide Minute No.).	..			180,000	0	0
,, Premium on Issue of Shares (being excess of value of Assets acquired over cash and nominal value of Shares issued)	..			83,621	0	0

NOTES.—*In the books of the Vendor Company it is best to take the Blackrod Shares at their market value. The accounts then give a fair idea of the effect of the transaction, which has (presumably) been carried through on the assumption that the Goodwill of the Vendor Company is worth £186,379; this, added to the Revenue balance and Reserves, give a total profit on the deal of £267,041, of which the debenture-holders take £28,000, leaving £239,041 for the shareholders. In the books of the Purchasing Company, on the other hand, the Company's own Shares can only be regarded as of par value. It appears that the property acquired is worth £83,631 more than the nominal value of the Shares in cash paid for it—the difference is the amount of premium actually realised on the issue. Another way of treating the matter would be to raise a Goodwill Account for £186,379, which would raise the premium on the issue to £270,000 = 30s. per Share on 180,000 Shares: as, however, the balance on Premium Account would probably be at once applied towards writing off the Goodwill Account, the first-named method seems simpler.*

AMALGAMATIONS.

It is, perhaps, unnecessary to point out that the closing entries in the Vendor's books are not affected by any consideration as to the exact constitution of the purchasing Company, while the mere fact that the latter may arrange to simultaneously acquire the undertakings of two or more different Companies presents no new feature, in that the opening entries in respect of each purchase will, of course, have to be kept entirely distinct. It remains, however, to consider the most convenient method of arranging the terms under which two separate Companies shall amalgamate their resources.

In practice, complications sometimes arise in the adjustment of .these amounts, owing to the amalgamations being the result of a bargain which has not taken into consideration any detailed examination of their respective positions, although in opening the books of the new Company such detailed investigation is essential. What is meant here will perhaps be best understood by considering in detail the following example : —

PROBLEM.—Two Mining Companies agree to amalgamate upon the basis that the value of their respective assets shall be taken at the figures appearing in the books. State what you think would be the best way of carrying out the amalgamation, the two Balance Sheets being as follow :—

" A " COMPANY, LIM.—BALANCE SHEET.

Liabilities.	£	s	d	Assets.	£	s	d
Capital, 100,000 Shares of £1 each ...	100,000	0	0	Property Account	95,000	0	0
Creditors	2,500	0	0	Debtors	3,000	0	0
Reserve Fund	20,000	0	0	Bullion in transit	10,000	0	0
Profit and Loss Account ...	5 000	0	0	Cash	19,500	0	0
	£127,500	0	0		£127,500	0	0

" B " COMPANY, LIM.—BALANCE SHEET.

Liabilities.	£	s	d	Assets.	£	s	d
Capital, 50,000 Shares of £2 each ...	100,000	0	0	Property Account	80,000	0	0
Creditors	1,000	0	0	Debtors	2,000	0	0
Profit and Loss Account ...	20,000	0	0	Consols	25,000	0	0
				Cash	14,000	0	0
	£121,000	0	0		£121,000	0	0

Show the Balance Sheet of the new Company.

In the above example, the problem has been intentionally simplified by the assumption that the book-values of the various assets and liabilities have been admitted. If they had not been admitted, it would have been necessary to prepare revised Balance Sheets setting forth the actual figures and adjusting the balance of undivided profit (or loss, as the case may be) accordingly. Again, had the basis of valuation been that the properties of both Companies were assumed to be of equal value, then either the undivided profits of the " A " Company must have been written down £15,000, or the undivided profits of the " B " Company written up by that amount. All necessary adjustments having been made, the next point is to equalise the position, as between the two sets of shareholders, so that the percentage of undivided Profits (including Reserves) to Capital may be the same in respect of both Companies. In the instance cited above it will be seen that this adjustment requires £5,000 in cash to be distributed among the shareholders of the " A " Company, or else £5,000 in cash to be contributed by the shareholders of the " B " Company. It will depend upon the available resources which course it is thought best to adopt. The following Balance Sheet shows the position of the amalgamated Company upon the assumption that the amalgamation has been carried through upon the basis of first making a return of 5 per cent. to the shareholders of " A " Company, and then issuing six fully-paid shares in the new Company to each holder of five shares in the " A " Company, and twelve shares in the new Company to each holder of five shares in the " B " Company. There being an ample cash balance, it has been assumed that the creditors' claims have been paid off, and the Balance Sheet then stands as follows :—

A. & B. UNITED, LIM.—BALANCE SHEET.

Liabilities.	£ s d	£ s d	Assets.	£ s d	£ s d
Nominal Capital, 240,000 Shares of £1 each	£240,000 0 0		Property Account	..	175 000 0 0
			Debtors	..	5,000 0 0
			Bullion in Transit	..	10,000 0 0
Capital Subscribed (240,000 Shares, fully paid up)	..	240,000 0 0	Consols	..	25,000 0 0
			Cash	..	25,000 0 0
		£240,000 0 0			£240,000 0 0

In practice, the terms of an amalgamation are frequently settled the other way round. That is to say, instead of any detailed valuation of the assets and liabilities being agreed upon, the intrinsic value of the *shares* in the Vendor Companies is agreed, and it is left for the amalgamating Company to adjust the details. When this course is pursued, it is necessary to proceed upon the assumption that the Capital *plus* undivided Profits of a Company are in fact at all times equal to the aggregate market value of its shares. Thus, if the shares of a Company stand at 1¼, the undivided Profits of that Company must be assumed to be equal to one-fourth of its paid-up Capital, and an adjusted Balance Sheet compiled upon this assumption. Liabilities and floating Assets would appear on this Balance Sheet at their actual value, and the difference would be assumed to be the value of the fixed assets in the case of a Mining Company, or the value of the Goodwill in the case of an industrial concern.

FRACTIONS OF SHARES.

Wherever distributions of shares are made, the difficulty will always arise in practice that an exact distribution requires fractions of shares to be distributed, which is, of course, impossible. In practice this difficulty is got over by setting upon one side the total number of shares which these fractions represent, realising them to the best advantage, and distributing the proceeds among the various parties in accordance with their respective rights. To take a very simple case:—Supposing it appears that 50 shareholders are each entitled to half a share, then there are 25 shares over that cannot be specifically allotted. If these 25 shares realised £10, each of the 50 shareholders would receive four shillings as representing the cash value of his half-share.

CHAPTER XVII.

FALSIFIED ACCOUNTS.

IN the present Chapter it is proposed to consider errors of all kinds in accounts, which have been deliberately made with the intention of misrepresenting the actual position of affairs. The usual object of such falsification is to conceal the fact that there has been an actual misappropriation of property belonging to the undertaking, but this is by no means necessarily the only motive. Cases sometimes arise in which the accounts have been falsified with a view to misrepresenting the actual profits made. Again, falsification is, as a rule, employed in connection with the record of cash, but not by any means necessarily. If, therefore, it is desired to effectively guard against, or detect, falsification, the matter must be viewed from a broad and comprehensive standpoint.

MISREPRESENTATION OF PROFITS.

Taking first of all the more unusual cases of falsification *not* employed as a cloak to conceal misappropriation, the commonest motives are—

(1) On the part of a vendor to overstate the profits of the undertaking to an intending purchaser;

(2) On the part of an intending purchaser, who has previously had charge of the books, to understate the profits of the undertaking he is about to acquire;

(3) On the part of a manager whose commission, or whose appointment, is dependent upon a certain standard of results, with a view to securing a continuance, or improvement, of his present position.

Taking each of these cases separately, the first may be more conveniently considered under the heading of " The Criticism of Accounts " (*vide* Chap. XXIII.) ; the second is of very common occurrence, although as a rule within somewhat narrow limits, but as it raises no special points it may be dismissed with the caution that the proprietor of a business should never think of selling it on the basis of accounts that have been prepared by—or exclusively in the interest of—the intending purchaser.

The third class named above calls for more careful consideration on account of its importance, and the variety of manners in which the falsification may be accomplished. Speaking generally, it may be stated, as being part of an effective system of internal check (*vide* Chap. III.), that no employee whose remuneration is based upon results should be allowed to in any way control the record of those results in the books ; this applies whether the basis of remuneration be a commission on sales, a commission on cash received, a commission on net profits, or upon any other form of transactions or results. It is clear that in such cases the employee is so directly interested that an effective system of control, and of internal check, requires the record of these figures to be entirely independent of the person whom they so directly affect. In most business houses this point is duly appreciated at its full value, and as a rule, therefore, falsifications of this description do not arise in practice ; but when the employee's remuneration is not in any way based upon results, there is a tendency to lose sight of the fact that he is still interested in those results proving favourable—first, because he may reasonably expect an increased remuneration if the business progresses; and, secondly, because if the business be found to be unprofitable, or otherwise unsatisfactory, there is at all events a risk of his services being dispensed with altogether. Under these circumstances, it is especially important that adequate precautions should be taken, partly because it would be often extremely difficult to prove fraudulent intent in connection with such cases, while immunity from a criminal prosecution must at all times remove a very effective automatic safeguard; but more particularly because many persons, who would under no circumstances think of directly applying to their own use monies belonging to their employers, would not scruple to misrepresent the position of affairs in order to avoid unpleasant consequences. Such misrepresentation may be absolute and deliberate, or it may merely arise through undue optimism (which is frequently another name for incompetence); but whatever the actual cause the result must, from the employer's point of view, be in all cases unsatisfactory. A typical example of falsification, arising possibly from undue optimism, is when the manager of a trading department values his stock-in-trade at balancing time at too high a figure; either because he is incompetent to estimate its true worth, or because, knowing the results of the past period have been somewhat unsatisfactory, he desires to postpone a certain portion of the loss, and bring it in to the next period. This latter form of falsification is only one step removed from the form of fraud which suppresses unpaid invoices, and thereby allows goods to be taken into stock as assets without their cost price being credited in the Bought Ledger; but to a certain extent it will be found to be a not altogether uncommon practice on the part of those whose honesty in other matters is unimpeachable. From one point of view, the practice of overvaluing stock-in-trade with a view to throwing losses into the next ensuing period is, of course, on a par with debiting losses, or unprofitable expenditure, to a Suspense Account, to be written over a term of years; but there is this essential difference between the two, that whereas employees when valuing the stock-in-trade are required to confine themselves strictly to the point at issue, directors and proprietors when finally settling draft accounts are reasonably entitled to look at the matter from every available standpoint.

FALSIFIED COST ACCOUNTS.

Another typical form of falsification that comes under this head, and which is very difficult of detection, may occur when the manager of a manufacturing or contracting firm is responsible for its profit-earning capacity. Upon such manager must necessarily devolve the task of estimating the cost of the work in progress, and as a rule it is difficult—if not impossible—to exhaustively verify the manager's calculations. If, under these circumstances, it should transpire that there has been a loss upon certain work completed during the period under review, there may be a danger of the loss being transferred to work in progress, and thus carried forward. A somewhat notorious case of this kind was brought to light a few years since in connection with the accounts of an important local authority. It was there found that such a system had been systematically carried on for a number of years past, with the result that whereas each contract as completed showed satisfactory results, much of the cost of the completed contracts had in point of fact been debited to those which from time to time remained uncompleted. This kind of falsification is rendered the more easy, because the records, upon the value of which work in progress is based, often form no part of the financial books. This emphasises the importance of all statistical records, which it is thought worth while to keep at all, being kept with the same care, and checked with the same amount of accuracy and systematisation, as the financial records themselves. The importance of this precaution is emphasised by the circumstance that whereas any material falsification of the financial accounts· is usually impossible without fraudulent collusion, it is often by no means a difficult matter to get statistical records passed and signed for by persons who, however careless, have no idea that they are lending themselves to the concealment of a fraud. For example, a foreman who would on no account allow Plant to go out of his yard without a proper authority might quite conceivably—whether through carelessness or for some other reason—sign vouchers that Plant had been forwarded to one contract, when in point of fact it had been forwarded to another. Such differentiations are somewhat difficult of comprehension to those who are trained in accounts, and who realise the importance of accuracy at all points, but the fact remains that falsifications of this kind are far more common than is generally supposed. And even when they are discovered, their reprehensible nature is but rarely duly appreciated, the general view being that the whole matter is a somewhat complicated " question of accounts," upon which those who are not experts may easily make mistakes without being in any way culpable.

That the exact nature of the class of falsification referred to may be clearly understood, the following example is appended. The group of accounts given first, and marked " A," are supposed to indicate the true position of affairs ; while the second group, marked " B," shows how the true position may be obscured by the passing of improper entries, which in the absence of careful supervision may readily remain undetected.

EXAMPLE "A":

Dr.   CONTRACT No. 1.   **Cr.**

		£ s d			£ s d
1900	To Wages	3,172 0 0	1900	By Contract Price	6.000 0 0
	„ Materials and Plant issued	3,400 0 0		„ Materials and Plant returned	160 0 0
				„ Loss	412 0 0
		£6,572 0 0			£6,572 0 0

Dr.   CONTRACT No. 2.   **Cr.**

		£ s d			£ s d
1900	To Wages	1,620 0 0	1900	By Balance down	3,691 0 0
	„ Materials and Plant issued	2,071 0 0			
		£3,691 0 0			£3,691 0 0
1901	To Balance down	3,691 0 0	1901	By Contract Price	6,150 0 0
	„ Wages	1,848 0 0		„ Materials and Plant returned	507 0 0
	„ Materials and Plant issued	975 0 0		„ Loss	57 0 0
		£6,514 0 0			£6,514 0 0

Dr.   CONTRACT No. 3.   **Cr.**

		£ s d			£ s d
1901	To Wages	813 0 0	1901	By Balance down	2,285 0 0
	„ Materials and Plant issued	1,472 0 0			
		£2,285 0 0			£2,285 0 0
1902	To Balance down	2 285 0 0			

EXAMPLE "B":

Dr.   CONTRACT No. 1.   Cr.

		£ s d			£ s d
1900	To Wages	3,172 0 0	1900	By Contract Price	6,000 0 0
	„ Materials and Plant issued	3,400 0 0		„ Materials and Plant returned	760 0 0
	„ Profit	188 0 0			
		£6,760 0 0			£6,760 0 0

Dr.   CONTRACT No. 2.   Cr.

		£ s d			£ s d
1900	To Wages	1,620 0 0	1900	By Balance down	4,291 9 0
	„ Materials and Plant issued	2,671 0 0			
		£4,291 0 0			£4,291 0 0
1901	To Balance down	4,291 0 0	1901	By Contract Price	6,150 0 0
	„ Wages	1,848 0 0		„ Materials and Plant returned	1,007 0 0
	„ Materials and Plant issued	975 0 0			
	„ Profit	43 0 0			
		£7,157 0 0			£7,157 0 0

Dr.   CONTRACT No. 3.   Cr.

		£ s d			£ s d
1901	To Wages	813 0 0	1901	By Balance down	2,985 0 0
	„ Materials and Plant issued	2,172 0 0			
		£2,985 0 0			£2,985 0 0
1902	To Balance down	2,985 0 0			

NOTE.—*The above example shows falsification by over crediting Contracts completed for the value of Materials and Plant returned, a corresponding sum being debited to works in progress. The like result might be achieved by debiting Cost to the wrong account.*

FALSIFICATION BY DIRECTORS.

So far the possibilities of fraud on the part of ordinary employees have alone been considered; but in connection with the accounts of Companies, it is important to bear in mind that the position of a Managing Director, and sometimes even of a Board of Directors, is somewhat analogous to that of the manager of a private undertaking. The continuance of a Director's appointment is, to some extent at least, dependent upon the continued profit-earning capacity of the undertaking; if, therefore, there is a falling-off in profits, there is a possibility that a tendency may arise to strain points in connection with accounts, with a view to making the apparent profits larger than the real profits. Within limits, this tendency may be permissible, for it is the recognised custom in the case of sound business undertakings to somewhat over-estimate such items as provision for Bad Debts, and the like, in profitable years, with a view to creating a secret reserve available in times of need. When, therefore, the need arises, it is perfectly legitimate to fall back upon any secret reserve that may be in existence. In practice, the only way of having recourse to a secret reserve is to under-estimate the expenses (or losses) for the current period; and so long as they are not so under-estimated as to turn the secret reserve into a minus quantity, this course is permissible on the part of Directors, although it would not be permissible on the part of subordinates.

DEFALCATIONS.

Turning now to the more direct forms of falsification, which have for their object the concealment of actual misappropriation, the nature of these false entries will (as might be expected) depend largely upon the exact form of misappropriation. As a rule, the misappropriation will take the form of money, but not necessarily, and it is important to bear in mind that an exhaustive check upon all receipts and payments is not always sufficient to afford an effective safeguard against all possible misappropriation. Taking, however, misapproriations of money first, these may take the form either of suppressing receipts, or of creating fictitious payments. With a proper system of internal check, coupled to an adequate system of bookkeeping by double-entry with self-balancing Ledgers, the suppression of cash received cannot reach serious proportions without detection. So far as Sold Ledger accounts are concerned, if the various Sold Ledgers are regularly balanced and independently checked, and if the Sold Ledger clerks have not the handling of the Sold Ledger cash, there is little or no risk of any peculation under this heading. So far as Cash Sales are concerned, it is usually practicable to devise a system which will render impossible the abstraction of moneys received under this heading without considerable collusion on the part of the employees. The risk of fraud in this direction is thus, as a rule, limited to unusual receipts on the one hand, or, on the other hand, to comparatively small undertakings which do not employ a sufficient staff to enable an effective system of internal check to be organised. In both these cases the best, and perhaps the only effective, safeguard is for the principal in the case of a private concern, or the Secretary (or Managing Director) in the case of a company, to himself devote sufficient personal time to the matter to enable him, in conjunction with the professional auditors, to establish a com-

plete system of check in all departments. It may be mentioned in passing, however, that serious frauds by way of omitting to account for cash received rarely occur, save when the system of accounting employed is quite primitive.

If the books be kept by single-entry, there is undoubtedly a somewhat serious risk that such omissions may remain undetected, for under such circumstances it is ·impossible to apply the check of balancing the Ledgers, either separately or collectively, and consequently moneys received from customers, but misappropriated, may quite conceivably be credited to the customers' accounts without being debited to Cash.

FICTITIOUS PAYMENTS.

Misappropriations by the creation of fictitious payments may, in the first place, be rendered extremely difficult by the adoption of a hard-and-fast rule that all payments, other than by Petty Cash, must be made by cheque, the person signing the cheques being responsible that the account is actually due, and that the cheque is so drawn as to (so far as possible) ensure its being only cashed by the persons entitled to it. " Bearer " cheques and " open " cheques should never be drawn without a sufficient explanation being obtained as to why this exceptional form of payment is necessary, and as an additional safeguard all " crossed " cheques should be marked " not negotiable," and, if for large sums, wherever practicable crossed " specially " to the bank of the payee. There should be a regular system in force for passing accounts for payment, rendering at least two persons responsible for the fact that the goods have been received, or the work performed, in respect of which payment is to be made, and at least two members of the counting-house staff responsible for the arithmetical accuracy of the account, and for the fact that the cheque put forward for signature agrees with the corresponding Personal Account in the Bought Ledger. A cheque should never be signed without these precautions being first adopted, and (save under exceptional circumstances) it ought to be possible to produce to the persons who are called upon to sign cheques accounts from the various creditors, showing that the amounts of such cheques are actually claimed by them respectively. If these precautions be adopted, the creation of fictitious payments is practically impossible, but with some undertakings such formalities could not be carried out in their entirety. For example, Banks have to pay large sums in cash, and it is not practicable for them to do so on anything better than the security of one cashier. Bank frauds are, however, of somewhat rare occurrence, and as all Bank employees are required to give guarantees for comparatively large sums, the risks incurred by a Bank that works upon a reasonable system of internal check are not serious. Recently, however, a somewhat notorious case occurred, in which a Bank lost large sums of money through the dishonesty of a clerk who was not entrusted with the handling of any monies or securities. This particular case is thus useful, as showing that it is not merely cashiers whom it is important to supervise. Here a clerk in charge of a Customers' Ledger forged cheques for large amounts in the name of one of the customers, which were duly paid through the Clearing House, but never debited by him to the account of the customer. The continuance of these frauds was, however, only rendered possible by the omission to provide some of the most usual and obvious safeguards. In the first place, the delinquent remained in undivided control of the same Customers' Ledger over an extended period, whereas an obvious precaution is to continually change the work devolving upon each of the various members of the staff; and, in the second place, he was, it appears, able to conceal the fact that his Ledger did not balance by making entries in a Journal which was not under his keeping, whereas every effective system should distinctly allocate the various books among the different members of the staff—not merely making each responsible for his own books, but also making it an invariable rule that no one *else* shall make any entries in those books. A clerk in charge of any book of account, whether a Cash Book, Journal, or Ledger, should be made responsible for the accuracy of that book as a whole, and also for every entry made therein. In the case of a Journal particularly, it is difficult to understand how fraudulent and improper entries could have been made from time to time without it being someone's business to verify those entries as being proper and duly authorised.

Fraudulent misappropriations are capable of being divided into classes upon yet another basis, and an examination of them from this new point of view will probably be found helpful. The actual misappropriation of assets, whether cash or otherwise, directly results in a corresponding amount of loss to the undertaking. When, therefore, the books come to be balanced, that loss must either fall against Revenue or be taken into the Balance Sheet. If it falls against Revenue, the Net Profits will be directly reduced to a corresponding extent; accordingly there is a distinct limit, beyond which misappropriations cannot be carried without their effect upon the profits being apparent. Consequently one frequently finds in practice that fraudulent entries are made in the books, with a view to concealing the loss by taking it into the Balance Sheet instead of into the Profit and Loss Account; that is to say, by some false entry the book value of the assets brought into the Balance Sheet is shown at a figure in excess of their proper valuation. A detailed examination of all the assets brought into the Balance Sheet would invariably result in the detection of such false entries. It is not always possible for such a detailed examination to be made by the professional auditors in the case of large concerns, but where—owing to the magnitude of the undertaking—it is unreasonable to expect so much to be done by the professional auditors, the bookkeeping staff can—with a reasonable amount of intelligent organisation—be so employed as to enable the various Ledger Accounts purporting to represent assets to be fully verified in the utmost detail.

THEFTS OF STOCK, &c.

Passing on to forms of misappropriation other than of cash, the most common of these is a theft of Stock-in-Trade, or Raw Materials, including Loose Tools. Unless the Stock-in-Trade be possessed of considerable intrinsic value, detailed Stock Accounts cannot be kept, and under such circumstances the only precautions that it is possible to adopt against this form of fraud are a careful actual inspection at frequent intervals by departmental managers, and the test which the periodical accounts afford of the percentage of gross profit actually realised, as compared with the percentage that might fairly be expected. It is not usually possible to go further in this direction than to hold the head of the department responsible for a certain percentage of gross profit, leaving him to bear the blame if that percentage be not realised either through careless buying or leakage. In the same way, with regard to Materials and Tools, foremen and heads of departments can (if they be competent) reduce the risk of losses under these headings to a minimum; if, therefore, competent persons be employed, and they be held responsible for the results that they achieve, it is probable that those results will be quite as satisfactory as though the most complete system of Stock and Stores Accounts could be devised and carried out in actual practice. As a rule, however, more or less incomplete Stores Accounts should be kept, to assist the persons held responsible in their supervision; and in the case of really valuable stocks (as, for example, a jewellery stock), complete Stock Accounts are, of course, absolutely essential.

CHAPTER XVIII.

BOOKKEEPING WITHOUT BOOKS.

UNTIL comparatively recently the science of systematically recording business transactions was invariably described as "Bookkeeping." Now, however, that further developments of that science have to an increasing extent substituted the use of loose sheets, or cards, for pages in bound books of account, the term "bookkeeping" appears to be too narrow to cover the whole subject, and accordingly the word "accounting" is coming into more general use. Bookkeeping without books is very commonly supposed to have originated in the United States of America, and until quite recently the necessary appliances for keeping accounts upon such a system were only manufactured there. The system is, however, so far as can be traced, not of American but of Chaldean origin, being the earliest known form of accounting, and perhaps the earliest ever employed. This, however, is less surprising when it is borne in mind that the science of accounting, in some form or another, was in general use long before bound books, or even paper, were thought of.

The Chaldean system of bookkeeping appears to have been very much upon the lines employed in public libraries at the present date. That is to say, a certain number of receptacles represented one class of accounts, and a certain number of portable articles another class of accounts, or transactions. The Chaldean worked this principle by supplying a wide-mouthed jar to represent the account with each person with whom he did business, placing in such jars from time to time tablets, each of which had a peculiar significance. The contents of the jar at any moment thus showed the balance of the account. The twentieth century librarian applies the same principle in a slightly different manner, using frames or sets of pigeon-holes instead of jars, and cards instead of tablets. These enable him to tell almost at a glance what persons have taken books out of the library, and what books are from time to time in their possession; and he thus carries the principle further than the Chaldean in all probability attempted, in that by the same mechanism he keeps a detailed set of Personal Accounts, and also a detailed set of Stock Accounts. A similar system might with great advantage be substituted for many of the elaborate bookkeeping methods employed for keeping tally of casks, packing cases, and other empties which are of sufficient value to render an accurate system of accounting imperative.

It has throughout the course of this work been assumed that the reader is well acquainted with the general principles of ordinary double-entry bookkeeping, and may therefore be taken to know that under the ordinary system of keeping accounts in books each transaction is in the first place recorded in a book of first entry, and that afterwards that record is again copied into the Ledger. If the transactions are complicated, the number of separate times that the record of the transaction has to be copied out is increased accordingly, with the result that in a concern of any importance a very large staff is kept exclusively employed in so multiplying copies of the record of transactions. The aim of the system of bookkeeping without books—which, for the sake of conciseness, may be referred to as the " Slip System "—is to (as far as possible) do away with the necessity for this continual recopying, by so framing the original record that it may, in turn, serve all the purposes that are ordinarily served by books of account.

If this system be adopted in its entirety it is sometimes practicable to obviate the necessity for any copying at all. Thus a carbon facsimile of an invoice for goods sold may in the first place perform the functions of a Day Book, and afterwards those of a Ledger Account; while in the same way the counterfoil of a Cheque Book, or of a receipt, may enable the Cash Book entries and Ledger postings of Cash to be dispensed with. The arrangement of systems of bookkeeping is, however, at all times very largely a matter of compromise between principle and convenience, and consequently it may often be thought undesirable to carry the Slip System to this extreme, while yet appreciating the advantages of employing it up to a point. The question as to how far it may be desirable to employ the Slip System, and as to how far it is better to retain what may conveniently—although inaccurately—be described as the " old " system of recording transactions in bound books of account, is a matter which can, in each case, be only finally determined after carefully considering all the attendant circumstances. No prudent accountant would think of laying down any general conclusions upon such a matter. In the present work, therefore, all that can usefully be attempted is to describe the possible applications of the Slip System to accounts, to indicate the manner in which these applications may be combined if thought desirable, and to point out in general terms some of the leading advantages, and most important disadvantages, that are likely to be experienced in consequence.

SLIP DAY BOOKS.

One of the most useful applications of the Slip System is undoubtedly that which does away with the necessity of copying every invoice sent out into a book of account, from which postings into the Sold Ledger have afterwards to be made. The chief disadvantages of the bound Day Book are the time occupied in compiling it, the great difficulty in dissecting the entries when dissection is necessary, and the risk that the entries actually made in the Day Book will not be a true copy of all the invoices forwarded to the customers. All these disadvantages are obviated by the Slip Day Book. The application of the system will naturally vary to some extent according to circumstances, but rudimentary examples have been in general use for a great number of years. Probably the commonest is to be found in most retail shops (c.f. page 32), where the counter-man makes out invoices for whatever he sells upon forms which, by means of a carbon sheet, enable an exact reproduction of the invoice handed to the customer to be retained. Simultaneously he enters in a summary at the end of his book against the corresponding distinctive number the total of each invoice, and these summaries should therefore show the total of his sales from time to time. The total shown by these summaries may be used as a check upon the Cash received by the Cashier (for Cash Sales and Credit Sales would be entered in different books, printed upon distinctively coloured paper) while, if the forms are systematically put away in consecutive order, there is frequently no occasion for any detailed entries to be made in the Day Book in connection even with Credit Sales. The work of the Dissecting Clerk is also greatly facilitated, the actual dissection being to a large extent readily performed by *sorting out* the duplicate invoices into groups according to the selling departments that have issued them. This system, as has already been stated, has been in very general operation for a number of years past; if, however, it be slightly amplified, its utility can be greatly increased. A somewhat larger form of invoice will usually be found desirable, and it is often convenient that the Invoice Form Books should be arranged upon the lines of a large Cheque Book, so that three or four forms may appear upon an opening. Unlike a Cheque Book, however, this book should be so arranged as—by the aid of a carbon sheet—to take a duplicate of all entries made upon the invoice form, which duplicate is also detachable, and should be sent to the counting-house at the same time that the original is despatched with the goods. The form of such a book may be readily gathered from the following—

EXAMPLE:

DUPLICATE INVOICE BOOKS
UPPER SHEET (on thin white paper).

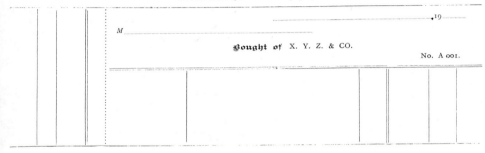

UNDER SHEET (on thicker paper, tinted according to Department, to facilitate dissection).

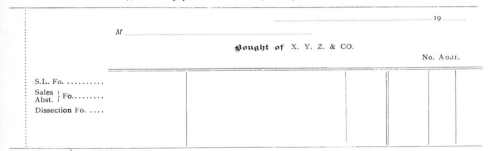

In addition to the advantages already enumerated, the employment of the above form of Invoice Book possesses another material advantage over the old-fashioned system of Day Book—namely, that it is absolutely impossible to prepare an invoice upon the properly headed form without at the same time bringing into existence a copy of such invoice. This effectively disposes of a risk that undoubtedly exists in practice—namely, that of inadvertently despatching goods accompanied by an invoice, without having first copied a record thereof in the Day Book.

It will be seen that the form given above contains certain reference spaces, the object of which has not yet been explained. These are required when it is decided to dispense even with a summarised form of bound Day Book, and to make the postings direct from the duplicate invoice slips. The counterfoils of the Invoice Book thus supply the functions of the Day Book so far as may be necessary—that is to say, they enable the total Sales from time to time to be readily ascertained for balancing purposes, and for the purpose of checking the dissection of such Sales, which doubtless takes place simultaneously. It is, of course, important that the slips should be carefully filed away in order, and that each Ledger entry should contain a reference which would enable the corresponding slip to be readily turned up at any moment when required; but so long as these precautions are attended to, no inconvenience will as a rule be found to result from posting direct from the copy invoice. The system possesses the material advantages of saving time, and of saving the risk of error in copying from the invoice into the Day Book—a matter which is the more important inasmuch as such an error would not disturb the balancing of the Ledger. This application of the Slip System has been for a great number of years employed by banks in connection with their customers' accounts, which are invariably posted up direct from the paying-in slips and cheques. An additional advantage of the system is that, if the original record contains bad or ambiguous figures, inasmuch as it has to pass through several hands, there is but little risk of those figures being mistaken in the first instance, and the error afterwards perpetuated throughout all the books. Practically the only disadvantage of the system is that reference to loose slips at a subsequent date would probably, under the best system of filing, occupy more time than reference to the Day Book. As a rule, however, such references would be sufficiently rare to make the point one of minor importance; while in those exceptional cases where, owing to the nature of the transactions, references are likely to be frequent, it would probably be thought better in any event to post full details of the entries into the Ledger, in which case the original slip would only have to be referred to if a dispute arose. Such cases may, however, be sometimes met by a further extension of the Slip System, under which the original invoice does duty for a Ledger Account as well.

SLIP LEDGERS.

Where it is desired to dispense with bound Ledgers as well as bound Day Books, and to make the original invoice slip serve all purposes, the underneath (or duplicate) slip requires to be slightly modified, and may take the following form:—

EXAMPLE:

		Particulars		Details		Dr.		Cr.	
									19
Name									
								No. A 000.	
		Forward ( )		£ s d		£ s d		£ s d	
								(NOTE.—The space occupied by this column must not be written upon on the upper sheet. It may be utilised for advertisements of specialities.)	
Sales Abst. Fo...... Dissection Fo......									
		Forward ( )							

Under these circumstances the slips, instead of being sorted out into consecutive order and carefully put away only to be referred to thereafter, under somewhat exceptional circumstances, are sorted out and put away in files or drawers, a separate space being set aside for the Personal Account of each customer. The account of that customer, therefore, instead of being comprised upon a single Ledger folio, or series of folios, is covered by a considerably greater number of loose slips, each of which contains only one entry, as well as the totals of the debits and credits both before and after that transaction was recorded. The number of slips in connection with any one Personal Account might under these circumstances easily reach inconvenient proportions; but this difficulty is to a very large extent obviated by providing two sets of filing mechanism, one of which contains all records of accounts that have been settled, leaving only the unsettled transactions in the filing frame that is being used and added to daily. The advantages of this development of the system are its absolute directness, and the impossibility of errors arising through incorrect copying. It is not particularly suitable where the number of transactions with each individual customer is likely to be very considerable, but it is of particular value in a business where the number of Sold Ledger Accounts is of necessity very large, although but comparatively few can be described as accounts of regular customers. The idea also provides a solution to what is often a most troublesome problem—namely, the most convenient method of dealing with small outstanding accounts in connection with cash businesses that are sometimes obliged to give credit to a known customer for a few days. There being no regular credit system, the Sold Ledgers will be non-existent; but a Sold Ledger *pro tem.* can be readily compiled from those invoice slips which represent unpaid accounts from time to time. By filing these slips upon a proper system, and dealing with them as transactions in accounts, it becomes possible to reduce the record to a proper and systematic basis; whereas, no matter

how carefully memoranda may be preserved until it is supposed that the occasion for further keeping them has gone by, there is always a likelihood of some oversight occurring. Moreover, such memoranda would at the best be of but little use for purposes of evidence in a Court of law, when it is, of course, open to the other side to call for the plaintiff's accounts dealing with the subject matter of dispute.

A very excellent device, framed upon these lines, has been produced by the Trading and Manufacturing Co., Lim., Temple Bar House, Fleet Street, E.C., from whose catalogue the following description is extracted:—

"**The Small Accounts Keeper** (illustrated below) is a simple, convenient, labour-saving, and economical device for keeping accounts of a small or transient nature.

EXAMPLE: *

" There is, perhaps, no greater difficulty in a retail business than the keeping in order of small accounts which are really not worth opening a Ledger Account for. Many are so small that a page of a Ledger or Account Book is wasted, or the items are so unimportant, or are paid so quickly, that booking into Memorandum or Day-book and posting to a Ledger is useless and altogether unnecessary labour. Besides that, your customer 'wants a bill.' With this system, the whole job is done at one writing.

" You cannot possibly mix your items, there being one account form for each customer, and the system is practically self-indexing.

" Where desired, they can be posted up from a day-book; but this is hardly necessary, except in a large business, or for purposes of checking.

---

* The above illustration is reproduced from the catalogue of the Trading & Manufacturing Co., Lim., from a block kindly lent by them.

" It will be found just the thing for customers who buy ' a few articles till Saturday night,' or ' till next week,' or ' till they pass again your way,' or ' come into the town again.'

" They perhaps leave a small balance over, or say ' don't charge it ; shall send it in.' Of course, they forget, but you can save loss by jotting it down on an ' S.A.K.' form.

" It consists of a thoroughly compact and substantially made file, having a patent swing twin-arch clip, fixed on a well-seasoned hard-wood back ; top cover-board well covered with cloth, and having eyeletted holes to prevent wearing in turning it over the arches.

" Indexing divisional sheets, made of glazed press-board, plainly lettered, can be supplied in 12's or 24's (one letter or two letters to each sheet), as may be considered necessary.

" Billheads or account forms are neatly ruled and printed on special paper in high-class style ; size 10¼in. by 5¼in., and are accurately punched to fit the twin arch. They are also made so that a duplicate copy can be taken at one writing, if desired.

EXAMPLE : *

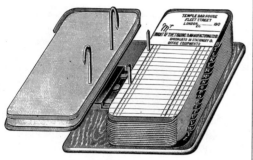

" Suppose a party named Jones buys an item, and, for any reason, does not pay. Take an account form and fill in name, and, if necessary, the address ; fill in the item, swing divisional at J open file and put the form on the uprights. When that party, or any other who may have had an account opened in the same way, has more goods to be charged, place them on the same sheet (without removing it from the file), and when they desire to pay, *the account is ready*, and can be opened up and removed in an instant. Think for a moment what an immense saving of labour and time this would be, instead of having to ' wade through ' leaves of a book or a stack of account forms. By placing accounts in absolutely alphabetical order, according to the vowel system (James before Jenkins, Smith before Smollett, and so on), the accounts are self-indexing.

" Any bill can be removed, or another inserted, in a moment, without disturbing the rest.

" This system will be found comparatively inexpensive, as Counter or Rough Day Books are dispensed with, besides the immense saving of time and labour."

The above remarks with regard to Slip Day Books are equally applicable to the initial record of all transactions other than Cash. In most businesses it will not be practicable to deal with any transactions other than Sales upon the Slip System, but individual ' cases may easily arise in which a further development of the system may be desirable. In this connection, it may be pointed out that the manner in which most solicitors keep their draft bills of costs contains in it the germs of the Slip System, and is capable of further amplification upon the same lines. It is not as a rule practicable to apply the system to Purchases, because the basis of the record in this case is an invoice received from outside, which naturally is not in the prescribed form suitable for such a purpose. It would not be impossible to annex slips to all invoices, as received, which would supply the omission ; but bearing in mind the fact that such invoices would be of all shapes and sizes, it is questionable whether it would often be found desirable to make the attempt, more especially in view of the fact that the number of Personal Accounts in connection with the Bought Ledger is never very great, and the demand therefore for labour-saving contrivances is thus less felt in this department than in connection with Sales.

SLIP CASH BOOKS.

Under this heading, as has already been foreshadowed, may be placed those developments of the Slip System which obviate the necessity of keeping subsidiary Cash Books for the sake of recording detailed postings into Trade Ledgers. Under all circumstances, it would doubtless be desirable to keep the General Cash Book as a bound book of account ; but in a concern of any magnitude, various subsidiary Cash Books would ordinarily be employed to record the entries affecting each of the several Trade Ledgers, and the Slip System may

---

* The above illustration is reproduced from the catalogue of the Trading & Manufacturing Co., Lim., from a block kindly lent by them.

often be usefully applied with a view to reducing work and saving unnecessary recopying in connection with these records.

Dealing first with Cash Received, as in the case of the old-fashioned Day Book, there is a risk of entries being omitted although goods have been sent out, so in the case of Cash is there a risk of money being acknowledged without the Cashier being debited with a corresponding sum. This risk is (to some extent at least) obviated by substituting carbon duplicate receipts for counterfoil receipts. The safeguard is, of course, not infallible, because such records being written in pencil might be tampered with subsequently; but this risk may be reduced to a minimum if careful supervision be insisted upon. The following form of Receipt Book will fully explain the general idea in connection with this part of the system.

EXAMPLE:

FORM OF THE CASH RECEIVED BOOK.

COUNTERFOIL FOR TOTALS ONLY.	DETACHABLE SLIP FOR LEDGER CLERK.	GUMMED RECEIPT FORM (Printed on reverse side to fold over).
001	**001** 19	**001** 19
	S L. Fo.	**Received** from .... 1d.
	Cash £ : :	Cash £ : : For X. Y. Z. & Co.
	Dis. £ : :	Dis. £ : : ....
002	**002**	**002**

In its most rudimentary form this system will be so applied that the carbon duplicates (which are facsimiles of the actual receipts issued to customers) are detached from the Receipt Book and handed to the Ledger clerks, to be posted by them to the Personal Accounts of the various customers. The counterfoils in the Receipt Book will enable a total of Cash Received to be arrived at which will serve the double purpose of enabling each Sold Ledger to be balanced, and of checking the cash debited in the General Cash Book as having been actually received from customers. If, however, the system be developed further (as previously explained) so that the original slips are employed to take the place of Ledger Accounts, then—like the Day Book slips— the duplicates must be somewhat altered in form, and will bear the same relationship to the above form, that the form on page 204 bears to that shown on page 203.

It is unnecessary to again go into the question of the relative advantages of the "old" and "new" systems at this point, as the matter has already been referred to in connection with the development of Day Book Slips into Ledger Accounts (page 205). It may be added, however, that it is very possible to over-estimate the disadvantage of receipts given from carbon books, and therefore in pencil. The possible risk that they might be fraudulently altered by the customer may, it is thought, be left out of account, because—apart from the evidence of the customer's cheque—the fact that a duplicate can be produced that *ought* to be an exact facsimile of the original reduces this risk to a minimum. The risk that the duplicate may be fraudulently altered to conceal a deficiency on the part of the Cashier is a contingency which, in the first place, will only seriously arise if the Cashier had control of the duplicates (a contingency that ought never to be possible) ; while, in the second place, given these undesirable conditions, the more common form of counterfoil receipt, although written in ink, affords even less protection than the carbon duplicate variety, for with the former there is nothing to prevent the body of the receipt and the counterfoil having been made out for different amounts *ab initio*, whereas with the carbon variety an alteration is a *sine quâ non* before any discrepancy is possible. It is, perhaps, just conceivable that the upper sheet might be filled up without any carbon sheet underneath, and the under sheet subsequently filled up by writing direct upon the carbon, but such irregularities as these would be too dangerous to be likely to occur in any well ordered office where a regular system of supervision applied. In the absence of supervision, irregularities of all kinds are, of course, not merely possible, but to be expected ; in such cases, however, their occurrence must in fairness be attributed, not to the system of accounting employed, but to the lack of system in connection with the supervision and the manner in which it is carried out.

Passing on to Cash Payments, a book containing particulars of remittances can be readily so framed (upon the lines already described) as to form the basis of postings to the debit of Ledger Accounts, without necessitating the intervention of a Bought Ledger Cash Book ; and, if thought desirable, such a book might be further extended so as to include the actual cheques themselves, although these would of necessity have to be written in ink, and it would be well therefore to so arrange the form that it was unnecessary to retain a carbon duplicate of this portion. It may be pointed out, however, that with most concerns Bought Ledger payments would not be so numerous as to make this particular development of the Slip System specially advantageous, while expenditure which had to be posted to the debit of Nominal Accounts would, it is thought, in all cases be better recorded upon the " old " system, through the medium of bound books. There is an obvious advantage to be gained by the application of the Slip System to Sold Ledger Cash, because it reduces to a minimum the risk of money being received and acknowledged upon the proper form without being afterwards duly accounted for. In the case of Bought Ledger Cash, however, and other payments by cheque, the counterfoils of the Cheque Book (which are themselves a rudimentary form of Slip System) afford a sufficient safeguard against such omissions.

SLIP LEDGERS.

The employment of the original record as a book of first entry, and also as a Ledger Account, has already been explained. It may be added, however, that there are other developments of the Slip System in connection with Ledgers, which may be used either in connection with Slip Day Books or Cash Books, or in connection with bound books of first-entry.

CARD LEDGERS.

With the ordinary bound Ledger, a page, or a certain number of pages, are in the first place set aside for each of the various accounts, and if the space so originally provided be filled up before the Ledger as a whole is full, the account has to be carried forward to some other portion of the same Ledger ; while eventually, when the whole Ledger has been completely filled, every account therein contained (except those which show no balance, and upon which no further transactions are expected) has to be simultaneously carried forward into a new Ledger, opened upon similar lines. The Card Ledger possesses the following advantages :—

(1) By keeping two sets of frames, for "open" and "closed" accounts respectively, the number of actual Ledger Accounts that have to be handled from time to time is reduced to a minimum, and the labour of extracting balances simplified to a corresponding extent.

(2) The record of transactions with each individual customer can be kept together, instead of being scattered over a number of different parts of a series of Ledgers.

(3) As the cards can be kept in any desired order, no Ledger Index is necessary.

(4) The time never arrives when a new Ledger and Index have to be prepared *in toto*. The Card Ledger is "perpetual."

(5) The cards being—for the sake of convenient handling—comparatively small, there is never any temptation to have recourse to the objectionable device of opening two or three accounts upon the same page.

The disadvantages of the Card System are:—

(1) A card may be displaced, or lost.

(2) A falsified card may be bodily substituted for one that the Ledger-keeper desires to suppress.

(3) An elaborate special ruling is impracticable upon a small-sized card.

(4) Objections might be raised to a Card Ledger, if produced as evidence in a Court of law.

Subject to the qualification that no development of the Slip System should ever be introduced, save where there is a competent staff of bookkeepers who are properly and effectively supervised, it is thought that the last-named is the only objection that need be seriously regarded. At the present time there might quite conceivably be some prejudice against Card Ledgers as evidence of transactions that actually took place at some previous date, but the Ledger posting is, of course, only one of several records that would be in existence to prove that the entry was made upon the date named. There ought, therefore, never to be any serious difficulty in producing sufficient evidence to show that the entries relied upon were actually made at the time stated, and this, of course, is the only material point.

The usual forms of Ledger Card, and of the framework in which such Cards may be arranged, are shown below:—

EXAMPLE: *

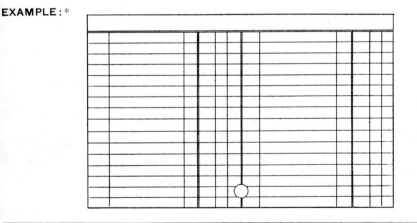

---

* *The above illustration is reproduced from the catalogue of the Library Supply Co., from a block kindly lent by them.*

EXAMPLE : *

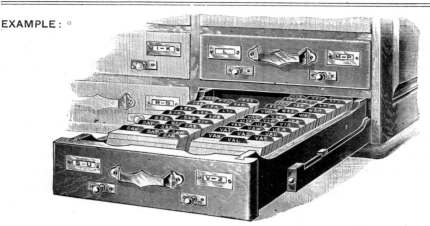

LOOSE-LEAF LEDGERS.

Loose-Leaf Ledgers occupy a place midway between Card Ledgers and Book Ledgers. In form they are like the latter, with the important exception that the leaves, instead of being permanently bound together, are merely held by a locking arrangement, which grips them tightly for the time being. As often as may be required the Ledger can be unlocked, filled up folios removed and placed in the "Old Accounts" binding cover, and their place taken by new sheets. The advantages of the Loose-Leaf Ledger over the Card Ledger would appear to be chiefly that it can be readily manipulated by those who have had no previous experience of the Slip System; and, further, that the sheets may be of any convenient size and ruling, whereas Cards cannot conveniently be larger than (say) five inches by eight inches, on account of the difficulty of quickly handling larger sizes. Under some circumstances, when it is desired that the Ledger postings should contain considerable detail, the advantage of being able to employ large Ledger Sheets of special ruling may be considerable. As a rule, however, for Bought or Sold Ledgers no very detailed postings are necessary. A form of Loose-Leaf Ledger is shown below :—

EXAMPLE : †

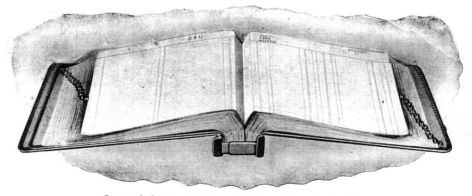

Open ready for use. Note the index distributed through the book.

     * The above illustration is reproduced from the catalogue of the Library Supply Co., from a block kindly lent by them.
     † The above illustration is reproduced from the catalogue of the Trading and Manufacturing Co. Lim., from a block kindly lent by them.

EXAMPLE: *

Sheet from Loose-Leaf Ledger.

SUMMARY.

From what has been ·stated above, it will be seen that the Slip System is—to some extent at least—a "reversion" to keeping records upon loose sheets of paper, instead of in bound books. If it is to retain its functions as a "system," it need hardly be pointed out that it is essential that especial care should be taken that everything is done properly and in order —in fact, systematically. It would probably never be safe to depute inexperienced or inefficient book-keepers to keep records upon the Slip System; but experience has shown that competent bookkeepers, if reasonably supervised, can produce excellent results from this system, and that a material saving of time—and, in consequence, of salaries—may result from its introduction. Another special convenience,

which in some cases is particularly valuable, is that the system readily lends itself to every possible sub-division of labour. With bound books it is not usually practicable for more than two clerks to be at work upon the same pair of books (Ledger and book of first-entry) at the same time. Under the Slip System, however, there is no difficulty whatever in any desired number of clerks being at work simultaneously. This naturally does away with one of the more important advantages of sub-dividing heavy Trade Ledgers; but the convenience of being able to balance each Ledger separately is such that a similar distinction should, as a rule, be observed in connection with Card or Slip Ledgers as much as with bound or Loose-Leaf Ledgers. This division can, however, be very readily marked by regarding each drawer or file in which the Cards, or Slips, are kept as a Ledger capable of being separately balanced. Alternatively, some houses prefer to abandon all attempt to divide, say, the Sold Ledger into sections, but balance the whole daily. So long as it is practicable to extract a Trial Balance each day, a sub-division is probably unnecessary; and—in connection with the Slip System—a per-manent record of the Ledger balances at the close of each day is undoubtedly of very considerable value; but if, for any reason, it is not practicable to balance the Ledger at such frequent intervals, some form of sub-division will doubtless be found desirable, in order to enable errors to be located when a difference in balancing is found to exist.

---

* The above illustration is reproduced from the catalogue of the Trading & Manufacturing Co., Lim., from a block kindly lent by them.

CHAPTER XIX.

COST ACCOUNTS.

COST ACCOUNTS are accounts supplemental, or subsidiary, to financial accounts, and are compiled for the purpose of giving additional information as to the detailed cost of working an undertaking, or any particular section thereof. It will thus be seen that, whereas the financial accounts are complete in themselves and independent of the Cost Accounts, the latter are of the very greatest importance and value to those responsible for the successful working of the undertaking. Speaking generally, a Cost Account may be said to be a section, or portion, of the Trading and Profit and Loss Accounts. It may sometimes represent some division of the latter in point of time or in departments (each section covering the same period as the combined account), or the divisions may be in both respects simultaneously, as when separate Cost Accounts are prepared of each contract undertaken, numerous contracts being worked upon at the same time, while the period occupied over each contract is a varying quantity.

The nature of the Cost Accounts, and also the manner in which they are compiled, will depend greatly upon the nature of the transactions embarked upon. Before discussing the matter further, therefore, it will perhaps be convenient to indicate the different classes of Cost Accounts most usually to be found. They are as follow :—

(1) Undertakings whose transactions are divisible into several distinct departments, each dealing with a separate class of goods, which are regularly being constructed.

(2) Undertakings whose transactions are divisible into distinct contracts, where the separate result of each contract is required.

(3) Undertakings whose transactions are divisible into separate contracts, each of which contracts is executed in part by various different departments, when it is desired to show separate departmental results, and also the results of each separate contract.

(4) Undertakings whose transactions consist of the manufacture of a single product, but where the conditions are such that the cost of manufacturing that product varies greatly from time to time.

(5) Undertakings whose transactions involve the manufacture of a great number of different articles, each consisting of two or more processes, where it is desired to show separate results, both departmentally and in respect of each article ; but where, owing to the number of the latter, complete Cost Accounts are impracticable.

The above classification of Cost Accounts has been suggested by a perusal of STRACHAN's " COST ACCOUNTS " (an interesting hand-book recently published by Messrs. Stevens & Haynes), and will serve the present purpose as well as any other. It will be readily understood, however, that in the nature of things Cost Accounts are hardly capable of exact division into distinct classes, on account of the widely varying requirements of different undertakings.

(1) DEPARTMENTAL COST ACCOUNTS.

The requirements under this heading are comparatively simple, inasmuch as all that is required is a number of detailed Trading Accounts—one for each department—all of which will cover the same period as the Trading Account which forms part of the system of financial books. Under these circumstances, it will be convenient that the financial Trading Account should include those items included in the Departmental Cost Accounts, and no others, so that the aggregate result of the Cost Accounts may agree with the balance transferred from the Trading Account to the Profit and Loss Account. This system of accounting will be found suitable to manufactures which include a number of comparatively simple and distinct articles, in which case the accounts are merely upon the lines of ordinary Departmental Accounts (already explained in Chap. V.) ; the system is also suitable where the manufacture consist of a number of distinct, and well-defined, processes through which every article has to be taken.

A typical example of such a condition of affairs will be found to obtain in a Boot and Shoe Factory. The procedure in such cases will be similar to the Departmental Accounts, save that each department, after the first, must be treated as purchasing from the preceding department its manufactured product. A definite scale of prices must therefore be arranged as between one department and another, each department being treated as having earned its profit as soon as it has completed its part of the whole process of manufacture. This system lends itself readily to the preparation of detailed and accurate accounts, and, speaking generally, infringes no fundamental principle of accounting. It is important, however, when preparing the financial accounts at the end of each period, to broadly review the general position with a view to guarding against partly-finished goods being taken into stock at a sum in excess of actual cost, unless there is every reason for supposing that the manufacture will in due course be completed and the articles then find a ready purchaser at the normal price. If there be any doubt under either of these headings, then clearly a reserve should be made against possible loss on the work already done in the earlier departments of manufacture.

(2) SIMPLE CONTRACT ACCOUNTS.

This, as a class of Cost Accounts, is not likely to occur often in practice ; but it is convenient to consider the simpler problems here provided before viewing them in their more practical, and more complicated, aspect as appearing under heading (3). The nature of the transactions is that certain simple articles, which can be completely manufactured in a single department, are contracted to be made at definite prices, and the object of the Cost Accounts is to show the actual cost of production, with a view to (a) checking the estimate upon which the contract was based ; (b) providing data for future estimates ; and (c) enabling leakages to be detected, thus paving the way for the introduction of further economies in the future. The principle in these cases is identical with the principle of Departmental Accounts, save that the division, instead of being upon definite lines that are invariably the same, varies from time to time according to the contracts then in hand, each account being closed up as soon as that contract is completed. The Cost Accounts do not thus run on for a period equal to the financial year of the undertaking, but for a period equal to the duration of the contract ; to enable the Cost Accounts to be reconciled with the financial accounts, however, each contract remaining uncompleted at the close of a financial year must be balanced up to that date, in addition to being balanced off when the work is finished.

(3) DEPARTMENTAL CONTRACT ACCOUNTS.

The distinction between the accounts that come under this heading and those referred to under the preceding is that the contract in each case consists of several " parts," or distinct processes, the results of each of which have to be definitely shown. The accounts therefore require still further sub-division in order to produce the required result. **Each** separate Cost Account should show not merely the result of that particular contract, but also the expenses incurred in connection with each department or process, and *per contra* that portion of the contract price which may be allocated thereto. The latter may be readily arrived at, in that the estimate would always be the aggregate of an estimate of each separate department, or process. Cost Accounts coming under this classification would be tabulated from time to time, so as to show not merely the separate result of each contract and the aggregate result of the contracts as a whole, but also the aggregate result of each separate department. The majority of manufacturers' accounts, where the work is contracted for in advance, will come under this heading.

(4) "SHORT-PERIOD" COST ACCOUNTS.

The requirements under this heading are comparatively simple, in that the account is practically neither more nor less than a Trading Account for a limited period, save that (as a rule) the particulars of cost will be fuller than is usually considered necessary in financial accounts. Examples of such accounts are afforded by Collieries, Iron and Steel Manufacturers, Gas Works, and the like, while accounts prepared upon exactly the same lines are compiled by Railways, Tramways, Hotels, and certain other undertakings, which, although not engaged in manufacture, require for their successful working to keep careful and constant supervision over their working expenses. The problem in such cases is comparatively simple, in that the analysis of expenditure follows exactly the same lines as that required for the financial accounts, save that perhaps some further dissection is necessary to provide the additional detail required. Assuming, however, that the Cost Accounts are prepared, say, fortnightly, then 13 such accounts should agree exactly in all particulars with the half-yearly Trading Account. The object of compiling the record at more frequent intervals is, in the first place, that leakages may be detected and rectified at the earliest possible moment; and, in the second place, that the output

may be controlled, by restricting it when conditions are unfavourable, and enlarging it when the value of the product is relatively high as compared with the cost of its production.

(5) MISCELLANEOUS COST ACCOUNTS.

Under this heading may be included the accounts of those manufacturers who deal with a vast number of different and continually varying articles, some of which are made for "stock" purposes, and some on contract, under such conditions that it is practically impossible to employ a complete system of Cost Accounts, such as those already described. In such cases naturally all that is possible is to compile the most complete accounts that are reasonably practicable in the difficult circumstances of the case. As a rule, it will not be practicable to do more than keep complete Departmental Accounts (as explained under paragraph (1)), and to supplement these by Cost Accounts in connection with certain articles, selected from time to time as tests; while occasionally it may be found practicable to keep complete particulars of all costing operations over a comparatively short period, although the cost of keeping such accounts continuously would be prohibitive. It is under this heading that the most difficult problems will arise in practice; but inasmuch as each must be dealt with upon its own merits, no general observations, such as could be made here, are likely to prove very useful in practice.

PREPARATION OF COST ACCOUNTS.

The general nature of Cost Accounts under varying circumstances having now been described, it will be seen that, in general, the process of compiling such accounts involves neither more nor less than an elaborate dissection of all expenditure into more or less numerous sub-divisions. Such expenditure may be broadly classified under four headings:—

(*a*) Wages.

(*b*) Materials specially acquired for that particular purpose, and capable of being directly charged thereto.

(c) Materials consumed from Stock.

(d) General Establishment Expenses.

The most convenient method of dissecting these four classes of expenditure will, in the nature of things, vary to a large extent according to the manner in which it is found convenient to record such expenditure in the financial books of account. The question is one that should always be carefully taken into consideration when the system of financial accounts is being designed; but, inasmuch as such systems will naturally vary enormously according to the requirements of each particular undertaking, only a few general indications can be given in the present work. This, it is thought, will be self-evident, when it is borne in mind that a volume at least the size of the present one might usefully be written on the Cost Accounts of any one representative industry.

(a) WAGES.—If the financial books are designed to show departmental results, the Wages Analyses may be readily framed to dissect the total wages paid from time to time into departments. When, however, it is desired to further sub-divide Wages so as to show the expenditure upon each of a number of different contracts, such dissection must (as a rule) take place outside the books necessary for financial purposes. Not infrequently the dissection may be best accomplished upon sheets ruled similar to the following

EXAMPLE : WAGES DISSECTION, for the Fortnight ended.................190..

Name	Total	Numbers of Contract										
	£ s d	£ s d	£ s d	£ s d	£ s d	£ s d	£ s d	£ s d	£ s d	£ s d	£ s d	£ s d
Contract Ledger fo.	....	....	....	....	....	....	....	....	....	....	....	....

If practicable, however, it will often be found to materially reduce the amount of work involved if some development of the Slip System (Chap. XVIII.) be applied to the analysis of Wages over the various contracts. The Slip System lends itself well to work of this description, in that there is rarely (if ever) any imperative necessity for keeping a permanent record of how the various details of Wages are made up, so long as the amount debited weekly (or fortnightly) to the various contracts then open is made to agree with the total of Wages paid.

It may be added that, under the general term "Wages" as employed here, it should be understood that all payments to workers and supervisors are included which are capable of being directly analysed over the various contracts in hand. Salaries paid to managers, and other similar expenses which cannot be so readily dissected, are best included under the heading of Establishment Expenses, and divided in the manner explained hereafter.

(*b*) MATERIALS DIRECTLY CHARGEABLE.—The expenditure under this heading may be readily arrived at if a suitable form of Purchase Book be employed for the record of invoices for all goods received, such as the following

EXAMPLE :

PURCHASE BOOK, for the month of.........................190 .

Date	No. of Invoice	Name	B. L. Fo.	Amount of Invoice	Miscellaneous Accounts			Stores	Contracts		
					Account	N. L. Fo.	Amount		No.	C. L. Fo.	Amount
				£ s d			£ s d	£ s d			£ s d

Here again, however, the principles of the Slip System may often be employed with advantage, the actual invoices themselves being handled, and charged up direct to the various contracts; or Analysis Sheets, supplementary to the Purchases Book, may be employed, such sheets being for all practical purposes "intermediate" Ledgers, collecting the materials directly chargeable against each contract, so that the periodical total only is posted to the Ledger Account opened in respect thereof in the Cost Ledger.

(*c*) STORES CONSUMED.—Under this heading may be included all Materials (including Plant) issued from the works for the use of any particular contract, each contract being afterwards credited with the value of such Materials and Plant as may be returned unconsumed. In the case of Plant, however, credit should be given at a reduced figure, to compensate for the wear and tear incurred during the time that the Plant remained at the disposal of that particular contract. To avoid confusion, it is perhaps desirable to add that this actual debiting and crediting of Plant to a contract would only be performed in cases where the work was done away from the factory; it is, then, most important to keep an accurate record of all Plant that may leave the factory premises, with a view to seeing that it finds its way back again to the factory yard after the contract has been completed.

There are numerous methods in general use of keeping a record of Stores; but many of these methods are unreliable owing to their unsystematic nature, and it is thought that some application of the Slip System is the only satisfactory method that can be employed. Under this system a requisition should be made out, and given to the Storekeeper in exchange for whatever may be required. This requisition should be recorded by the Storekeeper—

(1) To the debit of the contract;

(2) To the credit of that particular class of Stores or Plant.

On Stores (or Plant) being returned, the reverse process should be pursued. A good form of "Stores Issued Slip" for general purposes is the following :—

EXAMPLE :

(UPPER SHEET.)

ACME ENGINEERING COMPANY, LIM.

No. ooo. ....19..........

To the Storekeeper

Deliver to bearer

(This space

to be left

blank.)

Charge to

Contract No. .... (Signed)...

(LOWER SHEET.)

STORES ISSUED SLIP.

No. ooo. ....19..........

Debited fo.................Priced by...

Credited fo.................Passed by...

	Price	Amount
		£ s d

Debit to

Contract No..............

NOTE.—The Lower Sheet is forwarded from the office direct to the clerical staff in charge of Stores records, to be priced out and duly entered up by them.

The Stores Returned Slip might be upon the same lines, but should be printed on distinctively coloured paper, in order to guard against possible errors.

The Storekeeper should have charge of two Ledgers (each of which might usefully be of the Loose-Leaf, or Card, variety, as may be preferred), the first one to contain an account for each Contract to be debited with all Stores issued, and credited with all Stores returned; the second (or Stores Ledger) to contain an account for each distinctive class of Stores, to be credited with all Stores issued, and debited with all Stores returned into stock. The division of the Stores as a whole into separate Ledger Accounts is a matter that can only be usefully determined by someone practically acquainted with the nature of the goods to be handled. Speaking generally, all that can be said is that, while it is undesirable to multiply separate accounts unnecessarily, there should be a sufficient number of such accounts to enable them to provide a useful check upon the quantity of Stores in hand from time to time, and to enable such shortages as will doubtless of necessity arise to be carefully scrutinised, with a view to restricting losses within the narrowest possible compass. Each month the Storekeeper should compile a schedule of his total debits and credits to each account in both his Ledgers. The one set of figures will supply the monthly totals of Stores Issued and Stores Returned, to be debited and credited respectively to each Contract in the Cost Ledger; the other set will supply the totals of Stores Issued and Stores Returned to be credited and debited respectively to the Stores Account in the Nominal Ledger.

(*d*) ESTABLISHMENT CHARGES.—Under this heading must be included all those expenses that are not comprised in the three preceding ones, but which are included in the financial books as a debit to the Trading Account (or to the Trading and Profit and Loss Account, as the case may be). As the charge in respect of Establishment Expenses has to be made before the close of the financial year (and therefore before the exact total of such expenses has been ascertained), it is clear that the amount to be debited to each of the various accounts in the Cost Ledger in respect of Establishment Expenses can only be an estimated item. The estimate should, however, be compiled as carefully as possible, and should (if anything) err upon the side of being too heavy, rather than too light, so that the results shown by the Cost Ledger may be "conservative" estimates of the actual results achieved.

The best method of apportioning Establishment Expenses over the various accounts is a matter upon which some difference of opinion exists, and also one which must to some extent vary according to the circumstances of the case. Speaking generally, however, it may be stated that while certain Establishment Charges may be most accurately said to vary according to the total cost of the work performed, others will vary most closely according to the contract price, according to the amount of wages paid, or according to the amount of time occupied upon the job. As it is extremely desirable that the basis of apportionment should be as accurate as possible, it is desirable that Establishment Expenses should be sub-divided into two or more headings, and a separate amount for Establishment Expenses debited in respect of each group, upon the principle that appears to be the fairest. For the sake of more clearly showing what is intended here, the following sub-division is given. It must be understood, however, that each case should be carefully considered upon its own merits, in order that an accurate basis of apportionment may be arrived at.

(1) Establishment Expenses to be provided for by way of a percentage on the number of hours booked to the job—

Rent of Factory.

Rates, Taxes, and Insurance of Factory.

Salaries of Factory Managers.

(2) Establishment Expenses to be provided for by way of a percentage on the amount of Wages paid—

Depreciation of Machinery.

Motive Power.

(3) Establishment Expenses to be provided for by way of a percentage on total prime cost—

General Office Expenses.

Discounts and Bad Debts.

COST LEDGER ACCOUNTS.

So far the method of dissecting costs over distinct contracts has alone been dealt with. When, however, each contract has to be further sub-divided into separate processes for costing purposes, each such process must have allocated to it a separate Ledger Account. As a rule, it is convenient to let each contract as a whole bear a consecutive number rather than to allot a distinct number to each such process, the various processes being identified either by distinctive initials or secondary numbers; for example, 1562A. or 1562/1.

For marshalling the aggregate total of Cost Accounts at stated periods, an analysis of the Cost Ledger, ruled in tabular form, will be found extremely convenient. Where the contracts are numerous, it will usually be found best to give a separate line to each contract (or section thereof), the different classes of expenditure appearing in different columns; by this means the number of columns may be kept within reasonable limits. The following shows a useful form of ruling, which, however, will naturally require considerable modification according to circumstances.

EXAMPLE:

COST LEDGER SUMMARY for the year / half-year ended........................190

Cost Ledger Fo.	Contract No.	Sub-Contract No.	Wages	Special Materials	Stores and Plant	Total	Less Stores and Plant Returned	Prime Cost	Establishment Expenses			Total Cost	Contract Price	Profit	Loss	Remarks
									% on Time	% on Wages	% on Prime Cost					
			£ s d	£ s d	£ s d	£ s d	£ s d	£ s d	£ s d	£ s d	£ s d	£ s d	£ s d	£ s d	£ s d	

RECONCILIATION WITH FINANCIAL ACCOUNTS.

Cost records which are not capable of being reconciled, or agreed, with the actual results shown by the financial books are practically valueless, inasmuch as there can be no assurance even of their approximate accuracy. It is, therefore, an essential feature of every system of Cost Accounts which puts forward the least claim to completeness that the result should be capable of being—and should be—reconciled with the results shown by the financial books every time the latter are balanced. Of necessity, there will be some discrepancy between the two sets of results, for the following reasons :—

(1) Some portion of the actual expenditure upon Wages may not be directly chargeable against any Contract. Such portion should properly be included under the heading of " Establishment Expenses," but, owing to the difficulty of exactly estimating it in advance, there is certain to be some discrepancy under this item.

(2) In Materials directly chargeable there ought to be an exact agreement between the cost and financial records. Any Materials directly charged against a contract, but returned into stock because unconsumed, may be properly credited to the contract and debited to the appropriate Stores Account, and such entries ought not to interfere with an exact agreement under this heading.

(3) There should be no difficulty in obtaining an exact agreement between the general Stores actually debited to the various contracts, and those credited to the Stores Accounts ; but in practice there will always be a certain amount of shortages in the latter that have to be written off. Experience should show the amount of leakage that may fairly be expected under this heading—a leakage which ought to be entirely explainable as a loss of weight, or quantity, arising from the breaking of bulk, or from a loss of weight (e.g., through drying) while the goods remained in stock. Assuming, however, that an efficient supervision is kept over the Storekeeper, and that no improper leakages occur, a reserve sufficient to cover any loss under this heading may easily be provided for under " Establishment Expenses."

(4) Under the heading of Establishment Expenses there is bound to be some discrepancy between the estimates contained in the Cost records, and the actual facts recorded in the financial books. The most important factor in this discrepancy would be that, even supposing the correct amount of Establishment Expenses could be estimated in advance, it is practically impossible to estimate the output in advance, and therefore the percentage on the Prime Cost, &c., that must be added to the Prime Cost in order to cover Establishment Expenses cannot be absolutely determined beforehand. Such discrepancies as may arise under this heading, however, ought to be readily capable of being explained at the close of the financial period, and inasmuch as the total Establishment Expenses ought never in the case of normal industries to represent more than 5 per cent. or 6 per cent. of the total output, any difference that may legitimately occur under this heading ought not to be serious.

It has already been stated that the Cost records are, as a rule, best kept quite separate from the financial books. The most obvious advantages of so treating them are—

(1) That entirely different staffs may then be kept upon the two classes of records, when each will provide a check upon the accuracy of the other's work.

(2) The advantages that naturally obtain when Ledgers are sub-divided, namely, that an exact balance can be more readily arrived at, and (to

some extent, that each balance may be employed as a cheque upon the other.

The exact accounts to be opened in the financial books to record the cost transactions in total will naturally vary considerably according to circumstances. It may be mentioned, however, that often the most convenient plan will be to open in the Private Ledger a "Cost Ledger Account," which is virtually an "Adjustment Account," linking the financial books with the Cost Ledgers. At the close of each financial period the balance standing on the Cost Ledger Account in the Private Ledger should agree with the total of the outstanding balances in the Cost Ledger itself, as representing the value of Work in Progress. If it be thought desirable to make the Cost Ledger "self-balancing," with a view to enabling the accuracy of its postings to be checked at frequent intervals without reference to the financial books, this may be readily accomplished by introducing into that Ledger an "Adjustment Account" of the usual description.

CONCLUSION.

The subjoined *pro formâ* Cost Accounts provide examples of such accounts that have been found useful in actual practice in connection with the various industries named. Up to a point, they may be taken as an indication of the general requirements of these respective industries. It need hardly be pointed out, however, that the requirements of undertakings carrying on a similar business are by no means uniform. Special and local considerations have to be taken into account, and (as has been already stated) the most suitable system for any particular undertaking can only be ascertained after a full and detailed enquiry has been made into its peculiar circumstances and conditions.

EXAMPLES:

FOR IRON FOUNDERS, STEEL MANUFACTURERS, &c.

COST OF MANUFACTURE.

Tons Cwts. Qrs. lbs.

Dr.   Make   639   13   1   12

	Weight	Average price per Ton	Amount	Cost per Ton	Consumption of materials per Ton of Iron
	Ts cts. qs. lbs.	£ s d	£ s d	£ s d	Ts. cts. qs. lbs.
To Puddled Bars ..	316 9 3 0	3 5 7	1,037 8 10	1 12 5·25	9 3 16
„ Scrap Iron ..	413 11 0 14	2 11 0	1,054 2 4	1 12 11·25	12 3 11
„ Coal ..	730 0 3 14	—	2,091 11 2	3 5 4·50	1 2 3 9
	564 18 0 0	7 8	214 5 5	6 8·40	17 2 18
„ Firebricks, Clay, and Sand ..	..	..	33 3 4	1 0·44	
„ Stores ..	..	..	57 8 11	1 9·55	
„ Repairs—Materials ..	..	..	41 15 2	1 3·67	
„ Do. Labour ..	..	..	22 5 10	8·36	
„ Trade Charges ..	..	..	32 12 8	1 0·24	
„ Rent, Rates, and Taxes ..	..	..	54 18 6	1 8·60	
„ Gas and Water ..	..	..	10 17 6	4·08	
„ Office Expenses ..	..	..	31 13 6	11·90	
„ Wages and Salaries ..	..	..	467 11 4	14 7·43	
Total Cost ..	..	..	£3,058 3 4	4 15 7·17	
„ Balance, being Profit (carried to Profit and Loss Account) ..	..	..	249 8 8	7 9·85	
			£3,307 12 0	£5 3 5·02	

Cr.

		Ts. cts. qs. lbs.	£ s d	£ s d
By Bar Iron ..		646 14 1 21	3,593 2 9	Value per ton
Less	Ts. cts. qs. lbs.	£ s d		
Discounts and Allowances ..	6 1 0 9	94 10 7		
Carriage, Freight, &c. ..	..	105 14 3		
Commission ..	..	47 10 0		
	6 1 0 9	307 14 10		
		640 13 1 12	3,285 7 11	5 2 6·77
Deduct				
Decrease in Stock of Bar Iron :—	19 0 0 0	104 10 0		
Stock at 1 Jan. 1892 ..	18 0 0 0	90 0 0		
Do. 31 July 1892 ..		1 0 0 0	14 10 0	
By Mill Cinder Scale, &c. .. 145 tons 10 cwt. ..	..		3,270 17 11	5 2 3·22
			36 14 1	
Total make and value of same ..	..	639 13 1 12	£3,307 12 0	£5 3 5·02

FOR COLLIERIES.   PIT No. ....

Summary Cost Sheet, 4 weeks ending............ 19....

	£ s d	This Month — Average per Saleable Ton	Last Month
			This is for the corresponding figures of the previous 4 weeks
Tons Raised	14,000 0 0		
Tons Saleable	12,600 0 0		
(On which Costs are calculated.)			
	Tons. £ s d	s d	
Sales, Coal and Slack	12,000 3,912 10 0	6 6·25	
Coal Stock, Increase	600 150 12 6	5 0·23	
Total Credits	12,600 £4,063 2 6	6 5·39	

	£ s d	£ s d	s d	s d
Wages: Colliers	1,050 0 0		1 8	
„ Underground	551 5 0		0 10·5	
„ Surface	498 15 0	2,100 0 0	0 9·5	3 4
Timber used	315 0 0		0 6	
Rails „	13 2 6		0 0·25	
Stores „	52 10 0	380 12 6	0 1	0 7·25
Repairs and Renewals, exclusive of Wages	78 15 0		0 1·5	
Horse-keep and Stables	91 17 6	170 12 6	0 1·75	0 3·25
Royalty, Freehold and Leasehold	315 0 0		0 6	
Depreciation	157 10 0	472 10 0	0 3	0 9
Cost Loaded		3,123 15 0		4 11·5
Management	105 0 0		0 2	
Salaries and Travelling	91 17 6		0 1·75	
Office Expenses	52 10 0		0 1	
Rents, Rates, Taxes, Insurance and Employers' Liability	91 17 6	341 5 0	0 1·75	0 6·5
Discounts and Bad Debts		52 10 0		0 1
Total Cost		3,517 10 0		5 7
Apparent Profit, 4 weeks		545 12 6		0 10·39
		£4,063 2 6		6 5·39

FOR GAS COMPANIES.

.... GAS COMPANY.

WORKING STATEMENT for the Year ended .... 19....

	Cubic Feet
Gas made, as per Station Meter..	156,288,000
Gas Sold—Private Lighting..	137,963,400
Public Lighting ..	10,953,450
	148,916,850 or 95·28 per cent. on make
	7,371,150
Gas used on Works and Office, as per Meters ..	2,500,000 or 1·60 „ „
Gas unaccounted for ..	4,871,150 or 3·12 „ „
	100·00

Capital Employed ..	£76,689 0s. 0d.
„ „ per Ton of Coal Carbonized	£5 6s. 0d.
„ „ per 1,000 cubic feet of Gas sold	10s. 3d.
Coal Carbonized—Common ..	14,117 Tons or 97·62 per cent.
Cannel ..	344 „ „ 2·38 „
	14,461 „ „ 100·00

Gas made per Ton of Coal Carbonized	10,807 cubic feet
Gas sold per Ton of Coal Carbonized..	10,298 „
Coke made ..	14,460 chaldrons
Coke made per Ton of Coal Carbonized	36 bushels
Coke used for fuel per cent. on make ..	22·18
Tar made ..	150,180 gallons
Tar made per Ton of Coal Carbonized	11 „
Liquor made ..	405,594 „
Liquor made per Ton of Coal Carbonized	28 „
Net average price realised for Coke sold	8s. 2¾d. per chaldron
„ „ „ Breeze sold	2s. 8¼d. „
„ „ „ Tar sold	1¼d. „ gallon
„ „ „ Liquor sold ..	34s. per 1,000 gallons
Net proceeds of Coke and other Residuals per cent. on cost of Coal ..	73·32

	£ s d	£ s d	Per ton of Coal Carbonised		Per 1,000 Cubic Feet Sold	
			s d	s d	Pence	Pence
Coal ..		8,791 0 11		12 1·90		14·17
Less Residuals—Coke ..	4,633 0 4		6 4·89	..	7·47	
Breeze ..	118 6 0		1·96		0·19	
Tar ..	1,002 10 3		1 4·64		1·62	
Liquor ..	692 3 0		11·49		1·11	
Total Residuals ..		6,445 19 7		8 10·98		10·39
Net for Coal ..		2,345 1 4		3 2·92		3·78
Purifying ..	443 7 11		7·36		0·71	
Salaries of Engineers ..	350 0 0		5·81		0·56	
Wages and Gratuities at Works ..	1,436 0 11		1 11·83		2·31	
Repair of Works and Plant ..	3,816 7 6		5 3·34		6·15	
Salaries of Inspectors and Clerks ..	341 0 0		5·66		0·55	
Repair of Mains and Services ..	115 7 3		1·91		0·19	
Repairing and Renewing Meters ..	687 10 6		11·41		1·11	
Lighting and Repairing Public Lamps ..	558 17 10		9·28		·0·90	
Rates and Taxes ..	738 16 3		1 0·26		1·19	
Directors' Allowances ..	420 0 0		6·97		0·68	
Salaries of Secretary, Accountant, and Clerks ..	148 5 0		2·46		0·24	
Collectors' Commission ..	400 0 0		6·64		0·65	
Stationery and Printing ..	119 11 8		1·99		0·19	
General Establishment Charges ..	170 14 7		2·83		0·28	
Auditor ..	31 10 0		0·52		0·05	
Bad Debts ..	60 8 11		1·00		0·10	
Allowances ..	20 2 5		0·33		0·03	
Total Working Expenses ..		9,858 0 9		13 7·60		15·89
Coal and Working Expenses, less Residuals ..		12,203 2 1		16 10·52		19·67
Sale of Gas—Private Lighting ..	17,245 8 6					
Public Lighting ..	1,848 13 3					
	19,094 1 9		26 4·89		30·77	
Rental of Meters ..	554 6 10		9·20		0·90	
Rents ..	92 19 2		1·54		0·15	
		19,741 7 9		27 3·63		31·82
Profit ..		£7,538 5 8		10 5·11		12·15

The form of Cost Sheet for Water Companies will be similar, except that the units of calculation will be per 1,000 gallons of water supplied and per £1 of rateable value of property in district.

CHAPTER XX.

DEPRECIATION, RESERVES, RESERVE FUNDS, AND SINKING FUNDS.

IN the present chapter it is proposed to consider those provisions which are very generally regarded by all prudent business men as being essential to the continued prosperity of an undertaking, but which do not arise as a necessary record of actual tangible transactions that have taken place. For the most part, these provisions are necessitated by an alteration of circumstances, which—from one point of view at least—might be regarded as an actual "transaction," which called for a proper record in the usual way. They differ, however, in that the money value of the transaction must at all times be estimated, its exact amount never being capable of absolute determination in advance. The money value attached to the record must thus of necessity be a matter of opinion, rather than a matter of absolute fact. For this reason, doubtless, many misapprehensions are rife as to the true significance of these transactions, and the proper method of recording them in accounts.

DEPRECIATION.

In order to place any business undertaking in such a position that it may be regarded (so far as is humanly possible) as permanent, and able for an indefinite period to continue earning revenue, it is necessary—as has already been explained in Chapter II.—to provide from time to time for the maintenance of the Fixed Assets comprised therein, and for their renewal out of Revenue as and when such renewal is required by the circumstances of the case. In the meanwhile, repairs and partial renewals will in most cases be required in addition. The necessity for these latter, however, is but rarely overlooked, and attention may therefore be profitably concentrated upon that heavy expenditure which from time to time becomes necessary, when further tinkering with, and repairing of, an asset becomes impracticable, and the occasion arises to entirely replace it by another of similar description. The term "similar" is employed advisedly, for, in the nature of things, with the normal progress of science and invention, it is usually desirable, when the time comes to replace a worn-out asset, to replace it not by another of identical description, but by one of improved form, designed to better carry out a similar class of work. It need hardly be stated that in some industries the evolution of the most approved designs is far more rapid than in others.

From what has been stated, it will be seen that, over an indefinitely long period, the actual *cash* expended to repair, partially renew, and eventually to replace, assets as they become worn out (such as is necessary to maintain the undertaking as a whole), will, in a sense, cover such provision as may be necessary for Depreciation; but that at no moment of time, after a concern has been once started in going order, will the actual expenditure that can have been usefully made in this direction cover the actual shrinkage in value arising from wear and tear,

Q

the lapse of time, and the progress of modern invention. In the case of any single asset the total expenditure incurred up to the time that it is cast aside as useless, and replaced by another of a similar description (including, of course, the original cost of that asset), will be the cost chargeable against Revenue for Maintenance—a comprehensive term which includes Depreciation. But, taken as a whole, inasmuch as all of the assets comprised in any given undertaking will naturally not all wear out at once, the actual expenditure that can be usefully incurred will never be sufficient to cover the amount properly chargeable against Revenue under this heading. Consequently, for this reason if for none other, it is necessary, in addition to charging actual expenditure upon repairs and replacements to Revenue, to charge against the Revenue Account of each year a further sum, with a view to (as far as possible) averaging the expenditure on Revenue Account over a term of years, and that provision which it is so necessary to charge is usually called by the name of "Depreciation."

The essential factors to be borne in mind when making provision for Depreciation are—

(a) That during the life of an asset its original cost (*plus* all expenditure incurred in keeping it going) is a charge against Revenue ;

(b) That, in order to state as accurately as possible the net profit earned in each year during the period covered by the life of such asset, it is important that the aggregate charge for repairs and maintenance (including Depreciation) be spread over those years in the fairest possible manner.

In practice there are six different methods of apportioning these charges from year to year : —

(1) Charging each year with the actual cost of repairs and small renewals, and an equal fraction of the original cost of the asset.

(2) Charging each year with the actual cost of repairs and small renewals, and, in addition, with a sum for Depreciation, arrived at by way of a percentage on the reducing annual balance of the Asset Account, the percentage being calculated at such rate as to reduce the asset to its then actual realisable value by the time that it becomes useless for revenue-earning purposes.

By this means, the direct charge for Depreciation becomes gradually reduced from year to year, and thus affords a rough sort of compensation for the facts (a) that repairs and partial renewals will probably steadily increase, (b) that the earning capacity of the asset will also probably decrease as it becomes older.

(3) By estimating in advance the total sum that will be chargeable against Revenue during the life of the asset in respect of repairs, partial renewals, and original cost, and charging each year with an equal fraction of such total.

This method has the advantage of " levelling up " the charges against Revenue in respect of repairs and small renewals better than either of the two preceding ; but, inasmuch as it is based more than either of these upon estimates, it can in practice only be adopted with caution, save in cases where the experience of the past affords a really reliable indication as to the future.

(4) By charging Revenue with such a sum as will, at the expiration of the life of the asset, write off the original cost thereof, *plus* interest on the capital from time to time invested therein.

When the asset has more than a few years' life, this factor of interest is one that, in strictness, ought never to be lost sight of ; but in practice it is not as a rule thought necessary to take interest into consideration, save in connection with Leases, where (as has already been explained on page 6) the question of interest must of necessity be taken into account in order that each year's Revenue Account may be charged with the proper sum for the use of the premises occupied.

(5) By charging against Revenue in each year such a sum as will cover either the actual, or the average, expenditure upon repairs and small renewals, and also such a further sum as will, if set aside and invested at compound interest, accumulate to the original cost of the asset at the expiration of its estimated life.

This last-named is a very desirable method of providing for Depreciation where a comparatively limited number of assets are held, and it is therefore especially desirable to take steps to provide an actual sum of money readily available to replace them when they become worn out. Concerns owning a large number of assets of varying terms of life, each of a value relatively unimportant, need not go to the trouble of thus providing funds wherewith to replace assets when they become worn out; but when the cost of such assets is considerable, as compared with the assets of the undertaking as a whole, it is very desirable that special provision should be made, as otherwise, when the time comes to replace worn-out assets, it may be found that the provision that has been made for that purpose is represented by monies sunk in assets that cannot be readily realised at short notice without incurring considerable loss. If the sum to be provided is large, the actual accumulation of investments in high-class securities is probably the most desirable

means to adopt; but in cases where the sum required is small, although perhaps relatively large as compared with the undertaking as a whole, the most convenient and economical means of building up such a fund will probably be found to be by effecting a Sinking Fund, or Leasehold Assurance, Policy with one of the leading insurance companies, as the rate of interest allowed by these companies is probably higher than could in practice be earned upon small sums, although doubtless lower than large undertakings might earn for themselves, were they prepared to give the necessary time and attention to the matter, and to run the risk of a shrinkage in the capital value of the investments selected.

(6) By charging to Revenue in each year such a sum as represents the difference between the book value of the asset, and its actual value at the present time, as ascertained by a revaluation made by an expert valuer.

This last method, while theoretically the most perfect, as enabling the assets to be brought into the Balance Sheet at a more theoretically correct basis of valuation, is as a rule very defective in practice, on account of the uneven sums that it charges against Revenue from year to year in respect of practically identical services rendered to Revenue by the assets in question. As a check upon the rate of Depreciation employed, it is, however, very useful occasionally.

The application of the above-mentioned six methods of making provision for the depreciation of assets is well shown by the following

PROBLEM.—Show the different means by which provision may be made for charging against Revenue the cost of an asset having an estimated life of five years, the original cost being £1,000; assuming, further, that it is estimated that during the five years the expenditure on Repairs and small Renewals will be £120, the actual expenditure being subsequently ascertained to be as follows:—First year, nil; second year, £10; third year, £20; fourth year, £60; fifth year, £40.

METHOD I.—Under this method the asset is written-off out of Revenue by equal instalments of £200 per annum. The cost of Repairs, &c., is also debited to Revenue as incurred, so that the total charges to Revenue are :—

							£	s	d
1899	..	..	..	..	..		£200	0	0
1900							210	0	0
1901							220	0	0
1902							260	0	0
1903							240	0	0
				Total	..	..	£1,130	0	0

METHOD II.—Under this method it is necessary to charge Depreciation at the rate of (say) 50 per cent. per annum to arrive at anything approaching zero at the end of five years. (In practice this method would never be employed unless (*a*) the assumed life of the asset exceeded ten years, (*b*) some residual value remained at the end of the term which rendered the absolute zero unnecessary.)

The annual charges against Revenue (including repairs, &c.) are :—

							£	s	d
1899	..	..	..	..	..		£500	0	0
1900							260	0	0
1901							145	0	0
1902							122	10	0
1903							102	10	0
				Total	..	..	£1,130	0	0

METHOD III.—Under this method the total charge against Revenue during the five years is estimated at £1,120. One-fifth of this is accordingly written off each year, any difference between the estimate and the actual result being corrected in the last year. Thus :—

							£	s	d
1899	..	..	..	..	..		£224	0	0
1900							224	0	0
1901							224	0	0
1902							224	0	0
1903							234	0	0
				Total	..	..	£1,130	0	0

METHOD IV.—This method has already been mentioned upon page 6. The Asset Account in the Ledger appears as follows (assuming interest at 5 per cent.) :—

Dr.										ASSET ACCOUNT.										Cr.		
							£	s	d									£	s	d
1899	To Cost ..	..	..	..	..		1,000	0	0	1899	By Depreciation ..	..	..	..		231	0	0
	„ Interest ..	..	..	..	..		50	0	0		„ Balance	..	..	..		819	0	0
							£1,050	0	0							£1,050	0	0
1900	To Balance	..	..	..	..		819	0	0	1900	By Depreciation ..	..	..	..		231	0	0
	„ Interest..	..	..	..	..		40	19	0		„ Balance..	..	..	..		628	19	0
							£859	19	0							£859	19	0
1901	To Balance	..	..	..	..		628	19	0	1901	By Depreciation ..	..	..	..		231	0	0
	„ Interest..	..	..	..	..		31	9	0		„ Balance	..	..	..		429	8	0
							£660	8	0							£660	8	0
1902	To Balance	..	..	..	..		429	8	0	1902	By Depreciation ..	..	..	..		231	0	0
	„ Interest..	..	..	..	..		21	9	0		„ Balance	..	..	..		219	17	0
							£450	17	0							£450	17	0
1903	To Balance	..	..	..	..		219	17	0	1903	By Depreciation ..	..	..	..		231	0	0
	„ Interest..	..	..	..	..		11	3	0									
							£231	0	0							£231	0	0

NOTE.—Following the usual practice, Depreciation has been reckoned only approximately, leaving a small balance to be adjusted in the last year.

The net charge to Revenue in each year is the difference between the Depreciation and the Interest, *plus* provision for Repairs. If repairs be dealt with under Method I., the total charges to Revenue are :—

1899	..	..	..	..	..	£181	0	0
1900	..	..	..	..	..	200	1	0
1901	..	..	..	...	..	219	11	0
1902	..	..	..	..	..	269	11	0
1903	..	..	Total	..	..	259	17	0
						£1,130	0	0

If Method III. be adopted as to Repairs, the annual charges work out thus :—

1899	..	..	..	..	..	£205	0	0
1900	..	..	..	..	..	214	1	0
1901	..	..	..	..	..	223	11	0
1902	..	..	..	..	..	233	11	0
1903	..	..	Total	..	..	253	17	0
						£1,130	0	0

METHOD V.—This is the " Sinking Fund " method, and is fully described under that heading (*vide* page 234), excluding repairs, etc., the annual charge against Revenue, at 3 per cent., works out at about £196.

METHOD VI.—Under this method the charges against Revenue will be very unequal, and might quite conceivably be as follows :—

1899	..	..	..	..	..	£400	0	0
1900	..	..	..	..	..	200	0	0
1901	..	..	..	..	..	120	0	0
1902	..	..	..	..	..	180	0	0
1903	..	..	Total	..	..	230	0	0
						£1,130	0	0

NECESSITY FOR DEPRECIATION.

The question as to whether it is invariably necessary to provide for the Depreciation of Wasting Assets may be usefully considered at this stage. That the matter may be clearly comprehended in its true light, it may be pointed out that practically all assets are in the nature of things non-permanent. That is to say, at some future date—more or less removed according to the nature of the assets—the time will come when they are either worn out, superseded by others of more modern type, or lost to the present holder. All assets are subject to the operations of wear and tear, but in addition certain assets—as, for example, Leaseholds and Patents—cease to be of value after the expiration of a certain number of years, because the benefit of them can no longer be enjoyed by the former owner. Thus, when a lease expires, the premises revert to the superior landlord; and when a patent lapses, the monopoly formerly enjoyed by the owner ceases, and although he may still retain a valuable asset in the shape of Goodwill, he can under no circumstances expect to continue to derive an income from royalties paid by licensees. Certain assets—as, for example, Freehold Lands—are of such a character that for all practical purposes they are not subject to Depreciation, while certain other assets (*e.g.*, Loose Tools) are of so ephemeral a character that they have to be continually replaced at short intervals, and, so long as they are so replaced, their depreciation in value during their short spell of life is so unimportant that it may safely be ignored. But, with these exceptions, it may be stated in general terms that all assets are liable to Depreciation.

This being the position of affairs, it is clear that, if provision be not made for Depreciation by charging a proper sum against Revenue in each year, the time will eventually come when the undertaking must either be abandoned, or further Capital introduced into the business to enable new assets to be acquired for its continuance. The latter contingency ought never to arise if a proper system of accounting be employed, save under wholly exceptional circumstances—as, for instance, where an accident has destroyed certain assets owned by an undertaking, or when a new invention has suddenly and unexpectedly rendered valueless much valuable plant. The possibilities of this latter contingency ought never to be overlooked by business men, and so far as they can be reasonably foreseen they should be taken into account as a factor in Depreciation; but, inasmuch as loss under this heading can only be provided for by way of estimates, cases of insufficient provision may occur without anyone being seriously at fault, and under such circumstances the necessity may arise for introducing fresh capital to make good the ravages of Depreciation. Save, however, under this purely exceptional circumstance, all losses coming under this heading ought properly to be borne out of Revenue, for the true profits of an undertaking can only be that surplus which remains after providing for all expenses of carrying on that undertaking upon a permanent basis.

Some undertakings, however, are of such a nature that it is not to be expected that they can be profitably carried on for an indefinite period. Their very object is ephemeral in its nature, and at the outset it was clearly foreseen that at some future date the business would naturally and automatically come to an end. Under this heading may be included such concerns as the following:—A Single-ship Company, a Mine, Colliery, or Quarry, a Company (or partnership) formed to develop and sell a landed estate, to build upon and let leasehold lands, to work a patent or a few patents, or any novelty which by its nature cannot be expected to prove permanently attractive. In the case of all these undertakings, the proprietors must have foreseen at the outset that the venture upon which they were embarked had only a limited span of life, and that therefore the concern would not last beyond a certain number of years; while in many cases it would be absolutely impossible for anyone to put, in advance, a definite limit upon its actual duration.

In such cases, it is practically impossible to make such a provision for Depreciation as will insure that the capital of the undertaking will be returned intact to the proprietors at the end of the venture, on account of the impossibility of accurately estimating in advance the rate at which Depreciation will take place; and under these circumstances—and these alone—the attempt to provide for Depreciation *at all* may be legitimately abandoned, so long as it is made clear that this course is being pursued, and that (a) at the expiration of the venture the whole or the bulk of the capital will have been dissipated, (b) the distributions made to proprietors during the continuance of the venture are not true net profits, but a surplus of incomings over outgoings, which includes the gradual distribution of capital.

One of the most obvious objections to this course of procedure is that it is inconvenient to investors to receive periodically sums which are compounded of Capital and Income, in that if they spend all dividends as received their capital becomes gradually dissipated; while a further objection that may be raised is that, under these circumstances, the instalments of Capital as well as the pure profit have to bear Income Tax. On the other hand, if the attempt were made in all good faith to provide for Depreciation, it is quite likely that such provision as might be made would be subsequently found to be insufficient, so that, in spite of all endeavours, the dividends distributed might exceed the true profits earned. Moreover, the accumulation in the hands of the managers of large funds to compensate for the wastage in the value of Fixed Assets might in many cases present undesirable features, as those who may safely be entrusted with the business management of undertakings of this description may not necessarily be possessed of sufficient financial ability to invest such funds to the best advantage. If, therefore, an undertaking is by its nature of a non-permanent character, provision for Depreciation may not improperly be ignored, so long as the inevitable consequences of so doing are clearly appreciated. If, however, the company, or partnership, is intended to be permanent, even although its objects be ephemeral, proper provision for Depreciation must in all cases be made in order to ensure the permanence of the undertaking. Thus, if a company be formed to carry on a general shipping business, provision must be made for Depreciation, so that new ships may be purchased as the old ones become worn out, without the necessity of raising further capital; and similarly of a company being formed for the general purpose of speculating in land, and blocks of land are developed and sold, only the profit on such sales may be distributed after providing for all known and expected losses and shrinkages, as otherwise the capital will gradually become depleted, and the time will eventually arrive when future operations are impossible, on account of insufficiency of funds.

A question that is at the present time exercising the minds of many is as to whether Local Authorities need provide for the Depreciation of Fixed Assets acquired by them for trading purposes. In a general work of this description it is impossible to deal otherwise than generally with this particular matter. It may be pointed out, however, that the principles of accounting are of general application, and that if a trading business be so conducted that *no* provision is made for the Depreciation of its Fixed Assets, the accounts will show a balance in excess of the true Net Profit earned; and if, therefore, the whole of that balance be distributed from year to year, the capital of the undertaking will be gradually depleted, and the time will eventually come when either the venture has to be abandoned or fresh capital raised to enable it to be continued. On the grounds, therefore, of business common-sense and prudence, every argument would appear to be in favour of due provision being made for Depreciation, here as elsewhere. It may be added, moreover, that Local Authorities are, in general, required, as a condition of the power given them to raise capital, to "maintain" the assets acquired by them out of Revenue, and it has already been pointed out that the term "maintenance," rightly

understood, includes provision for Depreciation, as, unless such provision be included, the time must inevitably come when the assets can no longer be maintained, save by further capital expenditure.

RESERVES AND RESERVE FUNDS.

It would appear that these terms are in practice used somewhat loosely, different meanings being attached to them by different persons. In his work on "Auditors: their Duties and Responsibilities," Mr. Francis W. Pixley, F.C.A., states that there is "a distinct difference" between the two terms. "A Reserve," he considers, "is merely the surplus of "the credit side of the Balance Sheet over its debit "side, although perhaps the Reserve may be divided "under two or three different headings, such as "'Reserve' and 'Balance of Profit and Loss "'Account carried forward.' A Reserve of this "nature is either a provision against loss of Capital, ",or a Reserve for the equalisation of dividends, or "a Reserve as an extra inducement to those with "whom the company may do business to give credit. "A Reserve Fund, however, is not merely a surplus "shown on the debit side of the Balance Sheet, but "must be represented by special investments which "may, or may not, be shown distinctly on the credit "side of the Balance Sheet. If, therefore, the "Reserve is used in the general business of the "company it is not a Reserve Fund, although "perhaps the term might be properly so used, if "some stock used in the ordinary course of the "business were specially set aside, and when made "use of represented by cash set aside until "reinvested in further stocks specially ear-marked."

The above view is one that is very prominent in certain quarters, and it must be admitted that, inasmuch as there is a very general impression on the part of the public that the term "Reserve Fund" signifies that a corresponding amount of profits has been retained by the company, *and invested* to provide against future contingencies, it is perhaps desirable that more care should be devoted to the nomenclature of this important item than is generally observed. It will be noted, however, that Mr. Pixley advances no specific authority in support of his definitions of the terms "Reserve" and "Reserve Fund," and it may be added that his views upon the subject are by no means universally accepted. In particular, Mr. T. A. Welton, F.C.A., holds the view that, so long as divisible profits are not divided, they may properly be described as "Reserve Fund," no matter what the form of the assets may be; and as a matter of account this would appear to be the sounder view, in that it is impossible to state that any particular credit balance on a Ledger is represented by, or represents, any particular debit balance on that Ledger. That is to say, short of actually lodging assets with creditors as security, it is impossible to ear-mark certain assets, as in any way "representing" certain liabilities: the whole of the assets must be marshalled against the whole of the liabilities in the form in which they appear in a Balance Sheet, as ordinarily constructed.

For these reasons, the writer favours the view endorsed by Mr. Welton, that the term "Reserve Fund," properly understood, means neither more nor less than undivided profits which have been formally "reserved" when they might have been divided; while the term "Reserve" means a provision for an expected loss or liability that has not as yet been definitely ascertained. At the same time, it must be admitted that the uncertainty with regard to the exact meaning in any particular case of these important terms is greatly to be regretted. In considering further the nature of Reserves and Reserve Funds, and their respective functions in accounts, however, it must be understood that the former term is applied to those provisions which are properly charges *against* profits, and which have to be made before arriving at true Net Profits that are properly divisible; while the latter term will be employed to designate true Net Profits, that might have been divided as such, but which have been reserved, or capitalised *pro tem.*

RESERVES.

Following the lines indicated in the preceding paragraph, the necessity for providing for Reserves arises whenever it is required to charge something against profits, to represent an expense, or loss, which is known (or believed) to have been incurred. Thus a Reserve may be made to provide against loss from Bad and Doubtful Debts, to provide for Depreciation, or to provide against loss incurred in connection with a pending claim or action. Debts known to be irrecoverable would naturally be written off to the debit of Bad Debts in the ordinary way; but in addition it is generally necessary to make some further provision for loss under this heading, while it is clearly undesirable to actually write off debts so long as there remains any probability of their being eventually collected. Again, in some cases, with a view to averaging the charges against successive years, it is thought that the best way of providing against loss under this heading is by way of a percentage on the Sales which experience has shown to be reasonable and sufficient. Under these circumstances, it becomes necessary to pass an entry through the Journal, debiting Bad Debts Account with the estimated loss; but because there is no other Ledger Account that can be conveniently credited, an account has to be opened, entitled "Reserve for Bad and Doubtful Debts Account." The balance of this latter may appear upon the liabilities' side of the Balance Sheet; it is preferable, however, in the case of Reserve Accounts raised to provide for shrinkage in the value of specific assets, to deduct them from those particular assets, in which case, of course, no entry whatever will appear upon the liabilities' side of the Balance Sheet. The amount of the Reserve may, if thought desirable, be shown in detail upon the face of the Balance Sheet as a deduction, or, if preferred, the net value placed upon the Book Debts may alone appear there.

With regard to Reserves for Depreciation, the more usual course is to credit the Asset Account with such provision as it may be thought necessary to charge against Revenue; but sometimes this course is inconvenient—as, for example, when Depreciation is provided for by way of a fixed percentage upon the original cost of the assets, and further additions have to be debited to the Ledger Account from time to time. If, under these circumstances, Depreciation were credited to the Ledger Account, the balance periodically brought down would not show the total cost, but the total cost *less* Depreciation, and a calculation would have to be made every time in order to arrive at the amount upon which Depreciation must be charged. In such cases it is better to open a Reserve Account, to which the provision for Depreciation may be credited. In the Balance Sheet the credit balance of this account should in all cases be deducted from the asset against which the provision is being accumulated; but the practice of showing the credit balance separately upon the liabilities' side of the Balance Sheet is not uncommon. This is especially to be deprecated when the item bears the undistinctive title of "Reserve Account," for under such circumstances it might readily be supposed that the balance of the Reserve Account represented undivided profits, whereas it represents in fact admitted *losses* that should have been deducted from the assets which are found to be of less value than their respective Ledger balances. If, therefore, a Reserve for Depreciation be placed upon the liabilities' side of the Balance Sheet at all (as may sometimes be necessary, if it includes provision against a loss arising from several different classes of assets), it should be clearly stated as "Reserve for Depreciation," and not as "Reserve" or "Reserve Account."

The third kind of Reserve is neither more nor less than a Suspense Account, and, if it is separately shown upon the liabilities' side of the Balance Sheet, should be so styled, in order to avoid any possibility of its being confused with undivided profits. Unless, however, the item is a relatively large one,

it might reasonably be added to the "Sundry Creditors," instead of being separately shown.

RESERVE FUNDS.

A Reserve Fund, as has already been stated, is an item appearing upon the liabilities' side of a Balance Sheet, represented by a credit balance upon a corresponding Ledger Account which has been formed by the transfer to this account of items which from time to time have been debited to Net Profit Account. It intimates that there are in existence undivided profits of a corresponding amount, and, in the view of the writer, so long as these profits remain in existence the item is correctly described, no matter what form the assets of the undertaking may take from time to time. If, however, a loss is subsequently experienced which throws the balance of Profit and Loss Account to the debit side, then any balance of profits carried forward from the previous period must forthwith be applied towards the reduction or extinction of this debit balance, and any deficiency remaining thereafter must be debited to the Reserve Fund, to record the fact that these profits are no longer in existence, they having been eaten up by subsequent losses. This, it is conceived, is the true nature of a Reserve Fund. Its continued existence depends upon the continued existence of a corresponding surplus of assets over liabilities and capital, without being in any way concerned with the form—as contrasted with the value—of those assets. It may be added that a Reserve Fund may cease to exist owing to subsequent losses, notwithstanding the fact that there still remains in existence a specific investment of the value of the amount originally standing to the credit of Reserve Fund Account; and *per contra* fluctuations in the value of an investment supposed to represent the Reserve Fund would not automatically and directly affect the balance of the Reserve Fund Account, but would (if taken into account at all) be properly debited, or credited, to Revenue.

But although it is thought that the idea of any intimate connection between the Reserve Fund and a corresponding investment in " gilt-edged " securities is based upon an illusion, it must not be supposed that it is sought to discourage the practice, very general among prudent business men, of investing surplus assets in such a form that they are readily available in case of need. The whole object of refraining from dividing profits up to the hilt is to place the company in a more advantageous position, and it is a question of business policy as to how that end may be best achieved. Usually it is desirable to invest in Consols, or some other high-class security, a sum equal to the amount of profits reserved, as such a sum is thus rendered readily available in case of need, while in the meantime it earns a fair—although not very tempting—rate of interest. But cases may easily arise in which the reason for reserving profits is because, owing to increasing business, the working capital of the undertaking is found to be insufficient, and it is not thought desirable to raise further capital. Under such circumstances it is not only perfectly legitimate, but actually wise, to employ the assets represented by the undivided profits as working capital, or (as it is commonly termed) to invest the Reserve Fund in the business itself. It would be manifestly bad management to invest, say, £1,000, in Consols at a time when interest at 4 or 5 per cent. was being paid to debenture-holders, or upon a bank overdraft. But unless there is any specific reason why reserved profits should *not* be invested, it is always desirable that they should be so invested; otherwise the working capital will be in excess of the legitimate requirements of the business, when due attention may not perhaps be given to the prompt turning of floating assets into cash. The whole matter, however, as has already been stated, is one of administration rather than of general principle.

SINKING FUNDS.

When it is desired to accumulate a certain specific sum at the end of a definite period, in such a manner that the withdrawal of a corresponding amount of money from the business will cause no inconvenience, recourse is had to a Sinking Fund.

An estimate is made of the amount of interest that can be earned upon outside investments, and the amount that must be annually invested to produce the required sum is ascertained, upon the footing that the income derived from the investments is to be reinvested so that the whole may accumulate at compound interest. In practice, however, a certain margin must invariably be allowed to compensate for the loss of time in effecting such reinvestments, and it is prudent also to provide a further margin in case of a possible decline in the market price of the securities selected when the whole of the investment has to be sold.

When the object of accumulating the monies in question is to provide for the replacement of assets that will then be worn out, or otherwise valueless, the cost of making such provision is a charge against profits in the nature of Depreciation. But when the object is to provide for the repayment of borrowed money—as, for example, an issue of debentures—the cost is not properly chargeable against Revenue, for the payment of debts as they become due is not *per se* a Revenue charge. If, however, the liability (for the eventual repayment of which provision is being made) was originally incurred for the sake of providing working capital, then it is clear that when it is repaid working capital will to a corresponding extent be depleted, and if it be proposed to avoid this undesirable contingency the only possible alternatives are either (1) to re-borrow in the future, or (2) to provide for the repayment of loans out of profits. If it were desired to re-borrow in the future, no Sinking Fund would be necessary, for the old loan might in that case be paid off out of the new one; but if it be desired to pay off borrowed working capital out of profits, it is clear that profits must be specifically allocated to that purpose and not otherwise employed. Hence the necessity of providing a Sinking Fund, which, under these circumstances, is similar to a Reserve Fund systematically formed and invested outside the business, save that the income derived from the investments is credited to the Sinking Fund Account instead of being credited to Revenue.

It will thus be seen that the formation of a Sinking Fund involves two distinct sets of operations. In the first place, Sinking Fund must be credited annually with the prescribed instalments, which must be debited either to Profit and Loss Account or to Net Profit Account, according to whether the Fund is raised to replace wasting assets or to discharge liabilities; and, in the second place, Cash must be credited and Sinking Fund Investment Account debited with a corresponding sum, which must be taken out of the business and invested. Income received from investments must be debited to Cash and credited to Sinking Fund Account, and from time to time a corresponding sum must be reinvested, being credited to Cash Account and debited to Sinking Fund Investment Account. Theoretically, the Sinking Fund instalments may be accurately determined in advance, but in practice they will probably have to be modified from time to time, in order to ensure the realisable value of the investments reaching the prescribed sum at the future date already determined upon. When that date arrives, the investments will be sold, Sinking Fund Investment Account credited, and Cash debited. There is thus money in hand, available for the purpose for which the Sinking Fund was originally created. If that purpose was the replacement of assets, entries should be passed through the books writing off the amount standing to the debit of the various assets that have now become valueless, and debiting Sinking Fund Account therewith. If the Sinking Fund Account then shows a debit balance, the provision made in the past will have been insufficient to cover the realised loss, and the balance must therefore now be written off as an ascertained loss. If, on the other hand, the account shows a credit balance, the provision is in excess of the actual requirements, and such balance might be credited to Revenue, although it would doubtless be more prudent to transfer it to the credit of Reserve Fund. When the Sinking Fund has been created for the purpose of redeeming liabilities at a future date out of profits, and that end has been achieved, the balance to the credit of Sinking Fund Account should be transferred to the credit of Reserve Fund, representing—as it does—profits that have been reserved, instead of being distributed among the proprietors by way of dividend.

The employment of Sinking Funds for the purpose of providing for the repayment of liabilities is common in the accounts of Local Authorities, which are authorised to raise such funds as may be necessary for their purposes by terminable loans, on the condition that they create a Sinking Fund, charging the annual instalments against Revenue. As has already been stated, the repayment of liabilities is not a Revenue charge from the point of view of strict accounting; but in the case of these undertakings, which start operations with no capital of their own, it is clear that by no other means can the due repayment of loans be assured. In the case of trading departments, Local Authorities are required to charge Sinking Fund instalments against Revenue before arriving at a balance of surplus profits available for the relief of general rates. In some quarters it has been thought that this requirement absolves these authorities from the necessity of providing for Depreciation, while in others it has been urged that the due provision for Depreciation absolves the authorities from providing in addition for the repayment of loans. The judicial interpretations upon matters of account are in general so curious that it would be unwise to hazard an opinion as to the legal responsibility of Local Authorities under these circumstances. It may be mentioned, however, that the requirement that they shall provide out of Revenue for the maintenance of assets, and for Sinking Fund instalments, before arriving at a balance of surplus profits available for general purposes, will doubtless be regarded by accountants as conclusive on the point. It may be mentioned, however, that, as has already been stated, if Depreciation be ignored, these under-takings must of necessity be of a non-permanent character; if, on the other hand, Sinking Fund instalments be ignored, they must remain per-petually in debt. Moreover, assuming that only profitable enterprises be undertaken, and that they are ably and economically administered, there should (bearing in mind the low rate of interest at which Local Authorities are enabled to borrow money) be no difficulty in their providing for both Depreciation and Sinking Fund, while yet realising sufficient surplus profits (available for general purposes) to compensate the ratepayers for the financial risk of the enterprise. A trading venture that cannot produce such a result as this can, it is thought, hardly be regarded as offering sufficient inducements for it to be undertaken at all—unless, of course, the enterprise be regarded as necessary, quite apart from the question of possible profits.

CHAPTER XXI.

PAYMENTS BY INSTALMENTS AND INTEREST.

IN certain classes of undertakings the transactions —or a considerable part thereof—involve dealings on credit extending for a term of years, the indebtedness so created being liquidated by equal periodical instalments. Unless the period be quite a short one, it becomes, under these circumstances, important to consider the question of interest if the profits of successive years are to be accurately determined. In some cases the transactions are clearly stated to involve the question of interest—as, for example, when money is lent out on mortgage by a Building Society, or when a manufacturer of railway wagons disposes of them under a hire-purchase agreement—while in other cases (as, for example, in the Musical Instrument and Bicycle trades) a higher price is charged for credit transactions, which covers interest without any exact rate being prescribed. In both cases, however, the question of interest must be carefully taken into consideration.

It will be convenient in the first instance to describe the general principles involved, as exemplified in the case of hire-purchase agreements for railway wagons, as the problem here is of especial significance both to the manufacturer and to the hirer. The manufacturer is concerned in distinguishing between the Gross Profit on trading, which (with a reasonable reserve for contingencies) may fairly be stated to have been earned upon the execution of the hire-purchase agreement, and the income that he derives from interest charged to customers as compensation for the extended terms of credit given. To the hirer the question of interest is of importance, in that the aggregate amount of instalments paid by him under the hire-purchase agreement is naturally in excess of the intrinsic value of the assets acquired. It would consequently be improper for him to capitalise the whole amount of such instalments; while, for the purpose of debiting each year's Revenue Account with its proper charges, it becomes important to ascertain how much of each instalment represents interest, and how much may properly be capitalised. The necessity for going into the matter thus exhaustively arises from the fact that those industries which acquire wagons on the hire-purchase system at all (Colleries, Quarries, and the like) usually engage upon those transactions to an extent which—as compared with their transactions as a whole—renders the matter one of serious import, if the true result of those transactions in the aggregate is to be correctly shown by the accounts. On the other hand, some transactions of a similar nature—e.g., the acquisition of a Musical Instrument, a Bicycle, or an Encyclopædia on terms of deferred payment—are as a rule relatively unimportant to the hirer, and in consequence such a nice distinction between Capital and

Revenue—and especially between the Revenue charges of successive years—need not be made. Exceptions, however, will arise even here. Thus if a hotel, or a boarding-house, be furnished on the hire-purchase system, the transaction is of sufficient importance to merit being treated upon scientific lines in the accounts of these undertakings; and similarly, if a musical academy were to acquire its pianos upon these terms, the matter would be of sufficient importance, as compared with the transactions as a whole, to call for proper treatment. In such cases, the record of the transactions, from the hirer's point of view, will be the converse of the record from the point of view of the manufacturer, and it is therefore unnecessary to deal with the matter in further detail, as the record in connection with Colliery Accounts is fully described.

WAGON HIRE-PURCHASE AGREEMENTS.

The general nature of a contract of this description is that, if the "tenant" (*i.e.*, the hirer) makes the necessary periodical payments regularly, the manufacturer agrees to hand over the ownership of the articles in question to him at the end of the prescribed term upon the payment of a further nominal sum. There are various other conditions which, in practice, may have some bearing upon the contract, but these are the main features that have to be taken into consideration in connection with the treatment of the contract as a matter of account.

IN MANUFACTURERS' ACCOUNTS.—It is obvious that, from the point of view of the manufacturer, it would be most improper—even although it might perhaps be technically correct—to treat these instalments as simple hire, and at the end of the term (if they have been punctually paid and a further nominal consideration paid) to treat the articles in question as a *gift* from the manufacturer to the tenant. The right treatment for the manufacturer is unquestionably for him to regard all these transactions as *sales* of the articles in question, he at the same time lending to the purchaser the whole of the purchase-money, upon consideration of its being paid back to him by instalments with interest.

All the material information which would be expressed in any hire-purchase agreement would be (1) the number of instalments, (2) the period over which they are extended, and (3) the amount of each instalment. It is obvious, however, that the manufacturer cannot treat the transaction as being a sale to the extent of the aggregate amount of the instalments, inasmuch as interest has been added and the amounts of the instalments equalised. It is, therefore, only proper for him to credit his Trading Account at the outset with the "present value" of these future repayments. In order to arrive at this figure it is, of course, absolutely essential to first of all assess the rate of interest which the manufacturer reckons to get, as a consideration for the delay in payment of the purchase-price. This is, under ordinary circumstances, either 5 per cent. or 6 per cent.; but usually the calculations are not worked out accurately, the instalments being taken at some more or less round sum approximating to what the amount would come to if worked out exactly. Still, the proper course to pursue is, no doubt, to assume a fixed rate of interest, and upon this basis to arrive at the present value of the sum of the future instalments. This present value may be taken as the cash value of the article sold, and the transaction may be treated as a sale for that amount; *per contra*, it must be regarded as an advance to the purchaser for a corresponding amount. To the debit of this Advance Account, interest at 6 per cent. (or whatever the rate may be) will be added from time to time, and the actual instalments received will be credited; so that by the time the agreement expires there is no balance to either the debit or credit of the account.

EXAMPLE:

A. JONES.   CONTRA.

Dr.   Agreement No. 4,061 (10 half-yearly payments of £7 0s. 8d.)   *Cr.*

1892		£ s d	1892		£ s d
Jan. 1	To Sales Account	60 0 0	June 30	By Cash	7 0 8
June 30	,, Interest	1 16 0	Dec. 31	,, ,,	7 0 8
Dec. 31	,, ,,	1 12 10	,,	,, Balance	49 7 6
		£63 8 10			£63 8 10
1893			1893		
Jan. 1	To Balance	49 7 6	June 30	By Cash	7 0 8
June 30	,, Interest	1 9 8	Dec. 31	,, ,,	7 0 8
Dec. 31	,, ,,	1 6 3	,,	,, Balance	38 2 1
		£52 3 5			£52 3 5
1894			1894		
Jan. 1	To Balance	38 2 1	June 30	By Cash	7 0 8
June 30	,, Interest	1 2 10	Dec. 31	,, ,,	7 0 8
Dec. 31	,, ,,	0 19 3	,,	,, Balance	26 2 10
		£40 4 2			£40 4 2
1895			1895		
Jan. 1	To Balance	26 2 10	June 30	By Cash	7 0 8
June 30	,, Interest	0 15 8	Dec. 31	,, ,,	7 0 8
Dec. 31	,, ,,	0 11 11	,,	,, Balance	13 9 1
		£27 10 5			£27 10 5
1896			1896		
Jan. 1	To Balance	13 9 1	June 30	By Cash	7 0 8
June 30	,, Interest	0 8 1	Dec. 31	,, ,,	7 0 8
Dec. 31	,, ,,	0 4 2			
		£14 1 4			£14 1 4

In the above example the interest is worked out at half-yearly rests, but it may be added that many manufacturers use yearly rests, even when the instalments are payable half-yearly or quarterly.

It will be seen that the arrangement which is embodied in the above account is for the payment of half-yearly instalments, the first taking place six months after the execution of the agreement. It is not always, however, that this is the nature of the transaction. It frequently happens that the manufacturer requires the first instalment to be paid on the signing of the agreement. When this course is adopted it will be found to very materially affect the "cash value" of the article, inasmuch as there are by this means only *nine* instalments of interest to be debited instead of ten, and these in each case upon a smaller amount. For practical purposes it may be taken that, instead of the "cash value" being £60, as stated in our *pro forma* example, the

"cash value" will be £63 (approximately), if the instalments were required to be made in advance for each half-year. It will thus be seen how very important it is that these transactions should be treated upon a proper basis at the outset, for obviously a difference of £3 or more in the price of a single railway wagon would make a very considerable difference in the amount to be taken to the credit of Profit and Loss Account, as being the gross profit upon the sales.

Attention has already been drawn to the fact that this treatment of hire-purchase transactions is a purely artificial one. There is no compulsion on the part of the tenant to continue paying the instalments if it suits his purpose better to cancel the agreement and return the wagons. While the agreement continues, however, he is liable for the wagons being kept in good repair, and has to continue to punctually pay the instalments arranged. The result of this is that, even if the tenant chooses at some subsequent date to cancel the agreement and return the wagons, in the majority of cases the result will be an additional profit to the manufacturer. But this would not necessarily follow if the wagons were new at the date of executing the agreement and were returned, say, one year from that date. In that case there might be a loss, and to that extent the treatment just described may be said to be unduly favourable, having regard to the worst possible contingencies. But it is so rarely that these agreements are cancelled in the first year or so that this consideration may be disregarded, it being practically certain that the few cases in which it occurs will be very much more than averaged by those in which default is made at a later period of the currency of the agreement, in which case the manufacturer reaps a profit.

In point of fact, it is generally admitted that—at all events after the first two years have been completed—the tenant possesses some value in his agreement, even if he decide to discontinue the payments; and it is by no means unusual for him either to sell his rights under the agreement to some other person who is desirous of acquiring the wagons upon a hire-purchase system (obtaining the manufacturer's consent to the transfer), or for the manufacturer himself to pay some cash consideration to the tenant if the latter decides to abandon his rights under the agreement and return the wagons in good condition. That being so, it may be taken that the asset standing in the manufacturer's books, as being the amount due upon the loan of the purchase-money for the wagons, is a good asset for that amount, even if default should be made by the tenant.

IN HIRERS' ACCOUNTS.—It now becomes necessary to consider how these transactions should be dealt with in the books of the tenant or hirer. In view of the fact already mentioned, that the ownership of the goods remains with the manufacturer until the completion of the whole transaction, it might be argued that, strictly speaking, the whole of

the instalments should be charged against Revenue. On the other hand, it is obvious that this would very unduly affect the profits of the earlier years, for the simple reason that the instalments on a hire-purchase agreement are very much heavier than upon a simple hiring agreement (being, as a rule, something more than twice the amount), so that during the earlier years the undertaking would appear to be losing money by entering into hire-purchase agreements at all; whereas this is by no means the case in reality, the instalments being a wise capital outlay for the purpose of acquiring fixed assets at a future date. It will thus be seen that, even if the very strictest view of the position of affairs be taken, it is not necessary to charge against Revenue a larger proportion of the hire-purchase instalment than the amount for which the use of the wagons in question could have been obtained upon simple hire. Even this is really too much to charge, because the wagon companies naturally look to make a larger profit out of hiring than out of hire-purchase agreements. It therefore becomes necessary to go into the matter very much more exhaustively; and, assuming that almost all these transactions are negotiated upon a basis of 6 per cent. interest by half-yearly rests, it is thought that the following table, which shows the cash value of a wagon upon which half-yearly instalments of £5 are payable for any period from one to five years, will be found of use. As already stated, the usual term of these agreements is five years, but a very considerable number are for 3, 3½, or 4 years.

EXAMPLE :

TABLE showing cash value of debt repayable by half-yearly instalments of £5 each (rate of interest = 6 per cent., calculated at half-yearly rests).

Number of Instalments unpaid					Cash Value		
					£	s	d
2	(Agreement one year to run)		..	..	9	11	5
4	(,, two years ,,)		..	..	18	11	9
6	(,, three ,, ,,)		..	..	27	1	8
8	(,, four ,, ,,)		..	..	35	1	11
10	(,, five ,, ,,)		..	..	42	13	0

From the above table it will be seen that, assuming a hire-purchase agreement were entered into under which the tenant paid £10 per annum by half-yearly instalments during five years, the cash value of the wagon must be taken as being £42 13s., allowing interest at the rate of 6 per cent. with half-yearly rests. At the end of the first year (that is to say, after two instalments have been paid) the amount standing to the debit of Loan Account in the manufacturer's books will be reduced to £35 1s. 11d., at the end of the second year to £27 1s. 8d., at the end of the third year to £18 11s. 9d., and at the end of the fourth year to £9 11s. 5d., which amount would be altogether extinguished at the end of the fifth year. To a certain extent, this position of affairs may be taken as reciprocal—i.e., the difference between the original cash value and the reduced cash value in the manufacturer's books from time to time may be taken as being the investment of capital by the tenant in the property in question.

There are, however, other considerations to be borne in mind ; and for the sake of bringing these more prominently forward, it seems desirable to take a concrete example. Take the case of an agreement entered into on the 1st January 1903, by which the tenant agrees to make seven half-yearly payments at £8 6s. 6d. (the first being due on the 30th June 1903), the interest being assumed to be 6 per cent. with half-yearly rests. By reference to the foregoing table it will be found that the cash value of the wagon in this case is £51 17s. 6d. The following table may now be compiled, showing what proportion of the instalments paid during each year is in respect of interest upon the outstanding debt due to the manufacturer, the balance of the instalments being consequently the proportion which has to be capitalised. The column upon the extreme right in the following example shows the accumula-

tions upon the "Wagons Purchase Account" at the close of each year :—

Date	Amount of Instalment			Interest on Outstanding Debt			Proportion to Capital			Total to Wagon Purchase Account to date		
	£	s	d	£	s	d	£	s	d	£	s	d
31st December 1903	16	13	0	2	18	2	13	14	10	13	14	10
,, ,, 1904	16	13	0	2	1	5	14	11	7	28	6	5
,, ,, 1905	16	13	0	1	3	7	15	9	5	43	15	10
30th June 1906	8	6	6	0	4	10	8	1	8	51	17	6
	£58	5	6	£6	8	0	£51	17	6			

A careful examination of the above table will show that when the agreement is completed on the 30th June 1906 the tenant will have paid in all £58 5s. 6d., of which £51 17s. 6d. has been allocated to Capital, and £6 8s. to Revenue. The point which next claims attention is as to whether any further charge to Revenue is necessary, and, if so, how much.

REPAIRS.—The question of repairs should on no account be allowed to confuse the treatment of the hire-purchase agreement itself. The proper course is either to debit each year's Profit and Loss Account with the actual repairs incurred, or else to debit the Profit and Loss Account and credit Reserve for Repairs Account with the best estimate of the normal charge for repairs, and to debit the latter account with the cost of such repairs as are actually executed. This course has the advantage of averaging—as far as possible—the charge to Revenue in respect of these items ; but, in view of the fact that both the railway companies themselves and the Board of Trade regulations are very strict as to wagons being kept in a thoroughly effective state of repair, it is probable that in the long run these repairs will be found to average themselves, particularly when the tenant possesses wagons of different ages. But whichever method be adopted, the treatment of the repairs should be kept quite distinct from the statement of the gradual purchase of the wagons on a hire-purchase agreement.

R

DEPRECIATION.—The next question which calls for consideration is that of Depreciation. Up to the present the treatment indicated has been a question of right and wrong, rather than one of individual preference or discretion, but Depreciation is largely a question of individual discretion. In the first place, there is the precedent afforded by the statutory form of accounts with regard to railway companies, which suggests that *no Depreciation whatever need be provided for*, but that the proper course is to renew worn-out wagons out of Revenue. When any large number of wagons are held by the same owner this is no doubt the simplest course to pursue, as the charges to Revenue will be found to average themselves fairly closely. But if only a few wagons are owned, it may be found that the charges to Profit and Loss arising from their renewal are unequal, and it will then be found preferable to adopt some means which will have the effect of averaging them. Then, again, there arises the consideration that railway wagons—when owned by the class of persons who would naturally acquire them upon hire-purchase agreements—are " fixed assets," and not " floating assets "; therefore, even in the case of ordinary joint-stock companies, there is no statutory obligation requiring that Depreciation should be provided for from year to year. It will thus be seen that the whole matter is (subject to the articles of association of the paticular Company concerned) entirely one of separate choice, but that is no reason why the effect of the various methods which may be adopted under different circumstances should not be considered and their respective merits contrasted.

It may be taken at the outset that a railway wagon has a very long span of life. Being made up of a number of inter-changeable parts, it is quite possible, in the ordinary course of repairing, to entirely renew the wagon from time to time ; thus the time never really arises when the asset itself is absolutely worthless and cannot be tinkered with any longer. But those who are desirous of making ample reserves against Revenue for every possible risk will probably prefer not to rely too much upon this fact, but will assume a length of life upon the part of the wagons which is likely to be realised in all but abnormal cases—as, for instance, where accidents occur. So far as the author has been able to ascertain, the minimum life of a wagon may be put down at sixteen years, and many are used for a very much longer time. But, for those who wish to provide an ample reserve in the nature of Depreciation, it is worth while to regard the limit as sixteen years, because by this means they will be building up a Reserve which will be available in the event of that particular pattern becoming obsolete by reason of further improvements, and also in the event of the destruction of one or more wagons by accident. There are various methods by which the " cash value " of a wagon may be written off, and it is desirable that the precise effect of each should be fully studied.

Perhaps the most favourite method of writing off Depreciation, in the case of articles which from time to time require repairs, is to adopt a fixed percentage upon the amount of the reducing annual balance. The effect of this method is to write off much heavier sums in the earlier years, and smaller sums in later years of the asset's life, the object of this being to compensate for the fact that the amount of necessary annual repairs will probably be upon the increase. If it is desired to extinguish the value of an article in sixteen years by writing a fixed percentage off the reducing balance, it will be necessary to adopt a rate of depreciation of about 17½ per cent. The following table is prepared upon this basis with regard to the example already shown above : —

EXAMPLE :

Date	Interest	Depreciation	Total Charge to Revenue	"Book" Value of Wagon at close of year
	£ s d	£ s d	£ s d	£ s d
1903	2 18 2	9 1 6	11 19 8	4 13 4
1904	2 1 5	7 9 10	9 11 3	11 15 1
1905	1 3 7	6 3 7	7 7 2	21 0 11
1906	0 4 10	5 1 11	5 6 9	24 0 8
1907	..	4 4 1	4 4 1	19 16 7
1908	..	3 9 5	3 9 5	16 7 2
1909 &c.	..	2 17 2	2 17 2	13 10 0

With reference to the figures appearing in the last money column above, it will be noted that for the first four years the amount is increasing, while afterwards it is reduced. The reason for this is that during the continuation of the hire-purchase agreement a portion of the instalments is in respect of Capital, therefore the amount of the capital asset is increased during this period in spite of the amounts which are credited to that account and debited to Profit and Loss for Depreciation. It will further be noticed that at no time does the value of the wagon appear in the books at more than £24 0s. 8d., although the original value of the wagon when new was £51 17s. 6d., and, further, that during each of the first three years the total charge to Revenue exceeds £7. This figure of £7 is mentioned in this connection because that is approximately the amount which would be charged for simple hire, and it is obvious that under no circumstances can it be really proper to charge more against Revenue than the amount of simple hire, because, in addition to getting the use of the wagon, which is all that is paid for in the case of simple hire, the tenant is also gradually acquiring the ownership of the wagons themselves. It will thus be seen that the above system is one which operates very unfairly upon the earlier years' profits, and is also one which unnecessarily reduces the value of the wagons, for it cannot be said that the value of a wagon which is kept in thorough repair is reduced more than 50 per cent. in the course of four years.

Another method of providing for Depreciation is to write off annually one-sixteenth of the original "cash value" of the wagons. If this method be adopted in the present case it will be found that the rate of Depreciation must be approximately 6¼ per cent. per annum upon the original value, and the following table shows the figures corresponding to those already mentioned, if this alternative system be adopted:—

EXAMPLE:

Date	Interest	Depreciation	Total Charge to Revenue	"Book" Value of Wagon at close of year
	£ s d	£ s d	£ s d	£ s d
1903	2 18 2	3 4 10	6 3 0	10 10 0
1904	2 1 5	3 4 10	5 6 3	21 16 9
1905	1 3 7	3 4 10	4 8 5	34 1 4
1906	0 4 10	3 4 10	3 9 8	38 18 2
1907	..	3 4 10	3 4 10	35 13 4
1908	..	3 4 10	3 4 10	32 8 6
1909 &c.	..	3 4 10	3 4 10	29 3 8

Upon this system the total charge to Revenue does not in any year exceed the amount which would have to be paid for simple hire; but during the continuance of the hire-purchase agreement the charges to Revenue are very much larger than afterwards, being during the first year nearly twice what they become after the agreement has run out. It will further be noticed that the maximum value at which the wagon appears in the tenant's books is £38 18s. 2d., or about 75 per cent. of its original value when new. From many points of view this is a very much better method to adopt than the preceding, seeing that apparently the assets are not overstated in the hirer's books, nor are the charges to Revenue liable to serious fluctuations; but even this system is one which cannot be looked upon as being so correct as to leave no room for alternative methods.

A third method is, during the continuance of the hire-purchase agreement to only write off Depreciation upon the instalments debited to Capital. This method can certainly be justified in theory by the argument that it is obviously unreasonable that the tenant should be expected to provide in his own Profit and Loss Account against Depreciation of property which does not belong to him; and, although this view might be thought to be somewhat specious, it is well worth while to consider how the various annual charges to Revenue will work out if this basis of calculation be adopted. It will be found that, in order to extinguish the asset entirely at the end of 16 years, it will be necessary to some-

R 2

what raise the rate of Depreciation if this system be adopted, as compared with the 6¼ per cent. which was necessary when each instalment of Depreciation was equal. A simple calculation shows that 10 per cent. during the continuance of the agreement will produce approximately the desired result.

The obvious objection to this method—and, indeed, the only one which can be seriously raised—is that the charges to Revenue *increase* during each of the first three years (that is to say, during the continuance of the agreement), for, although the charge for interest decreases as the amount due to the manufacturer is reduced, the charges for Depreciation naturally become heavier and to a much more largely increasing extent.

In order to avoid this, the method has sometimes been adopted of averaging the instalments to Revenue during the period of the agreement, so that at its expiration the same amount stands to the debit of the Asset Account as upon this last-mentioned method, but that the instalments *during* the continuance of the agreement are equal.

From many points of view it is thought that this last is really the most convenient method to adopt under normal circumstances; but, as already stated, the question of apportioning Revenue charges among the various years of the estimated life of the asset is entirely a matter of individual discretion, and one in which the greatest latitude must be allowed, provided the apportionment is made in good faith.

OTHER HIRE-PURCHASE TRANSACTIONS.

As has already been stated, hire-purchase transactions in connection with railway wagons generally run into very large figures, thus emphasising the importance of accurate treatment. The "loading" of the cash price is also calculated (at all events approximately) at a definite rate of interest, which may reasonably be regarded as compensation for the money lent. In connection, however, with the furniture, musical instrument, bicycle, and other trades, the difference between the cash and credit prices is often such as to clearly show that the "loading" covers more than a reasonable charge for interest upon money lent, the industry being subject to other risks, and in particular to bad debts and to failure on the part of the hirers to continue their instalments, in which case the manufacturer, at the best, only becomes repossessed of an asset, which in this case has greatly depreciated in value. The enormous number of transactions involved also not infrequently precludes the possibility of any very accurate apportionment as between Capital and Revenue being made in the books of the manufacturer, and in such cases the following simplified method will be found useful, while at the same time answering all practical purposes. In order to describe this system in detail it has been thought best to take a particular case, afterwards showing how the principles involved may be applied to any given set of facts.

PROBLEM.—A piano costing £17 10s. is catalogued at £36, and may be purchased by twelve quarterly instalments of £3 each, or it may be bought for cash (at a discount of 20 per cent.) for £28 16s. Show how the instalments of £3 per quarter may be correctly apportioned between Capital and Revenue, and describe how such transactions may be conveniently recorded in the books of the manufacturer, assuming that they are of frequent occurrence.

In this case, if the piano were sold for cash the gross profit would be £11 6s., and this may be taken as the basis upon which to proceed. It will thus be seen that the £36, which represents the aggregate of the instalments, is made up as follows:—

Cost	..	..	..	..	£17 10 0	or 48·6 per cent.
Gross Profit	..	..	..	11 6 0	,, 31·4 ,,
Interest, &c.	..	..	..	7 4 0	,, 20·0 ,,
					£36 0 0	100·0 ,,

A special Day Book should be provided for the record of hire-purchase agreement transactions, through which each hirer is debited with the aggregate amount of instalments receivable from him. At the end of each month the total of this Day Book should be posted to an account in the Nominal Ledger entitled "Sales on Hire-purchase," and when the books are balanced 80 per cent. (48 6 % + 31·4 %) of the amount standing to the credit of this Account may be transferred to Sales Account, and 20 per cent. to Hire-Purchase Interest Suspense Account.

It remains to be considered how the amount standing to the credit of Hire-Purchase Interest Suspense Account should be dealt with at balancing. It may be mentioned in passing, however, that as for convenience sake these transactions have to be dealt with in totals, it may be found that the percentage of Gross Profit is not in all cases uniform, and that, therefore, the 80 per cent. already referred to may require some adjustment, so that the amount to be transferred to Sales Account may represent (as nearly as can be ascertained) the cash value of the instruments dealt with during the current period.

Assuming for present purposes, however, that 20 per cent. of the total is the proper amount to credit to "Hire-Purchase Interest Suspense Account," it will be found that this represents a charge of somewhat less than 12½ per cent. per annum on the amount of debts outstanding at the commencement of each year, and upon this basis the £7 4s. that represents loading for interest, &c., may be apportioned as follows :—

First year	..	..	..	..	..	£3 9 7
Second year	..	..	..	..	..	2 8 9
Third year	..	..	..	..	..	1 5 8
						£7 4 0

Or, in the form of a percentage, as follows :—

First year	..	..	..	..	..	48·3 per cent.
Second year	..	..	..	..	..	33·9 ,,
Third year	..	..	..	..	..	17·8 ,,
						100·0 ,,

Consequently, if all the transactions were entered into on the first day of each year, at the conclusion of the first year 48 3 per cent. of the balance standing to the credit of Hire-Purchase Interest Suspense Account might properly be credited to Revenue as interest earned, and in the second and third years 33·9 per cent. and 17·8 per cent. respectively of the original balance. As a matter of fact, however, transactions of course take place throughout the whole of the year, and consequently all the hire-purchase agreements entered into during, say, the year 1900 will not have come to an end by the 31st December 1902. Assuming that the transactions are usually evenly spread throughout the whole twelve months, the proper credit to Revenue during the first year would be only one-half of 48·3 per cent., or 24·15 per cent.; during the second year the remaining half of the 48·3 per cent. and half of 33·9 per cent.; and so on. Disregarding fractions, therefore, the proper transfers from Hire-Purchase Interest Suspense Account to the credit of Revenue might be taken to be as follows :—

End of the First year	..	..	..	..	..	24 per cent.
,, ,, Second year	..	..	..	..	..	41 ,,
,, ,, Third year	..	..	..	..	..	25 ,,
,, ,, Fourth year	..	..	..	..	..	10 ,,
						100 ,,

In order that these calculations may readily and correctly be made, it is desirable that a separate Hire-Purchase Interest Suspense Account should be opened in the Ledger for the transactions that take place in each financial year. Each such account will, therefore, remain open for four years, and (assuming the business has been established so long) there will always be four such accounts open at the same time.

The above calculations are, as has already been stated, based upon the assumption that 20 per cent. of the aggregate value of the instalments represents loading for interest, &c.; but the same principle will apply whatever the exact amount of loading may be.

So far, it has been assumed that the whole of the loading may fairly be regarded as interest charged as compensation for deferred payment; but, as has already been stated, in industries of this description it is but reasonable to suppose that some part of the loading is to cover other losses. These, however, for the sake of simplicity, are best dealt with quite independently of the apportionment of the instalments received as between Capital and Revenue. As to the exact Reserve to be made for Bad Debts and other losses arising from Depreciation in connection with uncompleted contracts, each manufacturer would be guided largely by his own individual experience. It is suggested, however, that until the business has been sufficiently established to enable a safe opinion to be formed, a Reserve against loss should be created by debiting Revenue Account and crediting "Reserve for Bad Debts and Depreciation Account" with, say, 10 per cent. of the Gross Profits arising from hire-purchase transactions. Losses actually realised should from time to time be transferred to the debit of this account, and care should be taken to see that the credit balance remaining is sufficiently large to provide a reasonable Reserve against all likely contingencies.

BUILDING SOCIETY MORTGAGES.

The proper treatment of accounts in respect of Building Society mortgages follows closely upon the lines already explained in connection with the hire-purchase of railway wagons, save that in some cases the interest is calculated at shorter "rests" than is customary with the latter transactions. Every Building Society, however, issues tables showing the amount outstanding from time to time on the mortgages which it takes, and these will enable the annual balance upon each Mortgage Account to be readily determined. Such an account would in all respects be identical with that shown upon page 239, save that the first item to the debit would represent the amount of the original advance, while the cash postings to the credit of the account would be the instalments received from time to time from the borrower, which instalments would (as a rule) be paid at more frequent intervals. The general principle, however, is absolutely identical in all other respects.

ANNUITY AND SINKING FUND SYSTEMS OF DEPRECIATION.

As explained in Chapter XX., one method of providing for Depreciation is to charge Revenue with such a sum as will at the expiration of the life of the asset write off the original cost thereof, *plus* interest on the capital from time to time invested therein. The object of this method is to compensate for the fact that as the assets become of less value, and as certain sums are from time to time set aside out of Revenue to compensate for such wastage, the Working Capital of the undertaking becomes to a corresponding extent increased, and the amount invested in Fixed Assets reduced. This method—the "Annuity" method, as it is called—compensates for this circumstance by charging each successive year with a gradually increasing sum as a gradually increasing amount of the undertaking's resources is released from Fixed Assets and—being placed among the Floating Assets—is thus available to earn profits in other directions. When the Sink-

ing Fund system is adopted, and the Depreciation instalments are invested outside the business, no such compensation is required, and (assuming that the Sinking Fund investments can be accumulated at the same rate of interest) it would be sufficient to charge against each year's profits the net amount charged against the *first* year's profits under the Annuity system.

Referring again to the *pro formâ* Ledger Account given upon page 239, by altering the heading, this may be assumed to be an account of a five years' Lease which originally cost £60, and which it is desired to write off under the Annuity system, reckoning interest at 6 per cent. upon the half yearly balances. The postings to the credit side of the account must in that case be taken as representing the charges for Depreciation, instead of being postings from the Cash Book. This gives a fixed charge of £14 1s. 4d. per annum (which might be indifferently described as "Depreciation of Lease" or "Rent" charged against Revenue for the use by the business of the Leasehold Premises); while the Interest charges—which amount to £3 8s. 10d in the first year and are gradually reduced to 12s. 3d. in the fifth year—represent Interest on the amount of Capital from time to time remaining sunk in this asset during the term of its life. Inasmuch as the £14 1s. 4d. per annum is not actually paid away, but accumulated in the business, it is assumed that its utilisation in this manner will produce profits compensating the business for the decreasing amounts credited to Revenue Account in respect of Interest.

If, however, the half-yearly instalments by way of Depreciation were to be taken out of the business and could be re-invested elsewhere at 6 per cent., would be sufficient to provide Sinking Fund instalments of (£7 0s. 8d. − £1 16s. =) £5 4s. 8d. per half-year, as this sum, invested at 6 per cent. compound interest, would at the end of the five years accumulate to the original £60. *Primâ facie*, therefore, the employment of a Sinking Fund would appear to effect an economy; but *per contra* it must be borne in mind that, had the Sinking Fund instalments remained in the business as Working Capital, they would presumably have been earning profits at least equal to any rate of interest that may be earned from outside investments of a suitable character. The advantage of employing a Sinking Fund lies not in any direct economy of Revenue charges that it may effect, but in the assurance which it gives that, when the wasting asset against which it has been created has become valueless, there will be monies in hand available for the purchase of another asset of equal cost.

CHAPTER XXII.

FORM OF PUBLISHED ACCOUNTS.

IT is usual for all undertakings carrying on operations over an extended period to balance their books, and prepare accounts showing the position of affairs and the progress made during the current period, at regular intervals. In the case of Partnerships, and other private ventures, the partnership articles generally state when, and how often, such accounts are to be prepared, it being customary to stipulate for the preparation of annual accounts, the financial year running from the commencement of the partnership. When, however, that date is—for any particular reason—inconvenient, some other date may be substituted, and in this, as in all other, respects the terms of the articles of partnership may be modified from time to time with the consent of all the partners. These periodical accounts are, of course, prepared solely for the information of the partners, and consequently in such form as they may mutually agree.

In the case of Public Companies, the shareholders may for many purposes be regarded as the partners in the undertaking, while the Articles of Association, or special Act of Parliament under which the Company is incorporated, may be regarded as analogous to articles of partnership. It is usual for Companies to prepare accounts annually for the purpose of submission to the proprietors in general meeting assembled, but in the case of some few undertakings —as, for example, Banks and Railway Companies—the accounts are prepared half-yearly. In other cases also the books are actually balanced half-yearly for the information of directors, although the information which is obtained is not published. It is usual for the annual, or other, accounts of the Company to be printed and circulated among the shareholders, although in the case of Companies registered under the Companies Acts there is no statutory provision to this effect, and the matter is accordingly regulated by the Articles of Association of each individual Company. The Articles also to some extent determine the amount of information that shall be given in the published accounts, although this is a matter that is in all cases very largely within the discretion of the directors, who, within very wide limits, have power to determine the form that the accounts shall take.

This question of form is one upon which it would be difficult to lay down any hard and fast rules of universal application. The varying circumstances determining the position of different undertakings renders the adoption of any stereotyped form practically impossible, although concerns carrying on similar classes of business might, as a rule, have their accounts framed upon very much the same lines. Opinions, however, vary greatly as to the amount of information which it is desirable to publicly disclose, and the precise form that that information should take, with the result that in practice the published accounts of almost every concern present some points of difference. Doubtless some nearer approach to uniformity would from most points of view be desirable, and in the case of clearly defined industries would be by no means impracticable, as is shown by the fact that Railways, Gas Companies, Life Assurance Companies, Building Societies, and certain other undertakings are required to publish their accounts in the form prescribed by the Legislature, and are enabled to adhere very closely to that form without inconvenience. But until something more nearly approaching uniformity is reached, it is thought that little would be gained in the present work by dogmatising upon the question as to the best form of accounts for different classes of representative undertakings. It has, on the other hand, been thought that a collection of a number of representative published accounts will prove at once more interesting and more instructive. Such a collection has accordingly been appended at the close of this chapter. Some of the accounts have been selected on account of the excellence of their form, some for the opposite reason, and others on account of special circumstances which render it probable that their careful study may be found of value. The accounts have accordingly been given in their published form without any alterations whatever, and the published certificates and reports of the Auditors have been appended. The names of the Auditors have been added, with a view to showing the practice of certain firms as to the wording of their Certificates and Reports. It must not, however, be supposed that in this respect the information afforded can be regarded as anything like complete, and in particular it must be borne in mind that the responsibility for the form in which the accounts of a Company are published rests primarily with the directors, rather than with the Auditors. It does not therefore necessarily follow that the forms reproduced are regarded by the respective firms of Auditors as being, in their opinion, the most suitable that might have been designed to meet the circumstances of that particular case.

The BALANCE SHEET of Messrs. FURNESS, WITHY & COMPANY, LTD., West Hartlepool, 30th April 1901.

Capital and Liabilities.	£ s d	£ s d	Property and Assets.	£ s d	£ s d
Share Capital—			Steamships, Freeholds, Lease-		
Total Authorised Issue :			holds, Buildings, Dry Dock,		
30,000 5% Preference Shares			Machinery, Plant, Stocks and		
@ £10 each	300,000 0 0		Work in progress at Shipyard	..	838,879 8 7
7,000 Ordinary Shares @ £100			Investments—		
each..	700,000 0 0		In Government and Railway		
	£1,000,000 0 0		Securities, Banks and In-		
			dustrial Companies	..	1,236,198 18 8
The whole of which have been			In Steamships and Shipping		
issued and fully paid	..	1,000,000 0 0	Companies	..	270,196 9 8
4½% Debentures	..	380,600 0 0	Sundry Debtors—		
			On Open Accounts and Steam-		
Creditors—			ers' uncompleted voyages ..	..	182,898 6 1
On open accounts at Head Office,			Cash and Bills—		
Shipyard and Branch Offices ..	82,441 14 11		Bank Deposits, Loans at Inter-		
On Bills payable for new Steam-			est, Cash in hand and Bills		
ers, Engines, &c. ..	499,836 9 4		Receivable (undiscounted) at		
			Banks, Head Office and		
	582,278 4 3		Branches	..	424,601 14 2
Add Amounts received on account					
of Steamers, less payments to					
Builders	211,113 14 9				
		793,391 19 0			
Reserve Fund for Depreciation, &c.	..	600,000 0 0			
Insurance Fund	..	75,000 0 0			
Profit and Loss Balance as per last					
Account	134,803 5 9				
Less—Dividend paid					
16th July 1900, at					
10% on £700,000 70,000 0 0					
Less Transfer to					
Insurance Fund.. 50,000 0 0					
	120,000 0 0				
	14,803 5 9				
Add Profit this year as per account	263,979 12 5				
	278,782 18 2				
Less—Written off to					
Reserve Fund 150,000 0 0					
Less—Written off to					
Insurance Fund 25,000 0 0					
	175,000 0 0	103,782 18 2			
		£2,952,774 17 2			£2,952,774 17 2

Profit and Loss Account for Twelve Months ending April 30th 1901.

	£ s d	£ s d		£ s d	£ s d
To Directors' Fees	..	5,600 0 0	By Profits—		
„ Income Tax	..	7,583 18 4	On Steamers Voyages, Purchase		
„ Interest on Debentures and			and Sale of Steamers, Ship		
Preference Shares	..	30,565 10 9	building Yard, Head Office		
„ Balance carried down	..	263,979 12 5	and Branches	..	184,658 11 6
		£307,729 1 6	„ Dividends on Investments ..	..	118,934 19 5
			„ Government Subsidy for Postal		
			Services	..	4,135 10 7
Proposed Appropriation.					£307,729 1 6
To Reserve Fund—					
For Depreciation, &c. ..	..	150,000 0 0	By Balance brought forward from		
„ Insurance Fund	..	25,000 0 0	1900	64,803 5 9	
„ Dividend—			Less—Transfer to Insurance		
At 10% on £700,000 ..	..	70,000 0 0	Fund	50,000 0 0	
„ Balance carried forward to next					14,803 5 9
year's Account..	..	33,782 18 2	Balance brought down, being		
		£278,782 18 2	profit for the year	..	263,979 12 5
					£278,782 18 2

West Hartlepool,   CHRISTOPHER FURNESS, Chairman.
July 19th 1901   HENRY WITHY,
     R. W. VICK, } Directors.
     STEPHEN W. FURNESS,
     F. W. LEWIS,

In accordance with the provisions of the Companies Act 1900, we certify that all our requirements as Auditors have been complied with. We have audited the books and accounts of Furness, Withy & Co., Ltd., kept at the Head Office and Branches in the United Kingdom, for the year ended 30th April 1901, in which are incorporated the Statements for the same period relating to the American and Canadian Branches as certified by local Accountants. We certify that, subject to the valuations of Stocks and Investments, the above Balance Sheet is, in our opinion, properly drawn up so as to exhibit a true and correct view of the state of the Company's affairs as shown by the books of the Company.

West Hartlepool,   MONKHOUSE, GODDARD & Co.,
19th July 1901.   Chartered Accountants.

LEVINSTEIN LIMITED.

BALANCE SHEET (Abridged), 30th June 1901.

Capital and Liabilities.	£ s d	£ s d
Nominal Capital	90,000 0 0	
Subscribed Capital, £90,000.		
6 per Cent. Cumulative Preference Shares of £10 each :—		
2,000 Shares, issued as fully paid ..	20,000 0 0	
1,000 Shares, fully paid..	10,000 0 0	
3,000 Shares	30,000 0 0	
Ordinary Shares of £10 each, fully paid :—		
6,000 Shares, of which 5,330 Shares were issued as £7 10s. per Share paid	60,000 0 0	
		90,000 0 0
4½ per Cent. First Mortgage Debenture Stock	70,000 0 0	
Add Interest accrued thereon to date (less Income Tax)	1,489 13 9	
		71,489 13 9
5 per Cent. Mortgage Debenture Stock (authorised issue £50,000)	30,000 0 0	
Add Interest accrued thereon to date (less Income Tax)	709 7 6	
		30,709 7 6
The balance of £20,000 5 per Cent. Debenture Stock unissued is reserved to the Bank as security for an overdraft up to £15,000 0s. 0d.		
Sundry Creditors (less Discount) ..	10,115 13 11	
Reserve for Outstanding Liabilities..	782 6 6	
		10,898 0 5
Liability on Bills Discounted, not matured ..	4,329 15 10	
Amount owing to Bankers		3,049 18 8
Reserve Fund		3,000 0 0
Interest on Investments held by the Trustees for the 4½ per Cent. Debenture Stockholders :—		
Amount at 30th June 1900	600 1 11	
Add Further Interest received by the Trustees to date	379 1 4	
		979 3 3
	£210,126 3 7	

Property and other Assets, &c.	£ s d	£ s d
Freehold Lands, Water Rights, Reservoirs, Buildings, Machinery and Plant, and Office Furniture:—		
Amount at 30th June 1900 .. £	105,742 2 6	
Less Depreciation of Buildings, Plant and Machinery, and Furniture ..	3,787 4 10	
	101,954 17 8	
Add Outlay during the year	4,104 17 5	
		106,059 15 1
Stock of Raw Materials and Colours on hand, and on Consignment, and Stores, &c., per Certified Stock Sheets		64,569 3 2
Sundry Debtors, less Reserve for Discount and Doubtful Debts		18,385 8 2
Cash in hand and at Foreign Bankers		262 1 0
Rates and Insurances paid in advance		98 14 1
Trustees for the 4½ per Cent. Debenture Stockholders :—		
Investments at cost and Cash held by them..	10,579 3 3	
Goodwill (Original Amount, £7,084 3s. 5d.)	5,000 0 0	
Suspense Account, being Law Costs and Expenses in Test Cases under the Patent Acts:—		
Amount at 30th June 1900 ..	902 2 3	
Deduct Amount now written off ..	165 16 8	
		736 5 7
Patents and Library Account :—		
Amount at 30th June 1900 ..	932 11 4	
Add Total expenditure since that date	563 9 9	
		1,496 1 1
Expenses of Issue of 5 per Cent. Debenture Stock :—		
Amount at 30th June 1900 ..	1,350 0 0	
Balance of Claim and Costs in John Campbell & Co.'s Action against the Company,		
Amount at 30th June 1900 ..	683 12 8	
Add Balance of Debt and Costs, since paid	347 8 8	
	1,031 1 4	
Less Amount now written off	100 0 0	
		931 1
Profit and Loss Account :—		
Balance brought forward from 30th June 1900, per Directors' Report £647 9 1		
Add Profit for the year ended 30 June 1901 .. 4,056 16 4		
	4,704 5 5	
Less Interest on Debenture Stocks ..	4,407 16 3	
	296 9 2	
Deduct Interim Dividend on Preference Shares paid for the half-year ended 31st December 1900 (*less* Income Tax) £855 0 0		
Amount written off John Campbell & Co.'s Action Account .. 100 0 0		
	955 0 0	
Balance at debit		658 10 10
		£210,126 3 7

We certify that all our requirements as Auditors have been complied with, and we report to the Shareholders that we have examined the Books Accounts, and Vouchers of the Company for the year ending 30th June 1901, and certify to the correctness thereof, and that, subject to the Stock being of the value stated, the foregoing Balance Sheet is, in our opinion, properly drawn up so as to exhibit a true and correct view of the state of the Company's affairs as shown by the Books of the Company.

MANCHESTER, 15th August 1901.

ASHWORTH, MOSLEY & Co., CHARTERED ACCOUNTANTS, Auditors.

LONDON AND ST. KATHARINE DOCKS COMPANY.

Dr.   **1.—RECEIPTS AND EXPENDITURE** for the Half-Year ending 31st December 1897.   Cr.

	31st Dec., 1896 £ s d	£ s d		31st Dec., 1896 £ s d	£ s d
To Salaries	504 6 8	500 17 9	By Proportion of Profits from the London and India Docks Joint Committee, per Accounts ..	156,809 7 1	153,055 4 6
„ Management, including Directors' Fees	1,493 1 7	1,537 2 9	„ Rents of Premises	239 15 1	389 13 8
„ Income Tax	2,098 7 4	2,364 9 2	„ Interest on advance to Joint Committee on account of Sundry Works	5,080 0 2	6,211 4 1
„ Superannuation Allowances ..	2,659 11 9	2,560 11 8	„ Interest from Bankers, &c. ..	184 2 3	113 7 6
„ Law Charges	136 16 8	19 10 3	„ Adjustment of Local Rates to end of 1896, repaid by Joint Committee		1,125 8 9
„ Losses, Allowances, and Incidental Expenses	1,758 3 3	71 3 4			
	8,650 7 3	7,053 14 11			
„ Interest on Debentures and Loans	5,917 19 4	5,187 0 6			
„ Ditto Debenture Stock ..	59,524 3 1	60,324 19 1			
„ Dividend on 4½ per cent. Preferential Stock	9,450 0 0	9,450 0 0			
„ Dividend on New 4½ per cent. Preference Stock (Act 1878)	13,500 0 0	13,500 0 0			
„ Dividend on New 4½ per cent. Preference Stock (Act 1882)	13,500 0 0	13,500 0 0			
	110,542 9 8	109,015 14 6			
Balance carried to Profit and Loss ..	51,760 14 11	51,879 4 0			
	£162,303 4 7	£160,894 18 6		£162,303 4 7	£160,894 18 6

Dr.   **2.—PROFIT AND LOSS.**   Cr.

	£ s d		£ s d
To Dividend 30th June 1897	71,958 14 4	By Balance from 30th June 1897	100,010 19 8
„ Balance	79,931 9 4	„ „ „ Receipts and Expenditure Account..	51,879 4 0
	£151,890 3 8		£151,890 3 8

Dr.   **3.—CAPITAL.**   Cr.

	£ s d			£ s d
To Cost of Docks, Warehouses, Land, Premises, and Works	10,919,408 5 1	By Capital Stock £5,756,697 5 10		
		„ 4 per cent. Debenture Stock .. 3,016,218 18 1		
		„ 4½ per cent. Preferential Stock .. 420,000 0 0		
		„ New 4½ per cent. Preference Stock (Act 1878)	600,000 0 0	
		„ New 4½ per cent. Preference Stock (Act 1882)	600,000 0 0	
				10,392,946 3 11
		„ Debentures		396,517 1 11
		„ Realised Property Account		62,061 5 8
		„ Premium on issue of Stock		67,883 13 7
	£ 10,919,408 5 1		£	10,919,408 5 1

Dr.   **4.—RESERVE FUND.**   Cr.

	£ s d		£ s d
To Advance to Joint Committee on Account of New Entrance, West India Dock ..	169,175 19 7	By Balance from 30th June 1897	323,033 6 11
„ Ditto New Shed, Royal Albert Dock ..	14,562 12 1	„ Premium on Issue of Stock	7,510 2 10
„ Ditto Frozen Meat Store, West Smithfield ..	70,156 16 0		
„ Ditto New Cold Air Store, W. India Dock ..	10,022 15 10		
„ Ditto Victoria Graving Dock	26,652 9 0		
„ Balance, being Debentures Redeemed	39,972 17 3		
	£330,543 9 9		£330,543 9 9

Dr.   **5.—ASSETS AND LIABILITIES.**   Cr.

	£ s d		£ s d
To Outstanding Rental, &c.	6,092 0 0	By Unclaimed Dividends	19,162 16 8
„ The London and India Docks Joint Committee ..	151,615 0 2	„ Unpaid Interest on Debentures and Preference Stocks	97,880 0 9
„ Bankers' Balances	2,057 18 1	„ Properties Purchased and not conveyed	655 10 0
„ Cash in Hand	100 0 0	„ Unpaid Accounts	8,604 6 2
„ Deposit at Bankers	13,000 0 0	„ Balance of Profit and Loss	79,931 9 4
„ Debentures Redeemed	33,369 4 8		
	£206,234 2 11		£206,234 2 11

Examined with the Books of the London and St. Katharine Docks Company, and found correct.

DOCK HOUSE, 109 LEADENHALL STREET,
January 1898.

SAMUEL PETO,
A. M. BETHUNE, } Auditors.

THE NEW ZEALAND MIDLAND RAILWAY COMPANY, LIMITED.

Dr.   BALANCE SHEET, 30th June 1895.   *Cr.*

	£ s d	£ s d
To Capital—		
Authorised—		
50,000 Shares of £10 each	500,000 0 0	
Issued—		
25,000 Shares of £10 each, fully called up .	250,000 0 0	
Deduct Arrears of Calls	575 0 0	
		249,425 0 0
To Five per Cent. First Mortgage Debentures	745,000 0 0	
Bonds forfeited	1,200 0 0	
		743,800 0 0
To Creditors—		
Sundry Accounts	4,223 14 1	
National Bank of New Zealand, Limited, Overdrawn Account	735 17 9	
Loans secured by Mortgages on Land, including £20,000 Loan from National Bank of New Zealand, Limited ..	79,300 6 8	
Debenture Interest accrued to 30th June 1895, including £562 10s. on Bonds held per contra	26,342 18 4	
		110,602 16 10
To Sundry Receipts and Land earned, as per last account, 30th June 1894	427,604 10 1	
Add—Receipts for the year ending the 30th June 1895:—		
Increased value of Land sold £1,026 17 7		
Land Mortgage Interest .. 7,288 18 7		
Land Rents 1,830 14 9		
Coal Royalty 875 1 6		
Timber Royalty 1,385 2 9		
*Traffic Receipts up to 25th May 1895 .. .. £13,567 0 1		
Less Working Expenses .. 10,310 8 7		
3,256 11 6		
Transfer and other Fees .. 2 5 0		
	15,665 11 8	
		443,270 1 9
To Liability on Contracts for Construction .. £158 15 0		
Note.—In addition to the above £743,800 of Debentures, an issue of £80,000 (part of £100,000) has been made as collateral security.		
* The Railway was seized by the New Zealand Government on the 25th May 1895.		
		£1,547,097 18 7

	£ s d	£ s d
By Cash—		
At Bankers and in hand (London) ..	5,185 3 7	
Do. do. (New Zealand) .	42 3 9	
		5,227 7 4
By Cash for Interest, in hands of the Trustees for the 5 per cent. First Mortgage Debenture Holders		99 13 3
By Debtors—		
For Land sold (secured by Mortgage and Agreements to Mortgage) of which £117,980 13s. 3d. have been pledged to secure loans, see per contra	118,915 11 5	
Sundry Accounts	3,546 2 1	
		122,461 13 6
By Investments—		
£15,900 New Zealand Midland Railway Company, Lim., Five per Cent. First Mortgage Debentures, of which £10,000 have been given as additional security for part of "Loans secured by Mortgages on Land," see per contra ..	14,131 8 7	
100 £10 Shares of the Black Ball Coal Mining Company of New Zealand, Limited, fully paid..	1,000 0 0	
		15,131 8 7
By Office Furniture, *less* Depreciation..		540 4 0
By Land, selected in New Zealand, portions of which have been sold, but definite particulars have not been received from New Zealand, at Contract valuation, of which £36,882 have been pledged to secure Loans, see per contra		53,289 1 3
By New Zealand Government, for Land earned but not selected, at Contract valuation		11,704 16 10
By Stock of Timber, *less* Depreciation ..		76 17 5
By Timber Drying Sheds, *less* Depreciation		122 11 2
By Working Railway Stores on hand on 25th May 1895		129 7 1
By Sundry Expenditure—		
As per last Account, 30th June 1894 ..	1,273,546 15 11	
Add—Expenditure for the year ending 30th June 1895:—		
Cost of Construction, Rolling Stock, Surveys, Engineering Fees, Compensation, &c., including £9,838 0s. 2d. arbitration fees and expenses .. £16,381 0 2		
Directors' Fees for three months to 30th September 1894 .. .. .. 437 10 0		
Trustees' Fees (Debenture) 300 0 0		
Law Charges 293 5 10		
Salaries, Rent, and other Current Expenses .. 5,303 9 9		
Rates and Taxes (New Zealand) 1,838 1 10		
Debenture Interest .. 10,847 1 8		
Debenture Interest to be funded 26,342 18 4		
Land Grant Expenses .. 2,489 4 5		
Further Expenses in connection with Timber Trade, *less* Sales .. 535 10 3		
64,768 2 3		
		1,338,314 18
		£1,547,097 18 7

We have compared the above Balance Sheet with the Books, Accounts, and Vouchers in London and the Accounts signed by the Local Auditors in New Zealand, and find the same to agree therewith. We are unable to verify the value of the Debts, Investments and Land.

London, 23rd December 1896.

COOPER BROTHERS & CO.,
Chartered Accountants, } Auditors.

JEREMIAH ROTHERHAM & Co., Limited.

BALANCE SHEET, 15th January 1902.

Liabilities.	£ s d	£ s d	Assets.	£ s d	£ s d
Share Capital—			Freehold and Leasehold Premises and Goodwill—		
Authorised and Issued :			Amount at 15th January 1901	270,484 13 6	
200,000 Preference Shares of £1 each fully paid	200,000 0 0		Added during the year—		
300,000 Ordinary Shares of £1 each fully paid	300,000 0 0		Outlay on New Buildings and Fixtures on Freehold and Leasehold Sites, *less* Depreciation on Lease-holds	63,087 10 8	
		500,000 0 0			333,572 4 2
			Fixtures and Fittings (Original Buildings)..	10,285 3 7	
Mortgage Debenture Stock		200,000 0 0	Moveable Plant, Furniture, Horses, Vans, &c. ..	4,146 18 5	
Bills Payable		4,613 6 1	Stock at Cost or Valuation	178,592 14 2	
Trade Liabilities	33,392 0 8		Book Debts 257,293 11 1		
Less—Discount 2½ per cent. ..	834 16 0		*Less* – Discount 2½ per cent... .. 6,432 6 9		
		32,557 4 8			250,861 4 4
Deposits		18,376 19 4			
Sundry Liabilities due or accrued ..		8,714 19 2	Sundry Debtors, including Advances on Security ..	10,147 12 6	
Dividend Warrants, &c., not presented ..		24 16 8	Fire Insurance, &c., paid in advance	820 0 7	
Reserve for Contingencies on Book Debts	3,500 0 0		Bills Receivable, in hand	4,548 9 11	
Capital Reserve Account	18,681 6 7		Cash at Bankers and in hand—		
General Reserve Account	17,000 0 0		On Deposit Account 20,000 0 0		
		39,181 6 7	On Current Accounts and in hand 17,514 9 3		
					37,514 9 3
Profit and Loss Account—					
Balance brought forward from last year	7,937 15 2				
Add—Profits for the year ending 15th January 1902, as per annexed account	34,582 9 3				
	42,520 4 5				
Deduct – Interim Dividends paid 31st August 1901, viz.:					
Preference Shares at 5% per annum £5,000					
Ordinary Shares at 7% per annum 10,500					
	15,500 0 0				
		27,020 4 5			
		£830,488 16 11			£830,488 16 11

Dr.	PROFIT AND LOSS ACCOUNT, Year ending 15th January 1902.		Cr.	
	£ s d			£ s d
Interest on Debenture Stock	7,729 9 11	Profit on Trading for the Year, after providing for bad and doubtful Debts and deducting Depreciation on Leaseholds, Fixtures and Moveable Plant		44,633 7 3
Directors', Trustees', and Auditors' Fees	2,220 0 0	Transfer Fees		110 7 6
Income Tax	211 15 7			
Balance, carried to Balance Sheet	34,582 9 3			
	£44,743 14 9			£44,743 14 9

HERBERT H. PIGGIN, *Secretary.*

FREDERICK SNOWDEN, } *Directors.*
ROBERT DUMMETT,

AUDITORS' REPORT.

To the Shareholders of JEREMIAH ROTHERHAM & CO., LIMITED.

We certify that we have examined the foregoing Balance Sheet and Profit and Loss Account, with the Company's Books, and that they are in accordance therewith. The Cash and Bills on hand and the Bank Balances and Book Debts have been verified by us, and the Stocks of Goods on hand have been valued and certified by the Managers of each Department.

We also report that in our opinion the above Balance Sheet is properly drawn up so as to exhibit a true and correct view of the state of the Company's affairs as shown by the Books of the Company, and we certify that all our requirements as Auditors have been complied with.

99 CHEAPSIDE, LONDON, E.C.
14th February 1902.

VINEY, PRICE & GOODYEAR,
Chartered Accountants.

THE WHITE FEATHER MAIN REEFS, LIMITED.

Dr.   BALANCE SHEET, 31st January 1899.   *Cr.*

	£ s d	£ s d		£ s d	£ s d	£ s d
To Share Capital—			**By Property—**			
Authorised—			Purchase Price of four			
160,000 Shares of £1 each	160,000 0 0		Mining Leases (48 Acres) situate at Kanowna, Western Australia, including all Developments, Ore at Grass and Tailings on Dump		126,110 17 9	
Issued—			„ **Plant and Machinery—**			
140,300 Shares of £1 each, with 18s. per Share, credited as paid thereon	126,270 0 0		Winding, Pumping Engine, Boiler and 20-Stamp Battery, complete, &c. ..		6,808 18 6	
Assessment of 2s. per Share on 140,300 Shares, all called up, making fully paid ..	14,030 0 0		„ **Buildings**		604 19 1	
7 Signatories Shares of £1 each	7 0 0		*NOTE.*—The above property was bought from the White Feather Main Reef Gold Mining Company, Limited, under Reconstruction Agreement of the 7th February 1898, and satisfied by the issue of 140,300 Shares of £1 each, credited with 18s. per Share as paid thereon, and by the payment of £7,254 15s. 4d. in cash.		133,524 15 4	
140,307 Total Shares issued	140,307 0 0					
Less Calls in Arrear ..	6 13 0					
		140,300 7 0				
„ **Sundry Creditors**	1,690 8 2					
„ **Unclaimed Dividends**—London ..	86 10 0					
		1,776 18 2	„ **Capital Expenditure** from 4th February 1898 to 31st January 1899—			
„ **Profit and Loss Account:—**			On Developments at Mine	4,449 6 10		
Profit from 4th February 1898, to 31st January 1899, as per Account ..	17,759 10 1		„ Plant and Machinery, including Cyanide Plant	2,146 7 5		
Deduct— £ s d			„ Buildings & Furniture	710 19 7		
No. 1 Dividend 1s. per Share.. .. 7,015 7 0					7,306 13 10	
No. 2 Dividend 6d. per Share.. .. 3,507 13 6			*Deduct—*Depreciation of 10% Plant & Machinery, £8,955 5 11= £895 10 7 Buildings, &c. 1,315 18 8= 131 11 10		140,831 9 2	
	10,523 0 6		£10,271 4 7			
		7,236 9 7			1,027 2 5	
						139,804 6 9
			„ **Sundry Debtors** and Payments in advance			487 13 5
			„ **Gold in Transit—**			
			From Kanowna to London		6,115 19 2	
			„ **Cash—**			
			At Commercial Bank of Scotland, Lim.—			
			Current Account ..	2,812 19 3		
			Dividend Account ..	86 10 0		
			In hand	6 6 2		
					2,905 15 5	
						9,021 14 7
		£149,313 14 9				£149,313 14 9

AUDITORS' REPORT.

We have examined the foregoing Balance Sheet, with the Books and Vouchers in London and with the Accounts received from Australia, and subject to the production of the Vouchers for the Colonial Dividends, it is, in our opinion, a full and fair Balance Sheet, properly drawn up so as to exhibit a true and correct view of the state of the Company's affairs. The arrangements for Transfer of the Property from the Liquidators into the Name of the Company are now in progress but have not yet been completed.

LONDON, *June 3rd 1899.*

WOODTHORPE, BEVAN & CO., *Auditors.*
Chartered Accountants.

THE WHITE FEATHER MAIN REEFS, LIMITED.

PROFIT AND LOSS ACCOUNT from 4th February 1898 (the date of the Incorporation of the Company) to 31st January 1899.

Dr.   Cr.

	£ s d	£ s d		£ s d	£ s d
To General Expenses—			**By Amount Realised on Gold Sales—**		
			On 9,476 tons Ore Crushed—		
London—			Fine Gold, 9,586·238 ozs.	37,322 11 10	
Directors' Remuneration, including			Silver, 606·19 ozs.	69 3 7	
percentage on Profits..	1,587 19 4			37,391 15 5	
Office Expenses,—Rent, and Secretarial Fee	373 12 6		„ **Public Crushing** ..	140 12 6	
Printing and Stationery	125 16 3			37,532 7 11	
Cables, Telegrams, and Postages	120 2 1				
Advertising	60 6 6		*Deduct—*		
Audit Fees..	52 10 0		Cost of Raising Ore.. £10,482 3 3		
Law Costs ..	66 10 0		Cost of Milling Ore .. 3,405 1 10		
Subscription to "West Australian			Bank Escort, Mint and		
Chamber of Mines"..	5 5 0		Brokerage on Gold	959 9 3	
Bank Charges	25 9 5		Repairs and Renewals		
Sundries	64 18 7		of Plant &Machinery	289 1 8	
		2,482 9 8	Freight and Carriage		
Australia—			on do.	19 14 6	
Rent of Leases	109 2 0			15,155 10 6	
Cables, Telegrams, and Postages	197 2 7				22,376 17 5
Printing and Stationery	72 17 6				
Advertising	32 10 9		„ **Interest** on Deposit at Bank		17 5 5
Cost of Assaying ..	26 0 6		„ **Transfer Fees**, London ..		73 12 6
Travelling Expenses	25 6 0				
Insurance Premium — Employers'					
Accident Liability	48 0 0				
Sundries	54 15 0				
Survey Fees	15 0 0				
Fees—Local Director at Coolgardie..	93 15 0				
Adelaide Office — Secretary, Local					
Attorney, and Rent	150 0 0				
		824 9 4			
„ **Difference in Exchange..**		24 3 10			
„ **Income Tax** (estimated)..		350 0 0			
„ **Depreciation on Plant**, Machinery and Buildings—					
10 per cent. off £10,271 4s. 7d.		1,027 2 5			
„ **Balance**—Being Profit as per Balance Sheet		17,759 10 1			
		£22,467 15 4			£22,467 15 4

LONDON GENERAL OMNIBUS COMPANY, LIMITED.

BALANCE SHEET, made up to December 31st 1901.

Dr.

Half-year ending Dec. 31st 1900 £ s d		£ s d	£ s d
773,592 0 0	**1. Capital.**		
45,149 8 10	Capital £1,000,000 0 0		
	Stock Issued	45,149 8 10	773,592 0 0
	Premiums	100,000 0 0	145,149 8 10
	From Reserve Fund		
300,000 0 0	**2. Debts and Liabilities.**		
	4% Mortgage Debentures ..		300,000 0 0
79,599 3 3	Loan from Parr's Bank, Limited	40,000 0 0	
812 18 8	Sundry Creditors	57,669 7 3	
2,850 0 0	Law Expenses and Compensation	1,039 13 4	
3,102 4 9	Debenture Interest, No. 15 Coupon..	2,825 0 0	
160 0 3	Unclaimed Dividends ..	2,315 0 0	
	Do. Debenture Interest	116 15 3	
86,624 6 8			103,965 19 8
210,000 0 0	**3. Reserves.**		
10,000 0 0	General Fund	85,000 0 0	
220,000 0 0	Horse Stock Reserve Fund ..	10,000 0 0	95,000 0 0
45,960 9 1	**4. Profit and Loss.**		
	Balance of Account		26,566 17 6
£1,471,326 4 7	Amount carried forward		£1,444,274 6 0

Cr.

Half-year ending Dec. 31st 1900 £ s d		£ s d	£ s d	£ s d
48,582 7 8	**5. Property held by the Company.**			
216,611 17 6	Freehold Land £48,532 7 8			
	Do. Buildings 228,843 19 5	277,376 7 1		
342,655 16 1	Leaseholds	388,683 19 6	666,060 6 7	
	Stock-in-Trade—			
607,850 1 3	Omnibuses, Horses, Harness and Yard Stock	482,550 14 1		
4,7,783 3 4	Office Furniture and Fixtures..	576 11 11	483,127 1 0	
	Revenue Departments—			
478,344 14 11	Plant and Stores, as per Valuations		1,149,187 7 7	
1,086,194 16 2	Horses in Training at Special Depôts	69,447 18 6		
67,546 14 3	Provender at Depôts and Granaries	8,995 0 0		
9,530 0 0		20,929 5 9		
21,797 2 9				
98,863 17 0	Unexpired Value of Police Licences	99,372 4 3		
528 17 0		470 0 0	99,842 4 3	
99,391 17 0				
1,185,586 13 4				1,249,029 11 10
	6. Good Debts owing to the Company.			
2,281 1 8	Interest and Dividends	800 0 0		
800 0 0	Deposits in Cash and Consols	727 5 6	1,655 7 6	
727 5 6	Sundry Trade Debtors for Manure, Rent, Carcases, Advertising and Stores for which no security is held		1,527 5 6	
12,992 11 2			10,766 16 9	
	7. Cash and Investments.			
16,800 18 4	Cash—Parr's Bank, Limited—			
	Current Account ..£6,856 5 4			
8,495 18 5	District Offices .. 2,246 19 7			
2,311 2 7	Head Office	9,103 4 11		
74 10 5	Paris Office	96 10 11		
24 16 8		25 3 4	9,224 19 2	
	Investments—			
10,906 8 1	£ s d			
110,167 5 0	80,000 0 0 Consolidated 2¾% Consols ..	80,122 1 1		
55,916 15 10	50,000 0 0 India 3½% Stock			
1,000 0 0	1,000 0 0 East India Railway 4½% Debenture Stock	1,738 4 9		
1,738 4 9	12,000 0 0 L.B. & S.C. Railway 5% Preference Stock	22,153 2 2		
22,153 2 2	10,000 0 0 L.&N.W. Railway 4% Preference Stock	14,144 14 7		
14,144 14 7				9,224 19 2
£204,120 2 4	Amount carried forward ..	118,158 2 7	9,224 19 2	13,949 9 9
				£1,262,979 1 7

LONDON GENERAL OMNIBUS COMPANY, LIMITED.

BALANCE SHEET, made up to December 31st 1901 (*continued*).

Dr.

Half-year ending Dec. 31st 1900				£	s	d	£	s	d
1,471,326 4 7	Amount brought forward	..	..				1,444,274	6	0

Contingent Liability.

| £5,000 0 0 | Leases Indemnity Fund | .. | .. | .. | | £5,000 | 0 | 0 |

| £1,471,326 4 7 | | £1,444,274 | 6 | 0 |

Cr.

Half-year ending Dec. 31st 1900				£	s	d	£	s	d	£	s	d
204,120 2 4	Amount brought forward	..	118,158	2	7	9,224	19	2	1,262,979	1	7
	INVESTMENTS—											
	4,000 0 0 Metropolitan Railway 4 % Debenture Stock											
6,428 2 6	Midland Railway 2½ % Preference Stock	6,428	2	6								
31,593 8 1	South Eastern Railway 5 % Debenture Stock	34,000	0	0								
10,890 12 1		6,200	0	0								
		31,593	8	1								
253,032 5 0		10,890	12	1								
5,000 0 0	Leases Indemnity Fund 2¾ % Consols	167,070	5	3								
258,032 5 0		5,333	6	8								
		5,000	0	0								
					172,070	5	3	181,295	4	5
268,938 13 1												

| £1,471,326 4 7 | | £1,444,274 | 6 | 0 |

Examined and found correct,

FREDK. HORNCASTLE,
RICHARD SEDGWICK, } Auditors.

REVENUE ACCOUNT, from July 1st to December 31st 1901.

Dr.

Half-year ending Dec. 31st 1900 £ s d				£	s	d	£	s	d	£	s	d
3,072 2 7	1. To General Expenses of Administration.											
2,500 0 0	General Law Charges, Travelling, Valuations, and administration generally	..	..	1,914	2	0						
	Directors' Fees	..	..	2,000	0	0						
							3,914	2	0			
871 9 3	Allowance to Wives and Children of Reservists	..	..				476	10	10			
552 1 4	Printing, Stationery, and Advertising	..	..				586	7	3			
9,716 7 2	Rent	..	..	10,661	19	2						
2,964 10 11	„ Leases Renewal	..	..	3,142	9	10						
							13,804	9	0			
5,982 13 5	Rates and Taxes	..	..				6,004	1	9			
255 13 3	Insurance	..	..				319	9	5			
	Office Expenses—											
3,488 6 2	Staff	..	..	3,490	15	8						
93 7 11	Gas and Water	..	..	83	0	6						
	Sundry, including Postage, Cleaning, and Messengers' Wages	..	..	283	6	1						
290 3 2							3,857	2	3			
29,776 15 2										28,962	2	6

| £29,776 15 2 | Amount carried forward | .. | .. | £28,962 | 2 | 6 |

Cr.

Half-year ending Dec. 31st 1900 £ s d				£	s	d	£	s	d	£	s	d
598,361 3 11	1. By Traffic—											
15 7 3	Ordinary	..	..				584,480	17	6			
	Private Hire	..	..				16	3	0			
598,376 11 2										584,497	0	6
273 12 11	2. By Sales of Manure	..	..							328	10	8
18,006 17 8	3. By Advertising in Omnibuses	..	..							18,629	18	4

| £616,657 1 9 | Amount carried forward | .. | .. | | | | | | | £603,455 | 9 | 6 |

LONDON GENERAL OMNIBUS COMPANY, LIMITED.

REVENUE ACCOUNT, from July 1st to December 31st 1901 (*continued*).

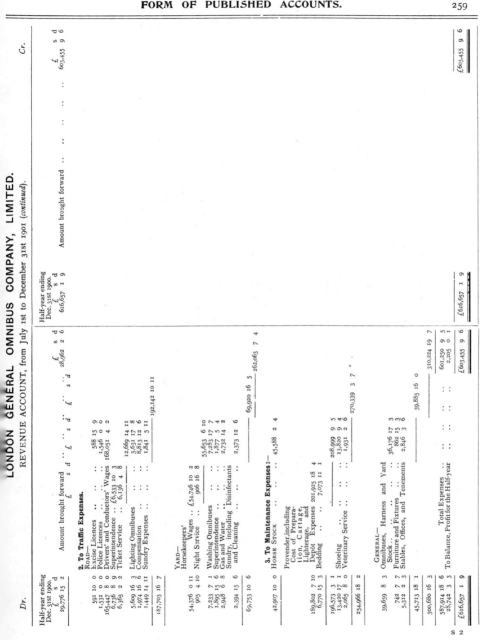

Dr.

Half-year ending Dec. 31st 1900. £ s d		£ s d	£ s d	£ s d	£ s d	£ s d
29,776 15 2	Amount brought forward					28,962 2 6
	2. To Traffic Expenses.					
	ROAD—					
591 10 0	Excise Licences		588 15 9			
1,531 0 0	Police Licences		1,546 0 0			
166,447 8 9	Drivers' and Conductors' Wages		168,051 4 2			
6,736 8 9	Superintendence ... £6,533 10 3					
6,363 2 2	Ticket Service ... 6,136 4 8		12,669 14 11			
5,609 16 3	Lighting Omnibuses		3,631 17 8			
1,974 16 6	Compensation		8,813 12 6			
1,449 14 11	Sundry Expenses		1,841 5 11	192,142 10 11		
187,703 16 7						
	YARD—					
54,376 0 11	Horsekeepers' Wages ... £54,746 10 2					
995 4 10	Night Service ... 966 16 8		55,653 6 10			
7,233 7 1	Washing Omnibuses		7,283 17 7			
1,895 15 6	Superintendence		1,877 5 4			
2,948 6 8	Gas and Water		2,732 14 2			
2,394 15 6	Sundry, including Disinfectants and Cleaning		2,373 12 6	69,920 16 5	262,063 7 4	
69,753 10 6						
	3. To Maintenance Expenses:—					
43,997 10 0	HORSE STOCK		45,588 2 4			
189,802 7 10	Provender, including Cost of Preparation, Cartage, Lighterage, and Depôt Expenses 201,925 18 4					
6,770 15 3	Bedding ... 7,073 11 1		208,999 9 5			
196,573 3 1	Shoeing		13,820 9 4			
13,420 17 1	Veterinary Service		1,931 2 6	270,339 3 7		
2,065 18 2						
254,966 18 2						
	GENERAL—Omnibuses, Harness and Yard Stock		36,176 17 3			
39,659 8 3	Furniture and Fixtures		862 15 3			
742 7 7	Stables, Offices, and Tenements		2,846 3 6	39,885 16 0		
5,312 2 3						
45,713 18 1						
300,680 16 3						
	Total Expenses				601,250 9 5	
	To Balance, Profit for the Half-year				2,205 0 1	
587,914 18 6						£603,455 9 6
28,742 3 3						
£616,657 1 9						£616,657 1 9

Cr.

Half-year ending Dec. 31st 1900. £ s d		£ s d
616,657 1 9	Amount brought forward	603,455 9 6
		£603,455 9 6

S 2

LONDON GENERAL OMNIBUS COMPANY, LIMITED.

PROFIT AND LOSS ACCOUNT.

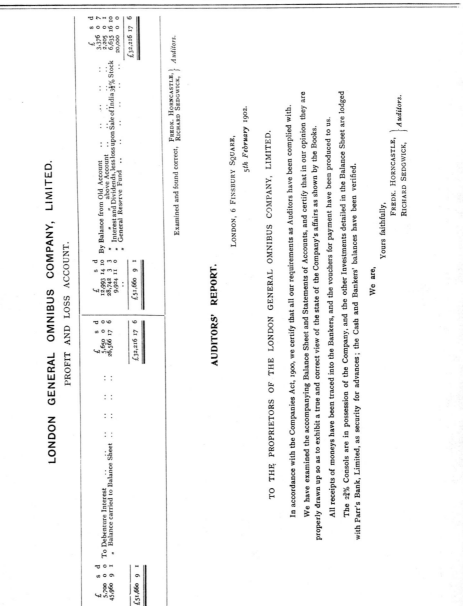

	£	s	d			£	s	d		£	s	d
To Debenture Interest	5,700	0	0	By Balance from Old Account	.. .. ..	12,993	14	10		3,376	0	7
" Balance carried to Balance Sheet	26,566	17	6	" " above Account	.. ..	28,742	3	3		2,205	0	1
				" Interest and Dividends, less loss upon Sale of India 3½% Stock	9,924	11	0		6,635	16	10
				" General Reserve Fund					20,000	0	0
	£32,216	17	6			£51,660	9	1		£32,216	17	6

	£	s	d
	5,650	0	0
	26,566	17	6
	£51,660	9	1

Examined and found correct, FREDK. HORNCASTLE,   } Auditors.
                                   RICHARD SEDGWICK, }

AUDITORS' REPORT.

LONDON, 6 FINSBURY SQUARE,

5th February 1902.

TO THE PROPRIETORS OF THE LONDON GENERAL OMNIBUS COMPANY, LIMITED.

In accordance with the Companies Act, 1900, we certify that all our requirements as Auditors have been complied with.

We have examined the accompanying Balance Sheet and Statements of Accounts, and certify that in our opinion they are properly drawn up so as to exhibit a true and correct view of the state of the Company's affairs as shown by the Books.

All receipts of moneys have been traced into the Bankers, and the vouchers for payment have been produced to us.

The 2¾% Consols are in possession of the Company, and the other Investments detailed in the Balance Sheet are lodged with Parr's Bank, Limited, as security for advances ; the Cash and Bankers' balances have been verified.

We are,

Yours faithfully,

FREDK. HORNCASTLE,   } Auditors.
RICHARD SEDGWICK,   }

ROCHDALE CANAL COMPANY.

STATEMENT OF ACCOUNTS for the Half-Year ended 31st December 1901.

Dr.   *A.* - CAPITAL ACCOUNT.   *Cr.*

	£ s d	£ s d		£ s d
To Capital Expenditure on Parliamentary Costs, Purchase of Lands, Construction of Canal and Works, and Improvements to 30th June 1901 ..	772,922 19 6		By Consolidated Ordinary Stock (Rochdale Canal Act, 1899)	752,780 0 0
Additional Expenditure this half-year	131 4 0		„ Debenture Stock—Issue of 1888 @ 3½%	48,000 0 0
	773,054 3 6		„ Premium on Debenture Stock	2,056 9 9
Less Sale of Land	100 0 0	772,954 3 6		
„ Capital Expenditure on Boats, Horses, Stabling, and Carrying Plant to 30th June 1901..	.. .. ..	25,980 1 6		
		798,934 5 0		
„ Balance carried down	.. .. ..	3,902 4 9		
		£802,836 9 9		£802,836 9 9
			„ Balance brought down	3,902 4 9

Dr.   *B.*—REVENUE ACCOUNT.   *Cr.*

	1900	£ s d		1900	£ s d
To Maintenance, Dredging, and Ice Breaking	..£3,223	3,163 2 8	By Toll Traffic Receipts	£6,574	6,589 8 5
„ General Charges	.. 1,082	1,066 17 3	„ Freight ditto	.. 14,029	13,048 14 6
„ Rents Payable..	.. 1,693	1,716 3 0		20,603	19,638 2 11
„ Rates, Taxes, and Insurance	.. 1,493	1,577 13 1	*Less* Traffic Expenses	..13,775	13,305 18 3
„ Law and Parliamentary Costs	.. 568	1,237 0 10	Nett Traffic Receipts	.. 6,828	6,332 4 8
„ Directors' Fees	.. 400	400 0 0	„ Rents Receivable	.. 5,223	4,564 2 9
„ Auditor and Accountant's Fees	.. 48	48 0 0	„ Miscellaneous Receipts	10	97 13 11
„ Interest on Debenture Stock	.. 840	840 0 0	„ Bank Interest, *less* Commission	..	31 8 8
„ Depreciation of Plant	.. 897	991 2 11	„ Balance at Debit of Revenue Account	..	14 9 9
		£11,039 19 9			£11,039 19 9

Dr.   *C.*—GENERAL BALANCE SHEET.   *Cr.*

Capital and Liabilities	£ s d	£ s d	*Property and Assets.*	£ s d
Proprietors' Capital, Loans and Debenture Stock, including Premium— per Account *A*		802,836 9 9	Expenditure on Land, Buildings, Construction of Canal, Plant, &c.—per Account *A*	798,934 5 0
Outstanding Accounts	12,823 13 10		Stores on hand	3,308 0 8
Dividends Unpaid	62 3 8		Accounts owing to the Company	8,010 5 5
		12,885 17 6	Cash at Bank £6,445 0 5	
Renewals Account—			Ditto in hands of Cashier and Agents .. 359 14 4	6,804 14 9
Amount, 30th June 1901	1,175 0 6		Fractions of Stock purchased under Rochdale Canal Act, 1899	52 18 8
Add Amount set aside this half-year ..	991 2 11			
	2,166 3 5			
Deduct Outlay on Renewals this half-year..	1,582 19 0			
		583 4 5		
Revenue Account—				
Balance, 30th June 1901 ..£3,642 1 1				
Less Dividend paid 24th August 1901 .. .. 2,822 18 6				
	819 2 7			
Less Debit Balance this half-year—per Account *B*	14 9 9			
Balance available		804 12 10		
		£817,110 4 6		£817,110 4 6

I have examined the foregoing Accounts and Balance Sheet, and certify, that in my opinion, they are correct, and exhibit the true position of the Company's affairs on the 31st December 1901.

MANCHESTER,   A. MURRAY, *Auditor.*

     10th February 1902.

C. M. ROYDS, *Chairman.*

THE FINE COTTON SPINNERS' AND DOUBLERS' ASSOCIATION LIMITED.

Dr. PROFIT AND LOSS ACCOUNT, for the Year ended 31st March 1903. **Cr.**

	£ s d		£ s d
To Interest on Debenture Stock	110,000 0 0	By Balance brought forward from last year's Account ..	13,899 13 5
„ Balance carried to Balance Sheet	320,739 4 3	„ Profits for the Year, including undistributed Profits of Subsidiary Companies, after charging Central Office Expenses, Management Salaries, and Directors' Fees, and after provision for Depreciation, Income Tax, and Bonuses to Management and Auditors' Remuneration	416,749 10 10
	£430,739 4 3		£430,739 4 3

BALANCE SHEET, 31st March 1903.

Liabilities.	£ s d	*Assets.*	£ s d
SHARE CAPITAL:— Nominal Capital—		Properties comprising Land, Mills, Buildings, Machinery, and Goodwill of Associated Concerns, at cost, as per last Balance Sheet	4,896,725 4 4
3,000,000 Five per Cent. Cumulative Preference Shares, £1 each £3,000,000 0 0		*Add*—Additions to Properties during the Year ended 31st March 1903, *less* Realisations	114,121 10 4
3,000,000 Ordinary Shares, £1 each 3,000,000 0 0			5,010,846 14 8
	£6,000,000 0 0	*Less* Depreciation Fund:— Balance at 31st March 1902 .. ..£233,771 2 5	
Capital issued and subscribed— 2,000,000 Preference Shares, £1 each, fully paid £2,000,000 0 0		*Add*—Depreciation for Year ended 31st March 1903 .. .. .. 140,000 0 0	
1,900,000 Ordinary Shares, £1 each, fully paid 1,900,000 0 0	3,900,000 0 0		373,771 2 5
Four per Cent. First Mortgage Debenture Stock :— Amount authorised and issued	2,000,000 0 0	*Deduct*—Outlay on Renewals of Properties during the Year, in addition to Ordinary Repairs charged against Profits	132,707 2 11
Four per Cent. First Mortgage Extension Debenture Stock :— Amount authorised and issued	750,000 0 0		241,063 19 6
Interest on Debenture Stock (*less* Tax)	51,562 9 1		4,769,782 15 2
Reserves :—		Sundry Investments, Loans and Shares in Subsidiary Companies	1,321,719 8 4
Amount set apart out of Profits .. £330,075 0 0		Central Office Furniture, Fixtures, &c. .. £2,822 8 9	
Premium on Shares issued .. 319,925 0 0	650,000 0 0	*Less* Depreciation 300 0 0	2,522 8 9
Insurance Fund	888 8 1	Stock-in-Trade :—Cotton £642,273 6 10	
Superannuation and Pension Fund ..	3,257 14 8	Yarn and Stores .. 858,322 8 1	1,500,595 14 11
Loans	53,876 7 1	Trade Debtors £508,408 18 4	
Sundry Creditors, on Bills and Open Accounts	558,518 5 7	Rents, Rates, Insurance, &c., paid in advance 7,555 7 9	515,964 6 1
Profit and Loss Account—Balance from Profit and Loss Account £320,739 4 3		Profits of Subsidiary Companies not yet distributed	65,546 1 11
Deduct Interim Dividends paid— On Preference Shares at 5 per cent. per annum £50,000 0 0		Cash at Bankers and in hand	5,711 13 7
On Ordinary Shares at 6 per cent. per annum 57,000 0 0	107,000 0 0		
Balance available for appropriation ..	213,739 4 3		
	£8,181,842 8 9		£8,181,842 8 9

To THE SHAREHOLDERS OF THE FINE COTTON SPINNERS' AND DOUBLERS' ASSOCIATION, LIMITED.

In conformity with the requirements of the Companies Act, 1900, we hereby certify that all our requirements as Auditors have been complied with. We have to Report that we have examined the Books, Accounts, and Vouchers of the Company in respect of the twelve months ended 31st March 1903, and that, in our opinion, the foregoing Balance Sheet is properly drawn up so as to exhibit a true and correct view of the Company's affairs as shown by the Books of the Company.

7 King Street, Manchester,
19th May 1903.

EDWIN GUTHRIE & Co.,
Chartered Accountants.

HAYES, CANDY & COMPANY, LIMITED.

Dr. BALANCE SHEET, 19th January 1903. *Cr.*

Liabilities	£ s d	£ s d	Assets	£ s d	£ s d
To Nominal Capital –			By Goodwill, as per Prospectus	..	50,000 0 0
20,000 Cumulative 5½ per cent.			„ Leasehold Premises	1,350 0 0	
Preference Shares, £5 each ..	100,000 0 0		*Less* Depreciation	75 0 0	
100,000 Ordinary Shares, £1 each ..	100,000 0 0				1,275 0 0
		200,000 0 0	„ Fixtures, Fittings and Office Furniture	.. ..	2,935 12 5
„ Issued Capital—			„ Stock in hand, after deduction of 2½ per		
16,000 Cumulative 5½ per cent.			cent. for discount..	.. ..	65,168 15 5
Preference Shares, £5 each, fully			„ Sundry Debtors, less 2½ per cent. ..	.. ..	59,450 8 0
paid	80,000 0 0		„ Reserve Fund Investments, at cost—		
80,000 Ordinary Shares, £1 each,			£2,269 3 0 National War Loan, 2¾%	2,199 18 0	
fully paid	80,000 0 0		£4,297 2 6 Nottingham Corpora-		
		160,000 0 0	tion, 3% Redeemable		
„ Reserve Fund— (*see cont'd*)			Stock	4,118 4 11	
As per last Balance Sheet ..	2,142 5 7				6,318 2 11
Proportion of Profits for year ending			„ Bills Receivable in hand..	.. ..	11,580 13 8
19th Jan. 1902 (as per Prospectus).	4,000 0 0		„ Cash at Bankers and in hand	.. ..	5,949 10 3
Add Interest received on Invest-					
ments re-invested	175 17 4				
		6,318 2 11			
„ Trade Creditors, Rebate and Sundry					
Accounts	.. ..	24,994 6 6			
„ Unclaimed Dividends	.. ..	28 14 1			
„ Profit and Loss Account—					
Balance as at 19th Jan. 1902 ..	14,114 1 3				
Less Preference Divi-					
dend paid 31st March					
1902	2,200 0 0				
Ordinary Dividend pa'd					
11th March 1902 ..	7,000 0 0				
Reserve Fund	4,000 0 0				
	13,200 0 0				
	914 1 3				
Add as per Account annexed ..	15,622 17 11				
	16,536 19 2				
Less Interim Dividends—					
5½% per annum on					
Preference Shares					
paid 1st Aug. 1902 ..	2,200 0 0				
7½% per annum on					
Ordinary Shares paid					
7th Aug. 1902 ..	3,000 0 0				
	5,200 0 0				
		11,336 19 2			
		£202,678 2 8			£202,678 2 8

Bills Receivable under Discount £5,342 4 3

Dr. PROFIT AND LOSS ACCOUNT for Year ending 19th January 1903. *Cr.*

	£ s d	£ s d		£ s d
To Managing Directors' Salaries	3,600 0 0		By Net Trading Profit	20,133 15 9
„ Directors' Fees	562 4 7		„ Transfer Fees	11 0 0
		4,162 4 7		
„ Income Tax	.. ..	359 13 3		
„ Balance carried to Balance Sheet ..	.. ..	15,622 17 11		
		£20,144 15 9		£20,144 15 9

JAMES C. HAYES, } *Directors.*
WILLIAM M. CANDY, }

JOHN P. GILLOCH, *Secretary.*

AUDITORS' CERTIFICATE AND REPORT.

In accordance with the provisions of the Companies Act, 1900, we certify that all our requirements as Auditors have been complied with. We report to the Shareholders that we have examined the above Balance Sheet with the Books and Vouchers of the Company, and in our opinion the Balance Sheet is properly drawn up so as to exhibit a true and correct view of the state of the Company's affairs as shown by the Books of the Company.

3 Frederick's Place, Old Jewry, E.C.

PRICE, WATERHOUSE & Co.

10th February 1903.

THE NATAL LAND AND COLONIZATION COMPANY, LIMITED.

BALANCE SHEET, 31st December 1895.

Dr.

Capital and Liabilities.	£ s d	1895 £ s d	1894
To Capital:—			
34,033 Ordinary Shares of £10 each	340,330 0 0		
9,906 Preference Shares of £5 each	49,530 0 0	389,860 0 0	389,860 0 0
" **Debenture Bonds:—**5 per cent.	6,250 0 0		
" 4½ "	2,400 0 0		
" 4 "	37,050 0 0		
" 3½ "	100 0 0	45,800 0 0	47,950 0 0
" Deposit at 2½ per cent.		4,500 0 0	
" Sundry Accounts due by the Company		1,521 9 10	4,389 6 5
" Interest accrued on Debenture Bonds		722 12 2	769 18 4
" Fencing Reserve Account		1,298 13 8	1,298 13 8
" Reserve Account		6,656 6 8	4,479 18 2
" Balance of Profit and Loss Account from the year 1894, as per last Balance Sheet		9,234 12 5	
" Balance Dividend of 8s. a Share on Preference Shares for 1894 £1,981 4 0			
Dividend of 4s. a Share on Ordinary Shares for 1894	6,806 12 0		
Added to Reserve	300 0 0	9,087 16 0	
" Profit and Loss Account for the year 1895..	146 16 5	17,559 2 9	17,715 19 2
Interim Dividend on Preference Shares paid 1st October last..	£1,981 4 0		
Added to Reserve	2,000 0 0	3,981 4 0	
		13,734 15 2	9,234 12 5
		£464,073 17 6	

Cr.

Assets.	1895 £ s d	1894
By Landed Property:—		
394,142 Acres of Land, House and Town Properties, &c., including Fixed Machinery thereon	425,950 13 4	490,218 1 11
" Fencing Expenditure	2,145 3 0	2,062 15 2
" Loans on Mortgage	1,300 0 0	425 17 5
" Balance payable by Purchasers of Properties	14,257 13 5	10,888 16 7
" Sundry Accounts due to the Company	497 11 0	658 15 0
" Furniture in Natal and London	252 3 2	369 1 4
" Agricultural Machinery and Diamond Drill	134 1 7	134 1 7
" Bills Receivable	3,968 17 9	1,504 7 7
" Cash at Bankers, in hand, and on deposit in London and Natal	6,968 2 1	3,347 0 7
" Mortgage Debenture Bonds of the Natal Plantations Company, Limited (£19,000)	8,599 12 4	8,599 12 4
	£464,073 17 6	

PROFIT AND LOSS, from 1st January to 31st December 1895.

Dr.

	1895 £ s d	1894
To Interest on Debenture Bonds	1,971 14 9	2,113 10 0
" London Office Expenses	1,031 3 2	1,098 2 11
" Durban Office Expenses	1,634 7 11	1,577 12 3
" Debenture Bond, Law, and other Expenses	81 11 3	
" Income Tax	253 10 2	274 10 8
" Land Department Charges:—		
Quit Rents, Rates, Repairs, Insurance, &c.	2,423 1 8	2,220 3 11
" Directors' and Auditors' Fees	640 0 0	640 0 0
" Balance carried to Balance Sheet	17,559 2 9	10,928 13 9
	£25,660 3 6	

Cr.

	1895 £ s d	1894
By Rents of Land and Town Properties	16,348 3 10	15,906 8 0
(Exclusive of arrears considered good, £1,375 19s. 5d., and of accruing rents)		
" Interest, Commissions, and Transfer Fees	731 8 6	752 18 5
" Profit on Properties Sold	8,580 11 2	9,354 6 3
	£25,660 3 6	

We have examined the above Balance Sheet and Profit and Loss Account with the Audited Statements transmitted from Durban, and with the Books and Vouchers in London, and certify they are in accordance therewith, and that in our opinion the above Balance Sheet, containing the particulars required by the Articles of Association, is properly drawn up, so as to exhibit a true and correct view of the state of the Company's affairs.

London, 5th March 1896.

TURQUAND, YOUNGS, BISHOP & CLARKE, *Auditors.*

BLACKPOOL LAND, BUILDING, AND HOTEL COMPANY, LIMITED.

BALANCE SHEET made up to 30th September 1901.

Capital and Liabilities.	£ s d	£ s d	Property, Assets, and Expenses.	£ s d	£ s d
Capital. Share Capital— Amount received from Shareholders, 8,123 Shares of 10s. each, fully paid		4,061 10 0	**Property.** Property— Balance of Cost of Property, as per last Account ..	2,127 5 11½	
			Add Expenditure during the year upon New Roads and Sewers	315 3 7	
Debts and Liabilities. Sundry Liabilities— Sundry Debts owing for Salaries, Law Charges, Directors' Fees, Rates and Taxes, &c.	303 6 9		Add Tithe Redemption ..	33 1 2	2,475 10 8½
Unclaimed Dividends ..	10 15 2	314 1 11	**Debts due to the Company.** Debts Due to the Co.— Sundry Tenants for Rent, &c.	47 13 0	
Realisation of Property. Realisation of Property—	£ s d		Sundry Debts for uncompleted Purchases and Interest thereon	6,833 0 0	6,880 13 0
As per last Account	5,410 1 10		**Cash.** Cash— In Bank	54 5 11	
Add Purchase Money of Land sold during year, and Sundry Receipts ..	404 12 8	5,814 14 6	In hands of Secretary ..	5 4 1	59 10 0
Less Bonus of 2s. 6d. per Share paid May 1901	1,015 7 6				
Law Charges, Directors' Fees, &c.	213 14 2	1,229 1 8			
		4,585 12 10			
Revenue. Available Balance— Balance available as per Revenue Account		454 8 11½			
		£9,415 13 8½			£9,415 13 8½

REVENUE ACCOUNT for the Year ended 30th September 1901.

Expenses.	£ s d	£ s d	Receipts.	£ s d	£ s d
Salaries of Secretary, Auditor, and Commission on Rents	58 16 10		Balance from last year ..	398 4 10½	
Rent of Office, Rates and Taxes	11 5 7		Less Dividend of 5% paid October 1900	203 1 6	195 3 4½
Travelling Expenses	18 5 0		Chief Rent and Rents of Land	52 15 0	
Advertising, Printing, and Stationery	3 13 8		Interest on Investments and on incomplete purchases	301 15 2	354 10 2
Stamps, Postages, and Petty Expenses	2 5 6				
Repairs and Maintenance ..	0 18 0	95 4 7			
Balance Available		454 8 11½			
		£549 13 6½			£549 13 6½

AUDITOR'S CERTIFICATE AND REPORT.

I hereby certify, in accordance with the provisions of the Companies' Act, 1900, that all my requirements as Auditor have been complied with. I beg to report to the Shareholders that I have audited the above Accounts and Balance Sheet, and that, in my opinion, the Balance Sheet is properly drawn up so as to exhibit a true and correct view of the state of the Company's affairs as shown by the books.

H. GARDNER, *Auditor.*

THAMES AND MERSEY MARINE INSURANCE COMPANY, LIMITED.

PROFIT AND LOSS ACCOUNT, 31st December 1901.

	£ s d		£ s d	£ s d
Balance, 1st January 1901	42,285 14 1	Dividends paid February and July 1901 ..		40,000 0 0
Balance of Underwriting Account, 1900, at 31st December		Claims, Returns, and Re-insurances paid		
1900	234,183 13 6	on 1900 Account, from 1st January 1901		
Interest on Investments	34,378 5 11	to date, and Underwriters' Commission	162,770 13 0	
Transfer Fees	43 17 0	Amount carried to Suspense Account on		
		closing 1900 Account	39,500 0 0	
		Bad Debts, 1900 Account	35 10 1	
		Income Tax, 1900 Account	988 17 9	
				203,295 0 10
		Loss on Exchange of Securities in con-		
		nection with United States Deposits ..		457 5 5
		Balance carried down		67,139 4 3
	£310,891 10 6			£310,891 10 6

UNDERWRITING ACCOUNT, 1901.

	£ s d		£ s d	£ s d
Premiums—Less Returns and Re-insurances	475,731 2 4	Claims paid		125,791 1 1
		Office Expenses, including Salaries, &c.,		
		London, Liverpool, and Manchester ..	25,481 5 5	
		Directors and Auditors' Fees	5,174 13 2	
		General Law Charges	6 7 10	
			30,662 6 5	
		Less proportion char̠ed to Internal Re-		
		insurance Account	1,270 5 11	
				29,392 0 6
		Expenses of Branches and Agencies ..		17,568 9 6
		Bad Debts		3 4 8
		Balance carried down		302,976 6 7
	£475,731 2 4			£475,731 2 4

GENERAL BALANCE SHEET, 31st December 1901.

	£ s d		£ s d	£ s d
To CAPITAL Subscribed — 100,000		By Investments (at Market Value on 31st December)		
Shares, @ £20 per Share £2,000,000 0 0		and Loans		1,148,745 9 9
		„ Debtors for Premiums, &c.		99,039 6 7
Paid up—£2 per Share	200,000 0 0	„ Interest accrued, but not received		14,495 1 6
„ Reserve Fund	450,000 0 0	„ Office Furniture and Fixtures		628 5 11
„ Outstanding Accounts	11,229 5 6	„ Stamps on hand		419 15 5
„ Internal Re-insurance Account	97,526 16 3	„ Bills Receivable		3,745 19 7
„ Investment Fluctuation Account, being the differ-		„ Cash on Deposit .. £12,000 0 0		
ence between Cost and Market Value of Securities		„ Do. at Bankers and in hand .. 16,748 4 10		
at 31st December	111,412 2 0			28,748 4 10
„ Suspense Account	54,965 16 0			
„ Dividends not yet claimed	572 13 0			
„ Balance of Profit and Loss Account	67,139 4 3			
„ Do. Underwriting Account, 1901	302,976 6 7			
	£1,295,822 3 7			£1,295,822 3 7

In accordance with the provisions of the Companies Act, 1900, we certify that all our requirements as Auditors have been complied with.

     J. F. CLARKE, London, ⎫
     J. S. H. BANNER, Liverpool, ⎬ *Auditors.*
     WM. ASHWORTH, Manchester, ⎭

We beg to report that we have each in our respective Districts examined the accounts of the Company, and that the above Balance Sheet compiled therefrom is in our opinion properly drawn up so as to exhibit a true and correct view of the state of the Company's affairs as shown by the Books of the Company.

We also report that we have individually satisfied ourselves of the existence of the Securities belonging to our respective Offices.

     J. F. CLARKE, London, ⎫
     J. S. H. BANNER, Liverpool, ⎬ *Auditors.*
     WM. ASHWORTH, Manchester, ⎭

LONDON AND GLOBE FINANCE CORPORATION, LIMITED.

Dr. BALANCE SHEET, 29th January 1897. *Cr.*

	£ s d	£ s d			£ s d	£ s d
To Capital	200,000 0 0		By Shares held in various Companies, those purchased being taken at cost, and those otherwise acquired taken at their par value			818,022 18 3
In 195,000 Ordinary Shares of £1 each, and 100,000 Deferred Shares of 1s. each.			(NOTE.—There is a liability in respect of calls not yet made, amounting to £47,845 6s. 7d. upon certain of the above Shares.)			
Issued—			" Sundry Debtors			209,537 18 1
165,000 Ordinary Shares upon which the full amount of £1 per Share has been called up	165,000 0 0		" Freehold Property in London ..			16,250 0 0
30,000 Ordinary Shares issued fully paid	30,000 0 0		" Loans in Stock Exchange—from Account to Account			70,312 8 0
100,000 Deferred Shares of 1s. each, upon which the full amount has been paid up	5,000 0 0		" Cash, at Bankers and in hand ..			254,770 0 8
295,000 Shares	200,000 0 0					
Less Calls in arrear..	1,172 10 0					
		198,827 10 0				
" Sundry Creditors		232,247 0 8				
" Unclaimed Dividends		167 17 6				
" Profit and Loss Account	952,650 16 10					
Less Interim Dividend paid ..	15,000 0 0					
		937,650 16 10				
		£1,368,893 5 0				£1,368,893 5 0

We have examined the above Balance Sheet and Profit and Loss Account, with the Books, accounts and vouchers relating thereto, and certify the same to be in accordance therewith. We are of opinion that the Balance Sheet represents the position of the Company's affairs, subject to such sum being set aside as may be considered the necessary reserve in respect to Shares held in various Companies, the value of which we are unable to assess. We have verified the balance of cash at the Bankers and in hand.

FORD, RHODES & FORD,
Chartered Accountants.
81 CANNON STREET, LONDON, E.C.

Dr. PROFIT AND LOSS ACCOUNT, from Incorporation to 29th January 1897. *Cr.*

	£ s d	£ s d		£ s d
To General Expenses	2,902 10 4		By Profit on Mining Properties, purchased, developed, and resold for considerations partly in Shares ..	482,146 5 5
" Directors' Fees	1,898 0 2		" Profits on Securities realised	463,889 17 7
" Salaries	2,892 14 7		" Underwriting Commissions	13,937 10 0
" Postages	605 13 10		" Transfer Fees	673 12 6
" Advertising	3,095 19 11		" Interest, &c...	6,099 19 11
" Printing and Stationery	1,194 19 8			
" Office Rent	566 16 4			
" Law Costs	796 18 4			
" Rates and Taxes	142 10 5			
		14,096 8 7		
" Balance		952,650 16 10		
		£966,747 5 5		£966,747 5 5

Dr. PROPOSED APPROPRIATION OF PROFITS. *Cr.*

	£ s d		£ s d
To Interim Dividend of 10 per cent. or 2/- per Share on 150,000 Ordinary Shares	15,000 0 0	By Balance brought down	952,650 16 10
" Further Dividend of 40 per cent. or 8/- per Share on 195,000 Ordinary Shares	78,000 0 0		
" Dividend of 15s. 7½d. per Share on 100,000 Deferred Shares, as per Memorandum of Association	78,000 0 0		
* Carried forward	781,650 16 10		
	£952,650 16 10		£952,650 16 10

* Subject to deduction for Income Tax upon Profits and Directors' percentage on Dividend.

THE VERNON COTTON SPINNING COMPANY, STOCKPORT, LIMITED,
Year ending 25th June 1903.

Dr.   TRADING ACCOUNT.   *Cr.*

	£ s d	£ s d		£ s d
To Cotton		114,906 4 8	By Yarn	143,001 4 2
Brokerage and Charges	673 2 8		Waste	3,093 19 9
Carriage	1,284 14 3		Sundry Sales	96 4 1
Coals	2,681 9 1		Transfer Fees	2 5 6
Oil and Tallow	365 16 6		Balance to Profit and Loss	5,291 12 3
Brushes	33 15 9			
Banding	476 10 4			
Paper and Twine	107 15 10			
Strapping	247 11 7			
Roller Leather	189 13 0			
„ Cloth	23 18 11			
Repairs—Buildings, Engines, Boilers, and Gearing	117 15 6			
Repairs—Machinery	353 0 3			
Card Clothing	200 0 0			
Skips and Bobbins	244 16 10			
Mill Charges	331 0 0			
Stores	200 10 10			
Gas, Electric Light, and Water	81 8 1			
Chief Rent	66 15 0			
Insurance	486 9 5			
Interest	1,587 7 8			
Bank Charges	69 10 0			
Commission	1,478 19 1			
Discount	3,033 2 9			
Rates and Taxes	756 17 7			
Depreciation	3,284 0 0			
Printing and Stationery	27 12 0			
Petty Cash	33 16 6			
		18,437 9 5		
Wages	17,975 1 8			
Directors' Remuneration	166 10 0			
		18,141 11 8		
		£151,485 5 9		£151,485 5 9

Dr.   PROFIT AND LOSS ACCOUNT.   *Cr.*

1902		£ s d	1902		£ s d
June 26.	To Balance	1,865 0 10	Aug. 6.	By Reserve Fund	4,000 0 0
Aug. 6.	Dividend	1,875 0 0	1903		
1903			June 25.	„	2,000 0 0
June 25.	Trading Account	5,291 12 3	„ „	Balance „	3,031 13 1
		£9,031 13 1			£9,031 13 1
June 25.	Balance	3,031 13 1			

Dr.   DIVIDEND ACCOUNT.   *Cr.*

1903		£ s d	1902		£ s d
June 25.	To Payments	1,898 4 6	June 26.	By Balance	52 12 0
„ „	Balance	29 7 6	Aug. 6.	Dividend	1,875 0 0
		£1,927 12 0			£1,927 12 0
			1903		
			June 25.	By Balance	29 7 6

Dr.   DEPRECIATION ACCOUNT.   **Cr.**

	£ s d		£ s d
1903		1902	
June 25. To Balance	52,997 2 5	June 26. By Balance	49,713 2 5
		1903	
		June 25. Depreciation on Buildings	1,419 0 0
		" " Ditto on Machinery	1,865 0 0
	£52,997 2 5		£52,997 2 5
		By Balance	52,997 2 5

Dr.   LOAN ACCOUNT.   **Cr.**

	£ s d		£ s d
1903		1902	
June 25. To Cash withdrawn	4,560 15 2	June 26. By Balance	28,575 5 8
" " Balance	27,518 2 10	1903	
		June 25. Cash Deposited..	2,509 6 11
		" " Interest	994 5 5
	£32,078 18 0		£32,078 18 0
		By Balance	27,518 2 10

Dr.   RESERVE FUND.   **Cr.**

	£ s d		£ s d
1903		1902	
June 25. To Profit and Loss	2,000 0 0	June 26. By Balance	2,000 0 0

Dr.   GENERAL BALANCE.   **Cr.**

	£ s d	£ s d		£ s d	£ s d
To Share Capital	75,000 0 0		By No. 1 Mill Account	..	10,195 16 11
Loan Capital	27,518 2 10		No. 2.		
		102,518 2 10	Buildings	52,601 11 7	
Sundry Creditors		2,360 3 5	*Less* Depreciation	15,571 3 4	
Unclaimed Dividends		29 7 6	No. 2.		37,030 8 3
Due to the Bank		6,569 3 3	Machinery	53,105 3 4	
			Less Depreciation	37,425 19 1	
					15,679 4 3
			Stock Cotton	29,268 1 0	
			" Yarn	7,218 3 9	
			" Waste	16 7 0	
			" Stores	400 12 10	
					36,903 4 7
			Sundry Debtors		8,631 9 11
			One Share Manchester Cotton Association	..	5 0 0
			Balance from Profit and Loss Account	..	3,031 13 1
		£111,476 17 0			£111,476 17 0

AUDITORS' REPORT AND CERTIFICATE.

To the Shareholders—

    We have audited the above Balance Sheet dated the 25th day of June 1903, and in our opinion such Balance Sheet is properly drawn up, so as to exhibit a true and correct view of the state of the Company's affairs, and is as shown by the books of the Company.

    In accordance with the provisions of the Companies Act, 1900, we certify that all our requirements as Auditors have been complied with.

                                                  W. CHARLESWORTH & Co., Chartered Accountants.

Stockport, 4th July 1903.

MEREBANK BRICK AND TILE COMPANY, LIMITED.

BALANCE SHEET, as at 30th June 1902.

Capital and Liabilities.	£ s d	£ s d	Property and Assets.	£ s d	£ s
To Authorised Capital	18,000 0 0		By Cash in Natal Bank Limited	10 8 4	
(in 18,000 Shares of £1 each.)			„ „ on hand .. £5 15 6		
Less Reserve Shares unissued—245	245 0 0		*Less* due to Petty Cashier.. 0 10 8		
		17,755 0 0		5 4 10	
„ Bills Payable	2,300 0 0		„ Bricks in Stock	1,650 19 6	
Sundry Creditors, as per Schedule ..	875 9 6		„ Stores on hand	31 0 6	
		3,175 9 6	„ Coal „	157 2 6	
		20,930 9 6	„ Rations „	32 18 3	
„ Balance carried to Profit and Loss Account		3,240 15 9	„ Freehold Property at Cost	5,637 17 7	
			„ Buildings—at cost :—		
			Manager's House .. 845 5 0		
			Sub-Manager's House.. 324 15 5		
			Engine Shed .. 275 5 5		
			Machine Shed .. 666 13 2		
			Office and Store.. 57 0 9		
			Drying Sheds .. 1,027 13 9		
			European Cottage .. 7 10 0		
			Indian Quarters.. 19 19 6		
				3,224 3 0	
			„ Kilns 5,442 0 8		
			Less Depreciation .. 212 4 0		
				5,229 16 8	
			„ Livestock and Vehicles at Cost..	43 1 0	
			„ Machinery 5,276 11 8		
			Less Depreciation .. 1,069 0 0		
				4,207 11 8	
			„ Plant 2,263 9 3		
			Less Depreciation .. 23 12 0		
				2,239 17 3	
			„ Pumping Plant at Cost ..	208 13 6	
			„ Main Drain—Cost of Cutting ..	61 19 2	
			„ Railway Siding—Cost at date ..	11 2 6	
			„ Clay Excavations—Cost of unused	175 0 0	
			„ Sundry Debtors, as per Schedule ..	1,244 9 0	
		£24,171 5 3			£24,171 5 3

MANUFACTURING AND TRADING ACCOUNT for the Year ended 30th June 1902.

	£ s d	£ s d		£ s d	£ s d
To Coal Consumed	2,143 7 9		By Brick Account—		
„ Clay Excavation	367 5 5		Stock at date at Cost .. £1,650 19 6		
„ Rations—Native, Indians	647 10 4		Sales for the Year .. 7,090 11 3		
„ Rent of Ground	175 0 0			8,741 10 9	
„ Wages for the Year ..	2,740 19 2		*Less*—		
„ Stores used	108 6 10		Stock at beginning of Year		
		6,182 9 6	taken over 197 0 0		
„ Balance, being Net Profit carried to Profit			Railway Freight and Allow-		
and Loss Account		2,159 19 0	ances 202 2 3		
				399 2 3	
		£8,342 8 6			£8,342 8 6

PROFIT AND LOSS ACCOUNT.

	£ s d	£ s d		£ s d	£ s d
To Directors' Fees	73 3 0		By Premiums on Shares—		
„ General Charges.. ..	294 8 1		1,000 Reserve Shares .. 732 10 0		
„ Insurance	70 18 7		6,000 Shares Increased Capi-		
„ Interest	47 8 9		tal, taken up at 30s. per		
„ Salaries	395 0 0		share 3,000 0 0		
„ Depreciation—			1,255 Shares taken up by		
Kilns £212 4 0			Directors at 30s. per share 627 10 0		
Machinery 1,069 0 0				4,360 0 0	
Plant 23 12 0			„ Transfer Fees	19 17 6	
	1,304 16 0		„ Manufacturing and Trading Account	2,159 19 0	
„ Preliminary Expenses — Total					6,539 16 6
written off	88 6 4				
„ Goodwill and Leases — Total					
written off	500 0 0				
		1,893 2 4			
„ Dividend paid, 21st October 1901	525 0 0				
		3,299 0 9			
„ Balance, being Net Profit	3,765 15 9				
Less Dividend paid ..	525 0 0				
		£6,539 16 6			£6,539 16 6

Audited, compared with Books and Vouchers, and certified correct,

Durban, 21st July 1902.

F. W. DORE, F.I.A.N., *Auditor.*

CRÉDIT LYONNAIS.

RÉSUMÉ DU BILAN GÉNÉRAL DÉFINITIF AU 31 DÉCEMBRE 1902.

Actif.			Passif.		
Espèces en Caisse et dans les Banques	134,686,424	13	Depôts et Bons à vue	555,421,079	62
Portefeuille	801,698,476	99	Comptes courants	689,778,608	94
Reports	173,366,146	62	Acceptations	123,590,292	94
Comptes courants	369,436,439	82	Bons à échéance	28,162,462	87
Avances sur garanties	249,755,700	28	Comptes d'ordre et Divers	21,914,645	89
Actions, Bons, Obligations et Rentes	8,299,148	73	Profits et Pertes " Bénéfices de l'Exercice 1902 "	28,121,309	23
Comptes d'ordre et Divers	7,650,173	79	Solde du compte " Profits et Pertes " des Exercices		
Immeubles { anciens .. .. .. 30,000,000 }	35,000,000	"	antérieurs	2,904,110	87
{ nouveaux .. .. .. 5,000,000 }			Réserves diverses	100,000,000	"
			Capital entièrement versé	250,000,000	"
Total .. .. Fr.	1,779,892,510	36	Total .. .. Fr.	1,779,892,510	36

RÉSUMÉ DE L'INVENTAIRE.

Solde crèancier .. .. Fr.	28,121,309	23	Bénéfice net de l'Exercice 1902 .. .. Fr.	28,121,309	23

THE TRUSTEE, INDUSTRIAL AND INVESTMENT CORPORATION, LIMITED.

Dr. BALANCE SHEET, June 30th 1892. *Cr.*

	£ s d	£ s d		£ s d	£ s d
To Share Capital Account—			By Cash at Bankers	8,268 3 3	
250 Founders' Shares of £10 each, issued as fully paid	2,500 0 0		Do. in Hand	12 15 11	
35,000 Ordinary Shares of £10 each, £2 per Share called up	70,000 0 0				8,280 19 2
			„ Exchequer Bills	4,914 2 9	
	72,500 0 0		„ Debentures and Shares in other Companies	63,941 15 3	
Less Arrears	2,992 0 0				68,855 18 0
		69,508 0 0	„ Sundry Loans on Securities deposited	..	31,467 6 8
„ Deposits and Loans	..	24,943 0 0	„ Sundry Debtors	..	1,893 6 10
„ Sundry Creditors	..	21 19 0	„ Bills Receivable	..	1,140 3 0
„ Reserve Fund	..	15,000 0 0	„ Preliminary Expenses—		
„ Profit and Loss Account—			250 Founders' Shares, issued as fully paid	2,500 0 0	
Balance at the credit thereof ..	..	5,734 9 8	Registration Fees, &c.	1,069 15 0	
					3,569 15 0
		£115,207 8 8			£115,207 8 8

REVENUE AND PROFIT AND LOSS ACCOUNT, from May 7th 1891 (the date of Incorporation),

Dr. to June 30th 1892. *Cr.*

	£ s d		£ s d
To Expenses of Management, including Directors' Fees, Salaries, Rent of Offices. and General Charges ..	4,383 1 6	By Dividends, Interest, &c.	4,905 6 6
„ Printing, Stationery and Stamps	207 19 1	„ Commissions Earned	20,375 0 0
„ Law Charges	87 5 2	„ Remuneration as Trustees	347 16 3
„ Commissions Payable	60 13 2	„ Insurance Premiums	213 7 10
„ Deposit Interest	70 7 0	„ Transfer Fees	2 5 0
„ Bad Debt	300 0 0		
„ Reserve Fund, under Article 142	15,000 0 0		
„ Balance	5,734 9 8		
	£25,843 15 7		£25,843 15 7

We have examined the above Accounts with the Books and Vouchers of the Corporation, and the Securities held, and find them correct.

August 11th 1892.

(Signed) Turquand, Youngs, Weise, Bishop & Clarke, } *Auditors.*
Thomson, Jackson, Gourlay & Taylor,

THE LONDON JOINT STOCK BANK, LIMITED.

Dr.   LIABILITIES AND ASSETS, 30th June 1902.   *Cr.*

	£	s	d		£	s	d
To Capital paid up, viz., 120,000 Shares at £15 per Share	1,800,000	0	0	By Government Stock, valued in accordance with the Resolution passed by the General Meeting of Shareholders, on the 19th of January 1865, viz.:—			
„ Amount of the Guarantee Fund	1,200,000	0	0	£1,500,000 Consols, taken at 90	1,350,000	0	0
„ Amount due by the Bank on Current Accounts, Deposit Receipts, Circular Notes, &c.	18,773,124	12	5	„ Other British Government Securities	904,251	5	0
„ Acceptances	909,532	4	6	„ Indian, Colonial Government and other Securities	1,476,577	4	6
„ Rebate of Interest on Bills Discounted, not yet due, carried to New Account	25,062	7	4	„ Securities lodged with Public Bodies	39,867	10	0
„ Amount of Net Profit for the Half-year ended 30th June, including £31,974 16s. 3d. balance of Profit and Loss Account, 31st December 1901 £158,606 0 3				„ Cash in hand and at the Bank of England	2,286,846	6	0
Less Reduction of Premises Account.. £10,000 0 0				„ Money at Call and Short Notice	5,555,070	0	0
Less Amount transferred to Superannuation Allowance Fund.. 5,000 0 0				„ Bills Discounted, Loans and other Securities	9,916,388	0	10
15,000 0 0	143,606	0	3	„ Liabilities of Customers for Acceptances as per contra	909,532	4	6
				„ Freehold and Leasehold Premises	412,792	13	8
	£22,851,325	4	6		£22,851,325	4	6

Dr.   PROFIT AND LOSS ACCOUNT for the Half-year ended 30th June 1902.   *Cr.*

	£	s	d		£	s	d
To Current Expenses, Directors' Remuneration, and Superannuation Allowances	108,055	6	9	By Amount of Gross Profit for the Half-year ended 30th June, including £31,974 16s. 3d. balance of Profit and Loss Account, 31st December 1901, after making provision for Reduction of Premises Account, for Bad and Doubtful Debts and payment of Income Tax	291,723	14	4
„ Rebate of Interest on Bills Discounted, not yet due, carried to New Account	25,062	7	4				
„ Dividend Account for the payment of Half-a-year's Dividend at the rate of 12 per cent. per annum on £1,800,000, amount of paid-up Capital on 120,000 Shares	108,000	0	0				
„ Reduction of Premises Account	10,000	0	0				
„ Superannuation Allowance Fund	5,000	0	0				
„ Amount carried to Profit and Loss New Account	35,606	0	3				
	£291,723	14	4		£291,723	14	4

Dr.   GUARANTEE FUND ACCOUNT, 30th June 1902.   *Cr*

	£	s	d		£	s	d
To Present Amount	£1,200,000	0	0	By Amount on 32st December 1901	£1,200,000	0	0

In accordance with the provisions of the Companies Act, 1900, we certify that all our requirements as Auditors have been complied with, and we report to the Shareholders that we have audited the above Accounts and Balance Sheet, and, in our opinion, such Balance Sheet is a full and fair statement, properly drawn up so as to exhibit a true and correct view of the state of the Bank's affairs, as shown by the Books of the Bank.

H. GILLIAT,
D. MEINERTZHAGEN, } *Directors.*
F. J. JOHNSTON,
      CHARLES GOW, *General Manager.*

JOHN G. GRIFFITHS,
    (*Deloittte, Dever, Griffiths & Co.*) } *Auditors.*
W. A. STONE,
    (*Cash, Stone & Co.*)

T

THE PLANTERS' STORES AND AGENCY COMPANY, LIMITED.

Dr.   BALANCE SHEET, 30th September 1900.   Cr.

Capital and Liabilities. — DIBRUGARH (ASSAM).

	Rs. as. p.	Rs. as. p.	£ s d
To Amount due to Calcutta Office	87,747 9 0		
Less amount in transit	3,565 10 6		
	84,181 14 6		
Add amount of Profit for this half-year ..	5,173 1 6		
		89,355 13 0	
„ Contingency Fund		8,700 0 0	
„ Deposit Account		89,414 0 1	
„ Sundry Creditors		40,998 4 11	
„ Furlough Account		1,000 0 0	
		Rs. 229,467 5 0	17,210 1 0

Property and Assets. — DIBRUGARH (ASSAM).

	Rs. as. p.	£ s d
IMMOVABLE PROPERTY—		
By Value of Manager's Bungalow Land and Out-houses	3,304 4 0	
„ Ditto of Assistants' Bungalow ditto ditto	1,837 2 0	
„ Ditto of Painted Iron Roof Godown complete, Pucka, asphalted, 250 feet long, 33 feet wide, height of apex 22 feet 10 inches	21,883 15 0	
„ Ditto of Pucka, Stock Godown	3,410 15 0	
„ Ditto of Book-keeper's House	140 11 0	
„ Ditto of Jorhât, Nazira, Moriani and Margherita Block	4,859 9 0	
MOVABLE PROPERTY—		
„ Ditto of Machinery, Fixtures and General Plant	2,518 1 9	
STOCKS—		
„ Ditto of Stock-in-Trade in hand and *en route*	104,265 3 0	
DEBTORS—		
„ Customers' Outstandings	63,293 11 10	
„ Sundry Debtors	10,937 10 0	
CASH—		
„ Cash in hand	13,016 2 5	
	Rs. 229,467 5 0	17,210 1 0

CALCUTTA.

	Rs. as. p.	Rs. as. p.	£ s d
To Amount due to London Office	289,736 15 1		
Add amount of Profit for this half-year ..	20,097 7 11		
		309,834 7 0	
„ Bills Payable		118,168 15 7	
„ Deposit Account ..		228,579 8 11	
„ Sundry Creditors ..		529,376 0 11	
„ Contingency Fund..		25,208 11 6	
„ Furlough Account ..		6,625 0 0	
		Rs. 1,217,792 11 11	91,334 9 1

CALCUTTA.

	Rs. as. p.	£ s d
By Value of Office Furniture and Fixtures ..	3,987 14 6	
„ Ditto of Goods in hand and Shipments Afloat	323,860 15 3	
„ Trade Outstandings	218,430 1 3	
„ Sundry Debtors	538,602 8 1	
„ Amount due by Dibrugarh Branch ..	87,747 9 0	
„ Cash in hand and at Bankers	45,163 11 10	
	Rs. 1,217,792 11 11	91,334 9 1

LONDON.

	£ s d	£ s d
SHARE CAPITAL—		
To Amount of 3,250 Ordinary Shares of £10 each, fully paid up	32,500 0 0	
„ Amount of 750 Deferred Shares of £10 each, fully paid up	7,500 0 0	
		40,000 0 0
LOAN CAPITAL—		
To Amount of sixty-three 5 per cent. Debentures of £100 each	6,300 0 0	
„ Deposit Account	19,337 0 4	
„ Exchange (in suspense) .. .·.	569 13 9	
„ Sundry Creditors	5,496 14 1	
„ Profit and Loss, as per separate statement	2,841 3 7	
		74,544 11 9
		£183,089 1 10

LONDON.

	£ s d	£ s d
By Amount due by Calcutta Office	21,730 5 5	
Add amount in transit..	1,862 18 0	
		23,593 3 5
„ Ditto paid for Goodwill	10,000 0 0	
„ Sundry Debtors	11,327 2 6	
„ Value of Office Furniture	78 2 5	
„ Amount Invested in Shares and other Securities	6,510 16 5	
„ Amount advanced on Mortgage of Property in Ceylon	6,900 15 8	
„ Cost of Deohall Tea Estate ..12,812 16 9		
„ „ Rytok Tea Estate (adjoining) 1,527 7 1		
	14,340 3 10	
„ Cash at Bankers and in hand	1,794 7 6	
		74,544 11 9
		£183,089 1 10

Exchange, 1s. 6d. per Rupee.

THE PLANTERS' STORES AND AGENCY COMPANY, LIMITED.

Dr. PROFIT AND LOSS ACCOUNT, 1st April to 30th September 1900. *Cr.*

	£ s d	£ s d
By Balance brought forward from 31st March 1900	2,879 3 0	
Less Dividend, the 33rd, paid 27th August 1900	1,200 0 0	
		1,679 3 0

DIBRUGARH. (Working Expenses)

WORKING EXPENSES—	Rs. as. p.	£ s d
To Establishment	11,648 4 9	
„ Charges and other Accounts	3,553 3 1	
„ Interest on Capital	3,114 10 10	
„ Moriani Branch Loss	131 11 4	
„ Depreciation	4,414 13 6	
„ Contingency Fund	1,980 1 10	
„ Commission	1,725 7 0	
	Rs. 26,568 4 4	1,992 12 5

DIBRUGARH. (Gross Profit)

	Rs. as. p.	
By Gross Profit on Merchandise Account ..	27,139 11 2	
„ Gross Profit on other Accounts	3,374 4 10	
„ Agency Department Profit	867 12 6	
„ Nazira Branch Profit	1,140 14 8	
„ Margherita ditto	86 7 2	
	Rs. 32,609 2 4	2,445 13 9

CALCUTTA. (Working Expenses)

WORKING EXPENSES—	Rs. as. p.	£ s d
To Establishment	33,670 0 10	
„ Charges, Rent, &c.	20,280 7 0	
„ Interest on Capital	711 1 2	
„ Contingency Fund	500 0 0	
„ Furlough Account	500 0 0	
	Rs. 55,661 9 0	4,174 12 4

CALCUTTA. (Gross Profit)

	Rs. as. p.	
By Gross Profit on Merchandise Account ..	23,728 10 4	
„ Gross Profit on Commission Account ..	42,013 3 0	
„ Gross Profit on Agency Account ..	9,094 7 11	
„ Gross Profit on other Accounts	922 11 8	
	Rs. 75,759 0 11	5,681 18 7

LONDON. (Working Expenses)

WORKING EXPENSES—	£ s d	£ s d
To General Charges	173 17 8	
„ Rent	87 10 0	
„ Directors' Fees	250 0 0	
„ Debenture Interest	157 10 0	
„ Passage Money	100 11 3	
„ Office Salaries and Auditor's Fee	599 0 0	
„ Interest	81 3 3	
„ Income Tax	92 16 0	
„ Half-year's Annuity to Mrs. Jefferson ..	25 0 0	
		1,567 8 2
„ Amount written off Investments		1,000 0 0
„ Balance		2,841 3 7
		£11,575 16 6

LONDON. (Commission)

	£ s d	£ s d
By Commission	1,310 18 1	
„ Interest on Capital	458 3 1	
		1,769 1 2
		£11,575 16 6

By Balance .. .. •• •• ..		£2,841 3 7

Exchange, 1s. 6d. per Rupee.

In accordance with the provisions of the Companies Act, 1900, I certify that all my requirements as Auditor have been complied with, and I report to the Shareholders that I have audited the Company's Balance Sheet, dated 30th September 1900, and in my opinion such Balance Sheet is properly drawn up so as to exhibit a true and correct view of the state of the Company's affairs as shown by the Books of the Company, subject to the accuracy of the valuation as given by the Directors to the Investments in Tea Estates and other undertakings.

LEWIS HARDY, F.C.A., *Auditor,*

22nd February 1901.

2 Creed Lane, Ludgate Hill, London, E.C.

T 2

ADMIRAL STEAM TRAWLING COMPANY, SCARBOROUGH.

STATEMENT OF ACCOUNTS for Half-year ending June 30th 1896.

The "Admiral" is insured against total loss for £1,200.

CAPITAL ACCOUNT.

		£ s d			£ s d
1895 Dec. 31	To "Admiral"	2,250 0 0	1896 June 30	By "Admiral"	2,250 0 0

REVENUE ACCOUNT.

		£ s d	£ s d			£ s d	£ s d
1896 June 30	Commission	67 4 8		1896 June 30	By Sales	889 13 0	
"	Landing Dues	9 3 10		"	" Sale of Old Rope, &c.	0 11 0	
"	Harbour { Scarborough	2 4 6		"	" Insurance Club's proportion of		
	Dues { Hartlepool	3 9 2			Salvage Claim	10 13 4	
			82 2 2				900 17 4
"	Fishermen	170 15 2					
"	Wages	179 13 0					
"	Labour	21 17 5					
			372 5 7				
"	Coals	119 0 0					
"	Oils	14 2 4					
			133 2 4				
"	Engineers, Repairs, &c.	92 6 7					
"	Ropes, Stores, &c...	51 9 5					
"	Net Braiding, Mending, and Tarring ..	11 11 2					
"	Carpenters	1 8 0					
"	Painting	2 11 0					
"	Salvage Claim	20 0 0					
			179 6 2				
"	Insurance	12 0 0					
"	Management	10 0 0					
"	Sundries	2 7 0					
"	Printing and Stamps	0 9 3					
"	Bankers' Charge	0 5 0					
			25 1 3				
"	Profit and Loss Account	44 19 10					
"	Dividends	64 0 0					
			108 19 10				
			£900 17 4				£900 17 4

PROFIT AND LOSS ACCOUNT.

		£ s d			£ s d
Dec. 31 1895	To Balance Due to Bank	21 15 10	Dec. 31 1895	By Cash in hand	0 10 6
June 30 1896	" Cash in hand	1 12 11	June 30 1896	" Revenue Account	44 19 10
	" Balance at Bank	22 1 7			
		£45 10 4			£45 10 4

Examined with Vouchers and found correct—SAMUEL SMITH, Merchant and Broker, Scarborough.

THE DUNLOP PNEUMATIC TYRE COMPANY, LIMITED.

Dr. PROFIT AND LOSS ACCOUNT to 31st March 1897. *Cr.*

1897 March 31	£ s d	1897. March 31	£ s d
To Interest on Debentures to 31st March 1897	18,392 16 5	By Royalties, Net Profit on Trading, including Dividends on Investments and Profit realised on Sale of Securities and issue of License, *less* Preliminary Expenses and Expenses incidental to Allotment	610,437 8 6
„ Plant, Furniture and Fittings. Amount written off	3,487 0 0	„ Transfer Fees	4,061 6 0
„ Balance carried to Balance Sheet, subject to Managing Director's Commission	592,618 18 1		
	£614,498 14 6		£614,498 14 6

Dr. BALANCE SHEET, 31st March 1897. *Cr.*

Capital and Liabilities.	£ s d	£ s d	£ s d	*Property and Assets.*	£ s d	£ s d	£ s d
1897 March 31				**1897. March 31**			
Capital—Preference Shares, 1,000,000 Shares of £1 each	1,000,000 0 0			Freehold and Leasehold Premises at cost			65,764 13 5
Ordinary Shares, 1,000,000 Shares of £1 each	1,000,000 0 0			Plant, Machinery, Fittings and Furnishing	34,873 18 11		
Deferred Shares, 2,000,000 Shares of £1 each	2,000,000 0 0			*Less* Amount written off ..	3,487 0 0		
	4,000,000 0 0					31,386 18 11	
Less Unpaid Calls..	982 10 0			Patent Rights and Goodwill..		4,261,322 7 8	
		3,999,017 10 0		Sundry Debtors		404,913 10 6	
Debentures—Nominal Amount, 10,000 Debentures of £100 each	1,000,000 0 0			Stock on hands..		182,793 4 3	
Less—Debentures purchased by the Company	450,000 0 0			Investments		259,795 1 9	
		550,000 0 0		Cash and Bills at Bankers and on hands..		36,797 10 4	
Sundry Creditors		211,846 5 11					
Reserve for Rebates ..		32,358 7 6					
Profit and Loss Account to 31st March 1897 ..	592,618 18 1						
Less Interim Dividend..£110,709 7 2 Reserve for Rebates 32,358 7 6							
	143,067 14 8						
		449,551 3 5					
		£5,242,773 6 10					£5,242,773 6 10

Auditors' Report.—We have examined the above Accounts, and consider. they correctly represent the position of the Company on the 31st March last.

8th July 1897. TURQUAND, YOUNGS, BISHOP & CLARKE.

ENGLISH SEWING COTTON COMPANY LIMITED.

Dr. BALANCE SHEET, 31st March 1903. *Cr.*

	£ s d		£ s d	£ s d
To Share Capital authorised, issued, and paid up:—		By Freehold and Leasehold Properties, Plant, Machinery, &c. (including capital outlay on same since their acquisition), and Goodwill of original purchases, also fully-paid shares in Subsidiary Companies, fully-paid preference and Ordinary Shares in R. F. & J. Alexander & Co., Limited, and 1,200,000 Shares of $5 each ($3½ per share paid up) of the Common Stock of the American Thread Company (as per Balance Sheet 31st March 1902)		2,342,515 3 0
1,000,000 5% Cumulative Preference Shares of £1 each	1,000,000 0 0	*Deduct* Amount of Interest previously included in purchase of Messrs. R. F. & J. Alexander & Co., Limited, in error	1,240 10 11	
1,000,000 Ordinary Shares of £1 each	1,000,000 0 0			2,341,274 12 1
" Debenture Stock authorised, issued, and paid up:—		*Add* Capital Expenditure during year ended 31st March 1903, less Sales (exclusive of £21,480 5s. od. expended by Subsidiary Companies). £6,272 9 4		
4% First Mortgage Debenture Stock £1,000,000 0 0		Amounts expended on Strutt Branch, 1901,1902, and 1903, now transferred .. 13,681 0 3		
Interest accrued thereon to 31st March 1903 10,000 0 0				19,953 9 7
	1,010,000 0 0	" English Thread Co., Limited—Purchase of 120 Guaranteed Preference Shares of £10 each	1,200 0 0	
" Loan on security of the Common Stock of the American Thread Co. and Interest	134,986 6 0	" The Thread Agency—250 Shares of $100 each, fully paid = $25,000	5,137 3 3	
" Capital Reserve Account	112,601 13 6	" The Yarn Agency—100 Shares of $100 each, fully paid = $10,000	2,054 17 4	
" Sundry Creditors	82,075 12 9			2,369,620 2 3
		Less Depreciation on English Plants, Furniture, and Fittings for the year	33,869 9 4	
		" Total Properties, &c. (including "Closed Works Account," £27,533 12s. 3d.), at 31st March 1903		2,335,750 12 11
		" The American Thread Company, Current Account		104,360 7 2
		" Subsidiary Companies—Balance of amounts due, and Dividends and Profit yet to receive		146,127 5 9
		" Stocks-in-Trade valued on basis of Cost or Net Realisation whichever is lower		435,787 8 10
		" Sundry Debtors (*less* Provision for Discounts and Bad Debts)		202,656 5 3
		" Cash at Bankers and in hand		50,204 6 4
		PROFIT AND LOSS ACCOUNT.		
		" Balance brought forward as per Directors' Report dated 8th September 1902	110,792 15 8	
		Add amount of interest previously included in the purchase price of Messrs. R. F. & J. Alexander & Co., Limited, in error	1,240 10 11	
		Amount previously credited to Profit and Loss Account as "Profits of and incident to the flotation of the American Thread Co.," now written back and credited to Capital Reserve Account	112,601 13 6	
			224,635 0 1	
		Deduct Reserve Account now transferred to Profit and Loss Account	124,620 17 3	
			100,014 2 10	
		Less Profit for the year as per Account	35,236 16 10	
		Leaving a net debit to be carried forward of		64,777 6 0
£3,339,663 12 3				£3,339,663 12 3

ENGLISH SEWING COTTON COMPANY LIMITED.

Dr. PROFIT AND LOSS ACCOUNT, for year ended 31st March 1903. Cr.

	£ s d	£ s d		£ s d	£ s d
To Directors' Fees—March to September 1902	2,082 3 9		By Manufacturing Profits	85,863 14 4	
„ „ September 1902 to March 1903 ..	2,058 6 8		Dividends from The American Thread Company, The Thread Agency, and The Yarn Agency	35,035 19 1	
		4,140 10 5			120,899 13 5
Law Charges and Accountancy ..		2,060 15 10	Income Tax—Balance of Account ..	2,773 14 11	
Depreciation on English Plants, Furniture, and Fittings	33,869 9 4		Transfer Fees	435 5 4	
Depreciation on Barcelona Plant, Furniture, and Fittings	4,691 10 4				3,209 0 3
		38,560 19 8			
Debenture Interest for one year ..		40,000 0 0			
Special Payments made during the year :—					
C. Diamond—Amount voted by Shareholders .. £2,000 0 0					
Awarded by the Manchester Chamber of Commerce (for services from April to September 1902) .. 500 0 0					
	2,500 0 0				
John Edward Lawton (for half-year to 31st March 1903, as per agreement) .	1,500 0 0				
Expenses of Shareholders' Investigation Committee	109 10 11				
		4,109 10 11			
Balance carried down		35,236 16 10			
		£124,108 13 8			£124,108 13 8
			By Balance brought down, being Profit for the year transferred to Balance Sheet		£35,236 16 10

In accordance with the provisions of the Companies Act, 1900, we certify that all our requirements as Auditors have been complied with. Our Report to the Shareholders accompanies this Balance Sheet.

WM. ASHWORTH,
JNO. P. GARNETT, } *Joint Auditors,*
JOHN E. HALLIDAY,

Manchester, 29th July 1903.

Chartered Accountants.

MANCHESTER, *29th July* 1903.

To the Shareholders of

THE ENGLISH SEWING COTTON COMPANY LIMITED.

GENTLEMEN,

We have audited the Accounts of the Company for the year ending 31st March 1903, and the Balance Sheet of that date, and have to report that such Balance Sheet is, is our opinion, properly drawn up so as to exhibit a true and correct view of the state of the Company's affairs as shown by the books of the Company.

PROPERTIES, &c.—The item £2,335,750 12s. 11d. is explained in the Balance Sheet itself, and the remarks we desire to make upon it are, that the Closed Works now stand at £27,533 12s. 3d., that the item of "Goodwill and Trademarks" remains unaltered at the sum of £448,941 15s. 3d., and that the sum of £13,681 0s. 3d., Capital Expenditure at the Strutt Branch, includes expenditure incurred up to 31st March 1902 amounting to £12,470.

Depreciation has been charged at the following rates :—

On Buildings, including Sprinklers	..	..	..	at 2½ per cent.	
,, Fixed Plant	..	..	..	,, 5	,,
,, Loose Plant and Machinery	..	..	..	,, 7½	,,
,, Office and Warehouse Furniture and Fittings, a sum exceeding				,, 10	,,

The item of Depreciation, £33,869 9s. 4d., in the Balance Sheet is in respect of English plant only, and does not include the depreciation charged on the plants of R. F. & J. Alexander & Company, Limited, and Ermen & Roby (Armentières), Limited, which are separately dealt with in the accounts of those companies. In addition to the item of £33,869 9s. 4d., the depreciation on the Barcelona Mills, amounting to £4,691 10s. 4d., has been charged against the Profit and Loss Account.

SUBSIDIARY COMPANIES.—Balance of amounts due and dividends and profits yet to receive, £146,127 5s. 9d., comprises sums advanced to R. F. & J. Alexander & Company, Limited, and Ermen & Roby (Armentières), Limited, (less a credit balance of account with the English Thread Company), as well as the dividend of £34,720 to be received from the American Thread Company.

STOCKS-IN-TRADE.—Printed instructions are issued by the Head Office as to the manner in which the stocks are to be valued, and some responsible person at each of the branches has certified that the quantities and prices are correct, and are taken in accordance with such printed instructions.

The Stock Sheets are, in all cases, signed as approved by a member of the Executive Committee. As stated in the Balance Sheet, the mode of valuation is "at cost or net realisation (whichever is lower)," and we are of opinion that the lines laid down in the printed instructions are fair and reasonable.

SUNDRY DEBTORS.—This item includes the foreign trade debtors, the accounts of which are kept by the Company's agents for foreign trade, the Central Agency, Limited. Summarised statements thereof, certified by Mr. David W. Kidston, one of the auditors of the Central Agency, Limited, have been produced to us.

Proper provision has, in our opinion, been made for Bad and Doubtful Debts and for Discounts.

CASH AT BANKERS AND IN HAND.—We have verified the cash at Bankers and at the Head Office and at some of the branches. With regard to cash at foreign banks and agencies under the control of the Central Agency, our remarks under the head of Sundry Debtors also apply.

PROFIT AND LOSS.—The net profit on the year's working, after paying £40,000 interest on Debentures, is £35,236 16s. 10d.

In the last Report of the Directors, the question was raised as to whether the sum of £112,601, representing "profits of and incident to the promotion and formation of the American Thread Company," which had been taken to the credit of Profit and Loss Account for the year ending 31st March 1899, should have been so dealt with.

At the request of the Company's Solicitors we considered the matter, and on the 2nd April last wrote them that in our opinion the sum of £112,601 could not be properly treated as profit. Subsequently the opinion of Counsel was obtained, who advised that the account should be amended by debiting the said sum of £112,601 to Profit and Loss, and passing a corresponding amount to the credit of a "Capital Reserve Account." Counsel further advised that the whole of the sum appearing in the Balance Sheet of 31st March 1902 to the credit of "Reserve Account" might properly be applied in reduction of any sum standing to the debit of Profit and Loss Account. In the present accounts the opinion of Counsel on both these points has been given effect to.

There has also been debited to Profit and Loss Account a sum of £1,240 10s. 11d., interest paid on the purchase-money for the Ordinary Shares in R. F. & J. Alexander & Company, Limited, which had been erroneously taken in the Balance Sheet at 31st March 1899, and subsequent Balance Sheets, as part of the cost of those Shares, and the like amount has been deducted from the Capital Expenditure.

After making these adjustments the amount at the debit of Profit and Loss Account is £64,777 6s. 0d.

We are, Gentlemen,

Your obedient Servants,

WM. ASHWORTH
JNO. P. GARNETT   } *Auditors.*
JOHN E. HALLIDAY

Chartered Accountants.

CHAPTER XXIII.

THE CRITICISM OF ACCOUNTS.

A CRITICISM of accounts' in detail—such as involves an inquiry into the detailed record of individual transactions, or even such as involves an inquiry into the summarised effect of such transactions with a view to verifying the periodical summaries (as exemplified by Balance Sheets and by various forms of Revenue Accounts)—comes properly under the heading of Auditing, and can therefore only be dealt with superficially in the course of the present work. For the same obvious reason it is impossible to discuss at length the importance of such an inquiry being conducted only by those who, by their previous training, are properly qualified to undertake the discharge of duties which, it must be admitted, are of a highly technical and responsible nature. At the same time, the present work would not be complete without some brief reference to the subject, if only for the reason that those who do not pose as being expert Auditors may require some guidance as to the circumstances under which it is expedient that they should seek the aid of professional assistance.

In approaching this portion of our subject, it is perhaps desirable to draw attention to the exact nature of those accounts that would, under ordinary circumstances, fall into the hands of a layman, upon which he might require to exercise his critical faculties, with or without professional assistance. Shortly stated, such a position of affairs may arise when (1) the proprietor (or proprietors) of an existing business contemplate a sale of the whole, or a portion, thereof to a purchaser, or to an incoming partner; (2) when a proposed partner is contem-plating joining an existing undertaking; (3) when those interested in the formation of a new company (or when those contemplating the purchase of an existing business) are desirous of acquiring a specified undertaking; (4) when a shareholder in an existing company is desirous of forming a reliable opinion as to its position, with a view (a) to increasing, or (b) to reducing his present holding. Under any of the above circumstances, it is obvious that there is legitimate ground for a critical inquiry into the position of affairs. Under other circumstances there may for various reasons be a desire to become intimately acquainted with the position, and, according to the point of view, other special questions may possibly have a bearing upon such an inquiry; but the circumstances recited above comprise, it is thought, the legitimate grounds of *bonâ fide* inquiry into the position and prospects of an existing undertaking, and for the purposes of this work attention may therefore be usefully confined within these limits.

NATURE AND LIMITATIONS OF ACCOUNTS.

Having, for the sake of convenience, thus to some extent limited the possible basis of inquiry, it may be pointed out that a criticism of the position and prospects of an undertaking based upon any of the objects above-mentioned must of necessity to a very large extent be confined to a more or less detailed —and in almost all cases (if the inquiry is to be useful) expert—inquiry into the accounts, which are the record of the transactions engaged upon and a summary of their result.

In cases where the accounts relate to business ventures that have been entirely completed, the record can, as a rule, be very conveniently summarised in the form of a simple Cash statement of summarised receipts and payments. This, as has already been mentioned, is the form of accounts almost exclusively required by the Courts from accounting parties; and, inasmuch as accounting parties are not as a rule called upon to furnish interim accounts, the requirements in this respect are perhaps less inadequate than might at first sight have appeared to be the case. Every completed venture of a business nature is capable of being recorded with something approaching completeness in the form of a Cash statement, and being in that form it is capable of the nearest approach to verification that is ever possible in connection with matters relating to accounts. That being so, the conservatism of the Courts in adhering to the Cash Account may to some extent at least be readily understood, for although the Cash Account, unsupported by other accounts, is rarely capable of completely disclosing the whole position of affairs, it does at least possess the merit of being capable of being absolutely verified—a quality which is not possessed by Balance Sheets, and only to a limited extent by Revenue, Profit & Loss, or Income & Expenditure, Accounts.

Very little reflection as to the nature of business transactions and accounts will, however, suffice to show that while a business venture is still being continued a Cash Account is insufficient to enable any definite opinion to be formed either as to its position or prospects, in that the Cash Account only records transactions that have been actually completed, while at any given moment while the venture as a whole remains a going concern numerous uncompleted transactions must remain pending which will materially affect, and may entirely alter, the position of affairs as disclosed by the simple Cash Account recording the effect of completed transactions. The general scheme of the science of accounting is such that when a business venture as a whole has been completed all the Ledger Accounts will of necessity be closed, and therefore show no balance, for the function of the various Ledger Accounts is to weigh the various transactions of different classes *pro* and *con*, and to show, in the form of Ledger balances under different headings, the nature and money value of those which at any given moment may remain uncompleted. These uncompleted transactions are recorded by means of Ledger balances of Real or Personal Accounts, and as such may, at any time when the books have been completely written up and balanced, be marshalled together into a Balance Sheet, which will then summarise the position of affairs at that date. But because the undertaking is a going concern, and because the various Ledger balances that comprise the Balance Sheet do represent the position of a series of uncompleted business transactions, it must necessarily follow that in the vast majority of cases absolute accuracy is hardly to be looked for, and the best which can under any normal circumstances be expected is that the figures comprised in a Balance Sheet may represent a fair valuation of the financial effect of the various transactions remaining uncompleted, as estimated by capable and reasonably prudent business men. As has already been stated, it is customary for going concerns to prepare at regular intervals (generally annually) Balance Sheets for the information of interested parties, and these Balance Sheets, if properly compiled, should enable competent persons to form a reliable idea as to the position of affairs. It cannot, however, be too strongly insisted upon that under no circumstances can they be regarded as statements of fact, or statements which it is possible for the most skilful or impartial person to absolutely *verify*, in the strict sense of the term. They are but estimates which, according to the nature of the circumstances, may sometimes be expected to be very closely borne out by actual results in the future, but which, on the other hand, in some cases cannot reasonably be expected to afford more than a rough indication of the possible course of subsequent events. This is a point which it is important should be borne in mind by all who take upon themselves the task of criticising the published Balance Sheets of going concerns.

On the other hand, Revenue Accounts (the term being used in its generic sense, as comprising Trading Accounts, Profit & Loss Accounts, Manufacturing Accounts, Income & Expenditure Accounts, &c.) are summaries of Nominal Accounts which record under convenient headings transactions that have taken place during the period under review. In so far as these transactions are absolutely completed, the figures in the Revenue Account may be relied upon, so far as they go, as absolute statements of fact ; but in so far as they comprise uncompleted transactions—and the Revenue Account of any going concern will to a large extent be made up of such—they suffer of necessity from the limitations already referred to in connection with Balance Sheets. In this connection, it will perhaps not be amiss to remind the reader that (as described on page 20) a Revenue Account is in fact a combination of a Cash Account and of the Balance Sheets of the commencement and close of the period covered by that account. It therefore possesses in a measure the advantages and drawbacks of both the sources from which it is compiled.

GOODWILL.

In criticising accounts from any of the points of view enumerated at the commencement of this chapter, it is well to bear in mind that any inaccuracies that may be discovered in the record (including under this heading any differences of opinion between the critic and the compiler of the accounts) affect not merely the estimate of the profitable nature of the business and the value of its net tangible assets, but also—and to the uninitiated to an unexpectedly large extent—the value of the Goodwill. The question of Goodwill lies somewhat outside the scope of the present work, and no attempt can therefore be made to deal exhaustively with the subject in these pages. It may be pointed out, however, that whenever a business changes hands, if it be of such a nature as to produce a profit

in excess of a reasonable rate of interest on the Capital invested and reasonable remuneration for the proprietor's time in managing it, it possesses a Goodwill of some value, varying from one to perhaps five years' purchase of the surplus profits so indicated. In special cases the valuation might possibly range even higher. It must thus be obvious that it would be worth the while of a dishonest vendor (or proposed vendor) to pay necessary expenses, or to fictitiously increase business profits, out of his own pocket, if by so doing he could secure a purchaser for the undertaking who would pay him from one to five times the amount by which he had falsified the accounts in question. From the point of view of an intending purchaser it is, therefore, especially important that accounts should be carefully criticised ; and the same remark, it need hardly be pointed out, applies to the intending investor in a company formed to take over an existing undertaking.

COMPENSATION CASES.

Another occasion upon which careful criticism of accounts is called for is when some public body— as, for example, a local authority or a railway—has obtained the sanction of the Legislature to compulsorily acquire the premises occupied by a business, upon condition of compensating those whom it displaces. The amount of compensation to be paid in these cases is (in default of mutual arrangement) fixed by arbitration, and not infrequently a difficulty arises, in that the accounts which have been kept in the past are incomplete, and therefore fail to fully and clearly disclose the actual position of affairs. Such data as is available under these circumstances may naturally, like most other things, be regarded from two points of view, and the following account of a *pro formâ* arbitration, organised by the Edinburgh Chartered Accountants Students' Society a short time since, will, it is thought, be especially instructive to the reader, as indicating the normal procedure under such cases, and the manner in which such incomplete accounts may be approached by the parties upon both sides, with a view to ascertaining the true value of the business comprised in the reference.

NOTE OF ARBITRATION PROCEEDINGS, carried out at Meeting of the Chartered Accountants Students' Society of Edinburgh, held in the HALL of the SOCIETY OF ACCOUNTANTS, 27 Queen Street, Edinburgh, on THURSDAY, 12th MARCH 1903, at 8 p.m.

Claimant—A. BLACK, Wine and Spirit Merchant, North Bridge, Edinburgh.

Respondents—THE NORTHERN RAILWAY CO.

Arbiter—FRANCIS MORE, ESQ., C.A.

Counsel for Claimant—W. ROSS TAYLOR, ESQ., Advocate.

Counsel for Respondents—J. HOSSELL HENDERSON, ESQ., Advocate.

Accountant for Claimant—J. MILNE HENDERSON, ESQ., C.A.

Accountant for Respondents—W. D. STEWART, ESQ., C.A.

Under powers contained in a special Act of Parliament, the Northern Railway Company, by notice dated 11th November 1902, took over the property in North Bridge, Edinburgh, consisting *inter alia* of a Shop in which A. Black had carried on the business of Wine and Spirit Merchant since 1890. The Respondents offered the Claimant £3,000 as compensation, but this was declined, and accordingly the amount fell to be ascertained by Arbitration.

The parties, by a Joint Minute dated 1st December 1902, appointed Mr. Francis More, C.A., to be sole Arbiter. Mr. More accepted the Office of Arbiter on 2nd December, and on that date issued an Order calling upon the Claimant to lodge a written statement of his Claim within 14 days, and allowing the Respondents to see and answer the same within 14 days thereafter.

In response to the Order the Claimant lodged the following Claim, viz. :—

1. For the Goodwill of the said business, which cost the Claimant £5,000 in 1890, and which has increased in value owing to the successful business carried on by the Claimant, and is now lost through the compulsory removal of the Claimant from the premises	£9,000	0	0
2. Loss arising through the compulsory realisation of Stock ...	500	0	0
3. Loss on realisation of Fittings and Utensils	500	0	0
Total	£10,000	0	0

Answers were lodged for the Respondents to the effect that the Claim was excessive.

The Arbiter, on the motion of parties, fixed Thursday, 12th March, at 8 p.m., for the commencement of the Proof.

The Accountant Witnesses for the parties had respectively prepared the Profit and Loss Accounts shown overpage—

I.—PROFIT AND LOSS ACCOUNT for the Five Years ended 11th November 1902, prepared for the Claimant.

	Year 1897-8	Year 1898-9	Year 1899-1900	Year 1900-1	Year 1901-2	Total.
By Shop Drawings...	£6,240 1 6	£6,500 2 10	£7,176 1 9	£7,280 11 4	£7,020 6 8	£34,217 4 1
To Purchases ...	£3,975 6 2	£4,191 19 6	£4,326 1 5	£4,642 18 2	£4,510 5 3	£21,646 10 6
,, Wages	431 10 6	428 9 0	442 7 9	447 0 1	460 1 8	2,209 9 0
,, Rent	300 0 0	300 0 0	350 0 0	350 0 0	350 0 0	1,650 0 0
,, Taxes, Rates, Licence, and Insurance ...	94 10 0	95 1 6	96 1 9	97 2 9	98 10 0	481 6 0
,, Coals and Gas...	33 5 6	34 15 9	35 0 7	37 1 6	31 2 9	171 6 1
,, Repairs... ...	13 6 7	20 7 6	14 19 1	35 1 2	14 1 5	97 15 9
,, Petty Expenses..	70 3 5	62 17 4	80 2 9	71 4 3	82 6 2	366 13 11
,, Balance, Net Profits ...	1,321 19 4	1,366 12 3	1,831 8 5	1,600 3 5	1,473 19 5	7,594 2 10
	£6,240 1 6	£6,500 2 10	£7,176 1 9	£7,280 11 4	£7,020 6 8	£34,217 4 1

Average Profits of Five Years, £1,518 16s. 7d.

Note.—The Stock is assumed to be the same at the beginning and end of each year.

J. MILNE HENDERSON, C.A.

II.—PROFIT AND LOSS ACCOUNT for the Three Years ended 11th November 1902, on the basis of percentage on Cash Drawings prepared for the Respondents.

	Year 1899-1900	Year 1900-1	Year 1901-2	Total
Shop Drawings	£7,176 1 9	£7,280 11 4	£7,020 6 8	£21,476 19 9
By Estimated Gross Profits, 33⅓ per cent. on above Drawings	£2,392 0 7	£2,426 17 1	£2,340 2 3	£7,158 19 11
To Wages (including £4 per week paid to Proprietor)	£650 7 9	£655 0 1	£668 1 8	£1,973 9 6
,, Rent	350 0 0	350 0 0	350 0 0	1,050 0 0
,, Rates, Taxes, and Insurance	56 1 9	57 2 9	58 10 0	171 14 6
,, Excise Duty	40 0 0	40 0 0	40 0 0	120 0 0
,, Business Expenses	130 2 5	143 6 11	127 10 4	400 19 8
,, Interest on Capital ... ... 5 per cent. on £7,000 (being price of Goodwill £5,000, and Stock and Fittings, &c., *less* Liabilities, £2,000).	350 0 0	350 0 0	350 0 0	1,050 0 0
To Balance, being Estimated Net Profits	815 8 8	831 7 4	746 0 3	2,392 16 3
	£2,392 0 7	£2,426 17 1	£2,340 2 3	£7,158 19 11

Average Profits of Three Years, £797 12s. 1d.

W. D. STEWART, C.A.

The books kept were :—

1. Excise Stock Book, kept according to law, to record the quantities and particulars of all Spirits received into Stock.

2. Shop Drawings Books, in which were entered at the end of each day the cash received in cash payments.

3. Bank Pass Books.

4. Cheque Counterfoil Books.

The Invoices and Receipted Accounts were kept and bundled each year.

The Cash Book was never balanced. It did not contain entries of :—(1) Bank Cheques and payments made by same ; (2) Payments into Bank; (3) Cash drawn by Proprietor other than £4 entered in name of Salary weekly.

No Stock Sheets were ever made up by Claimant.

The Premises were held under lease expiring on 11th November 1906, rent £350 per annum.

The following is a copy of the Precognition Report by J. MILNE HENDERSON, C.A., Edinburgh :—

I have examined the Books of A. B., Wine and Spirit Merchant, North Bridge, Edinburgh.

The books consisted of Excise Stock Books, Shop Drawings Books, Bank Pass Books, and Cheque Counterfoil Book. There were also produced to me the Invoices and receipted Accounts for the whole period of A. B.'s occupancy. From these sources I have prepared the following Statements.

1. *List of Shop Drawings* from March 1890 when A. B. took over the business. The Drawings are as follows, viz. :—

				£					£
1.	For year to	11th November	1891	5,206	8.	For year to	11th November	1898	6,240
2.	,,	,,	1892	5,354	9.	,,	,,	1899	6,500
3.	,,	,,	1893	5,491	10.	,,	,,	1900	7,176
4.	,,	,,	1894	5,891	11.	,,	,,	1901	7,280
5.	,,	,,	1895	5,710	12.	,,	,,	1902	7,020
6.	,,	,,	1896	5,994					
7.	,,	,,	1897	6,080					£34,216

Average of five years 1898-1902, £6,843.

The daily Drawings were arrived at by taking the amount in the till at the close of business, and allowing for cash payments and money put in for change in the morning. The Drawings have increased from £100 per week in the year 1890-91 to £140 per week in the year 1900-01 an increase of 40 per cent. The Drawings show a remarkably steady increase, the only decreases being in 1894-5 and 1901-2. I cannot account for the former year's decrease, but I understand the great increase in Working-men's Clubs, and the war have something to do with the fall in 1901-2. As these Clubs are sure to be reduced in the near future, I do not attribute any importance to the decrease in the year 1901-2. I think that in fixing the Compensation in this case the Profits for that year should not be made the basis, but that the average Profits of the five years to 11th November 1902 should be taken.

(2) *Purchases.*—These were made up from the Invoices and Receipted Accounts. The amounts shown in the Profit and Loss Account are the payments for Stock made in each of the five years ending 11th November 1902.

The difference between the Purchases and the Drawings show a Gross Profit of 36·74 per cent., and the accuracy of this I have tested in the following way :—

I ascertained from the Excise Book and from the Brewers' and other invoices the total quantity of liquor brought into the business during the five years and the cost of same.

Against this I put what the liquor yielded at so many glasses to the gallon, and so much per glass of Spirits and Beer respectively

				£
The total cost was (agreeing with the Profit and Loss Account)	..			21,646
And the estimated yield on this basis was	..	..	..	33,500
				£11,854

Equal to a gross profit of 35·38 per cent.

Over a period of five years I consider this a satisfactory test of the correctness of the Gross Profit brought out in the Profit and Loss Account.

I have assumed the Stock at the beginning and end of the period to be the same. Stock was taken on A. B.'s entry in 1890 and amounted to £2,000, but I understand this was too small a Stock to work the business, and it had to be increased by £200 or £300. Stock was not taken again, but last week it was sold off and realised only £1,700. I consider, therefore, that by leaving the Stock out of account in the Profit and Loss Account that the Profits are under rather than over-stated, moreover the State which I prepared to test the accuracy of the Drawings, proves that the Stock could not have increased.

(3) *Business Expenses.*—The Wages are those shown in the Cash Book with the exception of £208 per annum (£4 per week) drawn by the Proprietor in respect of salary. I consider that the Proprietor's salary does not form a charge against the Profits in estimating the amount payable for the Goodwill of a Business to be fixed under an Arbitration. The Rent, Taxes, and other expenses are the actual sums paid as shown by the Cash and Cheque Counterfoil Books, and in numerous cases vouched by receipted Accounts. I have found from the receipts the Claimant paid for Fittings at his entry £600, and that he has kept them in full repair since. These Fittings are practically of no value if removed.

The result shown by the Profit and Loss Account is as follows :—

						£	s	d
Net Profit for year	1897-8	..	..	..	..	1,321	19	4
,, ,,	1898-9	..	..	..	..	1,366	12	3
,, ,,	1899-0	..	..	..	..	1,831	8	5
,, ,,	1900-1	..	..	..	..	1,600	3	5
,, ,,	1901-2	..	..	..	..	1,473	19	5
				Total	..	£7,594	2	10

Average of five years £1,516 16s. 7d.

	£	s	d
I consider that a fair sum to be allowed to the Claimant for Compensation is six years profits on the above average, say	9,000	0	0
I also consider that Claimant is entitled to Compensation for loss on Fittings	500	0	0
And for loss on forced realisation of Stock	500	0	0
	£10,000	0	0

The Precognition of WILLIAM DANIEL STEWART, C.A. (Accountant for the Respondents), was as follows :—

I am a Chartered Accountant in Edinburgh, and have been in practice for the past six years. I have examined the Books kept by the Claimant, Mr. A. Black, Wine and Spirit Merchant, North Bridge, Edinburgh. These were as follows :—

(1) The Excise Stock Book, commonly called the Permit Book, showing the quantities of Spirits received in stock.
(2) The Shop Cash Book, showing the daily Cash Drawings and Cash Payments.
(3) The Bank Pass Books, and
(4) The Cheque Counterfoil Books.

The Bookkeeping was of a very elementary nature, the Cash Book never being balanced, while it did not show any Bank transactions. In my opinion the Claimant ought to have kept the following books :—

(1) Cash Book, incorporating the Bank transactions, balanced weekly.
(2) Invoice Book, recording the Goods purchased.
(3) Ledger, to which the Cash and Invoice Books would fall to be posted.

The Stock ought to have been taken at regular intervals, so as to show the Gross Profit on the business.

I have prepared a Statement from the Cash Book showing the Drawings and Expenses from 1899 to 1902.

In regard to the Drawings, I find, on the assumption that the Cash Book is correct, that they are as follows :—

	£	s	d
Year 1899-1900	7,176	1	9
,, 1900-1901	7,280	11	4
,, 1901-1902	7,020	6	8

Or average weekly Drawings of £137 13s. 1d.

It will be observed that the Drawings for the year 1901-2 are less than those of the previous year by £160 4s. 8d. The business would appear, therefore, to be a declining one.

As before stated, no Invoice Book was kept. The Claimant's Accountant has prepared his Statement of Purchases from the Invoices only. As no stock was taken either at the beginning or the end of the period, a proper Profit and Loss Account cannot be made up. The Stock cannot possibly be the same at all times. In a case of this kind, the Gross Profit can only be arrived at by taking a percentage on the Cash Drawings. I have had a great deal of experience in regard to Wine and Spirit Merchants' businesses both in Edinburgh and Glasgow, my connection being partly as Trustee on Estates having Interests in such businesses, and partly owing to my being connected with people in the trade. In my opinion 33⅓ per cent. on the Drawings would be a fair Gross Profit in a business of this kind. It would be a more exact method of arriving at the Gross Profit than by Invoices where some might be wanting. In this connection, I have made special enquiry regarding the Gross Profits of Public Houses, apart from those I have to do with professionally. The enquiries made confirm my views, for instance :—

A shop in the neighbourhood of Nicolson Street earns a Gross Profit of 6s. 6d. per £; a shop near Leith Street earns a Gross Profit of 6s. 6d. per £, and so on.

I believe that 33⅓ per cent. is the usual Gross Profit earned. In my knowledge the Inland Revenue authorities look upon 33⅓ per cent. as the usual Gross Profit earned in a Public House. They would be surprised if the Publican admitted he earned more. A great many Public Houses earn only from 25 per cent. to 36 per cent., especially where a very large carrying-out trade is done. In the average business 33⅓ per cent. is a fair Gross Profit. On this basis the Gross Profit would be as follows :—

	£	s	d
Year 1899-1900	2,392	0	7
,, 1900-1901	2,426	17	1
,, 1901-1902	2,340	2	3

Out of these Gross Profits have to be paid the Expenses These expenses are the same as those made up by the Claimant's Accountant with the exception of (1) Wages (which include £4 per week paid to the Proprietor), and (2) Interest on Capital.

In regard to Wages, in my experience, a business drawing £138 weekly cannot be worked under £13 weekly.

	£	s	d
Barman	4	0	0
4 Barmen	6	0	0
1 Cook	1	5	0
3 Boys	1	10	0
	£12	15	0

This business was worked by the Proprietor. It is proper, therefore, that his wages should be charged, as if he did not work, an experienced barman would have to be employed. I am aware that the Inland Revenue would not pass this sum as a charge on the business.

In Limited Companies, however, it is usual to charge against the Profits a sum for management to the Managing Director.

I have charged interest on Capital against the Profit.

This must be done before arriving at the Net Profit. The Capital involved is £5,000, the price of the Goodwill in 1890, and £2,000, the difference between the Assets consisting of Stock and Fittings and Liabilities. Interest on this sum of £7,000 is £350 per annum, at 5 per cent. It is the practice of Accountants to debit Profit and Loss with Interest on Capital before arriving at the Net Profit. This is done in the audit of the books of private firms. In view of the short Lease the Claimant ought to have charged Profit and Loss with such a sum each year as would give him back his whole Capital at its expiry. I have charged an exact sum of £350 as Interest on the assumption that the Capital involved always remained the same, viz., £7,000.

I consider that the rent paid by the Claimant for his premises (£350) as too high. A fair rent, in my opinion, would be £300. This would tell against the sale of the Goodwill in the open market. The Rents of Public Houses have been taken in cases of this kind at 2¼ times the week's drawings. This is also my experience of Public House Rents. In this case, with Drawings of £138, the Rent should be £310.

A most important point in connection with a Public House Business is the Lease. In this case there are only four years to run. A business with this short lease is not of much value to a purchaser unless the landlord agrees to a renewal.

There is no difficulty in selling the Goodwill of a Public House with a ten or fifteen years' lease. The rent has already been raised from £300 to £350, and would have probably been raised again at the expiry of the lease in Martinmas 1906. Landlords have a nasty habit of doing this. The Claimant would have been in a much stronger position if he had owned the property. In my opinion, the Goodwill of this business is of comparatively little value.

Magistrates have for some time had in view the reduction of licenses, and might possibly have done away with this one.

In Glasgow at the present time they are considering the reduction of licenses in a certain district. This shows the precariousness of licenses.

Again, many publicans insure their licenses with an Insurance Company of this kind. In a recent case, where a publican lost his license, which was insured, the Insurance Company denied liability without giving any reason for so doing. After charging all expenses as detailed, the Net Profits would be :—

						£	s	d
Year 1899-1900	..	..	..	..	..	815	8	8
,, 1900-1901	..	..	..	..	..	131	7	4
,, 1901-1902	..	..	..	..	..	746	0	3

Or an average Profit of £797 12s. 1d.

In regard to the amount of Compensation, I am of opinion that three years' purchase of the Net Profits would be ample :—

				£	s	d
That would amount to	..	..	..	2,392	16	3
To which add Loss on realisation of Fittings		..	..	200	0	0
Total Compensation	..	..	..	£2,592	16	3

I consider this a fair sum, looking to the fact that only four years of the lease have to run.

In recent cases the Claimant has been awarded about four years' purchase of the net Profits. In the case of *Taylor and the North British Railway Co.* the Claimant was awarded four years' purchase. Then, again, in the case of *Maclennan and the North British Railway Co.* the Claimant was awarded six years' purchase, but he owned the property. This puts a different complexion on the matter.

The main points on which the witnesses differed were as follows :—

(1) *Manager's Salary* (£4 per week), which had been drawn by the publican. It was argued for the Claimant that this should be looked on as drawings to account of Profit, and should not be charged in ascertaining the Net Profit which was to be the basis of compensation. It was argued for the Respondents that this salary could be earned elsewhere, and that it was drawn for work done, as otherwise a paid Manager would have been necessary. It was also argued that, had the Profits only been sufficient to meet this salary, no compensation in respect of Profit would have been payable.

(2) *Interest on Capital.*—The Claimant's witness held that this was not a proper charge in ascertaining Profits in a case of this kind. On the side of the Respondents it was argued that such Interest must be charged before arriving at the Profit.

Other points which were discussed were, how far should the expiry of the lease in four years affect the compensation, the falling off in the Profits, the defective system of bookkeeping, and whether this should tell against the Claimant. Many other points were brought out on which there is usually difference of opinion.

ARBITER'S AWARD.

The Claimant claims the sum of £10,000 in respect of compulsory removal from licensed premises of which he holds a lease expiring Martinmas 1906. The Respondents have tendered the sum of £3,000.

The Claimant has occupied the premises since 1890, and I am informed that he is now well up in years, which I take to mean that he is rather old to take kindly to a new venture.

It is admitted that he paid £5,000 in 1890 for the lease, and that since then the volume of business, as well as the Profits, have considerably increased. I do not think I am called upon to inquire what value attached to the premises in 1890. The Claimant may have made a good bargain, or he may have made a bad bargain ; that has, to my mind, little to do with the present question, which is, What value now attaches to the lease of the licensed premises which the Claimant, through the action of the Respondents, is forced to give up?

Both parties seem to think that the sum to be awarded under the head of what is called in the claim "Goodwill" should represent so many years' purchase of the Net Profits. The Claimant asks six years' purchase of an average yearly Profit of £1,500, being £9,000 : the Respondents say that three years' purchase of an average annual Profit of £797, being £2,391, would be ample.

The Accountant for the Respondents stated that the Claimant's bookkeeping was faulty, and that the rent of the premises was too high. Provided the Profits be correctly stated, the mode of bookkeeping adopted is of no moment, and if the rent had been smaller the Profits would have been larger, which would have been better for the Claimant.

Subject to what I have to say as to the average Profits brought out by the Claimant and Respondents respectively, I adopt the Profit and Loss statement submitted for the Claimant.

The Claimant states his average annual Profit at £1,518; the Respondents state it at only £798, being a difference of £720. To the extent of £170 this difference arises from the different modes adopted in arriving at the *gross* Profits. In bringing out the Gross Profits the Claimant deals with what I must hold to be actual figures, notwithstanding all that was said at the proof on behalf of the Respondents : the Respondents, on the other hand, assume 33⅓ per cent. of the Drawings to have been the Gross Profit. I prefer the Claimant's mode of arriving at the Gross Profits.

The remaining £550 of the difference arises from the Respondents charging against Profits interest on Capital and £4 per week which the Claimant paid to himself in name of wages.

I agree with the Respondents that interest on Capital and all expenses of management ought to be deducted before arriving at Net Profits. That is, I think, necessary when dealing with a Claim like the present, just as I think it would be necessary in dealing with a case of Goodwill pure and simple.

Suppose in the present case the business—notwithstanding its being well organised and managed—had only paid expenses and 4 or 5 per cent. on the Capital employed, no one, I think, would have said that there was any marketable Goodwill attaching to the business. I hold that it is only the *excess* earned, beyond fair interest on the Capital employed, that ought to count in any question as to the value of Goodwill.

In the case of a sale of the Business and Goodwill of a firm to, say, a limited liability company, it is a convenient and suitable mode of valuing the Goodwill to take it as worth so many years' purchase of the Net Profits. But I do not think the present case is one of Goodwill at all; it is simply a case for determining the Compensation to be paid to the Claimant for having his lease cut short by nearly four years. But I think it was quite essential to find out what Profit the Claimant had been deriving from his business, and therefore the evidence led on that point was very necessary.

The really important point to keep in view is, that the Claimant is to be deprived of a business from which he could confidently count on getting, not only fair interest on his Capital, but also something like £900 to £1,000 a-year of clear Profit during the next three or four years.

The Claimant was no doubt liable to be turned out of the premises without Compensation at the expiry of his lease; but the chances are that if the Respondents had not appeared he would have got a renewal. The Respondents might have acquired the premises under burden of the lease, and by waiting till 1906 could have entered free, but by that time the Claimant would have pocketed between three and four years' Profits.

It has also, however, to be kept in view that the Claimant is free to carry on his business elsewhere if he can secure licensed premises; and as he is in the position of a license holder who has been ejected from his premises under the powers conferred by an Act of Parliament, the licensing authorities would no doubt look favourably on any application he might make for leave to carry on business in new premises, especially as he has always conducted his business creditably. As, however, the Claimant is up in years, he may not care to start on a new venture : in that case he may be able to arrange a transfer of the license to another name, and receive a valuable consideration for the transfer.

Taking all the circumstances into account, I think a sum of £3,500 would be suitable Compensation to allow under this head of the Claim.

As regards the other two items of Claim, in respect of compulsory realisation of Stock, Fittings, and Utensils, I should have liked to have seen an Inventory and Valuation of the Stock, &c. A publican's Stock ought to be comparatively easy to realise at prices not much below cost; but the fittings and utensils would probably not yield much.

It was stated at the proof that the total sum realised for the Stock, Fittings, and Utensils, which were sold last week, was £1,700. I think if I allow £500 in place of the two sums of £500 claimed I will be doing substantial justice to the Claimant.

My award, which I shall write out in due course, will, therefore, be for a lump sum of £4,000. As this is more than the Respondents tendered, they must pay the whole expenses of the Arbitration.

U

In order to add to the completeness of this chapter, the author has been in communication with the Honorary Secretaries of the various Chartered Accountants Students' Societies, and through the courtesy of them and of their respective Committees, he is enabled to reproduce various *pro formâ* accounts which have engaged the attention of their respective Societies at meetings specially convened to instruct students in the science of criticising accounts. The *pro formâ* Balance Sheets, &c., appended have in all cases been carefully compiled, with a view to illustrating certain specific weak points which call for careful attention upon the part of critics. It is thought, therefore, that their careful study will be found instructive to those who may desire to follow the subject further. It may, however, be added that the only real basis upon which accounts may be usefully criticised is a complete audit, and that therefore those who may desire to go into the subject fully must of necessity master the subject of Auditing in all its manifold aspects.

THE LEEDS AND DISTRICT

Chartered Accountants Students' Association.

HIDES, LIMITED

(A Company registered without Articles of Association).

Directors:

H. GASKELL BLACKBURN (Chairman),

J. DAVIS,

C. A. WOOLSTONE.

Secretary: Auditor:

F. CLEMONS.   J. W. BURRELL.

DIRECTORS' REPORT,

To be submitted to the first Annual Meeting of Shareholders, to be held at the Board Room, Albion Place, Leeds, on Thursday, the 3rd day of March 1898.   The Directors have pleasure in presenting the Accounts of the Company to the Shareholders.

Full and satisfactory explanations of the Accounts and position of the Company will be given at the Meeting, which the Directors hope will be well attended.

Mr. C. A. Woolstone is the retiring Director and offers himself for re-election.

The Auditor, Mr. Burrell, also retires and offers himself for re-election.

H. GASKELL BLACKBURN .
Chairman.

U 2

THE LEEDS AND DISTRICT CHARTERED ACCOUNTANTS STUDENTS' ASSOCIATION.

HIDES, LIMITED.

BALANCE SHEET, December 31st 1897.

Capital and Liabilities.	£ s d	£ s d	Property and Assets		£ s d
To Nominal Capital —			By Plant, Machinery, Fixtures, and Tools, &c.,		
20,000 Shares of £5	100,000 0 0		at Cost		14,982 15 11
			„ Goodwill		11,231 4 7
„ Capital Account—			„ Stock-in-Trade		36,589 17 6
"A" 10,000 Ordinary Shares, £2 10s. paid	25,000 0 0		„ Sundry Debtors		8,756 5 3
"B" 10,000 Ordinary Shares, £5 paid	50,000 0 0		„ Preliminary Expenses		73 4 0
	75,000 0 0		„ Bills Receivable		422 10 6
Less Calls in arrear	30 0 0		„ Cash in Bank on Current Account	£8,221 4 8	
	74,970 0 0		Less Cheques not presented ..	301 4 8	
Less Forfeited Shares.. ..	270 0 0				7,920 0 0
		74,700 0 0	„ Cash and Bills in hand		855 12 11
„ Loan on Debenture Bonds, 4 per cent...		10,000 0 0	„ Cash in Bank on Deposit Account		5,000 0 0
„ Loan by Directors		5,000 0 0	„ Mr. Burrell, Auditor, in respect of future charges ..		300 0 0
„ Sundry Creditors		1,000 0 0	„ Deposit on Purchase of B. Ankrupt & Co.'s Tannery		4,700 0 0
„ Bills Payable		448 10 8			
„ Directors' Fees		1,000 0 0			
„ Reserve Fund		2,000 0 0			
„ Balance of Profit and Loss Account		289 0 0			
		£94,437 10 8			£94,437 10 8

PROFIT AND LOSS ACCOUNT for the Year ending December 31st 1897.

	£ s d	£ s d		£ s d	£ s d
To Stock-in-Trade, January 1st, 1897 ..		28,621 8 4	By Sales	80,091 12 4	
„ Purchases	48,234 1 7		Less Discount	1,902 10 2	
Less Discount	1,963 1 6				78,189 2 2
		46,271 0 1	„ Sale of Old Machines, &c.		509 11 3
„ Wages and Salaries		25,211 3 3	„ Stock-in-Trade, December 31st 1897		36,080 6 3
„ Balance, Gross Profit		15,175 8 0	„ Rent		500 0 0
		£115,278 19 8			£115,278 19 8
To Commission		8,231 3 1	By Gross Profit		15,175 8 0
„ Carriage and Freight		416 0 10	„ Transfer Fees		14 2 6
„ Rent		500 0 0			
„ Rates, Taxes, and Insurance		478 0 2			
„ Maintenance and Repairs		256 15 2			
„ Rope, Paper and Stationery		109 2 6			
„ Coal and Oil, &c.		165 10 9			
„ Bad Debts		525 1 7			
„ Depreciation of Machinery		496 16 5			
„ Interest and Bank Charges	1,924 4 3				
„ General Expenses, Auditor's Fee, Postages, and Petty Cash, &c.	204 11 8				
„ Interest on Debentures	400 0 0				
„ Balance carried to Balance Sheet ..	1,682 4 1				
„ Profit carried down..		4,211 0 0			
		£15,189 10 6			£15,189 10 6
June 30th. To Interim Dividend—			By Balance Profit		4,211 0 0
Ordinary Shares "A" £2 10s. od. paid 6 per cent. per annum ..	1,500 0 0		„ Loss on Year's Working		289 0 0
Ordinary Shares "B" £5 paid 6 per cent. per annum.. ..	3,000 0 0				
		4,500 0 0			
		£4,500 0 0			£4,500 0 0

MANCHESTER CHARTERED ACCOUNTANTS STUDENTS' SOCIETY.

THE HOLDFAST IRONWORKS COMPANY LIMITED.

Holdfast, near Barrow-in-Furness.

(A Company Registered without Articles of Association.)

Directors :

THOS. PLUMPTON, *Chairman.*　　C. H. WILLIAMS.
A. S. BREWIS.　　W. C. BARRETT, Junr.
S. LORD.　　ROGER N. CARTER.

Solicitors :
TAXED COSTS & CO.

Auditors :
GREGORY BLUNDERITT.　|　FRITZ CATCHEM.

Bankers :
WILDE THYME BANK, LIMITED.

Secretary :
CHARLES JORDAN.

Registered Offices :—STANDARD CHAMBERS, 65 KING STREET, MANCHESTER.

REPORT OF THE DIRECTORS.

To be submitted to the Eighth Annual Meeting of Shareholders.

Your Directors, in submitting herewith the Annual Balance Sheet, &c., at 30th June 1897, regret to report a loss of £12,346 2s. 9d., which increases the adverse balance to £18,331 0s. 2d. Under the circumstances, they advise that the Company be wound up voluntarily, and, at the Extraordinary Meeting to be held at the conclusion of the Annual Meeting, a resolution to that effect will be proposed.

The amount of £29,521 18s. 11d. added to Capital during the year includes all Renewals, but ordinary Repairs have been charged to Revenue. The amount of £10,467 3s. 5d. includes interest on the Debentures raised—to re-instate the Mine after the inburst of water—from the date of the receipt of the money up to the time when the damage was repaired, and this your Directors consider a proper charge to Capital.

T. PLUMPTON, Chairman.

MANCHESTER CHARTERED ACCOUNTANTS STUDENTS' SOCIETY.

THE HOLDFAST IRONWORKS COMPANY LIMITED.

Dr.   TRADING ACCOUNT for Year ending 30th June 1897.   Cr.

	£ s d	£ s d		£ s d	£ s d
To Purchases	408,619 5 3		By Sales	725,915 18 3	
„ Wages	250,397 14 11		Less Stock at 30th June 1896 ..	65,382 7 1	
„ Discounts, Allowances, &c. ..	30,451 8 4			660,533 11 2	
„ Balance carried to Profit and Loss		689,468 8 6	Add Stock at 30th June 1897 ..	70,241 9 5	
Account, being Gross Profit ..	..	41,306 12 1			730,775 0 7
		£730,770 5 7			£730,775 0 7

PROFIT AND LOSS ACCOUNT.

	£ s d	£ s d		£ s d
To Royalties	9,022 6 11		By Gross Profit, as per Trading Account	41,306 12 1
„ Carriage, Freight, &c... ..	5,114 3 2		„ Cottage Rents	227 14 11
„ Repairs, &c..	7,465 11 11		„ Interest on Unpaid Calls	45 19 3
„ Salaries, &c.	4,821 12 6		„ Suspense Account	269 7 10
„ Directors and Auditors ..	4,120 5 6		„ Loss during the Year	12,346 2 9
„ Travelling Expenses	2,610 7 2			
„ Rents, Rates, and Taxes ..	1,570 8 3			
„ Horses, Wagons, &c.	1,005 14 2			
„ Provision for Bad Debts ..	6,285 16 7			
„ Sundry Trade Expenses ..	4,026 7 5	46,042 13 7		
„ Interest on Debentures	4,500 0 0			
„ Provision for Income Tax ..	500 0 0			
„ Interest on Calls paid in advance ..	4 7 6			
„ Bank Interest	3,148 15 9	8,153 3 3		
		£54,195 16 10		£54,195 16 10

BALANCE SHEET, at 30th June 1897.

CAPITAL AND LIABILITIES.	£ s d	£ s d	£ s d	PROPERTY AND ASSETS.	£ s d	£ s d	£ s d
Nominal Capital—				Land, Buildings, Mines, Furnaces,			
20,000 Shares at £50 each ..	1,000,000 0 0			Mills, Machinery, Cottages, &c., on			
				30th June 1896	568,092 19 9		
Shares Issued—				Add Additions during the Year ..	29,521 18 11		
20,000 Shares at £35 called ..	700,000 0 0			„ Cost arising through Inburst			
Less 1,000 Shares forfeited £35,000				of Water	10,467 3 5		
Deduct Calls paid thereon 5,000						608,082 2 1	
	30,000			Stocks on hand, 30th June 1897 ..	..	70,141 9 5	
Less Calls in Arrear 2,500				Goodwill	..	40 000 0 0	
	27,500 0 0			Formation Expenses	..	1,6 0 0 0	
	672,500 0 0			Sundry Debtors—			
Add Calls paid in Advance	100 0 0			On Open Accounts	85,425 7 3		
		672,600 0 0		„ Bills Receivable	40,291 6 4		
Debentures—					125,716 13 7		
1st Issue at 5 per cent.	50,000 0 0			Less Provision for Bad Debts ..	6,285 16 7		
2nd „ at 6	50,000 0 0					119,430 17 0	
	100,000 0 0			Royalties paid in Advance	..	5,640 18 6	
Bank Overdraft	80,000 0 0			Loss arising through late Secretary's			
Less 2nd Issue Debentures ..	50,000 0 0			Defalcation, with Interest added ..	..	2,811 15 1	
	30,000 0 0			Profit and Loss Account—			
Sundry Creditors—				Loss at 30th June 1896	5,984 17 5		
On Open Accounts	40,564 2 1			„ this Year	12,346 2 9		
„ Bills Payable	20,725 9 6					18,331 0 2	
„ Provision for Income Tax ..	500 0 0			Cash in hand	..	35 14 1	
„ „ Wages, Rent, Taxes,							
&c.	1,784 4 9						
		63,573 16 4					
		£866,173 16 4				£866,173 16 4	

Audited and found correct, subject to Report.

G. BLUNDERITT.
FRITZ CATCHEM.

CHARTERED ACCOUNTANTS STUDENTS' SOCIETY OF LONDON.

THE FAIRWEATHER ENGINEERING COMPANY, LIMITED.

(Table " A " was adopted instead of drawing up special Articles of Association.)

Directors.

HORATIO BLUFFE, Esq., *Chairman* (HERBERT LANHAM).
DAVID QUERY, Esq. (SYDNEY G. COLE).
F. G. GINNY-PIGGE, Esq. (JAMES SAWERS).

Solicitor.	*Auditor.*
FOLEY O. DEED, Esq. (R. F. W. FINCHAM).	A. B. TICKEM, Esq. (E. C. PEGLER).
Secretary.	*Bankers.*
JAMES ROUTINE (G. P. CARTER).	BULLION & CO., LIMITED.

Registered Offices.

FAIRWEATHER, BLANKSHIRE.

REPORT OF DIRECTORS

To be submitted to First Annual General Meeting.

GENTLEMEN,—

Your Directors regret to have to report that the results of the Company's operations for the first year have been far from satisfactory. The great depression in trade, combined with the high prices of raw material, more especially coal and iron, have been the principal causes of this unlooked-for result. Further, we have been greatly hampered by the fact that the Cash Working Capital provided by the first issue of Shares has proved totally inadequate. However, your Directors feel confident that a far better result will be shown in the current year, provided that Shareholders will subscribe for more Preference Shares—it being the intention of the Board to issue 20,000 of these at once—and thus provide sufficient cash to enable us to complete the orders we have in hand, and enable us to buy on more favourable terms. The Company has a splendid stock of raw material on hand, and orders are coming in well; the price of coal is dropping daily, and everything points to a prosperous future. Your Directors therefore confidently recommend the Preference Shares as a sound investment, and it only remains for the Shareholders to subscribe liberally to the issue. full particulars of which will be sent you shortly.

The Auditor, Mr. A. B. TICKEM, retires, but offers himself for re-election.

HORATIO BLUFFE, *Chairman.*

MEMORANDA.

Extracts from original Prospectus :—

(1) All expenses incidental to the formation and registration of the Company, up to and including allotment, will be paid by the Vendor.

(2) The business will be taken over as a going concern as and from January 1st 1899.

The Company was registered on March 31st 1899, and went on allotment on April 21st 1899.

Table " A " was adopted, instead of drawing up special Articles of Association.

CHARTERED ACCOUNTANTS STUDENTS' SOCIETY OF LONDON.

THE FAIRWEATHER ENGINEERING COMPANY, LIMITED.

BALANCE SHEET, 31st December 1899.

Liabilities.	£ s d	£ s d	Assets.	£ s d	£ s d
To Share Capital—			By Sundry Debtors—		
Nominal—			Trade Loans and Calls	24,630 1 6	
150,000 Shares (Ordinary) of £1 each	150,000 0 0		Bills Receivable	4,010 0 0	
100,000 Shares (Preference) of £1 each	100,000 0 0				28,640 1 6
		£250,000 0 0	„ Suspense Account		856 4 8
			„ Cash at Bank	240 8 6	
			„ „ in hand	724 9 8	
Issued—					964 18 2
80,000 Ordinary Shares of £1 each (fully called up)	80,000 0 0		„ Leasehold Premises		20,000 0 0
40,000 Preference Shares (5%) of £1 each (fully called up).. ..	40,000 0 0		„ Plants and Machinery		12,480 3 6
		120,000 0 0	„ Stock, &c.—		
			Work in progress	8,100 5 2	
„ Sundry Creditors—			Completed Work in Store ..	18,021 0 4	
Trade	6,000 6 3		Stores and Materials	14,981 1 2	
Rent and Sundries	375 0 0		Stationery, &c.	500 1 4	
		6,375 6 3			41,602 8 0
			„ Investments at par		5,000 0 0
„ Loan at 5%, secured on Lease ..		500 0 0	„ Goodwill and Patent Rights, &c. ..		13,728 0 0
			„ Preliminary Expenses		642 8 3
			„ Profit and Loss Account		2,961 2 2
		£126,875 6 3			£126,875 6 3

I have examined the above Balance Sheet with the Books and Vouchers of the Company and certify them to be in accordance therewith. No Depreciation has been written off Leaseholds, Plants, and Machinery, and the correctness of the Balance Sheet is subject to this, and the value of the Investments being as stated above.

A. B. TICKEM, *Auditor.*

February 23rd 1900.

PROFIT AND LOSS ACCOUNT for the Year ended December 31st 1899.

	£ s d	£ s d		£ s d	£ s d
To Wages and Materials on Jobs completed	32,932 4 7		By Sales—		
„ Royalties	1,704 6 8		General	39,000 6 4	
„ Gross Profit	9,863 15 1		Patent Rights	5,000 0 0	
					44,000 6 4
			„ Profit on Uncompleted Contracts (Proportion)		500 0 0
		£44,500 6 4			£44,500 6 4
To Rent, Taxes, Gas, Accident Claims, &c.	2,906 1 1		By Gross Profit		9,863 15 1
„ Directors' and Auditors' Fees, Bad Debts and Salary of Managing Director, &c. ..	3,001 6 8		„ Balance, being Net Loss		1,961 2 2
„ Office Salaries and Expenses, Travellers', Postages and General Expenses, &c.	3,666 0 9				
„ Repairs	100 0 0				
„ Allowances off Sales..	1,964 2 1				
„ Bank Charges..	147 6 8				
„ Donation to War Fund .. .. '.. .. ,	100 0 0				
		£11,824 17 3			£11,824 17 3
To Balance, Net Loss	1,961 2 2				
Add Preference Dividend paid for the six months to June 30th	1,000 0 0				
		£2,961 2 2			

CHARTERED ACCOUNTANTS STUDENTS' SOCIETY OF LONDON.

THE FAIRWEATHER ENGINEERING COMPANY, LIMITED.

BALANCE SHEET, December 31st 1899.

Liabilities	£ s d	Revaluations, &c., made by Committee of Investigation £ s d	Assets	£ s d	Revaluations, &c., made by Committee of Investigation £ s d
To Share Capital—			By Sundry Debtors—		
Nominal—			Trade, Loans, and Calls	24,630 1 6	24,630 1 6
150,000 Shares (Ordinary) of £1 each	150,000 0 0		Bills Receivable	4,010 0 0	4,010 0 0
100,000 „ (Preference) „ „	100,000 0 0		„ Suspense Account	856 4 8	
	£250,000 0 0		„ Cash at Bank	240 8 6	240 8 6
			„ „ in Hand	724 9 8	724 9 8
Issued—			„ Leasehold Premises	20,000 0 0	19,500 0 0
80,000 Ordinary Shares of £1 each			„ Plant and Machinery	12,480 3 6	12,180 0 0
(fully called up)	80,000 0 0	80,000 0 0	„ Stocks, &c.—		
40,000 Preference Shares (5%) of £1			Work in Progress	8,100 5 2	8,100 5 2
each fully called up	40,000 0 0	40,000 0 0	Completed Work in Store ..	18,021 0 4	17,001 0 0
„ Sundry Creditors—			Stores and Materials	14,981 1 2	13,860 0 0
Trade	6,000 6 3	6,000 6 3	Stationery, &c.	500 1 4	400 0 0
Rent and Sundries	375 0 0	375 0 0	„ Investments at par	5,000 0 0	5,000 0 0
„ Loan @ 5% secured on Lease	500 0 0	500 0 0	„ Goodwill and Patent Rights, &c. ..	13,728 0 0	9,728 0 0
„ Reserve for Bad Debts	..	1,000 0 0	„ Preliminary Expenses	642 8 3	642 8 3
„ Reserve for Depreciation of Invest-			„ Profit and Loss Account	2,961 2 2	14,358 13 2
ments	..	2,500 0 0			
	£126,875 6 3	£130,375 6 3		£126,875 6 3	£130,375 6 3

I have examined the above Balance Sheet with the Books and Vouchers of the Company and certify them to be in accordance therewith. No Depreciation has been written off Leaseholds, Plant, and Machinery, and the correctness of the Balance Sheet is subject to this, and the value of the Investments being as stated above.

February 23rd 1900.

A. B. TICKEM,
Auditor.

PROFIT AND LOSS ACCOUNT for the Year ended December 31st 1899.

	£ s d	£ s d		£ s d	£ s d
To Wages and Materials on Jobs completed	32,932 4 7	32,932 4 7	By Sales—		
„ Royalties	1,704 6 8	1,704 6 8	General	39,000 6 4	37,036 4 3
„ Gross Profit	9,863 15 1	758 11 6	Patent Rights	5,000 0 0	
„ Amount written off Stock of Materials	..	1,121 1 2	„ Profits on Uncompleted Contracts		
„ Amount written off Completed Stock ..	..	1,020 0 4	(proportion)	500 0 0	500 0 0
	£44,500 6 4	£37,536 4 3		£44,500 6 4	£37,536 4 3
To Rent, Taxes, Gas, Accident Claims, &c.	2,906 1 1	2,906 1 1	By Gross Profit	9,863 15 1	758 11 6
„ Directors' and Auditors' Fees, Bad			„ Balance, being Net Loss	1,961 2 2	13,358 13 2
Debts, and Salary of Managing			„ Sale of Patent Rights (*less* £4,000,		
Director, &c.	3,001 6 8	4,001 6 8	cost of same estimated)	..	1,000 0 0
„ Office Salaries, and Expenses,					
Travellers', Postages, and General					
Expenses, &c.	3,606 0 9	3,706 2 1			
„ Repairs	100 0 0	100 0 0			
„ Allowances off Sales	1,964 2 1	..			
„ Bank Charges	147 6 8	147 6 8			
„ Donation to War Fund	100 0 0	100 0 0			
„ Suspense Account written off	..	856 4 8			
„ Depreciation off Lease	..	500 0 0			
„ „ „ Plant	..	300 3 6			
„ „ „ Investments	..	2,500 0 0			
	£11,824 17 3	£15,117 4 8		£11,824 17 3	£15,117 4 8
To Balance, Net Loss	1,961 2 2	13,358 13 2			
Add, Preference Dividend paid for					
the six months to June 30th ..	1,000 0 0	1,000 0 0			
	£2,961 2 2	£14,358 13 2			

THE CHARTERED ACCOUNTANTS STUDENTS' SOCIETY OF KINGSTON-UPON-HULL.

THE PHASTANLUCE ENGINEERING COMPANY, LIMITED,

PHASTANLUCE near GOOLE.

(A Company Registered without Articles of Association.)

Directors.
W. R. LOCKING, *Chairman.*
J. A. CARLILL.   W. SMAILES.

Solicitor.   *Auditor.*
J. J. T. FERENS.   PASS BARNEYS.

Bankers.
THE DOGGER BANK, LIMITED.

Secretary.
W. P. VICKERMAN.

Registered Offices—BOWLALLEY LANE, HULL.

REPORT OF THE DIRECTORS.

To be submitted to the Second Annual Meeting of Shareholders.

In submitting herewith the Balance Sheet and Relative Accounts as at 30th September last, your Directors desire to point out that, as anticipated when estimating the ensuing year's operations at the last General Meeting, the consistent advance in the prices of labour and material have had the effect of minimising to a considerable extent the profit on finished contracts which would otherwise have been realised. This advance in material still continues but will be in part compensated for during the coming year by the increased prices obtainable for every description of the Company's output.

An interim dividend of 5s. per share on the ordinary shares was distributed in March last, and the Board regrets that the available Balance of Profit as shown by the accompanying statements will not suffice after paying the Preference dividend to increase the dividend on the ordinary shares beyond the 5s. already received by the Shareholders. This 5s. was not distributed in cash, but was credited to the Capital Account in satisfaction of calls then due.

The Board recommend the declaration of a dividend of 6 per cent. on the Preference Shares and of 5s. per share on the Ordinary Shares, the latter to take effect as from March last.

Considerable Capital Expenditure has been incurred during the twelve months with the result of improving the Company's Assets in every way, and the Directors congratulate the Members of the Company on the splendid property they now possess and the complete efficiency of every department of the works.

The prospects for the ensuing year are very good but it must be inadvisable to give further detail here of the orders in hand on account of the keen rivalry of similar establishments and the necessity for secrecy.

Mr. J. A. CARLILL retires from the Board, but is eligible and offers himself for re-election.

Mr. PASS BARNEYS, the auditor, retires from office and does *not* offer himself for re-election on account of great pressure of professional work, which will cause prolonged absence abroad.

W. R. LOCKING,
Chairman.

CHARTERED ACCOUNTANTS STUDENTS' SOCIETY OF KINGSTON-UPON-HULL.

THE PHASTANLUCE ENGINEERING COMPANY, LIMITED.

Dr. TRADING ACCOUNT for the Twelve Months ended 30th September 1899. *Cr.*

	£ s d	£ s d		£ s d	£ s d
To Purchases 196,780 2 1			By Sales and Work done 438,966 11 3		
Less :			*Less :*		
Stock on hand at 30th Sept. 1899.. 44,603 10 9			Stock on hand at 30th Sept. 1898 21,306 11 4		
	152,176 11 4			417,659 19 11	
Less : Discounts 4,309 2 3		147,867 9 1	*Less :* Discounts 10,518 4 2		407 141 15
„ Wages.. .. .. 190,840 10 4					
„ Balance carried down, being Gross					
Profit for twelve months 68,433 16 4					
		£407,141 15 9			£407.141 15 9

Dr. PROFIT AND LOSS ACCOUNT. *Cr.*

	£ s d		£ s d
To Rents, Rates, and Taxes 3,280 9 4		By Gross Profit brought down 68,433 16 4	
„ Carriage and Freight 5,698 14 8		„ Rents, &c. 460 2 6	
„ Maintenance and Repairs, viz. :—Buildings, &c. .. 460 9 8		„ Interest on Unpaid Calls 175 0 0	
„ Do. do. Machinery and Plant 1,540 3 1			
„ General Expenses, including Stamps and Stationery.. 6,980 8 11			
„ Office Salaries 1.560 6 4			
„ Directors' Fees.. .. .. 5,000 0 0			
„ Audit Fee 5 5 0			
„ Travelling Expenses 1,860 6 9			
„ Stable Expenses 983 15 4			
„ Bank Interest and Charges 1,784 6 5			
„ Interest on Loans and Calls paid in advance 3,980 6 2			
„ Debenture Interest 2,100 0 0			
„ Income Tax 450 0 0			
„ Bad Debts 14,283 14 8			
„ Reserve 10,000 0 0			
„ Balance, being Profit for the Year carried down .. 9,100 12 6			
	£69,068 18 10		£69,068 18 10

	£ s d	£ s d
By Net Profit brought down 9,100 12 6		
„ Balance carried to next Account .. 199 7 6		
		9 300 0 0
Deduct :		
Interim Dividend on Ordinary Shares		
paid in March (5s. per Share) .. 7,500 0 0		
Preference Dividend at 6 per cent... 1,800 0 0		
		9,300 0 0

CHARTERED ACCOUNTANTS STUDENTS' SOCIETY OF KINGSTON-UPON-HULL

THE PHASTANLUCE ENGINEERING COMPANY, LIMITED.

BALANCE SHEET on the 30th September 1899.

Property and Assets.	£	s	d	£	s	d
LAND AND BUILDINGS: including Foundry Machine and Fitting Shops, Furnaces, Boiler Shops, &c.—						
As at 30th September 1898 .. .. 102,809 10 8						
Additions since 25,603 4 9						
Cost of Accident through Works Locomotive over-running Buffer Stops 2,709 11 2						
				131,122	6	7
FIXED PLANT AND MACHINERY, including Works Railway—						
As at 30th September 1898 .. .. 93,706 6 10						
Additions since 8,509 1 11						
				102,215	8	9
LOOSE PLANT AND TOOLS—						
As at 30th September 1898 .. .. 15,980 10 6						
Additions since 3,507 11 2						
				19,488	1	8
PATTERNS, MODELS, AND TEMPLATES—						
As at 30th September 1898 .. .. 4,200 0 0						
Additions since 950 10 2						
				5,150	10	2
PATENTS AND PATENT RIGHTS—						
As at 30th September 1898 .. .. 790 0 0						
Additions since 4,000 0 0						
				4,790	0	0
GOODWILL				30,000	0	0
FORMATION EXPENSES				2,920	0	0
INVESTMENTS IN OTHER COMPANIES, VIZ.—						
The Watho Hæmatite Steel Co., Ltd. 4,200 0 0						
The Goitblynde Boring & Exploration Co., Ltd., and reduced.. .. .. 5,775 0 0						
The Hallatcee Steam Ship Co., Ltd... 6,480 0 0						
The San Sanguinario and Vamoosino Sugar Crushing Co., Ltd., and reduced 7,983 0 0						
The Pretoria (Transvaal) Baths and Washhouses Co., Ltd. 5,562 0 0						
				30,000	0	0
SUNDRY DEBTORS—						
On Open Accounts 62,340 4 11						
Bills Receivable 93,583 4 9						
				155,923	9	8
Stocks on hand				44,603	10	9
Unexpired Values of Rents, Insurances, Rates, &c. ..				(789	10	11
Cash in Secretary's hands				1,990	10	6
				£528,993	9	0

Capital and Liabilities.	£	s	d	£	s	d
CAPITAL—						
AUTHORISED—						
30,000 6 per cent. Preference Shares of £5 each 150,000 0 0						
30,000 Ordinary Shares of £5 each.. 150,000 0 0						
				300,000	0	0
ISSUED—.						
30,000 6 per cent. Preference Shares £5 each fully paid 150,000 0 0						
30,000 Ordinary Shares £5 each. £3 10s. called 105,000 0 0						
				255,000	0	0
Less: 3,000 Shares forfeited 10,500 0 0						
Deduct Cash receiv'd thereon 3,000 0 0						
				7,500 0 0		
Less: Calls in Arrear .. 2,500 0 0				5,000	0	0
				250,000	0	0
Add: Calls paid in Advance.. .. 5,000 0 0						
				255,000	0	0
DEBENTURES—First Issue at 4 per cent. ... 25,000 0 0						
Second Issue at 6 per cent. 30,000 0 0						
				55,000	0	0
LOANS				15,000	0	0
BALANCE AT BANK				21,486	18	9
SUNDRY CREDITORS—						
On Open Accounts 90,600 2 4						
Bills Payable 43,406 7 11						
				134,006	10	3
RESERVE—						
As at 30th September 1898 .. .. 20,000 0 0						
Since added 10,000 0 0						
				30,000	0	0
VENDORS' ACCOUNT at 30th September 1899				18,500	0	0
				£528,993	9	0

MISLED MANSIONS,

LONDON, 5th February 1900.

Audited and left correct,

E. & O. E.

PASS BARNEYS, *Auditor.*

SHEFFIELD CHARTERED ACCOUNTANTS STUDENTS' SOCIETY.

THE RANMOOR COLLIERY COMPANY, LIMITED.

FULLWOOD near TINSLEY.

(A Company Registered without Articles of Association.)

Directors.

H. COOPER, *Chairman.*

J. T. BARR.   P. BEARD.   F. A. EYRE.   A. PLATT.   W. SILVESTER.

Trustee for Debenture Holders.

A. E. MERCER.

Solicitors.

CHEETHAM, FLEECEM & CO.

Auditors.

E. Y. BAUM & CO.

Bankers.

SHALESMOOR BANKING COMPANY, LIMITED.

Secretary.

M. WEBSTER JENKINSON.

Registered Office—HOOLE'S CHAMBERS, BANK STREET, SHEFFIELD.

REPORT OF THE DIRECTORS.

To be submitted to the Eighth Annual Meeting of Shareholders.

Your Directors, in submitting their Eighth Annual Report and Accounts, regret that, notwithstanding the recent high market price of Coal, they have to report a loss on the year's working of £2,846 16s. 8d., which, added to the Debenture Interest (as yet unpaid) and last year's balance, makes a total adverse balance of £29,528 3s. 1d. An amount of £16,100 has been added to Capital during the year. This includes all Renewals except ordinary repairs; also a sum of £8,985 13s. 4d., which was expended in putting the Mine into working order after the disastrous fire in October last, an expense which your Directors consider a proper charge to Capital.

The Company's affairs have been fully considered by your Directors, and they now advise that the Company be wound up voluntarily, and at the Extraordinary Meeting to be held at the conclusion of the Annual Meeting a resolution to that effect will be proposed.

H. COOPER, *Chairman*

SHEFFIELD CHARTERED ACCOUNTANTS STUDENTS' SOCIETY.

THE RANMOOR COLLIERY COMPANY, LIMITED.

Dr.   TRADING ACCOUNT for the Year ending 30th June 1900.   Cr.

1899		£ s d	£ s d	1900		£ s d	£ s d
July 1	To Stock	..	25,000 0 0	June 30	By Sales of Coal, Coke, &c. ..	..	209,021 13 9
1900					„ Wagon Hire Account		
June 30	„ Wages of Colliers, Top and				Surplus	..	600 0 10
	Bottom Daymen, Coke				„ Stock of Coal, Coke,		
	Burners, &c.	..	130,982 9 9		Material and Stores, &c.	..	12,000 0 0
	„ Coal Rents	..	14,854 10 2				
	„ Material, Stores. &c.	..	31,412 12 3				
	„ Gross Profit carried down ..	..	19,362 2 5				
			£221,621 14 7				£221,621 14 7
	To Salaries	9,760 9 8					
	„ Do. (Special)	20 0 0					
	„ Rates and Taxes	2,754 2 4					
	„ Accident Claims	1,340 10 3		By Gross Profit	..	19,362 2 5
	„ Travelling Expenses	967 6 5			„ Profit and Loss Account:		
	„ Manager's Commission ..	1,150 0 0			Loss for the year ..	..	2,846 16 8
	„ Insurance	534 3 7					
	„ Electric Light	673 4 11					
	„ Discounts, Allowances, &c...	289 7 7					
	„ Bank Charges	736 8 1					
	„ General Charges, Postage,						
	Stationery, Luncheons, Pit						
	Clothes, &c., less Cottage						
	Rents	1,018 6 3					
			19,248 19 1				
	„ Directors' and Auditor's Fees	2,460 0 0					
	„ Special Donations	500 0 0					
			2,960 0 0				
			£22,20· 19 1				£22,208 19 1

THE RANMOOR COLLIERY COMPANY, LIMITED.

Dr.   PROFIT AND LOSS ACCOUNT, 30th June 1900.   Cr.

1899		£ s d	1900		£ s d
July 1	To Balance	24,181 6 5	June 30	By Balance forward	29,528 3 1
1900					
June 30	„ Further Loss to date	2,846 16 8			
„	„ Debenture Interest	2,500 0 0			
		£29,528 3 1			£29,528 3 1
	To Balance	29,528 3 1			

SHEFFIELD CHARTERED ACCOUNTANTS STUDENTS' SOCIETY.

CAPITAL ACCOUNT.

	Expenditure to 30th June 1899	Expended this year	Total to 30th June 1900		Receipts to 30th June 1899	Received this year	Total to 30th June 1900
	£ s d	£ s d	£ s d		£ s d	£ s d	£ s d
To Freehold Land ..	30,000 0 0	..	30,000 0 0	By Ordinary Shares ..	250,000 0 0	..	250,000 0 0
„ Sinking Shaft and Opening-up Pit ..	285,000 0 0	10,000 0 0	295,000 0 0	„ Preference Shares ..	125,000 0 0	..	125,000 0 0
„ Plant and Machinery	63,000 0 0	5,000 0 0	68,000 0 0	„ Debenture Stock ..	50,000 0 0	..	50,000 0 0
„ Wagons	7,000 0 0	1,000 0 0	8,000 0 0				
„ Office Buildings, Cottages, &c. ..	2,500 0 0	100 0 0	2,600 0 0				
£	387,500 0 0	16,100 0 0	403,600 0 0				
„ Balance	..	..	21,400 0 0				
£			425,000 0 0				£425,000 0 0
				By Balance	..	..	21,400 0 0

BALANCE SHEET, 30th June 1900.

Liabilities.	£ s d	£ s d	Assets.	£ s d	£ s d
To Capital Account, balance	..	21,400 0 0	By Coal Rents Overpaid	..	29,624 3 11
„ Loans	..	10,970 3 6	„ Stock, viz. :—		
„ Debenture Interest	..	2,500 0 0	Coal and Coke	170 0 0	
			Materials, Stores, &c.	11,830 0 0	12,000 0 0
„ Sundry Creditors, viz. :—			„ Book Debts	..	12,681 11 4
Open Accounts, including Bills payable	23,759 8 10		„ Preliminary Expenses	..	1,800 0 0
Coal Rents and Royalties ..	16,622 16 11		„ Suspense Account, Amount of late Cashier's defalcations ..	..	2,600 0 0
Bank Overdraft	10,000 0 0	50,382 5 9	„ Cash in hand	..	18 10 11
„ Provision Account, viz. :—			„ Profit and Loss Account	..	29,528 3 1
Sundries	2,000 0 0				
Bad Debts	1,000 0 0	3,000 0 0			
		£88,252 9 3			£88,252 9 3

We have examined the above Balance Sheet with the Accounts and Vouchers relating thereto, and are of opinion that it is full and fair, and that it is properly drawn up so as to show a true and correct view of the state of the Company's affairs.

E. Y. BAUM & Co., *Auditors.*

MANCHESTER AND LIVERPOOL CHARTERED ACCOUNTANTS STUDENTS' SOCIETIES (JOINT MEETING).

THE WESSEX ENGINEERING COMPANY, LIMITED.

Incorporated 31st August 1897.

Directors.

Mr. R. N. CARTER, Manchester, *Chairman.*   Mr. A. F. DODD, Liverpool, *Deputy-Chairman.*

Mr. JOS. BELL, Junr., Manchester.   Mr. H. W. BOWLER, Liverpool.   Mr. H. L. RAWLINGS, Liverpool.

Mr. W. R. SHARP, Manchester.   Mr. S. S. DAWSON, Liverpool, *Managing Director.*

Secretary.

Mr. S. W. REDFEARN, Manchester.

REPORT OF THE DIRECTORS.

To be submitted to the Fourth Ordinary General Meeting of Shareholders.

Your Directors have pleasure in presenting the Accounts for the past year, which show an available profit (after payment of interest on Debentures and Interim Dividends on Ordinary and Preference Shares) of ..   .. £64,000 0 0 which they propose should be disposed of as follows:—

To Reserve Fund .. ..,	£10,000 0 0
Half-year's Dividend on Preference Shares	25,000 0 0
Final Dividend at the rate of 5 per cent. per annum on Ordinary Shares, making	
5 per cent. for the year	25,000 0 0
	60,000 0 0
Leaving a balance to carry forward of	£4,000 0 0

ROGER N. CARTER, *Chairman.*

MANCHESTER AND LIVERPOOL CHARTERED ACCOUNTANTS STUDENTS' SOCIETIES.

THE WESSEX ENGINEERING COMPANY, LIMITED.

TRADING AND PROFIT AND LOSS ACCOUNT for the Year ended 31st August 1900.

	£ s d	£ s d		£ s d	£ s d
To Purchases of Pig Iron, &c., net ..	550,000 0 0		By Sales	900,000 0 0	
Add Stock, 31st August 1899 ..	50,000 0 0		*Add* Stock of Finished Goods, at 31st August 1900	30,000 0 0	
	600,000 0 0			930,000 0 0	
Less Stock, 31st August 1900 ..	60,000 0 0		*Less* Stock of Finished Goods, at 31st August 1899	20,000 0 0	
		540,000 0 0			910,000 0 0
„ Wages..		160,000 0 0			
„ Carriage of Raw Materials		1,000 0 0			
„ Provision for Repairs, Renewals, and Depreciation of Machinery		50,000 0 0			
„ Royalties		1,000 0 0			
„ Balance, Manufacturing Profit		158,000 0 0			
		£910,000 0 0			£910,000 0 0

	£ s d	£ s d		£ s d
To Sundry Expenses	2,000 0 0		By Balance, Manufacturing Profit	158,000 0 0
Add Sundry Stock, 31st August 1899	500 0 0			
	£2,500 0 0			
Less Sundry Stock, 31st August 1900	1,500 0 0			
		1,000 0 0		
„ Travelling Expenses, Office Rent, Salaries, Audit Fees, &c. ..		12,500 0 0		
„ Workmen's Compensation Account, Amount set aside		300 0 0		
„ Amount paid to date in respect of Loss by Explosion		1,000 0 0		
„ Discount on Sales		20,000 0 0		
„ Bad Debts and Reserve for Doubtful Debts		700 0 0		
„ Interest on Debentures		2,500 0 0		
„ Managing Director's Commission on Net Profit at 5 per cent.		6,000 0 0		
„ Balance Profit	120,000 0 0			
Less Managing Director's Commission	6,000 0 0			
		114,000 0 0		
		£158,000 0 0		£158,000 0 0

MANCHESTER AND LIVERPOOL CHARTERED ACCOUNTANTS STUDENTS' SOCIETIES.

THE WESSEX ENGINEERING COMPANY, LIMITED.

BALANCE SHEET at 31st August 1900.

Capital and Liabilities.	£ s d	£ s d	Property and Assets	£ s d	£ s d
Nominal Capital—			Mining Concession, Land, and Buildings, at Cost ..		1,000,000 0 0
100,000 Ordinary Shares of £10 each ..	1,000,000 0 0		Goodwill		280,000 0 0
100,000 Five per cent. Preference Shares of £10 each	1,000,000 0 0		Machinery and Plant as at 31st August 1899	500,000 0 0	
		£2,000,000 0 0	*Add* repairs and renewals during the year	50,000 0 0	
Subscribed Capital—				550,000 0 0	
50,000 Ordinary A Shares of £10 each, fully paid	500,000 0 0		*Less* sale of old steam power fittings (cost £25,000)	10,000 0 0	
50,000 Ordinary B Shares of £10 each, £5 paid	250,000 0 0			540,000 0 0	
100,000 Preference Shares, fully paid ..	1,000,000 0 0		Reserve for Depreciation set aside in year ended 31st August 1898	50,000 0 0	
		1,750,000 0 0	Reserve for depreciation set aside in year ended 31st August 1899 ..	50,000 0 0	
Debentures—			Reserve for depreciation set aside this year ..	50,000 0 0	
1,000 Five per cent. Debentures of £100 each, issued 28th February 1900 at £95 per cent. and redeemable at par in 10 years..	95,000 0 0			150,000 0 0	390,000 0 0
Trade Creditors	70,600 0 0		Cost of installation of electric motive power, instead of steam..		30,000 0 0
Commission due to Managing Director.. ..	6,000 0 0		Stock of raw materials at market price (cost £50,000)..	60,000 0 0	
Reserve Fund..	10,000 0 0		Stock of finished goods at market price, *less* allowance to cover selling expenses	30,000 0 0	
Profit and Loss Account—			Stock of Sundries	1,500 0 0	
Profit for year..	114,000 0 0				91,500 0 0
Less Half-year's Dividend paid at 5 per cent. on Preference Shares .. £25,000 0 0			Trade debtors, *less* Reserve for doubtful debts and discounts	50,000 0 0	
„ Half-year's Dividend paid at 5 per cent. on A Ordinary Shares .. 12,500 0 0			Unworked dead rents	10,000 0 0	
„ Half-year's Dividend paid at 5 per cent. on B Ordinary Shares .. 12,500 0 0			Workmen's Compensation Account, claims paid this year	3,000 0 0	
	50,000 0 0	64,000 0 0	*Less* amount set aside to date at £300 per annum	900 0 0	
					2,100 0 0
			Cash at the Bank	40,000 0 0	
			Cash and Bills in hand	2,000 0 0	
					42,000 0 0
			Loss for year ended 31st August 1899 ..		100,000 0 0
		£1,995,600 0 0			£1,995,600 0 0

Subject to our report of even date the above Balance Sheet is, in our opinion, a full and fair Balance Sheet, containing the particulars required by the Company's regulations, and properly drawn up so as to exhibit a true and correct view of the state of the Company's affairs.

L. H. HARDMAN, Liverpool,
H. S. FERGUSON, Manchester,
Chartered Accountants, Auditors.

Manchester,
1st October 1900.

MANCHESTER AND LIVERPOOL CHARTERED ACCOUNTANTS STUDENTS' SOCIETIES (JOINT MEETING).

THE WESSEX ENGINEERING COMPANY, LIMITED, AND REDUCED.

NOTICE is hereby given that an Extraordinary General Meeting of the Company will be held on the 31st day of October 1901, at the CITY HALL, EBERLE STREET, LIVERPOOL, at the conclusion of the Ordinary General Meeting to be held at the same place on the same day, but not earlier than 7.30 P.M., for the purpose of considering—and if thought fit—passing the following resolutions, that is to say:—

    1.—That this Company be wound up voluntarily.

    2.—That MR. O. B. JUST, of Liverpool, Chartered Accountant, be, and he is hereby appointed Liquidator for the purposes of such winding-up.

    3.—That the Liquidator be, and he is hereby authorised to sell the whole of the Company's undertaking, property, and assets (exclusive of uncalled capital) to the X Syndicate for the sum of £1,141,600 payable as follows:—as to £1,074,250 in cash payable to the Liquidator within two months from the confirmation of these resolutions, and as to the balance of £67,350 by paying, satisfying, discharging, and fulfilling all the debts, liabilities, expenses, and engagements of this Company as disclosed in a schedule which for the purpose of identification has been signed by representatives of the Syndicate and of this Company.

    4.—That the sum of £500 be and it is hereby voted for the remuneration of the Liquidator, and all other expenses of the winding-up.

Should the above resolutions be passed by the requisite majority they will be submitted for confirmation as a Special Resolution to a Second Extraordinary General Meeting, which will be subsequently convened.

BY ORDER OF THE BOARD.

THE CITY HALL,
    EBERLE STREET,
        LIVERPOOL.

16th October 1901.

MANCHESTER AND LIVERPOOL CHARTERED ACCOUNTANTS STUDENTS' SOCIETIES.

THE WESSEX ENGINEERING COMPANY, LIMITED.

BALANCE SHEET as at 28th February 1901.

Capital and Liabilities.	£ s d	£ s d	Property and Assets.	£ s d	£ s d
NOMINAL CAPITAL—			Mining Concession, Land and Buildings at Cost	1,000,000 0 0	
100,000 Ordinary Shares of £10 each ..	1,000,000 0 0		Goodwill	280,000 0 0	
100,000 5 per cent. Preference Shares of £10 each	1,000,000 0 0		Machinery as at 31st August 1900 ..	£390,000 0 0	
	£2,000,000 0 0		Depreciation, ½-year	25,000 0 0	
					365,000 0 0
SUBSCRIBED CAPITAL—			Cost of Installation of Electric Motive Power, instead of Steam		30,000 0 0
50,000 Ordinary A Shares of £10 each, fully paid	500,000 0 0		Stocks on hand—		
50,000 Ordinary B Shares of £10 each, fully paid	250,000 0 0		Raw Materials and Finished Goods		76,650 0 0
100,000 Preference Shares, fully paid ..	1,000,000 0 0	1,750,000 0 0	Trade Debtors. less Provision against Loss		43,700 0 0
			Cash in hand and at Bank		12,300 0 0
DEBENTURES—			Profit and Loss Account—		
1,000 5 per cent. Debentures, of £100 each, issued 28th February 1900, at £95 per cent. and redeemable at par in 10 years	95,000 0 0		Balance, 31st August 1899	100,000 0 0	
Trade Creditors	53,500 0 0		Less Amount carried forward per Resolution of 29th October 1900 ..	4,000 0 0	
Reserve Fund as at 31st August 1900 ..	10,000 0 0			96,000 0 0	
Added per Resolution of 29th October 1900..	10,000 0 0		Loss for six months ending 28th February 1901..	14,850 0 0	
		20,000 0 0			110,850 0 0
		£1,918,500 0 0			£1,918,500 0 0

The above Account is supposed to have been laid before a Meeting of the Members in April 1901, when a Committee of Shareholders was appointed to investigate and report upon the Company's affairs.

RECONSTRUCTION SCHEME AS RECOMMENDED BY COMMITTEE OF SHAREHOLDERS.

Floating Assets having fallen below £150,000, Debentures are redeemable at 96 per cent. under terms of Trust Deed, and pressure is exercised by Trustee for Debenture Holders.

PROPOSALS.

Endeavour to settle with Debenture Holders at 96 per cent. free of accruing interest and expenses.

Reduce existing capital of Company thus :—

A Shares to £7 each fully paid.

B ,, ,, £7 ,, £3 10s. paid.

Preference ,, ,, £9 ,, fully paid.

Issue further Capital by way of First Preference Shares, viz. :—30,000 Shares of £5 each, and call the whole amount—*pro ratâ* allotment to all existing Members.

Write off the values of the fixed Assets and the adverse balance on Revenue Account to the extent of the reduction in the existing Capital.

Re-assess the value of the Machinery and Plant at £350,000.

Continue trading.

It is assumed that all these proposals were adopted and carried through ; the consent of the Court obtained to the reduction of the Capital ; the consent of the Debenture Holders and Shareholders obtained as regards their respective matters, and the issue of the First Preference Shares to existing Shareholders duly effected. The position of affairs would then be as annexed, dating the Accounts as 28th February 1901.

MANCHESTER AND LIVERPOOL CHARTERED ACCOUNTANTS STUDENTS' SOCIETIES.

THE WESSEX ENGINEERING COMPANY, LIMITED.

EFFECT OF RECONSTRUCTION SCHEME ON BALANCE SHEET, 28th February 1901.

Capital and Liabilities.	£ s d	£ s d	Property and Assets.	£ s d	£ s d
NOMINAL CAPITAL—			Mining Rights, &c.	1,000,000 0 0	
50,000 A Ordinary Shares of £7 each	350,000 0 0		Goodwill	28,000 0 0	
50,000 B Ordinary Shares of £7 each	350,000 0 0		Machinery and Plant	395,000 0 0	
100,000 Five per Cent. Preference			Profit and Loss Account	110,850 0 0	
Shares of £9 each	900,000 0 0		Debentures, 1 per cent. on Redemption	1,000 0 0	
30,000 First Preference Shares of £5					
each	150,000 0 0			1,786,850 0 0	
	£1,750,000 0 0		Less Reserve Fund	20,000 0 0	
				1,766,850 0 0	
SUBSCRIBED CAPITAL—			Less Reduction of Capital	325,000 0 0	
50,000 A Shares £7 each, fully paid ..	350,000 0 0			£1,441,850 0 0	
50,000 B Shares, £7 each, £3 10s. paid	175,000 0 0				
100,000 Preference Shares, £9 each,			Mining Rights and Goodwill		1,091,850 0 0
fully paid	900,000 0 0		Machinery and Plant		350,000 0 0
30,000 First Preference Shares, £5			Stocks		76,650 0 0
each, fully paid (new issue)	150,000 0 0		Trade Debtors		43,700 0 0
		1,575,000 0 0	Cash in hand and at Bank .. 12,300 0 0		
Trade Creditors		53,500 0 0	Add Cash for First Prefer-		
			ence Shares .. £150,000 0 0		
			Less Debentures redeemed 96,000 0 0		
				54,000 0 0	
					66,300 0 0
		£1,628,500 0 0			£1,628,500 0 0

BALANCE SHEET as at 31st August 1901.

Capital and Liabilities.	£ s d	£ s d	Property and Assets.	£ s d	£ s d
NOMINAL CAPITAL—			Mining Concession, Land, and Buildings at Cost ..	1,091,850 0 0	
50,000 A Ordinary Shares of £7 each ..	350,000 0 0		Machinery and Plant.. .. .. £350,000 0 0		
50,000 B Ordinary Shares of £7 each ..	350,000 0 0		Depreciation, ½-year 25,000 0 0		
100,000 Five per Cent. Preference				325,000 0 0	
Shares of £9 each	900,000 0 0		Stocks	87,500 0 0	
30,000 First Preference Shares of £5			Trade Debts	58,300 0 0	
each	150,000 0 0		Cash in hand and at Bank	3,600 0 0	
	£1,750,000 0 0		PROFIT AND LOSS ACCOUNT—		
SUBSCRIBED CAPITAL—			Loss 6 months to date ..	73,100 0 0	
50,000 A Shares, £7 each, fully paid ..	350,000 0 0		Reconstruction Expenses	3,000 0 0	
50,000 B Shares, £7 each, £3 10s. paid .	175,000 0 0				76,100 0 0
100,000 Preference Shares, £9 each,					
fully paid	900,000 0 0				
30,000 First Preference Shares, £5 each,					
fully paid (new issue)..	150,000 0 0				
		1,575,000 0 0			
Trade Creditors		67,350 0 0			
		£1,642,350 0 0			£1,642,350 0 0

AUDITORS' CERTIFICATE.

Pursuant to Section 23 of the Companies' Act, 1900, we hereby certify that all our requirements as Auditors have NOT been complied with.

A. B. } *Chartered Accountants.*
C. D. }
Auditors.

Liverpool, 9th October 1901.

AUDITORS' REPORT.

We have examined the above Balance Sheet with the Accounts and Vouchers relating thereto, and we have to report that subject to our Certificate annexed hereto, and to a further report which we have made to the Shareholders, the Balance Sheet is properly drawn up so as to show a true and correct view of the state of the Company's affairs on 31st August 1901, as shown by the books of the Company.

A. B. } *Chartered Accountants.*
C. D. }
Auditors.

Liverpool, 9th October 1901.

MANCHESTER AND LIVERPOOL CHARTERED ACCOUNTANTS STUDENTS' SOCIETIES.

THE WESSEX ENGINEERING COMPANY, LIMITED.

The Auditor's Report and Certificate will be read and discussed at the Ordinary Meeting of Shareholders, but the hopelessness of the Company is now generally admitted, and it is decided that steps be taken to wind up the Company voluntarily. A Syndicate has offered to take over the whole undertaking on the following terms,—the Capital to be repaid to the Shareholders in Cash.

Capital and Liabilities.	BALANCE SHEET.			SYNDICATE'S OFFER.			*Property and Assets.*	BALANCE SHEET.			SYNDICATE'S OFFER.		
	£	s	d	£	s	d		£	s	d	£	s	d
Capital	1,575,000	0	0	1,073,750	0	0	Mining Rights, &c.	1,091,850	0	0	750,000	0	0
Trade Creditors	67,350	0	0	67,350	0	0	Machinery and Plant ..	325,000	0	0	250,000	0	0
Expenses of Liquidation				500	0	0	Stocks	87,500	0	0	84,000	0	0
							Trade Debts	58,300	0	0	54,000	0	0
							Cash	3,600	0	0	3,600	0	0
							Profit and Loss Account	76,100	0	0			
	£ 1,642,350	0	0	£ 1,141,600	0	0		£ 1,642,350	0	0	£1,141,600	0	0

This offer has been accepted by the Directors subject to confirmation by the Shareholders.

PROPOSED DISTRIBUTION OF CAPITAL.

Both Classes of Preference Shares to be paid in full leaving £23,750.

But—

    (1).—If A. and B. Shares take proportionally to the Amounts

        paid up respectively then—

                A Shares receive 6s. 4d. per Share.

                and B Shares receive 3s. 2d. per Share.

Whereas—

    (2).—If B. Shareholders are asked to pay up their calls,

        and then rank with the A. Shareholders *pari passu*—

                A Shares receive £1 19s. 9d. per Share.

                and B. Shares pay £1·10s. 3d. per Share.

These Methods will be discussed at the Extraordinary Meeting of Shareholders, the Directors and several of the largest Ordinary Shareholders holding different views upon the method of division.

NOTE.—The general rule upon the point may be controlled by the regulations of a Company.

THE CHARTERED ACCOUNTANT STUDENTS' SOCIETY OF EDINBURGH.

THE NEW GUINEA GOLD MINING COMPANY LIMITED.

NOTICE IS HEREBY GIVEN, that the Second Annual General Meeting of Shareholders will be held within No. 27 Queen Street, Edinburgh, on Thursday, 23rd January 1902, at 8.30 p.m.

And Notice is hereby also given, that at the same place and on the same day, at 8.45 p.m., or as soon thereafter as the business of the above-mentioned Meeting is concluded, an Extraordinary General Meeting of Shareholders will be held for the purpose of considering, and, if approved of, passing the following resolutions :—

1. That an Agreement dated 9th January 1902, entered into between this Company and the Chartered Company of British New Guinea, relating to the transference of the business, property, and undertaking of this Company to the said Chartered Company, in exchange for Shares in the Chartered Company and Cash, is hereby approved and confirmed.

2. That in order to the carrying out of this Agreement, this Company is hereby required to be wound up voluntarily.

3. That this Company be wound up voluntarily.

4. That T. Quest, C.A., be appointed, and is hereby appointed, Liquidator of this Company, for the purpose of winding up the affairs and distributing the Assets thereof, and that with the powers conferred upon liquidators by The Companies Act 1862, and Acts amending and extending the same

5. That the Liquidator may make such modification in the terms of the Agreement mentioned in Resolution 1 as he may deem expedient, and do all things as he may find convenient or necessary for carrying the said Agreement into effect.

6. That the Liquidator may and shall receive the Ordinary Shares in the Chartered Company of British New Guinea, to be allotted in terms of the Agreement mentioned in Resolution 1, and may and shall distribute the same among the Members of this Company as follows, namely :—Every holder of Eight Ordinary Shares in this Company shall receive Nine Shares of the Chartered Company of British New Guinea, and the Liquidator shall, out of moneys to be received from the said Chartered Company, purchase all rights of the Shareholders of this Company to fractional holdings in the Chartered Company ; every holder of Founders' Shares in this Company shall receive Five Ordinary Shares in the Chartered Company for each Founders' Share held by him in this Company. Further, that the Liquidator shall receive in cash from the Chartered Company of British New Guinea, and shall distribute amongst the Shareholders of this Company according to their rights, the sum at the credit of Profit and Loss Account in this Company's Balance Sheet as at 30th June 1901.

By Order,

W. H. GRAY,
Secretary.

Registered Office,
Edinburgh, 15th January 1902.

THE CHARTERED ACCOUNTANTS STUDENTS' SOCIETY OF EDINBURGH.

THE NEW GUINEA GOLD MINING COMPANY LIMITED.

Directors.

H. P. MACMILLAN, Esq., Advocate, *Chairman.*

Admiral FLEET.   Hon. ANTHONY NOBLE.
Colonel CHARLES.   JEREMY SMART, Esq.

WILLIAM ANNAN, Esq., *Managing Director.*

Secretary—W. H. GRAY.

Law Agents—Messrs. MUTCH-MALEIND BROTHERS.

Auditor—T. QUEST, C.A.

REPORT BY THE DIRECTORS

To the Second Annual General Meeting of Shareholders,

to be held within No. 27 QUEEN STREET, EDINBURGH, on THURSDAY, 23rd JANUARY 1902.

The Directors have pleasure in reporting that the operations of the Company during the past year have been highly successful, and that the realised net profit for the year is £10,000. Out of this sum a dividend at the rate of five per cent. falls to be paid to the Ordinary Shareholders. This will absorb £4,500, and the Directors recommend that the balance (£5,500), together with interest on calls in arrear (£80), in all £5,580, be divided amongst the Shareholders, in accordance with the Memorandum of Association of the Company.

Notwithstanding the large profit on the past year's working, the Directors have had under their grave consideration the very serious outlay incurred for management in New Guinea. As a result of inquiries they have made, the Directors are satisfied that the Company cannot be continued in its present methods of work without heavy expenditure for management in New Guinea.

They have, therefore, opened negotiations with the Chartered Company of British New Guinea, which has large interests among the Owen Stanley Mountains, where the Company's mine is situated, and whose engineering and management staff will be able to control the working of the mine in a satisfactory and efficient fashion at a very great saving. After much correspondence and many meetings, the Chartered Company of British New Guinea has offered to purchase this Company's whole property, plant, and other assets, on the footing of the annexed Balance Sheet as at 30th June 1901, to assume liability for the Debentures, and to pay in cash to the Liquidator for distribution amongst the Shareholders, according to their respective rights, the balance of £10,000 appearing at the credit of Profit and Loss Account in that Balance Sheet.

The offer made by the Chartered Company is that for every Ordinary Share of this Company there should be given 1½ Share in the Chartered Company, and for every Founder's Share there should be given five Shares of the Chartered Company. Such portions of Shareholders' holdings in this Company as will result in fractional holdings in the Chartered Company will be paid off in cash at the rate of £1 1s. 3d. per Share of the Chartered Company to which the Shareholder is entitled. The present market value of the Shares of the Chartered Company is £1 1s. 3d., at which price they have stood for some months.

Arrangements have been made whereby all officials of the Company will be taken over by the Chartered Company at their present remuneration, and an understanding has been come to, that two Directors of this Company will be invited to join the Board of the Chartered Company.

In view of the strong position of the purchasing Company, and of the confidence of the public therein, as evidenced by the premium which its Shares command on the market, it has not been thought necessary to consult the Debenture Holders as to their wishes in connection with the proposed sale.

Provision has been made in the Agreement with the purchasing Company whereby it will issue free of charge Debenture Stock Securities for sums equal to the amounts of the principal moneys due on the present documents of debt, upon these being surrendered by the Debenture Holders. The Directors presume that the Debenture Holders will take advantage of this provision.

The Shareholders will, no doubt, be pleased to know that the Directors have succeeded in completing the purchase of the patent hydraulic extracting machine referred to in last Report. The price has, meantime, been entered in the Balance Sheet, partly under the heading Mining Rights and Plants, and partly under the heading Subsidiary Patent Rights.

In accordance with the provision of the new Companies Act, the Auditor's Report on the Accounts will be read to the Meeting. At the suggestion of the Auditor, the Report has not been printed, as in former years, at the foot of the Balance Sheet.

In terms of the Articles, two of the Directors, Admiral Fleet and Colonel Charles, retire at this time, but, being eligible, offer themselves for re-election.

The Auditor also retires, but is eligible for re-election.

By Order of the Directors,

W. H. GRAY,
Secretary.

EDINBURGH, 15*th January* 1902.

THE CHARTERED ACCOUNTANT STUDENTS' SOCIETY OF EDINBURGH.

THE NEW GUINEA GOLD MINING COMPANY LIMITED.

BALANCE SHEET, as at 30th June 1901.

Liabilities.			*Assets.*			
CAPITAL AUTHORISED AND ISSUED.			MINING RIGHTS AND PLANT—			
			Amount paid to Vendor			£50,000
Authorised—			Added during previous year £25,000			
90,000 Ordinary Shares of £1 each.			Do. do. this year 80,000			
10,000 Founders' Shares of £1 each.						105,000
The free surplus profits in each year, after 5 per cent. has been paid on the Ordinary Shares, is divisible, one-half among the holders of Ordinary Shares, and one-half among the holders of Founders' Shares.						155,000
			Subsidiary Patent Rights			4,500
			Preliminary Expenses			2,000
Issued—			Office Furniture, Fittings, &c.			100
90,000 Ordinary Shares of £1 each £90,000			Sums in hands of Officials in New Guinea			7,000
Less calls in Arrear 1,000			Cash at Bankers and in hand			600
		89,000				
10,000 Founders' Shares of £1 each, fully paid 10,000						
		99,000				
RESERVE—						
Premium received on issue of £50,000 5 per cent. Debentures £5,000						
Premium received on 30,000 Ordinary Shares issued during year 3,000						
Calls received and premium obtained on re-issue of 1,000 Ordinary Shares, 10s. paid, forfeited during the year 600						
		8,600				
DEBENTURES—						
Debentures bearing interest at 6 per cent. per annum, and repayable at par in 1910 50,000						
SINKING FUND FOR REDEMPTION OF DEBENTURES—						
Amount provided from out of profits last year.. £1,000						
Do. this year 1,000						
		2,000				
PROFIT AND LOSS ACCOUNT—						
Thus, profit on working for year 21,000						
Less Expenses of Management in New Guinea £9,000						
Expenses in Great Britain 1,000						
Sum set aside toward Sinking Fund for redemption of Debentures 1,000						
		11,000				
		10,000				
		£169,600				£169,000

EDINBURGH, 14*th January* 1902.—In accordance with the Companies Act, 1900, I hereby certify that all my requirements as Auditor have been complied with.

T. QUEST, C.A., *Auditor.*

CHAPTER XXIV.

MISCELLANEOUS PROBLEMS IN ACCOUNTS.

IN the preceding chapters the more usual problems arising in connection with general business undertakings have been considered at length in due sequence. It is proposed to devote the present chapter to the elucidation of certain matters which it has not been necessary to hitherto discuss in order to make clear the best treatment in connection with other problems afterwards described, but which on account of their intrinsic importance call for description in these pages, if the present work is to put forward any claim towards approaching completeness. The various matters that now remain to be described have been postponed, because they form no part of the sequence upon which the preceding pages are based: none the less are they matters which merit the careful attention of the student of accounting.

EMPTIES.

In the case of a number of industries, the most convenient treatment of Empties is a matter of very considerable importance. If an inadequate system be provided, the result will, in all probability, be that whereas the matter engages a considerable portion of the time of the bookkeeping staff, serious losses are yet experienced from this source, dissatisfaction given to customers, and perhaps in addition a misleading view of the position shown by the books. When the Empties are of considerable value a reliable system is, of course, especially important; but where Empties are charged for at all, it is essential that the method of account-ing employed in connection with them should be one that works smoothly in practice, shows reliable results, and at the same time does not make excessive demands on the time of the bookkeeping staff.

This being a general work, it is proposed to describe the various alternative systems of account-ing for Empties in general terms, indicating the principles upon which they are founded, and their relative advantages. In applying these principles to individual cases, it is, of course, important in the first instance to become fully acquainted with the practical requirements of those cases, and the systems described may require modification in detail in order that these requirements may be met to the best advantage. It is thought, however, that this task of adaptation may be readily accomplished so long as the general principles are made clear; whereas, had the alternative course been pursued of explaining in detail systems suitable to one or two specific industries, the formulation of a scheme suitable for other undertakings would not be so obvious.

First Method.—

When Empties are charged to customers at a price which is allowed in full upon their return in good condition, and the almost invariable practice is for them to be returned promptly (so that in point of fact customers never pay for Empties, except such as may be lost), the question arises as to whether it is worth while to make any record in the financial books until it becomes necessary to call upon a customer to pay for such Empties. This postponing of entries has the advantage of saving a considerable amount of clerical labour, but the extra trouble involved when it becomes necessary to make a charge militates against this system if such charges are likely to be numerous. When, however, the circumstances render its adoption suitable, the system may be readily worked in practice by treating the Empties on exactly the same lines as goods sent out on approval—the transactions being, indeed, for all practical purposes, identical. In the Nominal Ledger, Accounts should be opened to record transactions in each class of Empties, and these from time to time should show, as a debit balance, the value of the Empties in hand, or in the hands of customers pending return. Such accounts should be debited with the cost of further purchases and repairs (if any), and credited with the total sum charged for Empties not returned, the difference on the account from time to time showing the profit, or loss, as shown by the following

EXAMPLE:

Dr.						CASES ACCOUNT.						Cr.
1902					£ s d	1902			£ s d
Jan. 1	To Stock	2,000	200 0 0	Dec. 31	By Customers (for Cases not returned)	800	100 0 0
Dec. 31	" Purchases..	500	100 0 0		" Stock (carried down) ..	1,600	160 0 0
	" Repairs ..	..	20 0 0		" Loss transferred to Profit and Loss Account ..	100	60 0 0
		2,500	£320 0 0			2,500	£320 0 0
1903							
Jan. 1	To Stock	1,600	160 0 0				

Second Method.—

When the conditions are the same as under Method I., save that the necessity for charging customers is comparatively frequent, the balance of advantage is generally in favour of the Empties being at once charged up in the Sold Ledger in the ordinary way. The total charges for Empties must, however, of course be kept separate from the Day Book totals, in order that the nominal accounts may be correctly posted, and in the same way allowances for Empties Returned must be kept separate from Sales Returns. This separation is as a rule most readily performed by the addition of a special money column to the Day Book and Sales Return Book; but in some cases it may be found to sufficiently answer all practical requirements if the weekly, or monthly, totals be analysed before any postings are made to the nominal accounts. The entries in respect of Empties may either be posted in the ordinary way to the Sold Ledger Accounts, or in some cases it may be found convenient to employ a separate money column in the Ledger for these transactions. One advantage of such additional money columns is that the Empties have probably been charged to customers at a profit, which of course will not be realised (or only partially realised) if they are returned and allowed for in due course. At balancing time, therefore, it is generally necessary to make some Reserve against the amount charged to customers for Empties in their hands, in order to avoid undue inflation of profits. If the aggregate amount of outstanding debits in respect of Empties be ascertained (as is readily possible with the two-column Ledger), the amount of this Reserve may be at once arrived at; when, however, the introduction of a double column is considered undesirable, the amount of the Reserve can as a rule be readily gauged, if a statistical column be provided in the Ledger showing (in quantities only) the number of Empties in customers' hands from time to time. This latter plan, however, is only suitable where the Empties are all of the same description (*e.g.*, the bottles of a mineral water company, the sacks of a miller, &c.); in general businesses, where several different classes of Empties have to be accounted for, the statistical column is impracticable, as no reliable valuation could be placed upon Empties generally, and a separate column in the Ledger for the quantities of each class of Empty would be out of the question.

Third Method.—

Another plan that is often adopted in practice, and which is to some extent a variation of Method I., is to keep an "Empties Ledger," showing the amount of Empties in the hands of each customer in an account opened in his name. When there are numerous different kinds of Empties it will often be found that, in the long run, the keeping of a Statistical Ledger upon these lines is a saving, rather than an expenditure, of additional labour.

Fourth Method —

The system of accounts described in Chapter XVIII. is one that readily lends itself to the record of transactions in Empties, and may usefully be applied when the Empties are of sufficient value to make it really desirable that a careful record should be kept—as, for example, when they consist of specially constructed packing cases, casks, or mineral-water syphons. The plan adopted is somewhat upon the lines of the Card Ledger already described on page 208; but in reality it is practically identical with the "Chaldean" system, which (as stated upon page 201) is the basis upon which all classes of bookkeeping "without books" are founded. A certain number of cards, or tallies, are prepared, each of which has a distinctive number, corresponding with the number given to an Empty. While these Empties remain in the warehouse, the tallies corresponding to them remain in a corresponding division, or framwork, so arranged that any desired number can be at once taken out as required. As Empties are issued to customers, the corresponding tallies are taken out of the "warehouse" frame and placed in a division, or compartment, set aside to record the Empties in the hands of that particular customer. The tally remains in the customer's division until the Empty is either returned or charged for as missing. In the former case, the tally is returned to the Warehouse frame, in the latter case it is handed over to the clerk in charge of the department to be cancelled. The great advantage of this system is that, with only a very ordinary amount of care, it can be perfectly well undertaken by quite illiterate persons; while a further advantage is that it is just as simple to keep a record of a number of different classes of Empties as it would be if all were of the same description. When, however, the system is applied to the record of several different classes of entries, it is convenient that the tallies in respect of each class should be differently coloured, so that the distinctions may be readily discernible at a glance.

GOODS ON SALE OR RETURN.

If it be quite unusual for the business to send out goods on approval, no necessity arises for making any special provision in the books for the record of these transactions, any more than one would ordinarily provide special books for the record of any other transactions of a quite unusual nature. In such cases it will meet all practical requirements sufficiently well if the original entry on the forwarding of the goods be passed through the Day Book and posted to the Sold Ledger in the ordinary way, a note being appended to the Day Book entry (if necessary) to indicate that the customer has a right to return these goods if not approved of. In the event of the goods, or any portion of them, being returned, the record would be passed in the usual way through the Sales Returns Book, and credited to the customer's account in the Sold Ledger.

When, however, transactions of this description are numerous, it becomes necessary to provide a special means of recording them, in order (1) to save time, (2) to enable the goods out on "appro." to be readily watched, (3) to avoid the total of *bonâ fide* Sales being over-stated at balancing time by the inclusion of purely speculative transactions. In the case of a general business, the most convenient plan is to provide a separate Day Book for "appro." transactions, ruled as shown in the following

EXAMPLE:

"APPRO." BOOK.

Goods Forwarded				Goods Returned			Goods Charged	
Date	Particulars	Details	Amount	Date	Particulars	Amount	Fo.	Amount
		£ s d	£ s d			£ s d		£ s d

All goods sent out on approval are entered in this Day Book in the ordinary way, the columns on the right of the thick line, being, however, left blank. Goods returned are entered in the space provided for that purpose upon the right of the thick line, and the difference between the two entries (*i.e.*, the value of the goods retained) is extended into the extreme right-hand column and posted into the Sold Ledger. Only the extreme right-hand column, therefore, forms part of the financial system of accounts, and that column is treated as a Day Book. The rest of the "Appro." Book is for statistical purposes only. At balancing time the items representing goods remaining in the hands of customers may be brought forward to a new section of the book, so that the old section may be added up and the cross-totals agreed. The value of the goods remaining in the hands of customers, but not charged up, may be added to the inventory of Stock-in-trade, subject, of course, to deduction of the "loading" that represents the Gross Profit.

In the case of special industries, dealing perhaps with a single article which it may be necessary to send out on sale or return, it is often desirable to keep special tally of each such article. Under these circumstances, the tally system already described in connection with Empties may sometimes be found to meet the case. With others an adaptation of the Tabular System seems more convenient, a special book being kept, which combines the functions of a Stock Ledger and "Appro." Day Book, as shown in the following

EXAMPLE:

"APPRO." (AND STOCK) BOOK.

No. of Article	Sent to	No. of Appro. Note	Amount	Returned			Charged up	
				Date	No. of Credit Note	Amount	S. L. Fo.	Amount
			£ s d			£ s d		£ s d

ROYALTY ACCOUNTS.

Certain considerations arise in connection with the proper treatment of Royalties in accounts that call for attention here, by reason of the fact that a failure to understand the nature of these transactions may very easily cause an entire misapprehension as to the position of the undertaking. Royalties are paid to the owners of copyrights, and patent or mineral rights, in consideration of certain rights of user ceded by the owner. Thus publishers pay Royalties to authors for the right to produce and sell copyright works; manufacturers pay inventors Royalties for the right to embody patented inventions in their manufactures; and colliery, mine, and quarry owners pay Royalties for the right to extract from another's land the mineral of which they are in search.

Almost the only thing in common with these various classes of Royalties is that, as a rule, the amount payable, instead of being a fixed sum, varies with the extent to which the right is utilised—that is to say, with the *quantity* of business done of that particular description. When the Royalty paid is a fixed sum there is, from the point of view of accounting, no occasion to distinguish between Royalties and ordinary fixed expenses (*e.g.*, Rent, &c.), save that in a manufacturing business Royalties must always be regarded as an expense chargeable against Trading Account rather than Profit and Loss Account, forming (as they do) an essential item in the cost of production of the commodities dealt in. When, on the other hand, the amount of Royalty varies with the amount of business done, or with the output, the accounts must be so arranged as to lend themselves to a right calculation of the amount of such Royalty from time to time. Thus, in the case of a publisher, it is essential that detailed Stock Books should be kept, which will enable the number of copies sold of each work to be

readily ascertained and verified; and in the case of a manufacturer holding a license from a patentee, the accounts must be designed to readily show the number of articles upon which the benefit contained in the license has been employed, so that the holder of the patent-rights may receive the amount to which he is entitled. It is unnecessary to explain in detail how these ends may be achieved in practice in individual cases, as the precise method adopted will naturally vary greatly according to the general system of accounts in use. It may be mentioned, however, that as in all probability these records will be liable to be produced to the owner of the rights, to enable him to verify the correctness of the amount of Royalties payable, it is important to so arrange the books as to prevent the necessity of at the same time disclosing other information in connection with the business, which it may be thought desirable to keep private.

Occasionally the arrangement with regard to the payment of Royalties is such that no payment is due until the happening of a certain event—as, for example, until after the output has reached a certain figure; or *per contra* a fixed Minimum may be payable in any event, with a right to recover the excess of the Minimum over the Royalties out of future workings. In the first-named case it is important to bear in mind that the Royalties on the business actually done are at all times a charge against the profits of that business, even if (by special arrangement) they will not be immediately payable. Such Royalties should accordingly be credited to a "Royalty Suspense Account" and debited to Revenue as incurred: upon the happening of the event under which they become actually payable, the Royalty Suspense Account may be closed, and the balance transferred to the credit of the owner's Personal Account. In the second-named case, the record is upon the lines that ordinarily obtain in connection with Royalties payable on mineral rights, which will now be discussed in detail.

ROYALTIES ON MINERALS.

As already stated shortly, the usual arrangement between the owner of mineral rights and the owner. of the colliery, mine, or quarry engaged in exploiting those rights is upon the following lines : —

(1) A Royalty, based on the quantity of minerals raised, is payable to the owner.

(2) In any event a fixed minimum sum is payable to the owner annually.

(3) In the event of the Minimum Rent exceeding the Royalty on the output for the year, the excess of Royalties overpaid may be " redeemed " out of future workings, in later years when the amount of the Royalty exceeds the Minimum, or " Dead," Rent. In some localities, however, it is usual to qualify this right of recovery by limiting such a right to a period of three or five years : in other localities, the right may be exercised at any time during the continuance of the arrangement.

The agreement between owner and worker takes the form of a lease, and it will therefore be convenient to speak of those parties respectively as the lessor and the lessee.

The exact mode of assessing the Royalty payable depends partly upon the nature of the mineral and partly upon local custom, but in nearly all cases it is a fixed rate per ton, per cubic yard, or per acre of the mineral-bearing region worked. It is invariably based upon the quantity of the output. If it be at the rate of so much per ton, the amount of the Royalty may be readily computed from an inspection of the books, which will in all cases show the weight of mineral raised from day to day ; if,

however, the basis be by measure, it is usual for surveyors, appointed by the lessor and lessee respectively, to from time to time examine the workings, and agree as to the quantity of mineral extracted during the period under review.

These being the conditions obtaining, it will readily be perceived—

(a) That the Royalty upon the actual output is in all cases a proper charge against Revenue ;

(b) That under no circumstances must the amount paid to the lessor fall below the prescribed Minimum, or Dead, Rent ;

(c) That, so long as the actual payments to the lessor exceed the aggregate Royalties on the output up to that date, the excess is —from an accounting point of view— Royalties paid in advance, which may properly be carried to a Suspense Account and treated as an asset, *so long as the lessee retains the right to recover them out of future workings, and there is a reasonable probability that such future workings will enable the excess to be recovered ;*

(d) In no year must the actual payment to the lessor exceed the Minimum Rent, so long as any balance remains on the Royalties Suspense Account referred to above.

With this preliminary explanation, it is thought that the reader will experience no difficulty in following the working out of the problem given overpage, which fully illustrates the principles already described.

PROBLEM.—A Colliery is worked under a lease granted by Lord X., at a royalty of 8d. per ton, with a minimum yearly rent of £1,000, with power to recoup short workings. In the first year 25,000 tons are worked; in the second 26,500; in the third 24,600; in the fourth 31,000; and in the fifth 30,500 tons.

How would you deal with the respective years' royalties, both in Profit and Loss, and in the Balance Sheet?

Dr.   ROYALTIES ACCOUNT.   *Cr.*

I.	To Lord X...	£833 6 8		By Profit and Loss Account	£833 6 8
II.	To Lord X...	£883 6 8	I.	By Profit and Loss Account	£883 6 8
III.	To Lord X...	£820 0 0	III.	By Profit and Loss Account	£820 0 0
IV.	To Lord X...	1,000 0 0	IV.	By Profit and Loss Account	1,033 6 8
	„ Short-Workings Account	33 6 8			
		£1,033 6 8			£1,033 6 8
V.	To Lord X...	1,000 0 0	V.	By Profit and Loss Account	1,016 13 4
	„ Short-Workings Account ..	16 13 4			
		£1,016 13 4			£1,016 13 4

Dr.   LORD X.   *Cr.*

I.	To Cash	1,000 0 0	I.	By Royalties Account	833 6 8
				„ Short-Workings Account	166 13 4
		£1,000 0 0			£1,000 0 0
II.	To Cash	1,000 0 0	II.	By Royalties Account	883 6 8
				„ Short-Workings Account	116 13 4
		£1,000 0 0			£1,000 0 0
III.	To Cash	1,000 0 0	III.	By Royalties Account	820 0 0
				„ Short-Workings Account ..	180 0 0
		£1,000 0 0			£1,000 0 0
IV.	To Cash	£1,000 0 0	IV.	By Royalties Account	£1,000 0 0
V.	To Cash	£1,000 0 0	V.	By Royalties Account	£1,000 0 0

Dr.   SHORT-WORKINGS ACCOUNT.   Cr.

I.	To Lord X...	£166 13 4	I.	By Balance ..	£166 13 4
II.	To Balance..	166 13 4	II.	By Balance ..	283 6 8
	„ Lord X...	116 13 4			
		£283 6 8			£283 6 8
III.	To Balance..	283 6 8	III.	By Balance ..	463 6 8
	„ Lord X...	180 0 0			
		£463 6 8			£463 6 8
IV.	To Balance..	463 6 8	IV.	By Royalties Account ..	33 6 8
				„ Balance..	430 0 0
		£463 6 8			463 6 8
V.	To Balance..	430 0 0	V.	By Royalties Account ..	16 13 4
				„ Balance..	413 6 8
		£430 0 0			£430 0 0
VI.	To Balance..	£413 6 8			

NOTES.—*Other names for " Short-Workings Account " are " Redeemable Dead Rent Account," " Overpaid Royalties Account," " Royalties Suspense Account," &c. The balance standing to the debit of this account is shown as an asset in each annual Balance Sheet ; but it can only be properly so stated if there is good reason to suppose that it will be redeemed out of future workings, which in the above example seems somewhat doubtful.*

ACTUARIAL VALUATIONS AND ACCOUNTS.

In the case of the vast majority of undertakings, the only satisfactory system of accounting is by double-entry, under which it is possible to compile from time to time (*a*) a Revenue Account, showing the income and expenditure for the period under review, and the net profit (or loss) on the operations engaged upon ; (*b*) a Balance Sheet, showing (as nearly as may be ascertained in the case of a going concern, *i.e.*, an uncompleted venture) the position of affairs to date, which by its nature automatically checks the arithmetical accuracy of the Revenue Account. As has already been explained, single-entry, which does not provide this automatical check, is defective, because it lacks the useful information that a Revenue Account affords, and also because of the risk that errors in the compilation of the statement of assets and liabilities may remain undetected. For these reasons, double-entry bookkeeping is to be found in connection with the accounts of nearly every undertaking of importance, but in the case of some industries the system cannot be applied in its entirety, on account of the enormous labour that such a course would involve.

In particular is the application of a really complete system of double-entry impossible in connection with the accounts of Life Assurance Companies. In these concerns, the transactions may be roughly divided into two classes :—

(1) The earning of income by the investment of monies (this branch of the transactions can readily be, and is invariably, recorded by double-entry) ;

(2) The incurring of expenditure as the liabilities undertaken towards policy-holders increase from year to year, as the expectation of life of those policy-holders becomes shorter with the lapse of time.

Y

It would be practically impossible for a Life Assurance Company to determine annually the exact increase in its liability in respect of each policy, and to keep accounts in respect of each such policy, crediting the Policy Account and debiting Revenue with every such increase at the close of the year. Apart from the enormous amount of bookkeeping involved, to very little purpose, the cost of accurately ascertaining the " present value " of the liability in each case would, with these undertakings, be absolutely prohibitive, and would, moreover, involve great delay in the preparation of the annual accounts. These undertakings (which, it may be mentioned, are regulated by the Life Assurance Companies Act, 1870, which prescribes the form in which their accounts are to be kept) are worked upon the lines that their annual accounts are *interim*· accounts only, and do not attempt to estimate the profits of the year under review. The calculation of profits only takes place when what is called a " Valuation " Balance Sheet is prepared —once every three, five, or seven years, according to the constitution of the particular company concerned. The Valuation Balance Sheet is based upon an actuarial valuation of the liabilities of the undertaking in respect of all the policies then in force, the value of such liability in each case being arrived at as follows : —

Taking the expectation of life of the assured at n years, the gross liability is the present value of the amount of the policy, due n years hence.

From this must be deducted the present value of an annuity, payable for n years, of the net premium payable under the policy (*i.e.*, the actual premium, *minus* the " loading " that has been added to cover expenses of management).

Upon the above basis, the actuaries arrive at the total present value of the net liabilities of the undertaking to date, and the profits earned during the period are computed by single entry, as being the difference between the present value of the aggregate net liabilities, and the net assets available to meet those liabilities.

The profits of Friendly Societies having a benefit branch are computed upon the same lines, the actuarial valuation in their case being undertaken every five years.

A similar method of arriving at profits is frequently employed by Building Societies, to enable them to discover the gross profit earned from the lending of money on mortgages repayable over a term of years by equalised payments, and the liabilities incurred by agreeing to pay subscribing investors a fixed sum at the end of a term of years in return for a monthly (or other periodical) payment. As has already been explained in Chapter XXI., however, no difficulty need arise in the formulation of Building Societies,' and other similar, accounts upon a complete double-entry basis. The actual interest to be debited to each Mortgage Account, and credited to each Investment Account, may be readily ascertained from properly-designed tables. The essential advantage of keeping these accounts by double-entry arises from the fact that a complete and effective audit may by that means be far more readily accomplished; while the experience of the past has shown that, in connection with these particular undertakings, such an audit is absolutely essential for the security of all interested parties.

CHAPTER XXV.

PERIODICAL RETURNS.

UNDER this heading are included those records of business transactions which are made, either (1) for the purpose of supplying a branch (or the head office) with information as to what is taking place, to enable it to make the necessary records in its financial books; or (2) those records of transactions which are compiled from time to time, with a view to enabling interested parties to readily gauge the position of affairs without themselves performing any detailed or lengthy examination on the books of account. These two classes of Returns have in common the feature that they are independent of—but supplemental to—the financial books of account, and the system of bookkeeping comprised therein. They differ, however, in that while the first class forms the basis of records that have to be made in the financial books, Returns of the second class are but summaries in a convenient form of records that have already been made.

BOOKKEEPING RETURNS.

Dealing first with those Returns designed to convey information which is to form the basis of bookkeeping records, some of the most rudimentary examples of these Returns are the ordinary Invoice forwarded by the vendor to the purchaser of goods, and the Account Sales forwarded by a consignee to his principal the consignor. Other examples that frequently occur in practice are the daily, weekly, or monthly Reports of business done which are submitted by a branch to its head office. When, however, the transactions of the branch are completely recorded there, these Returns more properly come under the second class named above, as their object is not to form the basis of bookkeeping entries, but to supply managers and principals with accurate information as to what is taking place.

When a business undertaking is of such small dimensions that its operations are entirely carried out by a single person, it is clear that that person must become cognisant of all transactions as they transpire, and that Returns are not necessary to keep him informed upon the matter. If the exigencies of business would allow him to at once record these various transactions in the proper books of account, no records outside (or supplemental to) those books would be necessary; but in practice it is not always convenient, and perhaps not even always possible, to make such a record at once. Consequently, in even the very smallest businesses, something in the nature of Returns becomes necessary, to record transactions temporarily, pending their permanent record in the books. Formerly the Waste Book, in which a narrative of every transaction was entered as it took place, supplied this purpose, and in some businesses a memorandum book closely corresponding to the old-fashioned Waste Book is still employed; but in most concerns the Waste Book has shared the fate of the Journal—that is to say, it has been separated into a number of distinct sections, each of which records *pro tem.* transactions of a certain specified class. This separation of even the preliminary record is, of course, essential where business operations are conducted upon an extensive scale, and a number of persons are simultaneously engaged upon separate business transactions. In such cases it usually follows—to a greater or less extent according to circumstances—that those persons actually engaged upon the business transactions are *not* employed to keep the books in which the transactions are eventually recorded; hence arises the necessity of some form of Return, which will enable the Counting-House (where the books of account are kept) to be promptly advised from time to time of what has taken place, and what therefore has to be recorded.

A very little consideration will show that the most convenient mode of arriving at this result, of promptly and accurately advising the Counting-House of all transactions as they occur, must necessarily vary not merely according to the nature of the business, but also to the peculiar circumstances and conditions under which it is carried on. No one system would be equally suitable under all imaginable varying circumstances; consequently, in a general work of this description, the subject cannot be dealt with in full detail. It may be mentioned, however, that—here, as elsewhere, in connection with accounts—there are certain fundamental rules which may usefully be borne in mind, if the maximum of efficiency is to be produced with a minimum of effort. Foremost may be mentioned the desirability of, so far as possible, obviating the necessity of these records being recopied by hand. Any manual copy possesses the disadvantages of loss of time and liability to error. So far as possible, therefore, the original records should be utilised, rather than copied. This is a point that has already been mentioned at some length in Chapter XVIII., and it need only be added here that the Slip System is at least as applicable to Returns, and other statistical records, as it is to pure "bookkeeping" records, and that it may often be applied to these purposes, even in cases where its adoption, or partial adoption, for the accounts themselves seems undesirable.

In the case of Returns received from distant Branches, it is particularly convenient that the Return forwarded should be a mechanical, rather than a manual, copy of the record retained. All risk of any discrepancy between the two is thus avoided (save in the case of deliberate falsification), and consequently much discussion over differences in accounts may be saved. Moreover, if a duplicate of the original record be forwarded to the Head Office Counting-House, it is supplied with first-hand evidence of the actual nature of the transaction concerned, and is thus in a better position to detect errors of treatment on the part of the distant Branch than would be possible by any other means.

From the point of view of accounting, perhaps the most important Returns coming under this heading are the periodical Trial Balances remitted to the Head Office by a distant Branch, with a view to enabling the former to close its books embodying therein the effect of the Branch transactions. This, however, is a matter that has already been dealt with in Chapter V., where the treatment of Branch Accounts generally was very fully discussed.

STATISTICAL RETURNS.

Passing on to the second class of Returns, it will be convenient, perhaps, to consider in the first instance the exact circumstances under which these are called for, with a view to obtaining an insight into the special requirements of the position. In the case of a concern of any magnitude it may be safely stated that even those engaged in keeping the books would not be able, without subsequent reference to these books, to give any reliable idea as to the progress of the business and the position of affairs. Whenever information under these headings is sought for it becomes necessary to refer to the books, and to extract therefrom such information as may be required. At regular stated intervals this information is habitually extracted in the form of Balance Sheets, Trading and Profit and Loss Accounts, Cost Accounts, &c., but these are not as a rule compiled at sufficiently frequent intervals to answer all the purposes of practical business. A manufacturer or merchant who never refers to his accounts, save annually of half-yearly when the usual balance is struck, will, it may safely be said, be obtaining a very small fraction of the benefit that may fairly be expected from the keeping of accurate accounts upon a convenient and workable system. If these accounts are to be utilised to the fullest possible extent, the record that they build up must be examined, and carefully studied in all its bearings, at very frequent intervals. In the case of principals it is hardly to be expected that they will have either the time, or in many cases the skill, to pore over books of account from day to day with a view to discovering all that those books may have to tell; while, in the case of departmental managers, there might in addition be many objections to allowing them access to information that does not immediately and directly concern them. Hence arises the necessity of compiling periodical Returns, which will enable principals and managers to obtain such information as they may require from day to day, from week to week, or from month to month, with a minimum expenditure of time, while yet ensuring that such information shall be both reliable and sufficient for their several purposes.

Periodical Returns being thus eminently of a practical nature, it necessarily follows that, here again, the exact requirements of one concern will vary very greatly from the requirements of another, and it is thus only possible in the present work to refer to the matter in quite general terms. Speaking thus, it may be pointed out that, as a rule, those records that require to be most continually watched are—

(1) The finances of the business, with a view to seeing that Book Debts do not get unduly into arrear, and that sufficient moneys are got in to enable all current liabilities to be duly discharged.

(2) That the Output of the business is kept up.

(3) That the Capital invested in each department of the business is not increased without a corresponding increase of profits.

(4) That Standing Expenses are kept down.

In the case of large concerns, it is usually convenient that each of these matters should be dealt with in the form of a separate Return.

(1) Finances.

The information required under this heading will usually be provided by the Sold Ledger Adjustment Accounts, which show the total Book Debts outstanding; the Bought Ledger Adjustment Accounts, which show the total current liabilities (occasionally, however, special liabilities recorded in the Private Ledger must be added), and the Bank Balance. Often, however, it is convenient to add to these a summary of Cash receipts and payments during the current period, which may readily be compiled from the General Cash Book. When transactions in Bills are extensive, the Return should also show the balances of Bills Receivable and Bills Payable respectively outstanding, and the total of Bills Receivable and Payable accruing due during the next ensuing period.

(2) Turnover

The record under this heading may, as a rule, be readily arrived at from the Day Books, or whatever may be their equivalent in the case of a manufacturing business. The total Sales, or Output, of each department for the current period should be separately shown, and for purposes of comparison it is usually desirable to add (in parallel columns) the total from the date of the last stocktaking up to date, and also the same two sets of figures in the previous one, two, or three years. Such information may be very readily compiled from any ordinary set of books, and is of considerable value, more especially in connection with Return (3).

(3) **Interim Stock Accounts.**

These have already been dealt with in detail in Chapter VII., and *pro formâ* rulings will be found upon page 49. It only remains to be added that in most classes of business, and especially in connection with purely trading concerns, a definite percentage of Gross Profit is expected, not merely upon the Turnover of the business, but also upon the capital from time to time invested in Stock-in-trade. The information supplied by this Return enables those in authority to test (so far as is possible at interim periods, when no actual stocktaking is possible) the manner in which each department is being conducted, and the rate of Profit that is being earned, not merely upon the business done, but also upon the capital invested.

(4) **Expenses.**

The Return under this heading should show the Expenses for the current period in sufficient detail, and also the percentage that such Expenses bear to the Turnover of the business. The corresponding figures of the past two or three years should also be added in parallel columns. Especial care should be taken to see that this Return is really exhaustive, as in the nature of things accruing Expenses are often not recorded in the books of account, save at balancing time. With care, however, no difficulty should arise in arriving at the total expenses of each month or week. Most of the more important Standing Expenses can be accurately estimated in advance; while such items as Discounts, Salaries, Incidental Expenses, &c., can be readily arrived at from the Cash Book, due allowance being made for outstandings at the commencement and close of the current period. That the Return may be readily checked from time to time, however, it is often desirable to frame it upon the same lines as the Sales Return, providing additional columns for the total from the date of the last stocktaking to date. At the end of each financial period the Expenses Return can then be compared with the actual figures available, and discrepancies noted with a view (*a*) to discovering who is responsible for the error; (*b*) to, as far as possible, preventing its recurrence in the future.

SMALLER CONCERNS.

For small businesses separate Returns upon the above lines are often unnecessary, all material information being capable of being readily focussed upon a single statement. Inasmuch as conciseness is at least as much an object to be sought in these Returns as reliability, this focussing of results is in all cases desirable, and even where the business is of such a magnitude as to call for several detailed Returns, a Summary, combining the results upon some such lines as those shown in the following example, may be usefully appended. This example shows a form of Monthly Return which, with varying modifications of detail, may be usefully applied to most trading businesses.

EXAMPLE:

RETURN for 9 Months ending 30th September 1903.

	1903	1902	Compared with previous Year	
			Increase	Decrease
	£ s d	£ s d	£ s d	£ s d
Purchases for the Month	2,000 0 0	1,500 0 0	500 0 0	
Wages do.	900 0 0	650 0 0	250 0 0	
Sales do.	3,000 0 0	2,500 0 0	500 0 0	
Estimated Stock on 30th September	3,500 0 0	2,650 0 0	850 0 0	
Purchases from Stocktaking to Date	12,000 0 0	9,000 0 0	3,0 0 0 0	
Wages do. do.	5,000 0 0	3,750 0 0	1,250 0 0	
Sales do. do.	20,000 0 0	15,000 0 0	5,000 0 0	

APPROXIMATE PROFIT AND LOSS ACCOUNT, for the 9 Months to Date.

	1903		1902	
	£ s d	£ s d	£ s d	£ s d
Assumed Gross Profit @ 15% upon Sales	..	3,000 0 0	..	2,250 0 0
Salaries	1,000 0 0	..	950 0 0	..
Rent, Rates, &c.	400 0 0	..	400 0 0	..
Gas and Electric Light	100 0 0	..	85 0 0	..
Repairs	5 0 0	..	2 0 0	..
Housekeeping	2 0 0	..	2 0 0	..
Discounts	350 0 0	..	260 0 0	..
Fares and Carriage	90 0 0	..	60 0 0	..
Advertising	3 0 0	..	2 0 0	..
Postages	20 0 0	..	15 0 0	..
General Expenses	100 0 0	..	80 0 0	..
Commission	60 0 0	..	40 0 0	..
Travelling Expenses	50 0 0	2,180 0 0	25 0 0	1,921 0 0
Estimated Net Profit..	..	820 0 0	..	329 0 0

FINANCIAL STATEMENT, 30th September 1903.

	£ s d		£ s d
Liabilities on Bought Ledger Account	3,000 0 0	Book Debts Outstanding	2,700 0 0
„ „ Bills Payable	1,500 0 0	Bills Receivable on Hand	1,200 0 0
		Cash at Bank and in Hand	1,825 0 0
	£4,500 0 0		£5,725 0 0

CONCLUSION.

In the present chapter attention has been concentrated upon periodical Returns forming the basis for entries in, or extracted from, books of account. It must not, however, be supposed that these are the only Returns that are required for business purposes. In most undertakings reliable information is required, for comparative purposes, upon many matters which are incapable of being expressed in the form of £ s. d. For example, a railway company will require information as to the number of passengers under each class, the number of train-miles run, the amount of freight carried, &c., &c., all of which information is absolutely essential for the proper and economical management of the undertaking. To indicate even approximately, however, the desirable scope of non-financial Returns would involve a detailed inquiry into the practical working of each separate business considered, and is accordingly quite outside the scope of a work on accounting.

CHAPTER XXVI.

ACCOUNTS FOR LITIGATION.

IN the course of the present work, the subject of accounting has hitherto been considered chiefly, if not entirely, from the point of view of the requirements of business undertakings in this connection, with a view to showing how a full and complete record of the transactions of varying industries may be kept, in books of account, so as to provide at all times such information as may be necessary, or as may properly or reasonably be looked for as a result of keeping books. It remains, however, to be added that when disputes arise as to matters of account—whether or not such disputes lead to actual litigation—it often becomes necessary to deal with those accounts in a somewhat different manner, in order clearly to set forth the view taken by one, or other, of the disputants with regard to the matter at issue.

DISPUTES ON COMPLETED MATTERS.

When the dispute arises out of accounts relating to a concern which has been brought to an end by the discharge of all current liabilities, and the conversion of all outstanding assets into Cash, the dispute can, it is thought, only arise in one of three ways:—

(a) As to whether the account submitted is a correct and complete record of all receipts and payments;

(b) As to whether certain receipts ought not to have been larger, or certain payments smaller;

(c) As to who is entitled to the balance of Cash in hand.

In the first case, the matter is one of simple vouching of an ordinary Cash Account, accompanied perhaps by an inquiry into facts which cannot raise any real dispute on accounts *per se*. The second form of dispute would be analogous to an allegation against an executor or administrator of *devastavit* or abusive or improper administration, which might perhaps involve an inquiry into values, but not into accounts; while the third would be a matter of law pure and simple. It will thus be seen that such disputes as may arise in connection with the accounts of a completed venture, or other business undertaking, are not likely to raise any complicated questions of account at all, and therefore do not call for detailed consideration here.

DISPUTES ON UNCOMPLETED MATTERS.

When, however, the venture—so far from being completed—is still pending (that is to say, when the dispute arises out of the accounts of a going concern) complicated questions of account properly so-called may, and frequently do, arise, and it will probably be generally admitted that these are the questions which are (as a rule) least satisfactorily adjudicated upon in a Court of Law. For that reason, they are in practice frequently referred to Arbitration, and if the Arbitrator be a qualified accountant, such a tribunal is undoubtedly likely to be more satisfactory—assuming, of course, that the dispute on matters of account is not complicated by other disputes on important matters of law or fact. But whether recourse be had to the Courts of Law or to Arbitration, each of the parties to the dispute has to set out his own case, and it is as a rule thought desirable (even in arbitration cases) that this task should be entrusted to Counsel, who upon the whole are, in even the most complicated cases, likely to handle the matter better than the litigant himself could do.

To enable Counsel to do their clients justice, however, it becomes necessary that the whole position should be clearly and concisely laid before them, the strong points being drawn attention to, so that the case may be stated to the best advantage, and the weak points also enumerated, so that they may not be taken by surprise. In complicated cases of account it is often thought that the employment of Counsel places the client at a disadvantage, in that Counsel is under such circumstances called upon to argue upon technical matters with which he cannot reasonably be expected to be quite familiar. This is a view that is very generally entertained by business men, who often make no secret of their opinion that it is no use trying to get lawyers to understand accounts. It is thought, however, that—so far as there is any foundation at all for this grievance—it rests, not upon any lack of ability on the part of the Bar to grasp technical matters that may be clearly laid before them, but rather upon the inadequate manner in which those responsible for Counsel's briefs have discharged their duties. Where complicated questions of account are raised, that call for detailed inquiry in the course of the hearing of a dispute, it is thought that solicitors should in all cases seek professional advice as to the drafting of that portion at least of their brief; and, if necessary, a professional accountant should be retained to confer with Counsel upon this portion of the matter, and to attend with him at Court, with a view to keeping him posted from time to time as to the real effect of the points made by the other side, so far as they affect the accounts. When this course is pursued, it will usually be found that it is as easy

for Counsel effectively to handle questions of accounts as any other questions outside the immediate scope of their ordinary experience.

It is important, however, that, when proceeding upon these lines, accountants should remember that matters which seem fairly obvious to *them* will by no means necessarily be regarded as axioms by trained jurists. In particular is it desirable that the questions in dispute should be confined to the simplest and clearest issues possible, and especially is this the case if a jury are concerned. Accountants are, of course, aware that in the case of most business undertakings the Cash Book is not so much the backbone of the whole structure of accounts as many lawyers seem to think. They should bear in mind, however, that all completed transactions are capable of being verified, or refuted, by being reduced to a Cash basis, and whenever possible, therefore, this principle of reduction to the Cash basis should be employed. It is not merely more convincing to both the trained legal mind and the mind of the ordinary juryman, but also more reliable to all who are prepared to approach the matter without any professional bias. Uncompleted transactions cannot, of course, be always verified by having recourse to the Cash Book standard, but they are often capable of being far more clearly and distinctly explained than by a mere pedantic reference to some particular book of account, and a few of the ordinary academical rules of double-entry bookkeeping. Accountants would do well to bear in mind that what they have to prove is not that such and such a transaction has, or has not, been correctly recorded according to the accepted rules of accounting, but rather what are the actual facts in connection with the matter.

METHODS OF PROCEDURE.

It is quite impossible here to describe in detail the *modus operandi* that professional accountants should pursue in order to discharge to the best advantage their duty of assisting Counsel upon issues involving disputes in connection with accounts. The subject is far too wide a one to be dealt with adequately in a short compass, and indeed it may be questioned whether it would be really practicable to deal with it at all in a text-book. It may be mentioned, however, that one of the most common cases in which disputes arise in connection with accounts is when it is sought to establish a charge of misrepresentation or fraud in connection with accounts, or a charge of falsification of accounts. In these cases the matter is as a rule complicated by the number of the items challenged, and further by the fact that, even if the alleged offence has been committed, it has probably been committed by someone sufficiently experienced in accounts to have done all that lay in his power to cover up his tracks. If, therefore, the allegation is to be proved beyond reach of doubt, it is absolutely essential that the issue, which has been purposely obscured, be cleared not merely of all irrelevant, but also of all comparatively unimportant, items.

In criminal cases it will often be found that, whereas the accused has received money from a customer without debiting Cash (*i.e.*, himself) with the amount so received, the customer's cheque for the amount in question has been actually cleared through the prosecutor's banking account. *Primâ facie*, and without due consideration, anyone approaching the matter from the point of view of accounts might be tempted to charge the delinquent with stealing that specific sum of money received from the customer in question; but proof that the customer's cheque had been paid into the prosecutor's banking account would be a complete refutation of this charge. What has actually happened, in this hypothetical case, is that certain monies have been paid into the bank without being entered in the Cash Book: if, therefore, no monies have been improperly withdrawn, the bank balance should be over to a corresponding extent. The fact that the balance at bank exactly agrees with the balance shown by the Cash Book may suggest that a corresponding sum has been deliberately and improperly abstracted by the cashier; but a suspicion such as this is an entirely different thing from being in a position to *prove* that such money has been deliberately and feloniously abstracted, and what at first sight appeared to be a perfectly straightforward case becomes at once a doubtful and an extremely complicated one.

Another class of dispute in which the aid of professional accountants is often, and advisedly, sought is when the plaintiff seeks to recover money that he has invested in a business, on account of misrepresentations alleged to have been made by the defendant as to the state of that business. Here all that the accountant is concerned with is to show that the representations made by the defendant were false in material particulars, such as would naturally affect the decision of a reasonable business man. In such a case it is usually desirable for him to confine his attack to a comparatively small number of items that can readily and clearly be shown to be wrong. Other items, which in his opinion may be entirely incorrect, should as a rule be left alone, if there is any likelihood of the defendant being able to produce rebutting evidence showing that the matter at issue is one upon which the opinions of competent experts are divided. In such cases, the alleged misrepresentations will probably have taken the form of a Balance Sheet and Trading and Profit and Loss Account submitted by the defendant to the plaintiff, and it will become the duty of the accountant to point out certain specific items in these accounts where misrepresentations have occurred. Very probably the most convenient means of establishing these points will be by cross-examination of the defendant or one of his witnesses. To enable such cross-examination to be conducted by the plaintiff's Counsel conveniently, it is usually desirable to place in his hands a statement containing an exact copy of the accounts originally submitted to the plaintiff by the defendant, to which are appended—in such a manner as to be readily distinguishable from the accounts themselves—notes upon all points likely to arise at the hearing, their effect upon the ultimate result, along with references to the books or other records which must be produced to enable a detailed inquiry to be conducted. It is a great convenience to Counsel to have all this information upon the same sheet as the copy of the account, but it must, of course, be so supplied as to make it absolutely impossible for him to confuse the accountant's comments with the document as originally submitted. This separation can, however, be readily effected by placing a copy of the account in the inside of an open sheet, the various notes and memoranda being placed in margins outside and written in red ink. That it may be quite clear to which item the various marginal notes refer, the copy account should if necessary be spaced out, upon the lines shown in the following

EXAMPLE:

Dr.   PROFIT AND LOSS ACCOUNT,

	Add £ s d	Deduct £ s d			£ s d	£ s d
(A) *This item should include* ALL *expenses under these headings properly chargeable against the year's accounts. Nothing is included for liabilities outstanding under Prize Competition schemes (estimated at).. .. ..*	4,000 0 0		To Rent, Rates, Taxes, Advertising, Printing, Stationery, Wages, Salaries, Postages, Legal Expenses, Commissions, Discount, Lighting and General Expenses (A)		..	6,000 0 0
On 29th December 1900 Mr. A. paid B. C. & Co. £500 for advertising the Company's goods, this should be included to debit of Profit and Loss Account	500 0 0					
(B) *This is a debt due by Mr. A. to the Company (Sold Ledger K, fo. 69), and should be accounted for by him* .	..	20 0 0	„ Bad Debts (B)		..	20 0 0
C) *The Directors are entitled, under Article 69, to £500 per annum, no portion of this has been validly abandoned* ..	450 0 0		„ Directors' Fees (C)..		..	50 0 0
(D) *This item is quite debateable: enquire on what basis it was arrived at* ..	..		„ Depreciation (D)		..	2,000 0 0
			„ Balance carried to Balance Sheet, being Profit for Year		..	3,991 0 0
						£12,061 0 0

for the year ending June 30th 1901.   *Cr.*

	£ s d	£ s d		Add £ s d	Deduct £ s d
By Gross Trading Profits for Year (E) ..	..	12,000 0 0	(E) *Refer Nominal Ledger, fo. 261. See also Returns Book, fo. 79. On 1st July 1901 Goods returned amount to £1,267 10s. 0d.; should be deducted from Sales of current year (gross profit at 10 per cent., say)*	..	126 15 0
„ Transfer Fees (F)	..	1 0 0	(F) *Refer Register of Transfers, fo. 67-9. 72 transfers recorded. 72 × 2/6 = £9. Difference to be accounted for* ..	8 0 0	
„ Interest on Bank Account	..	50 0 0			
„ Profit on Investments Sold	..	10 0 0			
		£12,061 0 0			

BALANCE SHEET,

	Add £ s d	Deduct £ s d	Liabilities.	£ s d	£ s d
			NOMINAL CAPITAL—		
			50,000 6 per cent. Cumulative Preference		
			Shares of £1 each..	50,000 0 0	
			50,000 Ordinary Shares of £1 each ..	50,000 0 0	
			ISSUED CAPITAL—		
			50,000 6 per cent. Cumulative Preference		
			Shares of £1 each..	50,000 0 0	
			25,000 Ordinary Shares of £1 each ..	25,000 0 0	75,000 0 0
			Sundry Creditors	..	1,000 0 0
There is no means of verifying this			Unclaimed Dividends	..	1 0 0
amount, which seems a pure guess:			Customers' Deposits (G)	..	200 0 0
enquire how it is made up					
(¹I) *This item is, of course, subject to altera-*			Profit and Loss Account (H)	3,991 0 0	
tion as affected by items A–F.					
(I) *This deficiency included interim divi-*			*Less* Debit Balance from last Account (I)	3,292 0 0	
dend of 10 per cent. paid on Ordinary					699 0 0
Shares in January 1900. Get this					
admitted: also that there was a loss					
of £792 on the trading for year ended					
30th June 1900.					
					£76,900 0 0

June 30th 1901.

Assets.	£ s d	£ s d			Add £ s d	Deduct £ s
Cash at Bank (K)	..	5,000 0 0	(K)	*This includes a cheque for £7,500 paid to Company on 30th June 1901 by Mr. A.; on following day a correction entry was passed in book, and cheque not presented. The facts were—(1) Bank overdrawn, £2,500; (2) Due to Company from Mr. A., £5,000. Enquire as to how this arose: refer Private Ledger, fos. 11-13.*		
Sundry Debtors..	..	100 0 0				
Stock in Trade	..	4,800 0 0				
Leases, Goodwill, &c., as per Valuation of December 31st 1897, less Stock, and with subsequent additions at cost	82,000 0 0					
Written off to 30th June 1900 (L) £13,000 0 0			(L)	*This was never really written off out of Profits, but is a book entry correcting over-valuation of the item £82,000, which never really cost more than £69,000. Refer Private Ledger, fo. 120: get this admitted.*		
Written off to date (M) .. 2,000 0 0	15,000 0 0	67,000 0 0	(M)	*Only £2,000 really written off for Depreciation in 25 years, lease now only 8 years to run. Get this admitted.*		
		£76,900 0 0				

The foregoing example, it must be understood, is only intended to give some idea of the manner in which an accountant's notes may be conveniently placed in Counsel's hands. The *pro formâ* memoranda appearing in the margin are suggestive of matters that might possibly call for elucidation, with a view to establishing the allegation that the accounts, as submitted, were misleading in material particulars. They must not, however, of course be regarded as exhausting all possibilities of misrepresentation in connection with statements of account. Practically any item in a Balance Sheet, Trading Account, or Profit and Loss Account may, under some circumstances, be seriously misleading. The above example is merely intended to indicate the lines upon which accounts might usefully be framed for the convenience of Counsel at the hearing of a dispute.

It is worthy of notice that by Order LV., rule 37, of the Supreme Court the course of proceedings in Chambers in the Chancery Division is ordinarily the same as the course of proceedings in Court upon motions. Copies, abstracts, or extracts of or from accounts and other documents must, if directed, be supplied for the use of the Judge and his Chief Clerks, and, where so directed, copies must be handed over to the other parties. But copies cannot take the place of originals unless the Judge ·so directs. Where copies are supplied to the Judge, Counsel of the parties supplying the copies should also have them. As has been said, every care should be taken to give Counsel the fullest and clearest information possible as to the accounts which he has to support or attack, whether in Chambers or in Court, and it is generally desirable for the solicitor to confer (with or without the assistance of an accountant) with Counsel on the subject of the accounts before the hearing, in order that every possible point may be taken and all difficulties cleared up. Great confusion may occur through entirely new points being taken in Court, and this should be guarded against as much as possible. Of course, new points will very often arise in the course of cross-examination, but it ought to be made certain that they will not arise in the course of examination-in-chief through the previous reticence of the client, or carelessness of the solicitor. The practice in Chambers is dealt with under Heading viii., "Summonses to Proceed," of Rule LV., and other orders referred to in the Appendix hereto. It may be noted here that, though an accounting party is liable to be cross-examined upon his account, he is entitled to notice of the particular items and points on which he·is to be cross-examined. The cross-examination may take place before the account is touched. A Judge in Chambers can, as a rule of practice in his Chambers, exclude further evidence by a party who has cross-examined the evidence of the other side. (See *Williams* on "The Law of Accounts," p. 25.) It may further be remarked that interrogatories in writing for the examination of the accounting party—as, for instance, an inquiry whether any sums of money are due from a defendant administrator to the estate administered, and, if so, a demand that a particular account of such sums be set forth— may, by the leave of the Court, be delivered upon him. (See *Allfrey v. Allfrey*, 12 Beavan 292, and Order XXXI, rule 1.)

APPENDIX "A."

THE LAW RELATING TO

ACCOUNTS.

BY

J. E. G. DE MONTMORENCY, B.A., LL.B., (CANTAB.)

Of the Middle Temple, BARRISTER-AT-LAW.

APPENDIX A.

ACCOUNTS IN JUDICIAL PROCEEDINGS.

BEFORE dealing with the question of Accounts in specific branches of law, it will be convenient to refer generally to the taking of accounts by order in judicial proceedings.

All causes and matters dealing with the taking of Partnership or other Accounts are assigned to the Chancery Division of the High Court of Justice (Judicature Act, 1873, s. 34 (8)) if the accounts are complicated. If, however, they are simple, they may be dealt with in the King's Bench Division. (*Re Taylor*, 44 C.D. 128, in which case the judicial taking of accounts is very fully considered.) " In all cases in which " the plaintiff in the first instance, desires to have an account " taken, the writ of summons shall be endorsed with a claim " that such account be taken." (Order III., rule 8, of the " Supreme Court, and see *Re Gyhon*, 29 C.D. 834.)

Where a writ of summons has been endorsed for an account, under Ord. III., r. 8, or where the endorsement on a writ of summons involves taking an account, if the defendant either fails to appear, or does not after appearance, by affidavit or otherwise, satisfy the Court or a Judge that there is some preliminary question to be tried, an order for the proper accounts, with all necessary inquiries and directions now usual (see *infra*) in the Chancery Division in similar cases, shall be forthwith made. (Ord. XV., r. 1.) An application for such order as mentioned in this rule must be made by summons and be supported by an affidavit when necessary, filed on behalf of the plaintiff, stating concisely the grounds of his claim to an account. The application may be made at any time after the time for entering an appearance has expired. (Ord. XV., r. 2.)

The equitable principles that underlay the old suit and the modern action for an account are set forth in the following passage from the judgment of Lindley, L.J., in *L.C.D. Railway Co. v. S.E. Railway Co.* (1892, 1 Ch. 140) : " Before " the Judicature Acts a suit for an account could be main- " tained in equity in the following cases :—(1) Where the " plaintiff had a legal right to have money payable to him " ascertained and paid, but which right, owing to defective " legal machinery, he could not practically enforce at law.

" Suits for an account between principal and agent, and " between partners, are familiar instances of this class of " case. (2) Where the plaintiff would have had a legal " right to have money ascertained and paid to him by the " defendant, if the defendant had not wrongfully prevented " such right from accruing to the plaintiff. In such a case, " a Court of law could only give unliquidated damages for the " defendant's wrongful act ; and there was often no machinery " for satisfactorily ascertaining what would have been due " and payable if the defendant had acted properly. In such " a case, however, a Court of Equity decreed an account, " ascertained what would have been payable if the defendant " had acted as he ought to have done and ordered him to " pay the amount : *M'Intosh v. Great Western Railway Co.* " (4 Giff. 683) is the leading authority in this class of case. " (3) Where the plaintiff had no legal but only equitable " rights against the defendant, and where an account was " necessary to give effect to those equitable rights. Ordinary " suits by *cestuis que trustent* against their trustees and suits for " equitable waste fell within this class. (4) Combination of " the above cases." This division is still good if we bear in mind that the old distinction between equity and law has disappeared, and relief can be had in any division of the High Court, though in practice the Chancery Division alone has the machinery to deal with complicated cases of accounts. We may note here that a judgment or order for an account of what is due under a contract does not involve an inquiry as to damages in taking the account (*Manners v. Pearson & Son*, 1898, 1 Ch. 589) ; and also that an action for an account in equity is an action for the balance due on the taking of the account, and not for the several items to be included in it (*ibid.* p. 591 *per* Lindley, L.J.). It must be noticed that an order for an account under Order XV., rule 2, against an executor reserving further consideration but not ordering administration does not destroy the executor's power of preference, nor does it prevent other creditors from suing. (See *Re Barrett*, 43 C.D. p 70.) Nothing short of an order for administration can prevent this. (See Ord. LV., r. 10A (*b*).)

An order under Order XV., rule 1, would, in the case of the administration of an intestate's or a testator's personalty, include the following: An account of the intestate's (or testator's) personal estate, come to the hands of the defendants, B., C., and D., the administrators of his effects (or executors of his will), or of any (or if two only, either) of them ; or to the hands of any other person or persons by the order or for the use of the said defendants, or any (or either) of them ; an account of intestate's (or testator's) debts; an account of the intestate's (or testator's) funeral expenses ; an account of the legacies and annuities given by the testator's will. (See Seton's "Judgments and Orders," 6th edition, pp. 1465-6.) Forms of orders dealing with the administration of a testator's personalty at the suit of a person interested, or of personalty and realty in action by a person interested or by trustees and executors, and other similar orders, will be found set forth in Seton, pp. 1390-1693. Judgments or orders for account generally will be found in Seton, pp. 1352-89.

" The Court or a Judge may, at any stage of the proceed-" ings in a cause or matter, direct any necessary inquiries or " accounts to be made or taken, notwithstanding that it may " appear that there is some special or further relief sought " for or some special issue to be tried, as to which it may be " proper that the cause or matter should proceed in the " ordinary manner." (Ord. XXXIII., r. 2.) This rule only authorises the directing of such accounts and inquiries as are subsidiary to determining the rights of the parties, and which otherwise would be directed at the trial, and does not authorise the sending of the whole case to Chambers. (Garnham v. Skipper, 29 C.D. 566.) As a rule an order for an account cannot be made against a plaintiff. (Toulmin v. Reid, 14 Beav. 505.) As we shall see, questions of very complicated accounts may be referred to a referee. (Arbitration Act, 1889, s. 14, Rochefoucauld v. Boustead, 1897, 1 Ch. 196.)

" The Court or a Judge may, either by the judgment or " order directing the account to be taken or by any " subsequent order, give special directions with regard to the " mode in which the account is to be taken or vouched, and " in particular may direct that in taking the account, the " books of account in which the accounts in question have " been kept shall be taken as primâ facie evidence of the " truth of the matters therein contained (see Banks v. Cart-" wright, 15 W. R., 417 ; Gething v. Keighley, 9 C.D. 547), with " liberty to the parties interested to take such objections ' thereto as they may be advised." (Ord. XXXIII., r. 3.) Where vouchers have been lost, or the account cannot be taken in the ordinary way, the Court may give special directions, but such directions will not be given unless it appears that the ordinary evidence cannot be had. (Lodge v.

Prichard, 3 De G. M. & G. 906.) Audited accounts may be impeached for fraud, even though liberty to do so is not given in the order of the Court. (Holgate v. Shutt, 27 C.D. 111.) " Where any account is directed to be taken, the accounting " party, unless the Court or a Judge shall otherwise direct, " shall make out his account and verify the same by affidavit. " The items on each side of the account shall be numbered " consecutively, and the account shall be referred to by the " affidavit as an exhibit and be left in the Judge's Chambers, " or with the official or other referee, as the case may be." (Ord. XXXIII., r. 4.) Accounts for the Judge's Chambers, when required, may be charged at 8d. lower scale, 1s. higher scale per folio for copying, when costs are taxed on this scale or the scale is allowed. (See App. N to the Annual Practice 1904 ; and see Ord. LV., r. 37.) " Every alteration in an " account verified by affidavit to be left at Chambers shall " be marked with the initials of the Commissioner or " officer before whom the affidavit is sworn, and " such alterations shall not be made by erasure." (Ord. XXXVIII., r. 22.) Accounts shall be referred to as exhibits to affidavits. (Ord. XXXVIII., r. 23.) " Upon the taking of any account, the Court or a Judge may " direct that the vouchers shall be produced at the office of " the solicitor of the accounting party, or at any other " convenient place, and that only such items as may be con-" tested or surcharged shall be brought before the Judge in " Chambers." (Ord. XXXIII., r. 4A.) This rule is intended to prevent the enormous expense and delay which are continually incurred by directing the general accounts to be taken in the Chambers of a Chancery Judge. (Kay, L.J., in Re Fish, Bennett v. Bennett, 1893, 2 Ch., p. 427.) In this connection we may also refer to Ord. LV., r. 10A, which provides that " Upon an application for administration " or execution of trusts by a creditor or beneficiary under " a will, intestacy, or deed of trust, where no " accounts or insufficient accounts have been rendered, the " Court or a Judge may, in addition to the powers already " existing,—order that the application shall stand over for a " certain time, and that the executors, administrators, or " trustees in the meantime shall render to the applicant a " proper statement of their accounts, with an intimation that " if this is not done they may be made to pay the costs of " the proceedings." In the case (supra) of Re Fish the Court gave the plaintiffs, at their own risk as to costs, " the " power, if they like to examine those accounts, to contest " any items in them, including, of course, those pay sheets, " or day sheets (whichever they are called), which show the " charges made by Mr. Herbert Clifford Gosnell against " the estate, and also, if they think fit, entirely at their own " risk as to costs, to surcharge any item which may be " omitted in the accounts, and then if the contested items " are not arranged with the trustees, or if the surcharges

" are not arranged, liberty to bring any contested items
" before the Judge in Chambers, who is to be at liberty to
" refer any disputed items in the bills of costs to the Taxing
" Master to be taxed. And I beg to say that I understand
" that to mean that in those pay sheets of *Mr. Herbert
" Gosnell* every item which is contained in them, whether
" it be a charge for trustee's work or a charge for costs
" properly so called, is a charge which may, if contested, be
" moderated by the Chief Clerk, or by the Taxing Master
" before whom it goes. . . . If in the investigation of
" the accounts little or no change shall be made, then the
" Judge will have to consider how far the Plaintiffs' next
" friend and the adult Plaintiffs should pay the costs of that
" part of the action. If, on the other hand, considerable
" alteration is made, the Judge will have to consider whether
" the Defendants, or some of them, ought not to bear those
" costs or some part of them." (Pp. 427-8.) This important
judgment by Lord Justice Kay has been quoted at this length
as it throws considerable light on the practice of the Courts,
both with respect to accounts, and the costs—an important
matter—incurred in the preparation and investigation of
accounts. The " Annual Practice " (1904) states that the
practice of directing accounts to be furnished and vouched
out of Court is now largely followed. Trustees, it is added,
are entitled, on being required to furnish accounts in
respect of their trust estate, to demand that they should be
guaranteed against the expense of complying with the
requisition. (*Re Bosworth*, 58 L.J. Ch. 432.)

It is necessary to note that " any party seeking to charge
" any accounting party beyond what he has by his account
" admitted to have received shall give notice thereof to the
" accounting party, stating, so far as he is able, the amount
" sought to be charged and the particulars thereof in a short
" and succinct manner." (Ord. XXXIII., r. 5.) The
remaining three rules of this order are all of importance.
Rule 6 provides that " every judgment or order for a
" general account of the personal estate of a testator or
" intestate shall contain a direction for an inquiry what
" parts (if any) of such personal estate are outstanding or
" undisposed of, unless the Court or a Judge shall otherwise
" direct." It is obvious that such an inquiry is essential
for the completion of a general account. Rule 7 provides
that " where by any judgment or order, whether made in
" Court or in Chambers, any accounts are directed to be
" taken or inquiries to be made, each such direction shall
" be numbered so that, as far as may be, each distinct
" account and inquiry may be designated by a number, and
" such judgment or order shall be in the Form No. 28 in
" Appendix L., [to the Rules of the Supreme Court] with
" such variations as the nature of the case may require."
Form No. 28 is a form of ordering accounts and inquiries.
Form No. 11 in Appendix L is also of importance, as it gives
the form of an affidavit verifying accounts and answering
usual inquiries as to real and personal estate. (See Ord.
LV., r. 75, and also Daniel's " Chancery Forms," 5th
Edition, pp. 597-610.) The form of account verified by this
affidavit and called " Account A," is given in Form
No. 12, which contains a numbered list of dated receipts
and disbursements, while Form No. 13 is a similar account
of rents and profits referred to in Form 11 as " Account B."
Form 14 is an important form of Receiver's Account, to
which I shall have occasion to refer directly in connection
with the Rules of the Supreme Court dealing with Receivers.

Before doing so, I must complete my reference to
accounts generally :—" Where an account is directed, the
" certificate shall state the result of such account, and not
" set the same out by way of schedule, but shall refer to
" the account verified by the affidavit filed, and shall specify
" by the numbers attached to the items in the account
" which, if any, of such items have been disallowed or
" varied, and shall state what additions, if any, have been
" made by way of surcharge or otherwise, and where the
" account, verified by the affidavit has been so altered that
" it is necessary to have a fair transcript of the account as
" altered, such transcript may be required to be made by the
" party prosecuting the judgment or order, and shall then
" be referred to by the certificate. The accounts and the
" transcripts (if any) referred to by certificates shall be filed
" therewith or retained in Chambers and subsequently filed,
" as the Judge in Chambers may direct. No copy of any
" such account shall be required to be taken by any party."
(Ord. LV., r. 68.) It may be noted in connection with this
rule that no question could be raised by the certificate of the
Chief Clerk on matters with respect to which there is no
direction in the order under which the certificate is made.
(*In re Tillett*, 32 C.D. 639.) Also we may note that, in a
question of Partnership Accounts arising in an action of
administration of the estate of a deceased partner, the
certificate must distinguish between private and partnership
debts. (*Re Hodgson*, 31 C.D. 177.) In connection with the
certificate, it is necessary further to note that every certificate,
with the accounts, if any, to be filed therewith, shall be
transmitted by the Chief Clerk to the Central Office to be
filed, and shall thenceforth be binding on all the parties to
the proceedings, unless discharged or varied upon application by summons within eight clear days after the filing :
provided that the time for applying to discharge or vary
certificates, to be acted upon by the Paymaster-General
without further order, or certificates on passing receivers'
accounts, shall be two clear days after the filing thereof.
(Ord. LV., r. 70.) The Judge may, however, if the special
circumstances of the case require it, upon an application by
motion or summons for the purpose, direct a certificate to be
discharged or varied at any time after the same has become
binding on the parties. (Ord. LV., r. 71.)

We have still two remaining rules in Order XXXIII. that require notice : — " In taking any account directed by any " judgment or order, all just allowances shall be made " without any direction for that purpose." (Ord. XXXIII., r. 8.) Thus, in the case of an order dealing with the manage ment of a business carried on by an executor, though the executor cannot charge for time and work, he is entitled to all just allowances in the taking of an account of profits, even though he is a partner. (*Re Norrington*, 13 C.D. 654.) What are just allowances in particular cases may be gathered from the cases of the *Union Bank of London v. Ingram* (16 C.D. 53), *Rees v. Metro- politan Board of Works* (14 C.D. 372), *Vyse v. Foster* (L.R. 7 H.L. 318). Order XXXIII., r. 8B, directs that each Chief Clerk at the beginning of each sittings shall report to the Judge to whose Chambers he is attached all the cases in which he considers that there has been any undue delay in the proceedings before him. If (Ord. XXXIII., r. 9) it appears to the Court or Judge that there is any undue delay in the prosecution of any accounts or inquiries, the Court or Judge may require any party in the case to explain the delay, and may thereupon make such order with regard to expediting the proceedings as the circumstances of the case may require. (See also Order LV., r. 32.)

We may note generally with respect to the practice as to accounts in judicial proceedings that, if the Judge so directs, his Chief Clerks shall take such accounts and make such inquiries as have usually been taken and made by the Chief Clerks, and the Judge shall give such aid and directions in every such account or inquiry as he may think fit, but sub- ject to the right of the parties in certain cases to bring any particular point before the Judge. (Ord. LV., r. 15.) Of course, it must be remembered that in *all* cases the parties have a right to see the Judge personally, but where such an adjournment into Court is unnecessary, the party so adjourn- ing the case may have to pay the costs. It is important, moreover, to remember that in certain large classes of cases the Judge must deal personally with the matter. No order for accounts or inquiries concerning the property of a deceased person or other property held upon any trust or concerning the parties entitled thereto must be made, except by the Judge in person. (Ord. LV., r. 15A.) Moreover, where accounts are being taken in Chambers before the Chief Clerk, either party has a right to have an item which has been found against him adjourned before the Judge without taking out a summons for that purpose. And where a question of principle is involved in a particular item it may be necessary to do this. But the ordinary practice is to wait till the account is completed, and then take the adjournment once for all before the Judge. If a solicitor were so unreasonable as to insist on the adjournment of every item in an account to which he might object, the

Judge could punish the solicitor by making him pay the costs personally. (*Upton v. Brown*, 20 C.D. 731, *per* Jessel, M.R.) An adjournment to the Judge is not in the nature of an appeal, since there exists a right to have a point heard by the Judge personally. (*Smith v. Watts*, 22 C.D. 5.) It is further important to remember that the Judge in Chambers may, in such way as he thinks fit, obtain the assistance of accoun- tants, merchants, engineers, actuaries, and other scientific persons the better to enable any matter at once to be deter- mined, and he may act upon the certificate of any such person. (Ord. LV., r. 19.) The Judge cannot, however, delegate this power of calling in expert assistance to his Chief Clerks (*Mildmay v. Lord Methuen*, 1 Drew. 216) ; and when such an expert is called in by the Judge his evidence is merely material to guide the Judge, and he cannot call witnesses to support his evidence (see " Annual Practice," 1904 : *Morris v. Llanelly Railway Co.*, W.N. (1868) 46 ; *Ford v. Tynte*, 2 De G. J. & S. 127). An accountant so called in need not be employed in the presence of the parties (*Re London and Birmingham, etc., Railway Co.*, 6 W.R. 141), while the fact of such employment is additional to and not in substitution for the taking of accounts in Chambers. The allowance to such an accountant is in addition to the Court fee. (*Hutchinson v Norwood*, 32 W.R. 392.) The fees to be paid to such expert accountants and other experts called in by the Judge are to be regulated by the taxing officers, subject to appeal to the Court or Judge, whose decision shall be final. (Ord. LXV., r. 27 (36).) In the case of *Meymott v. Meymott* (33 Beav. 590), with respect to the general question of the payment of accountants, Sir John Romilly, M.R., said : " When the Chief Clerk appoints an " accountant, he always previously makes an arrangement " with him as to the amount of his remuneration ; but when " the accountant is employed by the parties themselves, the " Chief Clerk never interferes, but allows them to make their " own terms." This is still, there can be little doubt, the rule, and the further decision that the rule as to remunera- tion of accountants followed in bankruptcy proceedings is also followed in Chancery proceedings has never been overruled. Sir John Romilly, however, expressly declined to apply this rule in the case of official managers and liquidators employed in winding up companies. In this case, therefore, two guineas a day to the accountant for work done, one guinea a day to his chief clerk, and twelve to fifteen shillings a day to his junior clerk were allowed, as proper remuneration, by the Court. In this case the accountant was nominated by the parties and appointed by the Chief Clerk. We may also note here that if a plaintiff claims a general account he need not give particulars of the sums which it is alleged that the defendant has received to his use. But this is not the case if a specific sum be claimed. (*Blackie v. Osmaston*, 28 C.D. 123 ; *Augustinus v. Nerinckx*, 16 C.D. 17.) If the Court sees that an account must be taken it will not order particulars, but the mere asking for an account will not prevent the Court from ordering particulars. (*Kemp v. Goldberg*, 36 C.D. 505 ; Ord. XIX., r. 6, "Annual Practice," 1904.)

Finally, the Judge may order in proper cases accounts and inquiries to be referred to District Registrars. (Judicature Act, 1873, s. 66.) It must always be remembered in beginning legal proceedings for account that all actions for account must be brought within six years after the settlement of the account, or the time when the cause of action arose, or the last acknowledgment or part payment. (See Statutes, 21 Jac. 1, c. 16, s. 3, and 19 & 20 Vict. c. 97, s. 9, and Seton, pp. 1369-1370.)

Turning now to the question of Receivers' Accounts. Where a receiver is appointed for the purpose of equitable execution " with a direction that he shall pass accounts, the " Court or Judge shall fix the days upon which he shall " (annually or at longer or shorter periods) leave and pass " such accounts, and also the days upon which he shall pay " the balances appearing due on the accounts so left, or such " part thereof as shall be certified as proper to be paid by " him. And with respect to any such receiver as shall " neglect to leave and pass his accounts and pay the " balances thereof at the times so to be fixed for that purpose " as aforesaid, the Judge before whom any such receiver is " to account may from time to time, when his subsequent " accounts are produced to be examined and passed, disallow " the salary therein claimed by such receiver, and may also, " if he shall think fit, charge him with interest at " the rate of 5 per cent. per annum upon the balances " so neglected to be paid by him during the time " the same shall appear to have remained in the " hands of any such receiver." (Ord. L., r. 18.) If the question of Receivers' Accounts arises in the King's Bench Division, the practice of the Chancery Division is followed, as the receivers are appointed for an equitable purpose. (See *Walmsley v. Mundy*, 13 Q.B.D., 807.) It is to be noted that the jurisdiction over the receiver continues even after the accounts have been settled. At this late hour the penalties of the rule can be enforced. (*Hicks v. Hicks*, 3 Atk. 273 ; "Annual Practice," 1904.)

Receivers' Accounts have to be in the form No. 14 in Appendix L, with such variations as circumstances may require. (Ord. L., r. 19.) This form deals separately with receipts and payments and allowances on account of real estate and personal estate. Rule 20 directs that " every receiver " shall leave in the Chambers of the Judge to whom the cause " or matter is assigned his account, together with an affidavit " verifying the same in the form No. 22 in Appendix L., with " such variations as circumstances may require. An appoint-

" ment shall thereupon be obtained by the plaintiff or person " having the conduct of the cause for the purpose of passing " such account." It is further provided that " in case of any " receiver failing to leave any account or affidavit, or to pass " such account, or to make any payment, or otherwise, the " receiver or the parties, or any of them, may be required to " attend at Chambers to show cause why such account or " affidavit has not been left, or such account passed, or such " payment made, or any other proper proceeding taken, and " thereupon such directions as shall be proper may be given " at Chambers or by adjournment into Court, including the " discharge of any receiver and appointment of another, and " payment of costs." (Ord. L., r. 21.) It is necessary to note finally that a certificate of the Chief Clerk, stating the result of the receiver's account, is to be taken from time to time. (Ord. L., r. 22.)

The above rules as to Receivers' Accounts have an importance that extends beyond such accounts, for it is especially provided by the Rules of the Supreme Court that the accounts of liquidators and of guardians shall be passed and verified in the same manner as is by the above rules directed in the case of Receivers' Accounts. (Ord. L., rules 23, 24.)

Some reference must be made as to accounts in relation to the Arbitration Act 1889 (52 & 53 Vict. c. 49). Section 14 provides that in any cause or matter (other than a criminal proceeding by the Crown) if (*inter alia*) the question in dispute consists wholly or in part of matters of account, the Court or a Judge may at any time order the whole cause or matter, or any question or issue of fact arising therein, to be tried before a special referee or arbitrator respectively agreed on by the parties, or before an Official Referee or officer of the Court. We must note in passing that a Master of the Supreme Court may exercise all the jurisdiction and powers conferred upon the Court or a Judge by the Arbitration Act, 1899. (Ord. LIV., r. 12A.) The case cannot, however, be referred without the consent of the parties where the result depends partly on questions of law and fact, and partly on questions of account and scientific evidence. (*Case v. Willis*, 8 *Times*' Reports 610.) The expression " matters of account " is largely construed (*Re Leigh*, 3 C.D. 292) and " if the Court " can see that part of the dispute between the parties is " matter of account, that gives jurisdiction to refer the whole " case " (*Hurlbatt v. Barnett*, 1893, 1 Q.B. 79), except where there is a preliminary question as to the liability of the defendant. (*Ward v. Pilley*, 5 Q.B.D. 427, and see also *Case v. Willis* and the " Annual Practice," 1904.) As to the practice on trial as to accounts before a referee, reference must be made to Rules of the Supreme Court, Ord. XXXVI., part 8, rules 43-55C. The referee (subject to the order of the Court or a Judge) may hold the trial at or adjourn it to any place which he may deem most convenient, and have any inspection or view either by himself or with his assessors (if any), which he may deem expedient for the better disposal of the controversy before him. He must, moreover, unless otherwise directed by the Court or a Judge, proceed with the trial *de die in diem*, in a similar manner as in actions tried with a jury. (Ord. XXXVI., r. 48.) The Official Referees are to sit at least from 10 a.m. to 1 p.m. on Saturdays, and from 10 a.m. to 4 p.m. on other days during the sittings of the High Court. (Ord. LXIII., r. 16.) Subject to any order to be made by the Court or a Judge ordering the same, evidence shall be taken at any trial before a referee, and the attendance of witnesses may be enforced by *subpœna*, and every such trial to be conducted in the same manner, as nearly as circumstances will admit, as trials are conducted before a Judge. (Ord. XXXVI., r. 49.) Subject also to any such order, the referee is to have the same authority with respect to discovery and production of documents, and in the conduct of any reference or trial, and the same power to direct that judgment be entered for any or either party, as a Judge of the High Court (Ord. XXXVI., r. 50); but the referee cannot commit any person to prison or enforce any order by attachment or otherwise (Ord. XXXVI., r. 51). Moreover, before the conclusion of any trial before a referee, or by his report under the reference made to him, he may submit any question arising therein for the decision of the Court, or may state any facts specially for the Court to draw inferences therefrom, and in any such case the order to be made on such submission or statement shall be entered as the Court shall direct; and the Court shall have power to require any explanations or reasons from the referee, and to remit the cause or matter, or any part thereof, for retrial or further consideration to the same or any other referee; or the Court may decide the question referred to any referee on the evidence taken before him, either with or without additional evidence as the Court may direct. (Ord. XXXVI., r. 52.)

There is an appeal to the High Court (in the King's Bench Division to a Divisional Court) from a referee to whom a case is referred for trial, either by motion to set aside or vary the report or award and the judgment entered thereon, or by motion for a new trial. In the Chancery Division, the appeal would be to the Court of Appeal. (See the Judicature Act, 1894, s. 1 (15), and the Arbitration Act, 1889, s. 15 (2).) The report or award of any official or special referee or arbitrator on any such reference shall, unless set aside by the Court or a Judge, be equivalent to the verdict of the jury. (Arbitration Act, 1889, s. 15 (2).)

The remuneration to be paid to any special referee or arbitrator to whom the matter is referred under order of the Court or a Judge, shall be determined by the Court or a Judge (*ibid.*, s. 15 (3)); but an arbitrator under submission may fix his own fees, unless a contrary intention is expressed in the submission, and the costs of reference and of the award are in his discretion (Arbitration Act, 1889, s. 2 (*i*)).

It will be convenient here to notice certain cases where accounts can be compelled. An agent (but not apparently a principal) is liable to account where the course of dealing presumes the keeping of regular accounts. Where copyright is infringed, the right to account follows the obtaining of an injunction. (*Baily v. Taylor*, 1 Russ. & M. 73.) The right to account (if the case involves account) generally follows the right to an injunction, but of course it also arises otherwise. (See *Parrot v. Palmer*, 3 Myl. & K. 632.) An action for account will lie against a banker by his customers (*Bowles v. Orr*, 1 Y. & C. 464), and between tradesmen and their customers (*Courtenay v. Godschall*, 9 Ves. 473), and between merchants and commercial travellers to a certain extent (*Hunter v. Belcher*, 9 L.T. 501); also in the case of mines and tithes (*Pulteney v. Warren*, 6 Ves. 88), and between landlord and tenant (*O'Connor v. Spaight*, 1 Sch. & Lef. 305); also in the case of rents and profits arising from property alleged to be wrongly occupied (*Hicks v. Gallitt*, 3 De G. M. & G. 782). It is perhaps hardly necessary to state that merchants' accounts, after six years' total discontinuance, are barred (*Martin v. Heathcote*, 2 Eden 169); but, of course, if open accounts are continued by subsequent acts, they are not barred by length of time unless a settled balance can be presumed. As to what amounts to a settled and stated account depends upon the circumstances of the case. No precise form is necessary (*Sim v. Sim*, 11 Ir. Ch.Rep. 310), but it may be said generally that a clear statement of accounts signed by the parties may be regarded as a settled account, since it creates a single issue. (See *Attorney-General v. Brooksbank*, 2 Y. & J. 37.) But signature is not absolutely necessary (*Willis v. Jernegan*, 2 Atk. 252), nor need there be a minute settlement of items (see *Sewell v. Bridge*, 1 Ves. 297), and a merchant's account unchallenged for two years is regarded as stated (see *Tickel v. Short*, 2 Ves. 239). Settled accounts can only be re-opened on very strong grounds. (*Chambers v. Goldwin*, 5 Ves. 837.) The principles on which such accounts are re-opened are dealt with in the cases of *Coleman v. Mellersh* (2 Mac. & G. 309), *Buckeridge v. Whalley* (33 L.J. Ch. 649), *Newen v. Wellen* (31 L.J. Ch. 792), *Williamson v. Barbour* (9 C.D. 529), *Wier v. Tucker* (L.R. 14 Eq. 25), *Hickson v. Aylward* (3 Moll. 14), *Lewis v. Morgan* (5 Price 42), *M'Kellar v. Wallace* (8 Moore P.C. 378)

Partnership Accounts.

Section 28 of the Partnership Act, 1890 (53 & 54 Vict. c. 39), declares that "Partners are bound to render true "accounts and full information of all things affecting the "partnership to any partner or his legal representatives." This clause is usually inserted in partnership deeds, and it, apart from statute, represents a principle and an obligation —the obligation of *uberrima fides*—inherent in any partnership contract. The right to an account as between partners, or between a partner and the personal representatives, or the trustee in bankruptcy of a partner is undoubted. When a partner mortgages his share in a partnership and the mortgagee brings an action to realise his mortgage, the proper order is to direct an account of what the mortgagor's interest in the partnership was at the date when the mortgagee proceeded to take possession under his mortgage, that is, at the date of the writ; but if a dissolution of the partnership has previously taken place, the date of the dissolution is the date at which the account is to be taken. (*Whetham v. Davey*, 30 C.D. 574.) Again, if the partnership share is assigned with the consent of the other partners, the assignee is entitled to an account. (*Redmayne v. Forster*, 2 Eq. 467.) In certain cases the beneficiaries under the will of a deceased partner can have an account against the surviving partners (*Travis v. Milne*, 9 Hare 141), but, as a rule, their remedy is against the personal representatives of the deceased partner.

"The account which a partner may seek to have taken, "may be either a general account of the dealings and trans-"actions of the firm, with a view to a winding up of the "partnership; or a more limited account, directed to some "particular transaction as to which a dispute has risen." (Lindley, p. 496, 6th Edition.) There is no longer any iron rule that accounts can only be taken by the Court in partnership with a view to a dissolution, but the rule will be followed unless there is a good reason for departing from it. Lord Justice Lindley gives "three classes of cases in which actions for an account without a dissolution, are more particularly common " (p. 497).

"1. Where one partner has sought to withhold from his co-partner the profit arising from some secret transaction.

"2. Where the partnership is for a term of years still unexpired, and one partner has sought to exclude or expel his co-partner or to drive him to a dissolution.

"3. Where the partnership has proved a failure, and the partners are too numerous to be made parties to the action, and a limited account will result in justice to them all."

Where the partnerships of the various partners in one concern began at different dates, the Court will order, upon the bankruptcy of all the partners, the making of separate accounts, and that each estate shall first bear its own debts. (*Ex parte Marlin*, 2 Bro. C.C. 15.) In an action to take accounts of a partnership where the partnership is admitted, and no other question is in issue except the accounts, accounts of the partnership dealings may be ordered to be taken before the trial of the action. (*Turquand v. Wilson*, 1 C.D. 85.) If a partner's private transactions are mixed up with the partnership accounts the whole accounts must be produced, unless they can be satisfactorily severed. (*Pickering v. Pickering*, 25 C.D. 247.) It must, however, be noticed that a person cannot be compelled to produce books which belong jointly to himself and other persons who are not before the Court (see *Murray v. Walter*, Cr. & Ph. 114); but the doctrine laid down in this case "does not apply to cases in which the absent "parties interested in the books are in fact represented by "the defendants on the record, and have no interest in "conflict with theirs (*Glyn v. Cauldfeild*, 8 Mac. & G. 463); "nor it is said to an action by a *cestui que trust* against a "trustee who is charged with trading with trust monies in part-"nership with other persons not before the Court " (Lindley, pp. 505-6). We may note also that "the common order does "not entitle the person in whose favour it is made to "inspect by a professed accountant specially appointed "for the purpose; but if there is any necessity for so doing, a "special order for inspection by such a person will be made." (*Bonnardet v. Taylor*, 1 J. & H. 383.) "Books in use for "daily business are ordered to be produced at the place "where they are usually kept; and they will not be ordered "to be deposited in Court unless there is some special reason "for so doing (*Mertens v. Haigh Johns*, 735)," (Lindley, 506). We also note that accounts kept by a clerk who was the agent of all the members of the partnership, were received in evidence without his being called as a witness. (*Brierley v. Cripps*, 7 C. & P. 709.) This is also the place in which to notice the fact that "the partnership books are to be kept at the place of "business of the partnership (or the principal place, if "there is more than one), and every partner may, when he "thinks fit, have access to and inspect and copy any of "them." (Partnership Act, 1890, s. 24 (9).) A solvent partner is entitled to retain the partnership books when the other has become bankrupt. (*Ex parte Finch*, 1 Deac. & C. 274.) "Where a partnership has expired by efflux of time, and "in a suit for an account, &c., a receiver has been appointed "before decree, the Court will not compel defendant "(the former managing partner) to deliver up to receiver, "for the purpose of making out bills of costs, partnership "books and accounts, which have remained in his hands, "and title deeds belonging to a third person, which came "into the possession of the co-partners as solicitors, such "defendant offering the receiver free access thereto, and "to assist in making out such bills." ("Digest of English "Case Law," Vol. 10, cols. 494-5. *Dacie v. John*, 13 Price, 446.)

With respect to the defences to an action for an account and discovery between partners, Lord Justice Lindley in his book (p. 508) deals with six defences, in addition to "the "defence on the ground of illegality, of fraud, of laches on "the part of the plaintiff, and of want of proper parties to "the action." These six are:—(1) Denial of partnership; (2) Statute of Limitations; (3) Account stated; (4) Arbitrators' award already given on the matters of difference between the parties; (5) Payment and accord and satisfaction — *i.e.*, "payment of a sum of money and "acceptance of it in lieu of all demands"; (6) A release of all claims under seal. A release can, of course, be set aside on certain well-known grounds, and, if set aside, it ceases to be a defence.

A judgment for a partnership account in its simplest form is as follows: "Let an account be taken of all partnership "dealings and transactions between the plaintiff and "defendant as co-partners from ————. And let what, "upon taking the said account, shall be certified to be due "from either of the said parties to the other of them be within "(one month) from the date of the Master's certificate, paid by "the party from whom to the party to whom the same shall "be certified to be due. Liberty to apply." ("Seton on Decrees," 6th Ed., p. 2166.)

The question of Partnership Accounts is materially affected by Sections 29 and 30 of the Partnership Act, 1890.

Section 29 provides that "(1) Every partner must account to "the firm for any benefit derived by him without the consent "of the other partners from any transaction concerning the "partnership, or from any use by him of the partnership "property name, or business connexion. (2) This section "applies also to transactions undertaken after a partnership "has been dissolved by the death of a partner, and before "the affairs thereof have been completely wound up, either "by any surviving partner or by the representatives of the "deceased partner." Section 30 provides that "If a partner, "without the consent of the other partners, carries on any "business of the same nature as and competing with that of "the firm, he must account for and pay over to the firm "all profits made by him in that business." This does not, however, apply to profits made by a partner in a business that he carries on in breach of a covenant not to carry on any other business, but which is not in competition with the partnership business. (*Aas v. Benham*, 1891, 2 Ch. 244.)

The principles on which the accounts of a trading company should be kept and the profits ascertained, are laid down in *Lubbock v. British Bank of South America* (1892,

2 Ch. 198) and *Bolton v. Natal Land and Colonization Company* (1892, 2 Ch. 124). In the first case, a banking company, with a paid-up capital of £500,000, sold part of its undertaking for £875,000; after deducting the paid-up capital and other incidental expenses there remained a net balance of £205,000. This sum was held to be profit on capital and not part of the capital itself, and might be carried to Profit and Loss Account, and, after such an appropriation to the Reserve Fund as the directors thought proper, be distributed as dividends. Mr. Justice Chitty in this case dealt at length with the general principles on which the accounts of a trading company should be kept. On these questions of accounts the case of *Lee v. Neuchâtel Asphalte Company* (41 C.D. 1) should also be referred to, and Lindley on Companies, p. 429 *et seq.* (Ed. 5), together with Lindley on Partnership, p. 396, *et seq.* (Ed. 6).

The method of dealing with accounts on a dissolution of partnership is set forth in Section 44 of the Partnership Act, 1890. "In settling accounts between the partners after a "dissolution of partnership, the following rules shall, subject "to any agreement, be observed:—(a) Losses, including "losses and deficiencies of capital, shall be paid first out "of profits, next out of capital, and lastly, if necessary, by "the partners individually in the proportion in which they "were entitled to share profits: (b) the assets of the firm "including the sums, if any, contributed by the partners to "make up losses or deficiencies of capital, shall be applied "in the following manner and order:— (1) In paying the "debts and liabilities of the firm to persons who are not "partners therein: (2) In paying to each partner rateably "what is due from the firm to him for advances as dis-"tinguished from capital: (3) In paying to each partner "rateably what is due from the firm to him in respect of "capital: (4) The ultimate residue, if any, shall be divided "among the partners in the proportion in which profits are "divisible." (See Lindley on Partnership, pp. 599-601 and 633.)

The following form of judgment exhibts the process followed in the case of a dissolution caused by the death of a partner. (1) Let an account be taken of all dealings and transactions between W. deceased, the testator in the pleadings named, and the defendant, as bankers and co-partners; and Let what, upon taking the said account, shall be found due from the testator be answered by the plaintiffs, as the executors of his will, out of his assets; (2) And in case the plaintiffs shall not admit assets of the testator come to their hands — Account against them of his personalty—Settled accounts not to be disturbed. (Seton, p. 2813.)

The usual accounts of a deceased partner's personal estate in an action by beneficiaries are ascertained by "an inquiry

"what was the amount of the testator's capital, stock-in-
"trade, credits, debts, and liabilities in the partnership trade
"or business of, &c., in the pleadings mentioned, on the foot-
"ing of the deed of, &c. An inquiry whether any, and
"which, of the debts due to the said partnership at the date
"of the said deed remained unpaid, and under what circum-
"stances, and whether any, and what, steps ought to be taken
"for recovering the same; an account of the business, and
"of the profits and losses thereof, in each year since the
"testator's death; an inquiry what is the present amount of
"the capital, and of the credits, debts, and liabilities of the
"said business, and how much capital has been derived"
(Seton, p. 2200). It may finally be noted that to an action
by beneficiaries against the representatives of a deceased
partner for a general partnership account, all the surviving
partners must be made parties. (*Vyse v. Foster*, L.R. 7 H.L.,
318.)

Accounts in the Winding-up of Estates.

One of the first duties of an executor is to be prepared with
his accounts of the estate of the deceased, and to neglect this
duty is a ground for charging him with interest. (*Pearse v.
Green*, 1 J. and W. 140.) The accounts must be kept clear
and distinct, and if the executor allows these accounts to
become mixed with his own trading accounts he cannot
refuse to produce such account books. (*Freeman v. Fairlie*,
3 Mer. 44.) It must further be remembered that a legatee,
though he has no right to a copy of the estate accounts at the
expense of the estate, has a right to inspect such accounts and
to have a satisfactory explanation of the position of the estate
assets. (*Ottley v. Gilby*, 8 Beav. 602.)

It would seem in view of the provisions of the Land
Transfer Act, 1897 (Sections 1 (1) and 2 (2) and 2 (3)), that
this rule also applies to an heir and devisee of real estate.
These sections must be set out here, as it would certainly
appear that this Act has cast further duties as to accounts
upon the personal representatives of a deceased person :—

Section 1 (1) "Where real estate is vested in any person
without a right in any other person to take by survivorship
it shall, on his death, notwithstanding any testamentary
disposition, devolve to and become vested in his personal
representatives or representative from time to time as if it
were a chattel real vesting in them or him."

Section 2 (2) "All enactments and rules of law relating
to the effect of probate or letters of administration as
respects chattels real, and as respects the dealing with
chattels real before probate or administration, and as
respects the payment of costs of administration and other
matters in relation to the administration of personal estate,
and the powers, rights, duties, and liabilities of personal
representatives in respect of personal estate, shall apply
to real estate so far as the same are applicable, as if that
real estate were a chattel real vesting in them or him, save
that it shall not be lawful for some or one only of
several joint personal representatives, without the authority
of the court, to sell or transfer real estate."

Section 2 (3) "In the administration of the assets of a
person dying after the commencement of this Act, his
real estate shall be administered in the same manner,
subject to the same liabilities for debt, costs, and
expenses, and with the same incidents, as if it were
personal estate; provided that nothing herein contained
shall alter or affect the order in which real and personal
assets respectively are now applicable in or towards the
payment of funeral and testamentary expenses, debts,
or legacies, or the liability of real estate to be charged
with the payment of legacies."

It is therefore conceived that until the real estate is
vested in the heir or devisee the personal representatives
have the same duty to account for rents and profits as
in the case of leaseholds. This will frequently involve a
considerable increase of responsibility in the matter of
accounts on the part of the personal representatives. It
may be noted here that "trustees can, where they are
"required to furnish accounts in respect of their trust
"estate, demand to be paid or to be guaranteed the costs
"of doing so before complying: it makes no difference that
"one of the trustees is a solicitor." (*Re Bosworth*, 58 L.J.
Ch. 432); ("Williams on Executors," p. 1891.) An executor
"must account for all profits which have accrued in his
"own time, either spontaneously or by his acts, out of
"the estate of the deceased." (Williams, p. 1744.)
Thus profits may accrue after the death of the testator
by contract, by remainder, by increase, and by condition
("as where a lease for years . . . was granted by the
"testator, upon condition that if the grantee did not pay
"such a sum of money, or do other acts, &c., and this
"condition is broken or not performed after the testator's
"death, the chattel will be brought back to the executor
"and be assets." Williams, p. 1522.) Moreover, all profits
derived by the executor from his office, as where he
abandons it in favour of another for a valuable consideration, must be brought into account. All profits derived
from the carrying on of the testator's business or trade
must be brought into account. Moreover, "if a partner
"in a trading firm dies, and if he constitutes one or more
"of his co-partners his executors, and if there is nothing
"special in the contract of co-partnership, and if the assets
"of the testator are not withdrawn from the co-partnership

" but are left in it, and no liquidation is arrived at,
" no settlement of accounts come to, it is a trite and
" familiar rule in the Court of Chancery to hold that the
" estate of that testator is to all intents and purposes
" entitled to the benefit of a share of the profits which are
" made in the trade after his death." (Lord Cairns, L.R.
Vyse v. Foster, 7 H.L. 318.)

The general principle is that accrued profits in the
hands of an executor must be accounted for, while any
losses due to the laying out of the assets on private
securities cannot be recouped out of the assets. A Court
of equity " will compel an executor or administrator, in
" the same manner as it does an express trustee, to dis-
" cover and set forth an account of the assets, and of his
" application of them ; and, even in a case where the
" testator directed that the executor should not be com-
" pelled by law to declare the amount of a residue
" bequeathed to him, the Court directed an account
" against him." (*Gibbons v. Dawley*, 2 Ch. Cas. 198 ;
Williams, 1877.) In order to secure the assets, the
Chancery Court will, before probate or letters of administration have been granted, in exceptional circumstances
appoint a manager or receiver or both. Moreover, if " in
" the case of an executor or administrator, any miscon-
" duct, waste, or improper disposition of the assets is
" shown, the Court will instantly interfere and appoint a
" receiver. So the bankruptcy of a sole executor and trustee
" is a ground for such an appointment. The Court will
" not appoint a receiver because the executor may, and
" probably will, exercise his right of retainer to the pre-
" judice of the general body of creditors (*Re Wells*, 45
" Ch.D. 569), and the administration is not to be taken
" from the executor upon slight grounds. The Court
" has no jurisdiction to order, in a summary way, the
" executor of a deceased receiver to bring in and pass his
" testator's accounts, and pay the balance to be found due
" out of the assets." (*Jenkins v. Briant*, 7 Sim. 171 ;
Williams, 1881.)

One executor may settle an account with any person
accountable to the testator's estate, and in the absence of
fraud this settlement will bind the other (even though dis-
senting) executors (*Smith v. Everitt*, 27 Beav. 446); but
this does not seem to be the case where the executor personally gains by the settlement. (*Stott v. Lord*, 8 Jur. N.S.
249.) One of two executors may sue the other for an account
and payment of monies owing to the testator. (*Peake v.
Ledger*, 8 Ha. 213; " Walker's Law of Executors," 3rd
Ed., pp. 166-7.) It is further pointed out that, " where
" a residuary legatee brought an action to have executors'

" accounts taken, in consequence of their insisting on the
" correctness of the accounts rendered by them in spite of
" specific objections raised to them by the legatee, and
" such objections were sustained, the Court ordered the
" executors to pay the costs of the action." (*Pearce v.
Radclyffe*, 29 W.R. 420.) " A residuary legatee who asks
" an executor for his share of the residue, is like a person
" who brings an action for money had and received on his
" account. Being an executor, the defendant has a right to
" have the account taken : otherwise he is in no better
" position than if he were only a defendant to an action for
" money had and received." (*Ibid* 421 per Bacon, V.-C.)
" Where an accounting party destroys the accounts before
" the matters have been finally adjusted, and, still more,
" pending a litigation, the Court will presume everything
" most unfavourable to him consistent with the established
" facts." (*Gray v. Haig*, 20 Beav. 219 ; and see *White v.
Lady Lincoln*, 8 Ves. 363 ; Walker, p. 174.)

We now turn to the question of accounts for probate,
which must be referred to here, though it cannot be dealt
with fully. Reference should in cases of difficulty be made
to practice books—such as " Tristram and Coote's Probate
Practice " (13th Ed.) or " Bennett's Practitioner's Guide "
—on the subject.

In the executor's oath (swearing to the will) the
executors pledge themselves to " exhibit a true and perfect
" inventory of the said estate, and render a just and true
" account thereof whenever required by law so to do."
Where probate is granted, but power is reserved for other
executors to come in and prove, a copy of the account of
the estate identical with that to be attached to the Inland
Revenue affidavit must be brought in and annexed to the
oath. This affidavit varies in form to meet the special
circumstances of the case. Thus, in cases where the
deceased died after 1st August 1894, and only personal property passes on the death, the form used is the one known
as Form A-4. This form, in paragraph 3, runs as
follows :—" The account marked ' A ' hereto annexed, is
" a true account of the particulars and value, as at the date
" of the deceased's death, so far as I —— have been able
" to ascertain the same, of all the personal property of
" the deceased, whether in possession or reversion, within
" the United Kingdom, exclusive of what the deceased
" may have been possessed of or entitled to as a trustee
" and not beneficially, but including personal property
" over which the deceased had and exercised an absolute
" power of appointment." It is to be noted that in pursuance of the Finance Act, 1894, Section 8 (3), executors
must set forth in the accounts annexed to the affidavit *all*

the property liable to duty, though they are only responsible for estate duty in respect of the personal property (wherever situate) that the deceased could dispose of at his death. As we have noted above, the Land Transfer Act, 1897, affects the question of executors' accounts, but it throws no new responsibility for duty on the executors. The affidavits referred to above apply equally in the case of a will or an intestacy. The special account forms issued by the Inland Revenue under the Finance Acts, and known as forms C1, C2, C3, D2, should be referred to if it is desired to appreciate a method of accounts designed to secure a return of all kinds of property liable to duty. C1 deals with the property on which estate duty was not paid on the Inland Revenue affidavit. C2 is the account for settlement estate duty. C3 is the account that deals with the payment of estate duty and settlement estate duty by instalments. The one mercy vouchsafed to the rich by Sir William Harcourt, D2, is what is ominously known as a Corrective Account. The question of the carrying in of residuary accounts cannot be dealt with here; it is a special art, and is a peculiar branch of solicitors' work, and turns rather upon questions of arrangement than questions of form.

Under certain circumstances executors may be allowed to employ accountants. Thus, in the case of *Henderson v. M'Iver* (3 Madd. 275), the Vice-Chancellor held "that from the nature of the accounts the "Executor was justified in employing an Accomptant, and "that the Expense ought to be allowed in his Accounts." It must be remembered, however, that executors are only allowed to charge for the employment of an agent under very special circumstances. (*Weiss v. Dill*, 3 Myl. & K. 26.) In an administration action, the taking of elaborate accounts requiring the intervention of an accountant may be unavoidable. This class of action is provided for by Ord. LV., r. 3, of the Rules of the Supreme Court. Rule 3 declares that "the executors or adminis- "trators of a deceased person or any of them, and the "trustees under any deed or instrument or any of them, "and any person claiming to be interested in the relief "sought as creditor, devisee, legatee, next-of-kin, or heir "at law, or customary heir of a deceased person, or as "*cestui que trust* under the trust of any deed or instru- "ment, or as claiming by assignment or otherwise under "any such creditor or other person as aforesaid, may take "out, as of course, an originating summons returnable in "the Chambers of a Judge of the Chancery Division "for such relief of the nature or kind following, "as may by the summons be specified, and as the "circumstances of the case may require, (that is to say)

"the determination, without an administration of the "estate or trust, of any of the following questions or "matters : —

"(c) The furnishing of any particular accounts by the "executors or administrators or trustees, and the "vouching (when necessary) of such accounts."

It was held in the case of *Re Dartnell* (1895, 1 Ch. 474) that a beneficiary under a will expectant on the death of a tenant-for-life had a right to particulars of the trust estate, and the investment thereof. Under this order (LV.) Mr. Justice Kekewich has held that it is not necessary under an ordinary order for accounts in an administration action to vouch every item before the Chief Clerk, as any items can be waived by the parties taking the accounts. (*In re Brown; Benson v. Grant*, 1895, W.N. 115 (9).)

Finally, two cases relating to accounts in administration actions may here be referred to. In the case of *Jones v. Morgan* (1893, 1 Ch. 304), where a trustee, defendant to an administration summons, alleged that he had expended the whole of the residue in educating and maintaining A., the residuary legatee, during his minority, which expired in 1880, the Court held that the residuary legatee's right to an account was barred by Section 8 of the Trustee Act, 1888. This decision is of great importance to trustees. The second case, *Ellis v. Roberts* (1898, 2 Ch. 142), gives the form of order for account by trustees entitled to the protection given by Section 8 of the Trustee Act, 1888, against liability to render accounts extending beyond six years from the commencement of the action. The form was the form settled in the action of *How v. Earl Winterton* (1896, 2 Ch. 626), and approved by the Court of Appeal. It runs as follows : —

"And the defendant by his counsel admitting that on "the 9th August 1889"—six years before the issue of the writ—"there were moneys in his hands liable to the trust "for accumulation by the will of the testatrix directed, "This Court doth order that the following account be "taken, that is to say, (1.) an account of the monies in "the hands of the defendant on the 9th August 1889, "liable to the trusts for accumulation under the will of "the testatrix, Mary Rabett, and of the rents and profits "of the testatrix's estate subsequently received by him "in respect of the said term of fourteen years; but in "ascertaining the actual amount of the monies in the "hands of the defendant on the date aforesaid, any pay- "ments made before that date are to be allowed to the "defendant." This order was applied in the case of *Ellis v. Roberts* in view of the decision of the Court that the trustees' account should be limited to six years prior to the date of the summons.

LIABILITY TO ACCOUNT IN SPECIFIC CASES.

It will be convenient briefly to summarise here the more salient rules as to liability to account in specific cases, and as to the enforcement of such liability in the event of non-compliance.

(1) EXECUTORS AND ADMINISTRATORS.

An executor or administrator must keep clear and distinct accounts of the property which it is his duty to administer, and of all profits which, *in any way*, have accrued during his period of office. Executors and administrators are charged with interest on the assets in their hands at the rate of 4 per cent., if they have been negligent in laying out the money for the benefit of the estate, or the profits can be claimed or 5 per cent. charged (in certain cases at compound interest, or with " rests " giving double compound interest), if they have used the money or estate to their own interest. The right to an account is enforceable by an action brought in the High Court.

(2) TRUSTEES UNDER WILLS, SETTLEMENTS, AND TRUST DEEDS.

Trustees (including agents and receivers) must render accounts when called upon to do so by beneficiaries, and must be always ready to do so. If an action is rendered necessary by the neglect to keep accounts, the trustees will be liable in costs, at any rate up to the moment in the action when the accounts are produced. The beneficiaries are entitled to inspect the accounts and vouchers, but not to a copy of them, at the expense of the trust estate. Trustees must, moreover, account unconditionally, and not upon terms, as to expenses not legally chargeable by trustees, though in some cases they are entitled to a guarantee against the expenses of rendering accounts. A disclaiming trustee or executor must account for any money that may have come into his hands. New trustees have the same liability as the old trustees (in so far as liability is disclosed by the trust documents and papers, *Hallows v. Lloyd*, 39 C.D. 686), and therefore it is essential for a person about to be appointed a trustee to see that the deed of appointment sets out fully all dealings with the estate previous to his appointment, in order that his liability shall in fact only run from his appointment. New trustees are not, however, liable to account with respect to matters of which they have no notice, actual or constructive. A retiring trustee is, of course, not liable to account in respect of matters occurring after his retirement. A trustee who acquiesces in the mode in which accounts are kept by his co-trustee, and allows beneficiaries to believe he has sanctioned the mode, is responsible for the truth of the accounts, and, if the accounts are false, the Court can order him to make good the defalcations. If trustees can establish that a deceased trustee took an active part in the trust, an account may be ordered against his personal representatives. It must be remembered that concurrence by beneficiaries in breaches of trust is not a sufficient ground for a refusal to account on the part of the trustees.

Accounts must be rendered by trustees appointed under the Judicial Trustees Act, 1896. (See Seton, pp. 1278-1282.)

(3) LIQUIDATOR OF COMPANY WOUND UP BY THE COURT.

Such liquidator, under the Companies Act, 1890, must account to the Committee of Inspection. Accounts must be kept in the prescribed form, and the Cash Book must be in the form approved by the Board of Trade. An account of receipts and payments (in a prescribed form) must be sent to the Board of Trade at least twice a year (Section 20). Such vouchers and information as the Board require must be furnished, and the Board may at any time require the production for inspection of any books and accounts kept by the liquidator. The Board causes the accounts sent to be audited. The accounts are also certified by the Committee of Inspection, and, with the certificate of audit, are filed in the High Court.

A summary of such accounts is sent to all creditors and contributories. The inspection of books and papers of the company by creditors or contributories is regulated by Section 156 of the Companies Act, 1862, and Section 21 of the Companies Act, 1900.

(4) ACCOUNTS IN BANKRUPTCY.

Until a trustee in bankruptcy is appointed the Official Receiver must keep a record of receipts and payments in a Cash Book in the form directed by the Board of Trade. The trustee must submit his Record Book and Cash Book to the Committee of Inspection not less than once every three months, and the Committee must as often audit and certify the Cash Book. The trustee must every six months transmit to the Board of Trade a duplicate copy of the Cash Book for that period, with the necessary vouchers and copies of the certificates of audit by the Committee of Inspection. With the first accounts he must also send, in the prescribed form, a summary of the debtor's statement of affairs. When the estate has been fully realised and distributed, or the adjudication annulled, the trustee must at once send in his accounts to the Board of Trade. The accounts sent in by the trustee must be certified and verified by him in the prescribed form. When the trustee's account has been audited, the Board shall certify that the account has been duly passed, and thereupon the duplicate copy, bearing a like certificate, shall be transmitted to the Registrar, who shall file the same with the proceedings in bankruptcy. Each copy is open to the inspection of any creditor, or of the bankrupt, or of any person interested. (Bankruptcy Act, 1883, Section 78 (4).) Where a receiving order has been made against debtors in partnership, distinct accounts shall be kept of the joint estate, and of the separate estate or estates, and no transfer of a surplus from a separate estate to the joint estate on the ground that there are no creditors under such separate estate shall be made until notice of the intention to make such transfer has been gazetted. (Bankruptcy Rules, 293.)

(5) Trustee under Deed of Arrangement.

Deeds of arrangement must be registered under Acts of 1887 and 1890. They include—

(*a*) An assignment of property.

(*b*) A deed of or agreement for a composition.

(*c*) A deed of inspectorship by creditors, entered into for the purpose of carrying on or winding up a business.

(*d*) A letter of license from the creditors authorising the debtor, or any other person, to manage, carry on, realise, or dispose of a business, with a view to the payment of debts.

(*e*) Any agreement or instrument entered into by the creditors for the purpose of carrying on or winding up the debtor's business, or authorising the debtor, or any other person to manage, carry on, realise, or dispose of the debtor's business, with a view to the payment of debts.

By Section 25 of the Bankruptcy Act, 1890, every trustee under any deed of arrangement shall within thirty days of January 1st in each year transmit to the Board of Trade (or as they shall direct) an account of his receipts and payments as such trustee, in the prescribed form, and verified in the prescribed manner. This provision, on the application of the Board of Trade, may be enforced by the Judge of the High Court to whom bankruptcy business has been assigned. The term "trustee" includes any person appointed to distribute a composition, or act in any fiduciary capacity under any deed of arrangement. The accounts submitted to the Board of Trade in pursuance of this section shall be open to the inspection of any creditor on payment of the prescribed fee. The method of keeping the accounts by the trustee, with forms, is prescribed by rules issued under Section 25 of the Bankruptcy Act, 1890.

(6) Accounts between Mortgagor and Mortgagee.

A mortgagee is entitled to an immediate account of his principal, interest, and costs, and to have a day fixed for payment or foreclosure. Until the legal mortgagee takes possession, neither the mortgagor remaining in possession, nor his assignees in bankruptcy, nor a person holding under a mere voluntary trust for the mortgagor, need account to the mortgagee for the rents and profits. A mortgagee in possession must be diligent in realising the amount due on the mortgage. He is liable to account for the rents and other profits during his possession (and in taking such an account the Statute of Limitations is no bar), unless he can enter into possession under such an agreement with the mortgagor, for possession at a fixed rent, as the Court will uphold. The mortgagee must account to those who are interested in the equity of redemption, and he cannot by any dealing with the estate relieve himself from this liability. A mortgagee in possession is liable to account to a second mortgagee for so much of the surplus rent as he has paid to the mortgagor; but this is only from notice given of the subsequent mortgage. Any incumbrancer can, of course, ask for accounts against the mortgagor. An assignee or subsequent incumbrancer of the equity of redemption stands in the position of the mortgagor in the matter of accounts.

The purchaser in good faith of a mortgage debt is entitled to the entire debt, and not merely what he gave for it, and there is no right against him for an account of what he has paid for his purchase. So if the reversioner in fee purchases the first of several mortgages for less than is due on it, he may hold it for all that is due on it, and the puisné incumbrancers have no account against him (see "Fisher on Mortgages," 5th Edition, p. 826), save where the purchaser is in a fiduciary capacity. An assignee of a mortgage is bound by the state of accounts between mortgagee and mortgagor.

In conclusion, I may say that the Rules of the Supreme Court referred to at length above are intended to apply generally to all cases of account, whether they arise in the particular classes of cases with which I have dealt, or in other classes—such as questions of patents, copyright, designs, bankruptcy, winding-up of companies, or other matters. These rules and orders, and the statutes and cases quoted, contain the general principles of equity which the English Courts apply to the solution of the many difficult questions of account that almost daily arise for consideration.

J. E. G. DE MONTMORENCY.

APPENDIX "B."

MISCELLANEOUS QUESTIONS ON

ACCOUNTS.

MISCELLANEOUS QUESTIONS ON ACCOUNTING.

1.—From the following Trial Balance prepare Balance Sheet and Trading and Profit and Loss Accounts, as on 30th June 1902, of the business of W. Walker, silversmith and manufacturer :—

	£	£
Bills Payable		2,600
Rents from sub-Lettings		190
Incidental Expenses	500	
Withdrawals	1,650	
Wages	17,540	
Salaries	3,005	
Travelling Expenses	1,430	
Rent, Rates, and Taxes	1,850	
Insurance	90	
Advertising	650	
Commission	245	
Discounts and Allowances	700	
Bank Interest and charges	150	
Silverton Bank overdraft		950
Packing, &c.	350	
Sales		70,395
Goods Purchases	10,540	
Plating and Sundry Expenses	7,650	
Bad Debts	260	
Cash in Hand	105	
Sundry Debtors	20,250	
,, Creditors		2,300
Stock, 30th June 1895	9,560	
Bills Receivable	5,570	
Plant, Machinery, and Tools	4,250	
Capital		9,910
	£86,345	£86,345

Stock at June 30th 1896, £8,350.
Depreciation of Plant, &c., 5 per cent.

2.—Prepare Trading and Profit and Loss Accounts and Balance Sheet from the following Trial Balance at 30th June 1902 of the Pottery Company, Lim. Nominal Capital £10,000 in £10 Shares :—

	£	£
Subscribed Capital 900 Shares fully called		9,000
Calls in arrear	200	
Land and Buildings	2,000	
Machinery and Plant	2,500	
Loose Tools, &c.	500	
Horses, Carts, &c.	300	

2.—*(continued)*

Stock-in-Trade, 30th June 1901 :—

Earthenware	..	..	..	..	£1,000		
Cratewood, Packing, &c.		..	..	..	250		
Clay	..	..	..	..	1,000		
Coal and Sundries	..	..	..	..	250		
						2,500	
Profit and Loss Account	..	..	..	..	..		200
Debtors	..	..	..	..	..	3,000	
Creditors	..	..	..	..	..		1,000
Sales..	..	..	..	..	..		12,000
Packing &c.	..	..	..	..	..		1,000
Straw, Cratewood, &c.	..	:.	..	..	..	600	
Coal, Ccke, &c. ..	..	..	..	..	..	300	
Clay ..	..	..	..	..	..	2,500	
Wages	..	..	..	..	..	6,500	
Horse and Cart Expenses	..	..	..	..	..	300	
Carriage, &c.	..	..	..	..	..	500	
Repairing and Replacing Plant	..	..	..	..	150		
,, ,, Loose Tools		..	..	..	50		
,, ,, Buildings		..	..	..	100		
Rates and Taxes	..	..	..	..	..	50	
Gas and Water ..	..	..	..	..	..	50	
Bills Payable	..	..	..	..	..		800
,, Receivable	..	..	..	..	..	1,200	
Incidental Expenses	..	..	..	..	..	200	
Bank..	..	..	..	..	..	450	
Cash in hand	..	..	..	..	..	50	
						£24,000	£24,000

Stock-in-Trade 30th June 1902 was Earthenware, £800; Cratewood, &c., £200; Clay £800; Coal, &c., £200.

Write off Depreciations—Machinery and Plant, 5 per cent.; Land and Buildings, 2½ per cent.; Tools, &c., 5 per cent.; provision for Bad Debts and Discounts, 5 per cent. off Debtors.

3.—" A." sells to " B." goods to the value of £500, payable by draft of the former on the latter at four months' date from the 1st of May.

The drawer discounts his customer's bill with the County Bank at 5 per cent. per annum on the 1st of June. At maturity the bill is dishonoured. Give the entries in " A.'s" Day Book, Ledger, Bill Book, Cash Book and Journal, to duly record the transactions. Give also the corresponding entries in " B.'s books."

4.—" A." is a merchant who has transactions with " B." Give the entries in the books of " B." which you would make in respect of the following transactions:—On January 1st 1902 " A." draws on " B " at three months for £500, and discounts the Acceptance with the London and County Bank, Lim., receiving £495 in cash, of which he hands £247 10s. to " B." On 31st March, in order to provide funds to meet this bill, " B." draws on " A." for £550 at three months and discounts the Acceptance with J. & Co., receiving £545 in cash, of which he hands £22 to " A."

5.—Prepare Trading Account, Profit and Loss Account, and Balance Sheet for the year ended 31st December 1901, from the following Trial Balance of the books of Messrs. John Williamson & Company, Lim., manufacturers :—

	£	£
Nominal Capital, 100,000 Shares of £1 each		
Issued Capital (fully paid)		70,000
Freehold Land and Buildings	35,000	
Debentures		20,000
Machinery and Plant	27,000	
Loose Tools	1,000	
Stock at 1st January 1901	17,500	
Material Bought..	23,750	
Wages	9,000	
Office Salaries and Travellers	2,500	
Coal and Coke	1,300	
Rates and Taxes..	430	
Discounts	820	
Blankshire Banking Company, Lim.	3,500	
Sundry Debtors	6,800	
Sundry Creditors		2,070
Cash in hand	90	
Bad Debts	125	
Sales		53,000
Returns	1,880	
Repairs	405	
Interest on Debentures	800	
Patents (Cost)	13,170	
	£145,070	£145,070

Write off Depreciation on Patents and Machinery at 5 per cent. per annum, and on Loose Tools at 12½ per cent. per annum. Provide 5 per cent. on the Book Debts to cover Bad Debts The Stock at 31st December 1901 amounted to £16,350.

6.—From the following Trial Balance of a Manufacturing Company prepare a Trading Account, Profit and Loss Account, and Balance Sheet at December 31st 1900 :—

	£	s	d	£	s	d
Capital, Paid up—10,000 Shares at £10				100,000	0	0
Stock, January 1st 1900	32,400	12	6			
Cash in hand	120	6	0			
Bank	4,208	14	0			
Purchases and Sales	52,365	17	0	136,590	10	0
Manufacturing Charges	11,575	0	0			
Wages	28,555	4	0			
Salaries	1,525	0	0			
Sale Expenses	6,860	0	0			
Rates and Taxes	222	0	0			
Insurance	190	0	0			
General Expenses	2,640	10	0			
Discount	2,473	0	0	579	0	0
Bad Debts	575	0	0			
Interest and Bank Charges	387	17	6			
Land and Buildings	22,300	0	0			
Machinery and Plant	37,960	0	0			
Debtors and Creditors	52,640	0	0	20,862	4	6
Patents	7,700	0	0			
Bad Debts Reserve				888	0	0
Profit and Loss—Balance, December 31st 1899				779	6	6
Reserve Fund				5,000	0	0
	£264,699	1	0	£264,699	1	0

6.—*(continued)*

Charge Depreciation on Buildings at 3 per cent. per annum, on Machinery at 6 per cent.; credit to Bad Debts Reserve ½ per cent. on Sales, £136,600; write down Patents by 10 per cent.; carry forward £90 of Insurance; reserve 1½ per cent. Discount on Debtors. The value of Stock at December 31st 1900 is £22,600 18s. Charge 10 per cent. on Net Profits as remuneration to Managing Director, £500 as Directors' Fees.

7.—From the following Trial Balance prepare departmental Trading Accounts, General Profit and Loss Account, and Balance Sheet.

TRIAL BALANCE, 30th September 1902.

	£	£
William Blackley, Capital Account		15,000
,, Drawings Account	3,000	
Sundry Debtors	1,200	
Sundry Creditors		3,000
Business Premises	5,000	
Furniture and Fittings	4,000	
Bank		1,700
Cash	300	
Stock in Trade 31st March 1902—		
Department A.	2,000	
,, B.	4,000	
,, C.	3,000	
Purchases—		
Department A.	5,800	
,, B.	4,000	
,, C.	5,000	
Wages, Department A.	1,000	
Sales—		
Department A.		8,000
,, B.		5,000
,, C.		7,000
Salaries	700	
Trade Expenses	300	
Rent, Rates, &c.	500	
Discounts		300
Bad Debts	200	
	£40,000	£40,000

The Stock on 30th September 1902 was Department A., £2,000; Department B., £6,000; Department C., £2,000. Provide for depreciation of Furniture, £100; Doubtful Debts, £100; outstanding Rent, £150.

8.—What constitutes Capital Expenditure? Would you be justified in certifying to the accuracy of Accounts where such expenditure appeared without making inquiry into the real character of such expenditure? Give your reasons.

9.—What do you mean by "Fixed Assets" and "Floating Assets" in a Balance Sheet? Give two or three examples. Without any instructions being given by the Articles of Association of a Company, is there any legal difference between them as to providing a Depreciation Fund for known waste prior to striking a credit balance of the Profit and Loss Account and paying a dividend?

10.—You find in your annual audit of an Investment Company that Debentures of another Company are included amongst the Assets at their face-value, though purchased at a discount ; that such discount has been considered as commission earned and so credited to the Profit and Loss Account, and included in a larger sum carried to Reserve from the credit balance of the Profit and Loss Account. What is your opinion of this transaction ? What does it suggest ? If it does not meet with your approval, how would you have recorded the transaction ? What steps would you take to satisfy yourself as to the value placed upon the Debentures so purchased ?

11.—The following items are included in the Balance Sheet of a Company under the Companies Acts, under the head of Works and Plant :—

						£	s	d
Wages	..	..	..	..	..	13,712	9	3
Salary of Engineer	..	..	..	..	..	1,155	0	0
Two-thirds of Salary of Secretary, 1¾ years	..	..	..	..	466	13	4
Half Directors' Fees, 1¾ years	..	..	..	..	1,000	0	0
Interest on Bank Loan Account	..	..	..	..	327	12	6
Law Costs re Ancient Lights	..	..	..	..	832	15	11

Do you see anything objectionable, and if so, what, in these items being treated as Capital Outlay ?

12.—Define (a) Capital Expenditure, (b) Revenue Expenditure, (c) Fixed Assets, (d) Floating Assets. Give one typical example of each in connection with any business with which you are acquainted.

13.—Explain fully the distinction between Capital and Revenue in connection with the Accounts of three different classes of undertakings.

14.—Explain the reasons for any difference that may be observable between the examples you select.

15.—Are there, in your opinion, any circumstances which would justify the addition to actual cost of any anticipated Profit, in the case of partially Manufactured Goods, or of an uncompleted Engineering Contract, or in similar cases ?

16.—Give four examples of assets that are Fixed Assets in connection with some particular class of business, but generally Floating Assets.

17.—Give four examples of assets that are Floating Assets in connection with some particular class of business, but generally Fixed Assets.

18.—What is the proper basis of valuation for Fixed and Floating Assets respectively in a Balance Sheet ?

19.—A Finance Company which has paid £90,000 for six Patents of equal value, sold one of these Patents during the first year of its existence, and received as consideration for the sale 55,000 fully-paid Shares of £1 each in a subsidiary Company formed for the purpose of working the Patent.

19.—*(continued)*

In the second year the Finance Company sold the 55,000 Shares in the subsidiary Company for £30,000.

How would you, as Auditor, expect the 55,000 Shares or the proceeds of them to be treated in the accounts of the Finance Company at the end of the first and second years respectively?

20.—Do you consider that interest paid on Capital during the construction of the works of a Dock or Railway Company should be charged to Capital, or how otherwise; and what are the views generally held to be sound on this subject?

21.—Explain shortly the difference between a system of Internal Check and a Professional Audit.

22.—Give six typical examples of Fraud, of which only four involve the abstraction of actual money, and explain shortly what means you would suggest to reduce the risk of loss under each of these headings to a minimum.

23.—Give a list of the principal points that have to be considered in devising a system of Internal Check, and show what particular class of error each of these precautions is designed to avoid or detect.

24.—A. Kinet received from W. Leaf, of Montreal, 550 barrels of fine Flour at 18s. per barrel. A. Kinet paid Freight, £22; Insurance, £5; Storage, £6. He sold 300 barrels at 26s., and 250 barrels at 25s. Write out the records of the transactions as they would appear in A. Kinet's books.

25.—Write out an Account Sales to be furnished to W. Leaf in respect of the transactions stated in the last preceding question.

26.—Walters & Co. consign a shipment of Goods to Roy & Co., their agents in Dublin, on 30th January 1901, and draw upon them at six months for £1,000. They discount the acceptance with their Bankers on February 15th 1901, paying £13 15s. for discounting. On 28th February 1901 Roy & Co. advise that they have paid £33 for freight and landing charges on the consignment. On 30th April 1901 Roy & Co. remit £500 on account of proceeds, and on the 28th July 1901 they intimate that the Gross Sales have amounted to £1,340, and enclose debit note for Commission at 2½ per cent. on that amount.

Walters & Co. retire Roy & Co.'s Acceptance at maturity.

Show, by means of Ledger Accounts, how the foregoing transactions should be recorded in Walter & Co.'s books.

27.—Define an " Account Current " and make out such an account for North & Co., in respect of the following transactions with East & Co. : —

1902.	Sept.	16th.	Goods sold to E. & Co., £100, due October 1st.
	Oct.	1st.	Received Cash from E. & Co., £45.
	,,	21st.	Goods bought of E. & Co., £250, due December 1st.
	Nov.	1st.	Paid to E. & Co., cash £165.
	Dec.	1st.	,, ,, £150.
	,,	5th.	Goods bought of E. & Co., £250, due January 1st.
	,,	10th.	,, ,, £110, ,,
1903.	Jan.	1st.	Paid cash to E. & Co., £300.
	,,	9th.	Goods sold to E. & Co., £80, due February 1st.

The account to be made up to 1st February 1903. Interest to be at 6 per cent., which may be calculated by months instead of days.

28.—On January 20th 1902 Henry Brown forwarded to Thos. White & Co. on consignment 20 chests of Indigo at £60, paying £10 10s. for freight. On 15th April 1902 he receives an Account Sales, dated 18th March 1902, showing that the Goods realised £1,381 5s., and that the following expenses had been incurred :—

Dock Dues and Insurance	..	..	..	..	£6	4	5
Cartage	..	..	..	..	2	10	0
Storage	..	..	..	..	2	5	0
Del Credere at 1½ per cent.							
Commission at 2 per cent.							

and enclosing a Bill at three months for the balance.

(1) Show the entries in Brown's books.

(2)   Do.   do.   White & Co.'s books.

(3)   Do.   Account Sales.

29.—A. receives on account of B. the following :—

January 1st	..	..	..	..	..	£100
February 1st	..	..	..	..	..	200
March 1st	..	..	..	..	..	500

He pays on account of B. :—

February 1st	..	..	..	..	..	£50
April 1st	..	..	..	..	..	200

Make up an Account Current to 30th June, charging Interest at 5 per cent.

30.—On the 1st January 1902 a Firm possessed the following assets :—

Buildings	..	..	..	..	..	£3,000
Plant and Machinery	..	..	..	..	..	2,000
Stock-in-trade	..	..	..	..	..	2,000
Book Debts	..	..	..	..	..	2,500
Cash	..	..	..	..	..	500
						£10,000

30.—(continued)

The Book Debts were made up as follows :—

A.	..	..	..	..	..	..	£300
B.	..	..	..	..	..	..	400
C.	..	..	..	..	..	..	100
D.	..	..	..	..	..	..	500
E.	..	..	..	..	..	..	200
F.	..	..	..	..	..	..	300
G.	..	..	..	..	..	..	200
H.	..	..	..	..	..	..	500
							£2,500

The Creditors were made up as follows :—

I.	..	..	..	..	..	..	£1,000
J.	..	..	..	..	..	..	500
K.	..	..	..	..	..	..	200
L.	..	..	..	..	..	..	800
M.	..	..	..	..	..	..	500
							£3,000

The Capital of the firm belonged in equal shares to the partners X. and Y. During the month of January the following transactions occurred :—

Sales					Purchases				
A. ..	..	..	..	£100	I. ..	..	..	..	£200
B. ..	..	..	..	50	J. ..	..	..	..	700
C. ..	..	..	..	200	K. ..	..	..	..	100
D. ..	..	..	..	300	L. ..	..	..	..	500
E. ..	..	..	..	200	M. ..	..	..	..	200
F. ..	..	..	..	50					
G. ..	..	..	..	100					
H. ..	..	..	..	300					
				£1,300					£1,700

Cash Received					Cash Paid				
A. ..	..	..	..	£200	I. ..	..	..	..	£500
B. ..	..	..	..	400	J. ..	..	..	..	500
D. ..	..	..	..	500	K. ..	..	..	..	200
F. ..	..	..	..	200	L. ..	..	..	..	300
H. ..	..	..	..	500	M. ..	..	..	..	500
				£2,000					£2,000
					General Expenses	..	..	..	300
					X. ..	..	..	..	100
					Y. ..	..	..	..	100
									£2,500

You are required to record these transactions in Sold Ledger, Bought Ledger, and General Ledger, making each self-balancing. Take out a Trial Balance of each Ledger, and close the books as on 31st January 1902, taking the Stock-in-trade at that date at £3,500, reserving £200 for outstanding Trade Expenses, and £100 for possible loss on Doubtful Debts. Provide for Depreciation of Plant and Machinery at 12 per cent. per annum.

31.—State shortly how each Ledger in a set of books may be balanced separately, when no special provision had been made for that purpose when the system of accounts was originally designed.

32.—In the Trial Balance of a merchant's books, which are so arranged that the Bought and Sold Ledgers can be balanced separately, the debits exceed the credits by the sum of £2 3s. 6d. What would you suggest as the most likely explanation of the difference, and what steps would you take to find it?

33.—Does the fact that books are balanced indicate their absolute correctness? Give your views on the following items :—

	£	s	d
Debit Balances—			
E. White, Cash in full	74	0	0
P. Bull, Remittance ..	63	0	0
Credit Balances—			
O. Brown, Cash	91	3	6
Great Western Railway, Freight overcharged	24	10	0

34.—From books kept by Single-entry you extract the following as at 30th June 1901 :—

	£	s	d
Capital	3,850	0	0
Due from Customers	6,970	0	0
Cash in hand ..	54	0	0
Stocks (as per Stock Sheets)	2,790	0	0
Fixtures, Fittings, and Utensils	570	0	0
Creditors	2,760	0	0
Bank Overdraft	970	0	0
Bills Payable	340	0	0
Goods supplied to Private Residence	260	0	0

The amount of the Capital above-mentioned you find to be the balance after the sums of £300 for Drawings and £250 for Salary have been debited.

Prepare an Account showing the Profit earned during the year ended 30th June 1901.

35.—On the 1st of October 1902, A., a merchant carrying on business in Glasgow, consigns to his agent in New York 1,000 tons of Iron, which he invoices *pro formâ* at 50s. per ton. On the 1st of December he receives from the consignees, B. & Co., an Account Sales, showing that 200 tons have been sold at 14 dols., 250 tons at 14.20 dols., 150 tons at 14.25 dols., and 400 tons at 14.50 dols. B. & Co. deduct their Commission of 2 per cent., and remit a three months' bill in dols. for the balance. Show the necessary entries in A.'s books, assuming that the cost of freight, &c., amounted to £150. For facility of calculation it may be assumed that the average value of the dollar is 4s. 2d., but that on the date the bill was paid the rate of exchange was 5 dols. to the £.

36.—Taking the facts as stated in the previous question, show the entries necessary to record the transactions in B. & Co.'s Ledger, assuming that the Goods consigned were sold to four different customers and paid for by them in cash at one month.

37.—Explain how the books of a Branch business may be kept independently of the Head Office books, and yet in such a manner that the records may at any convenient time be included in the Head Office books. Illustrate your answer with a *pro formâ* Trial Balance of a Branch, and show the Journal entries necessary to close the books both of the Branch and Head Office.

38.—A manufacturer carrying on a business divided into departments receives an order for Goods which have to be supplied in part from different departments. What entries and office work would be involved in respect of such order from the moment of its receipt to the debiting of the Customers' Account in the Ledger ?

39.—A South Wales provision merchant has several Branches which are supplied from the Head Office. Each Branch has its own Sales Ledger, and hands over the total amount of the cash received to the Head Office every day. In the invoices for the Goods supplied by the Head Office to the Branches, 25 per cent. is added to the cost. All expenses are paid from the Head Office.

From the following particulars of the transactions of the Branches, raise the Ledger Accounts in the Head Office books, and prepare an Account showing the Gross Profit :—

	Cardiff	Newport	Bridgend
Goods received from Head Office	£5,000	£4,500	£3,500
Total Sales	5,200	4,300	3,100
Cash Sales	2,750	2,250	1,650
,, Received on Ledger Accounts	2,250	1,850	1,250
Debtors at commencement	1,555	1,665	1,350
,, Close	1,755	1,865	1,550
Stock at commencement	750	650	450
,, Close	1,060	960	760

40.—On December 31st 1900 the books of the X. Branch of Evans & Co., Oil Merchants, contain the following balances :—

	£ s d	£ s d
Book Debts	3,530 0 0	
Cash in hand	50 0 0	
Head Office Account		3,750 0 0
Office Expenses	780 0 0	
Oil Account		870 0 0
Tank Cars, Horses, &c.	260 0 0	
	£4,620 0 0	£4,620 0 0

The stock of Oil at the Branch amounted to £673.

Draft the necessary Journal entries to close the Branch books, and also the entries to be made in the books at the Head Office to incorporate the above.

41.—A Limited Company has a branch establishment at Brighton. On 31st December 1901 the following Trial Balance of the Branch books is forwarded to the Head Office :—

TRIAL BALANCE, 31st December 1901.

	£	£
Head Office..		2,400
Remittances	1,200	
Sold Ledger..	1,500	
Bought Ledger		500
Stock, 1st January 1901	2,000	
Purchases	6,500	
Sales		10,200
Rent	400	
Salaries	600	
Trade Expenses	500	
Bank	400	
	£13,100	£13,100

41.—*(continued)*

The Stock in hand on 31st December 1901 was £1,700. You are required to incorporate those transactions in the Head Office books, showing Branch Account and Branch Trading and Profit and Loss Accounts in the Head Office Ledger: also Branch Balance Sheet.

42.—

TRIAL BALANCE, 31st December 1903.

	Rs.	Rs.
Head Office..		84,000
Premises	50,000	
Fixtures	2,500	
Stock	25,000	
Debtors	75,000	
Bills Receivable	5,000	
Cash	12,500	
Creditors		60,000
Remittance Account	50,000	
Rent	2,000	
Bad Debts	5,000	
Salaries	12,000	
General Expenses	10,000	
Discounts		5,000
Sales		300,000
Purchases	200,000	
	449,000	449,000

Stock on December 31st 1903, 20,000 Rs.

Depreciation of Premises at 5 per cent.

Taking the above Trial Balance you are required —

(a) To close the Branch books and compile the usual Balance Sheet, Trading and Profit and Loss Accounts in rupees.

(b) To incorporate the Branch Trial Balance in the Head Office books, and close the latter, the Head Office Trial Balance being as follows :—

TRIAL BALANCE, 31st December 1902.

	£	£
Capital		5,000
Branch Account	6,100	
Remittance Account		3,300
Debentures		2,500
Cash	3,900	
Office Expenses	1,000	
Profit and Loss Account		200
	£11,000	£11,000

	s	d
Average Rate of Exchange	1	4
Rate 31st December 1901	1	3½
„ „ 1902	1	4½

(c) To show the Balance Sheet and Profit and Loss Accounts in the Head Office books, assuming that the rupee is to be converted at the uniform rate of 1s. 4d. for all Personal and Nominal Accounts.

43.—Explain what differences (if any) are necessary in the treatment of Branch Accounts with the Head Office situated abroad, and the Branch Office in this country.

44.—Explain shortly what you mean by the exchange value of a foreign currency, and why it varies from time to time.

45.—State how you would deal with a foreign currency when recording Consignment transactions (a) in the books of the Consignor, (b) in the books of the Consignee.

46.—Illustrate, by means of a short example, how you would record in the books of an English house the purchase of Goods from abroad in a foreign currency, and their subsequent payment in sterling.

47.—Illustrate how you would record, in the books of an English house, the sale of Goods to customers abroad, and the payment for such Goods by them in a foreign currency.

48.—What, in your opinion, would be the best method of dealing with Profit or Loss on exchange in the case of a London Company having its trading centre in South America ? Illustrate your method, and state whether it would apply alike to Capital and Revenue items.

49.—State briefly the general principles governing the question of Foreign Exchanges in Accounts.

50.—Explain quite shortly the effect of a fall in the exchange value of the Rupee on each of the following :—

(a) An English Company carrying on a general trading business in India.
(b) An English Company owning a Railway in India.
(c) An Anglo-Indian Bank.

Confine your answer to the effect that the variation in exchange should have on the published Accounts.

51.—Explain shortly what you understand by the Tabular System of Bookkeeping, and show, by means of *pro formâ* rulings, the application of this system (a) to a Ledger, (b) to a book of first entry.

52.—For what purposes does a Manufacturer require to keep a Stores Account ? Describe a simple system upon which such Accounts may be kept.

53.—How may a Trader approximately arrive at his Net Profit without taking Stock ?

54.—J. L. and W. D. enter into what may be termed a Limited Partnership for the purpose of buying at sales any railway rolling stock or machinery which could be obtained at a price cheap enough for a speculation, and sharing the risk—this being quite apart from their own proper businesses, in which they have no connection with each other. Sometimes one buys, sometimes the other, but Disbursements and Sales are made indifferently, including the receipt of money, on account of the Sales. There is no joint fund or bank account, and each works the individual transaction through his own business. The following transactions are recorded, and you are required to raise accounts for both parties, and show the completion and agreement of same,

including the equal division of profit and loss, and the balance carried to a general account.
Five per cent. per annum on all cash received or paid.

Jan. 1.	J. L.	buys Locomotive for £500.	
,, 12.	,.	pays cost of Transit, £10.	
Mar. 16.	W. D.	,, Rent for same, £1 6s. 8d.	
,, 18.	,,	,, Insurance, 10s.	
June 1.	,,	,, Repairs, £10.	
,, 30.	,,	sells Locomotive for £560.	
July 2.	,,	buys 500 tons Rails at £3 per ton.	
,, 30.	J. L.	pays Freight and Landing Charges, £25.	
Aug. 30.	,,	,, Rent, £2 5s.	
Sept. 1.	W. D.	sells same at £3 5s. per ton.	
,, 6.	J. L.	buys two Cranes, £50 each.	
,, 12.	,,	sells same for £108.	

Show how affairs stand on October 1st.

55.—A., B., and C. agree to purchase a business in New York and carry it on for a stated period. A. invested 4,000 dollars, B. 25,000 dollars, and C. 20,000 dollars. The Partnership Agreement provided that they should share profits and losses in the proportion of A. 5, B. 3, C. 1. At the end of the term the Balance Sheet was as follows:—

Liabilities.					Assets.			
Creditors—					Cash			$500.00
Trade Accounts			$69,000.00		Debts Receivable			68,000.00
Loan			16,000.00		Stock of Goods, as per Inventory ..			47,000.00
Partners' Capital—					Machinery and Plant			35,000.00
A...	$47,500.00				Shares and Bonds, at market price ..			22,000.00
B...	30,000.00							
C...	10,000.00		87,500.00					
			$172,500.00					$172,500.00

The business was sold and the Assets realised 140,000 dollars gross. The Costs and Expenses of the sale amounted to 5,000 dollars. Show the final accounts of the Partners, and convert the balance of each account into sterling, the rate of exchange being 4.80.

56.—P., Q., and R. have dissolved partnership, and, after realising all their assets, they find that they have for division the sum of £12,000. The Capital Accounts of the respective Partners at the dissolution were in credit, P. £4,000, Q. £3,000, R. £2,000. P. has advanced to the firm £500 apart from his Capital, and this had not been discharged. The Trade Creditors amount to £5,500. The Articles of Partnership provide that profits and losses shall be shared equally by the Partners. Show how the £12,000 should be distributed.

57.—A., B., and C. were Partners, and advanced the following Capital:—A. £4,000, B. £3,000, C., £2,000. Profits and losses were to be borne equally. At the end of the first twelve months each Partner had drawn £500. The Assets were then disposed of for £1,500, the purchaser discharging all the liabilities of the firm. How should this sum be apportioned among the Partners, and would any Partner or Partners have to advance any further sum? If so, state which Partner and how much, and prepare the necessary accounts showing the results.

58.—On the 1st July 1902 A. took B. into partnership. A. had the following assets:—

Leasehold Premises	..	..	..	..	..	£500
Stock in Trade	..	..	..	..	..	800
Book Debts ..	..	..	..	..	..	700
Cash at Bank	..	..	..	..	..	100

His liabilities (including £200 on Bills Payable) amounted in all to £800. B. brings in £1,500 in cash, and it is agreed that £500 of this shall be credited to A. as representing the price to be paid by B. for a half-share of Profits.

Open the books of the new Firm by means of Journal entries, and show the Balance Sheet at the commencement of the Partnership.

59.—The London Engineering Company, Lim., acquires on April 1st 1903, from William Brown, the following property:—

Stock in Trade	..	..	..	..	..	£10,000
Machinery ..	..	..	..	..	..	20,000
Freehold Buildings	..	..	..	..	..	47,500
Goodwill ..	..	..	..	..	..	22,500
						£100,000

Payment is made on the same day as follows:—

Cash ..	..	..	..	..	..	£20,000
Debentures	..	..	..	..	..	50,000
Preference Shares	..	..	..	..	..	10,000
Ordinary Shares	..	..	..	..	..	20,000
						£100,00

You are required to explain how the above arrangement may be carried into effect, and what entries should be made in the books of the Company?

60.—If a Company incorporated on 1st May buys a business on 1st May as from 1st January —i.e., the Company gets the Profits for a whole year up to 31st December—how would you apportion the Profits?

61.—A Company is about to apply for leave to reduce its Capital so as to wipe off past losses. The Directors suggest that a further sum should at the same time be written off its Plant and Machinery, so as to anticipate and provide for ordinary Depreciation, and thus for some years save this charge on Profit and Loss. Is this proposal sound? State reasons for your opinion.

62.—A Limited Company, registered on the 31st March 1900, takes over the Assets and Liabilities of a trading concern as on the 1st January 1900. The Profits for the six months ended on the 30th June 1900 amounted to £5,000. How would you deal with this sum in closing the books of the Company on the 30th June 1900? State whether you consider it available for distribution as dividend on the Shares, and give your reasons.

63.—On the 31st December 1902 the Assets of Arthur Jones appear in his books as follows :—

Freehold Premises	..	..	..	..	..	..	£2,000
Goodwill	..	..	..	..	..	..	1,500
Plant, Fixtures, &c.	..	..	..	..	..	..	750
Bills Receivable	..	..	..	..	..	..	550
Stock-in-Trade	..	..	..	..	..	..	2,500
Book Debts	..	..	..	..	..	..	2,000
Cash at Bank	..	..	..	..	..	..	700

His Creditors amount to £1,500. Jones decides to convert his business into a small Limited Company, with a nominal Capital of £12,000, divided into 12,000 Shares of £1 each, of which he agrees to accept 10,000 Shares, issued as fully-paid, as purchase consideration for his business, the Company taking over his liabilities. The remaining 2,000 Shares are issued to friends of Jones for cash, payable 5s. on Application, 5s. on Allotment, and the balance one month after Allotment. The purchase is completed, and the allotment takes place on the 8th January 1903.

Show the opening entries in the Journal of the new Company.

64.—A Company offers for subscription 100,000 Ordinary Shares and 100,000 5 per cent. Preference Shares of £1 each, payable 2s. 6d. on Application, 2s. 6d. on Allotment, 5s. one month after Allotment, and the balance as and when required. Explain how you would deal with the various applications that are received, and what records you would keep of the transactions between the Company and each separate applicant up to the time of opening the Share Ledger. Give *pro formâ* rulings of any special books that would be required.

65.—The following is the Trial Balance of the London Manufacturing Company, Lim., for the half-year ended 31st March last :—

TRIAL BALANCE, 31st March 1903.

	Dr.	Cr.
Capital Account		£25,000
Rent	£250	
Trade Creditors		4,800
Bills Payable		260
Stock, 1st October 1902	7,500	
Plant and Machinery	1,200	
Reserve for Bad Debts		25
Trade Debtors	10,500	
Bills Receivable	300	
Cash in hand	20	
Cash at Bank	1,650	
Carriage	250	
Travellers' Commission	150	
General Expenses	175	
Rates and Taxes	240	
Sales		30,000
Purchases	20,500	
Discounts	775	500
Wages	6,150	
Bad Debts	50	
Salaries	850	
Transfer Fees		25
Travelling Expenses	50	
Business Premises	10,000	
	£60,610	£60,610

The Nominal Capital of the Company is £50,000, divided into Shares of £1 each, of which 25,000 Shares have been issued and fully paid. You are required to prepare Balance Sheet, Trading Account, and Profit and Loss Account, making first the following adjustments:— Provide for Depreciation of Plant and Machinery at 10 per cent. per annum, for Depreciation of Business Premises at 2½ per cent. per annum; add £25 to Reserve for Doubtful Debts. The Stock on hand at 31st March last was £8,100.

66.—The Nominal Capital of the X. Y. Z. Company, Lim., is £250,000, divided into 250,000 Shares of £1 each. Of these 200,000 Shares have been issued at a premium of 2s. 6d. per Share. 15s. per Share has been called up, and the sum actually received from Shareholders (irrespective of premiums) amounts to £149,950. 100 Shares have, however, been forfeited for non-payment of Calls after 5s. per Share had been received thereon. State how the Capital Account of the Company should be shown on its Balance Sheet.

67.—On the 31st December 1900 the Accounts of a Limited Company showed a credit balance on Profit and Loss Account of £5,500. It was decided not to declare any dividend, but to apply these profits in the redemption of an issue of £5,000 worth of Debentures, which the Company was then empowered to pay off at 105.

You are required to show the Ledger Accounts affected by the carrying through of this transaction.

68.—A Company purchased a business as a going concern on January 1st 1900, with a right to the Profits from October 1st 1899.

Its Capital is:—

5 per cent. Preference Shares	...	...	...	£50,000
6 per cent. Preference Shares	...	...	...	50,000
Ordinary Shares	...	...	...	24,800

The year's Profits to September 30th 1900 are found to have been £7,664. What appropriation of such Profits would you consider to be correct?

69.—How should money received in respect of Shares which have been forfeited and re-issued be treated in the Accounts of a Company?

70.—A Limited Company was formed to take over the business of a private Firm which had Assets amounting to £640,000, represented as follows:—

Land, Buildings, and Plant	..	..	..	..	..	..	£420,000
Materials and Stores	..	..	..	..	..	..	23,500
Works in Progress	..	..	..	..	..	..	132,000
Book Debts	..	..	..	..	..	..	90,000
Cash in Bank	..	..	..	..	..	..	26,500
Cash in hand	..	..	..	..	..	..	500
							692,500
Less Trade Creditors			..	..	..		52,500
							£640,000

The purchase price is £800,000, payable £200,000 in fully-paid Preference Shares, £100,000 in fully-paid Ordinary Shares, £200,000 in Debentures, and the balance in cash.

The Share Capital of the Company was 300,000 Preference Shares of £1 each, 200,000 Ordinary Shares of £1 each, and the Debenture Capital £300,000 4 per cent. redeemable Stock the Share Capital other than that issued in payment of purchase-money is payable 2s. per Share on Application, 8s. per Share on Allotment, 10s. per Share six weeks after allotment, and the Debenture Stock, other than that issued in payment of purchase-money, 10 per cent. on Application, 50 per cent. on Allotment, and the balance six weeks after allotment.

Make the necessary entries in the Company's books.

71.—The London Engineering Company, Lim., invite subscriptions for 40,000 Preference Shares, being part of an issue of 50,000 such Shares of £1 each. The Subscription List closed on 25th March, when it was found that the following applications had been received, and the deposit of 2s. 6d. per Share thereon paid to the Company's bankers :—

		Shares.
A.	.. ..	5,000
B.	.. ..	10,000
C.	.. ..	5,000
D.	.. ..	2,000
E.	.. ..	10,000
F.	.. ..	10,000
G.	.. ..	10,000

On the 1st April the Board allotted Shares as follows :—

A.	.. ..	5,000
B.	.. ..	10,000
C.	.. ..	5,000
E.	.. ..	10,000
F.	.. ..	5,000
G.	.. ..	5,000

and intimated that a further 7s. 6d. per Share was payable on allotment.

You are required to show how the above would appear in the Applications and Allotments Book, and to explain what entries would be necessary in the financial books of the Company up to the point of sending out Allotment Letters and Letters of Regret.

72.—In the case of a Company which has issued Preference Shares carrying a cumulative dividend of 6 per cent., but which has not made any Profits for some years, how would you deal (if at all) with the arrears in a Balance Sheet of the Company ?

73.—Journalise the following transactions of a Limited Company.

The Company was registered on the 1st January 1902, with a Nominal Capital of £40,000, divided into 40,000 Shares of £1 each, of which 20,000 were issued as fully-paid to the Vendor as part of the purchase consideration, 10,000 offered for subscription to provide Working Capital, 5s. per Share payable on Application, 5s. per Share on Allotment, and the remainder in two Calls of 5s. each. 10,000 Shares to be held in reserve for future issue. The Vendor also received £5,000 in 5 per cent. Debentures, the balance of the purchase consideration.

1902		
January	5.	Applications, accompanied by 5s. per Share, were received for 5,000 Shares.
,,	6.	Allotment made of 5,000 Shares.
,,	10.	Amount due on Allotment of 5,000 Shares received.
February	10.	First Call of 5s. per Share, made payable 24th inst.
,,	,,	20,000 fully-paid Shares allotted to Vendor.
,,	,,	5 per cent. Debentures issued to Vendor for £5,000, balance of purchase-money.
,,	24.	Received on Account of First Call, £625.
,,	26.	Received Balance of First Call, £625.
March	10.	Second and Final Call of 5s. per Share made, payable on 24th inst.
,,	24.	Received on Account of Second and Final Call, £1,000.

74.—A private business, as carried on by John Smith, is converted on 1st January 1903 into a Limited Company under the title of "Smiths, Lim.," on the following terms :—The Company takes over the Cash and Bills in hand, but collects the Book Debts and discharges the Liabilities on behalf of the old firm ; it also purchases the Stock for £1,500, the Plant for £3,000, and the Goodwill for £5,000.

The purchase-money is payable as to £5,000 in 5 per cent. Debentures, as to £5,000 in fully-paid Shares, and the balance in cash. The Balance Sheet of the business on 31st December 1902 was as under :—

JOHN SMITH.

BALANCE SHEET, 31st December 1902.

	£ s d		£ s d
To Sundry Creditors	3,000 0 0	By Cash in hand	650 0 0
,, John Smith—Capital Account ..	11,150 0 0	,, Bills Receivable in hand	900 0 0
		,, Sundry Debtors, as per list £10,500	
		Less Reserve for Bad Debts 1,500	
			9,000 0 0
		,, Stock-in-Trade	1,600 0 0
		,, Plant	2,000 0 0
	£14,150 0 0		£14,150 0 0

The sums paid over by the Company in respect of Book Debts collected, over and above the amount used to pay off the Creditors, are as follows :—On 31st January, £2,000 ; 28th February, £2,000 ; on the 30th April an agreed sum of £1,350 in settlement of the balance and as purchase-money for the Book Debts then outstanding.

Show the Cash Book and Journal entries necessary to record the above transactions in the books of the new Company, open and post the Ledger Accounts, and take out a Trial Balance on the 30th April 1903.

75.—Write up the books of John Smith from 1st January to 30th April 1903, and close them at the latter date, and prepare a Balance Sheet.

76.—A Company was registered on 31st March 1900 for the purpose of acquiring the business of a firm from 1st January 1900, and its Share Capital, £75,000, and £20,000 4 per cent. Debenture Stock were all subscribed and paid on the day of registration. On making up the accounts on the 31st of December 1900 it was found that a Profit of £10,000, subject to interest on Debenture Stock, had been made, whereupon a dividend at the rate of 10 per cent. per annum, free of Income Tax, was declared.

Make the distribution, and say what becomes of the balance of Profit.

77.—M. stands in the books of the X. Co., Lim., as the holder of 100 fully-paid Shares of £1 each. M. dies, and probate of his will is granted to N. What must N. do before he can deal with the Shares, and what record should appear in the books of the X. Co., Lim.

78.—Give a list of the matters that have to be dealt with at the Statutory Meeting of a new Company.

79.—In what way would you advise that Premiums on the issue of new Shares in a Limited Company should be dealt with ? Give your reasons.

80.—What books is a Company under the Companies Acts required to keep, and what should they contain ?

81.—On the 1st January 1903 a Company offers for subscription its Capital of £100,000, divided into 100,000 Shares of £1 each. The Shares are offered at a premium of 2s. 6d. per Share, the whole being payable 5s. on Application, 7s. 6d. on Allotment, and the remainder, 10s., one month after allotment.

The whole of the Issue is applied for on the 2nd January, and the Company goes to allotment on January 8th.

Show the necessary entries in the financial books of the Company, assuming that all instalments of Capital are duly received.

82.—What special considerations arise in connection with Forfeited Shares ?

83.—W. & H. Falk agree to purchase from E. Sloe, trustee of T. Williams, deceased, a small Engineering business, for the sum of £7,000. The Assets, as they appeared in the books, were :—

1.	Engine, Boiler, Fixed Plant and Machinery	£3,000
2.	Stock-in-trade, comprising finished and unfinished Machines, Materials and Stores ..	2,500
3.	Loose Tools, Machines, and Office Furniture	1,000
4.	Pattern Models, &c.	650
5.	Book Debts	1,800
		£8,950

Messrs. Falk, in making their estimate of the value of the Assets, deducted the following percentages from the above items, namely :—(1) 25 per cent. (2) 20 per cent. (3) 10 per cent. (4) 50 per cent. (5) 10 per cent., being 2½ per cent. for Discounts, and 7½ per cent. for Bad Debts. They made a further deduction for expenses and contingencies, reducing the amount to £7,000, which was offered and accepted. On the 1st June 1900 the purchase was completed by the payment of £4,000 ; £2,500 being provided by W. Falk, and £1,500 by H. Falk, and for the balance W. and H. accepted three bills, each for £1,000, payable at three, six, and nine months respectively. Make the Journal entries for recording the above transactions.

84.—A. B. died on the 31st December 1900, leaving the following Estate :—

Cash in the House	£60
Cash at Bank	740
Household Furniture and effects, valued at	2,000
Consols, 2¾ per cent. valued at 95	5,000
Freehold Property (in occupation of deceased at time of death) valued at	2,200
Leasehold Property, let at £200 per annum, Rent payable quarterly on 25th March, 24th June, 29th September and 25th December, paid to 29th September 1900, valued at ..	2,500
£600 5 per cent. Debentures of the Charter Brewery, Lim., quoted at 31st December 1900, at £110 per cent. Interest payable half-yearly, 31st March and 30th September.	
£1,000 on deposit for 12 months, from 30th September 1900, with the Eastern Bank, at 4 per cent. per annum. Interest payable half-yearly, 31st March, and 30th September.	
5,000 Shares of £1 each in the South Wales Gold Co., Lim., 10s. per Share paid and 5s. more called up ; Call due 10th January 1901. No quotation for Shares, which are valued for Probate at £100.	
Sundry Debts owing to the deceased	750
Sundry Debts owing by the deceased	640

85.—A. B. was a partner in a business at the time of his death; and upon the accounts being made up it was found that he was entitled, in respect of his share of Profits, to £540, and as representing his Capital, to £5,000, but the Capital (£5,000) was to remain in the business, at 5 per cent. per annum interest.

The Funeral and Testamentary Expenses amounted to £100, and £800 was paid as Estate Duty.

The Income of the Estate to be paid quarterly to the Widow, who is to have the use of the Furniture and Freehold premises for life.

Assume the receipt of the Debts owing to the deceased, and of the Income as and when it becomes due, and assume also the payment of the Liabilities and of the Income to the Widow. Ignore Income Tax.

You are required to write up the necessary Estate Accounts to the 30th June 1901, and to prepare a Balance Sheet as on that date.

86.—A. died on 10th June 1902. The Estate and Liabilities at the date of Probate consisted of:—

	£	s	d
Freehold Property	20,000	0	0
2¾ per cent. Consols—£20,000 at 93	18,600	0	0
N.E. Railway Consols—£10,000 at 142	14,200	0	0
Leasehold Property	5,000	0	0
Book Debts due to Testator	1,100	0	0
Money out on Notes due to Testator	1,000	0	0
Cash in Bank on Deposit Account	20,000	0	0
„ „ Current Account	1,200	0	0
Cash in House	50	0	0
Household Effects	2,000	0	0
Reversionary Interest, present value	20,000	0	0
Life Policies and Bonuses	14,000	0	0
Interest and Rents Receivable accrued between 10th April 1902, and date of			
Affidavit for Probate on 10th August 1902	2,500	0	0
Tradesmen's Accounts due by Testator	1,300	0	0
Mortgage on the Freehold Property due by Testator	13,000	0	0
Interest Payable accrued from 10th April to date of Probate Affidavit on 10th			
August 1902 at 4 per cent. per annum	173	16	1

The Funeral Expenses amounted to £200, the Death and other Duties to £3,000, and the Executorship Expenses (all chargeable to Capital) to £1,200, while the Testator had misappropriated Trust Funds to the amount of £10,000 belonging to H. (excluding any question of interest to the latter).

Draw up the Journal entries necessary for opening the Estate books.

87.—Assuming the amounts stated in the above question to be those finally realised and paid, and the Estate distributed as on 10th August 1902, prepare Residuary Accounts showing:—

(a) The amount of Capital.

(b) The amount of Income.

88.—A Testator died December 31st 1899 leaving:—

Cash in the House, £30.
Consols, 2¾ per cent., £12,000, valued at 101 x.d.
Midland Railway Company's 4 per cent. Debentures £16,000, valued at 120 x.d. Dividend due January 1st.
Iron and Steel Company, 100 Ordinary Shares of £10 each, valued at £5, but paying no dividend.
Balance at the Bankers, £650.

There was due to Testator £4,000 on mortgage at 4 per cent. interest, due yearly on March 31st. His Debts to Tradesmen amounted to £500. The residue of the Estate is bequeathed half to his Widow and half to a Brother. He bequeathed to his two Executors (strangers in blood) £100 each. The Funeral Expenses were £75. The Stocks were realised at the valuation prices, and the Mortgage was called in on March 31st, on which day Probate was applied for.

Draw a Statement showing the residue on which Legacy Duty is chargeable.

89.—A , who was in partnership with B. and C. on equal terms, both as to Capital and share of Profits, died, leaving the following Estate:—

					£	s	d
Cash in the House	..	..	..	..	..		
Cash at the Bank	..	..	..	..	5	0	0
Freehold Property	..	..	..	..	500	0	0
Household Furniture, valued at	..	..	..	..	6,000	0	0
Shares in various Companies, valued at	..	..	..	700	0	0
					4,000	0	0

His Liabilities were £150.

The partnership Assets and Liabilities were as follows :—

Stock-in-Trade	..	..	..	..	..	10,000	0	0
Debts (Good) ..	..	..	..	..	3,000	0	0	
Cash at Bankers and in Hand	..	..	..	..	1,450	0	0	
Bills Receivable	..	..	..	..	..	300	0	0
Liabilities	..	..	..	..	..	4,500	0	0

Make up a Statement of the personal estate of which A. died possessed, showing the amount on which Estate Duty would have to be paid.

90.—The estate of George Washington, deceased, was left in trust equally to his two sons, but the elder, having arrived at his majority, has received his share, the moiety being still carried on in trust for the younger. The Trustees did not, however, convert the whole Estate into cash, but have taken over some of the Stocks at cost price, instead of the prices then current, and this has now to be rectified. From the following particulars draw up six months' accounts, and show what further sum is due to elder, and how younger's position is altered.

On January 1st younger's Account is :—

				Cost Price.	Present Price.
Pernambuco Water Works	..	..	..	£1,126 5 0	£1,220 0 0
Submarine Railway Co.	..	..	..	626 12 6	825 0 0
Arctic Railway Co. ..	..	..	..	500 0 0	579 10 0
British Funds	..	..	..	100 0 0	108 0 0
Mortgage..	..	..	..	1,750 0 0	
Cash at Bank	..	..	..	2,847 8 6	

The following items are younger's Income and Expenditure Account to June 30th:—

Sundry Dividends	..	..	..	..	£59 5 1	
Interest on Loan	..	..	..	..	53 6 0	
Purchase of Corporation Stock	..	..	..		£2,700 0 0
Maintenance	..	..	..	..		47 5 3
Cash Allowance	..	..	..	..		40 0 0

91.—A Testator bequeaths two Annuities. The Executors, under power granted by the Will, elect to satisfy the one by the purchase of a Government Annuity, and the other by annual or other instalments.

How should the two cases be dealt with in the books of the Trust ?

92.—A Testator leaves pure Personalty of the value of £10,000, Real Estate £25,000, and Leaseholds of the value of £20,000. He bequeaths Specific Legacies of Personalty to the value of £2,000, and Pecuniary Legacies to the value of £18,000. The Executorial Expenses, Debts, and Duties amount to £5,000.

The Real Estate falls into residue.

How is each Legacy to be satisfied, and state generally how Specific Legacies are to be dealt with in the books of a Trust.

93.—State fully the difference between the Double-Account System and the Single-Account System, and the general principles governing the valuation of Assets and Liabilities under each.

94.—To what classes of undertakings is the Double-Account System specially applicable, and why?

95.—What are the chief differences between the Double-Account System and the Single-Account System?

96.—How may provision be made for Depreciation when the Double-Account System is employed?

97.—How is Depreciation treated in the accounts of a Gas Company; and how would you deal with the rebuilding of works, originally costing £50,000, at a cost of £100,000, in a Gas Company's books? .

98.—Describe fully the correct method of dealing with (a) Repairs, (b) Renewals, (c) extensions under both the Single and Double-Account Systems.

99.—In the month of June 1902 A., B. & Co. made a return of Profit for Income Tax assessment under Schedule D, for the year ending 5th April 1903. The amount was £9,000, being the average of the three years ended 31st December 1901, namely:—1899, £9,000; 1900, £10,000; and 1901, £8,000. The assessment was duly made, and the tax on £9,000 paid in January 1903. Some months later, when the Accounts for the year 1902 were made up, the taxable Profit of that year was ascertained to be £6,900. State what adjustment and relief A., B. & Co. are entitled to, and how such relief is to be obtained; also state what difference it would have made in the amount of the relief if the Profits of the three years ended 31st December 1901 had been —for 1899, £13,800; 1900, £6,200; 1901, £7,000.

100.—Messrs. Field and Croft desire to know what return they ought to make of Profits chargeable with Income Tax under Schedule D, and what deductions they would be entitled to. Three years' Trading Accounts showed Profits of £90, £150, and £180, respectively, after charging against the Profits salary drawn by Partners at the rate of £3 per week each. The Profits were divisible, two-thirds to Field, and one-third to Croft. Neither Partner had income from any other source. Explain what steps should be taken to obtain proper assessments; and show the amounts payable by each Partner, the tax being a shilling in the £.

101.—Prepare the Income Tax Return of the Atlas Steel Company, Lim., for the year 1899-1900 from the following figures :—

Profit for the year 1896	...	...	...	£25,000
,, ,, 1897	...	...	...	23,740
,, ,, 1898	...	...	...	29,450

These Profits are, after bringing to credit net Income from Farms and Cottages £2,500, and £2,550 Income received from Investments, and after charging Income Tax paid, £600 ; Charitable Gifts, £500 ; Depreciation of Machinery, £1,600 ; and of Buildings, £1,000 ; and writing off £1,000 from the Colliery freehold each year. The property is the Company's own, and is assessed for Property Tax at £6,000.

102.—The following is the Profit and Loss Account of a Limited Company for the three years ended 31st December 1902.

You are required to prepare a Profit and Loss Account for the same period for Income Tax purposes, and to show what should be the amount of the first assessment of the Company for the year ended 5th April 1904 :—

Dr.					1900	1901	1902
Purchases..	..	..	..	..	£50,000	£51,000	£38,000
Salaries ..	..	..	..	..	3,500	3,500	3,500
Annuities ..	..	..	..	..	200	200	200
Charges ..	..	..	..	..	2,000	2,500	1,250
Donations to Charities	..	..	..		100	150	
Debenture Interest ..	..	..	..		5,000	5,000	5,000
Directors' percentage on Profits..	..	..		2,500	2,750	
Stationery..	..	..	..		250	260	225
Depreciation of Office Furniture	..	..		50	50	50
Telegrams..	..	..	..		150	148	126
Income Tax	..	..	..		1,500	1,520	1,670
Loss on Sale of Live Stock	..	..	..		100	..	20
Rent	..	..	..		200	200	200
Loss on Property Sold	..	..	..		..	..	600
Balance ..	..	..	..		19,450	22,722	
					£85,000	£90,000	£50,841

Cr.					1900	1901	1902
Sales ..	..	..	..	..	£84,525	£89,529	39,625
Dividends on Consols ..	..	..	..		380	377	375
Rents Received (£100 less Tax) ..	..	..		95	94	
Balance ..	..	..	..		..	..	10,841
					£85,000	£90,000	£50,841

103.—Prepare a Statement of Affairs and Deficiency Account, as on 10th October 1897, of William Corby, trading as William Corby & Son, from the following particulars :—

Cash in hand £85 ; Book Debts £3,472, estimated to produce £2,869 ; Unfinished Contract in hand, estimated to produce £3,000 over and above the cost of completing it ; Plant, Tools, &c., cost £1,880, estimated to realise £500 ; Office Furniture, estimated to realise £25 ; Stock-in-Trade £1,900 ; Investments valued at £6,200, of which are deposited with Bankers as security for Loan £5,460 ; Life Policies for £2,000 of the estimated Surrender Value of £1,470, subject to advances made by the Insurance Company amounting to £1,420 ; Unsecured Creditors on Trade Accounts £4,140 ; Unsecured Creditors for Cash advanced £5,308 ; W. Smith for 2 months' wages due to him £30; A. Compton, 6 months' salary due to him at £15 a month; Rent recoverable by distress £45; Bankers for Loans partly secured £10,134 (estimated value of Securities held by Bankers £7,460, viz.:—Investments £5,460 and Lease £2,000); Capital Account on 1st January 1897 as shown by the books, £189; Loss on Trading from 1st January to 10th October 1897, £374; Loss on Sale of Investments made on 13th June 1897, £200; Drawings, £750.

104.—Johnson & Caley, merchants, are unable to meet their obligations. From their books, papers, and information supplied by them, the following particulars relative to their affairs are ascertained:—

	£	s	d
Cash in hand..	250	0	0
Debtors—Good, £1,250; Doubtful, £600 : estimated to produce, £200; Bad, £1,000	2,850	0	0
Shares in the Straights Shipping Company, Lim., of par value	5,000	0	0
Property, estimated to produce £9,000	14,000	0	0
Bills Receivable (Good) ..	4,250	0	0
Other Securities—£3,000 pledged with partly secured Creditors, and the remainder with fully secured Creditors	28,000	0	0
Johnson's Drawings	9,000	0	0
Caley's do.	8,400	0	0
Sundry Losses	13,500	0	0
Trade Expenses	7,400	0	0
Creditors—Unsecured ..	25,000	0	0
„ Partly Secured	23,900	0	0
„ Fully Secured	17,000	0	0
Preferential Claims—Wages, Salaries, and Taxes	750	0	0
Johnson—Capital	10,000	0	0
Caley do.	16,000	0	0

Prepare a Statement of Affairs, showing the Assets, with respect to their realisation; also a Deficiency Account in respect of the deficiency shown by the Statement of Affairs.

105.—A Limited Company, having carried out its business objects, went into Voluntary Liquidation with the following Liabilities:—

			£	s	d
Trade Creditors			12,000	0	0
Bank Overdraft			20,000	0	0
Capital—					
10,000 Preference Shares of £10, £7 called ..			70,000	0	0
10,000 Ordinary Shares of £10, £9 called ..	£90,000 0 0				
Less Calls in arrear	2,000 0 0				
			88,000	0	0
Cash received from certain Shareholders in anticipation of Calls—					
On Preference Shares..	£24,000 0 0				
On Ordinary Shares ..	4,000 0 0				
			28,000	0	0

The Assets realised £200,000. Describe the Liquidator's process of winding-up, and prepare a General Liquidation Account, allowing £2,000 as the expenses of the Liquidation.

Note.—No Interest need be brought into account. The Preference Shares have no prior Capital rights.

106.—An Insurance Company, having a paid-up Capital of £80,000 in 80,000 fully-paid £1 Shares, and a Reserve of equal amount, invested in Securities to the amount of £150,000, and outstanding Balances and Cash £10,000, is absorbed by another Company, the consideration being £65,000 in Cash and the allotment of one Share of £25 (£2 10s. paid, and standing in the market at £19 per Share in the Purchasing Company) for every 16 Shares of their own Company.

Close the books of the Vendor Company, and show how the transactions will appear in those of the Purchasing Company.

107.—Describe the applications of the Slip System to Day Books, Returns Books, &c.

108.—Describe the applications of the Slip System to Cash Books.

109.—Instance a few of the applications of the Slip System which have been in general use for a number of years past.

110.—Indicate shortly what you think to be a few of the advantages and disadvantages of the Slip System.

111.—Describe fully the nature and method of keeping Card Ledgers.

112.—Describe the advantages and disadvantages of Card Ledgers as compared with Book Ledgers.

113.—Explain how slips of original entry may be employed as Ledgers, and mention any cases in which you think this form of accounting suitable.

114.—Describe quite shortly the essential features of the Slip System as applied to Ledgers.

115.—What is a Cost Sheet, what are its special advantages, and how is it made up? Give a specimen Cost Sheet of a Steel Manufactory.

116.—What is meant by the term " Depreciation "; is it the same as ordinary wear and tear?

Explain the object of charging Depreciation in the Profit and Loss Account as an expense.

117.—Explain shortly the various methods by which Depreciation on Buildings, Leases, Machinery, and Plant may be provided for, and give your comments on the working of the various methods

118.—On closing the books of a Firm the Trial Balance showed the following debit balances:—

A. & Co.	..	..	..	..	..	£1,260
B. & Co.	..	..	..	..	..	740
C. & Co.	..	..	..	..	..	600
D.	..	..	..	..	..	200

Since the date of the Trial Balance A. & Co. have become bankrupt, and their creditors have received 5s. in the £, and are to receive a second and final dividend of 2s. in the £.

The firm decide to create a Reserve of 10 per cent. in respect of B. & Co.'s debt, and a reserve of 20 per cent. in respect of the amount due from C. & Co. in consequence of disputes as to damaged Goods. D. has absconded, and it is decided to write off his entire indebtedness as being irrecoverable.

Draft Journal entries carrying out the above, and state the amount which will be charged against Profit and Loss Account.

119.—On 1st January 1899 a Company has a Reserve Fund amounting to £5,000 invested in Consols, and a balance to the credit of Profit and Loss Account amounting to £7,500. At the close of the year it is ascertained that the Company's operations have resulted in a loss of £10,000. You are required to show the effect of this result upon the accounts named.

120.—Explain the nature and operations of the Insurance Fund of a Company owning a fleet of Vessels. Is such a Fund applicable to all sorts of ship-owning, and, if not, for what reasons?

121.—Give your views as to the respective advantages under differing circumstances of providing for the expiration of Leasehold interests by a Company owning such property—

   (a) by the investment by the Company itself of a Sinking Fund;

   (b) by taking out a policy of Leasehold Assurance;

   (c) by writing down the value in successive Profit and Loss Accounts.

122.—What is the difference between a Reserve and a Reserve Fund? What is the object of creating the latter?

123.—A Firm expends large sums upon advertisements in order to form a business. Assuming that the expenditure thereon decreases annually until, in the seventh year, it reaches a point representing a normal annual cost under this head, how would you expect the amounts to be treated in each year's Balance Sheet? In your reply let £14,000 be the expenditure of the first year, and decrease £2,000 annually.

124.—State your views as to the principles upon which Leasehold Properties should be treated, and as to the manner in which their value as Assets should be determined for successive Balance Sheets.

125.—A fire partially destroys a Factory, and damages a quantity of Stock. The Insurance Company settles the claims thus:—By a lump sum in lieu of rebuilding, by a further sum in respect of the beneficial interest of the Insurers in the property during rebuilding, by selling the damaged Stock to the Insurers at an agreed sum, and deducting such sum from the gross claim for loss of Stock.

The rebuilding is effected at a lower cost than was anticipated, and a surplus remains. The damaged Stock is disposed of at a profit. How would you deal with the results of these transactions if you were certifying as to Trading Profits?

126.—What do you understand by the term "Sinking Fund"? How is initiated, and what is its operation from year to year?

127.—It has been stated that the Plant, &c., of a business cannot in a given year be depreciated unless sufficient profits have been made in that year wherewith to depreciate it. Show the fallacy of this statement, and the false issues involved.

128.—Explain the various uses of
   (a) Reserve Funds,
   (b) Suspense Accounts,

and furnish an example of each of the following cases :—

    (1) Banker.
    (2) Insurance Company.
    (3) A Firm of Merchants.
    (4) Trading Company.

129—Under what circumstances is it desirable that a Reserve Fund should specially be invested ? What class of Securities should it be invested in ?

130.—State precisely what you understand by the following terms :—

    (a) Reserve.
    (b) Reserve Fund.
    (c) Reserved Fund.
    (d) Permanent Reserve.
    (e) Depreciation Fund.
    (f) Depreciation Account.
    (g) Investment Fluctuation Account.
    (h) Investment Fluctuation Fund.
    (i) Dividend Equalisation Account.
    (j) Guarantee Fund.

Are any of these terms interchangeable ? Is the Auditor responsible for the correct use of the terms employed ?

131.—A. acquires for the sum of £200 the seven years' lease of certain Premises, which are let to B. for £40 per annum. The Ground Rent payable by A. is £4 3s. 4d. per annum. Show how the Leases Account should appear in A.'s Ledger during the remainder of the term.

132.—The facts being as stated in the previous question, with the exception of the circumstances that the premises are kept by A. himself, instead of being sublet to B., show the Leases Account, indicating clearly the proper amount to be charged annually against Revenue.

133.—Illustrate the difference between Depreciation at 6 per cent. yearly on the original value of Plant and Machinery, and 7½ per cent. yearly on the value remaining after deduction of the previous year's charge, say, at the end of six years on £20,000.

134.—A., a manufacturer, lets to B. 10 Wagons on a Hire-purchase Agreement, under which he is to receive half-yearly Instalments of £100 for five years. Show the necessary Accounts in A.'s books, reckoning interest at the rate of 6 per cent. per annum, calculated with half-yearly rests, assuming that the Wagons each cost A. £65 to make.

135.—The facts being as stated in the previous question, show the Accounts necessary in B.'s Ledger to record the transaction during the currency of the Hire-purchase Agreement.

136.—Under a Hire-purchase Agreement the value of the Assets in question would increase year by year. What method would you suggest should be adopted to set them forth correctly in the various Balance Sheets ? Take a term of seven years.

137.—Give a short example of an Account of Receipts and Payments, also of an Account of Income and Expenditure, and explain the difference between these two Accounts.

138.—Define what you understand by a Balance Sheet, state the sources and method of its preparation, and explain how a Balance Sheet differs from a Statement of Affairs.

139.—Define Trade Discount and Cash Discount, and give your views as to the manner in which they should be dealt with in the books.

140.—Would you defend, and if so on what grounds, the non-presentation by a Manufacturing Company of its Trading and Profit and Loss Accounts at its Annual Meetings ?

141.—What Accounts are usually presented to Auditors for the purpose of Audit

(a) When all the transactions during the period have been of a Cash nature, and

(b) When such transactions have been partly Cash and partly Credit ?

142.—From the following figures prepare a Trading Account upon the usual lines:—

Stock on 1st January 1902 ..	..	..	..	£3,000
Purchases	..	..	..	..	8,000
Wages..	..	.,	..	..	2,000
Sales ..	..	..	..	..	12,000
Stock-on-hand 31st December 1902	..	..	..	5,500

143.—Taking the figures given in the previous question. prepare separate Manufacturing and Trading Accounts with the aid of the following additional Information:—

Of the Stock on the 1st January £1,750 represents manufactured Goods ; £250 Goods unfinished, and £1,000 Materials.

Of the Stock on the 31st December £1,250 represents manufactured Goods; £2,750 Goods unfinished, and £1,500 Materials.

The Purchases consist of £6,000 Materials, and £2,000 manufactured Goods.

The trade price of the Goods manufactured during the year was £7,700.

144.—What is the advantage of arranging the Accounts so as to show a Gross Profit as well as the Net Profit ?

145.—Explain fully why it is that the Balance Sheet and Accounts of a business prepared from time to time are of necessity of a tentative character. When is it possible to prepare Accounts that are really final ?

146.—What special points in the Balance Sheet of a Company—apart from the correctness of figures—do you consider need careful consideration to afford due protection to Directors and Auditors ?

147.—What is " Goodwill," upon what is it based, and how should it be dealt with in a Trading Firm's books at the yearly closing ?

148.—The books of a Company close on the 30th June. How would you deal with the following items, and how would your method of dealing with them affect the Balance Sheet and Profit and Loss Account of the Company :—

(a) Premiums of Insurance on ship paid yearly on 31st March.

(b) Income Tax deducted from Interest on Debentures, paid on 30th June—date of closing.

(c) Wages accrued, but unpaid.

(d) Allowance of 1 per cent. on outstanding Book Debts to cover Discount allowances and Bad Debts.

(e) Stock in hand, and on what principle should it be valued as regards (1) Manufactured Goods, (2) Goods in process of manufacture, (3) Raw Material.

(f) Goods consigned in the hands of an Agent abroad.

(g) Wagons held on purchase lease.

(h) Patent rights purchased from Patentee.

(i) In the case of a Colliery, " shorts " redeemable within three years.

149.—A Limited Company having purchased Shares in another Company with the object of securing business connection, and there being no transactions or market quotations by which the value of the Shares may be fixed from year to year, state your opinion of the method which should be adopted by the Company holding the Shares for valuing them and stating this asset in its Accounts, first in the case of the benefits arising therefrom improving from year to year, and secondly on the assumption that the connection is becoming less profitable from year to year.

150.—What method would you adopt in auditing the Accounts of an English Trust Company, the Capital Investments of which are wholly in Stocks, Shares, and Bonds of other Companies ?

151.—How would you verify the Balance as shown in the Cash Book—

(a) Where no Banking Account is kept ;

(b) Where a Banking Account is kept, but all the transactions do not pass through the Bank ;

(c) Where all the transactions pass through the Bank, but the balances as shown in the Cash Book and the Bankers' Pass Book are not identical ?

152.—How should Bills Receivable discounted appear in the Balance Sheet of a Trader ?

153.—Distinguish between Depreciation and Fluctuation of Assets.

154.—A Company formed for promoting other Companies receives Cash and Shares in such Companies to cover its Disbursements and Profits. In auditing the Accounts of the Company, when it is proposed to pay a dividend, how would you satisfy yourself as to whether this dividend had been earned ? Give your reasons fully.

155.—In examining a number of Debtor Balances when making up the Accounts of a firm at the end of the year, what indications in the Ledger Accounts would you make use of to put you upon inquiry as to whether any of the Debts were Bad or Doubtful ? In drawing up the Accounts of a Trading Company, what is the best method to adopt in making a provision against Bad and Doubtful Debts ?

156.—If you found the Stock of a Manufacturing Company much larger at the end of the year than at the beginning, and also the percentage of Gross Profit larger than in previous years, and on referring to a previous year's accounts (when the Stock at the end was much less than the Stock at the beginning) you found the percentage of Gross Profit less than in other years when there was not a similar difference in the Stocks, what inference would you draw from the facts, and why ?

157.—The Trial Balance and Schedules of Debtors and Creditors in a Trading Company's books disclose :—

      (a) Debts owing to and by the same firms among the Debtors and Creditors.

      (b) Money owing by the Company to a Debtor for Calls unpaid and in arrear.

      (c) Money owing by the Company to the acceptor of a Bill Receivable discounted by the Company's Bank.

      (d) Money owing to the Company by the drawer of a Bill Payable accepted by the Company.

What considerations would guide you in deciding in each case whether these sums should respectively be set off and excluded from the Balance Sheet or not ? Assume for the purpose that they are all equal in amount.

158.—An Investment Company on December 1st last bought £10,000 of 4 per cent. Debentures of W. & Co., Lim., at 95 per cent. and paid a commission thereon of 15s. per cent. to cover all expenses. Between December 1st and 30th they sold and received payment for £7,000 of the Debentures at par.

The purchase-money of £10,000 was provided by the sale of £8,850 of 2¾ per cent. Consols, part of £20,000 Consols which had been purchased and stood in the Company's books at 110.

Set out in the Ledger Account with W. & Co., Lim., the transactions in the Debentures; also show in the Consols Account the entry of the transaction therein, and write up the Profit and Loss Account so far as it is affected by these transactions.

159.—A Company brought out a new Machine, and, for the purpose of getting it upon the market, sent to a large number of their customers Machines on sale or return. These Machines were debited in the Ledger Accounts of the several customers and included in the Ledger Balances at the end of the year. How would you deal with these Accounts in preparing a Profit and Loss Account and Balance Sheet ?

160.—Explain the method you would recommend for recording the transactions involved in supplying customers with Goods on sale or return as stated in the above question. Illustrate your answer by an example in which six Machines are sent out, four are sold and two are returned. If you prefer a special form of book give a specimen of the ruling.

161.—The Coal Mine Company, Lim., took a lease of a Colliery from G. Risch for 99 years from September 29th 1896, at a Ground Rent of £50 a year, payable half-yearly, and a Royalty of 6d. per ton, with a minimum Royalty of £80 a year payable half-yearly. During the first year the Company raised 2,500 tons, and during the second year ended September 29th 1898, 4,000 tons. The several amounts due to G. Risch were paid twenty-one days after becoming due.

Write up both Personal and Nominal Accounts, and balance them at the end of each year.

162.—How would you suggest that a Trader or Manufacturer should make provision in his books for known and uncertain losses by Bad Debts ?

163.—How would you deal in a Life Insurance Company's Accounts with Premiums received, bearing in mind the fact that Premiums are always paid in advance ? Should you apportion them ? If not, why not ?

164.—How would you deal in the books, and on compiling the Balance Sheet, with the Sacks sent out and returned by the customers of a firm of millers, having regard to the following facts :—

Sacks are debited when sent out at 1s.

An allowance is made for Sacks returned in good condition 6d., the estimated actual value of Sacks returned is 4d.

New Sacks purchased cost 7d.

The debit balances against customers may include the Sacks, which will either be paid for in full, or returned to claim the allowance ; or, again, customers may, having perhaps mislaid the Sacks, refuse to pay more than the estimated value of the Sacks missing.

165.—A. & B., colliery proprietors, take a Lease for 21 years at a Dead Rent of £600 a year, merging into a Royalty of 1s. a ton. The Dead Rents are recoverable out of Royalties paid within five years ; 800 tons were raised the first year, 4,600 tons the second year, and 75,000 tons the third year. 100 Colliery Wagons were purchased by the firm on the hire-purchase system, by which the wagons, at the end of ten years, became their absolute property in consideration of their paying 15s. a month for each wagon. It was assumed by the firm that each wagon would be worth £40 at the end of ten years. Show the Ledger Accounts for " Dead Rents," " Royalties," " Purchase of Wagons," for the first three years, the Accounts being balanced at the end of each year.

166.—A Mining Company, having its registered office in London, remitted to its Manager in South Africa during the year 1899 two sums of £3,000 each. The following were the payments during the year at the Mine :—

Wages, Development	..	..	..	..	..	£1,000
Do. Mining and Milling	..	..	..	..	..	1,000
Salaries..	..	..	..	..	..	800
Stores ..	..	..	..	..	..	2,000

N.B.—The Stores used during the year were £800 in Development and £700 in Mining and Milling.

Sundry Expenses ..	..	..	..	..	..	300

Bullion to the value of £3,600 was produced, and sent to the Standard Bank of South Africa, who advanced £3,500 on it, which they remitted direct to London.

Give the form in which the Manager's Accounts should be sent to London, and show how they should be entered in the London books.

167.—What do you understand by the term " Periodical Returns ? " By whom are such Returns prepared, and for what purposes ? Taking any concern with which you are acquainted, state what you consider such Returns should comprise.

cc

INDEX.

The History of Accounting

An Arno Press Collection

Bennet[t], James [Arlington]. **The American System of Practical Book-Keeping** and Foster, B[enjamin] F[ranklin], **The Origin and Progress of Book-Keeping.** 1842/1852. Two vols. in one

Brief, Richard P., editor. **The Late Nineteenth Century Debate Over Depreciation, Capital and Income.** 1976

Brief, Richard P. **Nineteenth Century Capital Accounting and Business Investment.** 1976

Bruchey, Stuart W[eems]. **Robert Oliver and Mercantile Bookkeeping in the Early Nineteenth Century.** 1976

Church, A[lexander] Hamilton. **Production Factors in Cost Accounting and Works Management.** 1910

Cole, William Morse. **Accounts:** Their Construction and Interpretation for Business Men and Students of Affairs. 1908

Dicksee, Lawrence R[obert]. **Advanced Accounting.** 1903

Dicksee, Lawrence R[obert]. **Auditing:** A Practical Manual for Auditors. 1892

Dicksee, Lawrence R[obert]. **Auditing:** A Practical Manual for Auditors. Authorized American Edition, Edited by Robert H. Montgomery. 1905

Dicksee, Lawrence R[obert]. **Depreciation, Reserves, and Reserve Funds.** 1903

Dicksee, Lawrence R[obert] and Frank Tillyard. **Goodwill and Its Treatment in Accounts.** 1906

Folsom, E[zekiel] G[ilman]. **Folsom's Logical Bookkeeping:** The Logic of Accounts. 1873

Garcke, Emile and J[ohn] M[anger] Fells. **Factory Accounts, Their Principles and Practice.** 1893

Hatfield, Henry Rand. **Modern Accounting:** Its Principles and Some of its Problems. 1916

Kehl, Donald. **Corporate Dividends:** Legal and Accounting Problems Pertaining to Corporate Distributions. 1941

Leake, P[ercy] D[ewe]. **Depreciation and Wasting Assets and Their Treatment in Assessing Annual Profit and Loss.** 1912

Lisle, George. **Accounting in Theory and Practice.** 1900

Matheson, Ewing. **The Depreciation of Factories, Mines and Industrial Undertakings and Their Valuation.** 1893

Montgomery, Robert H. **Auditing Theory and Practice.** 1912

Norton, George Pepler. **Textile Manufacturers' Book-Keeping for the Counting House, Mill and Warehouse.** 1894

Paton, William A[ndrew] and Russell A[lger] Stevenson. **Principles of Accounting.** 1916

Pixley, Francis W[illiam]. **Auditors:** Their Duties and Responsibilities Under the Joint-Stock Companies Acts and the Friendly Societies and Industrial and Provident Societies Acts. 1881

Reiter, Prosper, Jr. **Profits, Dividends and the Law.** 1926

Scott, DR. **Theory of Accounts.** 1925

Scovell, Clinton H. **Interest as a Cost.** 1924

Sells, Elijah Watt. **The Natural Business Year and Thirteen Other Themes.** 1924

Soulé, Geo[rge]. **Soulé's New Science and Practice of Accounts.** 1903

Sprouse, Robert T[homas]. **The Effect of the Concept of the Corporation on Accounting.** 1976

Zeff, Stephen A., editor. **Asset Appreciation, Business Income and Price-Level Accounting: 1918-1935.** 1976